T0295839

A History of the Reform and Opening Up of the People's Republic of China (1978–2021)

www.royalcollins.com

A History of the Reform and Opening Up of the People's Republic of China (1978–2021)

QI PENGFEI AND ZHOU JIABIN

Books Beyond Boundaries

ROYAL COLLINS

A History of the Reform and Opening Up of the People's Republic of China (1978–2021)

By Qi Pengfei and Zhou Jiabin
Translated by He Li, Feng Lei, and Ayinuer Yiganmu

First published in 2024 by Royal Collins Publishing Group Inc.
Groupe Publication Royal Collins Inc.
550-555 boul. René-Lévesque O Montréal (Québec) H2Z1B1 Canada

ISBN: 978-1-4878-1079-5

To find out more about our publications, please visit www.royalcollins.com.

Contents

Contents

List of Abbreviation

ACFIC	All-China Federation of Industry and Commerce
ADB	Asian Development Bank
APEC	Asia-Pacific Economic Cooperation
ARATS	Relations Across the Taiwan Straits
ASEAN	Association of Southeast Asian Nations
ASEM	Asia-Europe Meeting
BOCOG	Beijing Organizing Committee of Olympic Games
CASCF	China-Arab States Cooperation Forum
CCCPC	Central Committee of the Communist Party of China
CCDI	Central Commission for Discipline Inspection
CCTV	China Central Television
CEEC	Committee of European Economic Cooperation
CEPA	Closer Economic Partnership Arrangements
CIIE	China International Import Expo
CGTN	China Global Television Network
CMC	Central Military Commission
CNR	China National Radio
CPC	Communist Party of China
CPPCC	Chinese People's Political Consultative Conference
CRI	China Radio International

CSRC	China Securities Regulatory Commission
CTBT	Comprehensive Nuclear Test Ban Treaty
CWC	Chemical Weapons Convention
DOC	Declaration on the Conduct of Parties in the South China Sea
DPP	Democratic Progressive Party
DPRK	Democratic People's Republic of Korea
ESCAP	Economic and Social Commission for Asia and the Pacific
FOCAC	Forum on China-Africa Cooperation
GATT	General Agreement on Tariffs and Trade
GNP	Gross National Product
HKSAR	Hong Kong Special Administrative Region
ICAO	International Civil Aviation Organization
ICAPP	International Conference of Asian Political Parties
IMF	International Monetary Fund
IOC	International Olympic Committee
KFC	Kentucky Fried Chicken
KMT	Kuomintang
LAIA	Latin American Integration Association
LPRP	Lao People's Revolutionary Party
MCT	Ministry of Culture and Tourism
MFA	Ministry of Foreign Affairs
MHRSS	Ministry of Human Resources and Social Security
MINURSO	UN Mission on Referendum in Western Sahara
MSAR	Macao Special Administrative Region
NATO	North Atlantic Treaty Organization
NDRC	National Development and Reform Commission
NEVs	New Energy Vehicles
NPC	National People's Congress
NTA	National Tourism Administration
PLA	People's Liberation Army
PRC	People's Republic of China

PV	Photovoltaic
RCEP	Regional Comprehensive Economic Partnership
ROK	Republic of Korean
SCO	Shanghai Cooperation Organization
SEF	the Taiwan Strait Exchange Foundation
SEZs	Special Economic Zones
SMS	Small Message Service
SOEs	State-Owned Enterprises
SPNA	Shanghai Pudong New Area
SSEZ	Shenzhen Special Economic Zone
TAC	Taoist Association of China
UK	United Kingdom
UNAMIC	United Nations Advance Mission in Cambodia
UNAMSIL	United Nations Mission in Sierra Leone
UNESCO	United Nations Educational, Scientific and Cultural Organization
UNGA	United Nations General Assembly
UNIKOM	United Nations Iraq Kuwait Observation Mission
UNOMIL	United Nations Observer Mission in Liberia
UNOMOZ	United Nations Operation in Mozambique
UNTSO	United Nations Truce Supervision Organization
WHA	World Health Assembly
WHO	World Health Organization
WIC	World Internet Conference
WIPO	World Intellectual Property Organization
WMO	World Meteorological Organization
WTO	World Trade Organization

Preface

Whether from a grand historical view of the 100 years since the founding of the Communist Party of China (CPC), or from that of the more than 70 years since the founding of the People's Republic of China (PRC), the history of contemporary China's reform and opening-up, which has been more than 40 years so far (including the two major time periods: the new period of China's reform, opening-up and socialist modernization opened by the Third Plenary Session of the 11th Central Committee of the CPC (CCCPC) in December 1978 and the new era of socialism with Chinese characteristics opened by the 18th CPC in November 2012), is nothing less than the most dramatic and colorful chapter, the "China Story" most worthy of exploration and telling. In the past 40 years, from the beginning of the new era to the new century, and from standing at a new starting point to entering the new era, the CPC has united and led the Chinese people to explore and practice the cause of socialism with Chinese characteristics, creating earth-shaking miracles. In a few decades, we have completed the industrialization process that developed countries have undergone for hundreds of years, achieved a historic transformation from a highly centralized planned economic system to a dynamic socialist market economy, from a closed and semi-closed system to an all-round opening, made a historic breakthrough from a relatively backward state of productive forces to the second largest economy in the world, and realized a historic leap in people's living from inadequate subsistence to general well-off and comprehensive well-off. It has provided an increasingly perfect system, a solid material foundation and active spiritual power for the great rejuvenation of the Chinese nation, and greatly changed the face of China, the Chinese nation, the

Chinese people and the CPC, as well as influenced and changed the development process and pattern of the contemporary world. During these 40 years or so, we have created two historic achievements of rapid economic development and long-term social stability. The Chinese nation has risen and become prosperous and strong! Socialism with Chinese characteristics has ushered in a great leap from creation, development to perfection! General Secretary Xi Jinping solemnly declared that China's national rejuvenation has become a historical inevitability! The Chinese nation, with an entirely new posture, now stands tall and firm in the East! During these 40 years or so, as we have upheld and developed socialism with Chinese characteristics and driven coordinated progress in material, political, cultural-ethical, social, and ecological terms, we have pioneered a new and uniquely Chinese path to modernization, and created a new model for human advancement. We have expanded the avenues for developing countries to modernize, continuously contributed Chinese wisdom, Chinese solutions and Chinese power to promote human development and progress, and spread Chinese voices, Chinese theories and Chinese ideas, and significantly increased China's international influence, appeal and shaping power. That is to say, the history of reform and opening-up in contemporary China, or the history of reform and opening-up in the PRC during the 40 years or so, has become and should become the "top priority" and new growth point and new source of vitality in the study of the history of the CPC and the history of the PRC. The research on the history of reform and opening-up in China has basically become large-scale and systematic at the end of the last century, while the trend of becoming prosperous and gradually becoming "prominent" is since the new era of socialism with Chinese characteristics. On the one hand, since the end of the last century, the CPC and the Chinese government have discussed in an increasingly large space the major achievements and historical experiences of reform and opening-up, in the "political reports" of the five-yearly national congresses of the ruling party and the relevant "decisions" and "resolutions" adopted by the plenums of the Central Committee in their sessions, as well as in the "important speeches" of the leaders made publicly on the "fifth and tenth" years of the founding of the Party and the country (including the convening of the Third Plenary Session of the 11th CCCPC or the beginning of the new period of reform and opening-up). The basic guiding principles and ideological and theoretical foundations for the study of the history of reform and opening-up have been established (of course, the scientific understanding of the CPC and the Chinese government on the important discourse on the history of reform and opening-up has also fully absorbed, reflected and embodied the positive exploration results and academic wisdom of the academic community in this field of study). It should be especially noted that since the 18th National Congress of the CPC, the Party Central Committee, with Comrade Xi Jinping at its core, has issued a call to the whole Party and society to strengthen the study and education of the "four histories," namely the history of the Party, the history of New China, the history of reform and opening-up, and the history of socialist development, which has provided a new opportunity and impetus for specialized research on the history of reform and opening-up. On the other hand, during the same period, the academic community, from the perspective of the research law of the history of the CPC and the PRC, and from the perspective of the problem awareness and academic consciousness of speeding up the construction of the "three systems" of the discipline system, academic system and discourse system of philosophy and social science with Chinese characteristics based on the independent knowledge system and the core, also began to gradually and comprehensively and systematically delve into the research field of the history of reform and opening-up, exploring and releasing a large number of high-quality research results, promoting the research of the history of reform and opening-up to gradually become a new main direction, a new field of exploration and an important support point for the research of the history of the CPC and the PRC.

Compared with the "concentric circle" history of the CPC and the PRC, the history of reform and opening-up, as an organic part and an important content, still has a relatively clear and prominent development vein, development laws and phased characteristics of the special history. Its main theme is the reform and opening-up and socialist modernization as well as the exploration and practice of socialism with Chinese characteristics formed on this basis, which has a high ideological consensus and formed the mainstream opinion. It is precisely on this basis that we have divided the history of reform and opening-up for more than 40 years into four historical stages in this research result: first, from 1978 to 1992, which was the period of realizing the great historical transition and creating socialism with Chinese characteristics; second, from 1992 to 2002, which was a period when reform and opening-up entered a new stage and socialism with Chinese characteristics was successfully pushed into the 21st century; third, from 2002 to 2012, which is a period of continuous development of reform and opening-up and adherence to and development of socialism with Chinese characteristics under the new situation; fourth, from 2012 to 2021, which is a period when reform and opening-up has been comprehensively deepened and socialism with Chinese characteristics has entered a new era. This book formed the basic structure and framework of the four chapters, based on the "four-stage theory" of the history of reform and opening-up. The lower limit of the research time of this book is the relatively clear and prominent milestone of the centennial celebration of the founding of the CPC in 2021 and the third "Historical Resolution" of the centennial of the CPC adopted by the Sixth Plenary Session of the 19th CCCPC.

Of course, for the history of reform and opening-up, which, like the history of the CPC and the PRC, has an upper limit but no lower limit, and is still in the nature of "contemporary history" of "ongoing tense," its research cannot avoid the advantages and disadvantages of "contemporary history written by contemporary people." In this regard, we are holding a clear understanding and trying to explore the "strengths and weaknesses." We are well aware that the study of the history of reform and opening-up is a historical study of "vivisection" without distance, without precipitation and solidification, and is a live study of yesterday's "reality," which is today's "history," and today's "reality," which is tomorrow's "history." The basic shape of contemporary Chinese society is still in the process of growing, shaping, and maturing, and some major historical movements, historical events, historical phenomena, and historical influences are still developing and changing, and structural contradictions, regular checks and balances, and essential characteristics have not yet been fully revealed. The study of history is "what is near is fuzzy" and "what is far is clear." Without a "sense of distance," there is no "sense of history." Therefore, the study of the history of reform and opening-up is, and can only be, the pursuit of the relativity of historical truth. It is a process of constantly adjusting the focus, constantly correcting errors, constantly deepening understanding, and gradually approaching and entering the objective truth world.

Therefore, our personal opinion is that the research on the history of reform and opening-up is historical research with a certain "timeliness" and a foundational, cumulative, phased, open and sustainable research to "preserve historical records" for future "long-term" historical research. The study of the history of reform and opening-up must have a relaxed, generous and tolerant academic environment in which we can freely discuss and explore, and we should allow mistakes to be made and corrected. Of course, at the same time, there must be normal and healthy academic criticism and guidance that "do not cover up and do not disguise the wrong." In the same way, this academic exploration achievement also invites the criticism and correction of academic colleagues and readers.

This book is directly derived from the second half of the *History of the PRC*, which was first published in 2009 and revised and reprinted in 2021 by China Renmin University Press. Of course, after comprehensive and systematic rewriting and supplementary writing, I have consciously formed a relatively independent and complete new research system. Its nature is still the compilation of textbooks rather than academic research monographs. In order to make the writing coherent and smooth, the book also follows the "conventions" and "general rules" in the compilation of teaching materials. For the academic research results and research materials absorbed, used and referred to, including basic citations, the source is not indicated one by one, and only are to be fully reflected at the end of the book in references. I hereby express my apology and thanks.

A HISTORY OF THE REFORM AND OPENING UP OF THE PEOPLE'S REPUBLIC OF CHINA (1978–2021)

CHAPTER I

The Great Historical Turn

The Creation of Socialism with Chinese Characteristics (1978–1992)

Reform and opening up is a great awakening of the CPC and a great revolution in the history of the development of the Chinese people and the Chinese nation. It is this great awakening and great revolution that gave birth to the cause of socialism with Chinese characteristics and pushed the Chinese nation to find the right path for its great rejuvenation.

The Central Work Conference of the CPC and the Third Plenary Session of the 11th CCCPC held at the end of 1978 put an end to the two-year passive situation of moving forward in a wandering manner, realized a great turn of far-reaching significance since the founding of New China, and opened a new period of reform and opening-up and socialist modernization. Thus, China entered a brand-new stage of development, gradually creating socialism with Chinese characteristics. In terms of political development, China first gradually completed the historical task of rectifying the chaos, and then created a new situation of building socialist modernization in all aspects, elaborated the theory of the primary stage of socialism, clarified the basic line of the CPC in the primary stage of socialism, and formulated the "three-step" development strategy. In the process, the system of people's congresses was restored and developed, the socialist legal system was strengthened, and the new Constitution formulated in 1982 became the general constitution for governing the country in the new era. The system of CPC-led multiparty cooperation and political consultation, as well as the system of regional ethnic autonomy were consolidated and improved as the basic political system of contemporary China. The unification of China continued to advance, and remarkable achievements were made in religious work. The guiding ideology of national defense construction and the building of the people's army shifted to the track of peace-building; the people's army completed the "Great Disarmament" of one million military personnel; and the people's army moved towards revolutionization, modernization and standardization. In terms of economic development, the national economy was adjusted and restored under the guidance of the new "Eight-Character Policy," and the Sixth Five-Year Plan was completed ahead of schedule. Subsequently, the overheating of the economy was overcome, and a victory was achieved in the rectification of the situation, and the Seventh Five-Year Plan was completed. The five "No. 1 documents" of the Central Government pointed out the direction for the development and the reform of the economic system of the rural areas, which were flourishing. The reform of the urban economic system, with emphasis on State-owned Enterprises (SOEs), was in full swing, and the vitality of SOEs was enhanced. By conducting small-scale pilot programs from Special Economic Zones (SEZs) to open coastal cities and then to open economic zones, a comprehensive pattern of opening up along the coast, along the rivers and inland was formed. In terms of cultural development, the university entrance examination system was fully resumed, the National Science and Technology Conference was successfully convened, and rectification was carried out in the fields of education, science and technology. Subsequently, the reform of the science and technology education system was comprehensively promoted, leading to a flourishing of the cultural sphere. The cultural and ethical progress of the mass, with the "five things to emphasize, four things to beautify and three things to love" as its core, was vigorously carried out, and the promotion of socialist cultural and ethical progress was strengthened. With the boom of the sports and the five consecutive championships in women's volleyball greatly enhanced China's status in the international sports arena, and the breakthrough in China's gold medals at the Olympic Games marked the rebirth of a major sports nation. In terms of social undertakings, with the rapid economic growth and the rapid enhancement of comprehensive national strength, people's living standards were significantly improved, the quality of life was significantly improved, the problem of food and clothing was basically solved, and the country moved towards moderately prosperous society. The social welfare, social assistance and social insurance systems were gradually improved, and a new type of social security system was formed. The agricultural population moved to the secondary and tertiary sectors and urban-rural mobility intensified, which changed the social structure. At the same time, social life and social conducts were gradually changing, and a new system, a new ideology, a new life and a new order were established.

In terms of foreign affairs, China put forward the assertion that "peace and development remain the underlying theme of our times," formed an "independent foreign policy of peace" and achieved a strategic adjustment of foreign policy in the new era; China actively pursued the strategy of major-country diplomacy, normalized China-US and China-Soviet relations, and brought about closer relations with the developed countries of Western Europe, thereby maintaining world peace and promoting common development. China pursued the policy of good-neighborliness, significantly improved relations with neighboring countries, and basically formed a peaceful and friendly neighborhood environment conducive to China's development. Besides, China actively participated in international affairs and played an active role therein, establishing its diplomatic image as a responsible power and significantly improving its international status.

During this period, under the leadership of the CPC, China withstood the severe test of political turmoil and successfully completed the first step of the "three-step" strategy to solve the problem of food and clothing for the people, and steadily progressed towards the second strategic goal.

SECTION I

Initial Practice of Political System Reform and the Building of Socialist Democracy and the Legal System

1.1.1 The Realization of the Great Historical Turnaround and the Beginning of Reform and Opening Up

(1) The Introduction of the "Two Whatevers" and the Criticism of the "Two Whatevers" within the Party
During the special two-year historical development stage of "moving forward while wandering," the chaotic situation in the ideological, political, economic, cultural and social development areas caused by the "Great Cultural Revolution"

was not yet fundamentally reversed and resolved, the "leftist" mistakes were not yet comprehensively cleared up and corrected, and the "leftist" confinement in mind and theory in particular was still very serious; contemporary China needed a great emancipation of mind.

The victory in crushing the Gang of Four put an end to the 10 years of civil strife that had characterized the "Great Cultural Revolution." The CCCPC and the State Council, in response to the actual situation and the demands of the people, led a campaign to expose and criticize the crimes of the Gang of Four, to destroy their gang system and their residual forces, and to restore normal order in the country.

At that time, the world economy was developing rapidly, China was in urgent need of development in many areas, and the people were looking forward to the rise of the country from the crisis. In addition, the deepening of the work of exposing and criticizing the crimes of the Gang of Four and investigating its gang system inevitably touched upon the "leftist" mistakes of the "Great Cultural Revolution," and the cadres and the masses demanded that the "leftist" mistakes of the "Great Cultural Revolution" be seriously summarized and corrected. But the central leadership at that time failed to take up this important historical mission. On February 7, 1977, the *People's Daily*, the *Hongqi* magazine and the *People's Liberation Army (PLA) Daily* published an editorial entitled *Master File to Seize the Key Link*,[1] which put forward the guideline of "we will resolutely uphold whatever policy decisions Chairman Mao made, and unswervingly follow whatever instructions Chairman Mao gave. In theory, the "two whatevers" policy was contrary to the basic principles of Marxism, and in practice it created obstacles to upholding the truth and correcting mistakes in the new situation.

As soon as the policy of "two whatevers" was proposed, it was opposed and resisted by the old generation of proletarian revolutionaries represented by Deng Xiaoping. On April 10, 1977, Deng Xiaoping, who didn't resume his work yet, wrote to the CCCPC, stating his dissenting views on the "two whatevers." He proposed that "from generation to generation, we should use the genuine Mao Zedong Thought taken as an integral whole in guiding our Party, our army and our people." On May 24, in a conversation with Wang Zhen and Deng Liqun, he again pointed out that the "two whatevers" were not in line with Marxism, and that this was an important theoretical issue, a question of whether or not to adhere to historical materialism.

In July, the Third Plenary Session of the 10th CCCPC formally restored Deng Xiaoping to all his posts, which had been withdrawn in 1976. At this meeting, Deng once again stressed the need to understand Mao Zedong Thought completely and accurately, and to learn, master and apply the system of Mao Zedong Thought to guide our work. Only in this way could we not cut and distort Mao Zedong Thought and damage it. He also stressed the need to seek truth from facts, to restore Mao's doctrine of Party building and to carry forward the Party's fine style. Deng Xiaoping's speech was a powerful criticism of the "two whatevers" and a great impetus to the restoration and development of the CPC's mass line and the fine style of seeking truth from facts, to the emancipation of the mind, and to the realization of the rectification of the ideological line.

From August 12 to 18, 1977, the 11th National Congress of the CPC was held in Beijing. The Congress summarized the historical experience of the CPC and the Chinese people in their struggle against the Gang of Four, declared the end of the "Great Cultural Revolution," and reaffirmed the fundamental task of building China into a modern socialist power in the 20th century. On August 19, the Congress elected Hua Guofeng as Chairman of the Central Committee, and Ye Jianying, Deng Xiaoping, Li Xiannian and Wang Dongxing as Vice-Chairmen. However, due to the influence of "left" ideology, the congress failed to thoroughly correct the mistakes of the "Great Cultural Revolution" and continued to affirm the "theory of continuing revolution under the dictatorship of the proletariat." As a result, there were still many practical obstacles to breaking through the confines of the "two whatevers."

After the 11th Congress of the CPC, the old proletarian revolutionaries published articles and talks on the CPC's fine style of "seeking truth from facts" and criticized the erroneous policy of "two whatevers." In September, the *People's Daily* published Nie Rongzhen's *Revive and Pass on the Fine Conduct of our Party*, Xu Qianqian's "Always Adhere to the Principle of the Party Commanding the Gun," Chen Yun's "Adhere to the Revolutionary Style of Seeking Truth from Facts" and other articles. These articles expounded the importance of seeking truth from facts from different perspectives, forcefully criticized the "two whatevers" policy, and promoted the rectification of the ideological line. The First Session of the Fifth National People's Congress (NPC) held in February and March 1978 elected Ye Jianying as the Chairman of the Standing Committee of the NPC, and the First Session of the Fifth National Committee of the Chinese People's

Political Consultative Conference (CPPCC) elected Deng Xiaoping as Chairman of the CPPCC. The resumption of normal work by the NPC and the CPPCC played an important role in the normalization of China's political life.

(2) A Major Debate about the Criterion for Testing Truth

The theorists drafted an article on the issue of the criterion for testing truth in response to the policy of "two whatevers," and after repeated revisions, it was finally reviewed and finalized by Hu Yaobang, who was currently the vice-president of the Party School of the CCCPC. On May 10, 1978, the in-house journal of the Party School of the CCCPC, *Theoretical Trends*, No. 60, published the article "Practice is the Sole Criterion for Testing Truth." On May 11, *Guangming Daily* published the article as a special commentator, and Xinhua News Agency forwarded it in full. The following day, the *People's Daily* and the *People's Liberation Army Daily* reprinted the article in full. Subsequently, most provincial (regions and municipalities) Party newspapers across the country also reposted one after another. The article pointed out that the test of truth could only be social practice; the unity of theory and practice was one of the most fundamental principles of Marxism; the theoretical treasury of Marxism was not a pile of rigid and unchanging dogma, we needed to add new views and new conclusions to it constantly in practice, discard those old views and conclusions that were not suitable for the new situation; the spiritual shackles imposed on people by the Gang of Four must be broken. The article called on people to dare to challenge the ideological and theoretical no-go areas set by the Gang of Four, to clarify the rights and wrongs on major issues based on the Marxist principle that practice was the sole criterion for testing truth, and achieve a great emancipation of the mind.

The article was a fundamental theoretical rejection of the "two-whatevers" policy, which caused a huge reaction throughout the Party and the country, and in fact became the fuse for the debate about the criterion for testing truth. However, the discussion was suppressed from the very beginning. This brought enormous pressure on the discussion of the criteria for testing truth.

At this critical moment, Deng Xiaoping gave timely and clear support to the discussion. On June 2, 1978, he pointed out at an all-army conference on political work that seeking truth from facts was the starting point and fundamental point of Mao Zedong Thought, and focused on the important position of seeking truth from facts in Mao Zedong Thought and how to correctly treat Marxism-Leninism and Mao Zedong Thought. In response to the remarks and practices that suppressed the debate about the criterion for testing truth, he sharply criticized and called on the whole Party and army to purge the poison of Lin Biao and the Gang of Four, to set things right, to break the mental shackles and to bring about a great liberation of the mind. His speech was a strong support for the debate about the criterion for testing truth.

On June 24, with the support and guidance of Luo Ruiqing, Secretary general of the Central Military Commission (CMC) of CPC, the *PLA Daily* published an article entitled "*One of the Most Fundamental Principles of Marxism*" as a special commentator, further clarifying the basic Marxist view that practice was the sole criterion for testing truth, answering in a targeted manner the questions that had aroused controversy during the discussion, and promoting the debate about the criterion for testing truth.

Deng Xiaoping, Ye Jianying, Chen Yun, Li Xiannian, Hu Yaobang, Nie Rongzhen, Xu Xianqian, Luo Ruiqing, Tan Zhenlin and a number of other comrades all took a positive attitude towards this discussion. They spoke on various occasions, stressing the importance of seeking truth from facts, restoring the fine traditions of the CPC, overcoming the "leftist" mistakes that still exist, and promoting the rectification of the situation.

This extensive discussion on the criterion for testing truth, which had started in the theoretical circles and flourished in the press, gradually evolved into another nationwide ideological liberation movement. In the second half of 1978, the headquarters of various departments of the central Party and government organs and provinces and equivalent administrative units, as well as the headquarters of the PLA and the major military regions, and a large number of theoretical workers, published articles or talks, publicly expressing their support for the extensive discussion. Meanwhile, propaganda departments and Party schools around the country held seminars or training courses to participate in this extensive discussion, which gave a strong impetus to the deepening of this ideological liberation movement.

The extensive discussion on the criterion for testing truth was a profound Marxist education and ideological liberation movement. This extensive discussion not only thoroughly liquidated the theoretical and ideological pseudo-Marxist heresies of Lin Biao and the Gang of Four, but also broke the ideological fence of the "two whatevers" and re-established the basic Marxist principle that practice was the sole criterion for people to know the truth, pursue the truth and test the truth, which freed people from the bondage of cult of the individual and superstition, promoted the restoration of the Marxist line of thought of seeking truth from facts, and made the necessary ideological and theoretical preparations for the Third Plenary Session of the 11th CCCPC to realize the great turnaround of far-reaching significance in the history of the CPC, which had been in power since the founding of New China, and in the history of contemporary China.

(3) Central Work Conferences with Far-Reaching Implications

In December 1978, the CCCPC prepared to convene the Third Plenary Session of the 11th CCCPC. Prior to this session, the CCCPC held a 36-day Central Work Conference from November 10 to December 15 to prepare for the session. The conference first discussed the issue of shifting the focus of work of the ruling CPC and contemporary China to socialist modernization and construction. This issue was first raised by Deng Xiaoping during his visit to the three northeastern provinces in September 1978. He pointed out that China was a socialist country and that the fundamental manifestation of the superiority of the socialist system was that it allowed the social productive forces to develop rapidly at a rate not seen in the old society, so that the growing material and cultural needs of the people could be gradually met. Deng Xiaoping's opinion was endorsed by the Standing Committee of the Political Bureau of the CCCPC and was presented to the Central Work Conference as the collective opinion of the Standing Committee. During the discussion at the conference, Chen Yun and other old proletarian revolutionaries proposed that, in order to realize the shift of the focus of work, it was necessary to solve some of the major political events that had occurred during the "Great Cultural Revolution" and some of the major historical problems left behind before the "Great Cultural Revolution," which were of concern both inside and outside the Party. Based on the discussions at the meeting and the views of most of the comrades attending the conference, and after study by the Standing Committee of the Central Political Bureau, on November 25, Hua Guofeng announced on behalf of the Central Political Bureau that the CCCPC decided to vindicate several major cases in which the charges were false or which were unjustly or incorrectly dealt with, such as "Tiananmen Incident," "criticizing Deng and countering the Rightist Reversal Wind," "the February Reversal," "Bo Yibo and other 61 traitors group case," as well as the cases of Peng Dehuai, Tao Casting, Yang Shangkun and other people.

At the Central Work Conference, the comrades also discussed and made many proposals on a series of pressing issues, such as the guiding principle of shifting work priorities, rural policies, reform of the economic management system, the rush to success in economic work, the building of the ruling party and the building of democracy and the legal system in the country.

On December 13, Deng Xiaoping made an important speech entitled "Emancipate the Mind, Seek Truth from Facts and Unite Moving Forward in Unity." He first emphasized the importance of emancipating the mind, pointing out that emancipation of the mind was a major political issue at the present time and that in order to carry out the four modernizations, as in the case of the revolution in the past, it was necessary to rely on seeking truth from facts. At that time, in order to restore the tradition of seeking truth from facts, it was necessary to emancipate the mind and overcome the rigid state of thought that still seriously exists. He spoke highly of the significance of the discussions on the criterion for testing the truth, pointing out that it was indeed a political question of ideological line, and a question that concerned the future and fate of the Party and the country. Secondly, he elaborated that the implementation of democratic centralism was an important condition for the emancipation of the mind and suggested that now there was a special need to emphasize democracy to allow people to speak out and to trust that the vast majority of the masses had the ability to judge right and wrong. He also pointed out that in order to safeguard people's democracy, it was necessary to strengthen the rule of law and institutionalize and legalize democracy so that such a system and laws would not change with a change in leadership or with a change in the views and attention of leaders. What's more, he emphasized the need to deal with the problems left over from history, to distinguish clearly between the merits and demerits of some persons, and remedies have been made for a number of major cases in which the charges were false or the cases were unjustly or incorrectly dealt with. This lies in the aim of looking ahead, which is necessary for the emancipation of the mind, for stability and unity, and for the smooth shift in the focus of the Party's work.

Finally, he proposed to study new situations and solve new problems. He pointed out that new situations in all areas should be studied and new problems in all areas should be solved, with particular attention to studying and solving problems in the three areas of management methods, management systems and economic policies. He also proposed a "major policy" that would allow some regions and enterprises and some workers and peasants to earn more and enjoy more benefits sooner than others, in accordance with their hard work and greater contributions to society. He also proposed that the four modernizations represent a great and profound revolution in which we are moving forward by resolving one new contradiction after another. Therefore, all Party comrades must learn well and always keep on learning.

The speech not only raised and answered a series of fundamental questions facing the ruling CPC and contemporary China at a turning point in history, clarified the main tasks of the CPC in the future and the way forward, but also set the guidelines for the forthcoming Third Plenary Session of the 11th CCCPC, and in fact became the theme report of the conference and the manifesto for opening up a new road in a new period and creating a theory of building socialism with Chinese characteristics.

On December 15, the Central Work Conference ended. Thanks to the impetus of the old generation of proletarian revolutionaries and the joint efforts of the majority of the cadres present, the conference was freed from the shackles of the "two-whatevers" policy and turned a meeting originally intended for discussing economic work into a meeting for setting things right and breaking new ground.

(4) Achieving a Historic and Great Turnaround

From December 18 to 22, 1978, the Third Plenary Session of the 11th CCCPC was held in Beijing. The session discussed and adopted the proposal of the Political Bureau of the Central Committee to shift the focus of Party-wide work to socialist modernization from 1979 onwards, reviewed and adopted two documents on agricultural issues, the arrangements for the national economic plan for 1979 and 1980, and discussed personnel issues and established the Central Commission for Discipline Inspection (CCDI) through election.

The session re-established the ideological line of emancipating the mind and seeking truth from facts. What's more, the session thoroughly rejected the "two-whatevers" policy and clearly pointed out that Mao Zedong must be evaluated historically and scientifically and that the scientific system of Mao Zedong's thought must be grasped completely and accurately; it highly valued the far-reaching significance of the extensive discussion on the criterion for testing truth in emancipating the mind and correcting the line of thought; it stressed that only by emancipating the mind and adhering to the principles of seeking truth from facts, proceeding from reality in

everything and integrating theory with practice could the focus of work be successfully shifted.

The session made the strategic decision to shift the focus of the work of the Party and the country to socialist modernization, thus achieved rectification to restore order in the political line. The session called for the cessation of the slogan "taking class struggle as the key link "and made the decision to shift the focus of the Party's work to economic construction, thus realizing the strategic change of the CPC and contemporary China from "class struggle as the platform" to economic construction as the center. The strategic shift from "taking class struggle as the key link" to economic construction as the focus of the CPC and contemporary China was thus achieved, solving the long-standing problem of the strategic shift of the focus of work after the establishment of the basic social system.

The session made the great decision to implement reform and opening-up. The session held that the realization of the four modernizations required a substantial increase in the productive forces, which inevitably required a multifaceted change in the relations of production and the superstructure that were incompatible with the development of the productive forces and a change in all incompatible modes of management, activities and ways of thinking, so it can be seen that the reform was an extensive and profound revolution; it was proposed that the task of reforming the economic system and the political system that went with it should be accomplished, and the problem of the Party's lack of separation between the government and enterprises, the substitution of the Party for the government, and the substitution of the government for the enterprises should be seriously resolved; it was proposed that on the basis of self-reliance, we should actively develop equal and mutually beneficial economic cooperation with other countries in the world, and strive to adopt advanced technology and equipment from all over the world. It was also proposed that the guiding ideology of economic work should be corrected, the economic laws should be followed, and the role of the law of value should be emphasized. In the session, it was pointed out in a pragmatic manner the backwardness of Chinese agriculture, and policy and economic measures were proposed to speed up agricultural development, thus effectively launching rural reform.

The session reviewed and resolved a number of major issues left over from history and the merits and demerits of some important leaders. The session discussed and resolved some of the major political events that had occurred during the "Great Cultural Revolution" and the issues had left over from history before it, thus beginning the process of vindicating all unjust and false cases and comprehensively cleaning up and thoroughly resolving the controversies on major issues in history before and during "Great Cultural Revolution." The session also made a series of decisions to strengthen socialist democracy and the legal system. In order to safeguard people's democracy, it was necessary to strengthen the socialist legal system, institutionalize democracy and make it legal, ensure that there were laws to go by, the laws were observed and strictly enforced, and law-breakers were prosecuted, and ensure that all citizens are equal before the law and that no one was allowed to have privileges beyond the law.

The session achieved a reversal of the organizational line. The session decided to strengthen the Party's leadership institution, to improve the Party's democratic centralism, to improve Party rules and regulations, and to take Party discipline seriously, with particular emphasis on the collective leadership of the Party Central Committee and Party committees at all levels. It decided to set up the CCCPC for Discipline Inspection and elected Chen Yun as its first secretary. At this point, Deng Xiaoping became the actual core of the CCCPC leadership group in terms of embodying the correct guiding ideology of the ruling party and deciding on the major guidelines and policies of modernization.

The Third Plenary Session of the 11th CCCPC was a great turnaround of far-reaching significance in the history of the CPC since the founding of New China. The triumphal convening of the conference meant that the CPC had fundamentally broken the fetters of the "leftist" error and marked the end of the situation of "moving forward while wandering" since the Gang of Four had been crushed in 1976. The session re-established the ideological, political and organizational lines of Marxism and made the great decisions to shift the focus of work to socialist modernization and to implement reform and opening-up, which became the historical starting point for the great march of reform and opening-up and socialist modernization and the opening up of the great cause of socialism with Chinese characteristics.

After the Third Plenary Session of the 11th CCCPC, in the course of the ruling party's internal and external efforts to study new situations and solve new problems, some noteworthy phenomena emerged. On the one hand, some people were influenced by the "leftist" ideology and did not understand or even resisted the line, guidelines and policies of the ruling party since the Third Plenary Session of the 11th CCCPC; on the other hand, some people with ulterior motives took advantage of the time when the "leftist" mistakes were being corrected to doubt and deny the leadership of the ruling CPC and oppose the socialist system, Mao

Zedong Thought and the people's democratic dictatorship under the banner of "ideological liberation" and "democracy and freedom," and there were very few people in the ruling party who echoed them. If this situation was allowed to develop, it would inevitably lead to new ideological confusion and affect the stability and unity of the situation. In view of this, from January to April 1979, the CCCPC held a meeting on theoretical matters in Beijing to further sum up the lessons learned on the ideological and propaganda fronts and to study the fundamental tasks of theoretical propaganda work after the shift of work priorities. On March 30, Deng Xiaoping made an important speech entitled "Adhering to the Four Cardinal Principles," in which he raised the issue of adhering to the Four Cardinal Principles for the first time. He proposed that in order to realize the four modernizations in China, it was necessary to keep to the socialist road and to uphold the people's democratic dictatorship, leadership by the CPC, and Marxism-Leninism and Mao Zedong Thought. While criticizing the "leftist" erroneous ideas, he also criticized the wrong trend of denying the four cardinal principles from the right, forcefully refuted certain views advocating bourgeois liberalization at that time, clarified some ambiguous understandings in ideology and theory, and played an important guiding role in the rectification of guiding ideology.

The decision of the Third Plenary Session of the 11th CCCPC and the proposition of adhering to the four cardinal principles laid the foundation for the basic line of the CPC at the primary stage of socialism.

(5) Injustice Redressed, Order Restored

After the Third Plenary Session of the 11th CCCPC, the CCCPC, the State Council and Party and government organs at all levels, in accordance with the principle of seeking truth from facts and correcting any mistakes, had comprehensively vindicated the wrongful cases during the "Great Cultural Revolution" and since the founding of New China, and have properly resolved the problems left over from history.

The redress of unjust, false, and erroneous cases was mainly focused on the following aspects: the first was the public vindication and rehabilitation of some leaders of the Party, the State and the army who had been falsely accused or wrongly treated before and during the "Great Cultural Revolution," such as Peng Dehuai, He Long, Qu Qubai and Liu Shaoqi; the second was the vindication and rehabilitation of some departments that had been wrongly criticized or falsely accused during the "Great Cultural Revolution," such as the International Department of the CCCPC, the Publicity Department of the CCCPC, the United Front Work Department of CCCPC, the Ministry of Culture, the Ministry of Education and the General Political Department of the PLA; the third was the review and vindication of the wrongful cases that had occurred all over the country during the "Great Cultural Revolution;" the fourth was the review and rehabilitation the of wrongly classified counter-revolutionary incidents and criminal cases during the "Great Cultural Revolution" or to change their sentences; the fifth was the cleaning up and correction of the wrongful cases that had occurred before the "Great Cultural Revolution," such as the mistake of expanding the anti-Rightist struggle in 1957 and the mistakes made in the 1959 "anti-Rightist" political movement. By the end of 1982, the work of vindicating wrongful cases had basically been completed, wrongful cases involving 3 million cadres had been corrected, 470,000 Party members had been restored to Party membership, and tens of millions of cadres and people implicated in various wrongful cases had been freed.

At the same time, the CCCPC and the Chinese Government also adjusted social relations in many ways. In January 1979, the CCCPC issued the *Decision on the Question of Removing the Hats of Landlords and Rich Peasants and on the Composition of the Children of the Land and the Rich*. Subsequently, it forwarded the *on the issue of distinguishing workers from former industrialists and businessmen* of six departments including United Front Work Department of CPCC Central Committee, and promulgated the *Regulations of the CPC on Certain Specific Policies for Former Industrialists and Businessmen*, solved a series of problems left over from the past, and further implemented the ruling Party's various policies. By 1981, 700,000 people had regained their status as workers. This had a tremendous impact on the effective mobilization of all sectors of society, the consolidation and development of the united front under the leadership of the ruling CPC, and the mobilization of the entire Party and the entire nation to work with one heart and one mind for socialist modernization.

In order to fundamentally correct the "leftist" mistakes, the CCCPC considered it necessary to make a scientific summary of the history since the founding of New China and to make a correct evaluation of Mao Zedong and Mao Zedong Thought. In September 1979, Ye Jianying delivered a speech at a conference to celebrate the 30th anniversary of the founding of the PRC, in which he affirmed the achievements of New China in the past 30 years, made a preliminary analysis of the causes of the "Great Cultural Revolution" and its previous "left" mistakes, and summarized the main lessons of the "Great Cultural Revolution." It laid the foundation for the Party to correctly sum up its historical experience, especially to clarify some major issues of right and wrong since the founding of New China.

In November 1979, in accordance with the decision of the Fourth Plenary Session of the 11th CCCPC and under the chairmanship of Deng Xiaoping and Hu Yaobang, the CCCPC proceeded to draft the *Resolution on Certain Questions in the History of Our Party since the Founding of the PRC (Resolution)*. Deng Xiaoping, Chen Yun, Hu Yaobang and others devoted great efforts to the drafting of the *Resolution*, and after more than a year of drafting, discussion and repeated revisions, their views were gradually unified. On this basis, in June 1981, the Sixth Plenary Session of the 11th CCCPC considered and adopted the *Resolution on Certain Questions in the History of Our Party since the Founding of the PRC*.

The *Resolution* gave a correct summary of the major historical events since the founding of New China, especially the "Great Cultural Revolution." That is, while affirming the historic achievements of the socialist revolution and construction, it fundamentally rejected the "theory of continuing revolution under the dictatorship of the proletariat" and pointed out that the "Great Cultural Revolution" was a civil strife which was wrongly started by the leaders and exploited by the counter-revolutionary groups, and which brought untold sufferings to the Party, the country and the people of all ethnic groups; it also analyzed the subjective factors and social reasons for the mistakes. The *Resolution* evaluated the historical status of Mao Zedong in a factual manner and fully expounded the basic meaning, main content and guiding significance of Mao Zedong Thought. The *Resolution* pointed out that Mao Zedong was a great Marxist, a great proletarian revolutionary, strategist and theoretician. From the perspective of his life, his merits for the Chinese revolution far outweigh his faults. His merits were the first and his mistakes the second. Mao Zedong Thought was the application and development of Marxism-Leninism in China, the correct theoretical principles and summaries of experience on the Chinese revolution that had been proved in practice, the crystallization of the collective wisdom of the CPC. Mao Zedong Thought was the valuable spiritual wealth of our Party, and it would guide our actions for a long time. We must continue to adhere to Mao Zedong Thought and enrich and develop it with new principles and conclusions that were in line with reality. The *Resolution* affirmed the correct path of socialist modernization that has been gradually established since the Third Plenary Session of the 11th CCCPC, which was suitable for China's conditions, and made a summary of path from ten aspects, and put forward for the first time that "our socialist system is still at a primary stage" and that "the socialist system has to go through a long process from relatively imperfect to relatively perfect."[2] The adoption of the *Resolution* was of great significance in unifying the thinking of the Party and the people of China, maintaining the unity of the Party and the people of China and opening up the road to socialism with Chinese characteristics, and pointed the way to the healthy development of the Chinese socialist cause. The adoption of the *Resolution* marked the successful completion of the task of setting things right in terms of the guiding ideology of the CPC.

According to the recommendation of the Political Bureau of the CCCPC, this session also adjusted the main leading members of the CCCPC. Hua Guofeng resigned as Chairman of the CCCPC and Chairman of the CMC, and the session elected Hu Yaobang as Chairman of the Central Committee, re-elected Hua Guofeng, co-opted Zhao Ziyang as Vice Chairman of the Central Committee, and Deng Xiaoping as Chairman of the CMC. The Standing Committee of the Political Bureau of the CCCPC was composed of Hu Yaobang, Ye Jianying, Deng Xiaoping, Zhao Ziyang, Li Xiannian, Chen Yun and Hua Guofeng, and Xi Zhongxun was co-opted as the secretary of the Central Committee.

1.1.2 From the 12th to the 13th National Congress of the CPC

(1) The 12th National Congress of the CPC and "Building Socialism with Chinese Characteristics"

On September 1st to 11th, 1982, the 12th National Congress of the CPC was convened in Beijing. The Congress was attended by 1,545 official delegates and 145 alternate delegates, representing over 39 million members of the Party. The main agenda of the Congress was to consider the political report presented by the 11th Central Committee, to formulate a programme for the CPC in its endeavors to comprehensively initiate a new situation in socialist modernization, to adopt a new CPC Constitution, and to conduct elect ions for new central leadiership.

Deng Xiaoping presided over the opening ceremony of the Congress and delivered an opening speech, clarifying the historical status and tasks of the 12th National Congress of the CPC, and put forward the major proposition of integrateing the universal truth of Marxism with the concrete realities of China, "blazing a path of our own and building a socialism with Chinese characteristics."[3] This major proposition answered the important question of what direction to take and what road to take in reforming and opening up China. Since then, socialism with Chinese characteristics has become the theme of all the theories and practices of the CPC. He also put forward three major historical tasks facing the Chinese people in the 1980s: to intensify socialist modernization; to strive for the reunification of the motherland, including Taiwan; and to oppose hegemonism and safeguard world peace.

Hu Yaobang made a report entitled "Create a New Situation in All Fields of Socialist Modernization," setting forth the general task of the CPC in the new period: to unite the people of all ethnic groups, to be self-reliant and to struggle hard, to gradually modernize industry, agriculture, national defense and science and technology, and to build China into a highly civilized and democratic socialist country. The report put forward a programme of action to opened up new horizons for socialist modernization across in all fields, set goals and major policies for the end of the 20th century, called for a quadrupling of the country's gross industrial and agricultural output in the 20 years from 1981 to the end of the 20th century, and stressed a number of matters to which attention should be paid.

The Congress emphasized that, while promoting comprehensive economic development and building a high level of socialist material civilization, efforts must be made to build a high level of socialist cultural and ethical progress. A high level of socialist cultural and ethical progress was an important feature of socialism and an important manifestation of the superiority of the socialist system. The building of both socialist material civilizations and cultural and ethical progress was ensured and supported by the continued development of socialist democracy. Building a high level of socialist democracy was one of the fundamental goals and tasks of the ruling CPC and contemporary China. The building of socialist democracy must also be closely integrated with the building of the socialist legal system, so as to institutionalize and legalize socialist democracy.

The Congress decided to carry out a comprehensive rectification of the Party's style and organization in a planned and step-by-step manner from the second half of 1983, with the aim of achieving a fundamental improvement in Party discipline.

The Congress elected the 12th Central Committee, the Central Commission for Discipline Inspection and the Central Advisory Commission of the CPC.

The 12th National Congress of the CPC also adopted a new CPC Constitution, which included the general tasks of the CPC in the new period in its "General Principles" and served as a guideline for socialist modernization. The new CPC Constitution imposed stricter ideological, political and organizational requirements on Party members and Party cadres than those stipulated in previous CPC Constitutions, emphasizing that organizations at all levels, from the central to the local levels, must strictly abide by the principles of democratic centralism and collective leadership, stipulating that there should be no chairman of the CCCPC but only a general secretary, and that Advisory Commissions should be set up at the central and provincial levels as transitional bodies for the transition of old and new cadres, so as to give full play to the contribution of experienced veterans who had retired from the front line to the party's cause.

The First Plenary Session of the 12th CCCPC elected Hu Yaobang, Ye Jianying, Deng Xiaoping, Zhao Ziyang, Li Xiannian and Chen Yun as members of the Standing Committee of the Central Political Bureau, with Hu Yaobang as General Secretary of the Central Committee; decided that Deng Xiaoping would be Chairman of the CMC; approved Deng Xiaoping as Chairman of the Central Advisory Committee; and approved Chen Yun as First Secretary of the CCDI of the CPC.

In June 1983, the First Session of the Sixth NPC adopted elected Li Xiannian as President, Peng Zhen as Chairman of the Standing Committee of the NPC, and Deng Xiaoping as Chairman of the CMC.

The convening of the 12th National Congress of CPC marked the opening of a new era of comprehensive socialist modernization.

(2) The 13th National Congress of the CPC and the Basic Line for the Primary Stage of Socialism

From October 25 to November 1, 1987, the 13th National Congress of the CPC was held in Beijing. There were 1,936 official delegates and 61 specially invited delegates, representing more than 46 million Party members. The Congress approved the political report made by Zhao Ziyang on behalf of the 12th CCCPC and amended some articles of the Party Constitution.

The Congress expounded the theory of the primary stage of socialism and clarified the basic line of the CPC in the primary stage of socialism. The Congress pointed out that China was then in the primary stage of socialism. The basic meaning of the primary stage of socialism in China was: firstly, Chinese society was already a socialist society, and we must adhere to it and not leave it; secondly, Chinese socialist society was still in its primary stage, and we must proceed from this reality and not go beyond it. The two main characteristics of China's primary stage of socialism were: first, the socialist economic system based on public ownership of the means of production, the socialist political system of the people's democratic dictatorship and the Marxism as a guiding ideology were established, the system of exploitation and the exploiting classes died out, the country's economic strength grown tremendously, and there was considerable development in education, science and culture; second, with a huge population and a weak economy, the per capita gross national product was still among the lowest in the world.

The Congress formulated the basic line of the CPC at the primary stage of socialism: to lead and unite the people of all ethnic groups, to focus on economic construction, to adhere to the Four Cardinal Principles, to adhere to reform and opening-up, to be self-reliant, hardworking, and enterprising, and strive to build China into a modern socialist country that was prosperous, strong, democratic, culturally advanced. This basic guideline was summarized as "one center task, two basic points," which meant to keep economic development as our central task, uphold the Four Cardinal Principles and reform and opening-up. The Congress also clarified the guidelines for building socialism in China: first, we must focus on developing the productivity to carry out modernization; second, we must insist on comprehensive reform and make reform the driving force for all work; third, we must insist on opening up to the outside world, strive to absorb all the fruits of civilization in the world and gradually narrow the gap with the developed countries; fourth, we must insist on public ownership as the mainstay and develop a planned commodity economy; fifth, we must take stability and unity as the premise and strive to build democratic politics; sixth, we must take Marxism as the guide and strive to promote cultural and ethical progress. The theory of the primary stage of socialism is a summary of the experience of the CPC in carrying out the socialist revolution and construction, and is a major contribution by the Chinese Communists to the scientific theory of socialism.

The Congress proposed a Three-Step Strategy for Economic Development. The first step was to double the 1980 Gross National Product (GNP) to ensure the people have adequate food and clothing, which was basically achieved. The second step was to quadruple the 1980 GNP by the end of the 20th century to ensure the people live a relatively comfortable life. The third step was to increase the per capita GNP to the level of moderately developed countries by the mid-21st century to ensure the people live a well-off life and basically achieve modernization.

The Congress pointed out that, since the founding of the CPC, two historic leaps had been made in the process of combining Marxism with Chinese reality.

The first leap was made during the period of the new-democratic revolution, when a revolutionary road with Chinese characteristics was found and the revolution was led to victory; the second leap was made after the Third Plenary Session of the 11th CCCPC, when the Chinese Communists began to find a road for building socialism with Chinese characteristics on the basis of a summary of both positive and negative experiences over the 30 years since the founding of New China. The Congress generalized the outline of the theory of building socialism with Chinese characteristics and gave preliminary answers to such basic questions as the stages, tasks, dynamics, conditions, layout and international environment of socialist construction in China.[4]

The Congress elected the 13th Central Committee, the Central Commission for Discipline Inspection and the Central Advisory Committee.

On November 2, 1987, the First Plenary Session of the 13th CCCPC elected Zhao Ziyang, Li Peng, Qiao Shi, Hu Qili and Yao Yilin as members of the Standing Committee of the Political Bureau, with Zhao Ziyang as general secretary of the Central Committee; decided that Deng Xiaoping would be Chairman of the CMC, Zhao Ziyang as First Vice-Chairman and Yang Shangkun as Executive Vice-Chairman; approved Chen Yun as Chairman of the Central Advisory Commission of the CPC, Bo Yibo and Song Renqiong as Vice-Chairmen; approved Qiao Shi as Secretary of the CCDI of the CPC.

After the 13th National Congress of the CPC, Deng Xiaoping no longer held the position of member of the Standing Committee of the Political Bureau. However, he still followed the cause of reform, opening up and socialist modernization with a high sense of responsibility and mission, and continued to play an extremely important role.

(3) The Tests of Political Turbulences and the Formation of the New Central Leadership

The end of the 1980s was an "eventful period" at both the international and domestic levels. At the international level, anti-socialist forces were rampant, the interference of foreign hostile forces in socialist China did not stop for a moment, some communist countries in Eastern Europe were facing different degrees of crisis in power, and social upheavals occurred one after another; at the domestic level, there were also phenomena of improper Party conduct, corruption of cadres and deterioration of social conduct in political life, and there were outstanding problems such as price rises, market fluctuations, economic disorder and difficulties in governance and rectification in the economic sphere. Some bourgeois liberals took advantage of the opportunity to launch a wave of opposition to the Four Cardinal Principles, advocating political pluralism, "total westernization" and the capitalist road, which eventually led to a political turbulence. The Political Bureau of the CCCPC, with the support of Deng Xiaoping and other revolutionaries of the old generation, relied on the people to quell the turbulence.

After the turbulence, the question of where China was going became the focus of international and domestic attention. On June 9, 1989, when Deng Xiaoping met with the officers at the rank of general and above in command of the troops enforcing martial law in Beijing, he pointed out "that the line, guidelines and policies formulated by the Third Plenary Session of the 11th CCCPC, including the 'trilogy' of our development strategy, were they correct or not? Was it because of this turbulence that the correctness of the line, guidelines and policies we have formulated has come into question? Was our goal a 'leftist' one? Should we continue to use it as the goal of our future struggle? It should be said that the strategic goal we have set cannot be said to be a failure at least for the time being." He stressed that "if the 'one center task, two basic points' outlined by the 13th National Congress of the CPC was correct? Are the Two Basic Points, that is, the upholding of four principles and reform and opening-up, wrong? We are not wrong." He asked that "what should we do in the future? He thought that we should continue with the basic lines, guidelines and policies that we had originally formulated, and we should continue to do so unswervingly. Except for some changes in expression, the basic line and the basic guidelines and policies will remain unchanged."

From June 23 to 24, the Fourth Plenary Session of the 13th CCCPC was held in Beijing. The Plenary Session analyzed the nature and causes of the political turbulences that had taken place at home and abroad in the past two months, affirmed the decisions and major measures taken by the Party Central Committee in this serious political struggle, preliminary summarized the lessons learned and clarified the guidelines and tasks for the work of the CPC for the current and future period.

The Plenary Session elected Jiang Zemin as general secretary of the Central Committee; Jiang Zemin, Song Ping and Li Ruihuan were co-opted to the Standing Committee of the Central Political Bureau, and the Standing Committee of the Political Bureau was composed of Jiang Zemin, Li Peng, Qiao Shi, Yao Yilin, Song Ping and Li Ruihuan.

After the Fourth Plenary Session of the 13th CCCPC, the Chinese Communists, mainly represented by comrade Jiang Zemin, worked effectively and the domestic political situation stabilized, in which case Deng Xiaoping decided to resign from his then post while he was still in good health and hoped that this decision would be adopted at the Fifth Plenary Session. On September 4, 1989, Deng Xiaoping sent a letter to the Political Bureau of the CCCPC requesting the Central Committee to approve his resignation as chairman of the CMC of the CPC and indicating that he would also submit a request to the NPC to resign as chairman of the State Military Commission. On November 9, 1989, the Fifth Plenary Session of the 13th CCCPC adopted the *Decision on Agreeing to Comrade Deng Xiaoping's Resignation as Chairman of the CMC of the CCCPC* and confirmed Jiang Zemin as Chairman of the CMC. In March 1990, the Third Session of the Seventh NPC accepted Deng Xiaoping's request to resign as Chairman of the State Military Commission and elected Jiang Zemin as Chairman of the CMC.

After the Fourth and Fifth Plenary Sessions of the 13th CCCPC, the leadership of the CCCPC was smoothly handed over in a systematic and orderly manner, which was of great significance in ensuring the stability and continuity of the policies of the Party and the State and in achieving long-term national security; it also provided an important political and organizational guarantee for eliminating serious consequences of the political turbulences as soon as possible and pushing the socialist cause with Chinese characteristics into the 21st century. It was also a testimony to the high degree of political maturity and organizational strength of the CPC and a great achievement in the construction of socialist democracy and the reform of the political system in China.

1.1.3 Restoration and Development of the Basic Political System

(1) Restoration and Improvement of the Multi-Party Cooperation and Political Consultation System under the Leadership of the CPC

After the Third Plenary Session of the 11th CCCPC, the ruling CPC and the Chinese Government restored and improved the system of multi-party cooperation and political consultation and the system of regional ethnic autonomy under the leadership of the CPC, implemented the policy on overseas Chinese affairs and resumed work on overseas Chinese affairs, implemented the policy on religion and resumed work on religion, strengthened work on Taiwan, Hong Kong and Macao, and put forward the scientific concept of "One Country, Two Systems." The scientific concept of "One Country, Two Systems" and the basic State policy were put forward.

The multi-party cooperation and political consultation system under the leadership of the CPC is the basic political system of contemporary China, which was severely damaged during the "Great Cultural Revolution" and needs to be restored and strengthened urgently.

In October 1979, the Revolutionary Committee of the Chinese Kuomintang (KMT), the China Democratic League, the China National Democratic Construction Association, the China Association for the Promotion of Democracy, the China Peasants' and Workers' Democratic Party, the China Zhi Gong Party, the Jiu San Society, the Taiwan Democratic Self-Government League and other democratic parties and the All-China Federation of Industry and Commerce (ACFIC) held their national congresses to determine their future policies, tasks and organizational development, to amend their constitutions and to elect their respective The central leadership bodies were elected. On October 12, the CCCPC forwarded to the Organization Department and the United Front Work Department of the Central Committee the *Report on the Arrangement of Non-Party Personnel in Leadership Positions in Ministries and Commissions of the State Council and in Local People's Governments at All Levels*, emphasizing the need to overcome the "one-size-fits-all" mentality and to do a good job of arranging leadership positions for non-party members.

From December 1981 to January 1982, the CCCPC convened a national conference on united front work, calling for the democratic parties to be allowed to carry out their work independently and autonomously and to give full play to their initiative and creativity, so that multi-party cooperation under the leadership of the CPC could be further developed on the basis of the Four Cardinal Principles. In September 1982, the 12th National Congress of the CPC reaffirmed the CPC's consistent policy of multi-party cooperation and put forward the policy of "long-term coexistence, mutual supervision, mutual care, and sharing of honor and disgrace" between the CPC and the democratic parties. This is the basic policy of the patriotic united front in the new era and the guideline for the multi-party cooperation and political consultation system under the leadership of the CPC.

Under the guidance of this policy, the multi-party cooperation and political consultation system under the leadership of the CPC has been constantly improved, and the role of democratic parties and patriots without party affiliation in the political life of the country has been further brought into play. By October 1987, the number of democratic parties had grown to 239,000, and they had established permanent institutions in most provinces (autonomous regions and municipalities) and their own organizations in some cities and counties; many of them held leading positions at all levels, and some even served as leaders of the Party and the State, and they played an important role in actively participating in political affairs and deliberating on political issues.

The system of multi-party cooperation and political consultation under the leadership of the CPC is a basic political system of contemporary China and a socialist political party system with Chinese characteristics. As a patriotic united front organization at the present stage in China, the Political Consultative Conference is conducive to the development of socialist democracy, the realization of unity and friendship and cooperation between the ruling party and the participating parties, and the democratization and scientificization of decision-making by the ruling CPC and the Chinese Government.

(2) Gradual Improvement of the System of Regional Ethnic Autonomy
Beginning in 1978, the CPC and the Chinese Government gradually adjusted and implemented their ethnic policies and strengthened their ethnic work; the 1978 *Constitution* restored the provisions of the 1954 *Constitution* on ethnic issues. The CPC and the Chinese Government reinstated ethnic work institutions and established the State Ethnic Affairs Commission, which is in charge of national ethnic work. In May 1979, the State People's Committee held its first (enlarged) meeting to discuss and study the tasks of ethnic work in the new era; in October, the CCCPC and the State Council, in a report forwarded to the party group of the State People's Committee, called for better work for the mixed and scattered ethnic minorities. The CCCPC also forwarded the *Instruction of the United Front Work Department of the CCCPC on the Removal of Hats from Local Nationalists*, stipulating that all those classified as local nationalists during the 1957 anti-Rightist struggle and in subsequent years should have their hats removed; those who had indeed been wrongly classified should be corrected in a pragmatic manner.

In March 1980, April 1981 and July 1981, the Secretariat of the CCCPC convened the Symposium on Xizang Work, the Report on Ethnic Work in Yunnan and the Xinjiang Work Conference, respectively, to sum up the lessons learned from ethnic work since the founding of New China, correct the "left" mistakes in ethnic work and implement ethnic policies. In its practical work, the CPC paid special attention to solving the problems left over from history, vindicated a large number of unjust and false cases in ethnic areas and ethnic work, removed the label of "implementing the surrenderist line" from the national united front, ethnic and religious work departments, further strengthened ethnic unity, developed a new type of socialist ethnic relations, and accelerated the development of economic and cultural development in ethnic autonomous areas. It has further strengthened national unity, developed new socialist ethnic relations, accelerated the development of economic and cultural undertakings in ethnic autonomous areas, consolidated and developed the system of regional ethnic autonomy, and opened up a new situation in ethnic work.

The system of regional ethnic autonomy has been restored and developed; the 1982 *Constitution* fully restored the system of regional ethnic autonomy and, on the basis of the lessons learned from the positive and negative aspects of regional ethnic autonomy since the founding of New China, further expanded the autonomy of ethnic autonomous areas, providing for the autonomy of ethnic autonomous organs in such areas of social life as the economy, politics, language and writing, religious beliefs and habits of life. In May 1984, the *Law of the PRC on Regional ethnic Autonomy* was promulgated and decided to come into effect on October 1, 1984. This was an important achievement in the construction of the legal system of regional ethnic autonomy. Subsequently, various departments of the State Council and ethnic autonomous regions also enacted various special ethnic laws and regulations and autonomy regulations, building the basic framework of the legal system of ethnic autonomy. By December 1991, 100 autonomous prefectures and counties had enacted regulations on autonomy, and the provinces and autonomous regions concerned had also enacted regulations on the implementation of the law on regional ethnic autonomy.

From January 14 to 18, 1992, the CCCPC and the State Council held the Central Conference on Ethnic Work. At the conference, Jiang Zemin made a speech entitled "Strengthening the Great Unity of the Nationalities and Moving Forward Together for the Construction of Socialism with Chinese Characteristics." The speech emphasized that, in the new historical period, the core issue in improving ethnic work and strengthening ethnic unity was to actively create conditions to accelerate the development of economic and cultural undertakings of ethnic minorities and ethnic areas and to promote the common prosperity of all ethnic groups.

Selection and training of cadres from ethnic minorities. Since the Third Plenary Session of the 11th CCCPC, there has been a rapid increase in the number of cadres from ethnic minorities, as well as a significant improvement in their political quality, operational ability and cultural level. A large number of outstanding minority cadres of both virtue and talent have been selected for leadership positions at all levels and have become the backbone of the political, economic, cultural and social development of ethnic areas, enabling the leadership teams at all levels in ethnic autonomous areas to meet or approach the requirements of being "revolutionary, young, knowledgeable and professional." At the end of 1992, there were 29,000 ethnic minority cadres among cadres at the county (division) level or above in Party and government organs nationwide, of whom 10.5 percent were cadres at the provincial (ministerial) level, 7.9 percent were cadres at the prefectural (departmental) level, and 7.6 percent were cadres at the county (division) level. 7.6 percent.

The system of regional ethnic autonomy is one of the basic political systems of contemporary China, and its implementation and improvement have promoted political stability, social development and economic prosperity in ethnic areas, and the new type of socialist ethnic relations has been further developed.

(3) Implementing Policies on Overseas Chinese Affairs, Taiwan Compatriots and Taiwanese Families and Putting Forward the Scientific Concept of "One Country, Two Systems"

Adjustment and implementation of policies on overseas Chinese affairs, Taiwan compatriots and Taiwan dependents. "During the 'Great Cultural Revolution,' China's policy on overseas Chinese affairs, Taiwan compatriots and Taiwan dependents was undermined, causing adverse effects at home and abroad. In November, the CCCPC also made some provisions to further implement the policy of relatives of Taiwan residents in the motherland. The introduction and implementation of these policies have had a positive impact on overseas Chinese, Taiwanese compatriots and their families.

The adjustment and development of cross-Strait relations. The CPC and the Central Government have always been committed to the peaceful reunification of contemporary China. With the changes in the situation at home and abroad, the CPC, in response to the Taiwan issue, gradually formed the basic policy of peaceful settlement of the Taiwan issue and completion of the unification of the motherland during the negotiations on the establishment of diplomatic relations between China and the U.S. Starting from the second half of 1978, the Standing Committee of the NPC issued the *Massage to Compatriots in Taiwan* on January 1, 1979, proposing the "three links" and "four flows" of "commerce, navigation and postal services" and "scientific, economic, cultural and sports exchanges" with Taiwan. "On September 30, 1981, Ye Jianying, Chairman of the Standing Committee of the NPC, made a speech to the Xinhua News Agency, stating the "nine guidelines" of the CPC and the Central Government for the return of Taiwan to the motherland and the realization of peaceful reunification, which already included the meaning of "One Country, Two Systems."[5] At the same time, the CPC and the Central Government also took concrete measures and practical steps to ease cross-strait relations and advance the reunification process. Beginning in 1979, they stopped shelling the islands of Kinmen and Matsu; initiated the "Three Direct Links" across the Taiwan Strait and set up an agency specializing in Taiwan affairs to promote cross-strait exchanges; initiated the Communist Party negotiations; and welcomed Taiwan compatriots to return to the mainland to visit relatives, travel, study and do business. Although the Taiwan authorities have not abandoned the "three no's" policy of "no contact, no negotiation, no compromise," they have also relaxed. With the adjustment and relaxation of the relationship between the two parties, cross-strait relations have seen a new development, with the gradual expansion of civil exchanges, the gradual increase in the level of exchange personnel, the continuous expansion of exchange fields, the rapid development of economic and trade exchanges, and the growing investment boom. Through exchanges, the people on both sides of the Taiwan Strait have strengthened their feelings, reduced hostility and misunderstanding, enhanced the cohesion of Chinese culture, and deepened the understanding and love of Taiwan compatriots for the motherland.

"On September 30, 1981, Ye Jianying proposed that after national reunification, Taiwan could enjoy a high degree of autonomy as a special administrative region, and in January 1982, Deng Xiaoping summarized the above-mentioned talk: this "is in fact one country with two systems." In January 1982, Deng Xiaoping summarized the above talk: this "is in fact one country and two systems." The 1982 *Constitution* provides that the State may establish special administrative regions when necessary. In May 1984, the Second Session of the Sixth NPC officially used the phrase "One Country, Two Systems" to express the Chinese government's basic national policy for solving the issue of China's reunification. The content and meaning of the expression include: First, to uphold one China, that is, there is only one China in the world, namely the PRC, and Taiwan, Hong Kong and Macao are inseparable parts of the PRC. Second, to uphold two systems, that is, within the unified PRC, the main body of the country will adhere to the socialist system, while Taiwan, Hong Kong and Macao will maintain their original capitalist systems. Third, to maintain the capitalist system. Third, the high degree of autonomy, prosperity and stability of Taiwan, Hong Kong and Macao should be maintained. The scientific concept of "One Country, Two Systems" embodies the principle of safeguarding the unity of the motherland and national sovereignty, while taking into full consideration the history and reality of Taiwan, Hong Kong and Macao, and is highly flexible, and is the basic policy for advancing the cause of the peaceful reunification of the motherland.

The China-British and China-Portuguese diplomatic negotiations and their "agreements" to resolve the return of Hong Kong and Macao. The scientific concept of "One Country, Two Systems" and the basic State policy were originally designed to solve the Taiwan question. However, since the goodwill, sincerity and newness of the CPC and the Central Government in "peaceful reunification" did not receive a positive response from the Taiwan authorities, the deadlock in cross-strait relations could not be broken after a long time. Therefore, the CPC and the Central Government decided to choose the breakthrough point for "peaceful reunification and 'One Country, Two Systems'" on the issues of Hong Kong and Macao, which are relatively ripe in terms of conditions and timing, in order to "take the lead."

In September 1982, Deng Xiaoping made it clear to visiting British Prime Minister Margaret Thatcher that China would recover Hong Kong in 1997 and that the issue of sovereignty was not open for discussion. After that, China and Britain held diplomatic talks for two years (from September 1982 to June 1983, the "secret consultation" phase, during which China and Britain prepared for formal talks; from July 1983 to September 1984, the 22-round "formal talks" phase). "On December 19, 1984, the *Joint Declaration of the Government of the PRC and the Government of the United Kingdom of Great Britain and Northern Ireland on the Question of Hong Kong* and its three annexes. the *Specific Statement on the Basic Principles and Policies of the Government of the PRC regarding Hong Kong*, the *Sino-British Joint Liaison Group* and the *Land Deed*, were formally signed in Beijing. At the same time, the Chinese and British sides exchanged memoranda on nationality and travel documents.

The main elements of the *Sino-British Joint Declaration* are:

(1) The Chinese and British sides "separately" declared that Hong Kong would be "returned to China" on July 1, 1997. The Government of the PRC declares that it is the common wish of the Chinese people to recover Hong Kong (including Hong Kong Island, Kowloon and the New Territories) and that the Government of the PRC has decided to resume the exercise of sovereignty over Hong Kong on July 1, 1997. The Government of the United Kingdom (UK) declares that the Government of the UK surrendered Hong Kong to the PRC on July 1, 1997.

(2) China declares that it will implement the special policy of "One Country, Two Systems" in accordance with the Twelve Principles after the "reunification" of Hong Kong. 1) In order to maintain the unity and territorial integrity of the nation, and taking into account the historical and actual conditions of Hong Kong, the People's Republic of China has decided to establish the Hong Kong Special Administrative Region when resuming the exercise of sovereignty over Hong Kong, in accordance with Article 31 of the *Constitution of the People's Republic of China*. 2) The Hong Kong Special Administrative Region (HKSAR) shall come under the direct administration of the Central People's Government of the PRC. The HKSAR shall enjoy a high degree of autonomy, except that foreign and defense affairs shall be under the administration of the Central People's Government. 3) The HKSAR shall be vested with executive, legislative and independent judicial power, including that of final adjudication. The existing laws shall remain basically unchanged. 4) The Government of the HKSAR shall be composed of local people. The Chief Executive shall be selected locally by election or through consultations and shall be appointed by the Central People's Government. The principal officials shall be nominated by the Chief Executive of the HKSAR for appointment by the Central People's Government. Chinese and foreign public and police officers previously serving in government departments of the HKSAR may be retained. Government departments of the HKSAR may employ British or other foreign nationals as advisers or to fill certain public offices. 5) The existing social and economic systems and the way of life in Hong Kong shall remain unchanged. The HKSAR shall safeguard, in accordance with law, the rights and freedoms of the person, of speech, of publication, of assembly, of association, of travel, of movement, of communication, of strike, of choice of occupation and of academic research, and of religious belief. Private property, business ownership, legal rights of succession

and foreign investment shall be protected by law. 6) The HKSAR shall maintain its status as a free port and an independent customs territory. 7) The HKSAR shall maintain its status as an international financial centre, and shall continue to open its foreign exchange, gold, securities and futures markets, with free access to capital. The Hong Kong dollar shall continue to circulate and be freely convertible. 8) The HKSAR shall maintain its financial independence. The Central People's Government shall not levy taxes on the HKSAR. 9) The HKSAR may establish mutually beneficial economic relations with the UK and other countries. The economic interests of the UK and other countries in Hong Kong shall be taken care of. 10) The HKSAR may, individually and under the name of "Hong Kong, China," maintain and develop economic and cultural relations and enter into agreements with other countries, regions and relevant international organizations. The Government of the HKSAR may, on its own, issue travel documents for entry into and exit from Hong Kong. 11) The Government of the HKSAR shall be responsible for the maintenance of public order in the Region. 12) With regard to the above-mentioned basic policies of the PRC regarding Hong Kong and to Annex I to this Joint Declaration—a specific statement of the above-mentioned basic policies, shall be prescribed by the NPC of the PRC in the *Basic Law of the HKSAR of the PRC (Basic Law of HKSAR)* and shall remain unchanged for a period of 50 years.

(3) The British and Chinese sides declared that during the "transitional period" the British side would be "responsible for the administration of Hong Kong" subject to the "cooperation" of the Chinese side, On April 10, the Third Session of the Sixth NPC of China adopted the *Decision of the NPC on the Ratification of the Joint Declaration of the Government of the PRC and the Government of the United Kingdom of Great Britain and Northern Ireland on the Question of Hong Kong*. On May 27, Chinese Vice-Minister for Foreign Affairs Zhou Nan and British Ambassador Evans exchanged the instruments of ratification of the *Sino-British Joint Declaration* and its Annexes on behalf of the two Governments in Beijing, and jointly signed the certificate of the exchange of instruments of ratification. It was on this day that Hong Kong officially entered the "12-year transition period."

After entering the "12-year transitional period," the CPC and the Chinese Government focused on the drafting of the *Basic Law of the HKSAR* in order to achieve the strategic objectives of "smooth transition" and "smooth handover" before the reunification of Hong Kong in 1997 and "maintaining long-term stability and prosperity" afterwards. The drafting of the Basic Law of the HKSAR of the

PRC was one of the priorities of the CPC and the Chinese Government in order to achieve the strategic objectives of "smooth transition" and "smooth handover" before the return of Hong Kong in 1997 and "maintaining long-term stability and prosperity" after the return of Hong Kong in 1997. From the First Plenary Session of the Drafting Committee for the Basic Law of the HKSAR held from July 1 to 5, 1985 to the Nineth plenary session of the Drafting Committee for the Basic Law of the HKSAR held from February 13 to 17, 1990, the "Basic Law Drafting Committee" of Hong Kong The "Basic Law Drafting Committee" of Hong Kong worked for four years and eight months, with more than 1,700 days and nights. After nine plenary sessions, 25 meetings of the Chairman, 73 meetings of the working group and three meetings of the general working group, consultation with various regions and departments in Hong Kong and throughout the country, and repeated revisions, the Basic Law was finally published in the spring of 1990. On April 4, 1990, the Third Session of the Seventh NPC adopted the *Decision of the NPC on the Basic Law of the HKSAR of the PRC* and the *Decision of the NPC on the Establishment of the HKSAR. Decision of the NPC on the Establishment of the HKSAR, Decision of the NPC Approving the Proposal of the Drafting Committee for the Basic Law of the HKSAR on the Establishment of the Committee for the Basic Law of the HKSAR of the Standing Committee of the NPC, Decision of the NPC on the Method for the Formation of the First Government and the First Legislative Council of the HKSAR*, and adopted the design of the regional flag and regional emblem of the HKSAR of the PRC. On the same day, Chinese President Yang Shangkun signed Presidential Decree No. 26 of 1990 and promulgated it. The Basic Law of Hong Kong consists of the text and three annexes. The main text, the *Basic Law of the HKSAR of the PRC*, is basically structured as follows: Preamble; Chapter I, General Provisions; Chapter II, Relations between the Central Authorities and the HKSAR; Chapter III, Fundamental Rights and Duties of the Residents; Chapter IV, Political Structure; Chapter V, Economy; Chapter VI, Education, Science, Culture, Sports, Religion, Labour and Social Services; Chapter VII, External Affairs; and Chapter VIII, Interpretation and Amendment of this Law, Chapter IX, the Appendices. Annex I is the *Method for the Selection of the Chief Executive of the HKSAR*; Annex II is the *Method for the Formation of the Legislative Council of the HKSAR and its Voting Procedures*; and Annex III is the *National Laws in force in the HKSAR*.

Following the example of the diplomatic negotiations between China and the United Kingdom to resolve the issue of the return of Hong Kong, the process of the return of Macao to "One Country, Two Systems" was initiated in 1986. After four rounds of diplomatic negotiations between the Chinese and Portuguese Governments, the *Sino-Portuguese Joint Declaration on the Question of Macao* and its three annexes, the *Specific Statement on the Basic Policies of the Government of the PRC towards Macao* and the *Arrangement on the Transitional Period*, were officially signed on April 13, 1987. On March 31, 1993, the *Basic Law of the Macao Special Administrative Region (MSAR) of the PRC (Basic Law of MSAR)* was adopted at the First Session of the Eighth NPC, laying a solid legal foundation for the implementation of the "One Country, Two Systems" principle in Macao. This laid a solid legal foundation for the implementation of the "One Country, Two Systems" principle in Macao.

The diplomatic negotiations between China and Britain to resolve the issue of the return of Hong Kong, the signing of the *Sino-British Joint Declaration* and the introduction of the Basic Law of Hong Kong, and the diplomatic negotiations between China and Portugal to resolve the issue of the return of Macao, the signing of the *Sino-Portuguese Joint Declaration* and the introduction of the Basic Law of Macao, have opened the first page of the glorious history of "peaceful reunification and 'One Country, Two Systems'" in contemporary China. The first page of the glorious history of "peaceful reunification and 'One Country, Two Systems'" in contemporary China was opened.

(4) Reorientation and Implementation of Religious Policies, Restoration and Strengthening of Religious Work

In February 1979, the CCCPC approved the Report of the United Front Work Department of the CCCPC on *its proposal to remove the label of "carrying out the surrenderist and revisionist line" from the religious work departments of the country and to establish religious work agencies at all levels*. In June, the State Council approved the establishment of the Religious Affairs Bureau of the State Council, and subsequently, religious work agencies at all levels were restored, laying the organizational foundation for the implementation of religious policies and the development of religious work.

Reviewing and vindicating unjust and wrongful cases. In accordance with the spirit of the Central Government's policy of vindicating unjust and wrongful cases, it has conducted serious reviews of unjust and wrongful cases during the "Great Cultural Revolution," and has vindicated and restored the reputation of all those who were persecuted. "For example, the former president of the Chinese

Buddhist Association, Hirao Gyatso, was rehabilitated and rehabilitated. This has had a positive impact on uniting the religious community and the believing masses.

On July 16, 1980, the State Council transmitted to the Religious Affairs Bureau of the State Council, the State Construction Commission and other units *a report on the implementation of the property policy of religious groups*, in which the units occupying the properties were returned to the religious groups for use on a case-by-case basis. Subsequently, religious sites were restored and opened one after another in various places, providing material protection for the needs of religious groups and the faithful in their religious activities.

In March 1982, Document No. 19 of the CCCPC was promulgated, clarifying the basic meaning of religion, stating that religion consists of four aspects: religious beliefs, religious feelings, religious rituals and religious organizations, and revealing the essence and characteristics of religion; elaborating on the long-term nature of the existence of religion, and proposing a fundamental way to solve the religious problem under socialist conditions; clarifying the social nature of the religious problem in contemporary China, forming a programmatic document for dealing with the religious question at the primary stage of socialism.

Religious patriotic groups and organizations at all levels have been restored and established. Before and after the Third Plenary Session of the 11th CCCPC, religious groups such as the Buddhist Association of China, the Taoist Association of China (TAC), the Chinese Islamic Association, the Chinese Catholic Patriotic Association, the Chinese Catholic Bishops' Conference, the Chinese Christian Three-Self Patriotic Movement Committee and the Chinese Christian Association, as well as patriotic religious organizations in various places, resumed their activities one after another.

The implementation of religious policies and the implementation of religious work have stimulated the patriotic enthusiasm of religious people and believers, and Chinese religions have continued to play a positive role in the primary stage of socialism.

1.1.4 Initial Exploration of Political System Reform

The building of a democratic politics in which the people are the masters of the country is an essential requirement of socialism. Since the Third Plenary Session of the 11th CCCPC, China continued to strengthen the building of socialist democracy and made initial explorations of political system reform.

In July 1979, the Second Session of the Fifth NPC adopted the *Organic Law of the Local People's Congresses at All Levels and Local People's Governments at All Levels of the People's Republic of China*, and the *Election Law of the PRC for the National People's Congress and Local People's Congress at All Levels*, which made important changes to the construction of local power and the electoral system, eliminating the "revolutionary committee" system of the "Great Cultural Revolution" that had united the Party, government and military, and reforming the system of local power that had been unified with the administrative organs since 1954. On September 29, 1979, Ye Jianying proposed for the first time at a conference of celebrating the 30th anniversary of the founding of New China to "reform and improve the socialist political system." In order to strengthen and improve the leadership of the CPC, from September 5 to October 7, 1979, the Organization Department of the CCCPC convened a National Conference on Organizational Work, focusing on issues such as leadership building and reform of the cadre system, and putting forward specific requirements. From February 23 to 29, 1980, the Fifth Plenary Session of the 11th CCCPC studied and discussed the issues of strengthening and improving the leadership of the CPC. It proposed to adhere to the leadership of the Party, improve the leadership and capability of the Party. The Session decided to co-opt the Standing Committee of the Central Political Bureau and re-establish the Central Secretariat as a regular working body under the leadership of the Central Political Bureau and the Standing Committee of the Political Bureau; discussed and adopted the *Draft of Constitution of CPC*, which tightened the conditions of Party membership, improved the content of democratic centralism, made new provisions for the cadre system, and abolished the de facto lifelong system of leading cadres; discussed and adopted *The Code of Conduct for Intraparty Political Life Under New Circumstances*, which was a useful attempt to strengthen the building of the ruling party institutionally under the new circumstances.

In August 1980, at an expanded meeting of the Political Bureau of the CCCPC, Deng Xiaoping made a speech entitled "On the Reform of the System of Party and State Leadership." He pointed out that the first and foremost task of the reform of China's political system was to adjust and reform the leadership system of the Party and the State, in which power was excessively centralized, to develop socialist democratic politics, and to systematically ensure the democratization of the political life of the Party and the State, the democratization of economic management and the democratization of social life as a whole, so that the Party and the State would be energized from the top down. He pointed out that the main drawbacks of the then political system in China were bureaucratism, excessive centralization of power, paternalism, lifelong leadership of cadres and all kinds of privileges. On behalf of the Central Political Bureau, he also put forward six ideas for the reform of the Party and state leadership system. Deng Xiaoping's speech pointed out the direction for the reform of the leadership system of the Party and the State in the new era.

In September 1980, the Third Session of the Fifth NPC accepted the proposal of the CCCPC to restructure the leadership of the State Council, changing the phenomenon of too many part-time positions and deputy positions of party and government leaders, and ending the anomalous situation that had historically formed when the top positions of the party, government and military were combined under one roof. In January 1982, the Political Bureau of the CCCPC held a meeting to discuss the streamlining of the central organs. Deng Xiaoping proposed that "streamlining institutions is a revolution" and "realizing the revolutionization, rejuvenation, intellectualization and specialization of cadres is a strategic need for revolution and construction."[6] In February 1982, the CCCPC issued the *Decision on the Establishment of the Retirement System for Older Cadres*, stipulating that the chief cadres at the provincial and ministerial level should generally be no more than 65 years old, the deputy cadres no more than 60 years old, and the cadres at the departmental levels no more than 60 years old. This was the beginning of the Party and State's establishment of a retirement system for cadres and the replacement of the old with the new in the cadre force. In March of the same year, the 22nd and 23rd meetings of the Standing Committee of the Fifth NPC adopted the preliminary plan for institutional reform of the State Council and the implementation plan for institutional reform of ministries and commissions of the State Council. As a result of the institutional reform, the number of bureau-level agencies under the CCCPC was reduced by 11%, the total personnel establishment was reduced by 17.3%, and the number of senior and deputy posts in ministries and commissions was reduced by 15.7%. The number of ministries, commissions and their branches and offices under the State Council reduced from 100 to 69, with a reduction of about 30% in the total personnel establishment. According to the statistics of 38 ministries and institutions of the State Council, the number of ministers and deputy ministers and directors, except for those working part-time, reduced from 505 to 167, with a reduction of 67%. At the same time, a pilot reform of the enterprise leadership system started in the cities, with a view to resolving the problem of the lack of separation between Party and government and between government and enterprises; in some places in the countryside, experiments were conducted to abolish the people's communes, which integrated government administration and economic management, and to establish township governments.

In September 1982, the 12th National Congress of the CPC put forward the guiding ideology of building socialism with Chinese characteristics, identified for the first time the building of socialist democracy as one of the fundamental goals of the Party and the State in the new period of modernization, and formulated a programme for the building of the ruling party, and realized the reform of central leading bodies and the replacement of the old and the new. Since then, there was only a general secretary of the CCCPC, no longer a chairman or vice-chairman, and the Central Advisory Commission of the CPC was established as a form of transition from a lifelong leadership system to a retirement system.

In 1986, Deng Xiaoping made four consecutive speeches on the reform of the political system. He pointed out that: every step forward in the reform of the economic system now made us deeply feel the need for reform of the political system. Without reforming the political system, the achievements of the economic reform could not be safeguarded and the economic reform could not be carried forward, which would hinder the development of the productivity and the realization of the four modernizations. Deng Xiaoping advocated reform of the existing political system and put forward a clear vision of the tasks, objectives and basic contents of political system reform.

From March 25 to April 13, 1988, the First Session of the Seventh NPC was held in Beijing, and Premier Li Peng delivered the Report of the Work of the Government on behalf of the State Council. The report summarized the work of the past five years and set forth the goals, guidelines and tasks of construction and reform for the next five years. The session elected Yang Shangkun as President, Wan Li as Chairman of the Standing Committee of the NPC, Deng Xiaoping as Chairman of the CMC, and Li Peng as Premier of the State Council. From March 24 to April 10, Li Xiannian was elected chairman of the CCCPC at the First Session of the Seventh CPPCC National Committee.

In his report on the work of the Government, Li Peng set the reform of government institutions, the overcoming of bureaucratism, the improvement of efficiency and the seriousness of political discipline and law as the goals and tasks for the next five years. Since 1988, on the one hand, government agencies from the central to the local levels were reformed with the aim of transforming functions, streamlining institutions, reducing staff and improving administrative efficiency, and constantly improving the administrative system; on the other hand, a national civil service system was established, the personnel system for cadres was reformed, and ways and systems of talent management that are consistent with China's national conditions were explored.

As the fundamental political system of the new China, the system of people's congresses was also undergoing corresponding reforms. The NPC and its Standing Committee and local people's congresses at all levels were strengthening the exercise of the legislative, supervisory and decision-making powers conferred on them by the Constitution; strengthening the system of people's deputies, enacting the *Law of the PRC on Deputies to the National People's Congress and Local People's Congress at All Levels*, and further regulating and safeguarding the exercise of the powers of people's deputies; and strengthening the self-construction of the NPC and its Standing Committee. The reform of the political system in the new China continued to progress, and was increasingly improved in the course of that reform.

1.1.5 The 1982 *Constitution* and the Building of the Socialist Legal System

(1) The Strengthening of Socialist Democracy and the Rule of Law and the "Historical Trial" of the Gang of Four

After the founding of New China, the CPC led the nation in the exploration of democracy and the rule of law, and formulated the *Constitution of the PRC* and other basic laws. However, during the "Great Cultural Revolution," socialist democracy and the rule of law were destroyed and trampled upon, and with the end of the "Great Cultural Revolution," there is an urgent need to restore and strengthen the building of democracy and the rule of law.

From February 26 to March 5, 1978, the First Session of the Fifth NPC adopted the *Constitution of the PRC*, which restored some of the correct principles and institutions of the 1954 *Constitution*. However, because of the wrong guiding ideology, it failed to make substantive changes to the *Constitution* adopted at the First Session of the Fourth NPC during the "Great Cultural Revolution," and in many respects retained traces of the "left."

The Third Plenary Session of the 11th CCCPC clearly proposed that the socialist legal system should be strengthened, that democracy should be institutionalized and legalized, that its stability, continuity and authority should be maintained, to ensure that there were laws to go by, the laws were observed and strictly enforced, and law-breakers were prosecuted. The Session also proposed that, from then on, legislative work should be placed on the important agenda of the NPC and its Standing Committee.

In accordance with the requirements of the Third Plenary Session of the 11th CCCPC, the CCCPC and the NPC carried out a lot of fruitful work since 1979 to restore and improve democracy and the legal system. In February 1979, the Sixth Session of the Standing Committee of the Fifth NPC decided to establish the Legislative Affairs Committee of the Standing Committee of the NPC with Peng Zhen as its chairman and Hu Qiaomu and 9 others as deputy chairmen; in September, the Ministry of Justice of the PRC, which had been abolished in 1959, was restored to take charge of the administration of justice. In January 1980, the CCCPC decided to establish the Central Political and Legal Affairs Commission, with Peng Zhen as its secretary. The successive establishment of these specialized legal institutions provided a strong organizational guarantee for the construction of the socialist legal system.

Since 1979, the NPC gradually began systematic and comprehensive legislative work. On July 1, the Second Session of the Fifth NPC adopted the *Resolution on Amending Certain Provisions of the Constitution of the PRC*, and formulated and adopted seven important laws of the *Organic Law of the Local People's Congresses at All Levels and Local People's Governments at All Levels of the People's Republic of China*, the *Election Law of the PRC for the National People's Congress and Local People's Congress at All Levels*, *Organic Law of the People's Courts of the PRC*, *Organic Law of the People's Procuratorates of the PRC*, *Criminal Law of the PRC*, *Criminal Procedure Law of the PRC*, the *Law on Chinese-Foreign Equity Joint Ventures*. This was the first batch of laws enacted since the Third Plenary Session of the 11th CCCPC, which was of great significance for strengthening the construction of state power and the legal system. By the end of 1982, hundreds of new laws, decrees and administrative regulations had been promulgated, and the country had made significant progress in improving the socialist legal system and realizing the legalization of democracy.

(2) The Birth of the 1982 "Constitution"

With the development of socialist modernization, the 1978 *Constitution* obviously failed to adapt to the developing situation and must be comprehensively revised. On

September 10, 1980, the Third Session of the Fifth NPC accepted the proposal of the CCCPC and decided to set up a Constitutional Revision Committee, headed by Peng Zhen, to propose a new draft revision of the Constitution. After repeated studies and discussions, in February 1982, the Committee on Constitutional Revision put forward a discussion draft of the *Draft Amendment of the Constitution of the PRC*. Members of the Standing Committee of the NPC, some members of the Standing Committee of the National Committee of the CPPCC, leaders of democratic parties and people's groups, as well as the party and government department put forward views about amendments. In April, the Constitutional Revision Committee carried out serious discussions and revisions, and adopted the *Draft Amendment of the Constitution of the PRC*, which was published by the Standing Committee of the NPC and submitted to the people of China for discussion. After eight months of discussion, the Constitutional Revision Committee made several more amendments, which were adopted and submitted to the NPC for consideration on November 23.

On December 4, 1982, the Fifth Session of the Fifth NPC adopted and promulgated the fourth *Constitution of the PRC* since the founding of New China. It included the Preamble, the General Programme, the Basic Rights and Duties of Citizens, the State Institutions, the National Flag, the National Emblem and the Capital, etc., and was a relatively complete constitution for contemporary China during the period of socialist modernization.

The general guiding principle of the new *Constitution* was to adhere to the Four Cardinal Principles and to follow the path of socialism with Chinese characteristics. With the spirit of democracy and the rule of law as its main thread, the new *Constitution* reflected the reform of China's political system and the demands of the 12th National Congress of the CPC for the building of a high degree of socialist democracy, and stipulated that the fundamental task of the State in the future was to concentrate its efforts on socialist modernization. The new *Constitution* stipulated that China was a socialist State under the democratic dictatorship of the people, led by the working class and based on the alliance of workers and peasants. All power in the State belonged to the people, who, in accordance with the law, managed the affairs of the State and economic, cultural and social affairs through various channels and forms, which was the core content and basic principle of the Chinese State system.

The new *Constitution* made significant adjustments to the establishment, responsibilities and management system of state institutions: the system of people's congresses was strengthened and the powers of the Standing Committee of the NPC were expanded; the provisions of the 1954 *Constitution* for establishing the President of the State were restored; the State Central Military Commission was established to lead the national armed forces; the State Council adopted the system of responsibility of the premier, and ministries and commissions adopted the system of responsibility of ministers and directors; under the unified leadership of the central government, local power building was strengthened, the system of unity of government and society in Chinese people's communes was changed, and township power was established; direct democracy at the primary levels was expanded, and deputies to the NPC below the county level were directly elected; neighbourhood committees and villagers' committees were established at the primary levels as mass self-governance organizations, etc.

The new *Constitution* restored the provisions of the 1954 *Constitution* on the equality of citizens before the law, which was a fundamental principle that guaranteed the implementation of socialist democracy and the rule of law. The new *Constitution* also added new elements such as the inviolability of the human dignity of citizens and the legal protection of their personal freedom, freedom of religious belief, freedom of communication and privacy of communication. The provisions of the new *Constitution* concerning the fundamental rights and duties of citizens were an extension of the "General Programme" on the State system of the people's democratic dictatorship and the principles of socialism, and ensure that Chinese citizens extensive and genuine freedoms and rights, which were of great significance to the development of people's democracy.

The new *Constitution* stipulated that the both of the state operated economy, which was the dominant force in the national economy, and the collective economy, which was the main form of economy in rural areas of our country, were of socialist public ownership and they were the basis of China's socialist economic system. At the same time, it stipulated that the individual economy of urban and rural workers was a supplement to the socialist public ownership system and that the State protected their legitimate rights; the State protected investment in China by foreign economic organizations and individuals.

The new *Constitution* stipulated that there was a need for promoting cultural and ethical progress, building of culture, education and ideas, shaping new socialist ways and customs and cultivating of an uplifting spiritual outlook among the people.

The new *Constitution* contained provisions on the establishment of special administrative regions in individual localities and added new elements on the implementation of regional ethnic autonomy in minority areas.

The new *Constitution* inherited and developed the basic principles of the 1954 *Constitution*, summarized the rich practical experience of China's socialist construction and drew on the experience of foreign constitutional practice; it was based on the then reality of China and took into account the prospects for future development, and fully reflected the common will and fundamental interests of the entire Party and the people of the country, and was China's general constitution for the governance of the country in the new era. The promulgation and implementation of the new *Constitution* was of great significance for the people of all ethnic groups to live and work in peace and contentment, to promote socialist democracy, to improve the socialist legal system, to guarantee the long-term stability of the country and even to open up a new situation of socialist modernization and reform and opening-up.

(3) Socialist Legal Construction with Chinese Characteristics

With the strengthening of the rule of law, China began to change from relying mainly on policies to managing the country's affairs in tandem with policies and laws. In his political report to the 12th National Congress of the CPC, Hu Yaobang stressed in particular that the CPC should lead the people to continue to formulate and complete all kinds of laws, strengthen the Party's leadership of political and legal work, and ensure from all sides that the political and legal departments strictly enforce the law.

In July 1986, the CCCPC issued *a circular on the need for the entire Party to resolutely uphold the socialist legal system*, stressing that building a socialist legal system with Chinese characteristics was a great historical task for the Party. Under the new historical conditions, the idea of "construction with one hand and the rule of law with the other" should be seriously implemented, and the Party as a whole must attach importance to the building of the socialist legal system, and cadres and Party members at all levels should consciously accept the supervision of the masses and the restraint of the legal system, and develop the habit of acting in accordance with the law. At the same time, the Standing Committee of the NPC decided to popularize general knowledge of the law among all citizens and to carry out law-promoting education for the whole population. Since 1986, the State had implemented the "First Five-Year Plan" and the "Second Five-Year Plan" for the popularization of the law, through which cadres and masses had learned to use the weapons of the law to protect their legitimate rights and interests, and the concept of the legal system and legal awareness of the entire population had also strengthened, thus promoting the development of the legal system.

Legislative work was progressing well. In order to speed up the pace and improve the quality of legislation, a legislative plan was formulated at the First session of the Seventh NPC. Subsequently, further proposals were made to speed up the enactment of laws related to consolidation and deepening reform, such as the law on price control, the budget law, the banking law, the company law, the law on the suppression of unfair competition, etc. In order to complete the drafting work on schedule, the legislative plan was revised in 1991. In about 14 years from the end of 1978 to the 14th National Congress of the CPC in 1992, China initially formed a socialist legal system with Chinese characteristics.

Strict law enforcement achieved remarkable results. Judicial organs at all levels adhered to the leadership of the CPC and, with the support and supervision of the NPC and its Standing Committee, endeavoured to uphold the dignity of the law in accordance with the principle that "the laws are strictly enforced and law-breakers are prosecuted." Courts and procuratorates at all levels throughout the country insisted on basing their actions on facts and on the law, and adhered to the "two-pronged approach," cracking down on all kinds of criminal offences and on economic crimes such as corruption and bribery with obvious results, and the social security got improved significantly.

Team-building was continuously strengthened. The people's courts and the people's procuratorates attached great importance to the building of their judicial teams, and the political and operational quality of judges and procurators in particular continued to improve. Training centres for senior judges and prosecutors were established, and a number of young judges and prosecutors were trained as the backbone of the judiciary through multi-channel and multi-faceted training, and a management system for judges and prosecutors was established and improved to suit China's national conditions. In addition, judicial organs at all levels were "ruling the courts strictly" and "ruling the prosecution strictly," and were vigorously engaged in building the integrity of the judiciary, and the building of China's judicial team was significantly strengthened.

1.1.6 The "Great Disarmament" and the Modernization of the People's Army

(1) The Change in the Guiding Ideology of National Defense Construction and the Work of the People's Army and the "Great Disarmament"

With the shift in focus of the CPC and contemporary China, especially since the 1980s, when peace and development became the two major themes of the times, a strategic shift in the guiding ideology of national defense construction and the work of the people's army was also implemented.

In September 1981, Deng Xiaoping, chairman of the CMC, put forward the general policy of building a strong, modernized and formalized revolutionary army. On November 1, 1984, at a symposium of the Military Commission, he analyzed the correct relationship between domestic economic construction and national defense construction in that international situation and pointed out that the work of the army should be subordinated to the overall situation of national construction and vigorously support the development of the national economy. This marked the beginning of a fundamental shift in the guiding ideology of contemporary China's national defense construction and the work of the people's army. From May 23 to June 6, 1985, the CMC held an expanded meeting. The main task was to make a strategic change in the guiding ideology of national defense construction and the work of the army, which was a real shift from the past state of readiness for war based on "fighting early, fighting big, and fighting nuclear war" to the track of peace building. And it was important to make full use of the peaceful environment in which no major war would be fought for a long time in the future, and under the premise of obeying the overall situation of national economic construction, to strengthen the construction of the people's army in a systematic and orderly manner with modernization at the center, and to improve the military quality of the troops and enhance the self-defense capability of the people's army under modern war conditions. The expanded meeting of the CMC made it clear that within the next two to three years, the number of army quotas would be reduced by one million and the army would undergo streamlining, refurbishment and institutional reform. Prior to that, after two disarmament exercises in 1980 and 1982, the number of army posts had been reduced from 6.02 million to more than 4 million.

Beginning in the second half of 1985, the "Great Disarmament" was carried out in an organized manner from top to bottom in accordance with the deployment of the CMC, and was basically completed by the end of 1987.

Disarmament focused on streamlining institutions, particularly the organs and units directly under the headquarters, military regions, military services and arms, as well as the Nationaldefense Science and Industry Commission, by merging the military regions from 11 to 7; transferring the People's Armed Forces of counties and cities to the local establishment, with dual local and military leadership. Border guard forces and internal security, some of the forces on duty were transferred to the public security sector; the number of officers was reduced, and 76 types of cadre positions within the army were filled by soldiers after 1985, improving the ratio of officers to soldiers; the PLA field armies were transformed into group armies, increasing the degree of army synthesis; the proportion of special forces was increased, and new units such as army aviators and electronic countermeasures were formed, enabling the army forces to develop from a single service to multiple services and to a group army with a combination of all services to improve the technical level and combat capability of the units; the logistics system was reformed to improve its operational security capability. These reforms enabled the PLA to coordinate its combat capabilities and enhance its overall combat effectiveness, laying a solid foundation for the gradual establishment of an army system adapted to modern warfare.

In accordance with the policy that education should be oriented towards modernization, the world and the future, a three-tier training system for commanding officers was initially formed, consisting of junior, intermediate and senior command colleges. In January 1986, the National Defense University of the PLA was established on the basis of the merger of the Military Academy, the Political Science Academy and the Logistics Academy of the PLA, as a research base and personnel training base for the modernization of national defense.

The large-scale reform of the army system greatly improved the People's Army in terms of streamlining, synthesis and effectiveness. By 1987, the total number of posts in the PLA had been reduced from 4,238,000 to 3,325,000. After that, further reductions were made. By 1990, the total number of posts in the entire army was reduced to 3,199,000, with a total reduction of 1,039,000. After 1990, a series of adjustments were made and the size of the army was further reduced. At the same time, the overall quality of the army continued to improve, and the people's army continued to develop in the direction of modernization and regularization.

(2) The Modernization of the People's Army Was Highly Effective
Under the unified leadership and deployment of the CMC, contemporary China made significant achievements in national defense construction and the work of the people's army.

Political work was continuously strengthened. Since 1981, the CMC had issued a number of documents on political work. In the process of streamlining and integrating the People's Army, the entire army carried out active political work and conducted education on "lofty ideals, moral integrity, a good education and a strong sense of discipline" to complement the modernization and formalization of the army; in December 1986, the expanded meeting of the CMC formulated the *Decision on the Political Work of the Army in the New Era*; In 1991, the CMC promulgated the *Regulations on the Political Work of the Chinese PLA* to ensure the absolute leadership of the CPC over the armed forces and to keep the modernization and construction of the people's army in the right direction.

The level of education and training rose rapidly. Since 1978, troop training had been fully restored, and the PLA had seen a historically unprecedented training boom and a climax of scientific and technological training. The ground force, air force, navy, strategic missile units of the Second Artillery and other military services had intensified the process of comprehensive military training and modernization, as well as strengthening the cultural education of troops and improving the quality of military cadres. In 1990, the CMC issued the *Regulations on Military Training of the Chinese PLA*, the first basic regulation on military training for the entire army in New China, in order to continuously improve the level of basic training and contract battle tactics training of the troops.

Significant improvements in weaponry. Since 1978, with the recovery and development of the national defense industry, the modernization level of the weaponry of the People's Army had been further improved. In October 1982, China successfully launched its first launch vehicle from a submarine to a predetermined target area at sea, making it the fifth country to have the capability to launch strategic missiles underwater. In December 1983, China's first billion times ultra-high-speed giant computer "Galaxy-I" was successfully developed by the National University of Defense Technology and other units. In April 1984, China successfully launched its first experimental communication satellite, marking China's entry into the forefront of launch vehicle technology and satellite communication technology. The conventional weapons of the People's Army was gradually refined, and the limited strategic nuclear deterrent became more effective.

Further improvements were made in regulations and systems. Since 1978, the NPC and its Standing Committee promulgated 13 military laws, and the State Council and the CMC promulgated hundreds of military laws and rules and more than 1,000 military regulations, in order to reform the then military service system and the militia and reserve service system, and restored and established a new military rank system. At the same time, unprecedented achievements were made in the areas of military law enforcement, military justice, legal supervision, legal services and legal propaganda and education, which gave a strong impetus to the implementation of the policy of governing the military in accordance with the law.

The military strategic approach became clearer. In the late 1980s and early 1990s, the end of the Cold War and the end of the bipolar pattern brought about tremendous and far-reaching changes in the world landscape. After calm observation and scientific analysis, the ruling CPC and the Chinese government confirmed that the international situation in general was continuing to de-escalate, but that they had to remain fully alert to the danger of war, and that they had to take a long-term view and carry out the modernization of the army in a planned and systematic manner, while at the same time making good preparations for military struggle, combining and unifying the two correctly. According to Deng Xiaoping's general goal of building a strong, modernized, formalized revolutionary army and the development of the situation, in December 1990, Jiang Zemin put forward the general requirement of "being qualified politically and competent militarily and having a fine style of work, strict discipline and adequate logistic support"[7] to the troops at the military work conference as the general requirement for the army in the new period. He stressed the need to build the people's army into a revolutionary army with combat power.

The role of the People's Army in the economic construction of the country was obvious. In the light of the overall situation of national economic construction, the People's Army converted a large number of military facilities, such as institutions, docks and hospitals, to civilian use and directly supported local economic construction. In order to meet the needs of modernization and construction, the army carried out activities to learn about culture and cultivate talents for both military and local use, and trained a large number of talents for both military and local use, many of whom became the backbone of local economic construction after they had been demobilized. The PLA made great contributions to the protection of national property and the safety of people's lives and property, for example, in the floods in the southern Liaoning area in July and August 1985, in the fires in the Daxinganling area in May 1987, and in other major disaster relief and rescue activities.

The modernization of national defense and the reform of the army system not only significantly improved the military and political quality of the entire army and the command and operational level of its cadres, but also significantly strengthened the combat capability of the army, promoting the construction of revolutionization, modernization and formalization of the people's army, and directly supporting the economic construction of the country, making a new contribution to the socialist modernization of the new era.

Summary

The extensive discussions on the criterion for testing truth criticized the erroneous policy of the "two-whatevers," established the Marxist principle that practice was the sole criterion for people to know the truth, and began to set things right in the guiding ideology of the CPC. The Third Plenary Session of the 11th CCCPC re-established the ideological, political and organizational lines of Marxism, and made the historic decision to shift the work center of the Party and the state to socialist modernization and reform and opening-up. The adoption of the *Resolution on Certain Questions in the History of Our Party since the Founding of the PRC* marked the completion of the Party's rectification of its guiding ideology. The 12th National Congress of the CPC put forward the general tasks of the CPC in the new period and opened up a new situation of socialist modernization. The Constitution promulgated in 1982 became the general statute for the governance of the country in the new era. The 13th National Congress of the CPC put forward the theory of the primary stage of socialism and clarified the basic line of the CPC in the primary stage of socialism. The Fourth Plenary Session of the 13th CCCPC and the Fifth Plenary Session of the 13th CCCPC achieved a smooth transition between the second and third generations of the central leadership, which provided an important political and organizational guarantee for pushing the cause of socialism with Chinese characteristics into the 21st century. The multi-party cooperation and political consultation system under the leadership of the CPC was consolidated, which promoted the democratization and scientificization of decision-making by the CPC and the Chinese government. The system of regional ethnic autonomy was further improved, with political stability, economic development and social harmony in ethnic areas, and unprecedented unity among people of all ethnic groups. The policy on overseas Chinese, Taiwanese compatriots and Taiwanese families was implemented, the policy of peaceful reunification of the motherland and the scientific concept of "One Country, Two Systems" were clarified, and the great cause of reunification of the motherland was promoted. Religious policies were adjusted, religious work achieved remarkable results, and the religious believers and leaders became an active force in the construction of socialist modernization. The guiding ideology of national defense construction and the work of the people's army shifted to the track of peacetime construction. China completed the "Great Disarmament" of one million troop personnel, strengthened the political and ideological work of the people's army, standardized training and education, improved weapons and equipment, established and perfected various rules and regulations, and determined the strategic guidelines for the construction of the people's army in the new period.

SECTION 2

Breakthrough in Economic System Reform and the Construction of a Modern Socialist Economy

1.2.1 The Introduction of The New "Eight-character Policy" and the Recovery and Adjustment of the National Economy

(1) The Introduction of the New "Eight-character Policy" and the Recovery of the National Economy"

As the focus of the CPC and contemporary China shifted to economic construction, there was an urgent need to adjust and restore the national economy in order to change the difficult economic situation and to solve the new problems of lack of comprehensive balance and serious disproportion in the national economy brought about by the "the "Foreign Great Leap."

In March 1979, the CCCPC decided to establish the State Council Finance and Economy Committee under the responsibility of Chen Yun and Li Xiannian as the leading body in charge of overall financial and economic work. In April, the CCCPC held a working conference on the adjustment of the national economy, Li Xiannian made an important speech entitled "On the Adjustment of the National Economy," proposing a new "Eight-character Policy" of "adjustment, reform, rectification and improvement," emphasizing the adjustment while moving forward, reform in the adjustment, rectification in the adjustment, and improvement in the adjustment. He also proposed that the main task of adjustment was to resolutely and gradually adjust the seriously disproportionate relationship between various aspects, so that the entire national economy could really be put into the track of planned, proportional and healthy development; reform the industrial and economic management system, give full play to the enthusiasm of the central government, localities, enterprises and workers; continue to reorganize existing enterprises, establish and improve a good production order and work order; through adjustment, reform and reorganization, greatly improve the management and technical level, and better act according to objective economic laws.

The conference decided that from 1979, in accordance with the general policy of "adjustment, reform, rectification and improvement," three years would be spent on serious adjustment of the national economy. In June 1979, the Second Session of the Fifth NPC formally adopted the new "Eight-character Policy," and the economic adjustment work was in full swing.

Adjusting rural policies and focusing on restoring and developing agricultural production. In September 1979, the Fourth Plenary Session of the 11th CCCPC adopted the *Resolution of the CCCPC on Several Issues Concerning the Acceleration of Agricultural Development*, which introduced 25 policies. The state strengthened support for agriculture, relaxed rural policies, reduced and stabilized grain requisition, raised the prices of some agricultural products, conditionally liberalized the contracting of production to households, encouraged diversified business operations, and gradually opened the agricultural market. This mobilized the enthusiasm of farmers and greatly improved agricultural production. In 1979, the country's agricultural output increased by 8.6% over the previous year, and annual output of 664.2 billion jins of grain presented an increase of 9% over the previous year, and farmers' income increased by 10.8 billion yuan.

Accelerating the development of light textile industry, adjusting the internal proportion of industrial relations, so that the proportion of light and heavy industry could develop in harmony. In January 1980, the State Council decided to implement the "six priorities" for the light and textile industry to improve the production and circulation conditions of the light and textile industry, and to speed up the development of the light industry, textile industry and handicraft industry. The state also slowed down the development of heavy industry, adjusted the product structure, helped heavy industry strive to serve agriculture, light industry and the market, so that agriculture and industry, light industry and heavy industry, as well as the proportional relationship within industry tended to harmonize. In 1979, light industry grew by 9.6% compared with the previous year, while heavy industry grew by 7.7%; in 1980, light industry grew by 18.4% compared with the previous year, while heavy industry grew by only 1.46%.

Raising the proportion of consumption funds in the national economy to improve people's life. The state did everything possible to balance the fiscal balance, stabilize prices, so as to ensure economic stability and promote production development. Meanwhile, it increased the proportion of national consumption funds to ensure the improvement of people's consumption level. In addition, the state raised the purchase price of agricultural products and reduced some taxes in poor areas, which led to a certain increase in farmers' income and a significant change in their purchasing power and consumption level.

Compressing the scale of capital construction and reorganizing industrial enterprises. The state took into account the overall situation of economic construction and compresses the capital construction investment within the financial budget. In 1980, the state compressed the capital construction investment within the national budget in 1979 from 39.7 billion yuan to 30 billion yuan, and stopped or suspended the construction of hundreds of unplanned projects, and compressed the large and medium-sized projects under construction from more than 1,700 in 1978 to 904 by the end of 1980. The state also focused on shutting down and cutting a number of high-consumption, poor quality, small-scale, loss-making State-owned heavy industry enterprises to ease the contradictions of energy, raw material shortages and fiscal deficits. In 1981, the number of small enterprises in heavy industry was reduced by 4,400, including 367 metallurgical enterprises, 458 fertilizer and pesticide enterprises, and 3,172 machinery enterprises.

Although the adjustment began to bear fruit, on the one hand, however, the long-standing influence of the "leftist" mistakes in social life had not yet been completely eliminated, and the leading cadres of various departments and localities at all levels had deviations in their understanding of the adjusting policy, and the implementation was incomplete; on the other hand, the long-accumulated problems of abnormal economic development and the closed and rigid economic system could hardly be solved and changed within a short period of time, and the national economy was still lurking in an unforeseen crisis. The scale of national capital construction was not compressed in place, industrial reform and consolidation was weak, energy and transportation were tense, and the state treasury had a huge deficit of 17 billion yuan, reaching the highest point since the founding of New China. At the same time, problems such as inflation, rising prices, and various problems emerged, affecting the political stability and social development of the country.

In order to resolve these contradictions, the State Council held a national planning conference and a meeting of provincial governors, mayors and chairmen of autonomous regions from November 15 to December 21, 1980, to discuss and study the economic situation and economic adjustment work, and readjust the 1981 national economic plan. The CCCPC held a working conference from December 16 to 25, proposing further economic adjustment and political stability. Deng Xiaoping and other leaders of the Central Committee spoke firmly in support of the Central Committee's determination to "all be kept within the limits of financial capability so that expenditures remain equal to revenues"[8] to carry out "sober and healthy adjustment" in order to "stand firm and continue to move forward steadily."[9]

Therefore, from 1981, the adjustment work entered the second stage and started to implement the Sixth Five-Year Plan (1981–1985). Through unremitting efforts, the national economy made remarkable achievements in implementing the new "Eight-character Policy" of "adjustment, reform, consolidation and improvement." By the end of 1982, the long-standing problems of high accumulation rate and imbalance of the ratio of agriculture, light and heavy industries in the national economy had been significantly improved. The national economy reversed the instability caused by major disproportions and gradually embarked on a healthy development track.

The proportional relationships between agriculture and industry, light industry and heavy industry were basically reasonable, the structure of accumulation and consumption basically tended to be coordinated, and the national economy achieved stable, sustained and healthy development at a high rate. By the end of 1985, the total output value of industry and agriculture increased from 770.7 billion yuan to 1,333.5 billion yuan, an average annual growth of 11% at constant 1980 prices; the gross domestic product increased from 455.2 billion yuan to 9,040 yuan, an average annual growth of 10.7% at constant 1980 prices. This development situation basically returned to the level of the First Five-Year Plan period, and was also higher than the growth rate of many countries in the world in the same period. The most encouraging thing was that the development of agriculture in these five years was the fastest since the founding of New China. From 1953 to 1980, the average annual growth rate was 3.5%, with the faster growth rate of 4.5% in the First Five-Year Plan period. The average annual growth in the Fifth Five-Year Plan period was 5.1 percent, while the average annual growth in this period was 8.1 percent.

The country's financial situation improved year by year, and the people's living standards improved significantly. In the early years of adjustment, 1979 and 1980, the national fiscal deficit totaled 29.7 billion yuan. However, from 1981 to 1985, state revenue increased by an average of 15.9 billion yuan per year, an annual increase of 12 percent. The state's fiscal balance was basically balanced and the difficult financial and economic situation was improved. During this period, the average consumption level of the country's residents grew by 8.8% per year, compared with 2.6% from 1953 to 1980. Urban household consumption increased by 6.9% per person, and the per capita net income of farmers increased by 13.7% per year on average. The savings of urban and rural residents increased by hundreds of billions of yuan, from 21.06 billion yuan in 1978 to 121.47 billion yuan in 1984.

Major progress was made in the country's capital construction and technological progress, and foreign economic trade and technological exchanges and cooperation opened up a new situation. During the Sixth Five-Year Plan period, SOEs completed fixed asset investment of 533 billion yuan, with an increase of 67.3% over the Fifth Five-Year Plan period. New fixed assets amounted to 362.9 billion yuan, and 176,000 investment projects were completed, including 520 large-scale projects, and 200,000 renewal projects were completed. During these five years, the total volume of import and export trade of the country amounted to 252.4 billion U.S. dollars, an increase of 120% over the pre-adjustment period, and the export value rose from the 28th place in the world in 1980 to the 16th place in 1984. During the five years, the actual utilization of foreign investment in the country was 21.79 billion yuan, and 2,443 China-foreign joint ventures, 3,823 co-operative enterprises and 120 wholly foreign-owned enterprises were established in various places.

Through the joint efforts of the whole country, the Sixth Five-Year Plan was completed ahead of schedule in 1984, and was overfulfilled in 1985. The completion of the Sixth Five-Year Plan enabled some of the economic problems that had been plagued for a long time in the past to be solved relatively well. The substantial increase in grain and cotton production provided the conditions for solving the people's food and clothing problems. As the supply of consumer goods was relatively abundant, many commodities that were rationed and supplied by tickets in the past, except for grain and oil, were basically abolished and openly supplied, which showed a scene of prosperity throughout the country.

(2) Economic Overheating and the First Phase of Governance and Consolidation

From September 18 to 23, 1985, the National Congress of the CPC was held in Beijing and adopted the *Proposal for Formulating the Seventh Five-Year Program for National Economic and Social Development*, which put forward the basic guiding ideology of China's economic work during the Seventh Five-Year Plan period, and some important indicators on the overall situation and direction of economic and social development. It also set out the strategic guidelines and major policy measures for economic and social development, as well as the vision and steps for economic system reform. Based on the recommendations, the State Council formulated the *Seventh Five-Year Plan for National Economic and Social Development of the PRC*. This plan was approved by the Fourth Session of the Sixth NPC in April 1986. The Seventh Five-Year Plan stipulated that the total output value of industry and agriculture would reach 167.7 billion yuan in 1990 at constant 1980 prices, the total output value of the national economy would reach 111.7 billion yuan, and the per capita real consumption level of the country's residents would rise to 51.7 billion yuan. These targets are both positive and realistic, leaving room for maneuver.

During the Sixth Five-Year Plan period, there were also some shortcomings and mistakes in the economic development. The stipulation in the 12th National Congress of CPC about the first 10 years mainly to lay a good foundation was not seriously implemented. Starting from the second half of 1984, China experienced economic overheating, excessive currency issuance and over-distribution of national income. As industrial production grew too fast, fixed asset investment and consumption funds grew too much, and the prices of some commodities rose too much, some new factors of instability emerged in economic life.

In agriculture, after the bumper harvest in 1984, the guidance and input to agriculture were relaxed for a while, so that the grain output from 1985 to 1988 was lower than that in 1984 for several successive years. In industry, the processing industry developed blindly, and in the process of reforming the excessively controlled and over-regulated economic system, the necessary and appropriate concentration was neglected. The relationship between basic industries, infrastructure and processing industries within the industry was also out of proportion, and the supply capacity of energy and raw materials could not support the over-sized processing industries, which made a large amount of industrial production capacity be left idle for a long time. Inflation increased and the total demand of society greatly exceeded the total supply. From 1984 to 1988, national income increased by 70% (149% at current prices), while social investment in fixed assets increased by 214% and money income of urban and rural residents increased by 200%, resulting in an unbalanced and unreasonable structure of social production and consumption. Food production languished, the rapid population growth was not effectively controlled, the per capita level of food production fell, while the corresponding industrial production grew too fast, especially the processing industry spread bigger and bigger, making the proportional relationship between industrial and agricultural production out of balance. The chaos in the field of production and construction exacerbated the chaos in the field of circulation, which was highlighted by the fact that various companies were overrun, far exceeding the needs of normal commodity circulation. In particular, companies that did not distinguish the government and business, made use of the dual-track price system and resold important production materials from the circulation for profiteering, seriously disrupting the economic order. The blind development of the market should have been effectively curbed by the state macro-control, but at this time the share of state revenue in national income fell from 26.7% to 22% during 1984–1988, and the share of central revenue in the overall fiscal revenue fell from 56.1% to 47.2%, which greatly weakened the macro-control ability of the state.

From 1985 to 1988, inflation increased significantly. Especially in 1988, the national retail price index rose by 18.5% on top of the already significant increase, which was unprecedented since the founding of New China, causing serious anxiety among the people, but the Party and the government did not recognize the seriousness of this problem. On May 30, 1988, the Political Bureau of the CCCPC held a plenary meeting in Beijing and decided to start studying the price and wage reform programme to speed up the price reform. The meeting considered that it was now a critical stage for price reform, and although reform would be risky, there was no way out, so in addition to adjusting the purchase prices of some grains, oilseeds and cotton, the retail prices of four major foodstuffs, namely pork, cabbage, fresh eggs and sugar, were liberalized, and the prices of some production materials were also increased by a small amount. The 10th plenary meeting of the

Political Bureau of the CCCPC was held in Beidaihe from August 15 to 17, and adopted the *Preliminary Plan on Price and Wage Reform*, which led to the panic buying in Fuzhou, Tianjin, Shanghai, Chongqing, Chengdu, Beijing, Xi'an and other cities from late August.

Under the severe economic situation, in September 1988, the Third Plenary Session of the 13th CCCPC put forward the policy of managing the economic environment, rectifying the economic order and deepening reform in all aspects. For the economic work policy since 1984, especially for the price reform break-through, this was a relatively significant turnaround. The Session pointed out that in that period, China's economic situation was generally good, but there were some difficulties and problems, highlighted by the too much increase in price. In order to create conditions for rationalization of prices, so that economic development construction could be sustained, stable and healthy, it was necessary to seriously manage the economic environment and rectify the economic order while adhering to the general direction of reform and opening-up. In the specific program, the Session asked the local resolute implementation of the State Council on the second half of 1988 to introduce new measures to increase prices, all sectors of enterprises should not violate the provisions of the chaotic price increases, and decided to start the People's Bank of the value of savings business.

The Session pointed out that the main task of governance of the economic environment was to compress the total social demand and to curb inflation. To rectify the economic order was to rectify the various chaotic phenomena in economic life, especially in the field of circulation. Although the Session still adopted the *Preliminary Plan on Price and Wage Reform* in principle, it no longer called for its immediate implementation. Instead, it simply suggested that the State Council implement the plan gradually and steadily in accordance with the requirement of strictly controlling price increases in the next five years or a longer period of time and take into account the practical possibilities in all fields.

This governance and rectification went through two stages: the first stage, from the Third Plenary Session of the 13th CCCPC to the third quarter of 1989, was to reduce demand substantially, rectify order in the Circulation area and quickly reverse the trend of excessively rapid price increases. The second stage lasted from the fourth quarter of 1989 to September 1991. The whole process lasted for three years.

The main measures and achievements of the first stage were: 1) strengthening the regulation and control of prices by administrative means. The prices of daily necessities of the masses were stabilized, the indiscriminate price increase of agricultural production materials was stopped, the maximum price limit of unplanned production materials was strictly enforced, the prices in circulation, and the charges of urban public utilities and service industries were rectified. Through the above measures, the momentum of excessive price rises was checked. 2) Adjusting the interest rate of bank savings. Starting from September 10, 1988, the long-term value-protected savings of RMB was launched, and the interest rate of bank deposits was raised twice, which led to a significant increase in deposits and stabilized the financial situation. 3) Cleaning up and consolidating the circulation market. In August and September 1988, The State Council ordered the unified operation and purchase of cotton and grain, and specialized in important industrial and agricultural products. Companies that used administrative power or did not differentiate between government and enterprise were reorganized, their government functions were abolished, and their business scope was approved. 4) Compressing the scale of infrastructure. On September 24, 1988, the State Council requested that all localities should not only compress the scale of investment in fixed assets, but also adjust the development structure to ensure the sustainable development of the national economy. The construction of the buildings should be continued, postponed or suspended. The state's ability to regulate and control the macroeconomy was strengthened and improved, active intervention policies were implemented, and the attention of all parties was gradually directed from the blind pursuit and comparison of output growth rate to improve economic efficiency.

After about a year of economic consolidation, the excessive social demand was effectively controlled, the excessive industrial production rate dropped significantly, the consumer market tended to be balanced, the situation of currency investment improved significantly, and agricultural production turned around. Retail sales of social commodities amounted to 607.3 billion yuan, down 8.2% after deducting the price increase factor; annual grain production reached 407.45 billion kilograms, a record high. However, it also brought a weak market, business efficiency decline and other negative effects.

(3) Further Governance, Consolidation and Deepening Reform
The problems accumulated in 1988 made the economic situation in China very serious in the first half of 1989. From the fourth quarter of 1989 to September 1991, the main objective was to restore the normal growth rate of the national

economy by adjusting the economic structure, increasing the effective supply and activating the market, while continuing to compress the total demand.

From November 6 to 9, 1989, the Fifth Plenary Session of the 13th CCCPC was held to consider and adopt the *Decision of the CCCPC on Further Rectification and Deepening Reform*. The Session decided that it would take three years or a little longer, including 1989, to basically complete the task of rectification and consolidation. The Session believed that continuing to unswervingly implement the policy of rectification and deepening reform was the fundamental way to overcome economic difficulties and achieve sustained, stable and coordinated development of the national economy.

In terms of the objectives of rectification, the inflation rate should be gradually reduced, so that the rate of increase in retail prices nationwide would gradually drop to less than 10%. The situation of over-issuance of currency should be fundamentally reversed, so that the amount of currency issued would be in line with the reasonable needs of economic growth, efforts should be made to achieve fiscal balance, and fiscal deficit should be gradually eliminated; economic development should be accelerated on the basis of improving economic efficiency, quality and technology; the irrational situation of industrial structure should be improved to strive for a gradual increase in the production of major agricultural products; The CPC's leadership in the governance, rectification and deepening of reform should be strengthened.

In the governance and rectification policy, controlling social demand and adhering to the double-tight financial and credit policy should be continued, and basic industries such as agriculture and the adjustment of the economic structure should be strengthened. The economic order should be seriously reorganized, and continuous great efforts to clean up and reorganize all kinds of companies, especially in the field of circulation should be made to overcome the serious disorder in the field of production, construction, circulation, distribution. In-depth activities to increase production and save, and to increase revenue and cut costs should be carried out, and efforts to improve the management of enterprises should be made to tap the internal potential, improve the level of science and technology, and to take the road of less input, more output and high quality.

The Fifth Plenary Session of the 13th CCCPC clearly defined the objectives, tasks, guidelines and policies of the governance and rectification, coupled with the effective implementation, the second stage of governance and rectification achieved significant results.

The economy basically resumed normal growth, especially at the rate of normal years since the second half of 1990. The total industrial output grew by 8.5% in 1989, 7.8% in 1990 and 14.2% in 1991; grain production was abundant for two consecutive years in 1989 and 1990, reversing the hovering situation in the previous four years; inflation was controlled, excessive investment in fixed assets and excessive growth of consumer funds were curbed, and the contradiction that the total social demand was greater than the total social supply, which led to inflation, was significantly alleviated; the year-on-year increase in the national retail price dropped to 17.8% in 1989 and 2.1% in 1990; industrial restructuring began to take off. The proportion of investment in agriculture, energy, transportation and other infrastructure projects were increased, and that of productive investment was increased. Key projects were accelerated, and non-productive projects were brought under control; the chaos in the circulation field were rectified initially, and the work of cleaning up the companies linked to the state administration made obvious progress. By 1990, more than 100,000 companies had been abolished nationwide, and the problem of cadres of the authorities working part-time or holding posts in companies were basically solved, and the blind development of companies in the circulation field was controlled. The consumer psychology of the residents tended to be rationalized, prices were basically stable, and commodity resources were sufficient; foreign trade and foreign economic and technological exchanges continued to develop, with total exports increasing by 14.3% from 1989 to 1990, and China's foreign trade achieved a surplus in 1990, changing the situation of continuous deficit since 1984; science and technology, education and various social undertakings achieved further development, new progress were made in the popularization and promotion of new technological achievements, and many important achievements were made in key scientific and technological research and development; in 1991, foreign direct investment reached 11.977 billion U.S. dollars, more than double that of 1989.

In the case of internal difficulties and external pressure, three years of governance and rectification effectively curbed inflation, freeing the national economy from the plight of violent fluctuations and clearing the way for the further development of reform.

Governance and rectification and deepening reform were unified. During the period of governance and rectification, the reform of the economic system was around the governance and rectification and served for it. During this period, the socialized service system in rural areas began to develop; the system of responsibility for contract management of enterprises was continuously improved, and the organization of enterprise groups made obvious progress; the reform of the foreign trade system with gradual realization that foreign trade enterprises should be responsible for their own profits and losses, and the price reform with the adjustment of the prices of coal, transportation, grain and other important commodities and labor services, achieved the expected results. With the public economy as the main body, various economic components continued to develop, and the proportion of non-public economy in the national economy continued to rise, which played a great role in economic growth during the period of governance and rectification.

The Seventh Five-Year Plan had been successfully completed by the end of 1990 under the impetus of rectification and deepening reform. During the Seventh Five-Year Plan period, the average annual growth rate of GNP was 7.8%, and the average annual growth rate of national income was 7.5%, both of which exceeded the requirements of the Seventh Five-Year Plan. The average annual output of major industrial products increased significantly compared with the Sixth Five-Year Plan. The average annual output of major industrial products increased significantly over the Sixth Five-Year Plan period. During the five years of Seventh Five-Year Plan, the average annual growth of total agricultural output value was 4.7%, while agriculture, forestry, animal husbandry, sideline farming and fishery also grew across the board. The people's living standard further improved, with the average per capita income of urban residents increasing by 4.1% per year in real terms, the average per capita net income of farmers increasing by 2.4% per year, and the average consumption level of urban and rural residents reaching 720 yuan. The problem of food and clothing for the whole country was basically solved. The vast majority of the Seventh Five-Year Plan was completed and exceeded, laying the foundation for achieving the second strategic goal by the end of the 20th century.

At the completion of the Seventh Five-Year Plan, in December 1990, the Seventh Plenary Session of the 13th CCCPC considered and adopted the *Proposal of the CCCPC on the Formulation of the Ten-Year Plan for National Economic and Social Development and the Eighth Five-Year Plan.*

The *Proposal* set out the second strategic goal of modernization to be achieved in the next ten years: on the basis of vigorously improving economic efficiency and optimizing the economic structure, the GNP would quadruple that of 1980, with an average annual growth rate of about 6%; the people's livelihood would rise from subsistence to well-off; education would be developed, scientific and technological progress would be promoted, business management would be improved, the economic structure would be adjusted, and key construction would be strengthened to lay the material and technical foundation for the sustained development of the Chinese economy and society in the early 21st century; initially establish a socialist planned commodity economy based on public ownership, as well as an economic system and operating mechanism that combines planned economy and market regulation; The cultural and ethical progress would reach a new level, and socialist democracy and the legal system would be further improved.

The *Proposal* set out the basic guidelines for formulating and implementing the ten-year plan and the Eighth Five-Year Plan: unswervingly follow the road of building socialism with Chinese characteristics; unswervingly advance reform and opening-up; unswervingly implement the policy of sustained, stable and coordinated development of the national economy, and always take improving economic performance as the center of all economic work; unswervingly implement the principle of independence, self-reliance, hard work and thrift in building a country; unswervingly implement the policy of promoting both material and cultural-ethical progress.

According to the *Proposal,* The State Council formulated the ten-year plan for the period 1991–2000 and the outline of the Eighth Five-Year Plan. On April 9, 1991, the Fourth Session of the Seventh NPC approved the ten-year plan and outline.

In September 1991, the CCCPC held a working conference and declared that through the joint efforts of the Chinese government and people throughout the country for three years, remarkable results had been achieved in governance and rectification: economic overheating had been significantly decreased, and economic growth basically returned to normal. The double inflation of investment and consumer demand had been eased, and inflation had been effectively brought under control; market supply was sufficient, market order was obviously improved, and residents' consumption psychology tended to be normal; the contradiction of "bottleneck" in the industrial structure had been eased, and urban and rural residents had benefited from economic development. The main tasks of governance and rectification had been basically completed.

The successful completion of the Seventh Five-Year Plan, the formulation and implementation of the Ten-Year Plan and the Outline of the Eighth Five-Year Plan marked the emergence of China's socialist modernization from the difficult situation since 1989 to a new historical stage of struggle to achieve the second strategic goal of economic development in the 1990s.

1.2.2 The Five Central "No. 1 Document" and the Initial Breakthrough in the Reform of the Rural Economic System

(1) The First Step of Reform to Stabilize and Improve the Rural Economic System Centered on the Household Contract Responsibility System

For historical reasons, especially due to the influence of "left" mistakes, by 1978, more than 200 million people in China still had not solved the problem of food and clothing, and the CPC and the Chinese government were looking for countermeasures to solve the problems of agriculture, rural areas and farmers. In the winter of 1978, 18 peasant households in Xiaogang Village, Fengyang County, Anhui Province, took political risks and secretly made the choice of "all-round contract system" that was characterized by "work and production contracted to households." At the end of the next year, the agricultural production was bountiful and the grain output quadrupled, and the situation was very good. Wan Li, the first secretary of the CPC Anhui Provincial Committee, went to Fengyang for research and affirmed the enthusiasm and creativity of farmers. Subsequently, some communes in Sichuan, Guizhou, Gansu, Inner Mongolia, Henan and other places also followed suit secretly or semi-openly. This practice aroused great rection and controversy in the society. Deng Xiaoping explicitly expressed his support when he talked with the head of the central government on May 31, 1980, which played an important role in promoting rural reform. In September, the CCCPC held a forum with the first secretaries of the Party committees of all provinces, cities and autonomous regions to discuss the issue of strengthening and improving the responsibility system for agricultural production. After the forum, the Central Committee issued Document No. 75, which affirmed the existence of the household contract responsibility system, and the reform of rural areas entered a stage of great development of the household contract responsibility system.

January 1, 1982, the CCCPC approved the *Minutes of the National Rural Work Conference*, the first central "No. 1 document." The document pointed out that the various responsibility systems currently being implemented in rural areas, including the small package of work for a fixed amount of pay, professional contracting and joint production for pay, joint production to labor, fixing of farm output quotas for each household and group, and household-based and group-based contract system etc., were all socialist collective economic production responsibility systems. Since then, the comprehensive promotion and continuous improvement, summary and improvement of household-based contract system began throughout the country. In September 1982, the 12th National Congress of the CPC emphasized the importance of long-term adherence to the system of responsibility for agricultural production in the form of household-based contract system and its gradual improvement on the basis of summing up the practical experience of the masses. By the end of 1982, 78.7% of the production teams in the countryside had implemented the system of fixing of farm output quotas for each household, and the total national grain output had increased by 9%.

On January 2, 1983, the CCCPC issued a document entitled *Some Issues of Current Rural Economic Policy*, which was the second "Document No. 1" of Central Committee. The document pointed out that since the Third Plenary Session of the 11th CCCPC, many significant changes had taken place in rural China, the most far-reaching of which was the widespread implementation of various forms of agricultural production responsibility system, and the joint production contract system had become increasingly the main form. This was a great creation of the Chinese peasants under the leadership of the CPC, and a new development of the Marxist theory of agricultural cooperation in Chinese practice. The document also proposed to reform the system of the people's commune, which was a unified system of government and society, and to separate the administration from the communes, so as to eliminate the shortcomings of over-centralized management, "big hue and cry" of labor and egalitarianism, and to implement a combination of decentralized and unified management. By the end of 1983, 93% of the country's production teams had adopted the policy of the household contract responsibility system, and grain output increased by 9% over the previous year.

On the basis of the universal implementation of the household contract responsibility system, the reform of the Chinese people's commune system was also brewing. In October 1983, the CCCPC and the State Council issued the *Notice on the Separation of Government and Society and the Establishment of Township Governments*, stipulating the abolition of people's communes and the establishment of township/village governments as grassroots power and villagers' committees as the self-governance organizations of the masses. By the end of 1984, the separation of government and communes was basically completed, and 92,100 township/village governments and more than 820,000 villagers' committees had been established. By the spring of 1985, all rural areas had completed this work.

Since then, the system of Chinese people's communes had practically ceased to exist in contemporary China.

On January 1, 1984, the *Notice of the CCCPC on Rural Work in 1984* was issued as the third "Document No. 1" of the Central Committee. The document pointed out that the transformation from a subsistence economy to large-scale commodity production was an inevitable process for the development of China's socialist rural economy. Only by developing commodity production could we further promote the division of labor in society, raise productivity to a new level, make the countryside prosperous and rich, and accelerate the realization of socialist agricultural modernization. The document also proposed to extend the land contract period, generally should be more than 15 years. Long production cycle of development projects, such as trees, forests, barren hills, wastelands, etc., the contract period should be longer. The document stressed that specialized rural households, which had emerged on the basis of the implementation of the contract responsibility system, had taken the lead in getting rich through hard work and developing commodity production, which was a new thing in rural development. We should cherish and support them and provide them with necessary social services. The document also affirmed that township/village enterprises were an important pillar of agricultural production, an important way for the masses of farmers to common prosperity, and an important new source of national revenue. This played an important role in the stability of rural areas and the development of township/village enterprises.

The emergence of township and village enterprises. With the development of reform and opening-up, a special phenomenon emerged in rural China, that was, township and village enterprises blossomed in some developed areas, and the number and efficiency of these enterprises exceeded people's expectation. The CPC and the Chinese government gave clear support to this new development. In March 1984, the CCCPC and the State Council forwarded the *Report on Creating a New Situation for Communal Team Enterprises of the Ministry of Agriculture, Animal Husbandry and Fisheries and the Party Group of the Ministry*, and issued a notice stating that the development of diversified business operations was a strategic policy that China must adhere to in order to achieve agricultural modernization; township and village enterprises, namely the enterprises that organized by communes (townships) and groups (villages), cooperative enterprises run by some commune members, and other forms of joint industries and individual enterprises were an important part of diversification, an important pillar of agricultural production, an important way for the masses to achieve common prosperity, and an important source of national revenue. Party committees and governments at all levels should give positive guidance to township and village enterprises in the direction of development, in accordance with the relevant national policies for management, so that they could development in a healthy way. The great development of township and village enterprises was a major achievement of the reform of the rural economic system. By 1987, the number of employees in township and village enterprises reached 88.05 million, and the output value reached 476.4 billion yuan, accounting for 50.4% of the total output value of rural society, exceeding the total output value of agriculture for the first time. This was a historic change in the rural economy, which not only increased farmers' income, promoted agricultural development, prospered the rural economy, and renewed farmers' ideas, but also provided financial revenue, developed export trade, and advanced the process of China's industrialization.

The first step of the reform of the rural economic system that centered on the stabilization and improvement of the household contract responsibility system, made a historic breakthrough. The enthusiasm of peasants increased as never before, and agricultural production was bumper after bumper. From 1979 to 1984, the total agricultural output value increased by an average of 8.9% per year, and the per capita share of grain increased from 139 kg in 1978 to 395.5 kg in 1984, and the output of major agricultural and sideline products increased significantly, thus changing the passive situation of long-term shortage of agricultural products in contemporary China. The dissolution of nearly 40,000 people's communes nationwide, the rapid development of township and village enterprises and diversified business operations, and the vigorous development of rural markets led to the reform of the rural circulation system, and renewed the vitality of rural China. The success of the first step in reforming China's rural economic system strengthened people's belief in reform, laid the material foundation for comprehensive reform in various fields, and played and exemplary role.

(2) The Second Step of the Reform of the Rural Economic System Centered on Reforming the System of Unified Purchase and Distribution and Adjusting the Industrial Structure

The widespread implementation of the household contract responsibility system and the abolition of the people's commune system created conditions for the development of the rural commodity economy.

On January 1, 1985, the *Ten Policies of the CCCPC and the State Council on Further Revitalizing the Rural Economy* was issued as the fourth "Document No. 1" of the Central Committee. The document pointed out: reform the system of unified purchase and distribution of agricultural products; vigorously adjust the structure of rural industries, breaking the traditional pattern of agricultural economic development; further relax the policies of mountainous areas and forest areas; implement credit and tax preferences for township and village enterprises, and actively develop township and village enterprises; encourage the transfer of technology and the flow of talent; liberalize the financial policy of rural areas, and improve the efficiency of capital financing; in accordance with the requirements of the commodity economy, actively develop and improve the rural cooperative system; further expand the economic interaction between urban and rural areas, and strengthen the construction of small towns; etc. In 1985, the last 249 people's communes were disbanded, and the system of people's communes finally came to the end of its history, and the second step of industrial restructuring in rural areas was initiated.

January 1, 1986, *the CCCPC, the State Council on the 1986 Rural Work of the Deployment* was issued as the fifth "No. 1 document" of the Central Committee. The document pointed out that the difficulties encountered in the reform had to be solved by in-depth reform, and there was no way out by backtracking. It also pointed out that the reform should be carried on, the policy of taking agriculture as the foundation should be continued, and that agricultural stagnation must be avoided in the process of industrialization. Plus, the relevant policies should be implemented, inputs should be increased, agricultural production conditions should be improved, and production services should be organized to promote the sustained, stable and coordinated development of the rural economy.

From 1982 to 1986, the five "No. 1 documents" issued by the CCCPC promoted the development of the reform of the rural economic system and brought about a radical change in rural China. In 1987, China's grain output was nearly 400 million tons, an increase of 32% over 1978; cotton output was nearly 4.19 million tons, an increase of 93.3% over 1978; the total output value of agriculture reached 467.6 billion yuan, a threefold increase over 1978. The living standard of farmers gradually improved, and the problem of food and clothing of the majority of farmers was basically solved. The development of township and village enterprises accelerated the development of rural economy and the process of agricultural modernization, and the Chinese countryside showed a promising situation.

1.2.3 The Promotion of Urban Economic System Reform

(1) Initial Exploration of Urban Economic System Reform
The period of December 1978 to September 1984 was the initial stage of urban economic system reform. The basic idea of the reform was to expand enterprise autonomy, try out economic responsibility system and carry out the initial reform of ownership structure.

Expanding the autonomy of enterprises. After the Third Plenary Session of the 12th CCCPC, a basic understanding was formed within and outside the ruling Party that a serious defect of the contemporary Chinese economic management system was the concentration of too much power. Therefore, the reform of enterprises was mainly based on the needs of socialized production, adopting economic methods, managing the economy through economic organizations, combining planned management with market regulation, and expanding the autonomy of enterprises under the guidance of state planning. Previously, in October 1978, Sichuan began a pilot project to expand the autonomy of enterprises, allowing them to withdraw a small amount of profits to give bonuses to employees on the basis of achieving the goal of increasing production and revenue. The Third Plenary Session of the 11th CCCPC affirmed the Sichuan experience.

Starting from 1979, the state further implemented the pilot project of expanding the autonomy of enterprises, expanding the autonomy of management of State-owned industrial enterprises, implementing profit retention in SOEs, levying a tax on fixed assets, increasing the depreciation rate of fixed assets in State-owned industrial enterprises and improving the method of using the depreciation rate, and implementing full credit for working capital. By June 1980, the number of pilot enterprises in the country had reached 6,600, accounting for 16% of the total number of industrial enterprises in the national budget, with 60% of the output value and 70% of the profit. The market concept of these pilot enterprises generally enhanced, and the level of economic development of them was higher than the level before the pilot and the level of non-pilot enterprises, which showed that the experimental reform had achieved significant economic benefits.

In order to further lead the pilot work of expanding autonomy of enterprises, the 10 competent departments of the state economic issued the *Implementation of the*

State Council Documents on the Expansion of Power, Consolidation and Improvement of the Specific Implementation of the Expansion of Power Temporary Measures in May 1981 to further expand the autonomy of enterprises in the plan, profit retention and the use of retained funds, product sales, expansion of new products export and foreign exchange share, prices, taxes, bank loans and other aspects. However, only expanding enterprise autonomy couldn't solve all the problems in the economic system reform. There were two outstanding problems: the first was that the expansion of enterprise autonomy couldn't completely solve the problem of the relationships of responsibility (economic responsibility), power (economic power) and profit (economic interests) between the state and enterprises, and it also did not solve the problem of economic relations between enterprises and workers; the second was that the lag of economic system reform in other aspects of the city made it difficult to implement the autonomy of enterprises.

In order to make the reform of expanding the autonomy of enterprises strong, the economic responsibility system of industrial enterprises came into being. In April 1981, the State Council formally proposed the implementation of a pilot economic responsibility system for profit sharing at the National Work Conference of Industry and Transportation, namely, under the guidance of the state plan, with the aim of improving economic efficiency, putting responsibility in the first place, setting power and profit with responsibility, and closely combining the responsibility, power and profits of enterprises. In October, the State Council stressed that the implementation of the economic responsibility system should focus on the two aspects: first, the state to implement the economic responsibility system for enterprises, to deal with the relationships between the state and enterprises and solve the problem of no difference between good and bad business operation; second, establish the internal economic responsibility system for enterprises to deal with the internal relationships of enterprises and solve the problem of no difference between good and bad performance of employees. This economic responsibility system, which linked the economic responsibility of enterprises and employees to the state with their economic benefits and interests, effectively mobilized the enthusiasm of enterprises and employees. The economic responsibility system between the state and the enterprise mainly includes profit retention, responsibility for their own profits and losses, taxation for profit, enterprises' sole responsibility for their own profits and losses and other forms; the internal responsibility system of the enterprise mainly linked the job responsibility, assessment index, economic efficiency with the economic income of the employees, and realized comprehensive economic accounting. This allowed enterprises to establish a set of vertical and horizontal supporting, up and down combined complete system of economic responsibility. By the end of 1982, more than 80% of industrial enterprises and 30% of commercial enterprises had adopted various forms of economic responsibility system. Some enterprises began to implement the responsibility system of factory managers to ensure that enterprises really have the autonomy of production and management.

In order to solve the problem of profit distribution arose in the reform of the economic responsibility system, the state began to implement the first step of "profit to tax" in April 1983, namely, to levy 55% income tax on the profits realized by enterprises, and then to pay part of the profits after tax to the state and leave part to enterprises according to the standard approved by the state. This properly solved the problem of the distribution relationship between the state and enterprises, which had been difficult to regulate in the past, and used the taxation system to effectively regulate economic relations, so that enterprises began to become relatively independent economic entities with a combination of responsibilities and power, and profits, and gradually established a financial and taxation system of "independent accounting, state taxation, and sole responsibility for profits and losses" for SOEs, which changed the long-standing economic "pot-luck" situation of "unified collection and distribution" by the state to the enterprises.

Gradually, the single form of ownership was broken down, and the diversification of economic forms were realized. The reform of ownership structure should first solve the problem of returning to urban employment of a large number of educated youths who had been sent to the countryside during the "Great Cultural Revolution." In 1979, there were more than 20 million unemployed people in the country's cities and towns, and it was impossible to rely solely on enterprises or departments. From February 2 to 7, 1980, the CCCPC held a national conference on labor and employment, which called for the opening of employment channels and the implementation of the policy of combining the introduction of employment by labor and employment departments with voluntary organization and self-employment under the guidance of the government's overall planning. All places broke through the traditional ownership structure, relaxed the policies on urban and rural collective economy and individual economy, and encouraged and supported people to organize themselves for employment or individual self-employment. By the end of 1980, the number of individual industrial and commercial households reached 400,000, which not only effectively relieved the pressure of urban employment, but also further improved the ownership structure of China's economy. On October 17, 1981, the CCCPC and the State Council promulgated the *Decision on Opening Doors, Revitalizing the Economy and Solving the Employment Problem in Cities and Towns*, which clearly stated that it was a strategic policy of the Party to implement multiple forms of economy and multiple modes of business in the long term. The 1982 *Constitution* also affirmed the diversified economic forms with public ownership as the main body. On the basis of continuous development, contemporary China gradually formed a new ownership structure in which the State-owned economy was the mainstay and various forms of economy, such as collective, individual and private, coexist and develop together.

(2) The Full-Scale Reform of the Urban Economic System

In October 1984, the Third Plenary Session of the 12th CCCPC adopted the *Decision of the CCCPC on Economic System Reform*, which clarified the necessity and urgency of speeding up the reform of the entire economic system with emphasis on cities, and set out the direction, nature, tasks and basic policies of the reform.

The *Decision* broke through the traditional concept of opposing the planned economy to the commodity economy, and confirmed that the contemporary Chinese socialist economy was a planned commodity economy based on public ownership, and that the full development of the commodity economy was an insurmountable stage of the social economy and a necessary condition for the modernization of the contemporary Chinese economy. The *Decision* put forward three basic tasks of the reform: first, to further enhance the vitality of enterprises, especially the vitality of large and medium-sized enterprises owned by the people, so that they could really become relatively independent economic entities, which was the central link of the reform of the urban economic system; second, to further develop the socialist commodity economy and gradually improve the market system; third, to implement the separation of government and enterprises, to establish a system of economic responsibility, to use economic means and to improve the new socialist macroeconomic management system. In other words, the policy of revitalizing the economy internally and opening it up externally should be further implemented, so as to gradually establish a vibrant and dynamic socialist economic system with Chinese characteristics and promote the development of social productive forces.

This *Decision* was known as "the political economy combining the basic principles of Marxism and the practice of Chinese socialism." After that, the

CCCPC and the State Council issued a series of specific policies to promote the comprehensive economic system reform centering on cities from the perspective of the overall economic strategy.

Enterprise reform. Establishing and improving the combination of responsibility, power and profits of the enterprise management mechanism and enhancing the vitality of enterprises was the central part of the reform of the urban economic system. The general principle and idea were to further delegate power, surrender some of the profits, liven up, and to carry out explorations in contract management responsibility system, lease system, factory director (manager) responsibility system. In 1987, compared with 1978, the share of profit retained by SOEs in total profit rose from 3.7% to more than 40% (after deducting various taxes and fees, the actual profit retained accounted for about 20%), which enhanced the ability of enterprises to transform and develop themselves. Within the enterprises, the contract-based economic responsibility system was implemented to improve the efficiency of enterprises. By 1987, 80% of the country's SOEs had implemented various forms of contract responsibility system, and the factory director (manager) responsibility system from the pilot development to the full implementation. At the same time, an enterprise bankruptcy system was also introduced on a trial basis to promote the improvement of the business mechanism of enterprises.

Price reform. Before 1984, the price reform was based on planned price adjustment, focusing on raising the purchase prices of agricultural and sideline products; after 1984, the price reform was based on price liberalization, combined with liberalization and adjustment. The forms of prices gradually developed from a single form of fixed price in the past into the three forms of a national license price (fixed price), national guide price (activity price) and market-adjusted price (free price); the price management authority changed from a single form of state pricing in the past to the three forms of state pricing, enterprise pricing and free pricing. Prices increasingly reflected the value of goods and the relationship between supply and demand.

Reform of the scope and mode of macro-control. The state narrowed the scope of mandatory plans to expand the scope and proportion of guiding plans and market regulation, so as to transform the highly centralized single planning system into a multiple system where mandatory plans, guiding plans and market regulation coexist. In 1987, compared with the pre-reform period, the number of industrial products managed by the State Planning Commission under the directive plan was reduced from 120 kinds to 60 kinds, and the proportion of their output value in the total industrial output value fell from 40% to 17%, a decrease of 23%. The number of materials allocated by the state decreased from 259 kinds to 26 kinds, a decrease of 233 kinds. The number of commodities managed by the state plan decreased from 188 kinds to 23 kinds, a decrease of 165 kinds; the national funds for production and construction decreased from 76.6% to 31.2%, a decrease of 45.4% points, while the funds raised by banks increased from 23.4% to 68.8%, an increase of 45.4%. The planning and management system was reformed, the role of economic leverage in macro-control was significantly enhanced, and China's macro-control system begun to transition from direct to indirect regulation and control.

The reform of ownership structure and distribution method. On the premise of insisting on the main position of the public ownership economy, the policy of joint development of various economic components was further implemented, and the relatively homogeneous ownership structure changed greatly. In 1987, compared with 1978, the proportion of the national industrial output value of enterprises under national ownership fell from 77.6% to 59.7%, the proportion of the collective economy rose from 22.4% to 34.6%, and the proportion of non-public economic components in the national industrial output value rose from zero at the time of reform and opening-up to 5.6%; in the total retail sales of social commodities, the proportion of the national ownership of goods fell from 54.6% to 38.7%, the proportion of collective goods fell from 43.3% to 35.7%, and the proportion of non-public economic components rose from 2.1% to 25.6%; the number of workers in various industries such as individual industry and commerce in urban areas increased from 150,000 to 5.69 million. This change in the ownership structure led to a major reform of the distribution method, and a variety of distribution methods began to appear, gradually forming a pattern in which the public ownership system was the mainstay and a variety of economic components coexisted, and in which the distribution was based on labor and a variety of distribution methods coexisted.

Enterprise shareholding system reform began to pilot. In December 1986, the State Council promulgated the *Regulations on Deepening Enterprise Reform and Enhancing the Vitality of Enterprises*, stating that local governments might select a few large and medium-sized enterprises owned by the people for piloting the shareholding system. After that, the shareholding system reform started, and by October 1988, according to the incomplete statistics of 16 provinces and municipalities, there were 3,827 shareholding enterprises.

Fostering the market system and promoting reform in the circulation of commodities. The state required the active development of State-owned, collective, and individual business forms, and the implementation of multi-channel circulation; changing the wholesale system of unified purchase and supply of agricultural and sideline products at the administrative level, cutting out unreasonable business links, and accelerating the reform of the system of supply and marketing cooperation; vigorous development of transportation and commercial business facilities. The wholesale systems of commodities from the central to the local levels were changed one after another, and multi-functional trade centers and wholesale trade markets developed rapidly, and the number of farmers' markets, retail stores, service, maintenance and catering outlets increased greatly.

The comprehensive reform of the contemporary Chinese urban economic system broke through the long-standing rigid planned economic system, injected new vitality and vigor into the development of the national economy, and set the national economy on a path of sustained development. By 1988, the GNP had reached 1,385.3 billion yuan, an increase of 11.2% over the previous year; the national income was 115.33 billion yuan, an increase of 11.4% over the previous year; and the GNP had risen to the eighth place in the world. The output of some important industrial products jumped to the forefront of the world, including steel production of nearly 60 million tons and power generation of 540 billion kilowatt hours, which both jumped to the fourth place in the world; oil production rose to the fifth place in the world; coal production ranked first in the world. The reform of the economic system increased the income and living standard of urban residents, and the average salary of workers increased from 615 yuan in 1978 to 1,747 yuan in 1988.

With the further deepening of the reform of the urban economic system, the state also carried out extensive reforms of the fiscal system, the financial system, the foreign trade system, the commercial management system, and the labor and wage system, eliminating administrative constraints affecting the operation of the economy and promoting the vigorous development of the commodity economy; on the basis of adhering to the public ownership system as the main body, the state encouraged the development of the individual economy, the private economy, and foreign-funded enterprises and other economic components to change the single public ownership structure and activate the socialist commodity economy. In short, the reform of the urban economic system successfully broken through the ice of the rigid and closed planned economic system, and gave wings to the national economy to take off.

1.2.4 Special Economic Zones and the Pattern of Opening Up from "Point" to "Surface"

(1) Creation of Special Economic Zones

The establishment of SEZs was the first step in opening up to the outside world in contemporary China. A special economic zone is a specific area set aside by a sovereign state or region to attract foreign investment, technology and talents by adopting special policies and preferential measures that are more open than the general areas in foreign economic activities, in order to achieve certain economic objectives.

In 1978, the State Council sent two inspection teams to Hong Kong and Macao of China and some countries in Western Europe for inspection. After returning to Beijing, the Hong Kong and Macao group suggested to the Central Government at the end of May that Bao'an and Zhuhai counties in Guangdong, which were close to Hong Kong and Macao, should be turned into municipalities directly under the central government, and built them into production bases and foreign processing bases with a considerable level of industrial and agricultural integration, as well as a tourist area to attract tourists from Hong Kong and Macao. The suggestions were approved and supported by the leaders of the Central Government and the State Council. In January 1979, with the approval of the State Council, Bao'an County was changed to Shenzhen City and Zhuhai County was changed to Zhuhai City. In April 1979, the CCCPC held a working conference in Beijing. The main leaders of the Guangdong Provincial Party Committee, Xi Zhongxun and Yang Shangkun, reported to the Central Committee and proposed to take advantage of Guangdong's proximity to Hong Kong and Macao and the large number of overseas Chinese to open export processing zones in Shenzhen, Zhuhai and Shantou. Deng Xiaoping immediately instructed that some policies could be offered, so that they could make some attempts on their own. In July, the Central Government agreed to set up SEZs in Guangdong and Fujian provinces on a trial basis, and the "Export Special Zones" were set up in Shenzhen, Zhuhai, Shantou and Xiamen. In March 1980, the Central Government decided to change the name of "Export Special Zone" to "Special Economic Zone" according to the actual situation of the construction of special zones. On August 26, the 15th Meeting of the Standing Committee of the Fifth NPC formally approved the State Council's proposal to establish SEZs and considered and adopted the *Regulations on Special Economic Zones in Guangdong Province*. At this point, the procedures for establishing a special economic zone were completed.

From May 27 to June 14, 1981, the CCCPC and the State Council held a working conference for Guangdong and Fujian provinces and the SEZs, and the State Council further formulated 10 policies for running the SEZs. On November 26, the Standing Committee of the NPC decided to authorize the people's congresses of Guangdong and Fujian provinces and their standing committees to enact single economic laws and regulations for the SEZs in accordance with the actual situation of the SEZs and report them to the NPC Standing Committee and the State Council for record.

The establishment of Shenzhen, Zhuhai, Shantou and Xiamen SEZs began one after another. The economic construction of the SEZs was effective, basically opening up the situation of attracting foreign investment and opening up to the outside world, introducing a number of advanced technologies and equipment, and the infrastructure construction of the SEZs was also effective, with rapid development of industrial and agricultural production and continuous improvement of people's living standards. It is worth mentioning that the builders of the Shenzhen Special Economic Zone created the "Shenzhen Speed," which made the former frontier town on the deserted beach rise rapidly into a modern city. By 1983, the Shenzhen Special Economic Zone had signed more than 2,500 economic cooperation agreements with foreign investors, with a turnover of 1.8 billion U.S. dollars. In 1983, compared to 1978, Shenzhen's gross industrial and agricultural output value increased by 11 times, fiscal revenue increased by more than 10 times than before establishing the Special Economic Zone, foreign exchange earnings increased by two times, and capital investment increased by 20 times compared to the sum of 30 years after the founding of New China. The initial achievements of the Special Economic Zone accumulated experience for further opening up to the outside world.

(2) The Initial Formation of the Pattern of Opening Up Rolling from the Coast to the Mainland

The opening up to the outside world was in full swing in the reform of the economic system. In April 1983, the CCCPC and the State Council approved the *Discussion Minutes on Accelerating the Development and Construction of Hainan Island*, establishing the policy of opening up to the outside world to promote the development and construction of Hainan Island.

In order to further expand the opening up, push the policy of SEZs to the whole coastal area, give full play to the advantages of large and medium-sized coastal port cities, and accelerate the modernization of coastal provinces and cities, Deng Xiaoping visited Shenzhen, Zhuhai, Xiamen Special Economic Zone and Shanghai Baoshan General Iron and Steel Works from January 24 to February 15, 1984. On February 24, Deng Xiaoping pointed out: "we can consider opening up a few more points, adding a few port cities, and implementing some of the policies of the Special Economic Zones."

In late March, the CCCPC and the State Council held a forum with the heads of eight cities, including Tianjin, Shanghai and Dalian, and the heads of relevant provinces and regions. The forum focused on the experience and policies of the four special economic zones of Shenzhen, Zhuhai, Shantou and Xiamen and the development of Hainan Island, and demonstrated the conditions and ideas for the further opening of coastal port cities. On May 4, the CCCPC and the State Council on the approval of the *Notice of 'Minutes of the Symposium on Some Coastal Cities'* was issued as the No. 13 document of the central committee. The *Notice* pointed out that Deng Xiaoping's important talk on February 24 about opening up to the outside world and the work of special zones, as well as the views on the implementation put forward at the forum of some coastal cities, was an important step to give full play to the advantages of large and medium-sized coastal port cities, as well as to create a new situation of using foreign capital and introducing advanced technology to accelerate socialist modernization, and decided to open up 14 coastal port cities in Dalian, Qinhuangdao, Tianjin, Yantai, Qingdao, Lianyungang, Nantong, Shanghai, Ningbo, Wenzhou, Fuzhou, Guangzhou, Zhanjiang and Beihai, thus forming the golden coast of China's opening to the outside world. In November, the State Council issued a report entitled *Several Issues Concerning the Economic Development of Coastal Regions*. The report recommended "opening up the Pearl River Delta and the Yangtze River Delta, and then opening up the Liaodong Peninsula and the Jiaodong Peninsula one after another, to form an economic zone open to the outside world from Dalian Port in the north to Beihai City in the south."[10]

On the basis of the opening of coastal port cities, in February 1985, the CCCPC and the State Council forwarded the *Minutes of the Symposium on Yangtze River,*

Pearl River Delta and Minnan Xiamen-Zhangquan Triangle, and decided to open up the Yangtze River Delta, Pearl River Delta and Minnan Xiamen-Zhangquan Triangle as a coastal economic opening area, and pointed out that this was an important strategic layout for China to implement the policy of internal activation and external opening up, and was the layout of the socialist economic construction with important strategic significance. The open economic zones were independent economic areas approved by the state. They were established and governed by the open coastal cities and were supposed to attract foreign investment and introduce advanced technology for various developmental economic and technological activities by relying on their special resource conditions and preferential policies to achieve certain economic purposes. In April 1988, the First Session of the Seventh NPC formally approved the establishment of Hainan Province and decided to turn it into a special economic zone.

In this way, contemporary China formed an open zone from south to north consisting of 5 special economic zones, 14 open coastal cities, 3 open coastal regions, 2 open peninsulas and Hainan Province. The Yangtze River Delta Open Economic Zone mainly developed export-oriented industries and followed the path of "exporting to earn foreign exchange, introducing to improve and then expanding exports"; the Pearl River Delta Open Economic Zone developed export-oriented economy and sets up "Foreign-Funded Enterprises" and "Enterprises of Three Import and Compensation Trade," accelerated the development of processing industries and agricultural and sideline industries, broadened the product sales, to enter the market in Hong Kong and Macao; Fujian Xiamen Zhangzhouquan Economic Open Zone carried out innovation of light industry and food industry products, which was export-oriented and focused on food processing, clothing industry and other light industrial products, gradually entering the international market; Liaodong Peninsula and Jiaodong Peninsula vigorously developed export products to earn foreign exchange and entered the international market, while developing "foreign-funded enterprises"; Hainan Province was the largest special economic zone in contemporary China, which had taken shape by 1991.

With the vitality and development of the open economic zones in coastal areas, China's reform and opening-up policy and the influence of special economic zones were gradually expanding to inland provinces and cities and border areas. In April 1990, the opening of Pudong became a symbol of China's remarkable achievements in the 1990s. In 1992, China opened five cities along the Yangtze River, namely Wuhu, Jiujiang, Yueyang, Wuhan and Chongqing. At the same time, 17 provincial capitals, including Hefei, were identified as inland open cities, and border cities were gradually opened up from the northeast, northwest to southwest.

In this way, China's opening up to the outside world progressed from south to north and from east to west, basically forming a multi-level, focused and open pattern of special economic zones–coastal open cities–coastal economic open areas–open cities along rivers and inland–open cities along the border. By 1993, the total area of the country's open zone had reached 500,000 square kilometers, including 39 counties and cities with a population of 320 million. By this time, the cities opened to the outside world had covered all provinces, autonomous regions and municipalities directly under the central government, which gave a great impetus to China's economic and social development.

(3) Outstanding Achievements in Opening Up to the Outside World

At the beginning of opening up to the outside world, the CPC and the Chinese government took various ways to actively attract and utilize foreign investment and introduce advanced technology and management experience. 1) Introduction of foreign capital. At the early stage of reform and opening-up, the main problem China faced economically was the lack of capital, so the CPC and the Chinese government adopted international practices and made great efforts to introduce foreign investment. By the end of 1982, the Chinese government had officially signed 31 construction loan agreements with foreign governments and other financial organizations, with a cumulative amount of 2.83 billion U.S. dollars, and officially approved a number of Chinese-foreign joint ventures, Chinese-foreign cooperative ventures and wholly foreign-funded enterprises, which became a new component of China's economy and played a positive role in the construction of China. 2) Introduction of foreign technology. After 1979, China introduced 440 items of technology and imported equipment. After January 1982, the work of introducing technology into China was mainly on the track of technical transformation services. 3) Reform of the management system of foreign economic and trade. The export commodities were managed based on categorization and gradually formed a foreign trade development mode with multiple operations, multiple channels and multiple modes of operation. The total amount of China's export trade increased from 35.5 billion yuan in 1978 to 77.2 billion yuan in 1982;

the proportion of industrial products among export commodities increased from 46.5% in 1979 to 55% in 1982.

In 1982, the 12th National Congress of the CPC opened up a new dimension of China's modernization, and China's opening up to the outside world was further expanded with remarkable achievements. According to the statistics in 1988, the 10th year of opening up, China signed 16,377 agreements on the utilization of foreign investment, with a total amount of 78.51 billion U.S. dollars, and the actual utilization of foreign investment amounted to 36.663 billion U.S. dollars; 16,000 foreign-invested enterprises were approved, with an agreed investment of more than 28 billion U.S. dollars; 3,530 technology contracts were introduced, with a total amount of 20.55 billion U.S. dollars, and more than 20,000 technology projects were used to transform existing Chinese enterprises. The opening to the outside world contributed to the rapid development of China's foreign trade. In 1988, China's total import and export amounted to 102.8 billion U.S. dollars. China's position in international import and export trade rose rapidly, from 32nd place in 1978 to 16th place in 1988. In the 1990s, the situation of opening up to the outside world developed even more rapidly, and by the first half of 1993, the actual foreign investment brought in reached 9.4 billion U.S. dollars, nearly double the amount of the same period of the previous year. In about six months, the five special economic zones reached a gross domestic product of 48.4 billion U.S. dollars, with imports and exports reaching 12.1 billion U.S. dollars and foreign investment of 1.5 billion U.S. dollars.

The implementation of the strategy of opening up to the outside world greatly promoted China's economic development, made China's achievements world-renowned, shortened the gap between China and developed countries in terms of economic development level, and greatly accelerated the process of China's socialist modernization.

Summary

In the late 1970s, the introduction of the new "Eight-Character Policy" promoted the adjustment and recovery of the national economy, ensured the completion of the Sixth Five-Year Plan ahead of schedule, and enabled some of the problems that had long plagued the economic development of contemporary China to be better resolved. In the middle and late 1980s, in the face of the overheated economic situation, the CPC and the Chinese government took active measures to control and rectify the situation. The successful completion of the Seventh Five-Year Plan meant that China had achieved the first step of the "Three-Step" strategy and was steadily moving toward the second strategic goal. In this process, the five "No. 1 documents" of the Central Government promoted the revival and development of China's rural areas. The first step of the reform to stabilize and improve the rural economic system, centering on the household contract responsibility system mobilized farmers' enthusiasm for production and advanced the modernization of China's rural areas. The second step of reforming the rural economic system, centering on reforming the system of unified purchase and distribution and adjusting the industrial structure, promoted the adjustment of China's rural industrial structure and the sustained and stable development of the rural economy. Agricultural production was bountiful for years, and township and village enterprises emerged. The success of rural reform not only promoted the development of China's rural areas, but also strengthened people's belief in reform, laid the material foundation for reform in other areas, and exemplified the effect. The reform of SOEs was the focus of the reform of the urban economic system. The reform expanded the autonomy of enterprises, implemented the economic responsibility system, broken the "big pot of rice," changed the single ownership structure, and diversified the economic forms. The *Decision of the CCCPC on the Reform of the Economic System* broke new ground in the reform of China's urban economic system, and reforms in the fields of enterprises, prices, ownership and distribution, shareholding, and circulation were carried out comprehensively, breaking the shackles of the long-standing rigid planned economic system and injecting new vitality and vigor into the development of the national economy. With the establishment of special economic zones as the starting point, China's opening up to the outside world took a successful path in line with China's national conditions. It proved that reform and opening-up is the road to a strong nation.

Implementation of Cultural System Reform and Promotion of Socialist Cultural and Ethical Progress

1.3.1 "Resuming College Entrance Examination" and Educational System Reform

(1) Resuming College Entrance Examination

The cancellation of the college entrance examination system had affected the normal pace of national talent training. After the end of the "Great Cultural Revolution," the state began to eliminate the negative effects caused by the "two estimates" put forward by the Gang of Four, and realized the reform of the education system.

In March 1977, Deng Xiaoping pointed out: "The key to achieving modernization is the development of science and technology. And unless we pay special attention to education, it will be impossible to develop science and technology." In July, Deng Xiaoping, who officially resumed his work, volunteered to personally take charge of rectifying the field of science and education. On August 8, at the National Forum on Science and Education, he delivered his famous "Address on August 8," stating, "It must be affirmed that in the past 17 years, under the wise guidance of Mao Zedong Thought and the correct leadership of the Party, most intellectuals, whether in science or in education worked assiduously and achieved great success. People in the field of education worked especially harder."[11] He also put forward the need to respect knowledge and talents, and put forward opinions on six issues, including "two estimates." This speech evoked strong repercussions in China's educational and scientific circles. It was at this forum that Deng Xiaoping made up his mind to resume the college entrance examination.

On August 13, according to Deng Xiaoping's instructions, the Ministry of Education held the Second National Recruitment Work Conference. The participants had a heated debate on the "two estimates." The *People's Daily* wrote an internal reference material to expose the inside story of the "two estimates" and reported it to the Central Committee. On September 19, Deng Xiaoping specially talked to the person in charge of the Ministry of education, pointing out that the "two estimates" were not in line with reality, and proposed to seek truth from facts and set things right in the field of education. According to the spirit of Deng Xiaoping's talk, the Ministry of Education revised and improved the enrollment policy and reported it to the Central Committee. With the support of Deng Xiaoping, Ye Jianying, Li Xiannian and other central leaders, on October 5, the Political Bureau of the CCCPC approved the document on major reform of college enrollment. On October 12, the State Council officially approved and transmitted *The Opinions on the Enrollment of Colleges and Universities in 1977*. The major decision to resume the college entrance examination was born, and the college entrance examination system, which had been suspended for 11 years, was restored. In that year, 5.7 million young intellectuals took part in the college entrance examination, and 273,000 of them were admitted. In January 1978, the postgraduate enrollment system was restored and 10,000 postgraduate students were admitted. Higher education was the first to break away from the chain of "two whatevers" and regain a new life.

In April 1978, the Ministry of Education held a National Conference on Education. Deng Xiaoping addressed the issues of education serving socialist construction, creating a new generation with socialist consciousness and the need to adapt education to the requirements of national economic development, which pointed the way for the further development of education. The CPC and the Chinese government made education a major issue and restored and developed a large number of schools and colleges, especially key institutions of higher learning. At the same time, through rectifying school order, improving various school management systems, strengthening school teaching and ideological and political education, normal education was restored and developed, school management was strengthened, and the overall quality of teachers was improved.

(2) Reforming the Education System

After the Third Plenary Session of the 11th CCCPC, the CCCPC and the State Council had always regarded the reform of the education system as one of the key contents of the comprehensive reform to meet the needs of reform, opening up and modernization.

In January 1980, in his speech entitled *The Present Situation and The Present Situation and the Tasks*, Deng Xiaoping stressed that the development of economy and education was out of proportion, and in the future, we should vigorously increase the expenses of science, education, culture and public health. In September 1982, the 12th National Congress of the CPC pointed out that "the key to the four modernizations is the modernization of science and technology,"[12] and education was the foundation. Education should be regarded as one of the strategic priorities of economic development, and the strategic position of education in the socialist modernization construction should be initially established. On October 1, 1983, Deng Xiaoping wrote an inscription for Beijing Jingshan School: Education should be oriented to modernization, to the world and to the future. This put forward the general direction and policy for China's educational development and reform in the new period.

In order to further deepen the reform of the education system, in May 1985, the CCCPC and the State Council held a national education work conference in Beijing. At the meeting, Deng Xiaoping made a speech entitled *Devote Special Effort to Education.* he urged Party committees and governments at all levels to fully understand the importance of the reform of the educational system. The meeting discussed the *Decision of the CCCPC on the Reform of the Education System*, which was announced on May 27. The *Decision* put forward that education must serve socialist construction, and socialist construction must rely on education to raise education to a new strategic position; in order to reform the situation that the educational work does not meet the needs of socialist modernization, we must start with the educational system and carry out systematic reform; the fundamental purpose of the reform was to improve the quality of the nation, and to produce more and better talents quickly; by reforming the management system, expanding the autonomy of the school, adjusting the educational structure, correspondingly reforming the labor and personnel system, reforming the educational ideas, contents and methods that were incompatible with the socialist modernization, and creating a new situation in educational work.

In October 1987, the 13th National Congress of the CPC further proposed that the development of education must be placed in a prominent strategic position, and it was determined to shift economic construction from the "production movement" and "sea of people tactics" of the 1950s to the track of relying on scientific and technological progress and improving the quality of workers. This was a major strategic decision of China's modernization and promoted the deepening of the reform of the education system. The reform of the education system made great progress in China's education.

Adjusting the primary and secondary school system, universal primary education. The Ministry of Education successively proposed to reform the teaching plan of primary and secondary schools under the guidance of the

"Three Orientations," so as to reduce the burden of students and promote the comprehensive development of students. In December 1980, the central government proposed to gradually change the primary and secondary school system to a 12-year system, and basically realize the historical task of popularizing primary education in the 1980s. By 1984, there were 853,700 primary schools in China, with 135.77 million students. The average enrollment rate of school-age children reached 95%. On April 12, 1986, the Fourth Session of the Sixth NPC adopted *The Compulsory Education Law of the PRC*, and the country has started implementing nine-year compulsory education. By the end of 1991, 76% of the counties in the country had basically achieved universal primary education, and the cities had basically achieved universal junior high school education. China's basic education has reached a new level.

Adjusting the structure of higher education disciplines, reforming the management system, school system and enrollment allocation system. Since the resumption of the college entrance examination in 1977, China's higher education had rapidly recovered and developed. In 1988, the total number of students in school reached 2.06 million. Through the reform, the structure of higher education disciplines had been adjusted, and the proportion of liberal arts in higher education had been increased; the autonomy of colleges and universities had been expanded, joint schooling had been promoted, the single schooling system and education and teaching work had been reformed, and the teaching management system, talent training mode and the system of unified enrollment and unified distribution of graduates in the planning system had been improved; multiple channels of investment had been actively opened up, and a new investment, which was mainly run by the state and supplemented by social forces, had been formed to meet the requirements of socialist modernization.

Establishing a degree system and improving graduate education. In February 1980, the 13th Meeting of the Standing Committee of the Fifth NPC adopted the *Regulations of the PRC on Academic Degrees*, which came into force on January 1, 1981. In December 1980, the State Council approved the establishment of the Academic Degrees Committee of the State Council, and began to establish and improve the national degree awarding system. Graduate education gradually developed from mainly teaching and research to being oriented to economic construction at the same time. By the end of 1990, there were 580 colleges and universities with the right to confer bachelor's degrees; there were 586 units with the right to confer master's degrees, including 421 universities; there were 248 units with the right to confer doctoral degrees, including 199 universities; more than 2 million bachelor's degrees, 180,000 master's degrees and about 7,000 doctor's degrees were awarded, raising the proportion of high-level talents.

Restoring and developing vocational and technical education and adult education. In April 1978, National Conference on Education put forward the idea of reforming the structure of secondary education. In 1980, the CCCPC transmitted the documents of the national labor and employment conference and pointed out that it was necessary to change the unitary situation of secondary education. In May 1983, the Ministry of Education and other ministries jointly issued the *Opinions on Reforming the Structure of Urban Secondary Education and Developing Vocational Education*, which called for the development of vocational education to meet the needs of workers with specialized skills for socialist modernization. In May 1985, the *Decision of the CCCPC on the Reform of the Education System* pointed out that vocational and technical education was the weakest link in China's overall education, and that practical measures must be taken to change this situation and strive for a major development of vocational and technical education. Vocational and technical education developed rapidly, breaking through the single structure mode, and basically forming a "dual track" parallel pattern of basic education and vocational and technical education. At the same time, adult education was adjusted and restored, and the development process of continuing education and job training in the form of illiteracy eradication, establishment of higher education self-study examination system and radio and television universities, correspondence universities and night universities had been accelerated.

Reforming teacher education and building the teaching force. The key to cultivating qualified talents for socialism lies in the teaching staff. Teacher education and the construction of teaching force had always been the basic point of the development of education. Since 1978, China had gradually formed a relatively complete multi-channel, multi-level, multi-standard and multi-form teacher training network for basic education. In 1978, the qualification rates of teachers in primary schools, junior high schools and senior high schools were 47.1%, 9.8% and 45.9% respectively; By 1991, this proportion had become 89.6%, 56%, and 51.7%. In 1991, there were 257 higher normal colleges and universities with 470,000 students; there were 948 secondary normal schools (including 68 infant normal schools) with about 661,000 students (including 38,000 students in infant normal schools); there were 254 colleges of education with about 185,000 students; there were 2,061 schools for teachers' advanced studies with about 463,000 students. Through the reform, the overall quality of teachers was significantly improved.

Comprehensive reform of education in rural and urban areas. In May 1983, the central government issued the *Notice on Several Issues Concerning Strengthening and Reforming Rural School Education*, which called for accelerating the reform of the structure of urban and rural secondary education. Since 1986, the State Education Commission carried out the experiment of comprehensive education reform. In 1988, the "prairie fire plan" was implemented in rural areas, which improved the quality of workers and effectively promoted the development of rural economy. From 1988 to 1990, the state arranged special loans of 180 million yuan for the "prairie fire plan," mobilized local supporting funds of 594 million yuan, implemented more than 10,000 planned projects, popularized more than 10,000 practical technologies, increased new output value of 1.378 billion yuan, and total profits and taxes of 195 million yuan. A great feature of the comprehensive reform of urban education was to give play to the role of enterprises in vocational and technical education. The state tried to introduce the German "dual system" mode of schooling in six cities, including Suzhou, and achieved remarkable results.

The reform of the educational system not only injected new vitality into the educational cause of contemporary China and promoted the vigorous development of the educational cause, but also transported a large number of talents for China's socialist modernization and supported the construction of various fronts.

1.3.2 National Conference on Science and the "Spring of Science"

(1) The Convening of the National Conference on Science and the Implementation of the Intellectual Policy

During the "Great Cultural Revolution," the intellectual policies of the CPC and the Chinese government were seriously damaged. A large number of scientific research personnel left their scientific research posts, which greatly dampened their enthusiasm and caused huge losses to China's scientific research cause. It was urgent to restore order and reform the scientific and technological system.

In September 1977, the CCCPC issued a notice on convening the National Conference on Science and decided to restore the State Science and Technology

Commission and local science and technology management institutions at all levels, so that the science and technology departments paralyzed in the "Great Cultural Revolution" could regain vitality.

On March 18, 1978, the National Conference on Science was held in Beijing. At the opening ceremony, Deng Xiaoping pointed out that correctly understanding that science and technology were productive forces and correctly understanding that mental workers serving socialism were part of the working people was extremely closely related to the rapid development of our scientific cause. The rapid growth of China's science and technology depended on good Party leadership in these fields. When views diverge on scholarly questions, we must follow the policy of "letting a hundred schools of thought contend" and encourage free discussion. Deng Xiaoping's speech denied the long-standing "left" practice on the scientific and technological front, and promoted the rectification of chaos in the scientific and technological field. After the conference, the CPC and the Chinese government began to reverse the deviation in the policies towards intellectuals, which promoted the reform in the field of science and technology, and the scientific and technological work began to step onto the right track.

In 1980, when listening to the work report of the State Science and Technology Commission, Deng Xiaoping proposed that it was necessary to combine the economic and social development plans with the scientific and technological development plans to overcome the problem of disconnection between them. According to this instruction, in December 1980, the State Science and Technology Commission presided over the National Science and Technology Work Conference, which initially put forward the basic principles for the development of science and technology in the coming period, emphasizing that science and technology must serve economic construction and must develop in harmony with economic and social development, and reported it to the Central Committee. On April 16, 1981, the CCCPC and the State Council transmitted this policy, the main content of which were: first, science and technology should develop in harmony with the economy and society, and promote economic development as the primary task; second, we should focus on strengthening the research of production technology, correctly selecting technology and forming a reasonable technological structure; third, it was necessary to strengthen the technological development and popularization of scientific and technological achievements in the front line of industrial and agricultural production; fourth, to ensure the gradual development of basic research on a stable basis; fifth, to take learning, digesting and absorbing foreign scientific and technological achievements as an important way to develop China's science and technology. This was the first systematic and complete scientific and technological development policy since the founding of new China, which promoted the comprehensive progress of science and technology.

Adjusting and implementing the intellectual policy. After the Third Plenary Session of the 11th CCCPC, the CPC and the Chinese government restored the reputation of many intellectuals who had been persecuted in previous political movements, and constantly improved their working and living conditions. The assessment of academic and technical titles was resumed. By 1982, more than 1 million intellectuals across the country had won various high and medium-level titles, and their social status had been duly respected. At the same time, the State Council also promulgated the *Regulations of the PRC on Award of National Science*, which promoted the development of science and technology and greatly mobilized the enthusiasm of the vast number of scientific research personnel.

(2) Comprehensive Reform of the Science and Technology System

From 1980 to 1991, the scientific and technological system reform in contemporary China experienced three stages of development.

The first stage was from 1980 to 1985, mainly the pilot exploration of reform within the science and technology system. As early as December 1977, *National Science and Technology Development Plan 1978–1985 (Draft)* was formed at the National Conference on Science and Technology Planning. However, the "left" influence of the scientific and technological front had not been completely eliminated for a long time. Although the scientific and technological work was constantly recovering and developing, it was still difficult to meet the requirements of economic construction. In 1982, the CCCPC and the State Council put forward the guiding principle that "economic construction must rely on science and technology, and scientific and technological work must face economic construction."[13] In 1983, the State Council set up a leading group for scientific and technological work to lead the pilot reform of the scientific and technological system. Since 1979, a small number of scientific research institutions in Sichuan, Shanghai and other places had carried out pilot projects to expand the autonomy of scientific research institutions. The reform in this period mainly focused on the scientific research and production consortium, the paid transfer of technological achievements, the technology contract system, and the free combination of internal research groups of scientific research institutions, which accumulated experience for the comprehensive reform throughout the country.

The second stage was from 1985 to 1988, when the reform of the science and technology system entered a substantive stage. In March 1985, the CCCPC issued the *Decision on the Reform of the Science and Technology System*, pointing out that the fundamental purpose of the reform of the science and technology system was to enable scientific and technological achievements to be rapidly and widely applied in production, give full play to the role of scientific and technological personnel, liberate scientific and technological productivity, and promote economic and social development; the fundamental task was to eliminate flaws, establish a new system full of vitality and vigor, and form an operational mechanism that was compatible and coordinated with economic and social development. According to the requirements of the *Decision*, the reform of the scientific and technological system was carried out in many aspects around the center of strengthening the vitality of scientific and technological units and promoting the integration of science and technology with production. Various localities had successively opened up scientific and technological markets and encouraged various forms of scientific and technological trade activities.

In 1985, the CCCPC approved the "Spark Program" for rural areas, guiding farmers in science and technology, guiding township enterprises in science and technology, promoting rural economic development, accelerating the process of agricultural modernization, and creating a road of science and technology with Chinese characteristics to promote agriculture. In March 1986, the CCCPC adopted the *Proposals on Tracking Strategic High-Tech Developments in the World* put forward by four famous scientists. In November, the CCCPC and the State Council formally approved the *Outline of High Technology Research and Development Plan*, and launched China's high technology research and development plan, namely the "863 Plan." In accordance with the policy of combining military and civil affairs and focusing on the people, the plan mainly conducted research and development in seven high-tech fields that had a great impact on China's future economic and social development, including biotechnology, aerospace technology, information technology, laser technology, automation technology, energy technology and new materials. In January 1987, the State Council issued policies and measures to further liberalize scientific research institutions, scientific research personnel, relax policies and management, and promote the integration of science, technology and economy.

The third stage was from 1988 to 1991, which was the stage of deepening the reform of science and technology system. On May 3, 1988, the State Council issued the *Decision on Several Issues Concerning Deepening the Reform of the Science and Technology System*, which proposed the theory of "Science and Technology Growing into the Economy" to promote the integration of science and technology and economy. The main measures were as follows: first, to introduce competitive mechanism and actively implement various forms of contract management responsibility system. Second, to encourage scientific research institutions to grow into the economy in various forms, to develop a commodity economy with science and technology as the pillar, and to promote the technological transformation of traditional industries and the formation of new and high-tech industries with their technological advantages; to vigorously promote scientific and technological progress in enterprises and rural areas, and support the development of scientific research institutions under different forms of ownership, such as collectives and individuals. Third, to link the salaries of scientific research institutions and scientific research personnel with their actual contributions. This was another leap in theory and practice in the reform of China's science and technology system.

In 1988, the state launched the "Torch Program" to promote the commercialization, industrialization and internationalization of high-tech, and encouraged scientific and technological personnel of universities and scientific research institutions to "venture into business" to establish high-tech enterprises. The State Council also approved the establishment of the Beijing High-Tech Industrial Development Experimental Zone. Since then, it became a prairie fire. More than 50 national high-tech industrial development zones were established throughout the country. In April 1991, Deng Xiaoping put forward the idea of "Developing high technology and applying research results in production."[14] The thinking of China's scientific and technological modernization was becoming clearer and clearer, and the pace of reform was becoming stronger and stronger.

The scientific and technological reform brought great vitality to the development of science and technology, formed an independent and complete scientific system, and created a large scientific and technological team. According to statistics in 1990, there were 10.808 million scientific and technological personnel in the field of Natural Science in units owned by the people, 5,819 independent scientific research and technological development institutions at or above the county level, and 1,666 scientific research and technological development institutions in colleges and universities, with a total of more than 13,000 in the country; among the large and medium-sized enterprises, there were 1.943 million engineering and technical personnel, and 771,000 people engaged in technology development activities. The scientific research achievements were outstanding, and some have reached the world advanced level. In the 1980s, more than 110,000 major scientific research achievements were achieved, of which nearly 10,000 were awarded by the state, and scientific research in some fields reached or was close to the world's advanced level. In particular, major projects such as the electron positron collider, the heavy ion accelerator, and the synchrotron radiation laboratory were put into use one after another, the successful development of the "Yinhe" supercomputer, the successful launch of the underwater missile, the "Long March 2" high thrust bundled rocket, and the "Asia 1" communication satellite showed that China made new breakthroughs in high-energy physics, computer technology, carrier rocket technology, and satellite communication technology.

The exploration and practice of the reform of the scientific and technological system broke the previous single and closed planning and management system, changed the state of separation between science and technology and the economy, and enabled the scientific and technological forces to enter the main battlefield of economic construction, which not only promoted the progress of science and technology, but also led to economic development.

1.3.3 The Opening of the Cultural System Reform

(1) The Fourth "Congress of Chinese Writers and Artists" and the Preliminary Reform of the Cultural System

During the "Great Cultural Revolution," literary and artistic groups were dissolved, literary and artistic workers were attacked and persecuted, and literary and artistic works withered. In the new period of reform and opening-up and socialist modernization, the state made a rectification of the cultural field and carried out a drastic reform of the cultural system.

From October 30 to November 16, 1979, the Fourth Congress of the Association of Literature and Art was held. On behalf of the CCCPC and the State Council, Deng Xiaoping made a speech at the meeting, affirming the line of literature and art since the founding of new China and removing the hat of "dictatorship by the proponents of a sinister line of literature and art." He pointed out that in this noble cause, the development of literature and art was very wide world. Whether it was to meet the needs of the people's spiritual life in many ways, or for the training of new socialists, to improve the ideological, cultural and moral level of society as a whole, literature and art had an important responsibility that could not be replaced by other sectors. The Congress carried forward the past and opened the way for the future, and reestablished "letting a hundred flowers bloom and a hundred schools of thought contend" as the guiding principle for the construction, reform and development of cultural undertakings in the new period.

Since the founding of new China, China's cultural system had been deeply influenced by the Soviet model, and had never deviated from the stereotype of serving politics and central work. The government had always been completely responsible for the management of cultural organizations, which had to a great extent constrained the development of cultural undertakings. The cultural system was even more devastated and destroyed during the Great Cultural Revolution. At the end of 1979, on the basis of investigation and research, the Ministry of Culture proposed to rectify and adjust art performance groups and began to gradually relax the management system. Shanghai, Beijing, Anhui, Jiangsu and other places took the lead in implementing a team contracting system within some cultural organizations. Fujian implemented the management method of "four guarantees and one award" and begun to break through the confines of equalitarianism and having everybody "eat from the same big pot" in the management system, improved the management system, delegated the right to stage plays, a certain amount of financial rights and rights of employing staff, and to a certain extent mobilized the enthusiasm of some literary and art workers. By 1982, these reforms and adjustments had achieved initial results. However, the two most fundamental problems entangled in the reform of cultural organizations was not solved: unreasonable personnel structure and unreasonable distribution system.

On New Year's Day in 1983, Zhu Muzhi, Minister of Culture, pointed out in a speech published in *Guangming Daily* that the basic spirit and principles of agricultural reform were generally applicable to cultural and artistic undertakings, that was, to implement the responsibility system and contract responsibility system. This immediately triggered a reform of the contractual management responsibility system throughout the country, and most cultural organizations in the country quickly implemented various forms of contractual management responsibility system. By the first half of 1985, more than two-thirds of the national art performance groups had initially implemented the contract management responsibility system.

To a certain extent, the reform eliminated the existing shortcomings, brought into play the enthusiasm and creativity of literary and art workers, achieved the combination of responsibility, power and benefit, insisted on distribution according to work, overcome equalitarianism, and accumulated some experience in exploring the establishment and improvement of the system and mechanism for the development of socialist cultural undertakings.

(2) The Deepening of the Cultural System Reform

In April 1985, the CCCPC and the State Council approved the *Opinions on the Reform of Art Performance Groups* proposed by the Ministry of Culture, and the art performance groups began to gradually carry out a comprehensive reform from the operation mechanism to the management system. In accordance with the spirit of this plan and in combination with their own reality, all parts of the country implemented it one after another, taking social benefits as the guide, artistic tasks as the center, and economic tasks as the basis. They changed the phenomenon of one-sided pursuit of high performances, high income, physical strength and equipment, and opened a comprehensive benign competition in the creation, rehearsal, performance of excellent plays and training of talents, arrangement of performances and grassroots performances. This laid a foundation for the deepening of cultural system reform, and promoted cultural groups to gradually become more independent social and cultural groups.

In September 1988, the state further deepened the reform of the cultural system, gradually implemented the "dual track system" and the employment contract system or performance contract system in art performance groups, and established a sound cultural market system. The government indirectly managed these cultural groups and gradually realized the separation of ownership and management rights, thus establishing a new and dynamic system. This reform was a major institutional change that had a bearing on the entire cultural system and even cultural life. It covered all aspects from labor, personnel to planning, finance to taxation, industrial and commercial administration. The reform measures were more pragmatic and standardized, and a scientific, advanced, and dynamic socialist cultural system with Chinese characteristics was gradually established.

Through the joint efforts of all parties, great achievements were made in the reform of the cultural system and some experience was accumulated.

The cultural management system broke through the mode of national overall contracting and management, presenting a vivid situation in which the state, the collective and the individual run the culture together. At that time, it was still the state-run culture that dominated. Under the guidance of the policy of "a little from the central government, a little from the province, and a little from the local government," a large number of cultural venues such as mass art centers, libraries, cultural centers, cinemas, cultural palaces, youth palaces, children's palaces, workers' cultural palaces, clubs, recreation rooms, song and dance halls were built and expanded to meet the needs of the masses for a multi-level, multifaceted and diversified cultural life. By the end of 1990, there were 14,802 cinemas in China, five times that of 1980; there were 1,864 cinemas, an increase of 441 over 1980; 3,095 auditoriums and clubs were opened, 652 more than in 1980; there were 2,527 public libraries, 1.5 times that of 1980; there were 1,013 museums, 2.8 times that of 1980; there were 366 mass art galleries, 1.7 times that of 1980; there were 2,955 cultural centers and 52,000 cultural stations, twice that of 1980; there were 2,805 art performance groups. The content of cultural activities also became more colorful. Various lively and diverse forms that the people liked to see and hear entered cultural life. Cultural upsurge such as "reading fever," "music fever," "dance fever," "philately fever" and "tourism fever" sprung up, and the people's cultural living standards were significantly improved. The cultural undertakings in contemporary China began to glow with new vitality.

The management mechanism of having everybody "eat from the same big pot" was broken by the contract responsibility system, the personnel system of "iron rice bowl" was broken by the appointment system and the contract system, and the egalitarian distribution system was reformed by the system of distribution according to work. Reform and opening-up enabled the new mode of contract responsibility system to enter the field of cultural system, and enabled the state, the collective and the individual to organically integrate the position, power, benefit and efficiency in the internal management of cultural undertakings, thus promoting the liberation of productive forces in cultural undertakings. The emergence of the appointment system and the contract system strongly impacted on the "iron rice bowl" formed by the planned economy, making it possible for the rational flow of talents, and a lively situation in which people give full play to their talents and get their places had emerged. Adhering to the principle of distribution according to work will inevitably widen the income gap, thus breaking the egalitarian practice (of everyone taking food from the same big pot), and making a big step forward in exploring the reform of the distribution system.

The transformation of cultural management mode from a single service type to a business service type. Cultural enterprises and public institutions and other cultural groups carried out paid services and activities of "supplementing culture with culture," taking from "culture" and using it for "culture," constantly summed up experiences and lessons, and began to come out of a self-development and self-renewal way of survival, gradually became independent development of cultural entities. In 1988, there were 11,458 outlets in cultural institutions across the country that carried out paid services and the activities of "supplementing culture with culture." The annual net income was 180 million yuan, equivalent to 12% of the funds allocated by the state for cultural undertakings in that year; In 1989, the annual net income was 230 million yuan, equivalent to about 16% of the funds allocated by the state; In 1990, the annual net income reached 270 million yuan, accounting for 18.2% of the funds allocated by the state.

Beginning of the process of legalization and standardization of the management of cultural undertakings. The state accelerated the pace of cultural legislation and formulated a number of cultural laws and regulations and normative documents in a planned and step-by-step manner in accordance with the reform process. Cultural legal institutions were established and improved, cultural law enforcement was strengthened, and cultural affairs were managed and inspected in accordance with the law, so that contemporary Chinese culture gradually embarked on a path of rule-based, healthy competition and lively development.

The reform of the cultural system also promoted the enthusiasm and creativity of literary and artistic groups and workers in cultural undertakings, provided high-level literary and artistic works for the socialist modernization drive, trained a large number of outstanding literary and artistic talents, and constantly met the growing needs of the people for cultural life.

1.3.4 "Five Thing to Emphasize, Four Things to Beautify and Three Things to Love" and Promotion of Socialist Cultural and Ethical Progress

(1) "Five Thing to Emphasize, Four Things to Beautify and Three Things to Love"
Since the Third Plenary Session of the 11th CCCPC opened a new era of reform and opening-up and socialist modernization in contemporary China in 1978, the CPC and the Chinese government had always regarded strengthening the building of promotion of socialist cultural and ethical progress as an important content and task of building socialism with Chinese characteristics.

As early as March 1979, Deng Xiaoping put forward such issues as maintaining the lofty revolutionary ideal, improving the moral level of all the people, changing the social atmosphere and rectifying the Party style. In fact, he had put forward some basic requirements for promoting of socialist cultural and ethical progress. In September, Ye Jianying pointed out at a conference to celebrate the 30th anniversary of the founding of the PRC: "We must build a high level of material civilization, while improving the education, science and culture of the whole nation and the level of health, establish high revolutionary ideals and revolutionary moral style, develop a noble and colorful cultural life, and build a high level of socialist cultural and ethical progress."[15] On December 25, 1980, Deng Xiaoping pointed out at the Central Working Conference of the CPC that the socialist country we want to build must have not only a high degree of material civilization, but also a high degree of cultural and ethical progress. When he spoke of a civilization with a high cultural and ideological level, he referred not only to education, science and culture (which were of course indispensable) but also to communist thinking, ideals, beliefs, morality and discipline, as well as a revolutionary stand and revolutionary principles, comradely relations among people, and so on. This summarized the promotion of socialist cultural and ethical progress as the construction of education, science and culture as well as the construction of thinking and morality, and clarified the connotation of the construction of cultural and ethical progress. At the same time, Deng Xiaoping called on CPC members to set an example by spreading the various spirits formed during the long revolutionary war to all the people and the youth, making them the main pillars of the cultural and ethical progress of the PRC.

Under the initiative of the CPC and the Chinese government, the people throughout the country had a new understanding of socialist cultural and ethical progress and have gradually launched some mass activities to create civilization. On February 25, 1981, nine units including the All China Federation of Trade Unions, the Central Committee of the Communist Youth League, the All China Women's Federation, and the China Federation of Literary and Art Circles jointly issued the *Initiative on Civil and Courteous Activities*. Subsequently, the Publicity Department of the CCCPC, the Ministry of Education, the Ministry of Culture, the Ministry of Health, and the Ministry of Public Security also jointly issued a notice, calling for the development of civilized and polite activities as a major event in building socialist cultural and ethical progress. Therefore, a civilized and polite publicity and education activity with "five things to emphasize and four things to beautify" (stress on decorum, stress on manners, stress on hygiene, stress on discipline, stress on morals, beauty of the mind, beauty of the language, beauty of the behavior, beauty of the environment) as the main content was kicked off throughout the country.

In March 1981, the CCCPC and the State Council fully affirmed the mass activities of cultural and ethical progress, seriously summed up experience, proposed and advocated the first "National Ethics and Courtesy Month." Large and medium-sized cities and some rural areas across the country set off an upsurge of civilized and polite activities in various forms in combination with "learning from Lei Feng and establishing new trends." Many grass-roots units and schools organized activities with various themes, carried out a variety of competitions for establishing civilized new trends, and various industries also actively carried out various forms of education activities on professional ethics. For example, the PLA carried out the activities of "four haves" (having high ideals, moral integrity, a good education and ability), "three stresses" (stressing military appearance, courtesy, and discipline), and "two defies" (defying difficulties and hardships, defying bloodshed and sacrifice).

In February 1982, the General Office of the CCCPC forwarded the *Report on the In-Depth Implementation of the 'Five things to Emphasize and Four Things to Beautify' Campaign* of the Publicity Department of the Central Committee, which suggested that March of each year be regarded as the "National Ethics and Courtesy Month." This institutionalized and regularized the civilized and polite activities of "learning from Lei Feng and establishing new trends "and "five things to emphasize and four things to beautify," further promoted them nationwide, and started to establish a long-term mechanism for the construction of cultural and ethical progress. In the first "National Ethics and Courtesy Month," Hu Yaobang and other party and state leaders, together with more than 2 million people in the capital, actively participated in the rectification of "dirty, disorderly and poor," improved environmental sanitation, rectified public order, improved service quality, and initiated and led a good new socialist trend.

In September 1982, the report of the 12th National Congress of the CPC made a profound exposition on the socialist cultural and ethical progress from a theoretical perspective. The report pointed out that while building a high level of material civilization, building a high level of cultural and ethical progress was the strategic principle of building socialism; material civilization and cultural and ethical progress were conditions and purposes of each other; cultural and ethical progress was an important feature of socialism and an important manifestation of the superiority of socialism; the construction of cultural and ethical progress was divided into cultural construction and ideological construction. Ideological construction determined the socialist nature of cultural and ethical progress, of which the most important were the revolutionary ideal, morality and discipline; we should use revolutionary thinking and spirit to arouse the great enthusiasm of the masses for building socialism. The comprehensive exposition of socialist cultural and ethical progress at the 12th National Congress of the CPC marked the initial formation of the theory of socialist cultural and ethical progress construction as an important part of the theory of socialism with Chinese characteristics, and the construction of socialist cultural and ethical progress was determined as a strategic principle of China's socialist modernization.

In January 1983, the "five things to emphasize and four things to beautify" activity added the educational activities of "loving the motherland, loving social-ism and loving the CPC," thus further enriching the contents of activities of the cultural and ethical progress. In February, the CCCPC and the State Council decided to establish the Central Committee of "five things to emphasize, four things to beautify and three things to love" with Wan Li as the director to further promote the activities of "five things to emphasize, four things to beautify and three things to love." After that, all provinces, autonomous regions and municipalities also set up activity committees of "five things to emphasize, four things to beautify and three things to love." This raised the cultural and ethical progress activity of "five things to emphasize, four things to beautify and three things to love" to a new height and enabled it to be carried out more deeply and extensively. In 1984, Sanming City, Fujian Province was selected as a model of the "five things to emphasize, four things to beautify and three things to love" activity to promote the construction of urban cultural and ethical progress. In the process of cultural and ethical progress, advanced figures and outstanding deeds such as Zhu Boru, Zhang Haidi and Jiang Zhuying emerged throughout the country. Their communist fine morals and customs, as well as ideology and work style not only educated and guided the healthy growth of young people, but also infected and encouraged the people of all ethnic groups throughout the country to actively participate in the socialist cultural and ethical progress.

Since 1983, the "five things to emphasize, four things to beautify and three things to love" campaign had been popularized throughout the country. From schools and service departments to all walks of life, from large and medium-sized cities to rural grassroots units, from civilized life to civilized service and then to civilized production, all fields of social life were permeated with the wind of civilization, which played a positive role in strengthening the people's socialist ideals and beliefs, improving the social conduct and beautifying the social environment.

(2) The Establishment of the Guidelines for the Promotion of Cultural and Ethical Progress

After the reform and opening-up, the literary and art was rapidly activated, and a trend of bourgeois liberalization emerged. This was contrary to the socialist cultural and ethical progress and must be resolutely counterattacked.

As the fundamental guideline for promotion of socialist cultural and ethical progress, the Four Cardinal Principles required adherence to and maintenance of the basic socialist system on the ideological and theoretical front. In order to better grasp the adherence to the Four Cardinal Principles and the material civilizations as well as the cultural and ethical progress, especially to unify the thinking and actions of the whole party on the issue of cultural and ethical progress, in September 1986, the Sixth Plenary Session of the 12th CCCPC adopted the *Resolution on the Guiding Principles for Building Socialist Society with an Advanced Level of Culture and Ideology*, which, from the perspective of the overall layout of China's modernization drive, clarified the strategic position, fundamental tasks and basic guiding principles for the promotion of socialist cultural and ethical progress.

The *Resolution* pointed out that the overall layout of China's socialist modernization drive was to take economic construction as the center, unswervingly carry out the reform of the economic and political systems, unswervingly strengthen the promotion of socialist cultural and ethical progress, and make these aspects coordinate and promote each other.

The strategic position of the construction of socialist cultural and ethical progress determined that it must be the promotion of socialist cultural and ethical progress to promote socialist modernization, to promote comprehensive reform and opening-up, and to adhere to the Four Cardinal Principles.

The fundamental task of promotion of socialist cultural and ethical progress was to unite the people of all ethnic groups across the country with the common ideal of building socialism with Chinese characteristics, cultivate socialist citizens with high ideals and moral integrity and were cultured and disciplined, and improve the ideological and moral quality and scientific and cultural quality of the entire Chinese nation.

The guideline of the promotion of socialist cultural and ethical progress was that it must promote socialist modernization, promote comprehensive reform and opening-up, and adhere to the Four Cardinal Principles.

The *Resolution* was a programmatic document for China to strengthen the promotion of socialist cultural and ethical progress in the new period. It played an important guiding role in promoting the promotion of socialist cultural and ethical progress and ensuring the smooth progress of socialist modernization.

The 13th National Congress of the CPC stressed the importance of cultural and ethical progress construction under the guidance of Marxism. After the Fourth Plenary Session of the 13th CCCPC, the Chinese Communists, with Comrade Jiang Zemin as the main representative, profoundly summed up their experience, adhered to the principle of "doing two jobs at once" and constantly strengthened the promotion of socialist cultural and ethical progress. On July 1, 1991, in his speech at the meeting to celebrate the 70th anniversary of the founding of the CPC, Jiang Zemin further elaborated the basic principles for the promotion of socialist cultural and ethical progress from the perspective of building a socialist culture with Chinese characteristics, that was, we must adhere to Marxism-Leninism and Mao Zedong Thought as the guidance, and we must not diversify the guiding ideology; we must adhere to the direction of serving the people and socialism and the policy of "letting a hundred flowers bloom and a hundred schools of thought contend," prosper and develop socialist culture, and not allow things that poison the people, pollute society and oppose socialism to spread; we must inherit and carry forward the excellent traditional culture of the nation while fully reflecting the spirit of the socialist era, base ourselves on our own country while fully absorb the outstanding achievements of the world culture, and not allow national nihilism and total Westernization. This has pointed out the direction for the promotion of socialist cultural and ethical progress in the new period.

1.3.5 The Birth of China's First Olympic Champion and the Development of China's Sports in the New Era

(1) Recovery and Development of Sports
In the new period of reform and opening-up and socialist modernization, the sports cause in contemporary China radiated new vitality and made unprecedented

achievements. The reform of the sports system was also preliminarily explored, laying a foundation for the vigorous development of sports. From September 15 to September 30, 1979, the Fourth National Games was held in Beijing. The Games was the largest since the founding of new China. A total of 31 sports delegations (including Taiwan sports delegations) from all provinces (autonomous regions and municipalities) and the PLA and more than 4,000 sports athletes competed in 34 sports events in Beijing. Five people broke five World Records five times, three people leveled three world records three times, and 12 people broke eight Asian records 24 times. A number of modern sports equipment and facilities were used for the first time in the games, including the then internationally advanced electronic photographic timing equipment for track events, electronic timing equipment for swimming and laser ranging equipment for long-distance throwing events, which greatly improved the competition level and science and technology content in sports.

On November 26, 1979, the International Olympic Committee (IOC) officially announced the *Nagoya Resolution* at its headquarters in Lausanne, recognizing that the Olympic Committee of the PRC represented China to participate in the IOC, and the "Taipei Olympic Committee" of Taiwan participated in the IOC as a local organization of China. This properly solved the issue of China's legal seat in the IOC, which had been entangled since the 1950s.

In January 1980, the National Sports Work Conference was held in Beijing. The meeting summed up the experience and lessons of the development of sports in the 30 years since the founding of new China, and studied how to adapt to the new situation during the period of national economic adjustment and after China's participation in the Olympic Games, and accelerate the development of sports; it was believed that we should comprehensively improve the people's health level and sports technology level, and train more sports talents faster; it was believed that we should strive to create outstanding achievements on the world stage and promote sports to better serve the Four Modernizations.

In April 1981, the Chinese table tennis team took part in the 36th World Table Tennis Championships held in Yugoslavia, winning the championships in seven events, setting a new historical record of 55 years in the world table tennis championships, and establishing China's dominant position in the world table tennis arena. The Chinese women's volleyball team won the championship in the Third World Cup women's volleyball match in 1981, which was the first big ball world championship of China. Since then, the Chinese women's volleyball team had won the Nineth World Volleyball Championship in 1982, the 23rd Olympic Games in 1984, the Fourth World Cup Volleyball Tournament in 1985, and the 10th World Volleyball Championship in 1986, creating a miracle of "five consecutive championships," establishing a monument in the international volleyball arena and writing a new chapter in China's big ball sports. The Chinese women's volleyball team was the first group to win the championship among China's three major balls. It was a sign that China's competitive sports had entered the world sports arena after the reform and opening-up. "The Spirit of the Chinese Women's Volleyball Team" encouraged and promoted the continuous development of China's sports cause.

On March 30, 1982, IOC President Samaranch visited China. Deng Xiaoping met with Samaranch and his party. In April, when talking with some leading comrades, Deng Xiaoping pointed out that sports was an important aspect of the promotion of socialist cultural and ethical progress, and it was necessary to further study, put forward principles and formulate plans. With the great attention of the CPC and the Chinese government, China's sports cause had been developing vigorously and had made remarkable achievements one after another.

1982 was the most glorious year for Chinese gymnastics. At the Sixth Artistic Gymnastics World Cup held in Yugoslavia, the Chinese gymnastics team, which was not the favorite to win the championship, did not receive enough attention from other countries and media before the competition. However, in this event, Li Ning won six gold medals in floor exercise, pommel horse, rings, vault and all-round, and Tong Fei won the gold medal in the horizontal bar. This was not only the best result in Chinese history, but also the highest record in the history of world gymnastics. People exclaimed that the world gymnastics has entered the "Li Ning era."

In November 1982, the Nineth Asian Games was held in New Delhi, the capital of India. More than 3,300 athletes from 33 countries and regions participated in 21 events. China sent 445 delegations to participate in 18 of the 21 events. The Chinese team won 61 gold medals and the Japanese team won 56 gold medals. For the first time, China's number of gold medals exceeded that of Japan, which ranked first in the previous Asian Games, and became the new hegemon in the Asian sports arena.

Since it first participated in the Seventh Asian Games, China's sports achievements have been rising step by step. In the Seventh Asian Games, China ranked third with 33 gold medals, second with 56 in the eighth, and first with 61 in the nineth. This ended the 31-year history of Japan's dominance in Asian sports, realized the ambition of Chinese sports to break out of Asia and go global, and created a new era of Chinese sports dominance in Asia.

(2) China Won Its First Olympic Gold Medal

Since the restoration of the legitimate seat of the Olympic Committee in 1979, the Chinese sports delegation officially participated in the 23rd Olympic Games in 1984 for the first time, thus ending the era of isolation from the Olympic Games.

The 23rd Olympic Games was held in Los Angeles from July 28 to August 12, 1984. China sent a 353-member sports delegation, including 225 athletes, to participate in 16 events and a performance. On the first day of the competition on July 29, shooter Xu Haifeng won the first gold medal of the Olympic Games, which was the first time that the Chinese people climbed the podium of the Olympic champion. Xu Haifeng smashed the humiliation of "Sick Man of East Asia" and ushered in an exciting great breakthrough in Chinese sports. Then, Zeng Guoqiang, Wu Shude, Chen Weiqiang and Yao Jingyuan won the championship one after another; Li Ning won three gold medals at one stroke; China's women's volleyball team achieved "three consecutive championships"; Luan Jujie became the first Asian player to leap to the top of the world's foil; female diver Zhou Jihong also won the championship. The Chinese delegation finally wrote the glorious history of China's sports cause with 15 gold medals. The breakthrough of "zero" Olympic gold medal was an important milestone in China's sports cause.

From September 22 to October 7, 1990, the 11th Asian Games, which symbolized the "unity, friendship and progress" of the three billion people in Asia, was successfully held in Beijing. This was the first time that the Asian Games had been hosted by the PRC since its birth 40 years ago. It was also the first comprehensive international sports competition held by the PRC on its own land. More than 6,500 sports delegations from 37 countries and regions from the Olympic Council of Asia participated in the Asian Games. The number of delegations and the number of athletes participating in the games were unprecedented in the history of the Asian Games. The Chinese government gave great attention and support to this Asian Games, and the people of all ethnic groups also poured great enthusiasm into it. The success of the Asian Games not only enhanced the peace and friendship of Asian countries, but also achieved fruitful results in sports achievements: a total of four world records were broken, more than six world records were exceeded and five world records were leveled. The Chinese delegation won 183 of the 310 gold medals, breaking one world record and setting 30 Asian records, once again demonstrating the strength of a sports power. This was a magnificent monument in the history of Asian sports jointly built by the 1.1 billion Chinese people and the Asian people, and a brilliant stroke in the history of Chinese sports development.

The 14 years of reform and opening-up was also the initial stage of China's sports reform. The sports system began to break the previous mode of relying solely on state funding. Taking operation and income generation as a breakthrough point, it put forward the principles of "focusing on sports, accompanied by diversified business" and "supporting sports with sports and supplementing sports with subsidiary business," actively attracting social funds to finance the development of sports and supporting qualified institutions to carry out diversified business. Objectively, it tried to socialize and industrialize sports, and accumulated experience for further deepening the reform of sports.

Summary

Bringing order out of chaos in the field of education and the reform of the education system injected new vitality into contemporary China's education, promoted the development of education, trained various types of talents at all levels, supported the construction of various fronts, and improved the overall quality of the Chinese nation.

The convening of the National Conference on Science ushered in the "Spring of Science" in China.

The implementation of the intellectual policy and the comprehensive reform of the scientific and technological system promoted the progress of China's scientific undertakings, changed the situation where science and technology are separated from the economy, made scientific and technological forces enter the main battlefield of economic construction, promoted the development of China's economy, and strengthened China's comprehensive national strength.

The reorganization in the field of literature and art and the gradual reform of the cultural system revitalized and energized China's cultural undertakings, provided a high level of cultural and artistic works for socialist modernization, and cultivated a large number of excellent cultural and artistic talents. The establishment of the guidelines for the construction of cultural and ethical progress clarified the direction of the promotion of socialist cultural and ethical progress in the new period, promoted the continuous development of socialist cultural and ethical progress, and provided inexhaustible spiritual impetus for the construction of socialism with Chinese characteristics.

The mass cultural and ethical progress activities with "five things to emphasize, four things to beautify and three things to love" as the core content established a civilized social conduct.

The victory of the struggle against bourgeois liberalization ensured the guiding position of Marxism in the ideological field and laid a foundation for upholding the Four Cardinal Principles.

The restoration of China's seat in the IOC promoted the development of sports.

The breakthrough of zero gold medals in the Olympic Games improved China's position in the international sports arena.

The initial reform of the sports system brought about the prosperity of China's sports undertakings.

SECTION 4

Profound Changes in People's Lives and Construction of Socialist Undertakings with Chinese Characteristics

1.4.1 Living Standard and Quality of Life of Urban and Rural Residents in the New Period

(1) The Improvement of Material Standard of Living and Quality of Life of Urban and Rural Residents

In the New Period, with the development of economy, the material standard of living of urban and rural residents has been improved. China's per capita GNP increased from 379 yuan in 1978 to 1,879 yuan in 1991. Annual per capita disposable income of urban households rose from 343.4 yuan in 1978 to 1,700.6 yuan in 1991, and annual per capita net income of rural households rose from 133.6 yuan to 708.6 yuan during the same period. The consumption level of the national residents increased from 184 yuan in 1978 to 896 yuan in 1991, the consumption level of the urban residents increased from 405 yuan in 1978 to 1,925 yuan in 1991, and the consumption level of the rural residents increased from 138 yuan in

1978 to 621 yuan in 1991. Especially during the "Sixth Five-Year Plan" period, the average annual growth rate of the national residents' consumption level was 8.6%, and the growth rate of the rural residents reached 10.1%.

The withdrawal of the urban voucher-based supply system from the historical stage and the significant decrease of the proportion of farmers' self-sufficiency consumption. In 1985, the state abolished the system of unified purchase and sale of agricultural products, which had lasted for more than 30 years. By the end of the 1980s, the voucher-based supply system was basically ended, and the consumption pattern of Chinese people began to change from suppressed consumption to open supply and autonomous consumption. The consumption level of residents improved significantly. In 1990, the average consumption level of national residents reached 803 yuan, which was about 1.3 times higher than that of 1978 in terms of comparable prices. At the end of 1990, the balance of savings deposits of urban and rural residents increased from 21.06 billion yuan in 1978 to 703.42 billion yuan, an increase of 33.4 times. In 1991, it increased to 911.03 billion yuan, of which 74.53% were urban residents' deposits and 25.47% were rural residents' deposits. From 1978 to 1990, the per capita deposit balance increased from 89.8 yuan to 2,223.19 yuan for urban residents and from 7 yuan to 272.01 yuan for rural residents.

The number and quality of food, clothing and housing for urban and rural residents in China improved generally. In terms of food consumption, according to the statistics of the Food and Agriculture Organization of the United Nations (UN), in 1992, the average daily caloric intake of Chinese residents from food reached 2,727 kcal, higher than 2,439 kcal in 1978 and higher than the world average level of 2,631 kcal; The protein content intake reached 67.4g, higher than 63.4g in 1978 and close to the world average level of 68.7g; The fat content intake was 51.9 g, higher than 40 g in 1978 and higher than the average level of 51.1 g in Asian countries. Although there was a certain gap with developed countries, it was growing rapidly year after year. The Engel's coefficient of urban and rural residents was decreasing year by year. That is to say, the consumption structure of urban residents began to change from subsistence type and food and clothing type to quasi well-off type, and the consumption structure of rural residents began to change from subsistence type to food and clothing type. The consumption level of urban and rural residents in terms of clothing was also greatly improved in terms of quantity and quality, and the personalized trend of consumption was more obvious. In 1978, urban residents basically did not have color TV sets, and there were no TV sets in rural areas. By 1991, every 100 urban households had 68.41 color TV sets; every 100 rural residents had 52.4 TV sets, including 6.44 color TV sets. High-end consumer durables had started to move from the "old four pieces" (bicycles, watches, sewing machines, radios) to the "new six pieces" (televisions, washing machines, refrigerators, tape recorders, electric fans, and cameras). Housing conditions was greatly improved. The per capita living area of urban residents increased from 3.6 square meters in 1978 to 6.9 square meters in 1991, and the per capita living area of rural residents increased from 8.1 square meters to 18.5 square meters, further improving the quality of housing.

Conditions in medical and health care and sports and health care were continuously improved. The life expectancy of China's population increased continuously, from 67 years in 1978 to about 70 years in 1991. The infant mortality rate decreased from 39.33 ‰ in 1980–1985 to 32.45 ‰ in 1985–1990, a rate higher than the world average and the level of developing countries. The number of doctors nationwide increased from 1.033 million in 1978 to 1.78 million in 1991, the number of doctors per 1,000 people increased from 1.07 to 1.54, and the number of beds in hospitals and health centers increased from 1.856 million to 2.689 million. It is worth noting that during this period, China had already faced a serious population problem. The state had implemented a strict family planning policy since 1979, and had achieved certain results in controlling population growth. Since then, family planning policy remained a basic state policy for China.

Living environment and living conditions were protected and improved. At the beginning of reform and opening-up, the foundation of China's transportation was very weak, the total transportation volume was insufficient, the technical equipment was backward, and the transportation structure was not reasonable. In 1978, the total length of China's transport routes was only about 1.23 million kilometers, including 48,600 kilometers of railways, 890,200 kilometers of highways, 136,000 kilometers of inland waterways, 149,800 kilometers of civil aviation lines and 8,300 kilometers of pipelines. By 1991, the length of railways had increased to 53,400 kilometers, the length of highways was 1,041,100 kilometers, the length of civil aviation lines was 559,100 kilometers, and the length of pipelines was 16,200 kilometers. The transportation infrastructure had been greatly improved. However, the problem of environmental protection became increasingly prominent. Air pollution, industrial wastewater and dust constituted a great threat to the ecological environment. For example, in 1991, the country discharged 25 billion tons of industrial waste water, causing 85% of the cities in the country to lack clean water, more than 100 million people's drinking water was seriously polluted by industry, and 79% of the people in the country drank unclean water. Maintaining the harmony between man and nature, enabling people to have clean water sources, fresh air, green living places, comfortable space and green food became a necessary condition for building modern life and an important task of the Chinese government.

The employment rate of urban residents increased significantly. In 1978, the problem of urban unemployment became more prominent, with 5.3 million unemployed people registered in the labor department alone, and the unemployment rate reached 5.3%. In 1979, the number of unemployed people reached 5.68 million, and the urban unemployment rate climbed to a new high. In August 1980, the National Labor Work Conference put forward the policy of "Three Combinations," combining employment introduction by labor departments, employment through voluntary organizations and self-employment, making every effort to open up employment channels and solve the employment problem through multiple channels, thus more than 26 million people were employed within three years. By 1982, most areas in China had basically solved the urban unemployment problem accumulated before 1980, including that of the returning educated youth. After several years of efforts, the urban employment problem was further alleviated in 1984, and the urban unemployment rate dropped to 1.9%.

(2) The Improvement of Spiritual Life and Quality of Life of Urban and Rural Residents in the New Period

The people's cultural life became increasingly rich and colorful. "Nutrition, beautiful clothes, spacious living, high-end use and diversified play" gradually became a new trend for urban and rural residents to pursue a new life. Every change in material life brought traces of spiritual and cultural life to varying degrees. In terms of clothing, Western-style clothes made a comeback and entered the Chinese clothing industry; bell bottoms were also popular in line with the Chinese mentality of seeking freshness and novelty; jeans had entered China since the 1980s. They were free and unrestrained, and Chinese people gradually changed their dress orientation. In terms of diet, the consumption structure of Chinese people changed from a single subsistence consumption to diversification and fashion. Western diets such as McDonald's and Kentucky Fried Chicken (KFC) became popular in China, impacting on the eating habits of Chinese people. In terms of housing, the reform of housing commercialization was put forward and gradually implemented in the early 1980s. The "housing commercialization" gradually became a reality that Chinese people had to face. The special welfare of "housing distribution" enjoyed by urban residents was submerged by the housing commercialization. In terms of daily necessities, the consumption stratification of affordable consumption, middle-end consumption and high-end consumption was very obvious. People began to shift from single subsistence consumption to diversified consumption. High-end consumer durables such as computers, telephones, motorcycles, air conditioners and cars gradually replaced the "old four pieces" and "new six pieces" and entered the family life of some Chinese people who "got rich first." In terms of life and entertainment, TV, karaoke and rock music gradually entered the life of the Chinese people. Tourism also became a new way for people to pursue "fashionable" life, and people were more pursuing the richness of spiritual and cultural life.

With the development of modern communication tools, transportation tools and media, people's social interaction was expanded in space. The cross regional nature of communication was continuously enhanced, and the spiritual life style was more personalized and open. With the popularity of TV and radio in Chinese families, audio-visual culture with mass media as its content sprung up and gradually replaced the dominant printing culture in the past. People were more likely to choose cultural and entertainment life that met their individual needs, and they could also learn adaptively to meet their own development needs, so as to free themselves from the highly stressful working environment.

People's thirst for knowledge and technology became more urgent. In cities, since the early 1980s, many young workers participated in the "double supplement" learning of cultural and technical knowledge. According to statistics, in 1980, there were more than 76,000 schools directly run by enterprises and units across the country, and 1.738 million young employees participated in the "double supplement" program; there were 17,000 schools run by local trade unions, and 3.29 million young workers participated in the study. In addition, in 1983, more than 600,000 young people took part in the "Revitalizing China" reading activities. By June 1984, the number had reached 11 million. In 1992, there were more than 3.2 million students in various adult higher and secondary schools nationwide, and 49.59 million students graduated from adult technical training schools, most of whom were employees of enterprises and public institutions. During this period, the "old three kinds" (entertainment, reading, holiday activities) of workers' entertainment had been gradually replaced by new contents such as photography, art, calligraphy, philately, antique collection, sports competitions, fitness activities, music appreciation and tourism. In rural areas, the vast number of farmers who were no longer struggling for food and clothing also began to pursue a full spiritual life. Cultural and entertainment consumption and cultural service activities were no longer a distant luxury pursuit for the farmers. For example, in 1992, 35 townships and towns in Xishan City, Jiangsu Province established cultural facilities with their own characteristics, established 426 libraries with a collection of 900,000 books. Some townships and towns also established farmers' parks and farmers' cultural palaces, and 10 townships such as Ganlu and Xuelang built cultural buildings. There were 25 township theatres that can accommodate more than a thousand people in the city, 57 township film screening teams, and more than 400 village level cultural clubs, cultural rooms, youth homes, and elderly activity rooms. The proportion of the people's expenditure on cultural and educational services also increased year by year. Great changes took place in people's ways of leisure and entertainment. The cultural publishing industry developed rapidly. There were more and more newspapers, magazines and various books, and broadcasting, film and television undertakings also made considerable progress. In 1990, the national radio and TV population coverage reached 74.7% and 79.4% respectively.

The cultural level and education level of Chinese urban and rural residents improved significantly. In the third national census in 1982, 6.2 million people had university education, accounting for 0.6% of the total population; 68.34 million people had high school education, accounting for 6.8% of the total population; 180.38 million people had junior high school education, accounting for 17.9% of the total population; 355.25 million people had elementary school education, accounting for 35.2% of the total population; 229.96 million people were illiterate and semi-literate, accounting for 22.8% of the total population. In the fourth national census in 1990, 15.76 million people had university education, accounting for 1.4% of the total population; 89.888 million people had high school education, accounting for 8.0% of the total population; 263.385 million people had junior high school education, accounting for 23.3% of the total population; 420.205 million people had elementary school education, accounting for 37.2% of the total population; 181.609 million people were illiterate and semi-literate, accounting for 16.1% of the total population. The national school-age children enrollment rate increased from 94.0% in 1978 to 97.8% in 1991, the university enrollment rate increased from 5.9% in 1978 to 27.8% in 1991. The number of students in higher education increased from 856,000 in 1978 to 2,044,000 in 1991, and the number of university students per 10,000 population increased from 8.9 in 1978 to 18 in 1991. In 1992, the adult literacy rate was 73%, higher than the world average; the state's investment in education increased from 6.56 billion yuan in 1978 to 48.218 billion yuan in 1991, and its proportion in fiscal expenditure also increased from 5.9% to 10.2%; the total investment in education infrastructure also increased from 445 million yuan to 2.962 billion yuan, and its share in the total investment increased from 0.9% to 1.4%.

The improvement of the people's spiritual life and quality of life in the new period promoted the transformation of traditional social life style to modern life style. It was not only the product of reform and opening-up and modernization construction, but also promoted the deepening of reform and opening-up and the modernization process of Chinese society.

1.4.2 Reform of Social Welfare and Social Security System

Since the reform and opening-up, the reform and improvement of the social welfare and social security system had become an important work of the CPC and the Chinese government. As an important part of the redistribution of national income, social security, known as "economic stabilizer," refers to a social stability mechanism based on welfare means to ensure the basic living needs of every social member guaranteend by the state. China's traditional social security system was formed under the highly centralized planned economy, including the national security, unit security and rural collective security. It was not a social security in the full sense. From the early 1980s to the early 1990s, the reform of China's traditional social security system basically went through three stages and achieved certain results.

The first stage was from the early 1980s to 1984, when the State Council promulgated a number of administrative regulations to repair and improve the traditional social security system. This period was mainly for partial adjustments to solve problems left over by history, improve the imperfect retirement system for veteran cadres, and establish a poverty alleviation system.

In 1978, the State Council issued two documents, the *Interim Measures on the Resettlement of Elderly, Infirm, Sick and Disabled Cadres* and the *Interim Measures on the Retirement and Resignation of Workers*. Subsequently, the Organization

Department of the CCCPC and the State Labour Bureau put forward specific reform plans and carried out pilot projects according to the two interim measures, which was the beginning of the establishment of a old-age insurance system in China. From 1980 to 1983, the CPC issued a number of documents to further regulate the leaving of the posts to rest of veteran cadres, the retirement of military cadres, the retirement of workers, the retirement of veteran cadres, the labor insurance and welfare benefits of enterprise employees, and improve the imperfect retirement system of cadres and workers, which was clearly stipulated in the 1982 *constitution*.

In December 1979, the Ministry of Health, the Ministry of Agriculture, the Ministry of Finance, the State Administration of Medicine, and the National Supply and Marketing Cooperative General Agency jointly issued the *Constitution of Rural Cooperative Medical Service (Trial Draft)*, which proposed to comprehensively rectify and reform the rural grass-roots health organizations and the cooperative medical care system.

In 1983, the Ministry of Civil Affairs first proposed the establishment of a poverty alleviation system. On the one hand, the "large-scale poverty alleviation "would be implemented to help poor areas for economic development; on the other hand, the "small-scale poverty alleviation" would be emphasized to give economic assistance to poor households. This was a reform of the traditional social relief mode in the past. It changed the simple life relief in the past. It was a combination of relief and support for production, that was, the mode of changing "blood transfusion" into "hematopoiesis."

The second stage was from 1984 to 1991, which was the initial trial period of China's social security system reform. The contents of the reform include: first, the pilot reform of social pooling of the endowment insurance for enterprise employees; second, the pilot reform of social insurance for public medical care and labor insurance medical care; third, the attempt to establish an unemployment insurance system for state-owned enterprise employees; fourth, the reform of disaster relief methods; and fifth, the attempt to establish an endowment insurance system for farmers.

Since 1984, the reform of the endowment insurance system for urban employees had been gradually implemented. The first pilot of social pooling of retirement expenses was implemented in some State-owned enterprise employees in Jiangsu, Guangdong, Liaoning and other places. New steps were taken in the reform of endowment insurance system.

In April 1984, the Ministry of Health and the Ministry of Finance issued the *Notice on Further Strengthening the Administration of Public Health Care*, requiring all localities to strengthen leadership and establish and improve public medical management institutions; strengthen ideological education and correct misconducts; establish and improve various rules and regulations; actively and prudently reform the publicly funded medical system.

In September 1985, the CCCPC put forward for the first time in the *Recommendations of the CCCPC for the Seventh Five-Year Plan for Economic and Social Development* that it was necessary to adapt to the new situation of invigorating the domestic economy and further opening up to the outside world, and proceed from China's national conditions and strength, and gradually establish and improve various types of social insurance systems, improve and perfect social welfare, social relief and preferential treatment in accordance with the principle of benefiting production and ensuring life, so as to establish the rudiments of a socialist social security system with Chinese characteristics step by step. This recommendation was adopted at the National Congress of the CPC in September 1985 and became a programmatic document guiding the reform of the social security system.

Under the planned economic system, China implemented the policy of urban-rural dual division, which covered up the social unemployment phenomenon and there was no unemployment insurance. With the promotion of the reform of the labor employment system, the wage system and the labor insurance system and the promulgation of the *Bankruptcy Law of the PRC*, in July 1986, the State Council promulgated the *Interim Provisions on Unemployment Insurance for Employees of SOEs*, thus starting to establish an unemployment insurance system.

Since 1986, on the one hand, the state had stepped up its efforts to help the poor, providing 1 billion special interest discount loans every year for five consecutive years, focusing on supporting the economic construction of more than 300 poor counties, and trying to change the poverty alleviation system; on the other hand, the state had supported poor households with certain production capacity to escape from poverty in terms of policy, technology and employment, reducing the number of rural poor from nearly 100 million to 27 million. From 1987 to 1990, the state carried out pilot projects in more than 190 counties in 19 provinces (autonomous regions and municipalities) and explored the rural grassroots social security system based on old-age and medical security, which further developed the rural social security cause. However, it was still a long way to go to fundamentally realize "providing for the elderly" of the rural population. China's social insurance began to transform into a socialized social security, but the reform at this time was only tentative, with many limitations, and the effect of the reform was not obvious. Some measures of the reform were also in trouble for various reasons.

The third stage started from 1991, when China's social security system really began to enter the stage of partial reform. In 1991, the Eighth Five-Year Plan and the Ten-year Plan further put forward that efforts should be made to promote the reform of the social security system. To reform and establish the social endowment insurance and unemployment insurance system as the focus, to drive the development of other social insurance and social welfare, social relief and preferential treatment. In accordance with the principle that the state, collective and individual share a reasonable burden, a social endowment insurance system among all types of urban workers should be gradually established, the scope of unemployment insurance should be expanded, the method of unemployment insurance should be improved, and the multi-level social insurance should be implemented. In rural areas, the policy of active guidance should be taken to gradually establish different forms of old-age security system. At the same time, efforts should be made to reform the medical insurance and work-related injury insurance systems and continue to promote cooperative medical insurance.

In June 1991, the State Council promulgated the *"Decision on the Reform of the Endowment Insurance System for Enterprise Employees"* to comprehensively promote the reform of the endowment insurance system. This was a major reform of the endowment insurance system mode for enterprise employees, that was, to change the single national insurance system in the past, establish a new system combining the national basic endowment insurance, enterprise supplementary endowment insurance and personal savings endowment insurance, start to change the situation where the national compulsory basic security plays a single role in the social security field, and start to gradually implement a socialized and professional management system, as well as establish the basic framework of the endowment insurance system for urban workers, which was the basis for further reform. In short, during the 14 years from the Third Plenary Session of the 11th CCCPC in 1978 to the early 1990s, the reform of the social security system had made great achievements.

In terms of social insurance, great progress was made in the pilot reform of social insurance such as endowment insurance, unemployment insurance, public medical care, labor insurance, work-related injury insurance and maternity insurance for employees of urban enterprises. The basic endowment insurance system for employees of SOEs was initially established, the unemployment insurance system was established, and the insurance systems such as medical insurance, work-related injury insurance and maternity insurance were improved. The rural endowment insurance also developed rapidly, gradually establishing a rural social security system to protect the interests of farmers, relieve farmers' worries, and move towards standardized management.

In terms of social assistance, the state insisted on combining "big-scale poverty alleviation" and "small-scale poverty alleviation," combining poverty alleviation with assistance, relief and disaster relief, turning the "blood transfusion" mechanism into a "blood-making" mechanism, actively promoting the socialization of social assistance, insisting on relying on the masses, relying on the collective, production self-help, mutual aid, and supplemented by the necessary relief and support from the state. "When a disaster strikes in one location, help comes from all quarters," multi-channel and multi-level social assistance and relief of "state helps, collective subsidies and social donations" were adopted to improve the level of social assistance and ensure the basic livelihood of the people.

In terms of social welfare, with the advocacy and support of the government, the state adhered to the guiding ideology of "socialization of social welfare" and "social welfare, socially managed," and let the whole society participate in welfare undertakings. By 1991, there were 42,264 social welfare institutions in urban and rural areas, an increase of 370% over 1978; 645,856 people were adopted by welfare institutions, an increase of 248%; the number of social welfare enterprises increased to 43,071, an increase of 39 times over 1979; the number of disabled employees that resettled for employment reached 707,000, an increase of 15 times; the output value of social welfare enterprises reached 41.26 billion yuan, an increase of 57 times. The employment rate of disabled people with working ability in cities and towns reached more than 75%, and that in large cities reached more than 90%. Community services were more socialized. More than 75% of urban streets in China had carried out community services, and a total of 89,918 community service facilities had been built.

In terms of preferential treatment security, the work that the government and the people should support the military and give preferential treatment to the families of servicemen and martyrs, and that the military should support the government and cherishes the people was further strengthened the preferential treatment changed from simple living allowances to active support for production. In 1988, the State Council proposed to establish a pension and preferential treatment system combining the state, society and individuals, and initially formed a preferential treatment system with different standards and complete items. By the end of 1991, a total of 2.68 million military and civilian personnel had been trained, and the training and utilization rate reached 79%. In many places, it reached more than 90%. In 1991, the community self-raised preferential treatment funds from the masses reached 1.06 billion yuan. In the early 1990s, there was a greater upsurge of "double support" activities across the country. The Ministry of Civil Affairs and the General Political Department of the PLA jointly named 49 "national double support model cities (counties)."

1.4.3 Urban and Rural Mobility and Changes in Social Order

Since the 1950s, under the planned economic system, China chose the development strategy of giving priority to national industrialization, especially heavy industry, and implemented a strict urban and rural household registration system and a rigid labor employment system, thus gradually forming a dual economic structure in urban and rural areas and restricting the smooth transfer of rural surplus labor. The continuous accumulation of a large number of rural surplus labor not only hindered the process of industrialization, but also seriously affected the process of urbanization in China. With the pace of reform and opening-up, the changes of China's urban-rural mobility and social order also experienced a complicated and tortuous process over the past 14 years. The surging tide of urban-rural mobility and the change of social order were the inevitable product of China's system transformation and social transformation, and the only way for China to achieve industrialization, urbanization and modernization.

Looking at the characteristics and social impact of urban-rural mobility and social order changes in this period, there were mainly three stages of change.

The first stage was from 1978 to 1983, which was the initial development stage of urban-rural mobility. The Third Plenary Session of the 11th CCCPC opened the prelude to rural reform. Farmers began to become the main operators of the family economy and even the rural economy, which stimulated the enthusiasm of farmers. The broad masses of farmers began to shift from single operation to diversified operation. The rural surplus labor force gradually began to shift to the secondary and tertiary industries. Farmers opened a gap between urban and rural barriers, "going out to work" became a new way for Chinese farmers to seek a living and development. At the beginning of the reform, the situation of agricultural production was gratifying. The growth rate of farmers' income even exceeded the growth rate of urban residents' income. Farmers began to engage in agricultural production at ease. Moreover, the farmers seemed to be somewhat confused about the free mobility, and their willingness to move was still quite weak. In addition, the state's institutional space and the degree of urban system reform did not allow farmers to have more opportunities for free mobility. During this period, the mobility was mainly manifested as the short-distance mobility between the regions with relatively developed commodity economy in the eastern coastal areas, mainly the exploration of "leaving the land but not leaving the hometown." The scale of mobility was also very small, and the rural population with mobile employment nationwide did not exceed 2 million.

At this stage, the rural labor force was relatively fully utilized mainly through the development of diversified operations within the agriculture and the advancement to the depth and breadth of agricultural production. The establishment of the basic management system based on household contract greatly improved the production efficiency of agricultural labor, and the recessive surplus rural labor force under the previous old system began to become dominant. With the improvement of the supply of basic agricultural products and the improvement of rural accumulation capacity, the pattern of single grain production in the past was broken, and farmers began to actively develop diversified economy, which promoted the comprehensive development of agriculture. In 1978, the output value of forestry, animal husbandry and fishery accounted for 17.6% of the total agricultural output value, and increased to 20.5% in 1983. Rural labor resources were fully utilized within agriculture.

The second stage was from 1984 to 1988, which was the initial development stage of urban-rural mobility. This period was a period of rapid economic development in China. In March 1984, the CCCPC and the State Council forwarded the *report on creating a new situation for commune and brigade enterprises* issued by the Ministry of Agriculture, Animal Husbandry and Fisheries, which clearly put forward the policy of encouraging and supporting the development of township enterprises, established the important position of township enterprises in the national economy, and gave strong support in terms of policies, funds, taxes, etc. It promoted township enterprises to usher in the first climax since the reform and opening-up and brought the transfer of rural surplus labor and the mobility of urban and rural areas into a golden period of rapid development. Township enterprises sprung up and became the main channel for the transfer of rural surplus labor to non-agricultural industries. Rural labor was relatively fully utilized in rural areas through division of labor. The labor force absorbed by township enterprises increased from 52.08 million in 1984 to 95.45 million in 1988, with an average annual increase of 10.84 million and an average annual increase of 16.4%. The total number of employees in township enterprises across the country was close to the number of employees in units owned by the whole people (99.84 million).

At this stage, the urban-rural mobility began to open the channels of cross regional mobility.

The focus of economic reform shifted from rural areas to cities. The acceleration of urban economic system reform, especially the tertiary industry, which allowed the entry of rural surplus labor, attracted more and more labor to enter the cities. The gradual expansion of the regional gap in economic development between the East and the West provided a strong driving force for the flow of rural surplus labor. The rapid development of the economy in the eastern region enabled a large number of local rural surplus labor to achieve non-agricultural employment, transfer to the secondary and tertiary industries. It also absorbed foreign labor from near to far, providing a broader employment space and development space for the transfer of rural labor and urban-rural mobility. Therefore, the flow of rural surplus labor changed from short-distance and small-scale transfer to cross regional long-distance and large-scale flow.

Diversified economy and township enterprises were the main activating factors of urban-rural mobility, and the scale of cross regional mobility had been expanding. In the face of backward agricultural productivity and huge employment pressure, with the disintegration of the people's commune system and the acceleration of the pace of rural marketization and agricultural commercialization, the emergence of township enterprises, the opening of national policies, the further deepening of rural reform, and the promotion of diversified business in the development of production and marketing, it had become a bright road for farmers to go to cities to run businesses or to work in factories and provide various services. Farmers were no longer limited to the limited rural land, but continued to explore from near to far to expand employment, moved to a broader space, and sought a way to get rid of poverty and become rich.

Since 1985, the social and economic environment of urban-rural mobility in China had undergone irreversible changes. Affected by factors such as the gradual slowdown in agricultural production, especially in the planting industry, the rise in the prices of agricultural means of production, and the gradual expansion of the "scissors gap" of industrial and agricultural products, farmers had to leave their homes and go to cities to seek a source of livelihood. Farmers broke the shackles, gradually liberated the rural productivity by relying on their own efforts, and boldly embarked on a new path of "leaving the land and leaving the hometown," resulting in a large number of new social groups such as "farmer entrepreneurs," "farmer artists," "farmers cultural people" and "migrant workers" that were unique in the world.

With the establishment and development of special economic zones, more and more migrant workers gathered in the Pearl River Delta. During this period, farmers were still exploring ways to open up cross-regional mobility. However, the urban-rural mobility in this period was carried out in an orderly state, because the eastern coastal areas had a strong absorption capacity for rural surplus labor, and there was no serious contradiction between urban and rural mobility, and its impact on social order was not very strong.

The third stage was from 1989 to 1991, which was the slow adjustment stage of rural-urban mobility. Due to inflation and economic overheating in 1988, the state decided to rectify the economy, reduce the scale of economic construction and investment, and proposed that township enterprises should appropriately reduce the development speed during the rectification period according to the state's macro requirements and market needs. In three years, the rural non-agricultural employment labor force increased by only 2.9 million, and the average annual scale of urban-rural mobility was about 1 million, just 12% of the previous period. The new agricultural labor force only entered agricultural employment, so that the ratio of non-agricultural labor force to total rural labor force dropped from 21.5% in 1988 to 20.7% in 1991. The emergence of the "peasant worker rush" was an inevitable product of various historical and practical factors in the process of transformation of China from a traditional agricultural society with "political omnipotence" to a modern industrial society with "market deployment." It was not only a call for reforming the current labor and employment system, but also a social problem that must be faced squarely in the direction of modernization, and it should be realistically and advantageously guided by the situation to promote the positive development of urban-rural mobility and social order change.

Township enterprises, which once led the reform trend, had passed the golden period of development and entered a difficult adjustment period. To a certain extent, the rectification restrained the employment growth of township enterprises, the rural labor force returned to agriculture, and the transfer of rural surplus labor force was stagnated. However, it stimulated the impulse of farmers to go to the city to find employment opportunities. However, it objectively created a large number of rural workers who could not stay in the cities or return to rural areas, and brought new challenges to urban management, public security and employment.

The change of urban-rural mobility and social order was not only the product of economic reform and opening-up, but also the requirement of social progress; it not only promoted the urban economic and social construction, but also drove the rural economic and social development.

1.4.4 Social Life and Social Conducts

With the reform and opening-up, Chinese society was increasingly transforming into an open society. In modern society, material life was greatly enriched and cultural values were profoundly changed. People's ideas were based on science and rationality, and they held a scientific and secular attitude towards life. They did not stick to traditional constraints, but emphasize people's needs and life in this world.

However, the invasion of western lifestyles and the rapid development of commodity economy led to the transformation of people's lifestyles. People had more freedom to choose in their life. They emphasized the independence and freedom of individuals or families in social life, chose their own way of life independently, paid attention to meeting the legitimate natural desires of individuals and the needs of real life, and pursue their own happiness. The personal life space was gradually liberated from the traditional bondage. In the aspect of social communication, it had gradually turned from a closed type to an open type. The traditional social communication and interpersonal relationship between people gradually disintegrated. People began to develop their various relationships rationally, and social communication and interpersonal relationship became more rational.

In terms of values, more emphasis was placed on pioneering and innovation. In terms of love, family and marriage, people understood and pursued love with a more open mind. In particular, young men and women began to break the "mystery" of love, got rid of the taboos and constraints of traditional morality, and established a new outlook on love, marriage and family. Young people faced love with a more positive attitude.

Summary

Reform and opening-up had impact on the traditional system, changed people's values and lifestyles, reorganized the relationship between people, caused changes in the inherent system and order, and brought about drastic and profound changes in economic life, political life and ideological field. The living standards and quality of life of China's urban and rural residents improved significantly, the problem of food and clothing was basically solved, and China begun to move towards moderately prosperous society. From the early 1980s to 1991, China's social welfare and social insurance system began to reform, breaking the egalitarian practice (of everyone taking food from the same big pot) of the state in the past. A new social security system including social assistance, social insurance and social welfare was initially established. With the change of urban-rural mobility and social order, rural surplus labor gradually began to transfer to the secondary and tertiary industries, and farmers opened a gap between urban and rural barriers. "Out-migrating for work" began to become a new way for Chinese farmers to earn a living and seek development. The development of commodity economy promoted the "secularization" of social life and social conducts, changed the collectivization mode of previous life and the dependence of individuals on collectives and units, and accelerated the transformation of Chinese social life from tradition to modernity.

SECTION 5

All-Round Development of Chinese Diplomacy

1.5.1 The Underlying Theme of Peace and Development and the Strategic Adjustment of Foreign Policy

After the Third Plenary Session of the 11th CCCPC, with the shift of the focus of work and the new changes in the international situation, the CPC and the Chinese government adjusted their diplomatic principles and policies in a timely manner. While maintaining national independence and sovereignty and opposing hegemonism as always, the diplomatic work made it clear that its main task was to cooperate with the country's economic construction and the great cause of the reunification of the motherland, and to strive for a favorable and peaceful international environment and surrounding environment for contemporary China.

The change of the "one line" strategy of uniting with the United States to resist the Soviet Union. After the founding of new China, the Chinese government pursued a "one-sided" diplomatic strategy with the Soviet Union. After China and the Soviet Union became hostile, China opposed the United States and the Soviet Union at the same time. In the late 1970s, when considering diplomatic relations, China gave more consideration to "fighting for more time without war" and "delaying the outbreak of war" in order to seize time for construction. Especially after the establishment of diplomatic relations between China and the United States in January 1979, China once strengthened the "one line" strategy of uniting with the United States to resist the Soviet Union. In the 1980s, although the Chinese Communists, mainly represented by Comrade Deng Xiaoping, still emphasized the danger of war, they had made a new judgment on war and peace: the growth of world peace factors exceeded the growth of war factors, world war was avoidable, and it was possible to strive for a long-term peace. This was mainly based on Deng Xiaoping's correct grasp and objective analysis of the international situation: first, the strategic struggle between the two superpowers, the United States and the Soviet Union, had always been equal in strength, and the two sides had never broken their military balance, pinned down and confronted each other in the arms race; second, the United States and the Soviet Union dared not launch a war rashly. The aggressive wars launched by the two sides in local areas ended in failure and reached a stalemate; third, the people of the whole world, especially those of the third world countries, which account for three quarters of the world's population, loved peace and did not want war. This was a decisive factor in safeguarding world peace. China should of course make full use of this long period of peace to focus on socialist modernization, especially economic construction, to improve the country's comprehensive national power.

There had always been a Taiwan issue in China-US relations. In particular, shortly after the establishment of diplomatic relations between China and the United States, the US Congress passed the so-called "Taiwan Relations Act," which seriously damaged China-US relations. Although there had been some negotiations since then, the effect was not great. Under such circumstances, China began to change the "one line" strategy of uniting with the United States to resist the Soviet Union, abandoned the tendency of "drawing lines with the Soviet Union" and "drawing lines with the United States," and broke away from the cage of the cold war thinking of the East and the West. China began to turn to the international strategy of "all-round" diplomacy. It would not form alliances or establish strategic relations with any major country. It would not discuss affinity or estrangement based on the similarities and differences of social systems and ideologies. It would realistically proceed from China's national interests, open up to the outside world, actively develop relations with other countries in the world, and accelerate the process of China's socialist modernization.

The foreign policy of opposing hegemonism, maintaining world peace and strengthening solidarity and cooperation with the third world was defined. On August 21, 1982, Deng Xiaoping made it clear during his meeting with UN Secretary-General de Cuéllar that it was our true policy to oppose hegemony and maintain world peace, which was the foundation of our foreign policy. In September 1982, the report of the 12th National Congress of the CPC stated that the principles for developing relations between China and other countries were "mutual respect for sovereignty and territorial integrity, mutual non-aggression, non-interference in each other's internal affairs, equality and mutual benefit, and peaceful coexistence." The CPC should develop relations with the communist parties and other political parties of other countries in accordance with the four principles of "independence, equality, mutual respect and non-interference in internal affairs." Later, these four principles were expanded to the principle of developing relations between the CPC and various types of ruling parties and legitimate opposition parties around the world.

The assertion that peace and development were the themes of the times was put forward. On May 29, 1984, Deng Xiaoping clearly put forward the foothold of China's international strategy for the first time: China's foreign policy mainly consisted of two sentences: One sentence was to oppose hegemony and maintain world peace; the other sentence was that China would always belong to the Third World. China belonged to the Third World then, and it would do so even when it became prosperous and powerful, because it shared a common destiny with all Third World countries. China would never seek hegemony or bully others, but will always side with the Third World. He believed that the most prominent issues in the world were the peace issue and North-South issue, and proposed to strengthen cooperation among third world countries. On March 4, 1985, Deng Xiaoping further elaborated on the assertion that peace and development were the themes of the times: "Now the world's really big problems and global strategic issues, one is the issue of peace, one is the issue of economic or development.

The first involves East-West relations, while the second involves North-South relations. In short, countries in the East, West, North and South are all involved. But the North-South relations are the key question." This summary revealed the theme of the times in the world today, prospectively expounded the prospects of the development of the international situation, and provided a theoretical basis for the adjustment of China's international strategy and foreign policy.

By pursuing an "independent foreign policy of peace," the adjustment of China's foreign policy was basically completed. On June 4, 1985, Deng Xiaoping clearly pointed out two major changes in China's foreign policy at the enlarged meeting of the CMC. The first change was the understanding of war and peace. It was believed that the danger of world war still existed, but the growth of world peace forces exceeded the growth of war forces. It was possible that no large-scale world war would occur in a long time, and there was hope for safeguarding world peace. The second change was China's foreign policy, which clearly changed the "one line" strategy from Japan to Europe to the United States. On September 14, when meeting with the Austrian president, Deng Xiaoping pointed out: "our current judgment is that war can be avoided. Therefore, we have changed the strategy of 'one line.'" These two changes were of great significance to China's domestic and foreign affairs. The first change enabled China to truly shift the focus of its work to modernization. The second change made the characteristics of China's independent foreign policy of peace more distinct. In March 1986, the Fourth Session of the Sixth NPC summarized China's foreign policy as "an independent foreign policy of peace" for the first time, expounded it from ten aspects, and clarified the basic principles of its main contents. The adjustment of China's foreign policy was basically completed.

1.5.2 Normalization of China-US and China-Soviet Relations and Major-Country Diplomacy

(1) The Establishment of Diplomatic Relations between China and the United States and the Development of Bilateral Relations
In 1972, Nixon visited China and the *China-US Joint Communique* was issued, breaking the ice in China-US relations. However, the relations between the two countries soon fell into a state of stagnation. It was not until the end of the 1970s that US President Carter really expressed his willingness to normalize China-US relations. On the one hand, the U.S. wanted to rely on China to seek strategic

"balance" in the face of the Soviet Union's aggressive approach; on the other hand, the U.S. capitalists' desire for China, a market with great potential, was unstoppable. The U.S. accepted Deng Xiaoping's "three principles" for establishing diplomatic relations between China and the U.S., namely, abolishing treaties, withdrawing troops and breaking off diplomatic relations, and the two countries held diplomatic talks in Beijing in July 1978. On December 15, China and the United States signed the *Joint Communique between the PRC and the United States of America on the Establishment of Diplomatic Relations* (hereinafter referred to as the *Joint Communique on the Establishment of Diplomatic Relations between China and the United States*), which was announced to the world the next night. The United States took the position of recognizing the one-China principle and Taiwan as part of China's territory, acknowledging the PRC as the sole legitimate government of China, and reaffirming the basic principles of the 1972 *China-US Joint Communique*. From January 1, 1979, China and the United States formally established diplomatic relations. It was also on that day that the Carter Administration announced that it would sever the so-called "diplomatic relations" with Taiwan and formally terminate the so-called "Mutual Defense Treaty" signed with Taiwan; In April of the same year, the United States withdrew all US troops stationed in Taiwan. Of course, when China and the United States established diplomatic relations, there were still some outstanding issues, such as the United States did not give up its plot to interfere in China's internal affairs and continued to sell arms to Taiwan. Nevertheless, the establishment of diplomatic relations between China and the United States was still a major turning point of historical significance in the history of bilateral relations. The relations between the two countries entered a new stage, opening up a broad space for further exchanges and cooperation between the two countries in the political, economic, cultural, scientific and technological fields, and also conducive to peace and stability in the Asia-Pacific region and the world.

However, President Carter proposed the "Taiwan Relations Act" to the US Congress in January 1979. The act was passed by the Senate and the House of Representatives on March 26. Its basic spirit and many specific provisions violated the *Joint Communique on the Establishment of Diplomatic Relations between China and the United States* and the universally recognized norms of international law. In fact, it was an attempt to deny the one-China principle. The Chinese government was very indignant at this act of harming China's sovereignty and submitted a note of protest. The unilateral actions of the United States created a dark cloud on the issue of China-US relations and affected the development of China-US relations.

At the invitation of US President Jimmy Carter, Deng Xiaoping paid an official friendly visit to the United States from January 29 to February 5, 1979. This was the first visit by a Chinese leader to the United States since the founding of new China. During his visit to the United States, Deng Xiaoping had in-depth talks with President Carter on the Taiwan issue, China-US relations and international issues of common concern. Deng Xiaoping further clarified the Chinese government's position that the Taiwan issue is China's internal affair, saying: "China is willing to resolve the Taiwan issue in a peaceful way, but we will not tie our hands, because that will not be conducive to the peaceful settlement of the Taiwan issue; The United States can make contributions to China's peaceful settlement of the Taiwan issue and should not do anything detrimental to the peaceful settlement of the Taiwan issue."

Deng Xiaoping also had extensive talks with US congressmen, met with government officials and people from all walks of life, and visited Atlanta, Houston and Seattle. On January 31, the leaders of China and the United States signed the China-US Science and Technology Cooperation Agreement and the Cultural Agreement. On February 1, China and the United States issued a joint press communique, pointing out that the two sides reviewed the international situation and agreed that they share common interests and similar views in many aspects. The two sides reiterated their opposition to any country or group of countries seeking hegemony or domination over other countries and their determination to contribute to the maintenance of international peace, security and national independence. The two sides believed that the differences in social systems between the two countries should not prevent each other from strengthening friendly relations and cooperation. During his visit to the United States, Deng Xiaoping affirmed the common ground and narrowed the differences between the two sides in seeking common ground while reserving differences, and made great achievements, contributing to the development of bilateral relations under the new historical conditions.

In 1981, after taking office, President Reagan adopted a tough policy on the Taiwan issue, advocated the sale of weapons to the Taiwan region, and threatened that China had no right to interfere with the US policy toward Taiwan. China had always maintained that the issue of Taiwan was an internal affair of China that did not allow any foreign interference, and that the sale of weapons by the

United States to Taiwan was a dispute between China and the United States and an infringement of China's sovereignty by the United States. Although the US side agreed that the performance and quantity of arms sold to Taiwan in the future would not exceed the level since the establishment of diplomatic relations between China and the United States, it had never promised to draw up a timetable for completely stopping arms sales to Taiwan. Subsequently, China and the United States held many consultations and talks on this serious difference.

On February 28, 1982, the Chinese Premier and the US President exchanged letters and telegrams on the 10th anniversary of the publication of the *China-US Joint Communique*. The two sides reiterated the principles of the *China-US Joint Communique* and the *Joint Communique on the Establishment* of Diplomatic Relations between China and the United States, and emphasized overcoming obstacles in the development of bilateral relations, eliminating differences and strengthening the further development of China-US relations. US President Nixon also wrote an article on February 28 urging China and the United States not to go to extremes in dealing with Taiwan's status and arms sales to Taiwan. On March 2, Xinhua News Agency published a commentator's article entitled *A Critical Moment in the Development of Sino-US Relations*, pointing out that China's position was to strive for good, but it also had to make bad plans, indicating China's principled position on China-US relations.

Due to the deadlock in China-US negotiations, US President Reagan sent Vice President George H.W. Bush to visit Beijing on May 5, 1982 to hold talks with Deng Xiaoping and other Chinese Communist leaders. The two sides had an in-depth exchange of views on the issue of arms sales to Taiwan. After a long period of consultation and negotiation, China and the United States finally reached an agreement on August 15, 1982, and issued the *China-US Joint Communique* on August 17, that is, the "August 17 Communique." The two sides reiterated the principles confirmed in the *Joint Communique on the Establishment of Diplomatic Relations between China and the United States*. The United States once again affirmed that it had no intention to interfere in China's internal affairs or to implement the policy of "two Chinas" or "one China, one Taiwan." The two sides unanimously stressed that the principles of mutual respect for sovereignty and territorial integrity and non-interference in each other's internal affairs were the principles guiding China-US relations, including the handling of US arms sales to Taiwan. The United States promised that the performance and quantity of arms sold to Taiwan would not exceed the level since the establishment of diplomatic relations between China and the United States. It prepared to gradually reduce arms sales to Taiwan and finally resolve this issue. The United States expressed its recognition of China's principled position on thoroughly resolving this issue. The "August 17 Communique" took an important step in resolving the issue left over by history of US arms sales to Taiwan and pointed out the direction for the further development of China-US relations.

From January 7 to 10, 1984, Chinese Premier Zhao Ziyang paid an official visit to the United States at the invitation of U.S. President Ronald Reagan. This was another visit by a high-level Chinese leader to the United States after Deng Xiaoping's visit to the United States in 1979. During the talks between the leaders of the two countries, the Chinese side comprehensively expounded China's principled stand on the Taiwan issue and its principles and policies for the peaceful reunification of the motherland. China hopped that the United States would not set up obstacles to China's peaceful reunification. Although the US side said that it would abide by the China-US communiques and continue to implement the one-China policy, it also said that it could not abandon Taiwan and looked forward to a peaceful settlement of the Taiwan issue. The Chinese and US governments signed two agreements on cooperations in China-US industrial technology and China-US science and technology, and progress was made in negotiations on cooperation in the field of nuclear energy. This visit promoted the development of China-US friendly and cooperative relations. From April 26 to May 1 of the same year, US President Reagan paid a state visit to China, and thus the high-level leaders of China and the United States exchanged visits. President Reagan held talks with Chinese leaders Li Xiannian and Deng Xiaoping. The United States expressed support for China's modernization drive and was willing to strengthen economic, trade and cultural exchanges with China. However, the Taiwan issue was still an outstanding issue that affected the development of bilateral relations. In July 1985, Chinese President Li Xiannian visited the United States. During his visit to the United States, the two sides signed four important documents, including the *China-U.S. Agreement on Cooperation Concerning Peaceful Uses of Nuclear Energy, Annual Implementation Plan 2014–2016 of the Agreement on Cultural Exchange between the Governments of China and the United States, Protocol between the Government of the PRC and the Government of America for Cooperation in Educational Exchanges*, and the *Agreement between the Government of PRC and the Government of United States of America Concerning fisheries off the coast of the United States*. It was worth mentioning that the *China-US Agreement for Cooperation*

Concerning Peaceful Uses of Nuclear Energy was finally signed after more than a year of delay, which was an important breakthrough in Sino-US economic and technological cooperation. Despite occasional twists and turns in China-US relations, China-US economic and trade relations of mutual benefit developed in an all-round way, strategic security relations also developed by leaps and bounds, exchanges in culture, education, news and other fields became increasingly active, China-US friendly cooperation further developed, and bilateral relations improved and developed significantly.

In January 1989, George H. W. Bush became president of the United States, and China-US political relations once reached a new climax. In February, George H. W. Bush visited China at the invitation of Chinese President Yang Shangkun and Premier Li Peng. During Bush's visit to China, Chinese leaders expressed the hope that under the guidance of the Five Principles of Peaceful Coexistence and the principles of the three China-US joint communiques, mutual understanding and trust would be further enhanced, the potential of bilateral relations would be fully tapped, and cooperation in all fields would be continuously deepened, so as to achieve greater development of China-US relations. George H. W. Bush held that the United States and China have found a constructive and non-malicious way to discuss the Taiwan issue in accordance with the one-China principle as its basis. The United States had always paid attention to the Chinese people settling their own differences. The two sides reached consensus on many issues. However, the center of the US foreign policy was far from being friendly to China. In essence, it was a "peaceful evolution" strategy of "transcending containment" marked by ideology. Although the United States had repeatedly stated that it would abide by the principles of the three *Sino-US Joint Communiques* and pursue the one-China policy, it still continued to develop "substantive" relations with Taiwan in accordance with the Taiwan Relations Act.

(2) Normalization of China-Soviet Relations

The Soviet Union was the first country in the world to establish diplomatic relations with new China. However, since the 1960s, China-Soviet relations had been deteriorating. By the end of the 1970s, the improvement of China-US relations had made the China-Soviet contradiction more prominent. In April 1979, the Seventh Meeting of the Standing Committee of the Fifth NPC decided that the *Sino-Soviet Treaty of Friendship, Alliance and Mutual Assistance* would not be extended after its expiration. From September 1979, China and the Soviet Union began a new round of negotiations on state relations. However, at the end of 1979, the Soviet Union invaded Afghanistan adjacent to China, threatening China's national security, creating new difficulties for the normalization of China-Soviet relations and forcing the China-Soviet negotiations that had begun to be shelved for more than two years.

In March 1982, Brezhnev made a speech in Tashkent. Although he still attacked China's policies, he also sent a signal that he was willing to improve relations with China. China also expressed to the Soviet Union through diplomatic channels that it hoped that the Soviet Union would take practical actions to show its sincerity in improving bilateral relations. Therefore, after a long period of consultations, the two sides finally decided that starting from October 1982, the special envoys of the two governments (at the level of deputy foreign ministers) would take turns to hold political consultations in Beijing and Moscow. On October 5, 1982, the Deputy Foreign Minister of the Soviet Union led a delegation to Beijing to hold the first round of consultations between the special envoys of the Chinese and Soviet governments with the Chinese delegation headed by Vice Foreign Minister Qian Qichen, and frankly exchanged views on improving bilateral relations. From this time until June 1988, the special envoys of the two governments held 12 rounds of consultations, and China and the Soviet Union began to try to change the abnormal situation of China-Soviet relations for more than 20 years.

China had always insisted that the Soviet Union should take substantive actions to withdraw its troops from Mongolia and the China-Soviet border areas, withdraw its troops from Afghanistan, and urge Vietnam to withdraw its troops from Cambodia, so as to eliminate the security threat posed by the Soviet Union in the south, north and west of China and end political confrontation and military confrontation. However, for a long time, the Soviet Union avoided the practical problems hindering the normalization of relations between the two countries, and refused to take the three major obstacles to the normalization of relations between the two countries as a topic for discussion, thus causing the consultations to reach an impasse.

However, the deadlock in the relations between the two countries did not hindered the increasingly active political exchanges between the two sides. At the end of 1984, the first vice chairman of the Council of Ministers of the Soviet Union, Mr. Arshipov, paid an official visit to China. The two countries signed a series of agreements on developing China-Soviet economic and trade relations and decided to establish a China-Soviet economic, trade, scientific and technological cooperation committee. The Chinese foreign minister, the vice premier of the State Council and other senior officials also attended the state funeral of the Soviet Union leaders as Chinese envoys on three occasions, and made contact with the Soviet Union leaders, thus continuing the political exchanges between China and the Soviet Union, which had been interrupted for more than 20 years, and improving the cold political situation between the two countries.

After Gorbachev became general secretary of the CCCPC in 1985, he began to improve relations with China with a positive attitude. Deng Xiaoping also said that if the Soviet Union could remove the three major obstacles, it would be willing to hold a meeting with Gorbachev. The foreign ministries of China and the Soviet Union set up Consulates General in Beijing and Moscow respectively, and reached agreements on certain visa issues. In July 1985, Yao Yilin, vice premier of the State Council of China, visited the Soviet Union. The two sides signed an economic and technological cooperation agreement and a trade agreement. In 1986, Arshipov, vice chairman of the Council of Ministers of the Soviet Union, and Taretzin, first vice chairman of the Council of Ministers of the Soviet Union and chairman of the State Planning Commission of the Soviet Union, successively came to China to sign relevant agreements on expanding economic, trade, scientific and technological cooperation between China and the Soviet Union and on the contact and cooperation between the planning commissions of the two countries. This laid a good foundation for the normalization of China-Soviet relations.

In July 1986, Gorbachev made a speech in Vladivostok, saying that he was willing to discuss the issue of establishing good neighborly relations with China at any time and at any level, and announced that the Soviet Union was studying with Mongolian leaders the issue of withdrawing troops from Mongolia; the Soviet Union was also preparing to withdraw its troops from Afghanistan in stages, with six regiments to be withdrawn by the end of the year. In February 1987, China-Soviet border negotiations were officially resumed. In February 1988, Gorbachev issued a statement on the issue of Afghanistan, announcing the complete withdrawal of troops from Afghanistan within 10 months. The Soviet Union began to gradually make concessions on the three major obstacles to the normalization of China-Soviet relations, and China-Soviet political consultations began to develop in a positive direction. In June, the special envoys of the Chinese and Soviet governments focused on the Cambodian issue during the 12th round of consultations, and both sides expounded their respective positions. The Soviet

Union realized that the withdrawal of Vietnamese troops from Cambodia was an important factor in solving the Cambodian issue. After six years of political consultations between the special envoys of the two governments, the three major obstacles hindering the normalization of China-Soviet relations had been gradually removed, which had pushed forward the normalization of China-Soviet relations.

In December 1988, Chinese Foreign Minister Qian Qichen visited the Soviet Union, which was the first official visit of a Chinese foreign minister to the Soviet Union in nearly 30 years.

Qian Qichen had in-depth discussions with Soviet Foreign Minister Shevardnadze on China-Soviet relations and was received by Gorbachev. Subsequently, Shevardnadze paid an official visit to China in February 1989. Deng Xiaoping and Li Peng met with him respectively. Since Vietnam announced in January 1989 that it would completely withdraw its troops from Cambodia by September 1989 at the latest, at the end of the visit of the foreign minister of the Soviet Union, China and the Soviet Union issued a statement on the Cambodian issue. The exchange of visits between the foreign ministers of China and the Soviet Union and the issuance of the China-Soviet statement on the Cambodian issue showed that the three major obstacles to the normalization of China-Soviet relations had been clearly removed, making the high-level meeting between the leaders of China and the Soviet Union a reality.

In May 1989, Gorbachev, general secretary of the CCCPC and chairman of the presidium of the Supreme Soviet of the Soviet Union, visited Beijing and held a historic high-level meeting with Chinese leader Deng Xiaoping. Deng Xiaoping's proposal of "Let us put the past behind us and open up a new end"[16] became the consensus of the leaders of China and the Soviet Union. The two sides issued a joint communique in Beijing and agreed that the high-level meeting between China and the Soviet Union marked the normalization of state relations between China and the Soviet Union. China and the Soviet Union started a new type of state relations of good neighborliness, friendship, and mutually beneficial cooperation based on the Five Principles of Peaceful Coexistence.

(3) Strengthening of Relations with the European Community and Developed Countries in Western Europe
During the 14 years from 1978, when the Third Plenary Session of the 11th CCCPC opened a new period of reform and opening-up and socialist modernization in

contemporary China, to the early 1990s, China's relations with developed countries in Western Europe, such as the United Kingdom, France, Germany and Italy, had further developed, and the heads of state, heads of government and foreign ministers of China and Western European countries had frequently exchanged visits. In 1979, China established diplomatic relations with Portugal and Ireland. In November 1983, China established formal relations with the Coal and Steel Community and the Atomic Energy Community of the European Community, thus realizing the comprehensive establishment of diplomatic relations with the European Community (China established diplomatic relations with the European Economic Community in 1975).

From 1979 to 1984, the premier of the Chinese government visited Britain, France, Italy, the Federal Republic of Germany and other countries and the European Community. This was the first time that the premier of the Chinese government visited these countries and organizations. In 1986, Hu Yaobang, general secretary of the CCCPC, visited Britain, France, Italy and the Federal Republic of Germany. In 1987, Chinese President Li Xiannian visited France, Italy, Luxembourg and Belgium. This was also the first visit of a Chinese head of state to these countries. British Prime Minister Margaret Thatcher visited China twice in 1982 and 1984. She was the first serving British Prime Minister to visit China and promoted China and Britain to reach an agreement on the return of Hong Kong. During this period, 29 heads of states and governments from 17 Western European countries visited China more than 30 times, including Queen Elizabeth II of the United Kingdom, French Presidents d'Estaing and Mitterrand, Federal German President Carstens and Chancellor Kohl, Italian President Pertini and Prime Ministers Craxi and Andreotti, etc.

China and Western European developed countries established a good mechanism for high-level mutual visits and political consultations, which effectively promoted the in-depth development of all-round economic and trade cooperation and scientific, technological and cultural exchanges between China and Western Europe. Since 1978, China's trade volume with Western European countries had increased significantly from 6 billion U.S. dollars in 1981 to 19.835 billion U.S. dollars in 1992. In 1991, China's total import and export trade with the 12 countries of the European Community reached 15.141 billion U.S. dollars, accounting for 11.2% of China's total foreign trade, 4.6 times that of 1978. Preferential government loans and development assistance provided by Western European countries and the European Community to China were also increasing. Since 1984, the European

Community had been providing financial and technical assistance to China every year. The amount of assistance was 6 million European currency units per year, and increased to 8.6 million European currency units in 1988. In March 1988, China and the European Community signed an agreement on European Community's assistance to China's dairy development project. According to the agreement, the European Community provided nearly 100 million U.S. dollars in kind technical assistance to dairy development projects in more than 20 cities in China from 1988 to 1992. After 1987, the European Community provided emergency disaster relief assistance to some disaster-stricken areas in China for many times. By 1991, the total amount of assistance reached 2.53 million European currency units. In 1992, the European Community restored China's status as a recipient of development assistance and provided about 12 million U.S. dollars in development assistance funds to China.

Although there were some differences in social systems between China and Western European countries, the main theme of China's relations with them was still friendship and cooperation. Practice proved that developing political, economic and cultural exchanges and cooperation on the principles of seeking common ground while reserving differences, mutual respect, equality and mutual benefit could create a win-win situation of mutual benefit.

1.5.3 Good Neighborly Policy and Peripheral Diplomacy

(1) Strengthening and Improving the Relations with Japan
China attached great importance to and adhered to being good to its neighbors on the basis of the Five Principles of Peaceful Coexistence, pursued a good neighborly policy, and regarded the establishment and strengthening of good neighborly and friendly relations as the basic state policy of contemporary China and the focus of China's diplomatic work.

China and Japan were neighbors separated by a strip of water. The peoples of the two countries had forged profound friendship over a history of more than 2000 years. However, since modern times, especially since the Japanese War of aggression against China, the relations between the two countries had always been in an abnormal state. In 1972, the normalization of diplomatic relations between China and Japan opened a new chapter in the development of bilateral relations.

In August 1978, China and Japan signed the *Sino-Japanese Treaty of Peace and Friendship*. In October of the same year, Deng Xiaoping was invited to visit

Japan and attended the exchange ceremony of the instruments of ratification of the *Sino-Japanese Treaty of Peace and Friendship* in Tokyo on behalf of the Chinese government. This was also the first official friendly visit to Japan by a Chinese leader since the founding of new China. The conclusion and entry into force of the treaty brought China-Japanese good neighborly, friendly and cooperative relations to a new stage. In December 1979, Japanese Prime Minister Masayoshi Ohira visited China and announced that he would provide the first batch of government loans of 330 billion yen (about 1.5 billion U.S. dollars) to China, with a repayment period of 30 years. The Bank of Japan also provided 420 billion yen (about 2 billion U.S. dollars) of energy development loans to China. China and Japan signed agreements on cultural exchanges, scientific and technological cooperation, and cooperation in exploration and development of Bohai oil. Economic cooperation had gradually become the foundation of China-Japanese relations.

In 1982, the 10th anniversary of the normalization of diplomatic relations between China and Japan, the heads of government of the two countries exchanged visits, and the two sides put forward many constructive opinions on the development of China-Japanese relations. In November 1983, Hu Yaobang, General Secretary of the CCCPC, visited Japan to further exchange views with Japanese leaders. During these two years, the Chinese side gradually put forward the four principles of "peace and friendship, equality and mutual benefit, mutual dependence and long-term stability"[17] as the basis for developing friendly and cooperative relations between China and Japan. In March 1984, Prime Minister Nakasone Yasuhiro visited China. The leaders of China and Japan agreed to establish the China-Japan Friendship Committee for the 21st Century as an advisory body of the Chinese and Japanese governments. Nakasone said that he would follow the four principles to develop China-Japanese friendship from generation to generation. The Japanese government decided to provide China with a second tranche of government loans totaling 470 billion yen (about 2.1 billion U.S. dollars). In 1988, Japanese Prime Minister Noboru Takeshita visited China. He said that the development of relations with China was an important pillar of Japan's foreign affairs. Taking serious introspection of the past as the starting point, and took the *China-Japan Joint Statement*, the *Sino-Japanese Treaty of Peace and Friendship* and the four principles of China-Japanese relations as its basis, the Japanese government had not changed its policy of continuing to attach importance to and develop China-Japan relations. Prime Minister Noboru Takeshita announced a third batch of government loans of 810 billion yen (about

$6 billion) to China starting in 1990. In April 1989, Premier Li Peng visited Japan at invitation. The leaders of China and Japan reaffirmed that the *China-Japan Joint Statement*, the *Sino-Japanese Treaty of Peace and Friendship*, and the four principles of China-Japanese relations were the foundation of China-Japanese friendship.

With the development of political and economic relations between China and Japan, the two sides gradually presented a situation of simultaneous development of officials and people and multi-level, multi-channel and multi-form development in science, technology, culture and education exchanges and cooperation. In December 1979, the two countries signed the *"China-Japanese Cultural Exchange Agreement"*; in May 1980, the two countries signed the *"China-Japan Science and Technology Cooperation Agreement"*; In March 1981, the *Agreement between the Government of Japan and the Government of the PRC on Protection of Migratory Birds and Natural Habitats* was signed; in July 1985, the *"China-Japan Agreement for Cooperation Concerning Peaceful Uses of Nuclear Energy"* was signed. At the end of 1991, there were more than 28,000 Chinese students studying in Japan, including more than 4,700 government-sponsored students, more than 8,500 government-sponsored students and more than 15,700 self-funded students. Friendly exchanges between civilians and personnel exchanges became more frequent. Sister cities and tourism played an important role in promoting the understanding and exchanges between the two peoples and enhancing bilateral relations.

However, at the same time, China and Japan continued to disagree on issues left over by history. The extreme right-wing forces in Japan still had an attempt to revive militarism. The history textbook incidents in 1982 and 1986, the Japanese Prime Minister's visit to the "Yasukuni Shrine" in 1985, the "Guanghualiao" case in an attempt to create "two Chinas," and the isuue of sovereignty ownership of Diaoyu Islands had all affected the healthy development of China-Japanese relations.

(2) Relations with North Korea, Mongolia and India
Since the 1980s, China's peripheral diplomatic relations had improved and developed in an all-round way. In the northeast, China consolidated and strengthened its traditional friendship with the North Korea and Mongolia. North Korea is a country linked by mountains and rivers with China, and the two countries have traditional friendly and cooperative relations. Kim Il-Sung, the supreme leader of North Korea, paid three official friendly visits to China in September 1982, May 1987, and October 1991. Chinese party and state leaders Deng Xiaoping,

Peng Zhen, Li Xiannian, and Yang Shangkun also visited the North Korea one after another. Mongolia is a friendly neighbor with a common border of about 4,710 kilometers with China. Due to historical reasons, the relations between China and Mongolia underwent serious twists and turns. Through the joint efforts of the two countries, the normalization of the relations between the two countries was gradually realized in the 1980s.

At the same time, the Chinese government made unremitting efforts to restore and develop good neighborly and friendly relations with India. In 1979, Indian Foreign Minister Vajpayee visited China; in June 1981, Chinese vice premier and foreign minister Huang Hua visited India. Since then, China and India resumed high-level political exchanges between the two countries, which had been interrupted since the 1960s. In December 1988, Indian prime minister Rajiv Gandhi visited China at invitation, which was the first time that Indian prime minister visited China after Nehru's visit to China in 1954. The leaders of the two countries stressed that the Five Principles of Peaceful Coexistence advocated by China and India were the basic guiding principles for improving state to state relations and for establishing a new international political and economic order. The two sides held in—depth discussions on the China-Indian border issue and the Xizang issue. The two sides signed cooperation agreements on science and technology, civil aviation transportation and culture, and issued a joint communique. China was also actively improving and developing its traditional friendship and close cooperation with Pakistan, Bangladesh, Nepal, Sri Lanka, Bhutan, Maldives, Afghanistan and other countries.

(3) Relations with Vietnam, Laos and Other Southeast Asian Countries

China, Vietnam and Laos are neighbors linked by mountains and rivers, and have been friendly for generations. However, the relations with the two countries was tortuous for a time. At the end of 1978, Vietnam sent troops to Cambodia, worsening China-Vietnamese relations. From February to March 1979, serious armed conflicts occurred on the China-Vietnamese border. The Chinese border defense forces carried out a self-defense counterattack at the Guangxi and Yunnan borders, which dealt a blow to the arrogance of Vietnam's aggression. In 1988, China and Vietnam again had armed conflicts in the Chigua reef area of the Nansha Islands. China-Vietnamese relations were in a stalemate of confrontation during this period, which obviously did not accord with the interests of China and Vietnam. The Chinese side was actively working for the normalization of Sino-Vietnamese relations, and the two sides held constant consultations.

Since 1978, there was a rift in the relations between China and Laos. Laos demanded that China withdraw Chinese engineering and technical personnel and experts, and close Chinese diplomatic and news agencies in Laos. In the summer of 1980, China and Laos withdrew their ambassadors. In order to restore and develop the traditional friendship between China and Laos, since 1986, China and Laos began to seek ways to improve. In June 1988, the two countries resumed the exchange of ambassadors. In December, the minister of Trade and Foreign Economic Relations of Laos led a government trade delegation to visit China. The two sides signed the first trade agreement since the establishment of diplomatic relations between the two countries.

In the Southeast Asia region, China insisted on consolidating and developing its relations with Thailand, Malaysia, the Philippines, Myanmar and other countries of Association of Southeast Asian Nations (ASEAN) so as to make it reach a higher level.

The correct policies adopted by China in dealing with its relations with its neighboring countries greatly improved China's surrounding environment, changed China's passive posture of being besieged by enemies on all sides in the past, and many impending conflicts of interest were greatly resolved in the face of China's restraint and the principle of shelving disputes. Looking around China's neighbors, disputes and wars had become cooperation and exchanges. A peaceful, tranquil, good neighborly and friendly surrounding environment had basically taken shape. It was not only in the interests of Asian countries and peoples, but also conducive to world peace and tranquility.

1.5.4 Actively Participate in International Affairs and Create a New Situation in Diplomatic Work

(1) Actively Participates in International Affairs
Since the Third Plenary Session of the 11th CCCPC, China actively participated in international affairs. On the basis of upholding the supremacy of national interests, China closely grasped the profound changes in the international situation, sought common ground while reserving differences, adhered to the Five Principles of Peaceful Coexistence, and worked to establish a new international political and economic order and multilateral diplomacy.

Committing to the establishment of a new international political and economic order. As a permanent member of the UN Security Council, China firmly opposed power politics and hegemonism and was an important force in safeguarding world peace. In October 1987, China put forward the idea of political settlement of regional conflicts at the 42nd UN General Assembly (UNGA). Its basic principles were: first, it was necessary to stop aggression and expansion against other countries and end military occupation and interference against other countries. The sovereignty and independence of the aggrieved countries should be restored, and their internal affairs should not be interfered with. Second, regional conflicts must be resolved peacefully by the countries concerned through negotiations, and disputes within countries should be resolved by their own people. Third, all parties concerned must abide by the purposes of the *Charter of the United Nations (UN Charter)* and the norms of international relations, proceed from the overall interests of safeguarding peace and promoting development, respect and understand each other, and seek solutions acceptable to all parties. These ideas were well received in the international community. The Five Principles of Peaceful Coexistence, first proposed and advocated by China, were in the fundamental interests of the people of the world and conducive to world peace and development. With the continuous development of the multipolarization of the international pattern, the integration of the world economy, and the democratization of international relations, Deng Xiaoping proposed in December 1988 to adhere to the Five Principles of Peaceful Coexistence and establish a new international order. China's advocacy of mutual respect for sovereignty and territorial integrity was based on its understanding of the most essential features of a new type of international relations. The reason why the new order emphasized sovereign independence, territorial integrity, mutual non-aggression and non-interference in internal affairs was that any state's behavior must conform to the *UN Charter* and the norms of international relations. Each state had the right to choose its own social system, ideology, economic model and development path according to its own national conditions. Each state had the right to independently handle its own internal affairs. China's advocacy of equality and mutual benefit was aimed at hegemonism and power politics. All countries, big or small, strong or weak, rich or poor, had the right to participate in and consult international affairs. China opposed the practice of bullying the small with the big, bullying the weak with the strong, and suppressing the poor with the rich. All countries must be equal and mutually beneficial in economic, trade and other aspects, and must not propose any political conditions to interfere in the internal affairs of other countries. China advocated peaceful coexistence, which meant opposing territorial expansion and apartheid, opposing the threat or use of force to resolve international disputes, avoiding wars and conflicts, safeguarding world peace and security, creating a peaceful and stable international development environment, and establishing a just and rational new international political and economic order.

Multilateral diplomacy was extensively carried out. Before the 1980s, China's multilateral diplomatic activities were limited to the United Nations and its specialized agencies, and mainly in the field of political security. Since the 1980s, while strengthening its relations with the United Nations, China had strengthened its ties with global and regional economic, military, arms control, social, cultural and educational organizations and conferences. It had also vigorously supported multilateral diplomatic activities carried out by developing countries, safeguarded the legitimate rights and interests of developing countries, and further broadened the diplomatic field.

Multilateral diplomacy was an important component and concrete manifestation of new China's foreign strategy and foreign policy in the new period. It was a flexible and practical way of foreign activities adopted by China under the leadership of its independent foreign policy of peace and in light of the general trend of the current international situation and the needs of China's reform and opening-up. The CPC and the Chinese government repeatedly emphasized the importance of multilateral diplomacy when discussing their foreign strategies and policies. In 1986, the *Report on the Seventh Five-Year Plan* adopted by the Fourth Session of the Sixth NPC discussed the independent foreign policy of peace. It was the first time that multilateral diplomacy was explicitly listed as one of the important contents of China's foreign policy in the Report of the work of the Government work report. The report pointed out that China followed the purposes and principles of the *UN Charter*, supported the work of the United Nations Organization in accordance with the spirit of the *UN Charter*, and actively participated in the activities of the United Nations and its specialized agencies that were conducive to world peace and development. China extensively participated in various international organizations, carried out active multilateral diplomatic activities, and worked hard to enhance cooperation among countries in various fields. This was a clear-cut attitude adopted by the CPC and the Chinese government under the new domestic and international situation. Since then, China's multilateral diplomatic activities entered a new period of comprehensive development.

Among various intergovernmental international organizations, international conferences and international mechanisms, the United Nations system was the most important. Conducting multilateral diplomacy with the United Nations as the core was the most important component of China's diplomacy. As the largest and most universal international organization in the world today, with more than 190 members, the United Nations was the most important international forum and multilateral diplomatic arena. It was a stable form of organization for nation states to carry out international cooperation. It had more extensive, effective and global characteristics than any other international organization. Before the 1980s, China did not have a deep understanding of the UN affairs, so it focused on expressing its position in principle on major UN issues. In the new era, China adopted the policy of "taking the initiative and gradually deepening" in UN affairs, and became increasingly active in various international affairs. China always respected the purposes and principles of the *UN Charter*, supported the work of the UN organization in accordance with the spirit of the Charter, and actively participated in the activities of various organs of the UN system. By March 1986, China had participated in the activities of all UN economic commissions, development agencies and specialized economic agencies.

The Economic and Social Council was one of the six major organs of the United Nations. After China's legitimate seat in the general assembly was restored, its legitimate rights in the Economic and Social Council were restored. China had always been elected as a member of the Economic and Social Council and participated in the annual meetings and other work of the Economic and Social Council, making positive contributions to promoting the development of economic and social undertakings in various countries and promoting the progress of human civilization. The Economic and Social Commission for Asia and the Pacific (ESCAP) was one of the five regional economic commissions under the United Nations Economic and Social Council, and was the only inter-governmental comprehensive economic and social organization of the United Nations in the Asia-Pacific region. In July 1978, China sent a permanent representative to ESCAP. In the same year, the Chinese foreign minister visited the ESCAP headquarters in Bangkok. In 1981, China established a "permanent representative office to ESCAP" in its embassy in Thailand. The scope of cooperation had been expanding and the forms of cooperation had become increasingly diversified.

In April and May 1980, China resumed its legal seat in the International Monetary Fund (IMF) and the International Bank for Reconstruction and Development (the World Bank). China was one of the directors of the executive boards of the IMF and the World Bank respectively. China obtained a considerable amount of preferential loans from these financial institutions, which promoted the development of China's economy.

In 1981 China was elected a United Nations Commission on Human Rights member state at the first annual session of the Economic and Social Council. China actively participated in UN activities in the field of human rights. At the sessions of the Commission on Human Rights, China actively participated in the deliberations on human rights issues and directly participated in the drafting and formulation of United Nations Human rights instruments.

Before 1978, China's work in United Nations Educational, Scientific and Cultural Organization (UNESCO) was mainly to attend meetings of the general conference and the executive board, and basically did not participate in the operational activities or cooperation of the organization. Marked by the visit of the director general of UNESCO to China in 1978, China's cooperation with the organization entered a new era. In 1985, China donated 600,000 U.S. dollars to the organization to help it overcome its financial difficulties. China actively participated in various operational activities and various forms of cooperation of UNESCO. For example, in the early 1980s, with the support of UNESCO, various types of literacy training courses were held in some provinces and regions of China, which promoted the development of literacy in China. China actively undertook various academic seminars and research projects. Its cooperation with UNESCO had been constantly strengthened and expanded, and remarkable achievements were made. The cooperation projects of the two sides covered 29 provinces (autonomous regions and municipalities) and produced good social benefits. In 1980, China joined the World Intellectual Property Organization (WIPO). The WIPO had been giving strong support to China in the process of establishing a professional intellectual property team. China also undertook various meetings organized by the WIPO in China and sent personnel to participate in the work of its headquarters.

Arms control and disarmament were major issues of concern to people all over the world. The United Nations regarded the maintenance of international peace and security as its lofty goal, and regarded disarmament as one of the main means to achieve this goal. China had always supported comprehensive and complete disarmament. Since 1978, China had always advocated that the two superpowers bore special responsibilities on the issue of disarmament and should take the lead in taking action, which had been unanimously endorsed by the international community. Since 1986, China had put forward proposals on nuclear and conventional disarmament at the UNGA for five consecutive years, all of which had been unanimously adopted. China actively participated in international multilateral disarmament conferences and negotiations and made positive contributions to the conclusion of the *Chemical Weapons Convention (CWC)* and the *Comprehensive Nuclear Test Ban Treaty (CTBT)*. China actively participated in bilateral and multilateral security dialogue and cooperation in the Asia-Pacific region, advocated a new security concept, and actively supported the reasonable proposals and propositions of establishing nuclear free zones in various regions of the world. China successively acceded to a series of international arms control treaties. In 1985, China took large-scale disarmament action and announced the reduction of 1 million troops.

Since the 1980s, China had made constructive efforts in maintaining world peace and mediating regional conflicts through multilateral diplomacy, contributing to promoting global development and strengthening South-South cooperation. In the 1960s and 1970s, China's multilateral diplomatic activities were mainly based on political considerations. Therefore, although China restored its legal seat in the United Nations in the 1970s, it only regarded the United Nations as a forum for opposing hegemonism. In the 1980s, China's multilateral diplomacy was based on national interests. While abiding by international norms and practices, China assumed obligations and enjoyed rights. In a large number of multilateral diplomatic practices, China handled the relationship between the two well. China's position on UN peacekeeping operations had changed since the 1980s. Since the 36th session of the UNGA in 1981, China had clearly affirmed the role of UN peacekeeping operations and adopted a supportive position. Since 1982, China had begun to bear the cost of UN peacekeeping operations. It had made clear its international responsibilities and obligations, actively urged the settlement of global and regional hotspot issues, and tried its best to maintain international peace. In 1989, China formally applied to join the UN Special Committee on Peacekeeping Operations.

Apart from the United Nations, China also participated in many other important international organizations, and its relations with regional international organizations further developed. According to statistics, by 1988, China had acceded to more than 120 international conventions and multilateral conventions, of which three-quarters had acceded to since 1978. China increasingly attached importance to and made efforts to give play to the positive role of international multilateral relations, and devoted itself to a wide range of activities in multilateral relations, involving almost all aspects of international issues. In order to further expand the scope of its participation in international organizations, China formally submitted an application to the *General Agreement on Tariffs and Trade (GATT)* on July 11, 1986 to restore the status of a contracting party to the agreement. Although the progress of this negotiation was very slow, the submission of China's application for *GATT Resumption* and the development of its activities show that China was willing to bring many aspects of economic development into the norms of certain important international multilateral agreements. After the establishment of the World Trade Organization (WTO), the replacement of the *General Agreement on Tariffs and Trade*, in 1995, China formally applied for "WTO entry." After 15 years of arduous and tortuous negotiations on "GATT" and "WTO accession," China joined the WTO in 2001. China also gave active support to some organizations in developing countries. In the 1980s, China actively supported and directly participated in various activities of the non-aligned movement and the group of 77 meeting that embodied "South-South cooperation." China also participated as much as possible in the organizations and activities of some regional developing countries, such as the African Development Bank and its funds and the Pacific Cooperation Conference. China also insisted on opposing hegemonism and power politics in various forms on various occasions of multilateral relations and safeguarding the interests of the vast number of developing countries. The extensive multilateral cooperation not only enhanced China's status in the international arena, but also directly promoted China's economic and social development and progress.

(2) Developing Solidarity and Cooperation with Third World Countries in Asia, Africa and Latin America

While attaching importance to improving relations with developed countries, China also consolidated and strengthened its solidarity and cooperation with third world countries in Asia, Africa and Latin America. Since 1978, China had taken solidarity and cooperation with third world countries as the basic foothold of its foreign policy, further consolidated and expanded close cooperation with third world countries in Asia, Africa and Latin America in the political, economic, trade, cultural, educational, health and other fields, carried out friendly exchanges with multi-level and multi-channel comprehensive development, resolutely supported third world countries in their struggle against imperialism, hegemonism, colonialism and racism, respected their choice of social systems and development models in accordance with their national conditions, continued to provide them with new economic and technical assistance, helped them to develop their economies and pursue social progress, promoted South-South cooperation, which opened up bright prospects for world peace and development and the establishment of a new international political and economic order. For Arab countries in West Asia and North Africa, Premier Zhou Enlai put forward the "Five Principles" as early as when he visited Egypt in 1963. After the reform and opening-up, in 1983, China put forward the four principles of "Equality and Mutual Benefit, Practical Results, Diversity of Forms and Common Development" as the policy for expanding economic and technological cooperation with African and Arab countries in the new period. In 1990, during his visit to five Latin American countries, including Mexico, Brazil, Uruguay, Argentina and Chile, Chinese president Yang Shangkun put forward the four principles and five proposals, which promoted the further development of friendship and cooperation between China and Latin American countries.

In the 1980s, China formally established diplomatic relations with some countries in Africa, Latin America, West Asia and the South Pacific that had not yet established diplomatic relations.

(3) Opening Up a New Situation in Diplomatic Work
From the late 1980s to the early 1990s, the Soviet Union and Eastern Europe underwent drastic changes, and the bipolar international pattern ceased to exist. At the same time, western hostile forces were rampant, stepping up "peaceful evolution" in a vain attempt to bring the scourge of "political pluralism" and "multi-party system" to the east. Socialist China was pushed into the stormy waves of East-West and North-South contradictions.

After the political turmoil of 1989, at the instigation of the U.S., the Seven Western Countries Summit united to impose political and economic "sanctions" on China: "no senior official contacts" and cutting off political contacts with China; restricting economic and trade exchanges, not granting loans; prohibiting military cooperation; pressure was put on the Chinese government, and even billions of dollars of loans promised to China by the World Bank, the Asian Development Bank (ADB) and the Japanese government were put on hold. Facing the fierce offensive of "peaceful evolution" of the west, Deng Xiaoping put forward the calm and pragmatic strategic thinking of "calm observation, stable position and calm response,"[18] and required us to do our own things well. He also said that the last country in the world to be afraid of isolation, blockade or sanctions was China. The Chinese people were not afraid of isolation. No matter what changes take place in the international situation, China would be able to hold its ground. Calm observation meant being highly alert to the dynamics of the international and domestic political situation, soberly estimating the development of the world situation, using effective methods to control the development of China's political situation, facing squarely the anti-communist and anti-China waves launched by western hostile forces, resolutely cracking down on their arrogance, and avoiding political upheaval; to stabilize position meant to unswervingly adhere to the line of the 13th National Congress of the CPC, adhere to "one center task, two basic points," and stabilize China's political situation; to respond to the situation calmly meant to deal with the situation without fear, to be calm in the face of danger, to take things calmly, to put a brake on things with a static approach, to understand the direction of China's development in the face of twists and turns and adversity, and to continue to promote the modernization drive.

On September 29, 1989, at the conference commemorating the 40th anniversary of the founding of the PRC, Jiang Zemin clearly declared that economic sanctions against China could not in the least shake our determination to revitalize China and adhere to the socialist road, nor can it shake our desire to live in friendship with the people of all countries in the world. This was the attitude of the Chinese government and the Chinese people.

The western sanctions against China were a double-edged sword in itself. Shortly after the US government announced the sanctions, on July 2, 1989, Brent Scowcroft, special envoy of the US president and assistant to the president for security affairs, secretly visited China. Deng Xiaoping told him that Chinese leaders would not rashly take and make actions and statements to deal with bilateral relations, but they would never be vague in safeguarding China's independence, sovereignty and national dignity. In October, former US president

Nixon paid a friendly visit to China and expressed his desire to improve bilateral relations.

However, at this time, the international situation changed dramatically. Working class political parties in eastern European countries stepped down one after another. Then, at the end of 1991, the Communist Party of the Soviet Union lost its ruling position, the socialist camp ceased to exist, and the world socialist movement fell into a low tide. In the face of this complex situation, Deng Xiaoping put forward a series of guiding principles, such as "calm observation, stable position, calm response, hiding one's capacity and biding one's time, being good at self-defense, never taking the lead, and making a difference,"[19] and clearly pointed out that the fundamental intention of western countries was to ask China to give up socialism, but China would never give up the socialist system.

On the basis of scientific analysis of the international situation, the Chinese Communists with Comrade Jiang Zemin as the main representative clearly pointed out that peace and development were still the two major themes of the world today. China persisted in continuing to implement the basic foreign policy since reform and opening-up, persisted in opposing hegemonism and power politics, and persisted in developing friendly relations with all countries in the world on the basis of the Five Principles of Peaceful Coexistence. At the same time, the focus of diplomatic work in the early 1990s was clarified: first, to carry out good neighborly diplomacy, stabilize and actively develop relations with neighboring countries, and strengthen unity and cooperation with developing countries; second, break the sanctions imposed by western countries and restore and stabilize relations with western developed countries.

Since the second half of 1990, some western countries had gradually improved their relations with China. In July 1990, Japan first resumed loans to China. Subsequently, western European countries gradually resumed export credit guarantees, government loans, economic cooperation and scientific and technological exchanges with China. In October, the Foreign Ministers' Meeting of European Community decided to lift sanctions against China and restore normal relations with China. After 1987, the European Community provided emergency disaster relief assistance to some disaster-stricken areas in China for many times. By 1991, the total amount of assistance reached 2.53 million European currency units. In 1992, the European Community restored China's status as a recipient of development assistance and provided about 12 million U.S. dollars in development assistance funds to China.

The US government announced sanctions against China twice on June 5 and 20, and several anti-China climaxes occurred in the US Congress. China-US relations took a sharp turn for the worse, and there was a historic retrogression. After the end of the cold war, the United States' position on Taiwan's accession to the General Agreement on Tariffs and Trade undergone major changes, and it took the lead in playing the card of supporting Taiwan's "accession to the GATT," prompting some international economic organizations to express a "flexible" attitude toward Taiwan. In fact, it helped the Taiwan authorities "expand international space," also seriously affected China-US relations, and cast a shadow over the growing China-US relations. However, in 1990 and 1991, China and the United States realized the exchange of foreign ministers' visits, and the two countries also reached agreements on the intellectual property protection and market access. In 1992, the Chinese government proposed that China and the United States should develop friendly relations on the basis of the three Sino-US Joint Communique in accordance with the principle of "increasing trust, reducing troubles, developing cooperation and not engaging in confrontation." In November 1993, at the invitation of President Clinton, Jiang Zemin attended the informal meeting of leaders of the Asia-Pacific Economic Cooperation Organization held in Seattle, the United States, and had a formal meeting. The two sides reiterated that the three Sino-US Joint Communiques were the foundation of China-US relations, and stressed that China-US relations should be viewed from a global perspective, with an eye on the future and the 21st century. The meeting between the leaders of China and the United States marked the breaking of the so-called "sanctions" against China by the western countries headed by the United States.

China was actively improving and developing its relations with neighboring countries. In May 1989, Soviet Union leader Gorbachev visited China, realizing the normalization of China-Soviet relations and ending the confrontational relations since the 1960s. After the disintegration of the Soviet Union in December 1991, the Chinese government established friendly relations with Russia and other countries. During this period, China and the North Korea consolidated and strengthened their traditional friendship. China always actively supported the North Korea's socialist construction cause and provided assistance to the best of its ability. Since the reform and opening-up, economic and trade cooperation between the two countries was carried out smoothly, scientific and technological cooperation and exchanges were developed rapidly, and exchanges and cooperation in culture, education, art and sports were very active. In August 1992, China established formal diplomatic relations with South Korea. China actively supported the reconciliation between the north and the south and the denuclearization of the Korean Peninsula, and urged the two sides to continue to improve their relations through dialogue and consultation, so as to maintain peace and stability of the Korean Peninsula and promote the independent and peaceful reunification of the two Koreas. In 1991, North and South Korea joined the UXizang Nations at the same time and signed the *Agreement on Reconciliation, Non-aggression and Exchange and Cooperation between the South and North* and the *Joint Declaration on the Denuclearization of the Korean Peninsula*. In 1990, the supreme leader of Mongolia paid a visit to China and issued a joint communique guiding the development of bilateral relations, proposing to strengthen and develop the friendly and cooperative relations between the two countries in the political, economic, military, scientific, technological and cultural exchanges on the basis of the Five Principles of Peaceful Coexistence.

In October 1989, Kaysone Phomvihane, chairman of the Lao Council of Ministers and general secretary of the Lao People's Revolutionary Party, paid a friendly visit to China. In December 1990, Premier Li Peng paid an official friendly visit to Laos at the invitation of chairman Kaysone. This was the first visit of the Chinese Premier to Laos, marking a new stage in the development of China-Lao relations. In October 1991, the prime ministers of China and Laos formally signed the China-Lao border treaty in Beijing, which successfully solved the problems left over by history between the two countries and further promoted the development of bilateral relations in the direction of peace and friendship. In September 1991, the Vietnamese foreign minister paid an official visit to China and began to put the normalization of China-Vietnamese relations on the agenda. In October, the Paris International Conference officially signed the *Agreements on a Comprehensive Political Settlement of the Cambodia Conflict*. The Cambodian issue no longer became an obstacle to China-Vietnamese relations, and China and Vietnam began to carry out substantive diplomatic activities. In November, general secretary of the Central Committee of the Communist Party of Vietnam (CPV) Do Muoi and chairman of the Vietnamese Council of Ministers Vo Van Kiet led a high-level Vietnamese delegation to visit China. The high-level meeting between the top leaders of the party and government of the two countries became a major turning point in "ending the past and opening up the future," realizing the normalization of bilateral relations and making steady progress.

After 1989, Japan took part in the so-called "sanctions" imposed by the west against China, frozen high-level exchanges and some cooperation projects between the two countries at or above the ministerial level, restricted Japanese from coming to China, and postponed the negotiations on the third batch of government loans originally scheduled to start in autumn, which once brought the bilateral relations to a standstill. In September, Masayoshi Ito, president of the Japan-China Friendship Parliamentarians Alliance, led a delegation of the Japan-China Friendship Parliamentarians Alliance to visit China, reopening the door for the development of bilateral relations. In 1990, China-Japanese relations began to recover. Chinese State Councilors Zou Jiahua and Li Tieying, and Vice Premier Wu Xueqian of the State Council successively visited Japan and met with Japanese leaders such as Prime Minister Toshiki Kaifu. In July, the special envoy of the Japanese Prime Minister visited China and officially resumed the third batch of government loans. In April and June 1991, Japanese foreign minister Taro Nakayama and Chinese State Councilor and foreign minister Qian Qichen successively exchanged visits, further promoting the restoration and development of China-Japanese relations. In August 1991, on the eve of the 20th anniversary of the normalization of diplomatic relations between China and Japan, Japanese prime minister Toshiki Kaifu visited China, and China-Japanese relations were completely restored to normal. In 1992, Jiang Zemin and Wanli visited Japan one after another, and Emperor Akihito of Japan visited China for the first time, further developing China-Japanese relations.

In December 1991, Chinese premier Li Peng paid an official friendly visit to India. This was the first visit to India by a Chinese premier in more than 30 years. It was an important milestone in the development of China-Indian relations. During this visit, the two sides signed such important documents as the *Agreement Constituted by Exchange of Notes between the Government of the PRC and the Government of the Republic of India on Matters Concerning the Consular Convention between the PRC and the Republic of India*, the *1992 China-India Government Trade Protocol*, and the *Memorandum of Understanding between the Indian Space Research Organization and the China National Space Administration on Cooperation in the Peaceful Use of Outer Space*. They decided to resume the establishment of the Consulate General and bilateral trade, laying a solid foundation for expanding the fields of cooperation between the two countries. In 1992, Indian president Venkataraman visited China, and Sino-Indian relations improved significantly.

After years of efforts by both sides, China finally resumed its diplomatic relations with Indonesia in 1990, establishing diplomatic relations with Singapore in October 1990 and Brunei in September 1991. The development of diplomatic relations between China and ASEAN countries entered a new historical period, and various forms of exchanges and friendly cooperation were conducted in a wider range of fields.

In the 1980s, China formally established diplomatic relations with some countries in Africa, Latin America, West Asia and the South Pacific that had not yet established diplomatic relations. In 1990, China established diplomatic relations with Saudi Arabia. In 1992, China established diplomatic relations with Israel. In May 1990, president Yang Shangkun visited five Latin American countries: Mexico, Brazil, Uruguay, Argentina and Chile. In July 1992, Yang Shangkun visited Morocco, Tunisia and Cote d'Ivoire in Africa. At the same time, China's relations with countries in the South Pacific also developed greatly.

After the reform and opening-up, especially after the mid-1980s, China's diplomatic work achieved fruitful results. By 1992, China had established diplomatic relations with 154 countries, developed cooperation and exchanges with more than 200 countries and regions in economy, trade, science and technology, culture, etc., straightened out diplomatic relations with western countries and neighboring countries, strengthened relations with third world countries, and made a good start for the great cause of China's reunification; in an international environment full of stormy waves, China defended its independence, sovereignty and dignity, established the image of a responsible big country, won a favorable international environment for reform, opening up and modernization, and made positive contributions to the cause of world peace.

Summary

In accordance with the strategic shift of national priorities and new changes in the international situation, the CPC and the Chinese government grasped the theme of the times of peace and development and adjusted their foreign strategy at the right time, changing the "one-line" strategy of alliance with the United States and resistance to the Soviet Union and gradually forming a complete foreign policy with Chinese characteristics, with adherence to independence as the main goal, the Five Principles of Peaceful Coexistence as the fundamental criterion, the strengthening of solidarity and cooperation with Third World countries as the basic foothold, and the opening up to the outside world as the basic state policy. The CPC and the Chinese government actively promoted the normalization of China-American and China-Soviet relations, developed relations with developed countries in Western Europe, and established a steady and orderly major power diplomacy; strengthened and improved the policy of "good neighbor" and promoted neighborly and friendly neighboring diplomacy; actively improved relations with neighboring countries and changed the past situation of being enemies on all sides; worked to establish a new international political and economic order, actively promoted South-South cooperation, and further consolidated and developed diplomatic relations with Third World countries; actively participated in international affairs, carried out extensive multilateral diplomacy, and played an increasingly influential role in international affairs. After 1989, the Chinese government pursued a positive and rational diplomatic strategy and successfully broke the so-called "sanctions" imposed by Western countries, pushing China's diplomacy to a new level and opening up a new situation in China's diplomatic work.

CHAPTER II

A New Phase of Reform and Opening Up

Pushing Socialism with Chinese Characteristics to the 21st Century (1992–2002)

In 1992, the publication of Deng Xiaoping's "Southern Talks" and the convening of the 14th National Congress of the CPC marked that the cause of reform, opening up and socialist modernization had entered a new historical stage.

In the face of profound changes in the situation at home and abroad, under the guidance of Deng Xiaoping Theory, the CPC has led the people to defend socialism with Chinese characteristics and created a new situation of comprehensive reform and opening-up. In the aspect of political construction, the Chinese Communists has boldly carried out theoretical and practical exploration and established Deng Xiaoping Theory as their guiding ideology. The proposal of the general plan of "ruling the country by law" and the formation of the concept of building a socialist political civilization marked the new development of the ruling concept of the CPC. On this basis, China's various political systems have achieved new development, and the construction of socialist democratic politics has continued to advance. In terms of economic development, the CPC and the Chinese government have clearly defined the reform objectives of the socialist market economy, and have adopted a series of major measures to promote relevant reforms. They have established a basic economic system at the primary stage of socialism, in which public ownership is the mainstay and various forms of ownership develop together, and a distribution system in which distribution according to one's work is the mainstay and various forms of distribution coexist, and established the basic framework of the socialist market economy. At the same time, the realization of a "soft landing" of the economy, the successful response to the Asian financial crisis, China's accession to the WTO, the formation of an all-round layout of opening up to the outside world, and the formulation and implementation of development strategies such as the "large-scale development of the western region" have greatly improved China's economic development, comprehensive national strength and people's living standards. In terms of cultural construction, the deployment and implementation of the strategy for invigorating China through science and education have promoted the reform of China's science and technology system and education system and the vigorous development of various undertakings. The strategy of "the rule of virtue" has enriched the CPC's national governance thought and deepened people's understanding of the importance of strengthening socialist morals at the new stage and new situation. The proposition of vigorously prospering philosophy and social sciences and the implementation of relevant measures have created good conditions for the further development of philosophy and social sciences. In terms of social undertakings, with the transformation of the economic system, China's social and economic components, organizational forms, employment methods, interest relations and distribution forms have shown a new trend of diversification, and the social structure has undergone obvious changes. The issues relating to agriculture, rural areas and the wellbeing of farmers has become increasingly prominent. In this regard, the state has vigorously promoted the reform of the social security system, strengthened the comprehensive management of public security, and maintained long-term social stability. In terms of diplomatic work, under the guidance of the concept of "peaceful development," China's diplomatic strategy has undergone a major change from "hiding our capacity and biding our time" to "going out." China has established various forms of strategic partnership with major countries, actively developed friendly relations with neighboring countries from the standpoint of "implementing amity, sincerity, mutual benefit," further deepened its relations with the vast number of developing countries, gradually established a framework of "partnership" in diplomacy, participated in international organizations and activities with a positive attitude, and displayed China's image as a "responsible" major country. In terms of reunifying our motherland, through arduous work and struggle, the Chinese government successively resumed its exercise of sovereignty over Hong Kong and Macao, thus ending a century-long history of humiliation. Since Hong Kong and Macao's return to the motherland, the central government acted in strict compliance with China's Constitution and the basic laws of the special administrative regions and maintained lasting prosperity and stability in the two regions.

During this period, China successfully achieved the second step of the "three-step" strategy, and the people's living standards reached a well-off level on the whole. This is a new milestone in the history of the development of the Chinese nation. At the new historical starting point, China has planned and promoted the new "three-step" development strategy, and smoothly opened a new stage of building moderately prosperous society in an all-round way and accelerating modernization.

SECTION I

Opening Up of the New Stage and the Progress of Socialist Political Civilization

2.1.1 Deng Xiaoping's "South Talks" and the 14th National Congress of the CPC

(1) The Publication of Deng Xiaoping's "South Talks"
Since the 1990s, great and profound changes have taken place in the international and domestic situations. Internationally, the drastic changes in Eastern Europe, the disintegration of the Soviet Union, and the international communist movement suffered serious setbacks; with the end of the cold war, the world is moving towards multi-polarization; the development trend of economic globalization is increasingly obvious; some countries around China, especially some countries and regions in Southeast Asia, have witnessed a momentum of accelerated economic development. Domestically, in the early 1990s, the first strategic goal of China's economic development was basically realized, and by 1991, the three-year task of governance and rectification was basically completed. China's economic environment and economic order showed a momentum conducive to further reform. However, some economic and social problems have emerged in the course of China's development. In addition, some people have some misunderstanding of the implementation of the household contract responsibility system in rural areas,

the establishment of Special Economic Zones, the development of non-public economy, and what socialism is, how to build socialism, and the future and destiny of socialism. There has even been a dispute in China over whether the road is "capitalist" and "socialist." These incorrect understandings and debates actually involve the major issue of principle of whether or not to adhere to the basic line of "one center task, two basic points." Contemporary China's reform and opening-up and socialist modernization have entered a new critical moment.

From January 18 to February 21, 1992, 88-year-old Deng Xiaoping, who had retired from the leadership posts of the Party and the state, successively inspected and investigated Wuchang, Shenzhen, Zhuhai and Shanghai. During this period, he made a number of important speeches, incisively analyzed the international and domestic situations, scientifically summarized the basic practice and basic experience since the reform and opening-up, and clearly answered many major cognitive problems that often perplexed and bound people's minds in practice.

Deng Xiaoping's Southern Talks runs through a clear central thought, which was: we must unswervingly and comprehensively implement the CPC's basic line of "one center task, two basic points," emancipate our minds, seek truth from facts, leave enough room to demonstrate our capability, boldly carry out experiments, eliminate all kinds of interference, seize the favorable opportunity, accelerate the pace of reform and opening-up, and concentrate on economic development, and constantly push forward the cause of socialism with Chinese characteristics in an all-round way. Centering on this central idea, the main contents of Deng Xiaoping's Southern Talks include:

First, adhere to the CPC's basic line of "one center task, two basic points." We should adhere to the basic line for a hundred years, with no vacillation. That is the only way to win the trust and support of the people. Revolution means the emancipation of the productive forces, and so does reform.

Second, adhere to the "three favorables" standard. The chief criterion for making that judgement on reform and opening-up should be whether it promotes the growth of the productive forces in a socialist society, increases the overall strength of the socialist state and raises living standards.

Third, the proportion of planning to market forces is not the essential difference between socialism and capitalism. A planned economy is not equivalent to socialism, because there is planning under capitalism too; a market economy is not capitalism, because there are markets under socialism too. Planning and market forces are both means of controlling economic activity.

Fourth, the essence of socialism is liberation and development of the productive forces, elimination of exploitation and polarization, and the ultimate achievement of prosperity for all. If we want socialism to achieve superiority over capitalism, we should not hesitate to draw on the achievements of all cultures and to learn from other countries, including the developed capitalist countries, all advanced methods of operation and techniques of management that reflect the laws governing modern socialized production.

Fifth, we should maintain vigilance against the Right tendencies, but primarily against the "Left." At present, we are being affected by both Right and "Left" tendencies, but it is the "Left" tendencies that have the deepest roots. Right tendencies can destroy socialism, but so can "Left" ones.

Sixth, if we are to seize opportunities to promote China's all-round development, it is crucial to expand the economy. Slow growth equals stagnation and even retrogression. Where local conditions permit, development should proceed as fast as possible. Development is what really matters to all. Rapid development of the economy can only be based on science technology and education. Technology is a primary source of productivity,

Seventh, we need to follow the principle of "doing two jobs at once and attaching equal importance to each." There are two tasks we have to keep working at: on the one hand, the reform and opening process, and on the other, the crackdown on crime. We must be steadfast with regard to both. In the whole process of reform and opening-up, we should oppose corruption. Cadres and Party members should consider it of prime importance to build a clean government, always pay attention to and adhere to the four cardinal principles. The spread of bourgeois liberalization will have extremely serious consequences.

Eighth, we shall push ahead along the road to Chinese-style socialism. More and more people will come to believe in Marxism, because it is a science. The period from now to the middle of the next century will be crucial. We must immerse ourselves in hard work. We must immerse ourselves in hard work: we have difficult tasks to accomplish and bear a heavy responsibility.

Deng Xiaoping's Southern Talks, at a major historical juncture when the international and domestic political turmoil was severely tested, adhered to the theory and line since the Third Plenary Session of the 11th CCCPC, greatly encouraged the confidence of the CPC and the people of all ethnic groups to adhere to the basic line of the ruling party at the primary stage of socialism in China, gave a great impetus to speeding up the pace of reform and opening-up and modernization, and made sufficient ideological and theoretical preparations for the convening of the 14th National Congress of the CPC. It is another "manifesto" of emancipating the mind and seeking truth from facts to advance reform and opening-up and socialist modernization to a new stage.

In March, the Political Bureau of the CCCPC held a plenary meeting, which fully endorsed Deng Xiaoping's Southern Talks and fully affirmed its important practical and historical significance. Subsequently, the CCCPC and the State Council made a series of important decisions on accelerating reform, opening up and economic development. Shanghai and Shenzhen conducted pilot stock listings and accelerated the transformation of the business system of state-run enterprises. Foreign exchange futures trading began on a trial basis, some border cities and major central cities along the Yangtze River were opened to the outside world, and the development of the service sector accelerated. The whole cause of opening up and economic development has shown a strong momentum of development.

(2) The Convening of the 14th National Congress of the CPC

From October 12 to 18, 1992, the 14th National Congress of the CPC was convened in Beijing. There were 1,989 formal representatives and 46 specially invited representatives, representing more than 51 million Party members throughout the country. Jiang Zemin made a report entitled Accelerating the Pace of Reform, Opening up and Modernization, and Winning Greater Victory in the Cause of Socialism with Chinese Characteristics. Guided by Deng Xiaoping's theory of building socialism with Chinese characteristics, the Congress summed up the practice and basic experience of reform, opening up and socialist modernization in the past 14 years since the Third Plenary Session of the 11th CCCPC, summed up Deng Xiaoping's theory of building socialism with Chinese characteristics, and set the strategic plan for the coming period.

The Congress held that since the Third Plenary Session of the 11th CCCPC, we have been engaged in the cause of adhering to the basic line of the ruling party, liberating and developing the productive forces through reform and opening-up, and building socialism with Chinese characteristics. In terms of the breadth and depth of social changes it has caused, it has started a new revolution. Its essence and goal are to fundamentally change the economic system that constrains the development of China's productive forces, establish a new socialist economic system that is full of vitality and vigor, and at the same time, reform the political system and other systems accordingly to realize socialist modernization. The 14 years of great practice since the Third Plenary Session of the 11th CCCPC has opened up a new historical situation and made achievements that attract worldwide attention. The CPC has won the support of the broad masses of the people. The fundamental reason why the CPC has been able to achieve such a victory is that it has persisted in integrating the basic principles of Marxism with the specific realities of China, gradually formed and developed the theory of building socialism with Chinese characteristics, and formulated and implemented the basic line of the CPC at the primary stage of socialism.

The Congress systematically summarized the main contents and viewpoints of the theory of building socialism with Chinese characteristics from nine aspects: a) On the issue of the road of socialist development, we should stress following our own path, not taking books as dogma, not copying foreign models, taking Marxism as the guide, taking practice as the sole criterion for testing truth, emancipating the mind, seeking truth from facts, respecting the initiative of the masses, and building socialism with Chinese characteristics. b) On the issue of the development stage of socialism, the congress made a scientific conclusion that China is still at the primary stage of socialism, and stressed that this is a very long historical stage of at least one hundred years. All principles and policies must be formulated on the basis of this basic national condition, and cannot be divorced from reality and transcend the stage. c) the essence of socialism is liberation and development of the productive forces, elimination of exploitation and polarization, and the ultimate achievement of prosperity for all. The chief criterion for judging any action should be whether it promotes the growth of the productive forces in a socialist society, increases the overall strength of the socialist state and raises living standards. d) On the issue of the driving force of socialist development, it is emphasized that reform is also a revolution, and the only way to liberation of the productive forces and modernization. There is no way out for rigid stagnation. e) On the external conditions of socialist construction, the congress pointed out that peace and development are the two major themes in the world today. We must adhere to an independent foreign policy of peace and strive for a favorable international environment for China's modernization. f) On the issue of the socialist construction, the congress stressed the adherence to the Four Cardinal Principles—to keep to the path of socialism, to uphold the people's democratic dictatorship, to uphold the leadership of the CPC, and to uphold Marxism-Leninism and Mao Zedong Thought. g) On the issue of the strategic steps of socialist construction, it is proposed to basically realize modernization in three steps. h) On the issue of socialist leadership and reliance, it is emphasized that the CPC, as the vanguard of the working class, is the core of the leadership of the socialist cause. The CPC must adapt to the needs of reform, opening up and modernization, constantly improve and strengthen its leadership over all aspects of work, and improve and strengthen its own construction. i) On the issue of the reunification of the motherland, the congress put forward the creative idea of "One Country, Two Systems."

The Congress affirmed Deng Xiaoping's outstanding contribution to the theory of building socialism with Chinese characteristics. At the same time, it stressed that there are many other contents of this theory, which should be tested, enriched and improved in the practice of studying new situations, summing up new experiences and solving new problems. After discussion, the Congress decided to include this theory in the general program of the Party Constitution as the guiding principle for China's reform, opening up and socialist modernization. This is of great significance for unifying the thinking and actions of the whole Party of the ruling party and winning the great victory of socialism with Chinese characteristics.

The Congress clearly pointed out that the goal of China's economic reform is to build a socialist market economy, and formulated the decision-making and deployment to accelerate the pace of reform, opening up and modernization. It also put forward ten major tasks that must be completed in the 1990s:

First, speed up the development of economy on the goal of the building of socialist market economy.

Second, we should further open up to the outside world and make better use of foreign capital, resources, technology and management experience.

Third, adjust and optimize the industrial structure, attach great importance to agriculture, and accelerate the development of basic industry, infrastructure and the service sector.

Fourth, accelerate scientific and technological progress, vigorously develop education, and give full play to the role of intellectuals.

Fifth, give full play to the advantages of various regions, accelerate regional economic development, and promote the rationalization of the national economic layout.

Sixth, actively promote the reform of the political system so that socialist democracy and the legal system can achieve greater development.

Seventh, make up our minds to carry out the reform of the administrative system and institutions, so as to effectively transform our functions, straighten out relations, streamline our troops and simplify our administration, and improve efficiency.

Eighth, adhere to the principle of "doing two jobs at once and attaching equal importance to each" and pay very close attention to and strengthen socialist cultural and ethical progress.

Ninth, continuously improve people's living standards, strictly control population growth, and strengthen environmental protection.

Tenth, strengthen army building, enhance national defense strength, and ensure the smooth progress of reform, opening up, and economic development.[20]

The Congress also deliberated and adopted the *Resolution on the Work Report of the Central Advisory Committee*, the *Resolution on the Work Report of the CCDI*, and the *Resolution on the Report of the 13th Central Committee*. It was decided that the Central Committee would no longer establish an advisory committee after this Congress. The Congress elected the 14th Central Committee and the CCDI.

Subsequently, the First Plenary Session of the 14th CCCPC elected Jiang Zemin, Li Peng, Qiao Shi, Li Ruihuan, Zhu Rongji, Liu Huaqing, and Hu Jintao as members of the Standing Committee of the Political Bureau of the CCCPC, and Jiang Zemin as general secretary of the Central Committee; and decides that Jiang Zemin is chairman of the CMC and Liu Huaqing and Zhang Zhen are Vice-chairmen of the CMC; and approved Wei Jianxing as secretary of the CCDI.

The 14th National Congress of the CPC established a new theory for the forward development of China's reform and opening-up and socialist modernization, and pointed out the development direction of economic reform.

2.1.2 The 15th National Congress of the CPC and the Establishment of the Guiding Position of Deng Xiaoping Theory

Reform and opening-up is an unprecedented great and arduous socialist practice movement for the ruling Chinese Communists, and it is also a theoretical innovation activity. On February 19, 1997, Deng Xiaoping, the "chief designer" of reform and opening-up, died. After Deng Xiaoping, the ideals and convictions of the CPC has become the focus of attention at home and abroad.

At this important historical juncture, from September 12 to 18, 1997, the 15th National Congress of the CPC was held in Beijing. There were 2,048 official delegates, 60 specially invited delegates, and 58 million Party members throughout the country. Jiang Zemin made the report of *Hold High the Great Banner of Deng Xiaoping Theory for an All-round Advancement of the Cause of Building Socialism with Chinese Characteristics to the 21st Century*.

The congress pointed out the issue of the banner is of the utmost importance. The banner represents our orientation and image. The Congress first proposed and formally used the concept of "Deng Xiaoping Theory." The Congress proposed that the integration of Marxism-Leninism with China's reality has experienced two historic leaps, resulting in two great theories. The result of the first leap was a correct theory, a body of correct principles and a summary of experience that have been confirmed in the practice of the Chinese revolution and construction. Its main founder is Mao Zedong, and our Party calls it Mao Zedong thought. The result of the second leap was the theory of building socialism with Chinese characteristics. Its main founder is Deng Xiaoping. Our party calls it Deng Xiaoping Theory. These two great theories so achieved are the crystallization of the practical experience and collective wisdom of the Party and the people. The Congress pointed out that it has been gradually formed and developed under the historical conditions in which peace and development have become the main themes of the times, in the practice of China's reform, opening up and modernization drive, and on the basis of reviewing the historical experience of successes and setbacks of socialism in China and learning from the historical experience of the rise and fall of other socialist countries. For the first time it has given preliminary but systematic answers to a series of basic questions concerning the road to socialism in China, the stages of development, the fundamental tasks, the motive force, the external conditions, the political guarantee, the strategic steps, Party leadership, the forces to be relied on, and the reunification of the motherland. It has guided our party in formulating the basic line at the primary stage of socialism. It is a fairly complete scientific system which embraces philosophy, political economy and scientific socialism and covers, among other things, the economy, politics, science and technology, education, culture, ethnic, military and foreign affairs, the united front and Party building. It is also a scientific system which needs to be further enriched and developed in all aspects. The Congress stressed that firmly adhering to the line formulated since the Third Plenary Session of the 11th Central Committee means firmly holding high the banner of Deng Xiaoping Theory. After the death of Comrade Deng Xiaoping, it is all the more necessary for the whole Party to keep a high level of consciousness and staunchness on this issue.

The Congress proposed that the Party's program for the primary stage of socialism, and stressed that building a socialist economy with Chinese characteristics means developing a market economy under socialism and constantly emancipating and developing the productive forces, building a socialist culture with Chinese characteristics means taking Marxism as the guidance, aiming at training citizens so that they have high ideals, moral integrity, a good education and a strong sense of discipline, and developing a national, scientific and popular socialist culture geared to the needs of modernization, of the world and of the future. The Congress pointed out that this programme is an important part of Deng Xiaoping Theory, an elaboration of the Party's basic line in the economic, political and cultural fields and a summary of the major experience gained over the years.

At a time when the second step goal of the "three-step" strategy for China's economic development is about to be realized, the Congress made further plans on how to achieve the third step goal and put forward a new "three-step" development strategy: in the first decade of the 21st century, the gross national product would double that of 2000, making the people's well-off life more affluent, and forming a relatively complete socialist market economy system; with the efforts to be made in another decade when the Party celebrates its centenary, the national economy would be more developed and the various systems would be further improved; by the middle of the next century when the People's Republic celebrates its centenary, the modernization programme would have been accomplished by and large and China would have become a prosperous, strong, democratic and culturally advanced socialist country. Centering on this development strategy, the Congress made strategic arrangements for China's cross-century development.[21]

The Congress elected the 15th Central Committee and the CCDI.

The 15th National Congress of the CPC also established Deng Xiaoping Theory as the guiding ideology of the CPC in the Party Constitution. The newly revised Party Constitution clearly stipulates that the CPC takes Marxism-Leninism, Mao Zedong Thought and Deng Xiaoping Theory as its guides to action.

Deng Xiaoping Theory is the product of combining Marxism-Leninism's basic tenets with practice in contemporary China and the particular features of the era; it is a continuation and development of Mao Zedong Thought under new historical conditions; it represents a new stage for the development of Marxism in China; it is the Marxism of contemporary China and a crystallization of the collective wisdom of the CPC; and it guides the continuous progression of China's socialist modernization. Scientifically summarizing the scientific system connotation of Deng Xiaoping Theory and establishing the guiding ideology status of Deng Xiaoping Theory is a major event in the history of the CPC and the development history of contemporary China. It is of far-reaching historical significance for unifying the will of the whole Party and the whole people, continuing to push the cause of socialism with Chinese characteristics to a new stage of development and accomplishing greater achievements.

Subsequently, the First Plenary Session of the 15th CCCPC elected Jiang Zemin, Li Peng, Zhu Rongji, Li Ruihuan, Hu Jintao, Wei Jianxing, and Li Lanqing as members of the Standing Committee of the Political Bureau of the CCCPC, and Jiang Zemin as general secretary of the Central Committee; and decided that Jiang Zemin is chairman of the CMC; and approved Wei Jianxing as secretary of the CCDI.

On March 15, 1999, the Second Session of the Nineth NPC passed the amendment to the Constitution, which established the Deng Xiaoping Theory in national life as the guiding ideology.

2.1.3 Ruling the Country by Law and Building Political Civilization

(1) The Proposal of "Socialist Political Civilization"
After the Fourth Plenary Session of the 13th CCCPC, especially after the 14th National Congress of the CPC, in the process of establishing and improving the socialist market economy, and in the global wave of democratization, the CPC has a new understanding of socialist democracy.

First, on the essence of democracy, the Chinese Communists has believed that in real life, as a political phenomenon in a specific historical stage of mankind, democracy belongs to the superstructure of society, and its development is restricted by the development of social productive forces, social production relations, and economic foundation. In a class society, democracy in today's world can be divided into two different types of democracy, the bourgeoisie and the proletariat. In countries with different modernization processes, in addition to the development of commodity economy, historical culture, national psychology, even population size, ethnic distribution and other factors will have an impact on the development, nature and form of democracy. Jiang Zemin pointed out, "democracy belongs to the realm of politics and is part of the superstructure. There has never been any abstract superclass democracy in the world, nor has there been any absolute democracy. The development of democracy is always related to certain class interests, economic foundation and social and historical conditions. Every country has its own historical tradition and the actual situation of economic and social development. Democracy should suit its own national conditions. As far as contemporary China is concerned, "our socialist democracy embodies the broadest people's democracy and is the best democracy because it best suits China's national conditions." We can say whole heartedly that China's System of People's Congress is much more democratic and superior than the 'separation of three powers' system of western countries. Of course, our socialist democracy will also continue to develop and improve in practice with the progress of economy, culture and society.[22]

Second, on human rights, the Chinese Communists has adhered to the basic position of the Marxist concept of human rights and put forward the human rights viewpoint of the Chinese Communists in the new period and new stage. On the one hand, from the perspective of historical development, the Chinese people and the Chinese Communists have always been concerned about human rights. On the other hand, from the perspective of reality, the right to subsistence and the right to development are the most basic and important human rights of the Chinese people. It is meaningless for the Chinese people to talk about other aspects of human rights without the right to survival and development. The CPC and the Chinese government are the most resolute and loyal defenders of the basic rights of the Chinese people. In terms of space, the Chinese Communists believe that different countries have different national conditions and certainly face different human rights issues and concepts. They should carry out dialogue and cooperation on human rights on the basis of equality and mutual respect, oppose the politicization of the human rights issue, especially the behavior of some developed countries in using the human rights issue to interfere in the internal affairs of developing countries, and must guard against the new interventionism of "human rights above sovereignty" and "limited state sovereignty." National sovereignty is the premise and guarantee for the people of a country to fully enjoy human rights. Human rights are protected by sovereignty. Without sovereignty, there can be no human rights. The political report of the 15th National Congress of the CPC put forward for the first time that "respecting and protecting human rights" is an important content of "the Communist Party in power."

Third, on the importance of developing socialist democratic politics and the basic principles of building socialist democratic politics, at the beginning of the 21st century, the Chinese Communists emphasized that "developing socialist democracy and build a socialist political civilization is an important goal of socialist modernization.[23]

(2) Perfecting the Socialist Legal System and Putting Forward the General Plan of "Ruling the Country by Law"

With the continuous development of the reform to establish the socialist market economy and the rapid changes in China's economic and social life, the CPC has become more and more aware that under the new historical conditions, building a socialist country under the rule of law that coordinates with the economy and society has important practical significance and long-term historical significance. In 1992, the 14th National Congress of the CPC made a major strategic decision to establish a socialist market economy, and clearly stated that the establishment and improvement of the socialist market economy must be regulated and guaranteed by a complete legal system. In 1993, the Third Plenary Session of the 14th CCCPC adopted the *Decision of the CCCPC on some Issues Concerning Establishing of the Socialist Market Economy*, which clearly set forth the objectives of legal system construction: to follow the principles stipulated in the Constitution, accelerate economic legislation, further improve civil and commercial laws, criminal laws, laws related to state institutions and administrative management, and initially establish a legal system suitable for the socialist market economy by the end of the 20th century; reform and improve the judicial system and administrative law enforcement mechanism, and improve the level of judicial and administrative law enforcement; establish and improve law enforcement supervision mechanisms and legal service institutions, conduct in-depth legal education, and improve the legal awareness and legal concept of the whole society. The leadership of the CCCPC took the lead in studying the law. During the five years from the end of 1994 to the end of 1999, the CCCPC held ten lectures on the legal system.

In February 1996, Jiang Zemin made an important speech at the legal system lecture of the central leading comrades held by the CCCPC. He put forward the requirement of "ruling the country by law," and called on leading cadres at all levels to strengthen the study of law and legal knowledge, master and improve their ability to manage economic and social affairs by legal means, drive the broad masses of cadres and the masses with their own practical actions, and form a good atmosphere of studying and using law in the whole society, and lay a solid ideological foundation for upholding the rule of law. In March of the same year, the Fourth Session of the Eighth NPC took "ruling the country by law" as the goal and direction of the political system reform and included it in the *Outline of the Ninth Five-Year Plan for National Economic and Social Development and the Long-range Objectives to the Year 2010 approved by the meeting.* In September 1997, In the report of the 15th National Congress of the CPC, Jiang Zemin formally expounded the connotation of the political governance strategy of "ruling the country by law": "ruling the country by law" means that the broad masses of the people, under the leadership of the Party and in accordance with the Constitution and other laws, participate in one way or another and through all possible channels in managing state affairs, economic and cultural undertakings and social affairs, and see to it that all work of the state proceeds in keeping with law, and that socialist democracy is gradually institutionalized and codified so that such institutions and laws will not change with changes in the leadership or changes in the views or focus of attention of any leader. Ruling the country by law is the basic principle the Party pursues while it leads the people in running the country. It is the objective demand of a socialist market economy, an important hallmark of social and cultural progress, and a vital guarantee for lasting political stability of the country." The 15th National Congress of the CPC also clearly established "ruling the country by law" as the basic strategy for governing the country, decided on "building a socialist country ruled by law" as an important goal of socialist modernization, and put forward the major task of building a socialist legal system with Chinese characteristics. In March 1999, the amendment to the Constitution adopted at the Second Session of the Nineth NPC added a paragraph to Article 5 as the first paragraph, which reads, "The PRC governs the country according to law and makes it a socialist country under rule of law." The strategy of "ruling the country by law" has been formally written into the *Constitution.*

To govern the country according to law, we must first strengthen the legislative work and improve the quality of legislation. In 1993, the Standing Committee of the NPC proposed to enact more than 150 laws within five years, of which two-thirds were related to the building of the market economy. From March 1998 to the end of 2002, the Nineth NPC and its Standing Committee deliberated and adopted 112 decisions on laws and related legal issues, including 1 amendment to the Constitution, 74 laws (35 new laws and 39 amendments), 8 legal interpretations, and 29 decisions on legal issues. These laws and regulations basically cover the following seven categories of laws: the Constitution and laws relevant to the constitution, which mainly stipulate China's social system and state system, the basic rights and obligations of citizens, and the organization, duties and activities of state organs, such as the *Constitution* and *the State Council Organic Law;* civil law and commercial law, which mainly regulate civil and commercial relations between equal subjects, such as *General Principles of the Civil Law of the PRC* and *Contract Law of the PRC;* economic law, which mainly regulates the social and economic relations arising from the state's management of economic activities, such as the *Law on the Administration of Tax Collection of the PRC* and the *Customs Law of the PRC;* administrative laws, which mainly regulate the administrative activities of the state, such as the *Food Hygiene Law of the PRC* and the *State Compensation Law of the PRC;* social laws, which mainly regulates labor relations, social security and social welfare relations, such as the *Labor Law of the PRC* and *Workplace Safety Law of the PRC;* Penal Law, which mainly regulates crime and punishment; procedural laws related to litigation and non-litigation mainly regulate social relations arising from litigation and non-litigation activities, such as the *Civil Procedure Law of the PRC* and the *Arbitration Law of the PRC.* These seven legal categories have initially formed the framework of the Constitution-Centered Socialist Legal System of China. In March 2000, the Third Session of the Nineth NPC passed the *Legislative Law of the PRC,*[24] which enabled the legislative work to enter a new stage that was more scientific, democratic and standardized.

"Ruling the country by law" requires strengthening judicial work, safeguarding social fairness and justice, actively promoting judicial system reform, promoting and ensuring fair justice, and promoting judicial and procuratorial organs at all levels to independently and impartially exercise judicial and procuratorial powers according to law. The report of the 15th National Congress of the CPC clearly stated for the first time, "we shall promote the reform in judicial affairs, ensure institutionally that the judicial organs are in a position to exercise adjudicative and procuratorial powers independently and fairly according to law, and establish a system for investigating and prosecuting anyone who is held responsible for unjust or misjudged cases." On October 22, 1999, the Supreme People's Court promulgated outlines for *five-year reform of the people's courts,* which defined the guiding ideology, basic tasks and objectives of the People's Court to further deepen the reform, and proposed to comprehensively strengthen the judicial work and team building of the court. Since then, the People's Court has successfully carried out the reform of trial mode, trial procedure, evidence system, trial supervision system, court system, judge selection and judicial management.

"Ruling the country by law" requires administration according to law, further standardization and legalization of the methods and procedures for exercising power, and establishment of legal systems such as administrative reconsideration, administrative litigation and state compensation. In November 1999, the State Council issued the *Decision of the State Council on Comprehensively Promoting Administration According to Law*, which proposed that: further strengthen government legislative work, effectively improve the quality of government legislation, and lay a solid foundation for administration according to law; strengthen administrative law enforcement to ensure the smooth flow of government orders; strengthen supervision over administrative law enforcement. Under the guidance of the Decision, governments at all levels and their working departments have strengthened system construction, strictly enforced administrative law, strengthened supervision over administrative law enforcement, and constantly improved their ability and level of handling affairs according to law.

"Ruling the country by law" requires us to step up the education campaign to increase public awareness of law, and promote the spirit of the rule of law, creating a social environment in which people study, abide by and apply laws of their own accord.[25] From 1991 to 2000, the country successively implemented the "Second Five-Year Legal Education program" and the "Third Five-year Legal Education program" for law popularization. During the "Second Five-Year Plan" period of law popularization (1991–1995), 96 industries formulated plans for law popularization and organized the study of more than 200 professional laws and regulations. Through the "Second Five-Year Plan" for law popularization, about 700 million of the 810 million people nationwide have received law popularization education. 96 industry systems across the country have formulated professional law learning plans, and more than 200 laws have been included in the learning content. During the "Third Five-Year Plan" period (1996–2000), 30 provinces (autonomous regions and municipalities directly under the central government) carried out "ruling the country by law" in combination with law popularization activities, and 95% of prefecture-level cities, 87% of counties and 75% of grassroots units carried out governance according to law. More than 800 million people nationwide have received legal publicity and education to varying degrees. Various localities have held 242 lectures on the legal system for provincial-level leading cadres, and 9,752 people attended the lectures; thirty provinces (autonomous regions and municipalities directly under the central government) have carried out the work of administering provinces (autonomous regions and municipalities directly under the central government) by law. The whole society has formed a good habit of learning, abiding by, using and protecting the law, which has laid a solid foundation for administering the country according to law.

An important practical content of "ruling the country by law" is to govern according to law. It fully relies on the broad masses of the people, uses legal means to govern society, and realizes the legalization and standardization of the country's political, economic and social life. The work of governance according to law is a systematic project of legal system construction, which is composed of three governance projects connected to one another in "points," "lines" and "areas." "Point" refers to the grass-roots rule by law of villages, factories, schools, communities and shops. It is the basic project of the whole legal governance work and plays an important basic role in the process of "governing the country according to law" and building a law-based socialist country; "line" refers to rule the country by law of various industries such as land, water and tax. It is the pillar project of the whole "ruling the country by law work" and plays a connecting role in connecting "point" and "area" governance work; "area" refers to the "ruling the country by law" of provinces, cities, counties and townships. It is the main project of the "ruling the country by law" work and the concrete practice and component of the strategy of "ruling the country by law" in various places. Ruling the country by law of the grass-roots, ruling the country by law of the industry, and ruling the country by law of local affairs are interrelated and intertwined, and jointly build a skyscraper for law-based governing. During the implementation of the Nineth Five-Year Plan, 30 provinces (autonomous regions and municipalities directly under the central government) have carried out the work of administering the province by law. 95% of prefectural-level cities, 89% of counties, 75% of enterprises and institutions, and the whole industry departments with administrative law enforcement management functions have carried out the work of administering the province by law. Through the steady progress of the work of rule of law, the process of administering the country by has been vigorously promoted.

China has adhered to the practice of the rule of law in the light of its national conditions. At the same time, it has also paid attention to strengthening international exchanges and cooperation in the construction of the rule of law. In 2001, the *Shanghai Convention on Combating Terrorism, Separatism and Extremism* was signed between China and other members of the Shanghai Cooperation Organization (SCO).

(3) The Construction of Democracy at the Grassroots Level

China is a populous country with multi-layers of social management. The focus of people's production and life is at the grass-roots level. Developing grass-roots democracy is of great significance to upholding and consolidating the political status and pattern of the people as masters of the country, mobilizing all positive factors to serve reform and opening-up and socialist modernization, promoting social harmony, and achieving long-term peace and stability of the country.

In 1992, the 14th National Congress of the CPC put forward that "strengthening grass-roots democracy and giving full play to the role of workers' congress, residents' committee and villagers' committee"[26] was an important task of developing socialist democracy. The 15th National Congress of the CPC further affirmed the importance of grassroots democracy and stressed that "extending the scope of democracy at the grassroots level to make sure that people directly exercise their democratic rights, manage their own affairs according to law and create a happy life for themselves are the most extensive practices of socialist democracy."[27]

Since the new period, especially since the establishment and improvement of the reform of the socialist market economy, China's grass-roots democracy has gradually advanced and made considerable progress. a) In the countryside. Villager autonomy is a basic system in which the broad masses of farmers directly exercise their democratic rights, manage their own affairs, educate themselves and serve their own needs. It started in the early 1980s, developed in the 1980s, and was widely implemented in the 1990s. It has become an effective way to expand grass-roots democracy and improve rural governance in China's rural areas. Democratic election, decision-making, management and supervision are the main contents of villagers' autonomy. In November 1998, the Fifth Meeting of the Standing Committee of the Nineth NPC adopted the *Organic Law of the Villagers Committees of the PRC*, which promoted the rapid development of villagers' autonomy. According to incomplete statistics, the average participation rate of rural residents nationwide is over 80%, and in some places, it is as high as 90%. The Constitution stipulates the legal status of villagers' committees as grassroots mass autonomous organizations in rural areas. The Organic Law of the Villagers Committees has made clear provisions on the nature, functions, procedures and term of office of the villagers' committee, which has put the rural grassroots democratic autonomy on the track of healthy development. The successful practice of villagers' autonomy is a great pioneering work of the CPC in leading hundreds of millions of peasants to develop socialist democracy with Chinese characteristics. The expansion of rural grass-roots democracy and the implementation of villagers' autonomy have greatly stimulated the enthusiasm, creativity and sense of responsibility of the broad masses of farmers as masters of their own affairs, and opened a new chapter in China's rural democracy. b) In the city. The urban residents committee is a grass-roots mass autonomous organization for Chinese urban residents to realize self-management, self-education and self-service. It is an important form of direct democracy at the urban grassroots level. In 1982, the urban residents committee system was written into the Constitution for the first time. In 1989, the 11th Meeting of the Standing Committee of the Seventh NPC adopted the Organic Law of the Urban Residents Committees, which provided a legal basis and institutional guarantee for the development of urban residents' committees. In 1999, the state carried out pilot and experimental work of community construction in 26 urban areas throughout the country. Since then, community construction demonstration activities have been carried out throughout the country. The construction of urban communities has been promoted from point to area, from large cities to small and medium-sized cities, and from the eastern region to the western region, and has been gradually carried out throughout the country. Just like China's rural villagers' autonomy, the main content of urban community residents' autonomy is to implement democratic election, decision-making, management and supervision. In terms of democratic election, the form of election has gone through the process from candidate nomination to self-nomination, from equal amount election to differential election, and from indirect election to differential election. It has broken the geographical and identity restrictions, and the democracy has been continuously improved. In terms of democratic decision-making, community residents are the main body. They make democratic decisions on public affairs in the community through effective forms and channels such as community residents' meetings, consultations, hearings, etc. In terms of democratic management, the neighborhood committee handles affairs by law, regulates its work in by regulations and rules of community residents' autonomy, and strives to enhance the residents' sense of being the masters of their own affairs, so as to realize "everyone manages the affairs of the community." In terms of democratic supervision, the affairs of residents' committees shall be made public. All hotspot and difficult issues of residents' concern and major affairs involving the vital interests of all residents shall be made public to the residents in a timely manner, and residents' opinions shall be heard and residents' supervision shall be accepted through the convening of residents' appraisal meetings. c) In enterprises and institutions. The workers' congress is the basic system form to ensure that workers and staff implement democratic management over enterprises and institutions. In China, the workers' congress has a broad mass base. Among the representatives, there are not only workers, but also scientific and technological personnel, management personnel and other staff members. They can represent all the workers to manage the enterprise democratically. After the closing of the workers' congress, the trade union committee of the enterprise, as the working organization of the workers' congress, is responsible for the daily work of the workers' Congress. Since 1998, the opening of factory affairs has been implemented in SOEs, collective enterprises and their holding enterprises, and gradually expanded to non-public enterprises. The state has adheres to the principle of wholeheartedly relying on employees to run enterprises. With the deepening of reform and opening-up, it strives to promote enterprises and institutions of all types of ownership to establish and improve democratic management systems, effectively solve outstanding problems in this regard, and ensure that the democratic rights and legitimate rights and interests of employees are guaranteed.

(4) Reform of the Political Structure

In 1992, the 14th National Congress of the CPC set the goal of establishing and improving the socialist market economy, and pointed out that the goal of the political system reform was to develop socialist democratic politics with the improvement of the People's Congress system, the multi-party cooperation and political consultation system led by the Communist Party as the main content. In order to adapt to the economic reform and economic development, the 14th National Congress of the CPC made corresponding adjustments to the reform of the political structure and made four points clear: first, further improve the People's Congress system, strengthen the legislative and supervisory functions of the People's Congress and its Standing Committee, and better give play to the role of the people's representatives. We should improve the system of multi-party cooperation and political consultation under the leadership of the CPC and make the Chinese CCCPC serve as a major channel for conducting consultative democracy and democratic supervision. Second, leading organs and leading cadres should seriously listen to the opinions of the masses, give full play to the role of various experts and research and consulting institutions, and accelerate the establishment of a democratic and scientific decision-making system. Third, strengthen legislative work, strictly implement the Constitution and laws, strengthen law enforcement supervision, strengthen the building of legal departments, and enhance the democratic awareness and legal concept of the broad masses of cadres and the masses. Fourth, make up our minds to carry out the reform of the administrative system and institutions, so as to effectively transform our functions, straighten out relations, streamline our troops and simplify our administration, and improve efficiency. After the convening of the 14th National Congress of the CPC, new steps have been taken in political restructuring.

First, in order to adapt to the reform and development of the market economy, the government system and government functions began to change. In March 1993, the First Session of the Eighth NPC adopted *Decision on the State Council Institutional Reform Proposal*, and the work of institutional reform at the central level began. After the reform, the State Council set up a general office and 40 ministries and commissions, and the number of directly affiliated institutions and offices was reduced to 13 and 5 respectively. The national bureaus under the centralized management of directly affiliated institutions, offices and ministries and commissions have been greatly streamlined. Except for the reserved ones, some of them have been merged into ministries and commissions, or become functional bureaus within ministries and commissions, or changed to national bureaus under the management of ministries and commissions. The number of non-permanent organs of the State Council has also been greatly reduced from 85 to 26.

Secondly, the official implementation of the national civil service system. On April 24, 1993, the executive meeting of the State Council adopted the *Provisional Regulations on Public Servants of the State*, which came into effect on October 1, 1993. This marked that the construction of China's employment system has entered a new period. Since then, the State Council has also formulated 13 temporary provisions, 13 measures and a series of implementation plans and detailed rules.

Thirdly, the selection and appointment of cadres should be democratic, scientific and standardized. In order to make the selection and appointment of Party and government leading cadres more transparent, some localities have conducted public opinion polls during the selection of cadres, implemented a publicity system before official promotion, and implemented competition and open recruitment for some posts. In 1995, the CCCPC promulgated the *Interim Regulations on the Selection and Appointment of Party and Government Leading Cadres*, which stipulated the six principles that must be adhered to in the selection and appointment of Party and Government Leading Cadres: the principle of the Party managing cadres, the principle of having both political integrity and ability, the principle of appointing people on the basis of merit, the principle of being recognized by the masses and paying attention to actual achievements, the principle of openness, equality, competition and selection of the best, the principle of democratic centralism, and the principle of acting according to law. The Regulation has provided a policy and legal basis for establishing a scientific and standardized system for the selection and appointment of Party and government leading cadres, forming a vibrant and dynamic employment mechanism, and promoting the cultivation of younger, more revolutionary, better educated, and more specialized officials.

In 1997, in his report to the 15th National Congress of the CPC, Jiang Zemin further defined the phased tasks of the political restructuring: following the principle of simplification, uniformity and efficiency in the reform, we should establish a highly efficient, well-coordinated and standardized administrative system, with a view to improving their service for the people; we should reorganize comprehensive economic agencies into macroeconomic control authorities, reduce the number of industry-specific economic agencies and adjust their functions, strengthen law enforcement and regulatory authorities, and cultivate and expand social intermediary organizations; we should deepen the reform of the administrative system, statutorily delimiting the structures, functions, sizes and working procedures of the state organs and ensuring that their sizes are kept within authorized limits and their redundant personnel are reduced; we should also deepen the reform of the personnel system by introducing a competitive and incentive mechanism and improving the system of public servants to build up a contingent of administrators who are highly competent and professionally specialized.

After the 15th National Congress of the CPC, the institutional reform of the central and local governments at all levels was launched one after another. On March 10, 1998, the Plan for Restructuring submitted by the State Council to the First Session of the Nineth NPC was adopted. An unprecedented restructuring was launched in the State Council. In addition to the general office of the State

Council, the number of constituent departments of the State Council has been reduced from 40 to 29. Among them, the Ministry of Coal, the Ministry of Machinery, the Ministry of Metallurgical Industry, the Ministry of Domestic Trade, the Light Industry Federation and the Textile Federation have been downgraded to National Bureaus managed by the State Economic and Trade Commission; the Ministry of Electric Power was abolished and its functions were merged into the State Economic and Trade Commission; the Ministry of Chemical Industry, China National Petroleum and Natural Gas Corporation and China Petrochemical Corporation were merged into the State Bureau of Petroleum and Chemical Industry under the management of the State Economic and Trade Commission. After the restructuring of various departments of the State Council was basically completed, the restructuring of the departments of the CCCPC and the governments at the provincial, municipal, county and township levels began one after another. In the five years from 1998 to October 2002, the administrative establishment of Party, government and mass organizations at all levels throughout the country was reduced by 1.15 million. In the process of restructuring, cities, counties and townships reduced the number of overstaffed personnel by about 430,000, and the number of provincial-level government agencies was reduced from 28 to 18 on average. In terms of staffing, the departments of the CCCPC and provincial Party committees were reduced by 20%, the departments of the State Council by 47.5%, the provincial governments by 48.2%, and the Party, government, and mass organizations at the city, county, and township levels by 19.4%.

In order to coordinate with the reform of the national administrative institutions, and further improve the civil service system, the work to establish a high-quality and professional national administrative cadre team had been put on the agenda. In 2000, the CCCPC promulgated the Outline for Deepening Reform of the Cadre and Personnel System, which clearly explained the objectives, principles, and contents of the reform of the cadre and personnel system. In 2002, the CCCPC promulgated the Regulations on the Selection and Appointment of Party and Government Leading Cadres, which made comprehensive provisions on all aspects of the selection and appointment of leading cadres, making this work more complete.

(5) The System of Multi-Party Cooperation and Political Consultation Led by the CPC Has Been Constantly Improved

The multi-Party cooperation and political consultation system led by the CPC is one of the basic political systems of new China and a socialist political Party system with Chinese characteristics. After the reform and opening-up, the CPC has learned from historical experience and actively promoted the institutionalization of multi-party cooperation and political consultation. In December 1989, the CCCPC issued the Opinions on Upholding and Improving the System of CPC-led Multi-Party Cooperation and Political Consultation, which provides a comprehensive and systematic explanation of the principles for democratic parties to play their roles in deliberation and administration of state affairs, political consultation and democratic supervision in political life concretely and practically. In October 1992, the 14th National Congress of the CPC took the improvement of the multi-party cooperation and political consultation system led by the CPC as the main content of the political system reform. In March 1993, the First Session of the Eighth NPC formally wrote "the system of multi-party cooperation and political consultation led by the CPC will exist and develop for a long time" into the Amendment to the Constitution of the PRC, giving it a clear constitutional basis. In March 1994, the Second Session of the Eighth National Committee of the Chinese CCCPC adopted the Amendment to the Charter of the CPPCC, which for the first time included participation in and discussion of state affairs in the main functions of the CPPCC. In September 1999, Jiang Zemin pointed out at the speech at the meeting marking the 50th anniversary f the CPPCC: in the contemporary era, the Communist Party is in the ruling position and needs to always accept the supervision and criticism of the democratic parties that have always maintained close cooperation with it. We should adhere to the principle of "long-term coexistence, mutual oversight, sincere relations, and the sharing of both the good times and the bad" between the Communist Party and the democratic parties, give full play to the role of the democratic parties as political parties participating in state governance, and continue to strengthen cooperation and work with the democratic parties and people without party affiliation.

Driven by this series of policies, since the 1990s, the multi-party cooperation and political consultation system under the leadership of the CPC has become increasingly important in the political and social life of the country. The specific manifestations are as follows:

First, the political consultation between the CPC and various democratic parties and people without party affiliation has been gradually institutionalized and standardized. From 1990 to the end of 2002, the CCCPC and the State Council held or entrusted relevant departments to hold as many as 200 consultations, symposiums and briefings.

Second, members of democratic parties and people without party affiliation has played an important role in the People's Congress. Members of the democratic parties and people without party affiliation account for a certain number of people's congress deputies at all levels, members of the Standing Committee of the people's Congress and members of special committees.

Third, members of democratic parties and people without party affiliation hold leading positions in governments and judicial organs at all levels. They have the right to command the administrative management, to decide on the handling of problems, and to make suggestions on the appointment and removal of personnel.

Fourth, all democratic parties and people without party affiliation has played an important role in the CCCPC. In the organizational structure of the CPPCC, there is a large proportion of members of the democratic parties in the CPPCC members, standing committee members and leading members of the CPPCC at all levels, and there is a certain number of them in the heads and members of the special committees of the CPPCC and in the organs of the CPPCC. All democratic parties make full use of the various consultation methods of the CPPCC to carry out consultations and discussions and put forward opinions and suggestions on major national and local policies and important issues in political, economic, cultural and social life, as well as the common affairs of all democratic parties participating in the work of the CPPCC, important affairs within the CPPCC, and other important issues related to the patriotic united front.

Fifth, all democratic parties and people without party affiliation exercise democratic supervision over the work of the ruling party through various channels and forms. Government departments and judicial organs have further broadened the channels of democratic supervision and continuously strengthened the supervision work by employing members of democratic parties and people without party affiliation as special personnel and absorbing and organizing democratic parties and people without party affiliation to participate in the inspection of Party conduct and combating corruption, other special inspections and law enforcement supervision.

Sixth, all democratic parties and people without party affiliation actively participate in the cause of reform, opening up and modernization, and constantly make suggestions for promoting the great cause of the motherland's reunification and all-round social progress. All democratic parties actively participate in the formulation and implementation of national policies, carry out investigation and research on the overall, strategic and forward-looking major issues in the country's political, economic and social life, and put forward policy suggestions. The contents of these suggestions cover various fields such as economy, politics, culture, society, education, science and technology, health, national defense, foreign affairs, compatriots in China's Hong Kong, Macao and Taiwan regions. For example, they conducted investigations and studies on the Three Gorges Hydro-Power Project, farmland protection, the "three direct links" between the two sides of the Strait, and the Western Development, large-scale development of the western region. They had put forward opinions and suggestions to the CCCPC and the State Council, which were highly valued and many of them were adopted. Various democratic parties and local organizations have also carried out investigations and researches on local economic and social development issues. All these have effectively played the role of democratic parties in policy and intellectual consultation.

Practice has proved that as a basic political system of the country, the multi-party cooperation and political consultation system led by the CPC has historical inevitability, great creativity and great superiority. With the continuous advancement of China's political system reform and the development of socialist democracy, the multi-party cooperation and political consultation system led by the CPC is also in constant development.

Summary

Since 1992, the political development of contemporary China has entered a new historical stage. The profound changes in the world political pattern, the continuous advancement of the reform of the domestic socialist market economy, and the rapid improvement of the people's economic and cultural life have prompted the ruling CPC to make a theoretical response to the great changes in society and to use new theories to guide hundreds of millions of Chinese people in the great and arduous cause of socialist modernization. Deng Xiaoping Theory is the historical inheritance and development of Marxism in this era and in this nation, and it enriches the foundation for building contemporary China. On this basis, China has implemented the strategy of "ruling the country by law," which has made great progress in the national governance thinking of China. Grass roots democracy has advanced, political system reform has been carried out in depth, and the reform of the cadre and personnel system has been gradually carried out. The political status of the people as masters of the country has been effectively guaranteed.

SECTION 2

Opening of the Reform of the Socialist Market Economy and the Overall Acceleration of Economic Development

2.2.1 Establish and Improve the Socialist Market Economy

According to the traditional economic viewpoint, market economy is the unique feature of capitalism, and planned economy is the basic characteristic of socialism. After the reform and opening-up, with the new understanding of the essence and development stage of socialism, and with the gradual expansion of the scope of the contemporary Chinese market economy, the Chinese Communists' understanding of this concept has changed. The 12th National Congress of the CPC has put forward the economic development policy of "planned economy as the mainstay and market regulation as the supplement."[28] The Third Plenary Session of the 12th CCCPC established that China's socialist economy is a planned commodity economy based on public ownership, and the commodity economy is a stage of socialist development we cannot jump over. On October 23, 1985, when meeting with foreign guests, Deng Xiaoping said: "there is no fundamental contradiction between socialism and a market economy. The problem is how to develop the productive forces more effectively." The 13th National Congress of the CPC put forward that the socialist planned commodity economy should be a system of internal unity of planning and market. After the Fourth Plenary Session of the 13th CCCPC, it was proposed to establish an economy and operating mechanism that combines planned economy with market regulation to adapt to the development of a planned commodity economy. At the beginning of 1992, when inspecting the south, Deng Xiaoping pointed out: "the proportion of planning to market forces is not the essential difference between socialism and capitalism. A planned economy is not equivalent to socialism, because there is planning under capitalism too; a market economy is not capitalism, because there are markets under socialism, too. Planning and market forces are both means of controlling economic activities."[29]

This brilliant conclusion has fundamentally removed the ideological shackles of regarding planned economy and market economy as belonging to the category of social basic system, and has made a new major breakthrough in people's understanding of the relationship between planning and market.

The 14th National Congress of the CPC held in October 1992 formally put forward the idea of establishing and improving China's socialist market economy. The Congress held that the socialist market economy to be established in China is to enable the market to play a fundamental role in the allocation of resources under the macro-control of the socialist countries, so that economic activities follow the requirements of the law of value and adapt to changes in supply and demand relations; through the function of price lever and competition mechanism, resources are allocated to the links with good profits, and pressure and power are given to enterprises to achieve the survival of the fittest; take advantage of the market's sensitive response to various economic signals to promote the timely coordination of production and demand. At the same time, we should also see that the market has its own weaknesses and negative aspects. We must strengthen and improve the state's macro-control over the economy. At the same time, the Congress stressed that the establishment of a socialist market economy involves many areas of China's economic foundation and superstructure, and requires a series of corresponding restructuring and policy adjustments. It is necessary to pay close attention to the formulation of overall plans and implement them in a planned and step-by-step manner.

In order to implement the task of the reform of economy set by the 14th National Congress of the CPC, in November 1993, the Third Plenary Session of the 14th CCCPC adopted the *Decision of the CCCPC on some Issues Concerning Establishing of the Socialist Market Economy*, formulated the overall plan for the socialist market economy, and determined it as the action plan for reform of economy in the 1990s. The Decision clearly elaborates the basic framework of the socialist market economy: around the reform goal of establishing a socialist market economy, it is necessary to adhere to the policy of public ownership as the main body and the joint development of multiple economic components, further transform the operation mechanism of SOEs, establish a modern corporate system with clear property rights, clear powers and responsibilities, separation of government and enterprises, and scientific management that is adapted to the requirements of the market economy; necessary to establish a nationwide unified and open market system, realize close integration of urban and rural markets, and link the domestic market with the international market to promote the optimal allocation of resources; necessary to transform the government's functions of managing the economy, establish a sound macro-control system with indirect means, and promote the optimal allocation of resources; Open market system, realize the close integration of urban and rural markets, connect the domestic market with the international market, and promote the optimal allocation of resources; change the government's function of managing the economy, establish a perfect macro-control system with indirect means to ensure the healthy operation of the national economy; necessary to establish an income distribution system with the distribution according to one's work as the mainstay, giving priority to efficiency and taking into account fairness, and encourage some people in some regions to get rich first; necessary to establish a multi-level social security system to provide urban and rural residents with social security that is appropriate to China's national conditions and promote economic development and social stability.

In accordance with the spirit of the 14th National Congress of the CPC and the Third Plenary Session of the 14th CCCPC, China's reform of the socialist market economy was launched in an all-round way.

In the aspect of enterprise restructuring, the first entry point was the reform of SOEs. In November 1994, the State Council designated 100 large and medium-sized SOEs to establish a modern corporate system. In 1996, the pilot enterprises for the establishment of the modern corporate system had spread throughout 31 provinces (autonomous regions and municipalities directly under the central government), and the number of pilot enterprises was 2,343. Among the reformed companies, 71% established the board of directors, 63% established the board of supervisors, and 33% established the board of shareholders. The corporate governance structure of the company has initially taken shape. In September 1997, the 15th National Congress of the CPC reiterated that the establishment of a modern corporate system was the orientation of the reform of SOEs, and stressed that the majority of large and medium-sized state-owned backbone enterprises should initially establish a modern corporate system by the end of the 20th century. In September 1999, the Fourth Plenary Session of the 15th CCCPC further discussed the reform and development of SOEs and adopted the *Decision of the CCCPC on Major Issues Concerning the Reform and Development of State-Owned Enterprises (SOEs)*, which required that by 2010, which required that by 2010, the reform of the economy and the two fundamental changes in the pattern of economic growth and the expansion of foreign opening should be met. The strategic restructuring and reorganization of SOEs should be basically completed, and a more reasonable layout and structure of the state-owned economy should be formed. A more complete modern enterprise system should be established, economic efficiency should be significantly improved, the ability of scientific and technological development, market competition and the ability to resist risks should be significantly enhanced, and the state-owned economy should play a better leading role in the national economy. Subsequently, the SOEs continued to carry out reforms in many aspects and at a deeper level. In 2000, total profits from state-owned industrial enterprises and from the industrial enterprises with a controlling share held by the state reached 239.2 billion yuan, an increase of 190% over the 1997 figure. By the end of 2000, the number of large and medium-sized SOEs with losses of 6,599 in 1997 had decreased by 4,799, accounting for more than 70%. In 2000, small SOEs also realized a profit of 4.81 billion yuan, ending the situation of net loss for six consecutive years. Many SOEs in difficulties for a long time had started to get out of the trough, and their operating conditions had been improved significantly. They had basically realized the three-year goal of reforming and extricating large and medium-sized SOEs from difficulties put forward by the 15th National Congress of the CPC. Most large and medium-sized state-owned backbone enterprises had initially established a modern corporate system.

With regard to the reform of the fiscal and taxation system, in December 1993, the State Council issued the Decision on Implementing the Fiscal Management System of the Tax Division System, which decided to reform the contract system in the local financial work from January 1, 1994, and implemented the fiscal management system of the tax devision system for all provinces (autonomous regions, municipalities directly under the central government) and cities specifically designated in the state plan. The principles and main contents of the reform of the tax devision system are as follows: according to the division of powers between the central and local governments, the scope of fiscal expenditure at all levels should be reasonably determined; according to the principle of combining administrative power with financial power, the tax categories are uniformly divided into central tax, local tax and central local shared tax, and the central and local tax systems are established. Two sets of tax authorities are set up to collect and manage the taxes respectively; the amount of local revenue and expenditure should be verified scientificly, and a relatively standardized system of tax return and transfer payment from the central government to local governments should be implemented; a hierarchical budget system should be established and improved and budgetary constraints at all levels should be strengthened.

As for the reform of the financial system, on December 25, 1993, the State Council promulgated *Decision of the State Council on Reform of the Financial System*, which proposed that the objectives of the reform of the financial system were: to establish a macro-control system of the central bank that independently implements monetary policy under the leadership of the State Council; to establish a financial organization system in which policy finance and commercial finance are separated, with state-owned commercial banks as the main body and various financial institutions coexisting; to establish a unified, open, orderly, and strictly managed financial market system. Since 1994, a new round of financial system reform has been gradually carried out: (1) reform the means of control of the central bank, establish a strong macro-control system of the central bank, and exercise strict supervision over financial institutions. Establish a monetary policy committee to adjust monetary and credit policies in a timely manner. (2) Establish policy banks and separate policy businesses from commercial business. In 1994, the China Development Bank, the Export Import Bank and the Agricultural Development Bank of China were successively established. (3) turn national specialized banks into commercial banks actually owned by the state and separate policy finance from commercial finance. In 1995, the *Law of the PRC on Commercial Banks* was promulgated and implemented, which clarified the legal status of state-owned professional banks as enterprise legal persons. (4) Establish a unified, open, orderly and strictly managed financial market. (5) Reform the foreign exchange management system and implement a managed floating exchange rate system. In 1996, the RMB realized the convertibility under the current account, making a big step towards the goal of full convertibility. The success of the exchange rate integration has played an important role in further communicating the domestic and foreign markets, improving China's external economic environment, further attracting foreign investment, and developing an open economy.

In the investment and financing reforms, an investment restraint mechanism has been generally established, in which both the investors and the banks providing loans must bear the risk responsibility; the macro-control over investment scale and structure has been improved, investment decision-making has been standardized, and blindness in investment has been reduced.

Through a series of reforms, by 2000, China had successfully realized the transformation from a planned economy to a socialist market economy. The role of the market in the allocation of resources was increasingly strengthened, and the socialist market economy was initially established.

2.2.2 Economic "Soft Landing" and Successful Response to the Asian Financial Crisis

(1) Economic "Soft Landing"
In the early 1990s, due to the one-sided pursuit of high speed by some localities and departments, the gradual failure of the original macro-control mechanism and the unsound new control mechanism, China's economy was overheated, which was manifested in the excessive increase in fixed asset investment, the real estate fever, the Development Zone fever, the financial disorder, and the price rise.

In the first half of 1992, the CCCPC repeatedly reminded us to prevent the occurrence of economic overheating, and stressed the need to make great efforts in deepening reform, and avoid making a fuss about expanding the scale of investment, so as to prevent new redundant construction and product backlog.

In April 1993, the CCCPC held an economic briefing to discuss and solve the problems of indiscriminate fund-raising, indiscriminate lending, real estate fever and Development Zone fever. In June, the CCCPC and the State Council issued the *Opinions on the Current Economic Situation and Strengthening Macroeconomic Regulation and Control*, and decided to adopt 16 measures focusing on rectifying the financial order, mainly to strictly control currency issuance, resolutely correct illegal inter-bank lending, resolutely stop all kinds of indiscriminate fund-raising, strictly control the total scale of credit, and stabilize the foreign exchange market price. Accordingly, the State Council has successively convened the National Conference on Financial Work and the National Financial Work Conference and the National Taxation Work Conference to intensify the rectification of the financial and taxation fields. In July, the State Council held National Conferences on Financing, Finance and Taxation, and put forward two "three-point decisions."

In addition to adopting necessary administrative and organizational measures, the current macroeconomic regulation and control should mainly focus on the use of economic and legal means to find a way out of accelerating the transformation of the old and new systems, and turning the solution of outstanding problems in economic operation into a driving force for accelerating reform and establishing a socialist market economy. After three years of efforts, the macro-control achieved remarkable results, the investment overheat was effectively controlled, the growth rate of fixed asset investment has dropped from 62% in 1993 to 14.8% in 1996, the financial order was gradually restored, the total amount of credit was controlled, the prices was gradually liberalized and the growth rate was obviously decreased, and the retail price index of commodities had decreased from the highest 25.2% in October 1994 to 6.1% in 1996.

This macroeconomic regulation and control successfully suppressed inflation, while maintaining a rapid economic growth rate. From 1993 to 1996, the GDP grew at an average annual rate of 12%, achieving a "soft landing" from economic overheating and inflation to high growth and low inflation, avoiding major economic ups and downs, and laying a foundation for healthy economic development and successfully resisting the impact of the Asian financial crisis.

(2) Tackling the Asian Financial Crisis

In the second half of 1997, the financial crisis broke out in Southeast Asian countries and soon spread to the whole Asia and other parts of the world. Affected by this, China's total foreign trade import and export volume showed a downward trend, and economic development encountered serious difficulties. In the face of the impact of the financial crisis, in September 1997, Jiang Zemin proposed at the First Plenary Session of the 15th CCCPC that financial risks were sudden, widespread, and extremely harmful. we must maintain a high degree of vigilance. Preventing and resolving financial risks was an important and urgent task for China's economic work. In February 1998, the CCCPC clearly put forward the guiding principle of strengthening confidence, knowing what to do, preparing for the rainy day, coping calmly, working hard, seeking benefits and avoiding disadvantages. It stressed that we would resolutely adopt measures to expand domestic demand, implement a proactive fiscal policy and a prudent monetary policy, increase investment and strengthen infrastructure construction; we would increase the living security of low- and middle-income people and improve the people's livelihood; we would take measures such as raising the export rebate rates and cracking down on smuggling, and do everything possible to increase exports, so as to stimulate economic growth in many ways.

These countermeasures and measures took effect quickly. Since 1997, China's economy has continued to grow, and its foreign trade exports have rebounded significantly since the second half of 1999. Under the critical situation of economic recession and substantial devaluation of currencies in many countries, China fulfilled its commitment not to devalue the RMB, making contributions to alleviating the global financial crisis and promoting the economic recovery and development of Asian countries.

(3) Formulation and Implementation of the National Economic Plan

The Fourth Session of the Eighth NPC adopted the *Outline of the Nineth Five-Year Plan for National Economic and Social Development and the Long-range Objectives to the Year 2010*. This is the first medium- and long-term plan under the conditions of China's socialist market economy and a cross century development plan. According to the Outline, the period from 1996 to 2010 is an important period for China's reform, opening up and socialist modernization to carry forward the past and forge ahead into the future. China would stride into the 21st century with a brand-new attitude, establish a relatively complete socialist market economy, fully realize the second step strategic objective, and make major strides towards the third step strategic objective, so as to lay a solid foundation for basically realizing modernization in the middle of the next century. The main objectives of the Nineth Five-Year Plan for National Economic and Social Development are: comprehensively complete the second strategic deployment of the modernization drive, to control the population within 1.3 billion by the year of 2000, and to quadruple the per capita GNP over that of the year of 1980; basically eliminate poverty and the raise the people's living standards to a well-off level; accelerate the construction of a modern corporate system and initially establish a socialist market economy; lay a better material and technological foundation and economic system foundation for the implementation of the third step strategic deployment at the beginning of the next century. The main objectives of national economic and social development in 2010 were as follows: double the gross national product over that of the year of 2000, control the population within 1.4 billion, make the people's well-off life more comfortable, and form a relatively complete socialist market economy.

During the Nineth Five-Year Plan period, in the face of the complicated international and domestic economic environment, China made painstaking efforts to improve the quality and efficiency of economic operation, further strengthened its comprehensive national strength, and during this period, China's GDP grew at an average annual rate of 8.3%. The output of major industrial and agricultural products now stands in the front ranks of the world's economies, and commodity shortages were by and large eliminated. The quantities of grain and other major agricultural products we are capable of producing increased noticeably, marking a historic change from a long-term shortage of agricultural products to a basic balance in their total supply and demand, with even a surplus during good harvest years. Positive progress was made in industrial restructuring, high-tech industries such as the information industry grew rapidly, and achievements were made in eliminating backward and reducing excess industrial production capacity. The service sector continued to grow and the jobs increased. Marked success was achieved in infrastructure development, alleviating bottlenecks. The reform of the economic system was carried forward, and the socialist market economy was initially established. The three-year goal of reforming and extricating large and medium-sized SOEs from difficulties was basically achieved, major progress was made in adjusting and improving the ownership structure, the construction of the market system was comprehensively promoted, and the macro-control mechanism was further improved. The pattern of all-round opening-up has basically taken shape. Foreign trade and the use of foreign capital have expanded in scale, improved in structure and quality, and the open economy has developed rapidly. The people's living standards has continued to improve, the consumption structure is improved, and the problem of food and clothing for the rural poor is basically solved. We implemented the strategies of developing the country by relying on science and education and of achieving sustainable development. Culture, public health, sports and other social undertakings continued to develop. The Fourth Session of the Nineth NPC adopted the *Outline of the 10th Five-Year Plan for National Economic and Social Development* in March, 2001. The Outline pointed out that the main objectives of national economic and social development during the 10th Five-Year Plan period were: the national economy would maintain a relatively rapid development rate, the strategic adjustment of the economic structure would achieve remarkable results, the quality and efficiency of economic growth would be significantly improved, and a solid foundation would be laid for doubling the GDP by 2010 compared with 2000; major progress would be made in establishing a modern corporate system for SOEs, the social security system is relatively sound, substantive steps would be taken to improve the socialist market economy, and participation in international economic cooperation and competition would be made on a larger scale and to a deeper extent; employment channels would be broadened, the income of urban and rural residents would continue to increase, the material and cultural life would be greatly improved, and ecological construction and environmental protection would be strengthened; the development of science, technology and education would be accelerated, the quality of the people would be further improved, and remarkable progress would be made in the building of spiritual civilization and the building of democracy and the legal system. The "Outline" also set out the detailed objectives of macro-control, economic restructuring, development of science, technology and education, sustainable development and improvement of people's living standards during the 10th Five-Year Plan period, and puts forward a series of important measures to promote the implementation of the 10th Five-Year Plan.

2.2.3 "WTO Entry" and the Formation of All-Round Opening Up Pattern

Since the 1990s, China's opening to the outside world has been promoted from the coastal areas to the provinces and regions along the river, along the border and inland. Taking the development and opening up of Shanghai Pudong as a new starting point, the opening-up has been pushed forward in depth. While implementing the economic development strategy of the coastal areas, the opening-up along the border, the opening-up along the river and the opening-up in the inland have been carried out. The revitalization of the Yangtze River Delta and other regions has been accelerated, and the industrial belts such as the Pearl River Estuary have been comprehensively upgraded, gradually forming an all-round, multi-level and wide-ranging pattern of opening-up.

In 1992, the 14th National Congress of the CPC made it clear that we should further open up to the outside world and make better use of foreign capital, resources, technology and management experience. The area of opening up should be expanded to form a multi-level, multi-channel and all-round pattern; the field of utilizing foreign capital should be broadened; we should actively explore the international market, promote the diversification of foreign trade, and develop an export-oriented economy. The report also stressed in particular the need to deepen the reform of the foreign trade system and establish as soon as possible a new foreign trade system suitable for the development of the socialist market economy and compatible to international trade norms. The *Decision of the CCCPC on some Issues Concerning Establishing of the Socialist Market Economy* issued in 1993 also pointed out: unswervingly implement and accelerate the pace of the policy of opening up to the outside world, make full use of the international and domestic markets and resources, and optimize the allocation of resources; actively participate in international competition and international economic cooperation, give play to the comparative advantages of the economy, develop an open economy, and realize mutual complementarity between the domestic economy and the international economy; in accordance with the national conditions and the general norms of international economic activities, regulate foreign economic activities, correctly handle foreign economic relations, and constantly improve our international competitiveness. The "Decision" required: conscientiously sum up experience, constantly improve the degree of opening up, and guide the development of opening up in a high-level, wide-ranging, and vertical pattern.

According to these requirements, on December 25, 1993, the State Council made the *Decision of the State Council on Reform of the Financial System*, and realized the exchange rate integration from 1994. On January 11, 1994, the State Council made the *Decision on Further Deepening the Reform of the Foreign Trade System*. Starting from April 1, 1996, import tariffs on more than 4,000 commodities has been drastically reduced, and the total tariff rate was reduced to 23%. In September 1995, the Fifth Plenary Session of the 14th CCCPC decided to continue to opening up wider to the world and enhancing opening up. During the implementation of the Nineth Five-Year Plan, it was necessary to adapt to the needs of the development of the socialist market economy and the prevailing rules of the international economy, initially establish a unified and standardized foreign economic system, and expand foreign trade and foreign economic and technological exchanges and cooperation with the goal of promoting economic growth and improving quality and efficiency. Focusing on absorbing direct investment, we should improve the environment, expand areas, guide investment, optimize the structure, open more financing channels, and strengthen domestic supporting facilities.

In November 1996, at the Fourth Informal Meeting of Asian-Pacific Economic Cooperation (APEC) leaders, Jiang Zemin announced that the average tax rate of China's import and export commodities in 1996 would be reduced from the original 35.9% to 23%, and strive to reduce it to about 15% by 2000. Since December 1, 1996, the RMB has been convertible under the current account. After that, China also decided to reduce the import and export tariff rate from October 1, 1997. The average tariff rate was reduced from 23% to 17%, with a reduction of 26%. This tax reduction involves more than 4800 items, with a reduction of more than 73%. Since 1993, China has lowered its tariff rate on its own for many times, and the tariff rate has dropped by 60% in the past five years. This fully demonstrates China's determination and confidence to participate in international competition and cooperation with a more open attitude. In 1997, the 15th National Congress of the CPC further proposed that opening up is a long-term basic state policy. We should strive to do better in opening to the outside world, improve the pattern of opening up in all directions, at all levels and in a wide range, develop an open economy, enhance international competitiveness, and promote the optimization of the economic structure and the improvement of the quality of the national economy. This once again expressed the strong determination of the CPC and the Chinese government to continue to adhere to opening up.

By the end of 2001, China's accession to the WTO began a new stage in opening up. The WTO, founded on January 1, 1995, is one of the most important international economic organizations in the world. Its predecessor is the GATT established in 1948. China was a founding party to the GATT. However, after the founding of new China, due to internal and external reasons, it did not continue to participate in the GATT. The implementation of the state policy of reform and opening-up, especially the increasing trend of economic globalization, prompted the CPC and the Chinese government to decide to apply for the restoration of the status of the States Party to the GATT, and put forward an application for the "resumption of GATT" in July 1986. In March 1987, the GATT established a working group to deal with China's application for "GATT resumption." However, the initial negotiations encountered great obstacles in terms of economic system. It was not until 1992 when China established the goal of establishing a socialist market economy that the "GATT" negotiations entered a substantive stage, that is, the stage of opening up the market.

In November 1993, when Jiang Zemin first attended the APEC Informal Leaders' Retreat held in Seattle, the United States, he put forward three principles for China's "GATT resumption": first, GATT is an international organization, and it would be incomplete without the participation of China, the largest developing country; second, China will participate as a developing country; third, China's participation is based on the principle of the balance of rights and obligations. On the basis of adhering to these three principles, the Chinese government has made active efforts to "re-enter the GATT." In 1994, it introduced a series of major reform measures in foreign trade, foreign exchange, and the tax system, and substantially reduced tariffs on nearly 3000 items. However, due to the unreasonable obstruction of a few Western countries, China failed to become the founding country of the WTO in 1995. On June 3, 1995, China became an observer of the WTO. In July of the same year, China's "GATT resumption" negotiations were turned into negotiations on China's accession to the WTO. Due to the great differences between the two sides, no substantive progress was made in the negotiations in the following two years. In August 1997, at the fifth meeting of the WTO working group, China conducted bilateral market access negotiations with nearly 20 WTO members and reached agreements with New Zealand, the Republic of Korea, Hungary and other countries.

In April 1999, Zhu Rongji visited the United States, but the two sides failed to reach a comprehensive agreement. On November 15, China and the United States finally signed a bilateral agreement on China's accession to the WTO. China's "accession to the WTO" had made a breakthrough and decisive progress. Subsequently, China concluded negotiations with Canada, the European Union, Switzerland and Mexico on accession to the WTO. At that time, the bilateral market access negotiations between China and 36 of the 138 WTO members that had put forward negotiation requirements to China had been completed. On September 17, 2001, the 18th meeting of the working group of the WTO held formal talks at the headquarters of the WTO. All legal documents on China's accession to the WTO were adopted and submitted to the General Council for deliberation. In November, the Fourth Ministerial Conference of the WTO was held in Doha, the capital of Qatar. The meeting reviewed and adopted all legal documents on China's accession to the WTO. On the afternoon of November 11, the signing ceremony of the protocol on China's accession to the WTO was officially held. After signing the protocol, Shi Guangsheng, head of the delegation, submitted the instrument of ratification of China's accession to the WTO signed by President Jiang Zemin to the director general of the WTO. According to the provisions of the WTO, China became an official member of the WTO 30 days later, that was, from December 11, 2001.

After China's accession to the WTO, China's opening up has entered a new stage, from opening up in limited scope and fields to opening up in all directions; from the opening-up led by the policy characterized by pilot projects to the foreseeable opening-up under the legal framework; from unilateral self-opening to mutual opening with WTO members. China's accession to the WTO has given China's economy a favorable position to participate in the formulation of rules and competition in the process of globalization, thus opening up new horizons and to the outside world as well as gaining broader development space. It is of great significance to expanding China's opening up and promoting domestic reform and development.

2.2.4 Strategic Measures for Regional Coordinated Development

(1) The Strategy of Developing the Western Region.
At the beginning of the implementation of the reform and opening-up, Deng Xiaoping put forward the strategic thinking of "two overall situations" in the modernization, that is, the central and western regions should obey the overall situation that the eastern coastal areas develop first; after the development of the eastern coastal areas, we should obey and support the overall situation of the development of the central and western regions, so as to promote the development of the modernization of the whole country. At the turn of the century, the eastern coastal areas have the conditions to support the development of the central and western regions. The CCCPC has made the strategic decision of the development of the western region in a timely manner.

In 1995, in his famous speech entitled *Properly Handle Relationships between Major Areas of the Socialist Modernization,* Jiang Zemin elaborated more specifically on the issue of "the relationship between the eastern region and the central and western regions." He pointed out: narrowing regional disparities should be regarded as an important policy to be adhered to for a long time, and resolving regional development gaps and adhering to coordinated regional economic development is a strategic task for future reform and development.[30] In 1997, he pointed out in the report of the 15th National Congress of the CPC: the state should increase its support to the central and western regions and make efforts in various areas to gradually narrow the regional development gap.[31] In June 1999, Jiang Zemin stressed in Xi'an: accelerate the implementation of the strategy of the large-scale development of western region. Subsequently, several members of the Standing Committee of the Political Bureau of the CCCPC successively went to the western region for inspection. In September, at the Fourth Plenary Session of the 15th CCCPC, Jiang Zemin once again clearly pointed out that the state should implement the strategy of "large-scale development of the western region." On January 16, 2000, the State Council established a leading group for the development of the western region under the State Council, headed by Premier Zhu Rongji and Vice Premier Wen Jiabao.

On March 5, 2000, Premier Zhu Rongji of the State Council, in his Report on the Work of the Government work report to the Third Session of the Nineth NPC, explained the basic principles for the implementation of the "large-scale development of the western region" and the work in several major areas that need to be focused on: accelerate infrastructure construction; conserve and improve the ecological environment; in light of local geography, climate, resources and other conditions, different regions should focus on developing strong industries with local characteristics as well as high and new technology industries where conditions permit; make efforts in science, technology and education; the translation of scientific and technological advances into productive forces should be accelerated, people should be trained in different fields at different levels of expertise, and the overall quality of the workforce should be improved; further open up to the outside; improve the investment environment and actively introduce capital, technology and management experience. In October, the *Proposal of the CCCPC for the Formulation of the 10th Five-Year Plan for National Economic and Social Development* was adopted at the Fifth Plenary Session of the 15th CCCPC. It explained the strategy for the large-scale development of the western region and put forward its guiding ideology, and stressed that the large-scale development of the western region was an arduous historical task, which required both a sense of urgency and ideological preparation for long-term struggle. We should persist in proceeding from reality, be proactive, act according to our ability, make overall planning and scientific demonstration, highlight key points, and implement them step by step. We should strive to make breakthroughs in the infrastructure construction and ecological environment in the western region in five to ten years, and make a good start in the large-scale development of the western region.

According to the decision of the CCCPC, the State Council issued the *Circular of the State Council Concerning on Carrying out the Development of China's Vast Western Regions* on October 26, 2000, formally launching this century project. These measures can be summed up in the following five aspects: a) The principles of policy formulation and the focus of support. The implementation of the large-scale development of the western region is a grand systematic project and an arduous historical task, which requires both a sense of urgency and ideological preparation for long-term struggle. We should persist in proceeding from reality, be proactive, act according to our ability and realistic principles, make overall and long-term planning based on the present and make scientific demonstration, highlight key points, and implement them step by step. We should prevent a flurry, oppose wastefulness, and not engage in "big whoop." We should speed up the transformation of concepts, intensify reform and opening-up, implement the strategy of rejuvenating the country through science and education and sustainable development, integrate the role of the market mechanism with macroeconomic regulation and control, and integrate the spirit of self-reliance of the broad masses of cadres and people in the western region with the support of all quarters. At present and for a period to come, the key tasks of implementing the large-scale development of the western region were: accelerate the construction of infrastructure; strengthen ecological environment protection and construction; consolidate the basic position of agriculture, adjust the industrial structure, and develop characteristic and holistic tourism; work to develop science, technology, education, culture, and public health; strive to make breakthroughs in the infrastructure construction and ecological environment in the western region in five to ten years, and make a good start in the large-scale development of the western region. By the middle of the 21st century, we should build the western region into a new western region with economic prosperity, social progress, stable life, ethnic unity, and beautiful mountains and rivers. The scope of the policy of large-scale development of the western regions includes Chongqing, Sichuan, Guizhou, Yunnan, Xizang Autonomous Region, Shaanxi, Gansu, Ningxia Hui Autonomous Region, Qinghai, Xinjiang Uygur Autonomous Region, Inner Mongolia Autonomous Region and Guangxi Zhuang Autonomous Region. In developing the western region, we need to begin work at places along major transportation routes, such as the Eurasian Continental Bridge, the Yangtze River, and the routes in the southwestern part of the country leading to the sea. Major cities connected by such lines should serve as economic centers and play leading roles in the development of their adjacent areas, and gradually foster the economic zones along the Tongguan-Lanzhou-Urumqi line, the upper reaches of the Yangtze River, and the Nanning-Guiyang-Kunming line to promote development of the surrounding areas, drive the development of other regions, and promote the large-scale development of the western region in a step-by-step and focused manner. b) The Policy of Increasing Capital Input. More funds should be put in place to ensure implementation of this strategy. The proportion of central financial construction funds used in the western region should be increased. Priority should be given to construction projects. Water conservancy, transportation, energy and other infrastructure, development and utilization of advantageous resources, and characteristic high-tech and military to civilian technology industrialization projects should be given priority in the western region. The financial transfer payment should be increased. With the increase of the central financial resources, the scale of general transfer payments from the central government to the western region should be gradually increased. In the allocation of special subsidies for agriculture, social security, education, science and technology, health, family planning, culture and environmental protection, we should give preference to the western region. We should increase financial and credit support. According to the independent principle of commercial credit, the banks should the credit investment in the construction of basic industries in the western region, and focus on supporting the construction of large and medium-sized energy projects such as railways, trunk roads, electric power, oil and natural gas. c) Policies to improve investment environment. We need to improve the soft environment for investment. Implement preferential tax policies; implement preferential policies for land and mineral resources; use the price and charge mechanism to adjust the price, reasonably set the price of "transmitting gas from west to east China" and "west-to-east electricity transmission," and establish a price formation mechanism for the production and marketing of natural gas, electricity, oil and coal. d) Policies to open up China wider to the rest of the world. We should further expand the scope of foreign investment, further expand the channels for utilizing foreign capital, work to develop foreign trade and economic cooperation, and promote regional cooperation and counterpart support. e) Policies to attract talents and develop science, technology and education. formulate policies conducive to attracting, retaining and encouraging talents to start businesses in the western region; give play to the leading role of science and technology, increase the support of various science and technology plan funds to the western region, and gradually increase the amount of science and technology funds used in the western region; increase investment in education; accelerating the development of culture and health.

With the correct leadership of the CCCPC and the State Council and the joint efforts of all parties, the strategy of "developing the western region" has been pushed forward in a down-to-earth manner. In 2000, the "ten major projects" were newly started, namely, the Xi'an-Hefei section of the Xi'an Nanjing railway, the construction of Western highways, the construction of airports in the western region, the Chongqing elevated light rail, the Sebei-Xining-Lanzhou gas transmission pipeline, the 300,000 ton potassium fertilizer project in Qinghai, the project of returning farmland to forests and grasslands in the western region, the infrastructure construction of universities in the western region, the Zipingpu in Sichuan, and the Shapotou Water Conservancy Project on the Yellow River in Ningxia. In 2001, a number of key projects were started successively, including the landmark projects of the large scale development of the western region strategy— the Qinghai-Xizang railway, the west-to-east power transmission project, the west to east gas transmission project, the Baise water conservancy project in Guangxi, the Nierji water conservancy project in Inner Mongolia, the important sections of the five vertical and seven horizontal national trunk lines in the western region, and the Lanzhou Chongqing oil pipeline project.

The large-scale development strategy to speed up development of the central and western regions of the country is a major policy decision made by the CCCPC and the Chinese government for the new century in accordance with Deng Xiaoping's strategy for China's modernization drive, which encompasses the development of both the coastal areas and the interior. This is crucial to our efforts to boost domestic demand, promote sustained national economic growth and bring about coordinated development of regional economies for eventual common prosperity as well as to strengthen national unity, safeguard social stability and consolidate border defense.

(2) The Strategy for Sustainable Development

Environment and development are major issues of universal concern to the international community today. Protecting the ecological environment and achieving sustainable development has become an urgent and arduous task in the world. Protecting the environment and developing the economy have a bearing on the future and destiny of mankind, affecting every country, every nation and even every individual in the world. The whole world is very concerned about this. The CPC and the Chinese government are also extremely concerned about this issue. In 1991, China initiated the meeting of Ministers of Environment and Development of developing countries" and issued the *Beijing Declaration*. This is a positive contribution made by China and other developing countries to promoting the undertaking of the world environment and development.

In June 1992, the United Nations Conference on Environment and Development was held in Rio de Janeiro, Brazil. The conference adopted *Agenda 21*, namely the action plan for sustainable development worldwide. At the meeting, Premier Li Peng of the Chinese government made an important speech, expressing China's stand and attitude of actively participating in the environmental protection and development of the international community. At this meeting, the Chinese government solemnly signed the *Rio Declaration on Environment and Development*. On July 2, led by the State Planning Commission and the State Science and Technology Commission, functional government departments and social organizations began to prepare *China's Agenda 21*. After nearly one and a half years, *China's Agenda 21* was compiled and revised. On March 25, 1994, the 16th executive meeting of the State Council discussed and adopted the *China Agenda 21*, and China's "sustainable development" strategy began to be implemented.

China's Agenda 21 clarifies the specific contents of the strategy for "sustainable development": social sustainable development, mainly including population, residents' consumption and social services, poverty eradication, health, sustainable development of human settlements, disaster prevention and mitigation, etc. Economic sustainable development includes sustainable development of agriculture and rural economy, sustainable energy production and consumption, etc. Rational utilization of resources and environmental protection, includes the protection and sustainable use of natural resources such as water and soil, the protection of biodiversity, the prevention and control of land desertification, the protection of the atmosphere and the harmless management of solid wastes, etc.

In order to support the implementation of *China's Agenda 21*, the Chinese government also formulated the *Plan for Priority Programme for China's Agenda 21*. In 1995, the CCCPC and the State Council defined sustainable development as the basic development strategy of the country, formulated a series of principles and policies suitable for the national conditions, and called on the people of the whole country to actively participate in this great practice. Jiang Zemin made many important speeches on the strategy for sustainable development. At the conclusion of the Fifth Plenary Session of the 14th CCCPC on September 28, 1995, he pointed out: in the modernization drive, the realization of sustainable development must be regarded as a major strategy. We should put population control, resource conservation and environmental protection in an important position, make population growth compatible with the development of social productive forces, coordinate economic development with resources and the environment, and realize a virtuous cycle. In the report of the 15th National Congress of the CPC, he also stressed: as a populous country relatively short of natural resources, China must implement a sustainable development strategy in the modernization drive.[32]

After entering the new century, the CPC and the Chinese government have paid more attention to the issue of sustainable development. In July 2001, at the 80th anniversary of the founding of the CPC, Jiang Zemin once again emphasized the viewpoint of harmonious development between man and nature and the strategy for sustainable development, and proposed: we should promote the coordination and harmony between man and nature, so that people can work and live in a beautiful ecological environment; adhere to the strategy for sustainable development, properly handle the relationship between economic development and population, resources and the environment, improve the ecological environment and beautify the living environment, and improve public facilities and social welfare facilities; and take a positive path to development that ensures increased production, higher living standards, and healthy ecosystems."[33] On March 10, 2002, Jiang Zemin pointed out at the Central Forum on Population, Resources and Environment Work: the core of achieving sustainable development was to achieve coordinated development of economy, society, population, resources and environment. Now, there is an increasingly clear international consensus that development should not only depend on economic growth indicators, but also on cultural, resource and environmental indicators. In order to achieve sustainable economic and social development, and to ensure that future generations of the Chinese nation always have good conditions for survival and development, we must attach great importance to and effectively solve the problem of changing the pattern of economic growth, correctly handle the relationship between economic development and population, resources and environment, promote the coordination and harmony between man and nature, and strive to create a civilized development path of production, rich life and good ecology in accordance with the requirements of sustainable development."[34]

Subsequently, the State Council also issued the *Outline of Action for China's Sustainable Development at the Beginning of the 21st Century*, clarifying that the guiding ideology, overall objectives and basic principles of China's sustainable development strategy had been clearly defined. The guiding ideology for the implementation of the sustainable development strategy is to adhere to the people-oriented principle, take the harmony between man and nature as the main line, take economic development as the core, take the improvement of the people's quality of life as the fundamental starting point, and take scientific and technological and institutional innovation as the breakthrough point, persistently and comprehensively promote the coordination of economic society and population, resources and ecological environment, constantly improve China's comprehensive national strength and competitiveness, and lay a solid foundation for the realization of the third step strategic objective. The overall goal of China's sustainable development at the beginning of the 21st century is to continuously enhance the capacity for sustainable development, achieve remarkable results in economic restructuring, effectively control the total population, significantly improve the ecological environment, significantly improve the utilization rate of resources, promote the harmony between man and nature, and promote the whole society to embark on a civilized development path of production development, affluence and good ecology. The basic principles of sustainable development are: the principle of sustainable development and coordination, the principle of rejuvenating the country through science and education and continuous innovation, the principle of government control and market regulation, the principle of active participation and extensive cooperation, and the principle of key breakthroughs and comprehensive promotion.

Adhering to the path of sustainable development is an inevitable conclusion drawn by the CPC and the Chinese government after summing up the experience and lessons of economic and social development over the years. It is a strategic choice made by keep our feet firmly on the ground while setting our eyes to the long-term future. Since the 1990s, China has vigorously carried out river pollution control, land and resources control, desertification control, shelter forest system building, biodiversity protection and other projects. The "Nineth Five-Year Plan" determined in 1995 focused on the pollution prevention and control of the "three rivers" (Huaihe, Haihe and Liaohe rivers), "three lakes" (Tai, Chao and Dianchi lakes), "two areas" (carbon dioxide and acid rain pollution control areas), "one city" (Beijing) and "one sea" (Bohai sea) as the cross century green project. After the 15th National Congress of the CPC, the State Council successively promulgated the *National Plan for Ecological Environment Development* and the *National Plan for Nature Reserve Development*. In fact, these measures have achieved visible outcomes. But at the same time, we must be soberly aware that China is a country with a large population and inadequate resources. The per capita share of important resources is far below the world average, and the pressure on population, resources and environment is increasing. Therefore, we must further establish an economic operation mechanism and management system conducive to sustainable development through institutional reform, scientific and technological progress and strengthening management, gradually realize the transformation of the pattern of economic growth, and promote sustained, rapid and healthy economic development and comprehensive social progress.

Summary

Inspired by Deng Xiaoping's Southern Talks, the CPC and the Chinese government clearly put forward the reform goal of establishing a socialist market economy. On this basis, China has successfully responded to the problem of economic overheating and the Asian financial crisis. As a result, the economy has accelerated its development, the people's living standards have been significantly improved, and the comprehensive national strength has been greatly enhanced. By 2002, the GDP had increased from 2.4 trillion yuan in 1992 to 10.2 trillion yuan, the national fiscal revenue had increased from 0.35 trillion yuan to 1.89 trillion yuan, the state's foreign exchange reserves had increased from 19.6 billion U.S. dollars in 1992 to 286.4 billion U.S. dollars, and the total volume of foreign trade imports and exports had reached 620.8 billion U.S. dollars, ranking the fifth in the world. The per capita disposable income of urban households reached 7,703 yuan in 2002, and the per capita net income of rural households reached 2,476 yuan. At the same time, since its accession to the WTO, China has made important contribution to world economic Prosperity.

SECTION 3
Building a Socialist Culture with a Specifically Chinese Character

2.3.1 Strategy for Invigorating China through Science and Education

The strategy for invigorating China through science and education is the fundamental plan to realize China's economic revitalization and national modernization. It refers to comprehensively implementing the idea that science and technology is the primary force of productivity. We should adhere to education as the foundation, place science and technology and education in an important position in economic and social development, enhance the country's scientific and technological strength and its ability to transform into real productive forces, improve the scientific, technological and cultural quality of the whole nation, and shift economic development to the track of reliance on technological progress and improving labor quality, and accelerate the realization of national prosperity. Its ideological and theoretical basis is Deng Xiaoping's assertion that "science and technology constitute a primary productive force." In 1992, in the report of the 14th National Congress of the CPC, Jiang Zemin pointed out: to revitalize the economy, we must first revitalize science and technology. We must put education in a strategic position of priority development and strive to improve the ideological, moral, scientific and cultural level of the whole nation. This is the fundamental plan to realize China's modernization.[35] In February 1993, the CCCPC and the

State Council issued the *Outline of China's National Plan for Education Reform and Development*, which proposed that by the end of the 20th century, China should form a basic framework of a socialist education system with Chinese characteristics and suitable to the new era of the 21st century. In July of the same year, the Second Meeting of the Standing Committee of the Eighth NPC passed the *Law of the PRC on Scientific and Technological Progress*, the first law on science and technology since the founding of new China.

After entering the mid-1990s, the tide of economic globalization and industrial informatization in the world has gradually risen. The competition of comprehensive national strength is increasingly concentrated on the competition of science and technology, talents and education. On March 18, 1995, the Third Session of the Eighth NPC passed the *Education Law of the PRC*, which provides legal guarantee for the development of education. On May 6, 1995, the CCCPC and the State Council made the *Decision on Accelerating the Scientific and Technological Progress* on the basis of scientific analysis of the development trend of economy and science and technology and the situation at home and abroad, and proposed for the first time to implement the strategy for invigorating China through science and education throughout the country. After the release of the *Decision*, the CCCPC and the State Council held a national science and technology conference from May 26 to 30. This meeting is an important meeting in the history of China's scientific and technological development. At the opening ceremony of the national science and technology conference, Jiang Zemin delivered an important speech entitled "Striving to Implement the Strategy for Invigorating China Through Science and Education." He called on the ruling party, namely the whole Party and the people throughout the country to comprehensively implement Deng Xiaoping's idea that technology is a primary source of productivity, and to devote themselves to the great cause of implementing the strategy for invigorating China through science and education. In September, the Fifth Plenary Session of the 14th CCCPC adopted the *Proposal of the CCCPC on the Ninth Five-Year Plan for National Economic and Social Development and the Long-range Objectives to the Year 2010*, which takes "implementing the strategy for invigorating China through science and education and promoting the close integration of science, technology, education and economy" as one of the nine important principles that must be implemented in economic and social development in the next 15 years. In order to further implement the strategy for invigorating China through science and education and develop higher education, in November 1995, with the approval of the State Council, the State Planning Commission, the State Education Commission and the Ministry of Finance jointly issued the *Overall Construction Plan of the "211 Project,"* which officially launched the "211 Project," aiming at building about 100 universities and a number of key disciplines in the 21st century. In 1996, the Fourth Session of the Eighth NPC formally put forward the *Outline of the Ninth Five-Year Plan for National Economic and Social Development and the Long-range Objectives to the Year 2010.* "Invigorating China through science and education" has thus become the basic national policy of contemporary China.

In 1997, in the report of the 15th National Congress of the CPC, Jiang Zemin once again put forward the strategy of the strategy for invigorating China through science and education and the strategy for sustainable development as the cross century national development strategy, and stressed the need to fully assess the great impact of future scientific and technological development, especially high-tech development, on the comprehensive national strength, social and economic structure and people's lives. On March 4, 1998, Jiang Zemin further pointed out at a forum with members of the National Committee of the Chinese CCCPC on science and technology that "innovation is the soul of a nation's progress, and the inexhaustible force enhancing a country's prosperity."[36] The whole Party and the whole society should truly place scientific and technological progress and innovation in a more important strategic position, fully mobilize the enthusiasm of the vast number of scientific and technological personnel, and invigorate China through science and education. In order to strengthen the leadership of science, technology and education, in June 1998, the CCCPC and the State Council established a national leading group for science, technology and education (Premier Zhu Rongji as the group leader and Vice Premier Li Lanqing as the Deputy Group Leader). They made a series of decisions on deepening education reform, comprehensively promoting quality education, strengthening technological innovation, developing high technology, and realizing industrialization, which effectively promoted the development of science, technology and education. In that year, Jiang Zemin proposed at the meeting to celebrate the 100th anniversary of the founding of Peking University that in order to realize modernization, China should have a number of world-class universities. In December, the Ministry of Education formulated the *Action Plan for Invigorating Education in the 21st Century*, which is the construction blueprint for China's cross century education reform and development, and sets the development goals for the years of 2000 and 2010. The formulation and implementation of this plan have made a more solid step in the reform and development of China's education. In June 1999, the CCCPC and the State Council issued the *Decision on Deepening Education Reform and Comprehensively Promoting Quality Education*. In August, the National Technology and Innovation Conference was held. Jiang Zemin pointed out at the conference that the key to comprehensively implementing the strategy for invigorating China through science and education and accelerating the scientific and technological progress of the whole society is to strengthen and continuously promote knowledge and technological innovation. The meeting adopted the *Decision of the CCCPC* and the *State Council on Strengthening Technical Innovation, Developing of High Technology and Realization of Its Industrialization*. In order to commend and encourage the vast number of scientific and technological personnel to continuously promote scientific and technological innovation, the CCCPC and the State Council decided to establish the Highest Science and Technology Award of China from 2000. Since then, the Highest Science and Technology Award of China has been awarded once a year.

After the implementation of the strategy for invigorating China through science and education, major scientific and technological inventions and innovations have made new achievements. In agriculture, in 1997, Yuan Longping, an academician with the Chinese Academy of Engineering, put forward the technical route of "super high yield breeding of hybrid rice." The experimental field produced nearly 800 kilograms per mu and the rice quality was similar to that of Japonica rice, which attracted great attention in the world; in October 2001, the Chinese Academy of Sciences, the State Planning Commission and the Ministry of Science and Technology jointly announced that the "working framework map" and database of Chinese rice (indica rice) genome had been completed, and the data would be released for free sharing worldwide. In the field of biomedicine, in 2000, Chinese scientists participated in and completed with high quality one percent of the sequencing tasks in the "working draft of the human genome," indicating that Chinese scientists have the ability to rise to the forefront of international science and make important contributions. In the field of electronic information industry, in September 1998, China developed an all-digital high-definition TV system with independent intellectual property rights, which marks that China has systematically mastered this internationally competitive high technology and laid the technical foundation for upgrading the

TV industry. In the field of natural science exploration, from July to September 1999, China conducted its first Arctic expedition and research; in the same year, Chinese scientists discovered that there was an "Ozone Valley" over the Qinghai-Xizang Plateau, which attracted extensive attention from the global scientific community.

2.3.2 The Strategy of "the Rule of Virtue"

With the gradual transition of the economic system, it is increasingly urgent to build a moral system that is compatible with it. To build a new moral system, we should not only adhere to the Communist moral principles, inherit the fine traditions of the revolutionary era, and draw on the moral ideas of the traditional culture, but also take into account the contemporary national conditions and the trend of social development. The idea of "the rule of virtue" is put forward precisely to establish an ideological and moral system compatible with the development of the socialist market economy, so as to improve the national moral quality and promote the comprehensive development of society.

In October 1996, the Sixth Plenary Session of the 14th CCCPC adopted the *Resolution of the CCCPC on Several Important Issues Concerning Strengthening the Construction of Socialist Spiritual Civilization* on the basis of summing up the experience and lessons of China's spiritual civilization since the reform and opening-up and in combination with the needs of the new situation. The *Resolution* pointed out: in the whole process of reform, opening up and modernization, the basic task of ideological and moral construction is to adhere to patriotism, collectivism and socialist education, strengthen the construction of social ethics, professional ethics and family virtues, and guide people to establish the common ideal of building socialism with Chinese characteristics and to foster a sound world outlook and outlook on life and values. The *Resolution* also made detailed provisions on such issues as the great significance, guiding ideology, objectives, core contents and main means of spiritual civilization construction. These marked the initial formation of a framework system for socialist ideological and moral construction under the conditions of establishing a socialist market economy. In order to organizationally ensure the implementation of the Resolution of the Sixth Plenary Session of the 14th CCCPC, in May 1997, the CCCPC decided to establish the Central Commission for Guiding Cultural and Ethical Progress as the deliberative body of the Central Committee to guide the national spiritual civilization construction. In September, in the report of the 15th National Congress of the CPC, Jiang Zemin put forward the general requirements for socialist moral construction: advocating communist ideology and morality, combining the requirements of progressiveness and universality, and encouraging all ideology and morality conducive to national unity, ethnic unity, economic development and social progress.

In June 2000, Jiang Zemin expounded the role of law and morality in state management at a national conference on communication and outreach. He pointed out: as an integral part of the superstructure, law and morality are both important means to maintain social order and regulate people's thinking and behavior. They are interrelated and complementary to each other. The rule of law regulates the behavior of social members with its authority and coercive means, while the rule of virtue improves the ideological understanding and moral awareness of social members in a convincing way. Moral and legal norms should be combined to play a unified role. In January 2001, at the National Conference of Publicity Ministers of the CPC, he clearly put forward the strategy of "integrating the rule of law with rule by virtue. "In his "July 1st" speech in 2001, he once again stressed: it is necessary to integrate the rule of law with the rule by virtue, so as to create a noble ideological and moral foundation for maintaining good social order and fashion.

The so-called "ruling the country by virtue" means that we should take Marxism-Leninism, Mao Zedong Thought, Deng Xiaoping Theory and the important thought of the "Three Represents" as the guide, focus on establishing the common ideal of building socialism with Chinese characteristics and the sound world outlook, outlook on life and values, adhere to the integration of inheriting fine traditions and carrying forward the spirit of the times, respect the legitimate rights and interests of individuals and assume social responsibilities, pay attention to the coordination between efficiency and safeguarding social fairness, organically link the requirements of progressiveness with the requirements of universality, actively establish a socialist ideological and moral system that adapts to the development of the socialist market economy, and develop socialist spiritual civilization. This ideological and moral system regards serving the people as the core, collectivism as the principle, and love the motherland, the people, labor, science, and socialism as the basic requirements. By vigorously advocating social ethics such as civility, courtesy, helping others, caring for public property, protecting the environment, and abiding by laws and disciplines, and professional ethics such as loving one's post, being honest and trustworthy, doing things in a fair manner, serving the people, and contributing to society, and family virtues such as respecting the old and loving the young, equality between men and women, harmony between husband and wife, diligence and thrift in running the family, and unity among neighbors, we have formed a code of conduct that is generally recognized and consciously observed by all the people, and form an interpersonal relationship of solidarity and mutual assistance, equality and fraternity, and common progress in the entire society. The basic characteristics of "ruling the country by virtue" are: emphasizing the power of ideological education and spirit, emphasizing the role of role models in guiding people and society, curbing corruption, preventing and counteracting social evils by means of customs, public opinion, education and cultivation, good and evil judgment, conscience reflection, honesty and self-discipline.

In September 2001, the CCCPC issued the *Citizen Ethics Construction Program*. This Outline systematically expounds the guiding ideology, principles, main contents and methods of citizen moral construction, reflects the idea of "ruling the country by virtue," and is an outline document for the CPC and the Chinese government to guide the socialist moral construction at the new stage. The *Outline* pointed out: we should encourage all our people to develop the basic virtues of "patriotism and observance of law, courtesy and honesty, solidarity and friendship, diligence, frugality and self-improvement; and devotion and contribution."

After a period of practice, China has gradually formed some important regular and enlightening experiences in "ruling the country by virtue":

First, we should do a good job in the construction of political ethics, administer the Party and government strictly, and form a moral demonstration group. The *Decision of the CCCPC on Strengthening the Construction of the Party's Ruling Ability* adopted at the Fourth Plenary Session of the 16th CCCPC pointed out that it was necessary to strengthen ideological and moral education and discipline education, commend the typical examples of diligent and honest administration, urge Party members and leading cadres at all levels to strengthen the cultivation of Party spirit, often cultivate the virtue of government, always think of the harm of greed, and always be self-disciplined, and consciously withstand the test of long-term governance under the conditions of reform, opening up, and the development of the socialist market economy.

Second, in the promotion, appointment, removal, assessment, inspection, and reward of Party and government cadres, we should conscientiously implement the principle of having both political integrity and professional competence, and regard the moral quality and moral character of cadres as an important standard. Therefore, it is necessary to expand democracy in the selection and appointment of cadres, strengthen the construction of the system, effectively guarantee the fairness and equality of the operating procedures, avoid closed operation and dark box operation, and prevent and deal with the excessive concentration of cadres' appointment rights and the resulting patriarchal phenomenon, the bondage of serfs of superior and subordinate relations, and the phenomenon of buying and selling posts.

Third, it is necessary to establish a socialist ideological and ethical system compatible with the socialist market economy and the socialist legal standard and consistent with the traditional virtues of the Chinese nation.

Fourth, it is necessary to pay attention to improving citizens' moral awareness, cultivating citizens' moral feelings, and internalizing them into codes of conduct, especially focusing on teenagers.

Fifth, we should take the results of moral education and moral teachings for the masses as one of the important standards for measuring the construction of spiritual civilization in various regions and units, and strive to make moral education an important means to change the social atmosphere and improve the people's moral standards in ideological construction.

Sixth, we should combine "rule by virtue" with "rule of law." On the one hand, strengthen the moral construction; on the other hand, by cracking down on various illegal activities by law, we should curb the corruption in the ruling party and the society, maintain social order, and create a good social environment for socialist moral construction.

"Rule by virtue" is the crystallization of the thinking of the ruling Chinese Communists on how to manage state affairs and how to educate and guide the people to advocate a noble spiritual life under the new historical conditions by drawing lessons from the previous dynasties' ways of governing the country and foreign countries' experiences and lessons in state affairs management. It has important practical significance for China in the period of social transformation.

2.3.3 A New Situation of Prospering the Cause of Philosophy and Social Sciences

Philosophy and social science is an important tool for people to understand and transform the world, and an important force to promote historical development and social progress. The research ability and achievements of philosophy and social sciences are an important part of comprehensive national strength. With the deepening of reform, opening up and modernization, the CPC and the Chinese government have gradually deepened their understanding of the important role of philosophy and social sciences.

Since the 1990s, Jiang Zemin has repeatedly emphasized the important role of philosophy and social sciences in the cause of building socialism with Chinese characteristics. In August 2001, at the Beidaihe Meeting, he put forward the proposition of "philosophy and social sciences are as important as natural sciences in four ways," that is, philosophy and social sciences are as important as natural sciences; cultivating high-level philosophy and social scientists is as important as cultivating high-level natural scientists; improving the quality of philosophy and social sciences of the whole nation is as important as improving the quality of natural sciences of the whole nation; appointing and giving full play to the talents of philosophy and social sciences is as important as doing that in natural sciences. In April 2002, he delivered a speech at Renmin University of China, and put forward the conclusion that "five high values" should be attached to philosophy and social sciences: always attach great importance to the great role of philosophy and social sciences in the Party and country governance and the construction of socialism with Chinese characteristics; attach great importance to the reform and development of higher education in the field of philosophy and social sciences; attach great importance to improving the conditions for philosophical and social science research and talent training; attach great importance to tackling key issues in the field of philosophy and social sciences; attach great importance to the achievements and roles of scholars who have made outstanding contributions to the development of philosophy and social sciences. He also put forward "five hopes" for the vast number of philosophy and social science workers: everyone would innovate their thinking and constantly make new achievements in promoting theoretical innovation, institutional innovation, and scientific and technological innovation; everyone would deepen the practice of reform, opening up and modernization, and strive to make scientific theoretical answers to major issues of overall, strategic and forward-looking nature; everyone would not only base themselves on China but also face the world, strive to inherit and carry forward the excellent culture of the Chinese nation, and actively learn from the beneficial cultural achievements created by the people of other countries; everyone would adhere to the style of rigorous scholarship, seeking truth from facts, democracy and realism; everyone would adhere to the Marxist stand, viewpoint and method to guide the development of philosophy and social sciences. He called on Party committees and governments at all levels and the whole society to make joint efforts to vigorously promote the development and prosperity of China's philosophy and social sciences. In July of the same year, in his speech at the Chinese Academy of Social Sciences, he pointed: philosophy and social sciences have "two irreplaceable roles": in terms of the relationship between natural sciences and philosophy and social sciences, the roles of philosophy and social sciences and the workers in the fields are irreplaceable; the role of philosophy and social science in the development of socialist material civilization, political civilization and spiritual civilization is irreplaceable.

2.3.4 Development of Sports

After the publication of Deng Xiaoping's Southern Talks in 1992, China's reform and opening-up cause set off a new round of climax, and China's sports cause also entered a new historical period. The National Sports Commission Directors' Meeting held in 1993 formulated and issued the *Opinions on Deepening the Reform of Sport System* and five supporting documents of the National Sports Commission, with the goal of launching the life-based, universal, socialized, scientific, industrialized and legalized sports reform. With the gradual improvement of the system and the continuous improvement of the people's living standards, China's sports undertakings have developed rapidly at the new stage. Chinese athletes have made one historic breakthrough after another in various sports events, and more and more people are actively involved in national fitness activities.

The Chinese sports Corps has risen in an all-round way in the international sports arena. The development of a country's competitive sports is often an important indicator of its sports development. At the Barcelona Olympic Games in 1992, the Chinese delegation won 16 gold, 22 silver and 16 bronze medals, ranking fourth in the number of gold medals, surpassed the previous highest in the 1984 Olympic Games and archived the best result in history. At the Olympic Winter Games in Albertville, France, in the same year, the famous Chinese speed skater Ye Qiaobo ranked only second in the 500m race because she collided with a foreign player on the slide. Although she missed the gold medal, she still set a milestone for Chinese sports and won the first silver medal in the Olympic Winter Games for China. In May 1993, China held the first East Asian Game in Shanghai. The Game was a great success both in terms of the organization and the progress of the games, which showed the solid foundation for China to hold large-scale games. China made outstanding achievements, winning 102 gold medals and the first place with great advantages. At the Sydney Olympic Games in 2000, the Chinese Corp won 28 gold, 16 silver and 15 bronze medals, ranking third in both the gold medal table and the medal table. It was the first time that it entered the top three in the gold medal table of the Olympic Games, setting a record for the number of gold medals and the number of medals in previous Olympic Games. Among them, the Chinese men's gymnastics team realized the dream of winning a team gold medal. The Chinese table tennis team won all the gold medals in the Olympic Games for two consecutive times, and the women weightlifters won all the gold medals in all the four levels they participated in. All these have fully demonstrated the superiority of China's socialist political, economic, cultural and social development, and China's sports have become a force of world attention. At the Salt Lake City Winter Olympics held two years later, Chinese athlete Yang Yang beat players from other countries to win the women's 500m short track speed skating championship, winning the first gold medal of the Chinese Winter Olympics.

China's sports industry is booming. After the 14th National Congress of the CPC, with the establishment of the socialist market economy, China's sports development has gradually become to market-oriented and industry-oriented. The National Sports Commission has carried out great reform. All sports management functions have been separated from government management, and 20 sports management centers have been established. In particular, taking the football reform as a breakthrough, we should promote the process of the association's materialization and promote the football games to the market. In accordance with this, all football teams have become the market players who are responsible for their own profits and losses and operate independently according to the requirements of the establishment of professional clubs, which has driven the development of China's football industry. Since then, professional basketball, volleyball, table tennis clubs and other professional clubs have been set up to develop in an industrialized mode. In 1994, the National Sports Commission (now the General Administration of Sport of China) was officially established to uniformly administer, number, print and issue sports lottery tickets throughout the country, and officially named the tickets "China Sports Lottery." From 1994 to the end of 1999, a total of 10.2 billion yuan of sports lottery tickets were sold and 3.06 billion yuan of public welfare funds were raised, providing a financial guarantee for the continuous development of China's sports undertakings. In 2000, on the basis of the success of the pilot project, China's computer sports lottery began to be issued nationwide, which effectively promoted the rapid development of sports lottery.

The fitness for all initiative was steadily lauched. With the continuous improvement of living standards and the development of China's sports undertakings, the ordinary people's awareness of participating in sports activities is also growing. On June 20, 1995, the Chinese government promulgated the epoch-making *Outline of the National Scheme for Fitness for All*. This is a major decision of the state to develop social sports and an outline document for China's development of national fitness at the end of the 20th century and the beginning of the 21st century. The planned and purposeful mass sports activities of government organs, communities, factories and mining enterprises have been vigorously carried out. Rural sports, sports for the disabled, sports for ethnic minorities and sports for the elderly have made great progress. The enthusiasm and initiative of the masses to participate in sports activities have been enhanced. The sports population has increased continuously, reaching 37% of the total population, and the gap with developed countries has been significantly narrowed.

Sports is an important symbol of social development and human civilization progress, and an important embodiment of comprehensive national strength and social civilization. At the new stage of reform and opening-up and the development of socialism with Chinese characteristics, the continuous deepening of China's sports reform and the vigorous development of China's sports cause have had an important impact on the prosperity of socialist cultural undertakings and the promotion of economic and social development.

Summary

In the spring of 1989, when summing up the experience and lessons since the reform and opening-up, Deng Xiaoping said: Our biggest mistake has been in the area of education. Political and ideological work has been weakened, and we have not done enough to expand education.[37] Therefore, the Chinese Communists, with Comrade Jiang Zemin as the main representative, placed the building of spiritual civilization in a prominent position. Under the background of significant changes in people's ideas and behavior, the *Resolution of the CCCPC on Several Important Issues Concerning Strengthening the Construction of Socialist Spiritual Civilization* outlines the blueprint for the construction of socialist spiritual civilization under the new historical conditions. The strategy for "invigorating China through science and education" has responded to the development trend of the world's scientific and technological revolution and accelerated the historical process of China's modernization. The strategy of "ruling by virtue" has raised the socialist moral construction to the height of governing the country and is of great significance to China in the transition period. Vigorously prospering the cause of philosophy and social sciences and paying attention to the cultivation and promotion of the humanistic spirit and national spirit in the real society are not only the objective requirements of development, but also one of the symbols of the maturity of the ruling party. The vigorous development of China's sports cause has had an important impact on the prosperity of socialist cultural undertakings and the promotion of economic and social development.

SECTION 4
Achieving Moderately Prosperous Society in General While Coping with Risks and Challenges

2.4.1 Three Business Tides and "Four Diversities"
China's economic system reform has not only injected vitality into the development of the state-owned economy and the collective economy, but also brought a relatively relaxed environment for the development of the non-public economy. The implementation of several important economic system reform measures has prompted the rise of domestic business boom, and the non-public economy has thus seen several stages of development climaxes. With the development of non-public economy, the social life of contemporary China has become increasingly diversified.

Before the Third Plenary Session of the 11th CCCPC, there were no private enterprises in China, and the number of individual economy was 140,000. At that time, China was facing the huge employment pressure of a large number of educated youth returning to the city and the backlog of 7–8 million urban unemployed people. Not long after the meeting, Deng Xiaoping invited the former industrial and commercial leaders to have a discussion. He proposed to attract foreign capital and hoped that the former industrial and commercial leaders would use the funds after the implementation of the policy to set up private enterprises. In February 1979, the CCCPC and the State Council approved the report of the first meeting of directors of industry and commerce administrations after the end of the "Great Cultural Revolution." According to the report, all localities may, according to the needs of the local market and after obtaining the consent of the relevant competent departments, approve some idle workers with official hukou to engage in repair, service and handicrafts, but they are not allowed to hire workers. This provided a policy basis for the development of the individual economy. By the end of this year, the number of individual employees in China had increased to 310,000. On October 17, 1981, the CCCPC and the State Council issued *Several Decisions on Opening up Employment Channels, Invigorating the Economy and Solving the Urban Employment Problem*, which proposed that in the future, while adjusting the industrial structure, we must focus on opening up employment channels in the collective economy and the individual economy, and made it clear that this is a strategic decision, not an expedient measure. For individual industrial and commercial households, operators shall be allowed to hire no more than two helpers; those who have special skills may take up to five apprentices. By the end of 1981, the urban individual economy had grown to 1.83 million households with 2.27 million employees. The *Decision of the CCCPC on the Reform of the Economic System* promulgated in 1984 systematically expounded for the first time the basic guiding principles of the CPC and the Chinese government for the development of the individual economy. It was emphasized that China's current individual economy was connected with socialist public ownership, which was different from the individual economy connected with capitalist private ownership. It played an irreplaceable role in developing social production, facilitating people's life and expanding labor employment. It was a necessary and beneficial supplement to the socialist economy and was subordinate to the socialist economy. The *Decision* also called for "removing obstacles, creating conditions and giving legal protection to the development of the individual economy."[38] In 1985, the number of individual industrial and commercial households reached 11.71 million, with 17.66 million employees and a registered capital of 16.9 billion yuan. The first business upsurge emerged in contemporary China.

On January 20, 1987, the CCCPC and the State Council made *Several Provisions on Further Promoting the Reform of the Scientific and Technological System*, proposing to support and encourage some scientific and technological personnel to go out of scientific research institutions, institutions of higher learning and government institutions, contract and lease small and medium-sized enterprises owned by the entire people in cities, towns and rural areas, contract or lead collective township enterprises, set up and operate development of technologies, technical services and technology trading institutions, establish various small and medium-sized joint ventures, joint-stock companies, etc., and allow them to create wealth for the society while obtaining legal income and allow technology shareholders receive dividends according to their shares. This *Regulation* has encouraged some scientific and technological personnel to "venture into business." In November, the 13th National Congress of the CPC clearly put forward the policy of encouraging the development of individual economy and private economy. The report of the 13th National Congress pointed out: the development of the economy of various forms of ownership with public ownership as the main body, and even the existence and development of the private economy, should all be determined by the actual situation of the productive forces at the primary stage of socialism. Only in this way can we promote the development of productive forces. At present, other economic sectors other than ownership by the entire people have not developed enough rather than developed too much. We should continue to encourage the development of the urban-rural cooperative economy, the individual economy and the private economy. At the same time, it is emphasized that policies and laws concerning the private economy must be formulated as soon as possible to protect their legitimate interests and strengthen their guidance, supervision and management. The relatively loose external environment has promoted the development of the non-public economy. At the end of this year, there were 13.37 million individual industrial and commercial households in China, with 21.58 million employees and a registered capital of 23.6 billion yuan. These individual industrial and commercial households actually included some private enterprises. The First Session of the Seventh NPC held in April 1988 adopted the Amendment to the Constitution, which confirmed the legal status of the private economy in the socialist ownership structure. In this year, there were 90,581 private enterprises with 1.64 million employees and a registered capital of 8.4 billion yuan; There were 14.53 million individual industrial and commercial households, with 23.05 million employees and a registered capital of 31.2 billion yuan. This is the second business tide emerging in contemporary China.

In 1992, in his Southern Talks, Deng Xiaoping mentioned the old story of "the fool's melon seeds cannot be moved "eight years ago, and directly said that the CPC's policy on the development of the non-public economy cannot be changed, which brought great encouragement to all sectors of society. In October, Jiang Zemin pointed out in the report of the 14th National Congress of the CPC that China should establish a socialist market economy. State owned enterprises, collective enterprises and other enterprises should enter the market and play the leading role of SOEs through equal competition. Foreign capital, resources, technology, talents and the private economy as a beneficial supplement should and can be used by socialism. In terms of ownership structure, public ownership, including ownership by the entire people and collective ownership, was the main body, supplemented by the individual economy, the private economy and the foreign-funded economy. A variety of economic sectors developed together for a long time. Different economic sectors can also voluntarily carry out various forms of joint operations. This established the important position of the individual economy and the private economy, cleared away the ideological confusion and all kinds of obstacles for the development of the non-public economy. In accordance with the spirit of the central authorities, the State Administration for Industry and Commerce relaxed the scope and mode of operation of the private economy and simplified the registration procedures of private enterprises. By the end of 1992, the number of individual industrial and commercial households in China had reached 15.339 million, with 24.677 million employees; the number of private enterprises registered reached 139,000, an increase of 28.8% over 1991; there were 2.318 million employees, an increase of 26% over 1991. In April 1993, the State Administration of Industry and Commerce issued *Several Opinions on Promoting the Development of the Individual Economy and the Private Economy*, putting forward 20 policies of the Chinese government to promote the healthy development of the individual and private economy. In November, the Third Plenary Session of the 14th CCCPC adopted the *Decision of the CCCPC on some Issues Concerning Establishing of the Socialist Market Economy*, which proposed that the establishment of a socialist market economy was to enable the market to play a fundamental role in the allocation of resources under the state's macro-control. To achieve this goal, we must adhere to the principle of taking public ownership as the main body and developing various economic sectors together. As a result, the individual economy, private economy and foreign-funded enterprises have developed rapidly, and the number of registered companies has increased continuously. From 1993 to 1995, China's non-public economy had developed at a high speed, with an average speed of 66% in the three years, reaching 82% in the highest year and 51% in the lowest year. Contemporary China ushered in the third upsurge of doing business.

By the end of the 20th century, China's non-public economy showed a strong trend of rapid development. According to statistics, the number of private enterprises in China had reached 1.589 million, and the number of individual industrial and commercial households was 31.606 million, with 130 million employees. The registered capital of non-public enterprises had reached 1.35 trillion yuan, and became one of the important sources of tax revenues. Since the beginning of reform and opening-up, China's national economy has grown by an average rate of 9.5%, while the individual and private economy has grown at an annual rate of more than 20%, increasing production and creating 6 million jobs each year.

The rapid development of non-public economy has brought profound changes to China's social life. In September 1999, the CCCPC's Several *Opinions on Strengthening and Improving Ideological and Political Work* pointed out: China was at the critical stage of reform and great development, and the social situation had undergone complex and profound changes. The diversifications of economic components and economic interests, social life styles, social organization forms, and employment posts and employment methods were becoming increasingly obvious. This was called the "four diversifications." Diversification of economic components and interests: China has completely broken the single public ownership pattern under the planned economic system, and has formed a situation in which different economic components such as state-owned, collective, individual, private, wholly foreign-owned and China-foreign joint ventures develop together in market competition. With the adjustment of the ownership structure, a variety of interest subjects such as agricultural household contractors, individual industrial and commercial households, private enterprises, collective enterprises, SOEs, foreign-funded enterprises, and joint-stock enterprises have been formed; the reform of press and publication, literary and art groups, and scientific research institutes has made a large number of public institutions face the market, move towards enterprise management, and become relatively independent interest subjects. In addition, with the integration of distribution according to work and distribution according to production factors, the interest subjects have become more diverse. Diversification of social lifestyles: the diversification trend of economic interests, group ownership and access to means of life has promoted the changes of people's living habits, ways of living and values, and the changes of people's consumption, communication and daily life styles. Different groups and different interest subjects have gradually developed their own lifestyles. And because the field of material life is constantly changing, people's social life has to undergo more profound changes. Diversified forms of social organizations: on the one hand, the traditional trade unions, the Communist Youth League, the women's Federation, the Youth Federation, the students' Federation, the China Federation of Literary and Art Circles, the Writers' Association, the Association for Science and Technology, the All-China Journalists Association and other people's organizations and mass organizations are sound and well organized, and continue to play an important role in the construction of socialist material and spiritual civilization. On the other hand, various trade associations, self-employed workers' associations, consumer associations, chambers of Commerce, and a large number of societies, federations, research associations, and friendship associations have covered almost all aspects of social life. In addition, there are various unregistered social organizations that exist and operate. Diversification of employment posts and employment methods: the traditional "all inclusive" employment methods such as "egalitarian practice (of everyone taking food from the same big pot)" and "iron rice bowl" have been broken. The employment introduced by the labor department, the self-employment of workers and finding jobs on their own are combined and mutually complementary. As a result of the reform of the employment system and the cadre system, the number of fixed workers in enterprises has been gradually decreased, and the number of contract workers and temporary workers has been increased. The lifelong employment system of cadres and the principle of "cadres are only prepared to be promoted and not demoted" have been changed. The cadre appointment system, open recruitment and competition for posts have been gradually implemented. Many workers are engaged in secondary occupations in addition to their primary occupations.

The emergence of the "four diversities" trend is not only an inevitable and positive phenomenon brought about by the reform of China's economic, political and cultural systems, but also a positive reflection of people's all-round development. However, it also puts forward new requirements for the ideological and political work of the ruling party and the social management work of the government.

2.4.2 Issues Relating to Agriculture, Rural Areas and the Well-Being of Farmers

Agriculture, rural areas and farmers are of great importance to the reform, opening up and socialist modernization drive. Without stability in the countryside, there will be no stability in the whole country. Without moderately prosperous society for the farmers, there will be no well-off society for the whole people. Without agricultural modernization, there will be no modernization of the entire national economy. China has made remarkable achievements in Rural Reform. However, in the historical process of modernization, rural economic development, spiritual civilization construction, democracy and legal system construction and grass-roots organization construction are facing many new problems. In some places, the central government's rural policies have not been well implemented, and the growth of farmers' income has been slow, which has affected the full play of their enthusiasm. The agricultural infrastructure is weak, the ability to resist natural disasters is not strong, and the pressure on population, resources and environment is increasing. Especially after 1996, agriculture entered a difficult period, and the income gap between farmers and urban residents was widening. The Asian financial crisis in 1997 and the flood disaster in 1998 caused huge losses to the already fragile agricultural production. "Issues relating to agriculture, rural areas and the wellbeing of farmers" gradually surfaced and became the focus of the whole society.

In October 1998, the Third Plenary Session of the 15th CCCPC specially studied and formulated the Decision of the CCCPC on Several Major Issues Concerning Agriculture and Rural Work. The *Decision* fully affirmed the basic experience of rural reform since the Third Plenary Session of the 11th CCCPC, established the goals and principles for the cross century development of agriculture and rural areas, and made the strategic deployment for developing rural productivity and promoting agricultural and rural modernization. The "Decision" proposed that from 1998 to 2010, the goal of building a new socialist countryside with Chinese characteristics was: economically, adhere to the principle of public ownership as the mainstay and the common development of various ownership economies, and constantly emancipate and develop rural productive forces; politically, adhere to the leadership of the CPC, strengthen the building of socialist democratic politics in rural areas, further expand grassroots democracy, and ensure that farmers directly exercise their democratic rights according to law; culturally, continue to promote the building of socialist spiritual civilization in rural areas in an all-round way, and cultivate new farmers with with lofty ideals, moral integrity, intellectual abilities and a strong sense of discipline. To achieve this goal, we must adhere to ten principles: always put agriculture in the first place in the development of the national economy; adhere to the basic policy of long-term rural stability; pay close attention to grain production and actively develop diversified economy; develop agriculture by relying on science and education; promote the sustainable development of agriculture; vigorously develop township enterprises and transfer surplus agricultural labor through multiple channels; lighten farmers' burdens; implement the basic national policy of family planning; promote the construction of rural grassroots democratic politics; pay attention to both material and spiritual civilization. To develop the rural productive forces, we should achieve the following: adhere to a two-tier management system based on household contract management and combined with unification and division; deepen the reform of the circulation system of and improve the market system of agricultural products; speed up the construction of agricultural infrastructure focusing on water conservancy and improve the agricultural ecological environment; rely on scientific and technological progress to optimize the agricultural and rural economic structure; promote the building of moderately prosperous society in rural areas and intensify efforts to tackle key problems in poverty alleviation; strengthen the construction of democracy and legal system at the grass-roots level in rural areas; strengthen the construction of socialist spiritual civilization in rural areas; strengthen the building of grass-roots party organizations and the ranks of cadres in rural areas.

In order to solve the problems of "agriculture, rural areas and farmers" and realize moderately prosperous society in rural areas as soon as possible, in the 1990s, the CPC and the Chinese government took solving the problem of food and clothing for the rural poor as the focus of their work, and made a series of specific arrangements for poverty alleviation and development and tackling key problems. In 1994, the State Council formulated and began to implement the *Seven-Year Priority Poverty Alleviation Program*, which clearly stated that from 1994 to 2000, we should concentrate human, material and financial resources, mobilize the forces of all sectors of society, and strive to basically solve the problem of food and clothing for 80 million poor people in rural areas in about seven years.

The key points of the seven-year program to help 80 million people out of poverty are: (1) By the end of the 20th century, the annual per capita net income of the vast majority of poor households would reach more than 500 yuan, and the basic conditions for stable food and clothing would be met. (2) strengthen infrastructure construction and basically solve the problem of drinking water for people and animals, so that the vast majority of poor townships and towns and places where there are trade fairs and commodity producing areas would have access to roads, extend power grids to all the counties without electricity, and the vast majority of poor townships would have access to electricity. (3) Change the backward situation of education, culture and health, basically popularize primary education, and actively eliminate illiteracy among young and middle-aged people; carry out adult vocational and technical education and technical training so that the majority of young and middle-aged workers can master one or two practical skills; improve medical and health conditions, prevent and reduce endemic diseases and prevent disability; strictly implement family planning and control the natural population growth rate within the limits set by the state.

After seven years of efforts, by the year 2000, remarkable achievements had been made in poverty alleviation and development, and great changes had taken place in the face of poverty-stricken areas. The number of poor people in rural areas who had not solved the problem of food and clothing had decreased to 30 million, accounting for about 3% of the rural population. With the exception of a small number of social security recipients, especially poor people living in areas with poor natural conditions and some disabled people, the problem of food and clothing for the poor in rural areas was basically solved, and the poverty alleviation target set by the central government was basically realized.

While helping the poor, the CPC and the Chinese government have all along attached great importance to reducing the burden on farmers. In March and July 1993, the general office of the CCCPC and the general office of the State Council successively issued the *Emergency Notice on Effectively Reducing the Burden of Farmers* and the *Notice on the Opinions on the Examination and Approval of Projects Involving the Burden of Farmers*, cancelled 37 financing, fee collection and fund-raising projects and 43 activities of the central and state organs for reaching a certain standard or upgrading, and corrected 10 wrong fee collection methods, basically blocking the source of increasing the burden of farmers. The Decision of the CCCPC on Several Major Issues Concerning Agriculture and Rural Work adopted at the Third Plenary Session of the 15th CCCPC in 1998 took *giving more and taking less, so that farmers can get more benefits* as the policy guideline for reducing farmers' burdens. In the 21st century, in order to fundamentally lighten the farmers' burdens, the CCCPC has decided to carry out the tax reform. On March 2, 2000, the CCCPC and the State Council issued the Notice on Carrying out Experimental Reforms of Taxes and Administrative Charges in Rural Areas. The main content of the rural tax reform experimental project is: abolish the administrative fees, government funds and fund-raising specially collected for farmers, such as township overall planning fees and rural education fund-raising; abolish slaughter tax; abolish the labor accumulation workers and voluntary workers under unified regulations; adjust the agricultural tax and all taxes on special agricultural; reform the village retention, collection and use methods. Practice has proved that the central government's decision on the rural tax reform is completely correct and conforms to the rural reality. On this basis, the central authorities decided to further expand the scope of the rural tax reform experiment. In March 2001, the State Council issued the Notice on Further Carrying out Experimental Reforms of Taxes and Administrative Charges in Rural Areas. The general requirements and guidelines are: strengthen leadership and improve policies; expand experimental projects and accumulate experience; carry out the reform in a coordinated manner, steadily implement it, and effectively reduce the burden on farmers, so as to ensure the success of the rural tax reform. The continuous deepening of rural reform has effectively promoted the development of rural economy and the continuous increase of farmers' income, effectively promoted the sustained growth of the entire national economy, and safeguarded the overall situation of reform, development and stability.

The implementation of the above-mentioned measures to solve the "issues relating to agriculture, rural areas and the wellbeing of farmers" has produced great practical results. The country's grain production continuously increased by a large margin, the adjustment of the agricultural structure advanced in depth, the farmers' income increased rapidly, the comprehensive rural reform was gradually deepened, agricultural tax, livestock tax and taxes on special agricultural products were rescinded throughout the country, the rural tax reform achieved major results, social undertakings were further developed, the construction of rural grassroots organizations were strengthened, and the relationship between cadres and the masses were significantly improved. The good situation of agriculture and rural development has played an important supporting role in maintaining steady and rapid growth of the national economy and social stability. However, at the same time, it must also be noted that agriculture and rural development are still in a difficult climbing stage. The contradictions of weak agricultural infrastructure, lagging development of rural social undertakings, and widening income gap between urban and rural residents are still prominent. Solving the "issues relating to agriculture, rural areas and the wellbeing of farmers" is still a major and arduous historical task in the process of industrialization and urbanization.

2.4.3 Reform of Social Security System

Since the Third Plenary Session of the 11th CCCPC in 1978, China's social security system reform has made great achievements. However, the current social security system is far from meeting the objective requirements of the socialist market economy. With the establishment of the modern corporate system, the reform of the labor employment systems, the expansion of the scope of labor mobility, the aging of the population and other problems, the social security system is facing more and more serious challenges. Therefore, the task of further deepening the reform of the social security system is imminent.

In 1993, the Third Plenary Session of the 14th CCCPC adopted the *Decision of the CPC on the Establishing of the Socialist Market Economy*, which proposed that "the establishment of a multi-level social security system is of great significance for deepening the reform of enterprises and institutions, maintaining social stability, and successfully establishing a socialist market economy. The social security system includes social insurance, charities, social welfare, job placement for demobilized servicemen, social mutual aid, and personal savings accumulation.[39] The 15th National Congress of the CPC further proposed that we shall build a social security system, introducing old-age pension and medical insurance systems by combining social pools with individual accounts, and improve the unemployment insurance and social relief systems so as to provide the basic social security. These principles and policies are fully reflected in the reform of the social security system.

We will reform the basic old-age insurance and establish a unified system that combines social pools with individual accounts. On June 26, 1991, the State Council promulgated the *Decision on the Reform of the Old-age Insurance System for Employees of Enterprise*, requiring the implementation of the old-age insurance system jointly borne by the state, enterprises and individuals. In March 1995, the State Council issued the *Circular on Deepening the Reform of the Pension System for Staff and Workers of Enterprises* and the *Measures for the Implementation of the Combination of Social Pools and Personal Accounts of Basic Old-Age Insurance for Enterprise Employees*, which brought the reform of the old-age insurance system into a standardized operation stage. However, due to the differences in the situation of various regions and enterprises, there has been a problem that the contribution rate of basic old-age insurance funds has decreased year by year. In July 1997, the State Council promulgated the *Decision on Establishing the Basic old-age Insurance for Enterprise Employees*, requiring all localities to implement the merger as soon as possible in accordance with the unified plan for basic old-age insurance. In 1998, the CCCPC and the State Council decided to implement the "two guarantees" and establish the "three guarantee lines," taking ensuring the timely and full payment of pensions for enterprise retirees as the main work objective. After several years of promotion, the number of employees participating in basic old-age insurance had increased from 86.71 million at the end of 1997 to 108.02 million at the end of 2001; the number of people receiving basic old-age pensions increased from 25.33 million to 33.81 million, and the average monthly basic pension also increased from 430 yuan to 556 yuan. In order to ensure the timely and full payment of basic old-age pensions, the Chinese government has made efforts to improve the level of basic old-age insurance funds, gradually implemented provincial-level coordination, and constantly increased financial input to the basic old-age insurance funds. From 1998 to 2001, the central government's subsidy expenditure on basic old-age insurance alone reached 86.1 billion yuan. In 2001, the socialized distribution rate of basic pensions reached 98%. By 2001, pensions for retirees were basically be paid in full and on time. In addition, the original old-age security system is still implemented for employees and retirees of government organs and institutions.

On the basis of pilot projects, we promoted the reform of the medical insurance system. Accelerating the reform of the medical insurance system and ensuring the basic medical care of employees are the objective requirements and important guarantees for the establishment and improvement of the socialist market economy. On April 14, 1994, with the approval of the State Council, the System Reform Office of the State Council, the Ministry of Finance, the Ministry of Labor, and the Ministry of Health jointly issued the Opinions on the Pilot Reform of the Employee Medical System, and determined Zhenjiang City in Jiangsu Province and Jiujiang City in Jiangxi Province as the pilot cities for the reform of the medical insurance system for employees. On the basis of the pilot projects in Zhenjiang and Jiujiang, at the end of 1998, the State Council issued the *Decision of the State Council on Establishing the Urban Employee's Basic Medical*

Insurance System, and medical social insurance began to replace the public medical care and labor insurance medical care in the national (unit) security system. The "Decision" proposed that the main task of the reform of the medical insurance system is to establish a basic medical insurance system for urban workers, that is, to adapt to the socialist market economy and establish a social medical insurance system that guarantees the basic medical needs of workers according to the affordability of finance, enterprises and individuals. As for the payment method, the Decision stipulates that the basic medical insurance shall be jointly paid by the employer and the employees. The contributions of the employer shall be controlled at about 6% of the total wages of the employees, and the contribution of the employees is generally 2% of their own wages. With the development of economy, the payment rate of employers and employees can be adjusted accordingly. By the end of 2001, 97% of the prefectures and cities nationwide had initiated the reform of basic medical insurance, with 76.29 million employees participating in basic medical insurance. In addition, the public medical care and other forms of medical security system also covered more than 100 million urban population.

We need to improve the unemployment insurance system. With the continuous advancement of enterprise reform, the establishment of a modern corporate system, the adjustment of the economic structure, the implementation of the policies of the policy of encouraging mergers, standardizing bankruptcy, laying off and reassigning redundant workers, the emergence of a large number of laid-off workers, and the further improvement of China's unemployment insurance system have became important issues in China's labor security work and even the whole social and economic life in the new stage. In April 1993, the State Council promulgated the *Regulations on the Unemployment Insurance for Staff and Workers of the State-Owned Employees*, which marked that China began to re-establish the unemployment insurance system in the process of establishing a socialist market economy system. On January 22, 1999, Decree No. 258 of the State Council, promulgated the *Regulations on Unemployment Insurance*, which provided a strong legal guarantee for the sustained and healthy development of unemployment insurance. From 1998 to 2001, the number of people participating in unemployment insurance increased from 79.28 million to 103.55 million. At the end of 2001, the number of people receiving unemployment insurance benefits was 3.12 million. With the improvement of the unemployment insurance system, the subsistence allowance system for laid-off workers of SOEs was gradually included in the unemployment insurance. By 2001, the vast majority of laid-off workers from SOEs had received subsistence allowances.

We would implement a subsistence allowances system. This was a new form of urban social relief. In June 1993, Shanghai took the lead in establishing subsistence allowances system for urban residents, which was affirmed by the Ministry of Civil Affairs. On the basis of the pilot projects in the eastern coastal areas, in order to properly solve the living difficulties of the urban poor, the State Council decided to establish the system of subsistence allowances for urban residents throughout the country. On September 2, 1997, the State Council issued the *Notice on Establishing an Urban Basic Minimum Living Allowance System Nationwide*, which made clear provisions on the scope, standards, sources of security funds and relevant policies. The target of the system of subsistence allowances for urban residents is urban residents whose per capita family income have not met the standard of subsistence allowance for impoverished urban residents and hold a non-agricultural household registration, mainly including three types of personnel: (1) residents who have no source of income, no working ability, and no fixed or dependent person; (2) residents who have not been reemployed during the period of receiving unemployment benefits or the expiration of unemployment benefits, and whose per capita family income is lower than the standard of subsistence allowance for impoverished urban residents; (3) residents whose per capita family income is still lower than the standard of subsistence allowance for impoverished urban residents after the employees and laid-off workers receive their wages and basic living expenses and the retirees receive their pensions. The standard for subsistence allowances for urban residents shall be determined by the local people's governments independently. In 2001, the number of people receiving subsistence allowances nationwide reached 11.707 million, and the central government invested 2.301 billion yuan in issuing subsistence allowances.

In addition, in January 1994, the State Council promulgated the *Regulations on the Work of Providing Five Guarantees*, and the work of rural Five Guarantees program has been standardized since then. In the same year, the State Council also formulated and promulgated the *Seven-Year Priority Poverty Alleviation Program* and the *Decision on Deepening the Urban Housing System Reform*, which ushered in a new development period for poverty alleviation and housing system reform. Subsequently, the State Council promulgated the *Decision on Health Reform and Development*, which included health system reform in the reform agenda. In March

1998, while retaining the Ministry of Civil Affairs, the new central government established the Ministry of Labor and Social Security, which relatively unified the social security management system. Social security has gradually become a basic social system.

After years of exploration and practice, a social security system framework with Chinese characteristics was put in place. The coverage of social insurance has continued to expand, the subsistence allowances for urban residents have basically expanded the coverage of subsistence allowances to all those in need under dynamic management, and the scope of rural subsistence allowances and living assistance for people in extreme difficulty has been gradually expanded. The socialization of social welfare has been accelerated, and philanthropy has further developed. However, at the same time, we also need to see that the task of developing social security in China is still arduous.

2.4.4 "Flood Control" in 1998

After the flood season in the summer of 1998, due to the abnormal climate, the rainfall in most parts of the country was obviously excessive, and there was persistent heavy rainfall in some areas. The rainfall doubled, causing some places to suffer serious flood disasters. Another Basin-wide flood occurred in the Yangtze River since 1954, with eight flood peaks. The water level of the river section 360 km below Yichang, water level Dongting Lake and Poyang Lake exceeded the historical record for a long time. The Shashi River section once had a high-water level of 45.22 meters. The Nenjiang River and Songhua River had super historical floods, and there were three flood peaks. The Xijiang River in the Pearl River Basin and the Minjiang River in Fujian Province also once had major floods. The economic and social development and the safety of people's lives and property were seriously threatened by floods in many cities and vast rural areas along the rivers and lakes in Hubei, Hunan, Jiangxi, Anhui, Jiangsu, Heilongjiang, Jilin, Inner Mongolia and other provinces.

The CCCPC and the State Council have always paid close attention to the climate change and the flood situation of rivers, and made timely and careful arrangements for the flood control work throughout the country; according to the actual situation of the areas threatened by floods, the strategic principles of strict prevention and defense, ensuring the safety of the Yangtze River levees, important cities, and people's lives were clearly put forward, and the major decision of large-scale use of the PLA in flood control and rescue and coordinated operations of the military and civilians was made. At the most critical moment of flood control and rescue, the CCCPC and the State Council made a correct judgment, and issued a general mobilization order, requiring the broad masses of military and people to strengthen their confidence, persist until the final victory was achieved. The National Flood Control and Drought Relief Headquarters resolutely implemented the Decisions of the CCCPC and the State Council, fully prepared, comprehensively deployed, resolutely commanded and scientifically dispatched, and won the initiative of flood control.

In the whole flood control and rescue work, the CPC and the Chinese government have attached great importance to the lives and vital interests of the people in the disaster areas. The central leaders directly commanded this struggle and was linked with the hearts of the flood fighting troops and the people throughout the struggle. On August 13, at the decisive moment of the flood control and rescue, Jiang Zemin personally went to the front line of Hubei Province to express condolences to the military and people. On the 14th, after listening to the reports of the Hubei Provincial Party committee, the provincial government, and the Guangzhou Military Region on flood control and rescue work, Jiang Zemin delivered a speech entitled "Winning the Final Victory in the Decisive Battle of Flood Control and Rescue in the Yangtze River," and issued a general mobilization order to the flood control troops and people throughout the country. On the 16th, Jiang Zemin issued an order to the PLA participating in the flood control: all troops along the line should go up the embankment, the army and the people should unite to fight a decisive battle, and win a total victory. At the same time, local party and government cadres at all levels were required to lead the masses and work with the officers and men of the armed forces to strictly guard against and defend the levees of the Yangtze River.

In the fight against floods, the party committees and governments at all levels in the affected provinces and regions conscientiously implemented the principles and decisions of the CCCPC and the State Council, strengthened leadership in fighting floods and dealing with emergencies, and went all out to do a good job in mobilization and organization. The PLA and the armed police force dispatched more than 300,000 officers and men to control the flood and rescue. They carried forward the spirit of sacrifice of "fear neither hardship nor death" and the style of continuous fighting without fear of fatigue, and played the role of a mainstay. The people of the whole country carried forward the fine tradition of unity, friendship, mutual assistance of the Chinese nation and carried out various forms of assistance activities, and vigorously supported the front-line military and civilian. After several months of hard work, we have finally ensured the safety of the main embankments of major rivers and lakes, important cities and major traffic arteries, people's lives and property, and reduced the loss of this extraordinarily large natural disaster to the minimum.

In this struggle of flood control, the "great spirit of flood control" was also bred. This is: United as one, not afraid of difficulties, sparing no effort in forging ahead, perseverance, daring to win. This spirit is the development of patriotism, collectivism and the socialist spirit, the development of socialist spiritual civilization the glorious tradition and fine conduct of the CPC and the People's Army, and the concentrated embodiment and new development of the national spirit of the Chinese nation in contemporary China.

2.4.5 Comprehensive Management of Social Security

In the 1990s, China's society entered a period of rapid transformation, and the public security was a relatively severe situation. As the situation changes, the CPC and the Chinese government summed up the historical experience of social security and put forward a comprehensive management method. Comprehensive management of social security is the social system project under the unified leadership of party committees and governments at all levels, organize and rely on the power of the people in various departments and units, using political, economic, administrative, legal, cultural, educational and other means, through strengthening the fight, prevention, education, management, construction, transformation and other aspects of the work, to solve the problem of social security, achieve the fundamental prevention and combat crime, maintain law and order and guarantee social stability.

In February 1991, the CCCPC and the State Council issued the *Decision on Intensifying the Improvement of Social Security by Taking Comprehensive measures*. On March 2 of the same year, the Standing Committee of the NPC adopted the *Decision on Intensifying the Improvement of Social Security by Taking Comprehensive measures*. These two "Decisions" were outline documents for the comprehensive management of social security. They defined the status and role, nature and tasks, objectives and requirements, scope of work, leadership system, principles and guarantee measures of the comprehensive management of social security. They provided an important legal basis for the comprehensive management of social security and marked that the comprehensive management of social security in contemporary China entered a new stage of development.

The main contents of the two Decisions are as follows: (1) Strengthening the comprehensive management of social order is an important task of upholding the people's democratic dictatorship and also a fundamental way to solve the problems of social order in contemporary China. The problem of public security is a comprehensive reflection of various social contradictions. Therefore, we must mobilize and organize the forces of the entire society and use various means to comprehensively deal with it. (2) The comprehensive management of public security must adhere to the principle of striking and preventing at the same time, giving consideration to the symptoms and the root causes, and focusing on the root causes. Its major tasks are: to crack down on all kinds of illegal and criminal activities that endanger society; to strictly manage the system and strengthen public security prevention; strengthen ideological and political education and legal education for all citizens, especially for young people; encourage the masses to consciously maintain social order and fight against illegal and criminal acts; actively mediate civil disputes and alleviate social contradictions; strengthen the education, rescue and reform of those offenders. (3) Be good at using legal weapons to do a good job in the comprehensive management of public security. (4) All departments and units must establish a management responsibility system for comprehensive management objectives, so as to fulfill their duties and cooperate closely. People's governments at all levels should incorporate the comprehensive management of social security into the overall plan for the construction of the two civilizations, earnestly strengthen leadership, and provide support and guarantee in terms of human, material and financial resources. (5) To strengthen the comprehensive management of public security, we must mobilize and rely on the broad masses of the people. (6) We should closely integrate the responsibility for comprehensive management of public security with the political honor and economic interests of units and individuals, and establish a reward and punishment system. (7) People's governments at all levels should organize and implement the comprehensive management of public security, and all departments and all parties should work together and take an active part in it. The standing committees of the people's congresses at all levels shall regularly supervise and inspect the comprehensive management of public security.

Since then, Party committees, governments and "comprehensive management" organizations at all levels have conscientiously implemented the two "Decisions," mobilized the active participation of all sectors of society and the broad masses of the people, and promoted the comprehensive management of social order throughout the country. The Central Committee for the comprehensive management of public security has also successively issued regulations on performing the due responsibilities within the geographical jurisdiction and several regulations on the implementation of the leaders' responsibility system. On November 14, 1993, the Central Committee for the Comprehensive Management of Public Security, the Central Discipline Inspection Commission, the Organization Department of the CCCPC, the Ministry of Personnel, and the Ministry of Supervision jointly issued Several Provisions on the Implementation of the Leaders' Responsibility System for the Comprehensive Management of Public Security, providing a specific policy basis for the implementation of the leaders' responsibility system. All localities have also strengthened system construction around the comprehensive management of public security and established and improved a series of effective rules and regulations. The comprehensive management committees and offices at all levels have improved and perfected the system of regular committee meetings, the system of contact and cooperation among member units, and the system of work inspection, assessment, rewards and punishments. At present, all localities have basically formed a leadership pattern of comprehensive management of public security, with the principal leaders taking the charge personally, the authorized leaders in charge of specific work, and the relevant leaders jointly in charge, driving and promoting the comprehensive implementation of various measures for comprehensive management.

In 1997, Jiang Zemin put forward the guiding opinions on strengthening the comprehensive management of public security in the report of the 15th National Congress of the CPC, which was "to combine punishment with prevention and lay more stress on the latter." All regions across the country have gradually formed a clearer working idea: with the responsibility system taking the lead, the "crackdown" as the primary link, the prevention of crime as the focus, and the grass-roots security creation activities as the carrier, we should vigorously strengthen the grass-roots infrastructure for comprehensive management of public security, organize and coordinate all relevant departments to work together, mobilize the broad masses to actively participate, and effectively implement all measures for comprehensive management of public security to urban and rural grass-roots units. Under the guidance of this thinking, the Central Commission for Comprehensive Management for Public Security deployed special struggles such as "anti-theft," "cracking down on car bandits and road tyrants," "anti-trafficking and banning prostitution" and the rectification of rural public order, and organized and coordinated relevant departments to participate in the "anti-pornography and anti-illegal activities," "cleaning up and rectifying electronic game business places" and the anti-drug struggle. In particular, under the unified leadership of Party committees at all levels, we coordinated relevant departments and organized grassroots forces to fight against cult organizations, crack down on the illegal activities of cult organizations, and educate, rescue, and transform a large number of cult addicts. In 1996 and 2001, according to the unified deployment of the central authorities, the Comprehensive Management Commission carried out the nationwide crackdown throughout the country. On the basis of investigating areas with chaotic public security and serious public security problems, the commission mobilized all forces to carry out key rectification in key areas around railways, schools, enterprises and in areas with chaotic public security. In order to effectively prevent and reduce crimes, many localities set up a work system integrating attack, prevention and control based on their actual conditions. In 2000, the five central ministries and commissions jointly issued the Notice on Investigating the Leadership Responsibility of *Places Where Major Problems Seriously Endangering Social Stability Occurred.* They investigated the leadership responsibility of some places where major problems seriously endangering social stability occurred, issued the investigation notice, investigated the leadership responsibility of these places, and vetoed them. This method has produced good social effects and promoted the implementation of the responsibility system and the comprehensive management of public security.

Summary

In the 1990s, especially after China carried out the reform of the socialist market economy in 1992, Chinese society entered a period of social transformation, and the social structure changed significantly. In the wave of industrial innovation and system reform, the number of workers in traditional industries is decreasing, and their economic and social status cannot be compared with the past. Emerging industries have attracted a large number of young workers with knowledge to join them, and these people have become new forces in the working class. The farmer class under the collective ownership system has also changed. In some provinces, the number of rural migrant workers who leave the land and the hometown has accounted for half of the total rural labor force. The annual peak of the Spring Festival transportation constitutes a wonder in the world, which has truly reflected the mobility of the rural population in China. The traditional labor medical security system can no longer meet the needs of the reform of the socialist market economy. The state has begun to explore a new social security system. In the face of increasingly prominent public security problems, the state has gradually strengthened comprehensive social management, and the public security has been improved significantly.

SECTION 5
A New Diplomatic Pattern of "Peaceful Development"

2.5.1 From "Hiding One's Capacity and Biding One's Time" to "Going Global"

In the late 1990s, according to the development trend of economic globalization, China put forward the strategy of "going global" in a timely manner, forming a new pattern of opening up that combine "bringing in" and "going global."

After analyzing the overall characteristics of the international situation, the report of the 14th National Congress of the CPC believed that "endeavoring to develop a favorable international environment for China's reform, opening up, and making a greater contribution to world peace and development" is the general task of the diplomatic work in the new stage. It emphasizes that China will unswervingly pursue an independent foreign policy of peace, strive to build a peaceful, stable, just and reasonable new international political and economic order and is willing to play a positive role in the work of the UN. This was the beginning when China's diplomacy got rid of the predicament in the late 1980s and early 1990s and began to face the world in an all-round way.

In 1997, in the report of the 15th National Congress of the CPC, the CPC put forward ten propositions for China's Diplomacy: adhere to Deng Xiaoping's thinking on diplomatic work and firmly pursue an independent foreign policy of peace; oppose hegemonism and safeguarding world peace; work to bring about a just and rational new international political and economic order;

respect diversification; uphold good-neighborliness; further strengthen our solidarity and co-operation with other Third World countries; further improve and develop our relations with developed countries on the basis of the Five Principles of Peaceful Coexistence; uphold the principle of equality and mutual benefit, and conduct extensive trade, economic and technological cooperation and scientific and cultural exchanges with all countries and regions to promote common development; take an active part in multilateral activities and give full play to China's role in the United Nations and other international organizations; stay committed to developing friendly relations and cooperation with countries around the world on the basis of the Five Principles of Peaceful Coexistence. The report also said: China is a staunch force safeguarding world peace and regional stability; China's construction needs a long-term peaceful international environment, especially a good surrounding environment; China's development will not pose a threat to any country. If it develops in the future, it will never seek hegemony, because China has a history of being bullied by foreign powers; the development of China needs a long-term peaceful international environment, and above all, we need to maintain good relations with the surrounding countries; China's development will not pose a threat to any country, and when it becomes developed in the future, it will never claim hegemony, because China has a history of being bullied by the great powers.

In December 1997, when Jiang Zemin met with the representatives of the national foreign investment work conference, he put forward "going global" as the national development strategy for the first time. He stressed that it was not only necessary to actively attract foreign enterprises to invest in and set up factories in China, but also necessary to actively guide and organize domestic enterprises with strength to go global, invest and set up factories abroad, and make use of local markets and resources. At the Second Plenary Session of the 15th CCCPC, Jiang Zemin pointed out that in order to cope with the impact of the Asian financial crisis on China's economy and exports, it is necessary to lead and organize step by step and support a number of powerful and advantageous SOEs to go out; we should "bring in" and "go global." These are two closely related and mutually reinforcing aspects of our basic national policy of opening up to the outside world. The *Proposal of the CCCPC for the Formulation of the 10th Five-Year Plan for National Economic and Social Development* was adopted at the Fifth Plenary Session of the 15th CCCPC. It proposed that we should take a more active stance, seize the opportunity, meet the challenges, tend to avoid harm, continuously improve the competitiveness of enterprises, and strive to do better in opening to the outside world, improve the pattern of opening up in all directions, at all levels and in a wide range. We should implement the "going out" strategy and strive to make new breakthroughs in the utilization of domestic and foreign markets and resources.

Driven by the "going out" strategy, China's opening up to the outside world has further expanded, and the intensity of foreign investment has further increased. By the end of 2001, China had participated in 195 overseas resource cooperation projects with a total investment of 4.6 billion U.S. dollars; a total of 6,610 overseas enterprises had been established, of which the Chinese side invested 8.4 billion U.S. dollars. Foreign investment had gradually developed in various forms, such as cross-border mergers and acquisitions, equity exchange, overseas listing, and the establishment of overseas industrial parks. A number of overseas R&D centers and industrial parks had been gradually established, and a number of enterprises had emerged in the international market.

At the same time, from 1992 to 2001, China not only continued to maintain diplomatic exchanges between countries, consolidate good neighborly relations, and establish strategic relations with major countries, but also actively participated in the multilateral international system. For example, on the issue of human rights, China, on the one hand, upheld its own human rights position, and on the other, advocated active dialogue and participation in international human rights protection mechanisms; actively participated in the forming international organizations and tried to have its own influence on the forming rules; and began to gradually put forward its understanding and concepts on international politics.

All these showed that China started to "go out" from "hiding its capacity and biding its time" in the early 1990s, and actively exerted its influence in international affairs. This development and change of China's foreign strategy is mainly due to the fact that with the deepening development of globalization, China has gradually integrated into the process of globalization and has more and more frequent contacts with the international community. The future and destiny of contemporary China are increasingly closely linked with that of the world. China needs to "go out" to better understand the world. It also needs to open its mind to let the world better understand China. Especially in the 21st century, China's national strength has been continuously enhanced, and the international situation is also undergoing profound evolution. In order to make the international situation develop in a direction favorable to China, China needs to "go out," actively participate in international affairs, and expand its own space and room for maneuver on the international stage.

After China joined the WTO in November 2001, new breakthroughs were made in diplomatic thinking and strategy. China has participated in the construction of the multilateral system with a more active and positive attitude, and has really gone out.

China's pursuit of peaceful development is a strategic choice made by the Chinese government and people in accordance with the development trend of the times and their own fundamental interests. It also clarifies the important direction of China's efforts to promote world peace and development.

2.5.2 New Orientation of Major Country Relations

(1) China-US Relations

In China's diplomatic strategy, China-US relations play a very important role. Whether it is China's modernization drive, or the settlement of the Taiwan question and the reunification of the motherland, China-US relations are inevitably involved. After the political turmoil in 1989, China-US relations once reached a deadlock. It was not until 1993, when the first the informal meeting of the leaders of the APEC Organization was held in the United States, and the heads of state of China and the United States held a high-level meeting, that China-US relations began to show a momentum of improvement. However, on May 22, 1995, the US government decided to allow Lee Teng-Hui, leader of the Taiwan region, to pay a so-called "private" visit to the United States in disregard of China's protests. This violated the basic principles of the three Sino-US joint communiqués and led to the drop of Sino-US relations to the lowest point since 1989.

On November 24, 1996, Jiang Zemin and Clinton met in Manila. During the meeting, Clinton stressed: the United States is willing to see a strong, stable and secure China. Our two countries share common strategic interests on many issues. The United States is willing to establish a good cooperative partnership with China. Jiang Zemin also said to US secretary of state Albright, who visited China soon after, that "great changes have taken place in the current international situation. However, China and the United States, as two major countries with great influence in the world, share extensive common interests. In particular, the two countries have great potential for cooperation in developing complementary and mutually beneficial economic cooperation, jointly safeguarding global and regional peace, and promoting world economic prosperity. This is a solid foundation for bilateral relations. Of course, there are some differences between the two sides. The two sides should stand high and take a long view. Proceeding from safeguarding the fundamental interests of the two peoples and promoting peace, stability and prosperity in the world and the Asia Pacific region, the two sides should enhance understanding, seek common ground while reserving differences, and expand cooperation."[40] In such a political atmosphere, the heads of state and government of the two countries exchanged visits from 1997 to 1998.

From October 26 to November 3, 1997, Jiang Zemin paid his first state visit to the United States. During his visit to the United States, he put forward five principles for Developing China-US relations facing the 21st century: (1) persistently examine and handle China-US relations from a strategic perspective and a long-term perspective, and firmly grasp the overall situation of bilateral relations; (2) actively seek the convergence of common interests, and consider not only our own interests, but also the interests of the other side; (3) abiding by the three *Sino-US Joint Communiques* is the foundation for developing China-US relations; (4) correctly handle differences between the two countries in the spirit of mutual respect, equal consultation and seeking common ground while reserving differences; (5) properly handle the Taiwan question. The two sides issued the *Sino-US Joint Statement*, which stated that they would work together to establish a constructive strategic partnership between China and the United States. From June 25 to July 3, 1998, US President Clinton paid a return visit to China. The two sides once again defined the establishment of a constructive strategic partnership as the direction forward for China-US relations, and China-US relations were greatly improved.

On May 8, 1999, the US led North Atlantic Treaty Organization (NATO) brazenly bombed the Chinese Embassy in the Federal Republic of Yugoslavia, and China-US relations once again fell to a low point. In September, when attending the informal meeting of leaders of the APEC Organization in Singapore, President Jiang Zemin and President Clinton met and reached consensus on continuing to promote the constructive strategic partnership between China and the United States. At the end of the same year, China and the United States reached an agreement on China's accession to the WTO, and China-US relations began to develop on a healthy track. In 2001, after George W. Bush became president of the

United States, he pursued a unilateralist foreign policy and positioned Sino-US relations as a "strategic competitive partner," making China-US relations, which had just eased, tense. In April 2001, the plane collision incident between China and the United States made China-US relations face a severe test again. However, after the "9.11" incident in the same year, the common interests of China and the United States on the issue of counter-terrorism promoted the elimination of the shadow of China-US diplomacy. In October 2001, President Bush and President Jiang Zemin met in Shanghai during the informal meeting of leaders of the APEC Organization, which opened up new prospects for the development of bilateral relations. China-US relations have developed again under the framework of "building a constructive strategic partnership." Since then, China-US pragmatic cooperation has been further strengthened and developed.

(2) China-Russian Relations

After the disintegration of the Soviet Union, China was one of the first countries to recognize Russia's independence and appointed the former ambassador to the Soviet Union as the ambassador to Russia. In 1992, Russian President Yeltsin visited China for the first time. At the end of the talks, the two sides issued the *Joint Statement of the PRC and the Russian Federation on the Basis of Mutual Relations*, which established the state relations of non-alliance, non-confrontation, good neighborliness, friendship and mutually beneficial cooperation between the two countries. In 1994, Jiang Zemin successfully visited Russia. The two sides issued the *Joint Statement between the PRC and the Russian Federation*, which officially announced that China and Russia had established a "constructive partnership oriented to the 21st century," and expressed that the two sides were willing to continue to develop friendly and cooperative relations, believing that such relations are an important part of security, stability and economic prosperity in the Eurasian continent and the Pacific region. China Russia relations are not aimed at any third country. China and Russia neither seek hegemony nor expansion. In April 1996, Yeltsin visited China for the second time, and the relations between the two countries were further developed and upgraded to "a strategic partnership coordination oriented to the 21st century based on equality and mutual trust." In November 1998, during his visit to Russia, Jiang Zemin further explained this in his speech at the Science City of Novosibirsk: "China wishes to be Russia's good neighbor, good friend and good partner forever on the basis of equality and mutual benefit to promote common prosperity. This is the most fundamental and important significance of the strategic and cooperative partnership developed by our two countries-a partnership oriented toward the 21st century."[41]

After entering the 21st century, followed by the comprehensive construction of good neighborly and friendly relations in the 1990s, China-Russian relations have entered the best period of bilateral exchanges in history, showing the characteristics of the times and the state of seeking truth and pragmatism.

First, China-Russian political and strategic relations have continued to write new chapters.

In March 2000, Putin was elected president of Russia. He inherited Yeltsin's friendly policy toward China. In July, President Putin visited China for the first time. The two sides signed the *Beijing Declaration*, the *Joint Statement on the Anti-Ballistic Missile Issue* and the agreements between seven other government departments. The *Beijing Declaration* stressed that the strategic partnership coordination between China and Russia based on equality and trust and oriented to the 21st century fully conformed to the fundamental interests of the two peoples. In July 2001, President Jiang Zemin visited Russia, signed the *Treaty of Good-neighborliness and Friendly Cooperation between the PRC and Russian Federation* with President Putin, and issued the *Joint Statement of the Heads of State of China and Russia*. The statement pointed out that the *Treaty of Good-Neighborliness and Friendly Cooperation between China and Russia* was an important milestone in the history of bilateral relations, marking those bilateral relations have entered a new stage.

Second, the economic and trade relations between China and Russia are on the right track, showing a trend of in-depth development.

After Putin came to power in 2000, with the improvement of Russia's economic situation, China-Russian trade also entered the fast lane. According to the statistics of the General Administration of Customs of China, in 2000, the total trade volume between China and Russia was 8.003 billion U.S. dollars, an increase of 39.9% year on year. In 2001, the trade volume between China and Russia reached 10.67 billion U.S. dollars, compared with 11.927 billion U.S. dollars in 2002. More importantly, China-Russian trade has taken the form of multi-level and multi-channel. There is not only special trade between governments, but also border trade, barter trade, compensatory trade, the trade between the inhabitants of border areas and tourism shopping. The Russian-Chinese trade has been optimized, from the initial Russian exchange of raw materials and primary processed products for Chinese daily necessities to the trade for products with higher technological content. The fields of China-Russian economic cooperation have also been expanded to include industry, agriculture, forestry, energy, transportation, environmental protection, military industry, peaceful use of atomic energy and space. China and Russia have established a number of joint ventures and cooperative enterprises.

In addition, after entering the new century, China and Russia have become increasingly close in science and technology, culture, education, and a large number of non-governmental exchanges, which have enhanced mutual understanding and traditional friendship between the two peoples and added many new positive elements to the good neighborly and friendly bilateral relations.

(3) China-Japanese Relations

Japan is a close neighbor separated by a strip of water from China. After the end of the cold war, while China-Japan relations have been developing deeper and wider, some new contradictions and frictions between the two countries have been constantly emerging, and China-Japan relations have entered a historical stage in which competition and cooperation coexist.

The Chinese Communists, with Comrade Jiang Zemin as the main representative, have always attached importance to diplomatic work with Japan and stressed the need to climb high and look far to promote the steady development of China-Japan friendly cooperation. In November 1998, Jiang Zemin paid an official visit to Japan. China and Japan issued the *Sino-Japan Joint Declaration*, declaring that the two countries would establish a *friendly cooperative partnership committed to peace and development*. On the basis of the *Sino-Japanese Joint Statement* and the *China-Japan Treaty of Peace and Friendship*, the declaration comprehensively summed up the positive and negative experiences and lessons of bilateral exchanges, and pointed out the direction for the healthy and stable development of China-Japan relations in the new century. In the spirit of taking history as a mirror and facing the future, China and Japan agreed to establish a friendly and cooperative partnership committed to peace and development. The *Sino-Japan Joint Declaration* issued by the two countries was the third important document guiding bilateral relations after the *Sino-Japanese Joint Statement* of 1972 and the *China-Japan Treaty of Peace and Friendship* of 1978. It has a far-reaching impact on the long-term development of bilateral relations and reflected the fundamental interests and common aspirations of the two peoples, and conforms to the trend of the times of peace and development.

On the basis of adhering to the principles and spirit of the two political documents reached between China and Japan, Jiang Zemin also proposed that China and Japan should "take history as a mirror and face the future" in the light of the new situation and changes in China-Japan relations since the end of the cold war, and hoped that Japan would continue to follow the path of peaceful development. Jiang Zemin said that in recent years, the repeated statements in Japan that denied aggression and even beautified war and colonial rule cannot but arouse the severe condemnation and high vigilance of the Chinese people and the Asian people, and were bound to arouse the dissatisfaction of the Japanese people. Only by conscientiously drawing lessons from history, deeply repenting of its crimes of aggression, and adhering to the path of peaceful development can Japan win the understanding and trust of Asian countries and the international community, and prevent the recurrence of historical tragedies.

In dealing with the frictions and problems in the development of China-Japan relations, the Chinese Communists represented by Comrade Jiang Zemin had shown a high degree of principality. In response to the erroneous words and deeds of the Japanese government that violated the political commitments made on the Taiwan question after the cold war, Jiang Zemin solemnly pointed out that the Taiwan question concerned China's territorial sovereignty and the great cause of reunification, and affected the feelings of 1.2 billion Chinese people. We hoped that the Japanese side would earnestly respect the Chinese government's position on the Taiwan question, abide by its solemn commitments on the Taiwan question made in the *Sino-Japanese Joint Statement*, and properly handle the Taiwan question. In view of the fact that Japan US security cooperation included Taiwan in its scope and obstructed the process of China's peaceful reunification after the cold war, Jiang Zemin sharply pointed out that whether Japan-US security cooperation directly or indirectly includeded Taiwan in it was an infringement on China's territorial sovereignty and interference in China's internal affairs. The Chinese government and people firmly opposed this. On the Diaoyu Islands issue, on November 24, 1996, when attending the Fourth Informal Meeting of APEC leaders in Manila, Jiang Zemin stressed that "Diaoyu Islands are an inalienable part of Chinese territory ... It is hoped that the Japanese side can take further measures, especially to prevent Japanese right-wing forces from creating new incidents again."[42]

(4) China-EU Relations

After the end of the cold war, with the strengthening of European integration, the EU has gradually become an important force on the world stage. Since 1992, China's relations with the EU have made considerable progress. In July 1995, the EU put forward the Report *on the long-term policy of China-Europe relations*, stating that it would develop political, economic and trade relations with China in an all-round way. In November 1996, the EU issued the *New EU strategy for Cooperation with China*, which emphasized the "comprehensiveness, long-term nature and independence" of its China policy. Since 1998, China and the EU have established an annual summit mechanism. The two sides agreed to establish a long-term and stable China-EU constructive partnership oriented to the 21st century. In 2001, a comprehensive partnership was established between China and EU.

2.5.3 "Implementing Amity, Sincerity, Mutual Benefit"

After the end of the cold war, due to the profound changes in the world pattern, especially the disintegration of the Soviet Union and the outbreak of the Afghan war in 2001, China's surrounding environment is more complicated than in the past. It has become an extremely important issue in China's diplomatic strategy to properly handle relations with neighboring countries. Since 1992, because the Chinese government has developed relations with neighboring countries in the principle of peace, friendship, mutual benefit and cooperation, China's surrounding environment has maintained a good development trend on the whole. China has proven itself to be a good neighbor, good friend and good partner of its neighboring countries through practical actions.

In Northeast Asia, after the end of the cold war, the traditional friendly relations between China and the Democratic People's Republic of Korea (DPRK) have further developed. In 2001, Jiang Zemin successfully visited the DPRK and put forward the guiding principle of "inheriting the fine tradition and be future-oriented, good neighborliness and friendship, and strengthening cooperation" in bilateral relations. The traditional friendship between China and the DPRK has been consolidated and developed. After George W. Bush was elected president of the United States, he pursued the strategy of "unilateralism" and "preemption," interrupted the dialogue with the DPRK, and declared that the DPRK was an "axis of evil." On the other hand, the DPRK announced that it would accelerate the pace of manufacturing nuclear weapons, and the situation on the Korean

Peninsula suddenly became tense. Proceeding from the overall situation, China has made unremitting efforts to mediate actively, and has successfully facilitated the Three-Party and Six-Party Talks, thus avoiding the escalation of tension on the peninsula and playing a constructive role in maintaining peace and stability in Northeast Asia. In August 1992, China and the Republic of Korea (ROK) established diplomatic relations, and the relations between the two countries developed rapidly, with extensive cooperation in the political, economic, cultural, scientific and technological fields. In November 1998, ROK President Kim Dae-Jung visited China. The two sides agreed to establish a China-ROK cooperative partnership oriented to the 21st century on the basis of the principles of the *UN Charter*, the spirit of the communique on the establishment of diplomatic relations between China and the ROK, and good neighborly and friendly cooperation between the two countries.

After the end of the cold war, ASEAN has further become an integrated political, economic and security cooperation organization based on economic cooperation in Southeast Asia. China is committed to developing friendly relations and cooperation with ASEAN. In July 1991, Chinese State Councilor and Foreign Minister Qian Qichen was invited to participate in the relevant activities of the 24th ASEAN foreign ministers' meeting held in Kuala Lumpur for the first time, which opened the dialogue process between China and ASEAN. In 1996, after China became the comprehensive dialogue partner of ASEAN, the two sides established the ASEAN-China Joint Cooperation Committee in February 1997, which established the overall dialogue framework of the two sides. In December 1997, Jiang Zemin attended the first China-ASEAN informal summit meeting, which defined the direction and guiding principles of the China-ASEAN "good neighborly partnership of mutual trust oriented to the 21st century." In 2001, China proposed the establishment of a free trade area in Northeast Asia between China and ASEAN.

In South Asia, after the normalization of relations between China and India in the late 1980s, the exchanges between the two countries in the fields of economy, trade, science and technology, culture and so on have increased rapidly. In September 1993, Indian Prime Minister Rao visited China and the two sides signed the *Agreement between the Government of the PRC and the Government of the Republic of India on the Maintenance of Peace and Tranquility along the Line of Actual Control In china-India Border Areas*. In 1996, when Jiang Zemin visited India, the two sides unanimously agreed to establish a constructive cooperative partnership oriented to the 21st century on the basis of the Five Principles of Peaceful Coexistence. In March 2000, China and India held the first round of security dialogue. In May, Indian president Narayanan paid a state visit to China. The two sides exchanged views and reached consensus on bilateral relations and regional and international issues of common concern. In January 2002, Premier Zhu Rongji paid an official visit to India. The two sides signed six cooperation documents in tourism, science and technology, water conservancy, space and other fields to further promote the comprehensive development of China-India relations. In 1996, China and Pakistan announced to jointly build a comprehensive cooperative partnership oriented to the 21st century. After the establishment of the new Afghan government in December 2001, the Chinese government immediately recognized it.

At this stage of development, China has been playing an increasingly important role in maintaining regional peace and promoting common development. During the Asian financial crisis in 1997, China, proceeding from the common interests of Asian countries, insisted on the stability of the value of the RMB and provided assistance to relevant countries within its capacity, which played a major role in the final victory of Asian countries over the crisis.

In addition, it needs to be specially pointed out that at this stage of development, new China had also ushered in the "second climax" of diplomatic negotiations in the history of the Republic to solve the land border issues around it, and basically settled the issues left over from the history of new China.

At this stage of development, after decades of arduous development, new China's diplomacy has gone from "weak" to "strong" and from "difficult" to "open." It has come through all the ups and downs, and has been active in the international community and international relations system as a major country and "a responsible builder." It is against the background of this unprecedented good situation that the diplomatic negotiations and demarcation of the land border issue of new China made unprecedented breakthroughs and major progress in the same historical period, ushering in the "second climax" following the "first climax" from the second half of the 1950s to the first half of the 1960s. Diplomatic negotiations were held between China and the Soviet Union and its successor, Russia, and its new land neighbors, Kazakhstan, Kyrgyzstan, and Tajikistan, which became independent from the Soviet Union, as well as with Vietnam and Laos, to formally demarcate all bilateral land borders except for the China-Indian, China-Bhutan, and part of the China-Russian borders.

On May 16, 1991, the Chinese and Soviet governments formally signed the *Agreement on the Eastern Section of the China-Russia Boundary Line between the PRC and the Russian Federation*. So far, the eastern border line of the bilateral land border between China and the Soviet Union, which was about 4,300 km long, had been basically demarcated in the form of international treaties with bilateral and multilateral legal binding force. On September 3, 1994, the Chinese and Russian governments formally signed the *Agreement on the Eastern Section of the China-Russia Boundary Line between the PRC and the Russian Federation*. So far, the western border line of the bilateral land border between China and the Russia had been basically demarcated in the form of international treaties with bilateral and multilateral legal binding force. Through the *China Kazakhstan Border Agreement*, the *Supplementary Agreement on the Border between China and Kazakhstan* and the *Second Supplementary Agreement on the Border between China and Kazakhstan* signed successively in 1994, 1997 and 1998, the 1,783 km long China Kazakhstan border was officially demarcated. The 1084 km long China-Kyrgyz border was formally demarcated through the *Sino-Kyrgyz Border Agreement* and the *Sino-Kyrgyz Border Supplementary Agreement* signed in 1996 and 1999. Through the *China Tajikistan Border Agreement* and the *China Tajikistan Border Supplementary Agreement* signed in 1999 and 2002, the 490-kilometer-long China-Tajikistan border was formally demarcated. On December 30, 1999, the penultimate day before the end of the 20th century, the Chinese and Vietnamese governments formally signed the *Land Border Treaty between the PRC and the Socialist Republic of Vietnam*, which formally demarcated the 1,440 km long land border between China and Vietnam. As early as October 24, 1991, the governments of China and Laos formally signed the Border Treaty between the PRC and the Lao People's Democratic Republic, which formally demarcated the land border line between China and Laos, which was more than 500 kilometers long. In addition, in the "first climax" period, China formally demarcated and delineated the bilateral land border lines between China-Myanmar, China-Nepal, China-Pakistan, China-Arab Emirates, China-DPRK and China-Mongolia through diplomatic negotiations. New China signed border treaties with 12 of its 14 Land neighbors in succession, making more than 90% of China's 22,000-kilometer-long land border lines officially confirmed in modern international relations and the international law system. Only the remaining 2,000 kilometers of land borders between China and India and China and Bhutan remain to be resolved through bilateral diplomatic negotiations. That is to say, through the unremitting efforts of the CPC and the Chinese government, the land and territorial outline of the PRC, an emerging nation-state, is finally becoming clearer and clearer, and the "embarrassing" situation of "borders without boundary" in the history of Chinese civilization for thousands of years will finally turn over its last heavy page.

2.5.4 Write a New Chapter in Relations with Developing Countries

As the largest developing country in the world, China's relations with other developing countries in Asia, Africa and Latin America have witnessed new development since the 1990s.

After entering the new stage, the friendly relations between China and Arab countries had been further deepened. In August 1993, the Arab League office in Beijing was officially established. In the late 1990s, in order to reverse the unfavorable situation of the slow development of bilateral economic relations, China and Arab began to take positive and pragmatic measures to promote comprehensive cooperation and economic and trade development. In December 1997, the two sides put forward four suggestions on consolidating and developing the long-term and stable cooperative relations between China and Arab League facing the 21st century: Mutual respect and equal treatment; maintain dialogue and consultation; carry out mutually beneficial cooperation and seek common development; support each other in international affairs. In January 1999, China and Arab League signed a memorandum of understanding on the establishment of a political consultation mechanism. Subsequently, China established a diplomatic consultation mechanism with most Arab countries.

China-Africa friendship and cooperation goes way back. Since the 1980s, China-Africa relations have withstood the test of sudden changes in the international situation and continued to maintain strong vitality. In May 1996, Jiang Zemin visited Africa and put forward five suggestions for building long-term stability and comprehensive cooperation in China-Africa relations facing the 21st century: sincere friendship, equal treatment, unity and cooperation, common development, and facing the future. In the 21st century, it has become the consensus of both sides to enhance China-Africa cooperation. In October 2000, the "Forum on China-Africa Cooperation" was launched in Beijing, establishing a collective dialogue mechanism between China and African countries, thus injecting new vitality into the development of China-Africa relations in the new era. The first ministerial meeting of the Forum on China-Africa Cooperation announced that China and Africa would establish a new type of partnership featuring long-term stability, equality and mutual benefit. In 2000, China-Africa trade volume reached 10.6 billion U.S. dollars.

Since the 1990s, China's relations with Latin American countries have also continued to develop. China has always maintained dialogue relations at the foreign minister level with the Rio Group, one of the most representative regional political consultative bodies in Latin America. In 1994, China became an observer state of the Latin American Integration Association (LAIA). In May 1997, the Caribbean Development Bank officially accepted China as a member state of the bank. In October of the same year, the delegation of MERCOSUR, an important organization of South American integration, visited China and held the first dialogue with China. In April 2001, Chinese President Jiang Zemin put forward the direction for the development of China-Latin American friendly and cooperative relations: enhance understanding, treat each other as equals, and become friends of mutual trust; strengthen consultation, support each other and safeguard the legitimate rights and interests of China and Latin America internationally; mutual benefit and common development, and strive to expand economic and trade cooperation; face the future, look forward to the long term, and establish extensive and comprehensive cooperative relations.

2.5.5 Multilateral Diplomacy of a "Responsible Major Country"

At the beginning of the end of the cold war, the international environment faced by China was not optimistic. Some western countries-imposed sanctions on China on the pretext of the 1989 political turmoil in China, which affected the relations between China and Western powers. The 14th National Congress of the CPC in 1992 once again emphasized that opening up to the outside world was essential for reform and construction, and that all the advanced civilizational achievements created by all countries in the world, including developed capitalist countries, should be absorbed and utilized for the development of socialism, and that closure would only lead to backwardness. The report of the 15th National Congress of the CPC proposed that we should uphold the principle of equality and mutual benefit, and conduct extensive trade, economic and technological cooperation and scientific and cultural exchanges with all countries and regions to promote common development. We should take an active part in multilateral diplomatic activities and give full play to China's role in the United Nations and other international organizations. According to this guiding ideology, China has actively expanded multilateral diplomacy, further integrated into the international community. China has actively and extensively participated in various activities in the multilateral political, economic and social fields, promoted international development and cooperation, and is an important participant in many major global and regional issues. Its attitude and stance have important weight and have had a major international impact. Chinese leaders have increasingly participated in the discussions of major international issues in international organizations and focused on strengthening cooperation in the multilateral international field. More and more important world and regional international conferences have been held in China. China's multilateral diplomacy has shown the most active situation since the birth of new China, and has also shown distinct characteristics.

China has more comprehensively and deeply participated in the multilateral activities of international organizations with the United Nations as the focus, and played its role. As the center of international cooperation and the authoritative multilateral diplomatic arena, the United Nations is an important channel for China to observe, understand and influence the world. It is also an important place for China to state its own interests and propositions. The pace of China's active participation in UN peacekeeping operations has been further accelerated, and it has successively provided assistance by sending military observers, military liaison officers, military advisors, engineering units and other military personnel to the United Nations Truce Supervision Organization (UNTSO), the United Nations Iraq Kuwait Observation Mission (UNIKOM), the United Nations Advance Mission in Cambodia (UNAMIC), the UN Mission on Referendum in Western Sahara (MINURSO), the United Nations Operation in Mozambique (UNOMOZ) and the United Nations Observer Mission in Liberia (UNOMIL) and the United Nations Mission in Sierra Leone (UNAMSIL) and other UN peacekeeping organizations. China has extensively participated in UN activities in the multilateral economic field and actively promoted dialogue between the north and south and South-South cooperation. China has repeatedly called on developed countries to fulfill their official development assistance commitments to developing countries in full and on time, increase direct investment, reduce the debt burden of developing countries, reverse the flow back of funds, eliminate protectionism, and promote international economic and technological cooperation with developing countries. China actively promotes the reform of the United Nations. China has always believed that the United Nations plays an irreplaceable role in international affairs. China firmly supports the reform of the United Nations so as to strengthen the role of the United Nations and multilateral cooperation and better respond to global threats and challenges. In September 2000, at the initiative of China, the heads of the five permanent members of the Security Council, China, the United States, Russia, Britain and France, who attended the United Nations Millennium Summit, held their first meeting in the history of the United Nations.

We have extensively participated in various intergovernmental international organizations with the United Nations as the core, various global international conferences and international mechanisms, and actively participated in international affairs, providing favorable external conditions for China's accelerated development. With the enhancement of its comprehensive national strength, China's influence and leading role are also growing in the process of participating in international multilateral activities. Deepening its relations with international organizations is an important way for China to further move towards the world, safeguard and expand its own interests, and better assume its international responsibilities. It is also an inevitable choice for China to step onto the international multilateral diplomatic stage with a more active and open attitude. For example, in September 1995, China successfully hosted the Fourth World Conference on Women in Beijing, which was unprecedented in the history of the United Nations. The *Beijing Declaration and Action Plan* adopted by the conference have had a cross century impact on the development of the global women's cause and have further promoted the in-depth development of China's women's cause.

In addition to actively participating in the multilateral activities of the United Nations, China has also increasingly participated in the multilateral activities carried out by regional international organizations. China has actively participated in and vigorously promoted the development of regional international organizations, and is committed to building a regional system platform for multilateral diplomacy. China has initiated or established the SCO and the Boao Forum for Asia, established the China-ASEAN "10 + 1" cooperation mechanism and the China-EU summit regular meeting system, actively participated in and vigorously promoted the cooperation process between the APEC Organization and various Latin American subregional organizations, and promoted the formation and operation of the Six-Party Talks mechanism on the Korean nuclear issue. China has gradually established, actively expanded and effectively utilized various forms of multilateral cooperation mechanisms with more and more international organizations or conferences as carriers. Regional international organizations represented by the European Union and the North American Free Trade Area have become two major economic sectors in the world. China has increasingly strengthened economic and cultural exchanges and cooperation with them. The APEC is an important economic cooperation organization developed under the new historical conditions to adapt to the diversity of the Asia-Pacific region. China's multilateral diplomacy in this organization is extremely active. Since the Seattle Conference in 1993, the Chinese president has participated in the organization's informal leadership meetings for 15 consecutive times, which shows that China attaches great importance to the organization. At the Bogor Conference in 1994, Jiang Zemin advocated the convening of a meeting of ministers of ministries of science and technology in the Asia Pacific region. At the Subic Conference in 1996, Jiang Zemin put forward the famous "APEC approach," which has won wide consensus from other countries. In 1997, at the Manila meeting, Jiang Zemin proposed the establishment of a "Science and Technology Industrial Park oriented to the Asia-Pacific Economic Cooperation Forum" to promote cooperation and exchanges among industrial parks. In 1998, the Chinese government also set up a Science and Technology Industry Cooperation Fund with 1 million U.S. dollars. At the Olank Conference in 1999, China proposed to deepen the level of economic and technological cooperation. At the Brunei Conference in 2000, China initiated to hold the APEC high level meeting on human resources capacity building. In 2001, China, as the host, successfully hosted the 13th APEC Ministerial Meeting and the Nineth informal APEC leaders' meetings, and adopted such important documents as the Digital APEC Strategy and the Shanghai Consensus. By participating in APEC activities, China has further actively developed friendly and cooperative relations with Asia Pacific countries. Now, APEC has become an important international stage for China to exert its influence as a major country. More and more people have gradually enhanced their understanding of China's status as a regional power through China's participation in APEC affairs.

The multilateral diplomacy between China and EU countries began with the first Asia-Europe Meeting (ASEM) between the 15 EU countries and the 10 Asian countries held in March 1996. During the second ASEM meeting in 1998, EU countries and Chinese leaders met for the first time and decided to hold a China-EU summit every year, thus forming the annual China-EU summit mechanism. ASEM stipulates that a summit meeting be held every two years. Under the ASEM mechanism and the China-EU summit mechanism, China has actively participated in such multilateral meetings as the informal meeting of senior officials of Asia-Europe in Brussels, the Asia-Europe Business Forum, the Asia-Europe Business Conference, the Asia-Europe foreign ministers' meeting, and the Asia-Europe economic ministers' meeting. Since China and the EU both attach importance to the international multilateral system and global governance rules with the United Nations at the core, and share common interests in international politics, economy, security and sustainable development, bilateral and multilateral cooperation between the two sides has further promoted the China-EU comprehensive strategic partnership. Through the ASEM, China's influence in the world's politics and economy is growing.

Starting from the establishment of political mutual trust with neighboring countries, China has actively carried out multilateral diplomatic work. On the one hand, it has solved the historical problems left over by the cold war with relevant countries, and on the other hand, it has actively expanded new areas of cooperation with neighboring countries on the basis of good neighborliness and mutual trust. From 1992 to 1995, China and Russia, Kazakhstan, Kyrgyzstan, Tajikistan and other countries successively signed border agreements or agreements on strengthening trust in the military field. In 1991, China and ASEAN began the dialogue process; in July of that year, Chinese State Councilor and Foreign Minister Qian Qichen attended the opening ceremony of the 24th ASEAN foreign ministers' meeting, marking the beginning of China as an ASEAN's consultation partner. In 1997, China and ASEAN established a partnership of good neighborliness and mutual trust. In 2002, China and ASEAN countries signed the Declaration on the Conduct of Parties in the South China Sea (DOC), emphasizing the peaceful settlement of disputes in the South China Sea through friendly consultations and negotiations. Taking the opportunity of strengthening the cooperation mechanisms with China-ASEAN "10 + 1" and "10 + 3" (ASEAN-China, Japan, ROK), China has made great efforts to enhance the economic integration in East Asia and close economic cooperation with East Asian countries. In 2000, Zhu Rongji put forward the idea of establishing the China-ASEAN (10 + 1) free trade area at the fourth China ASEAN leaders' meeting, and put forward a series of constructive suggestions on how to strengthen mutually beneficial cooperation within the framework of "10 + 1" and "10 + 3." In 2001, China and ASEAN countries decided to establish a free trade area with a population of 1.7 billion, a GDP of 2 trillion U.S. dollars and a trade volume of 1.2 trillion U.S. dollars within 10 years. On November 4, 2002, leaders of China and ASEAN signed the *Framework Agreement on Comprehensive Economic Cooperation between the PRC and the Association of Southeast Asian Nations*, marking the formal launch of the process of establishing the China-ASEAN Free Trade Area. The establishment of China-ASEAN Free Trade Area not only has helped to build China's overall strategy of regional economic integration, but also helped to promote the process of regional economic cooperation in Southeast Asia and the formation of the East Asian economic circle, and ultimately created good external development conditions for China. In 2003, China and ASEAN established the strategic partnership for peace and prosperity. While strengthening political mutual trust and vigorously developing economic cooperation with neighboring countries and regions, China has also promoted regional security cooperation in the light of the new situation and achieved a series of positive results. The SCO is a typical example of China's initiative to establish a multilateral mechanism for the first time. It is also a product of Member States' demand to collectively safeguard regional security. It is developed on the basis of the Shanghai Five mechanism. After the disintegration of the Soviet Union, the border issue left over from history between China and the Soviet Union immediately became a common issue between China and Russia, Kazakhstan, Kyrgyzstan and Tajikistan. In 1996, the heads of state of China, Russia, Kazakhstan, Kyrgyzstan and Tajikistan held their first meeting in Shanghai, and the Shanghai Five mechanism was officially launched. The "Shanghai Five" cooperation began to expand from focusing on military security to focusing on military security as well as anti-terrorism cooperation. In July 1998, the leaders of the five countries issued the *Declaration of Alma-Ata*, stating that "any form of national separatism, ethnic exclusion and religious extremism is unacceptable." The five countries "will take measures to combat international terrorism, organized crime, smuggling of weapons, drug and narcotics trafficking and other transnational criminal activities." In June 2001, the SCO was officially established in Shanghai. The leaders of Uzbekistan and the heads of state of the "Shanghai Five" Member States jointly signed the Declaration on the Establishment of the SCO, which marked that the original "Shanghai Five" successfully realized its important function expansion. To a great extent, the SCO has improved the geo-security environment around China, making China in a very favorable strategic situation in the northeast and northwest for the first time.

In addition to establishing the SCO aimed at maintaining peace, stability and development, and promoting regional multilateral diplomatic practices such as ASEAN, China, Japan and South Korea (ASEAN Plus Three countries) cooperation, China has also actively carried out shuttle diplomacy to resolve the nuclear issue on the Korean Peninsula, promoted the establishment of a multilateral security mechanism in Northeast Asia, and is committed to maintaining peace and stability in Northeast Asia. In order to properly handle the conflicts and frictions in the surrounding regions with the attitude of seeking common ground while reserving differences, China has vigorously advocated the unity and mutual assistance of Asian countries. Through strengthening regional cooperation mechanisms, China has striven for "win-win" and strengthened communication and cooperation with its neighboring countries in global affairs, thus continuously enhancing the cohesion of Asia, especially East Asia.

The vast number of developing countries are the most firm allies and "all-weather" friends that China can rely on in carrying out multilateral diplomatic activities. The establishment of the emerging multilateral consultation and cooperative mechanism is a major measure for China to upgrade the cooperation with the vast number of developing countries in the new century. The Chinese government attaches great importance to multilateral friendly cooperation with existing regional and subregional organizations in Latin America and regards it as an important component of South-South cooperation. The foreign minister level dialogue between China and the Rio Group, one of the most influential regional political coordination and consultation institutions in Latin America, has formed a fixed mechanism. At the end of 2000, China established a system of political consultation between the ministries of foreign affairs with 12 Latin American countries and the Andean Community, and constantly raised the level of attendance at the Forum for East Asia-Latin America Cooperation. In addition, as an observer, China has participated in the activities of Latin American regional and subregional organizations such as the Inter-American Development Bank, the LAIA, and the UN Economic Commission for Latin America and the Caribbean. Following the principle of "abiding by the contract, ensuring quality and valuing justice," China's economic, trade and technological cooperation and trade relations with Latin American countries have witnessed a new situation. China-Africa cooperation is carried out under the institutional framework of the Forum on China-Africa Cooperation. The Chinese government has taken concrete actions to show that it attaches great importance to the China-Africa cooperation mechanism and strives to promote the in-depth development the cooperation. China has actively participated in the discussions of relevant multilateral economic organizations over the years on the world economic situation, the economic development and debt of developing countries, capital trade, technology transfer and other issues, and stands for giving priority to solving the urgent problems faced by developing countries. In the work of multilateral environment, food, crime prevention, drug control, refugees, women and other fields, China has actively participated in the drafting and consultation of relevant international conferences and documents, and made due contributions to the solution of major international issues facing mankind.

Since the 1990s, China's multilateral diplomacy has shown distinct characteristics, the most notable of which is the wide range of fields and diverse ways.

First, China's multilateral diplomacy has adopted more and more different forms such as multilateral summit diplomacy, government diplomacy, political Party diplomacy, military diplomacy and non-governmental diplomacy. For example, at the informal meeting of APEC leaders, Chinese leaders put forward a unique "APEC approach" that emphasized gradualness, flexibility and openness. It withstood the pressure of western countries eager to promote the process of trade and investment liberalization in the Asia Pacific region, created a cooperation model different from that of the west, and enriched the contents and methods of international multilateral cooperation. The increasingly active multilateral party diplomacy of the CPC has greatly enriched the content and form of China's multilateral diplomacy. These channels and forms of multilateral political party exchanges have enabled friends of political parties around the world to have a deeper understanding of the CPC's ruling philosophy and foreign policy propositions, further expanded the space for the CPC's foreign exchanges, and strengthened China's influence on the international stage. With its flexible and diverse ways and unique style, non-governmental diplomacy has opened up a broad diplomatic field for China, enhanced mutual understanding between China and foreign countries, promoted economic, trade, scientific and cultural exchanges between China and other countries in the world, and laid a more stable mass foundation for strengthening friendly relations between them. China has more extensively participated in various activities in the multilateral economic and social fields and played an increasingly active role in global issues such as the environment, food, crime prevention, drug control, refugees and women. Second, the combination of firmness in principle and flexibility in strategy is another major feature of China's multilateral diplomacy. Adherence to the principle of independence and autonomy, safeguarding the country's sovereignty, security and national interests is unshakeable and is a manifestation of the firmness of the principle. China has made clear its principled stand on various multilateral occasions, especially on some major issues. For example, on the issue of nuclear arms control and disarmament, China's ultimate goal is the complete prohibition and thorough destruction of nuclear weapons; on the issue of peace and military conflicts, China firmly opposes aggression and expansion in international conflicts; on the issue of the world economy, China advocates South-South cooperation and North-South dialogue to inject vitality into economic development; China advocates the principle of equality between large and small countries, mutual respect for independence and sovereignty, and opposes interference in the internal affairs of other countries under any name or pretext. On major issues involving national sovereignty and interests, China has always taken a firm and clear-cut stand and will never trade principles.

However, on the premise of not harming the long-term and fundamental interests of the country, China can also maintain a certain degree of flexibility in the way or means of dealing with specific international affairs. Adherence to combining principle with flexibility is an important part of China's diplomatic strategy. Third, the development of China's multilateral diplomatic activities can be said to be a rational process of deepening its participation in the international system. Geographically, intergovernmental and non-governmental organizations and forums ranging from international, regional to cross regional; in terms of categories, from politics, economy, security to culture, health, sports and other social aspects. China's expansion of multilateral diplomacy is a gradual and in-depth process, showing an all-round, multi-level and wide-ranging development scale. In this process, China has adhered to the principles of independence and sovereign equality, and decided on the scope, extent and speed of its participation according to its national conditions. China is always opposed to any international organization or country using international mechanisms to interfere in China's internal affairs, nor does it interfere in the internal affairs of any other country. On the Taiwan question, which involves China's sovereignty and territorial integrity, China opposes the admission of Taiwan by any intergovernmental international organization. China has always adhered to the policy of non-alignment in the process of participating in international organizations and systems. China does not participate in any bilateral or multilateral international organizations with military alliances. The multilateral organizations and mechanisms that China participates in and promotes are open, non-aligned, and non-targeted at third parties, and within these organizations and mechanisms China also pursues an independent and autonomous policy, deciding its own policy according to the merits of the matter. In the international community, China adheres to its position as a developing country, speaks for and always considers global issues from the position and position of developing countries. By expressing its views on major international issues in international organizations and mechanisms, China has played an unprecedented constructive role and a more important role in better safeguarding world peace and enhancing China's international status.

Summary

In the early 1990s, starting from the major principled position of taking economic development as the center, Deng Xiaoping drew lessons from the ideological debate of the international communist camp in the 1950s-1960s, and got rid of all kinds of political and public opinion pressure on the CPC and the Chinese government after the drastic changes in the Soviet Union and Eastern Europe at home and abroad, and put forward the strategic decision of "hiding one's capacity and biding one's time." On the one hand, China has focused on actively doing a good job in domestic economic development. On the other hand, it has sought breakthroughs from various conflicts of interest in the international community, breaking the western "sanctions" against China that harm others and do not benefit itself, thus winning an opportunity for diplomatic development. After the 14th National Congress of the CPC, China began to participate in international multilateral relations with a more positive attitude and tried to put forward its own ideas on international politics. After China joined the WTO in 2001, it has participated in various international political, economic and cultural activities with a more proactive attitude and a responsible major country stance. Multilateral diplomacy and summit diplomacy have become more active. The policy proposal of establishing a fair and reasonable new international political and economic order has been responded by more and more countries. The opening strategy of "going global" has achieved remarkable results. Contemporary China's comprehensive national strength has been greatly strengthened, its international environment has been greatly improved, and its international status has been greatly enhanced.

SECTION 6
"Peaceful Reunification, and One Country, Two Systems"

2.6.1 Hong Kong's Return

On May 27, 1985, the Chinese and British governments exchanged the instruments of ratification of the *Sino-British Joint Declaration* and its three annexes on the Hong Kong issue. Hong Kong officially entered the "12-year transition period." After entering the "transitional period," the drafting of the *Basic Law of the HKSAR of the PRC* and the legalization and institutionalization of the scientific concept of "One Country, Two Systems" have become the primary task faced by the Chinese government in solving the Hong Kong issue. After four years and eight months of hard work, the drafting of the Basic Law of Hong Kong has finally been completed. In April 1990, the Third Session of the Seventh NPC formally adopted and promulgated the Basic Law of Hong Kong, and Hong Kong entered the "post-transition period."

How Hong Kong develops in the "post-transition period" is not only related to Hong Kong's social stability and economic prosperity, but also to the smooth transition and smooth handover of Hong Kong around 1997. It is also a major issue related to China-British relations. However, since the 1990s, with the drastic changes in Eastern Europe and the disintegration of the Soviet Union and other changes in the international situation, the British government has adjusted its China policy and created obstacles to China-British cooperation on the Hong Kong issue in many ways. On April 24, 1992, the British government announced that Chris Patten was the 28th British Governor of Hong Kong. In October, Chris Patten, who had just been in Hong Kong for three months, delivered the policy address "Our Next Five Years" with its subtitle as "the Agenda For Hong Kong," and unilaterally introduced the "Hong Kong Political Reform Plan." This political reform plan obviously runs counter to the relevant provisions and spirit of the *Sino-British Joint Declaration*, violates the commitment of the British side to link the development of Hong Kong's political system with the Hong Kong Basic Law, violates the relevant understandings reached between China and the United Kingdom, and creates huge obstacles to the smooth transition and smooth handover of Hong Kong. In January 1993, Deng Xiaoping made a speech on the China-British confrontation triggered by Patten's political reform plan. He hoped that the British side would handle it according to the statement and agreement with less disputes and more cooperation; however, if the British government and the British Hong Kong authorities insist on confrontation, the Chinese government has no other choice but to follow through.

However, Chris Patten still insisted on his own course, and adopted a non-cooperative attitude on such issues as the negotiation of financial arrangements for the new airport and the arrangement of military land, which aggravated the tension in China-British relations. In view of this situation, the Chinese government decided to "start anew," adopted the policy of "focusing on ourselves" and rely on Hong Kong compatriots to ensure the smooth transition and smooth handover of Hong Kong.

In accordance with the spirit of Deng Xiaoping's instruction of "focusing on ourselves," the Chinese side accelerated the pace of preparations for the HKSAR.

The preparation of the HKSAR was carried out according to the procedure of "the formation of the Preliminary Working Committee, the Preparatory Committee, and the Selection Committee, the selection of the Chief Executive, and the formation of the executive, legislative, and judicial branches of the HKSAR headed by the Chief Executive, and the Handover Ceremony."

In July 1993, Preliminary Working Committee of the Preparatory Committee of the HKSAR was formally established. It consisted of 70 members (57 in the first group and 13 in the second group), including 32 mainland members and 38 Hong Kong members. The chairman was Qian Qichen, and the vice chairmen were An Zijie, Huo Yingdong, Li Fushan, Lu Ping, Zhou Nan, Jiang Enzhu and Zheng Yi. There were five special groups: the administrative group, the economic group, the legal group, the cultural group, and the social and security group. From July 1993 to January 1996, the "Preliminary Working Committee" worked for two and a half years, held six plenary meetings, and adopted 46 written suggestions and opinions on a series of major issues related to the smooth transition and smooth handover of Hong Kong.

In January 1996, the Preparatory Committee for the HKSAR was formally established, consisting of 150 members, including 56 mainland members and 94 Hong Kong members. The chairman was Qian Qichen, and the vice chairmen were An Zijie, Huo Yingdong, Li Fushan, Tung Chee-hwa, Liang Zhenying, Wang Hanbin, Lu Ping, Zhou Nan and Wang Yingfan. There were six working groups: the selection committee group, the first chief executive group, the provisional legislative council group, the legal group, the economic group and the celebration group. In one and a half years from the 1st Plenary Meeting in January 1996 to the Nineth Plenary Meeting in May 1997, the Preparatory Committee adopted a series of legal documents, basically completing the preparatory work for the HKSAR and laying a foundation for the establishment of the region.

In November 1996, the selection committee for the first government of the HKSAR was formally established. All 400 members were permanent residents of Hong Kong. The two functions of the "Selection Committee" were "to select the candidates for the first chief executive and to elect members of the provisional legislative council." On December 11, 1996, the Third Plenary Meeting of the "Selection Committee" elected Tung Chee Hwa as the candidate for the first Chief Executive by an absolute majority of 320 votes (on December 16, 1996, Premier Li Peng appointed him on behalf of the Central People's Government). On December 21, 1996, the Fourth Plenary Meeting of the "Selection Committee "elected 60 members of the Provisional Legislative Council by secret ballot (on January 5, 1997, the First Plenary Meeting of the "Provisional Legislative Council" elected Rita Fan as the president of the "Provisional Legislative Council" by secret ballot).

From June 30 to July 1, 1997, the handover ceremony between China and Britain and the Establishment Ceremony of the SAR and the SAR government were held successively. On July 1, President Jiang Zemin of the PRC solemnly announced to the world in Hong Kong: the national flag of the PRC and the regional flag of the HKSAR of the PRC is solemnly raised in Hong Kong. At this moment, people all over the world were turning their eyes to Hong Kong. According to the *Sino-British Joint Statement* on the Hong Kong issue, the two governments held the handover ceremony of Hong Kong's political power as scheduled, declaring that China resumed the exercise of sovereignty over Hong Kong and the Hong Kong SAR of the PRC was officially established. This was a grand event for the Chinese nation and a victory for the cause of world peace and justice. July 1, 1997 was recorded in history as a day worthy of people's eternal remembrance. The return of Hong Kong to the motherland after 100 years of vicissitudes marked that Hong Kong compatriots have become the true masters of the motherland and that Hong Kong's development has entered a new era. "

2.6.2 Macao's Return

After Hong Kong entered the "transitional period," the return of Macao also entered the agenda of the Chinese government on "peaceful reunification and One Country, Two Systems."

From June 1986 to March 1987, the diplomatic talks between the Chinese and Portuguese Governments on the Macao issue were held in Beijing (four rounds of formal talks, including Zhou Nan, head of the Chinese delegation, and Medina, head of the Portuguese delegation). On March 26, 1987, the heads of the delegations of China and Portugal initialled the *Sino-Portuguese Joint Declaration* on the Macao issue in Beijing; on April 13, the joint declaration was officially signed by the heads of government of both sides in Beijing. The joint declaration declares that the government of the PRC would resume the exercise of sovereignty over Macao on December 20, 1999. On January 15, 1988, the exchange of notes between the Chinese and Portuguese Governments on the Macao issue took effect, and Macao officially entered the "12-year transition period" (1988–1999) of preparing for the handover between China and Portugal and the MSAR.

After the settlement of the Hong Kong issue, the "historical legacy" between China and Britain, which was delayed for a century and a half, the Macau issue, the "historical legacy" between China and Portugal, which was delayed for four and a half centuries, was finally successfully resolved in the era of the Chinese Communists' rule, in the era of the PRC, where the people are the masters, and in the era of the peaceful development of the Chinese nation towards rejuvenation, and the shame of generations was wiped out, and the dream of reunification and reunion of generations was fulfilled.

The Drafting Committee for the Basic Law of the MSAR was formally established in October 1988 and consisted of 48 members, including 29 Mainland members, 19 Macao members, with chairman Ji Pengfei, vice chairmen Hu Sheng, Wang Hanbin, Ma Wanqi, Stanley Ho, Lei Jieqiong, Qian Weichang, Edmund Ho Hau Wah, Xue Shousheng, Li Hou and Zhou Ding. First, a drafting group on the structure of the basic law was organized, and then five special groups were set up: the special group on the relationship between the central authorities and the MSAR, the special group on the basic rights and obligations of residents, the special group on the political system, the special group on the economy, and the special group on cultural and social affairs. From October 1988 to January 1993, the "drafting committee" worked for 4 years and 4 months, 1,500 days and nights. After 9 plenary meetings, 16 chairman committee meetings, and 60 special group meetings, the structure (Draft) discussion draft, the draft for comments, and the draft were finalized, and "a word was worth a thousand gold." On March 31, 1993, the First Session of the Eighth NPC adopted the *Basic Law of the MSAR of the PRC*, including Annex I, *Method of the Selection of the Chief Executive of the*

MSAR, Annex II, *Method for the Formation of the Legislative Council of the MSAR and its Voting Procedures*, Annex III, *National Laws Be Applied in the MSAR*, and the patterns of the regional flag and regional emblem of the *MSAR*, Adopted the decision of the NPC on the *Method for the Formation of the First Government, the First Legislative Council and the First Judiciary of the MSAR*, the *Decision of the NPC on the Basic Law of MSAR of the PRC*, the *Decision on the Establishment of the MSAR*, and the *Decision on NPC Approving the Proposal by the Drafting Committee for the Basic Law of the MSAR on the Establishment of the Committee for the Basic Law of the MSAR Under the Standing Committee of the NPC*. On the same day, President Jiang Zemin issued Order No. 3 of 1993, which read "the basic law of Macao is hereby promulgated and shall come into effect as of December 20, 1999."

Since the nature and status of the MSAR established after the return of Macao in 1999 and the HKSAR established after the return of Hong Kong in 1997 were completely the same, and both were "models" of the scientific concept of "peaceful reunification and 'One Country, Two Systems,'" the Macao Basic Law issued in 1993 was based on the Hong Kong Basic Law issued in 1990 in terms of content, form, basic structure and main provisions. A high degree of consistency was maintained (both of the two basic laws were composed of the "preamble" plus the text of nine chapters, three annexes and the relevant decisions of the Four NPCes). However, the Macao Basic Law was not a simple copy of the Hong Kong Basic Law after all, but fully reflected the characteristics of Macao in terms of specific provisions according to the situation of Macao.

The preparation of the MSAR fully learned from the successful experience of Hong Kong's return to the motherland, and also followed the procedure of "the formation of the 'preparatory committee' and 'Selection Committee'—the formation of the chief executive and the formation of the legislative, executive and judicial bodies of the Special Administrative Region headed by the chief executive—the 'handover ceremony.' The only difference was that in the preparatory process of the MSAR, due to the cooperation between China and Portugal, there were no "variables" and "indispensable" transitional measures, such as "the preliminary working committee" and the "Provisional Legislative Council" that had to be taken in the preparatory process of the HKSAR due to the Sino-British confrontation.

In May 1998, the Preparatory Committee for the MSAR was formally established, consisting of 100 members, including 40 mainland members, 60 Macao members, chairman Qian Qichen, vice chairmen Ma Wanqi, Edmund Ho Hau Wah, Stanley Ho, Wu Fu, Cao Qizhen, Xie Fei, Liao Hui, Wang Qiren and Wang Yingfan. There were four special groups: the government affairs group, the legal group, the economic group, and the social and cultural group. In one and a half years from the First Plenary Meeting in May 1998 to the Nineth Plenary Meeting in July 1999, the Preparatory Committee adopted a series of legal documents, basically completing the preparatory work for the MSAR and laying a foundation for the establishment of the region.

In April 1999, the Selection Committee for the first government of the MSAR was formally established. All 200 members were permanent residents of Macao. The "top priority" of the work of the "Selection Committee" was to select the candidate for the first chief executive of the MSAR. On May 15, 1999, the Third Plenary Meeting of the "Selection Committee" elected Edmund Ho Hau Wah as the candidate for the first Chief Executive by an absolute majority of 163 votes (on June 20, 1999, Premier Zhu Rongji appointed him on behalf of the Central People's Government).

From December 19 to December 20, 1999, the handover ceremony of political power between China, Portugal and Macao and the Establishment Ceremony of the Special Administrative Region and the government of the special administrative region were held successively. On December 20, President Jiang Zemin of the PRC solemnly announced to the world in Macao: "The Chinese and Portuguese governments have just held the ceremony of the transfer of government of Macao, at which the Chinese government solemnly declared the resumption of its exercise of sovereignty over Macao and the official establishment of the MSAR of the People's Republic of China." "This signifies that henceforth our Macao compatriots have truly become the masters of this land and that Macao has entered a brand-new era in its development. This great event of the Chinese nation will shine forever in the annals of history!"[43]

The peaceful resolution of the historical territorial and dispute issues between countries through diplomatic negotiations and the peaceful resolution of the issue of national unification between regions with different social systems through "One Country, Two Systems" is an original contribution of the CPC and the Chinese government to the development of the Marxist theory and practice of the nation-state, to the history of human political civilization, and to the contemporary world where peace and development are the main themes. The "Hong Kong and Macao model" of "peaceful reunification and 'One Country, Two Systems'" and the successful practice of the return of Hong Kong and Macao have opened up a new path in the history of the development of Marxism, the history of the development of human political civilization, and the unification and integration of nation states in the contemporary world. It is not only beneficial for contemporary China to continue to solve the issue of national reunification, such as the Taiwan question, and to solve the border and territorial disputes, such as the China-Indian border issue. Moreover, it can also serve as a reference and inspiration for the contemporary world to continue to solve national reunification issues such as the Korean Peninsula issue and territorial disputes such as the British-Argentina Malvinas Islands issue.

After the reunification of Hong Kong and Macao, the Central Government has effectively implemented the principles of "One Country, Two Systems," "Hong Kong people governing Hong Kong," "Macao people governing Macao" and a high degree of autonomy, and has acted in strict accordance with the Basic Law of the Hong Kong and Macao Special Administrative Regions, firmly maintaining the prosperity and stability of Hong Kong and Macao. Hong Kong and Macao continue to maintain their original capitalist system and lifestyle, and fully exercise the administrative power, legislative power, independent judicial power and final adjudication power conferred by the Basic Laws of Hong Kong and Macao. Hong Kong and Macao residents enjoy extensive democratic rights and freedoms. "One Country, Two Systems," "Hong Kong people governing Hong Kong," "Macao people governing Macao," and a high degree of autonomy have become a reality from a scientific concept.

To realize China's complete reunification is the shared aspiration of all Chinese people and is in the fundamental interests of the Chinese nation. The core contents of the scientific concept and basic national policy of "peaceful reunification and 'One Country, Two Systems'" are:

First, one China. There is only one China in the world. The mainland and the Hong Kong, Macao and Chinese Taiwan are inseparable parts of China. China's sovereignty and territorial integrity are inseparable. The only legitimate govern-ment representing China in the international community is the government of the PRC. This is the premise and foundation for the peaceful reunification of the country.

Second, two systems. On the premise of one China, China's main body, namely the mainland, implements the socialist system. Hong Kong, Macao and Taiwan maintain the original capitalist system, the social and economic system, the lifestyle, and the laws will remain basically unchanged. Their economic and cultural ties with foreign countries remain unchanged, and they coexist and develop together for a long time.

Third, the SARs enjoy a high degree of autonomy. After the peaceful reunification of the country, Hong Kong, Macao established special administrative regions directly under the Central People's government (so will Chinese Taiwan), enjoying a high degree of autonomy, including administrative power, legislative power, independent judicial power, final adjudication power, and certain foreign affairs power. The Taiwan region can also retain its own military forces.

Fourth, peaceful negotiations and peaceful reunification. The peaceful reunification of the motherland should be realized through peaceful negotiations. But at the same time, it is not necessary for them make a commitment to renounce force. This is not aimed at our compatriots, but at the separatist schemes of various separatist forces at home and abroad.

Regarding the ideological origin and theoretical basis of the scientific concept and basic state policy of "peaceful reunification and one country, two basic points must be recognized: on the one hand, it is a modernized inheritance, development and innovation of the ideological heritage and traditional culture of national reunification in the history of Chinese civilization with a clear chronology; on the other hand, it is a "Chineseized" inheritance, development and innovation of the classical Marxist doctrine of the state. And the spiritual soul is "seeking truth from facts."

In the classical expositions of Marxist classical writers on the state theory, there is no direct and specific content related to the national unification of the nation-state and its realization path. However, their theoretical interpretation of the "world history" issue, of the state form (state structure) of the nation-state, including the "federalism" issue, of the function of "mediators" in the "special period" of the nation-state and "easing conflicts," of the peaceful coexistence of socialism and capitalism under specific conditions, and so on, have all provided rich and profound ideological enlightenment to the Chinese Communists who have been struggling to find a new path and a new model for realizing the great reunification and reunion of the Chinese nation. It is precisely from the classical expositions of Marxist classical writers on the state theory that the Chinese Communists adhere to the ideological line of seeking truth from facts, emancipating the mind and advancing with the times, and combine the basic principles of Marxism with China's historical development, traditional culture, basic national conditions and the concrete reality of the Chinese people's revolution, construction and reform led by the CPC. As a result, they creatively put forward the scientific concept and basic national policy of "peaceful reunification, 'One Country, Two Systems,'" which is a new thinking and new way for new China, which has been at the primary stage of socialism for a long time, to realize national reunification and the great reunion of the Chinese nation in the era of globalization. Practice has proved that "One Country, Two Systems" not only unswervingly upholds the one China principle, reflects the Chinese people's firm determination to realize the reunification of the motherland and safeguard national sovereignty and territorial integrity, but also respects the history and reality of Hong Kong, Macao and Taiwan. It is the creative strategic concept of the Party to realize the reunification of the motherland.

2.6.3 New Changes in Cross-Strait Relations

Solving the Taiwan question is the top priority of the great project of "peaceful reunification and 'One Country, Two Systems'" in contemporary China and the ultimate goal of the great project of "peaceful reunification and 'One Country, Two Systems'" in contemporary China. In the 1980s, "chief designer" Deng Xiaoping's scientific concept of "One Country, Two Systems" was originally designed to solve the Taiwan question. Only because the deadlock on the Taiwan question at that time was not easy to resolve in a short time, he chose to solve the Hong Kong and Macao issues with relatively mature conditions as a breakthrough, and through the "Hong Kong model" and "Macao model" of Hong Kong and Macao's return and "One Country, Two Systems," to accumulate experience and create conditions for the final settlement of the Taiwan question. After entering the 1990s and the new century, the Chinese Communists with Comrade Jiang Zemin as the main representative carried out theoretical and practical innovation of the important thinking of the new "Three Represents" on the basis of inheriting and developing Deng Xiaoping Theory, which is a precious "ideological heritage." On the one hand, they worked hard to realize the return of Hong Kong and Macao and build the "Hong Kong and Macao model" of "One Country, Two Systems." On the other hand, they gradually shift the strategic focus of the great project of "peaceful reunification and 'One Country, Two Systems'" in contemporary China to the settlement of the Taiwan question. According to the new changes in China's domestic and international situation in the "post-Cold War era," and in accordance with the evolution of the political ecology on Taiwan and the new changes in cross-strait relations, the strategic thinking and specific policies on Taiwan work have been comprehensively adjusted, from "anti-independence" and "promoting unification" to "anti-independence," from a "passive response" of "counting on the Taiwan authorities" to a "self-centered" approach of "counting on the people of Taiwan." The "active manipulation" of "soft and hard" and "softer and harder."

Through white papers such as *The Taiwan Question and Reunification of China* and *The One-China Principle and the Taiwan Issue*, and through the *Eight Points of Jiang*, a comprehensive and systematic set of theories and policies on Taiwan has been gradually formed, opening up a new situation for the normalization and peaceful development of cross-strait relations, which has laid a solid foundation for the resolution of the Taiwan question and the realization of the ultimate goal of the great project of "peaceful reunification and 'One Country, Two Systems'" in contemporary China.

Since the 1990s, cross-strait exchanges in all aspects have been increasing. First, we moved from open contact to negotiation and dialogue. In October 1992, the Association for Relations Across the Taiwan Straits (ARATS) and the Taiwan Strait Exchange Foundation (SEF) reached a consensus on the two sides' oral expression of "both sides of the Taiwan Strait adhere to the one China principle" in the business talks, that is, the "1992 Consensus." On this basis, in April 1993, Wang Daohan, chairman of the ARATS, and Koo Zhenfu, chairman of the SEF, held the "Wang-Koo Talks" in Singapore, which attracted worldwide attention. The talks achieved positive results. The two sides signed four agreements, including the *Joint Agreement of the Wang-Koo Talks*, which established a channel for normalization of cross-strait exchanges. Second, cross-strait economic and trade relations have developed rapidly. The mainland has formulated a series of policies and measures to effectively protect the interests of Taiwan businessmen on the mainland. In March 1994, the Sixth Meeting of the Standing Committee of the Eighth NPC adopted the Law of the PRC on the Protection of Investment of Taiwan Compatriots; in April, the CCCPC and the State Council held an economic work conference on Taiwan, which proposed the principle of "equal priority and appropriate relaxation" for Taiwan businessmen's investment. At the same time, it pointed out that on the one hand, efforts should be made to run the existing joint ventures well, and on the other hand, it should continue to actively promote comprehensive economic exchanges and cooperation between the two sides of the Strait. On December 5, 1999, the State Council promulgated *Rules for the Implementation of the PRC on the Protection of Investment of Taiwan Compatriots* to further guarantee and promote cross-strait business and trade exchanges.

However, the development of cross-strait relations during this period was not smooth sailing. In 1988, when Chiang Ching-Kuo died and Lee Teng Hui came to power, the "Taiwan independence" forces gradually rose. In particular, after Chen Shui-Bian, leader of the Democratic Progressive Party, who advocated "Taiwan independence" came to power in 2000, separatist activities of "Taiwan independence" became increasingly rampant.

In order to remove obstacles and promote the new development of cross-strait relations, on January 30, 1995, Jiang Zemin, on behalf of the CPC and the Chinese government, delivered an important speech entitled "Continue to Promote the Reunification of the Motherland." he put forward eight proposals for developing cross-strait relations and promoting the reunification of the motherland: (1) Upholding the one China principle is the basis and prerequisite for achieving peaceful reunification. (2) We have no objection to the development of non-governmental economic and cultural relations between Taiwan and foreign countries, but we oppose Taiwan's so-called "expansion of international living space" activities aimed at "two Chinas" and "one China, one Taiwan." (3) Hold talks on peaceful reunification between the two sides of the Strait. On the premise that there is only one China, we are prepared to talk about any matter. In the course of negotiations, representatives of various parties and organizations on both sides of the Strait may be invited to participate. (4) Strive to achieve peaceful reunification and the Chinese do not fight the Chinese. We are not committed to renouncing the use of force. This is not directed against our compatriots in Taiwan, but against the interference of foreign forces with China's reunification and against the schemes to bring about the "independence of Taiwan." (5) Facing the development of the world economy in the 21st century, it is necessary to vigorously develop cross-strait economic exchanges and cooperation, so as to facilitate the common prosperity of the cross-strait economy and benefit the entire Chinese nation. (6) The splendid culture of five thousand years jointly created by the sons and daughters of all ethnic groups in China has always been the spiritual bond for all Chinese people and an important foundation for achieving peaceful reunification. (7) The 21 million Taiwan compatriots, whether they are from Taiwan or other provinces, are all Chinese, and they are all flesh and blood compatriots and brothers. We fully respect Taiwan compatriots' life style and their wish to be the masters of our country. (8) Welcome the leader of the Taiwan authorities to visit in an appropriate capacity; we are also willing to accept Taiwan's invitation to visit Taiwan. This speech reflects the consistency and continuity of the principles and policies of the CPC and the Chinese government for resolving the Taiwan question, and the determination and sincerity to develop cross-strait relations and promote the reunification of the motherland.

On May 11, 1998, Jiang Zemin delivered a speech entitled "Tasks of Taiwan Work under the New Situation" at the Central Taiwan Work Conference, which further gave play to the importance of "upholding the one China principle": "we need to resolutely uphold the one China principle." "upholding to the one China principle is the foundation and prerequisite for developing cross-strait relations and achieving peaceful reunification as well as the most powerful weapon for us to oppose any attempt to separate Taiwan from China and opposing any foreign interference forces in the Taiwan question. It is also an important matter of principle concerning our country's sovereignty and territorial integrity, and we definitely cannot afford to vacillate on this issue."[44] After entering the 21st century, on February 21, 2000, the Taiwan Affairs Office of the CCCPC, the Taiwan Affairs Office of the State Council, and the Information Office of the State Council issued a white paper entitled "The One-China Principle and the Taiwan Issue," which addressed Jiang Zemin's proposal of "upholding the one China principle." It comprehensively and systematically explained from different angles and aspects such as "the factual and legal basis of one China," "the emergence and basic meaning of the one China principle," "several issues concerning the one China principle in cross-strait relations" and "several issues concerning the adherence to the one China principle in the international community" and specifically explained and emphasized that "the one China principle was the cornerstone of the Chinese government's Taiwan policy," "only by adhering to the one China principle can peaceful reunification be realized."[45]

During this period, in order to safeguard the fundamental interests of compatriots on both sides of the Strait and safeguard national sovereignty and territorial integrity, the CPC and the Chinese government always held high the banner of "upholding the one China principle" and waged a resolute and fruitful struggle against the increasingly serious and even rampant "Taiwan independence" separatist activities led by the leaders of the Taiwan authorities Lee Teng Hui and Chen Shui-Bian. Over the past decade or so, three major struggles had been waged: first, the struggle against separatism and "Taiwan independence" from June 1995 to March 1996; second, the struggle against Lee Teng Hui's "two-state theory" in 1999; and third, the struggle against Chen Shui-Bian's "one side, one country theory" from 2001 to 2002. These three major struggles have fully demonstrated the strong will and determination of the Chinese people to resolutely defend national sovereignty and territorial integrity, dealt a heavy blow to the arrogance of the "Taiwan independence" separatist forces, and safeguarded Taiwan's status as a part of Chinese territory. At the same time, the CPC and the Chinese government have also made every effort to promote "doing a good job of winning the hearts and minds of the people in Taiwan." In doing this, the most direct and effective way and approach is to develop cross-strait economic exchanges and cooperation, and promote cross-strait political negotiations on the basis of deeply-integrated and mutually-beneficial relationship between the two sides of the Strait, so as to create conditions for the final settlement of the Taiwan question and the realization of the peaceful reunification of contemporary China.

Summary

Before and after China's scientific concept and basic national policy of "peaceful reunification and 'One Country, Two Systems'" were put forward and put into practice, there have been various national unification models in the international community, such as the "Vietnam model" and the "Yemen model." They have two main points in common: one is "settlement by force" and the other is "one country, one system." Under the above model, the leading Party of unification has to use "force and power" and other means to realize and maintain the national unity of the nation-state. The proposal and practice of China's scientific concept of "peaceful reunification and 'One Country, Two Systems'" have opened up a new road and a new model for the realization of national reunification. It has creatively absorbed and borrowed from Chinese history and traditional culture and from world history and contemporary countries around the world to achieve national unity and national solidarity, fully revealing the institutional advantages and far-reaching influence of socialism with Chinese characteristics. The realization and maintenance of national reunification and national unity by means of peaceful reunification and "One Country, Two Systems" is in line with the theme of peace and development in the world, the trend of the times of economic globalization, political multipolarity and cultural diversification, the core, fundamental and long-term interests of the Chinese people and the common interests of the people of the world, a great initiative of the new socialist China in political civilization, and a great contribution of the new socialist China to the cause of peace and justice for mankind.

CHAPTER III

Continuous Development of Reform and Opening Up

Upholding and Developing Socialism with Chinese Characteristics under the New Situation (2002–2012)

When human society enters the 21st century, new China has also entered a new historical stage of implementing the third step of the "three-step" development strategy. At the new stage of the new century, looking at the international and domestic situation, China is in an important period of strategic opportunity and prominent contradictions. It can be said that challenges and opportunities, and difficulties and hopes coexist.

Facing the complicated international and domestic situation, the CPC and the Chinese government have always held high the great banner of socialism with Chinese characteristics, guided by Deng Xiaoping Theory and the important thought of "Three Represents," thoroughly implemented the scientific outlook on development, led the people of all ethnic groups across the country to write a new chapter in the cause of socialism with Chinese characteristics, and successfully adhered to and developed socialism with Chinese characteristics in the new situation. In terms of political progress, we should establish the important thought of "Three Represents" as the new guiding ideology, and put forward and implement the scientific outlook on development. The system of people's congresses, multiparty cooperation and political consultation under the leadership of the CPC, the urban and rural democracy at the grassroots level, and the system of regional ethnic autonomy have been continuously consolidated and improved, and socialist rule of law has been continuously strengthened. This is not only an important embodiment of deepening the construction of socialist democracy with Chinese characteristics, but also the proper meaning of building a moderately prosperous society in all respects. In terms of building the economy, in order to better promote the economic construction of socialism with Chinese characteristics, the CPC and the Chinese government have made strategic decisions to improve the socialist market economy and promote the sound and rapid development of the national economy. They have successively formulated and implemented the 11th Five-Year Plan and the 12th Five-Year Plan, and have successively issued nearly ten central "No. 1 documents" on the "issues relating to agriculture, rural areas and the wellbeing of farmers," striving to strengthen the construction of a new socialist countryside. In addition, it has effectively responded to the huge impact of the international financial crisis by seeking advantages and avoiding disadvantages and turning crises into opportunities, and has implemented major measures such as building an innovative country, so as to maintain sustained, rapid and healthy development of the national economy and continuously improve people's living standards. In terms of cultural development, the Party should put cultural development in a more prominent position, actively promote cultural restructuring, establish a socialist concept of honor and disgrace, and promote the construction of the system of core socialist values, firmly grasp the direction of the advanced socialist culture, vigorously develop cultural undertakings and cultural industries, explore a new path for the development of socialist culture with Chinese characteristics, and create a new situation in cultural development. In terms of social construction, the Party puts forward the strategic task of building a socialist harmonious society, actively promotes social construction focusing on improving people's livelihood, accelerates the reform of the system of social security, cancels agricultural taxes, improves people's lives, defeats the sudden "SARS" epidemic, resists Wenchuan earthquake and other serious natural disasters, and promotes social harmony and stability. In terms of diplomatic work, in order to strive for a peaceful and good international and domestic environment for building a moderately prosperous society in all respects, we should always adhere to the path of peaceful development, take the construction of a harmonious world as the goal, and carry out all-round foreign exchanges and actively participate in international affairs in accordance with the diplomatic work deployment of "a large country is the key, the surrounding is the primary, developing countries are the foundation, and multilateral is the stage." In terms of "One Country, Two Systems" and the reunification of the motherland, we should actively strengthen the construction of "One Country, Two Systems" in the HKSAR and the MSAR, and promote the peaceful development of cross-strait relations.

During this period, China successfully completed the first step of the "new three-step development" strategy, achieved a historic breakthrough as the world's second-largest economy, and laid a good foundation for building a moderately prosperous society in all respects.

SECTION I

New Starting Point, New Goal, and Political Progress of Socialism with Chinese Characteristics

3.1.1 The 16th National Congress of the CPC, the 17th National Congress of the CPC and the Theoretical Innovation of the Ruling Party

(1) The Convening of the 16th National Congress of the CPC and the Establishment of the Guiding Position of the Important Thought of "Three Represents"
When human society enters the 21st century, new China has entered a new development stage of building a moderately prosperous society in all respects and accelerating socialist modernization. New changes have taken place in the world conditions, national conditions and party conditions. Internationally, on the whole, peace and development as the theme of the times have not changed, but the international situation is undergoing profound changes. The trend of world multi-polarization and economic globalization is developing in twists and turns, scientific and technological progress is changing with each passing day, and the competition for comprehensive national strength is becoming increasingly fierce. At home, the fundamental reform of the economic and social system has achieved a new historic breakthrough in reform and opening-up, which has had a profound impact on all aspects of China's social life. The economic structure has changed dramatically, the social strata have been differentiated and reorganized, and the subjects of interest have become increasingly diverse. As far as the ruling party is concerned, significant changes have taken place in the historical position,

275

working environment and historical tasks of the CPC. The number of new party members has increased significantly, and the alternation of new and old cadres has continued, putting forward new and higher requirements for the continued governance of the CPC.

It is against this background that Jiang Zemin first put forward the important thought of "Three Represents" during his inspection in Guangdong in February 2000, emphasizing that: "summing up the history of our party for more than 70 years, we can draw an important conclusion, which is that our party has won the support of the people because it has represented the development trend of China's most advanced productive forces, the orientation of China's most advanced culture, and the fundamental interests of the overwhelming majority of the Chinese people in all historical periods of revolution, construction, and reform, and through the formulation of correct lines, principles, and policies to strive unremittingly for the fundamental interests of the country and the people. Mankind has come to the turn of a new century and the turn of a new millennium. Under the new historical conditions, how our party can better achieve these 'Three Represents' is a major topic that requires deep thinking by all Party comrades, especially the party's senior cadres.[46] "In October, 2000, at the Fifth Plenary Session of the 15th CCCPC, Jiang Zemin pointed out: "we should implement the requirements of the 'Three Represents' in all our work. We should see whether the measures we have taken and the work we have done meet the requirements of the 'Three Represents.' If they meet the requirements, we should unswervingly adhere to them, and if not, we should have the courage to correct them in a practical and realistic manner."[47] In July, 2001, at the annual meeting to celebrate the 80th anniversary of the founding of the party, Jiang Zemin made a comprehensive and in-depth exposition of the scientific connotation of the important thought of "Three Represents" from the height of the law of historical development and the requirements of the progress of the times, It is pointed out that "our party must always represent the development requirements of China's advanced productive forces, that is, the party's theories, lines, programs, principles, policies and all work must strive to conform to the laws of the development of productive forces, reflect the requirements of constantly promoting the liberation and development of social productive forces, especially the requirements of promoting the development of advanced productive forces, and constantly improve the living standards of the people through the development of productive forces." "Our party should always represent the orientation of China's most advanced culture. That is, the party's theory, line, program, principles, policies and all kinds of work must strive to reflect the requirements of developing a national, scientific and popular socialist culture that is oriented to modernization, the world and the future, promote the continuous improvement of the ideological and moral quality and scientific and cultural quality of the whole nation, and provide spiritual power and intellectual support for China's economic development and social progress." "Our party must always represent the fundamental interests of the overwhelming majority of the Chinese people. That is, the party's theory, line, program, principles, policies and all work must adhere to the fundamental interests of the people as the starting point and destination, give full play to the enthusiasm, initiative and creativity of the people, and enable the people to continuously obtain practical economic, political and cultural interests on the basis of continuous social development and progress."[48]

From November 8 to 14, 2002, the 16th National Congress of the CPC was held in Beijing. This is the first congress held by the CPC in the new century, and it is also a very important congress held by the CPC under the new situation of starting to implement the third step strategic deployment of socialist modernization. Jiang Zemin, general secretary of the CCCPC, delivered a report entitled *Build a Well-Off Society in All-Round Way and Create a New Situation in Building Socialism with Chinese Characteristics* to the Congress. In his report, Jiang Zemin profoundly summarized the achievements of the past five years and the basic experience of the past 13 years, comprehensively expounded the historical background, practical basis, theoretical basis, scientific connotation, ideological essence, spiritual essence and great significance of the important thought of "Three Represents," and clearly put forward China's goals for the next 20 years and the principles and policies to promote all aspects of work. He emphasized: "the important thought of 'Three Represents' is the inheritance and development of Marxism Leninism, Mao Zedong Thought and Deng Xiaoping theory, reflects the new requirements of the development and changes of the contemporary world and China on the work of the party and the state, is a powerful theoretical weapon to strengthen and improve Party building and promote the self-improvement and development of socialism in China, is the crystallization of the collective wisdom of the whole party, and is the guiding ideology that the Party must adhere to for a long time. Always adhering to the "Three Represents" the foundation for building our Party, the cornerstone for its governance and the source of its strength. "To implement the important thought of 'Three Represents,' the key lies in keeping pace with the times, the core lies in adhering to the party's progressive nature, and the essence lies in adhering to exercising power for the people. All Party comrades should grasp steadfastly this fundamental requirement and constantly enhance their consciousness and firmness in implementing the important thought of the 'Three Represents.'"[49] The Congress passed a resolution on the *Revised Constitution of the Communist Party of China*, which established the important thought of "Three Represents," together with Marxism Leninism, Mao Zedong Thought and Deng Xiaoping theory, as the guiding ideology that the CPC must adhere to for a long time, and stressed that to create a new situation in the cause of socialism with Chinese characteristics, we must hold high the great banner of Deng Xiaoping theory, fully implement the important thought of "Three Represents," carry forward the past and forge ahead, and keep pace with the times. We should earnestly implement the important thought of "Three Represents" in all fields of socialist modernization, which is embodied in all aspects of the construction of the ruling party.

To sum up, the important thought of "Three Represents" means that the CPC must always represent the development requirements of China's advanced productive forces, the orientation of China's advanced culture, and the fundamental interests of the overwhelming majority of the Chinese people. It has achieved fruitful results on major issues of building socialism with Chinese characteristics such as the ideological line, development path, development stage and development strategy, fundamental tasks, development momentum, relying on strength, international strategy, leadership and fundamental purpose. It has further answered the questions of what socialism is and how to build socialism with a series of closely linked and interconnected new ideas, new viewpoints and new judgments. It creatively answered the questions of what kind of party to build and how to build it. The important thought of "Three Represents" is the inheritance and development of Marxism Leninism, Mao Zedong Thought and Deng Xiaoping theory, reflects the new requirements of the development and changes of the contemporary world and China on the work of the party and the state, is a powerful theoretical weapon to strengthen and improve Party building and promote the self-improvement and development of socialism in China, is the crystallization of the collective wisdom of the whole party, and is the guiding ideology that the Party must adhere to for a long time. Always adhering to the "Three Represents" the foundation for building our Party, the cornerstone for its governance and the source of its strength."

(2) The Convening of the 17th National Congress of the CPC and the Scientific Outlook on Development

After the 16th National Congress of the CPC, the Chinese Communists represented by Comrade Hu Jintao, based on the basic national conditions of the primary stage of socialism, under the guidance of Marxism Leninism, Mao Zedong thought, Deng Xiaoping theory and the important thought of "Three Represents," summarized China's development practice, learned from foreign development experience, adapted to the new development requirements, and based on the new situation and tasks, especially the important enlightenment of the fight against SARS, clearly put forward the scientific outlook on development.

In April, 2003, Hu Jintao proposed to adhere to the comprehensive concept of development during his inspection in Guangdong. In July, 2003, Hu Jintao first put forward the concept of the scientific outlook on development at the National Conference on the prevention and control of SARS. Hu Jintao pointed out: "we should better adhere to the scientific development that is comprehensive, coordinated and sustainable, more consciously adhere to promoting the coordinated development of socialist material, political and spiritual civilizations, adhere to promoting the all-round development of man on the basis of economic and social development, and keep enhancing the harmony between man and nature."[50] This is the first expression on the scientific outlook on development by the leaders of the CPC. In October, 2003, the Third Plenary Session of the 16th CCCPC clearly put forward that we should "adhere to putting people first, and establish a comprehensive, coordinated and sustainable development." This is the first time that the scientific outlook on development has been completely put forward in the official document of the CPC.

On March 10, 2004, at the Symposium on population, resources and environment work of the CCCPC, Hu Jintao further elaborated on the profound connotation and basic requirements of the scientific outlook on development. In September, 2004, the Fourth Plenary Session of the 16th CCCPC was held. The meeting called for adhering to the scientific outlook on development of putting people first, comprehensive, coordinated and sustainable development to better promote economic and social development. In October, 2005, the Fifth Plenary Session of the 16th CCCPC passed the *suggestions of the CCCPC on formulating the 11th Five-Year Plan for National Economic and Social Development*, which clearly pointed out that the scientific outlook on development is the concentrated embodiment of the world outlook and methodology guiding the development, and adhere to the overall economic and social development under the guidance of the scientific outlook on development. In March, 2006, the outline of the 11th Five-Year Plan for national economic and social development, adopted at the Fourth Session of the 10th NPC, once again stressed the importance of using scientific outlook on development to guide the overall economic and social development.

From November 8 to 10, 2002, the 16th National Congress of the CPC was held in Beijing. In his report *Hold High the Great Banner of Socialism with Chinese Characteristics and Strive for New Victories in Building a Moderately Prosperous Society in All Respects* Hu Jintao profoundly expounded the era background, scientific connotation and spiritual essence of the scientific outlook on development, put forward clear requirements for the in-depth implementation of the scientific outlook on development, and made it clear that it is the fundamental ideology guiding economic society. He clearly pointed out: "the first priority of the scientific outlook on development is development, the core is putting people first, the basic requirement is comprehensive, coordinated and sustainable development, and the fundamental method is overall consideration." "The scientific outlook on development is the inheritance and development of the important thoughts of the three generations of the party's central collective leadership on development, the concentrated embodiment of the Marxist world outlook and methodology on development, a scientific theory that is in line with Marxism Leninism, Mao Zedong thought, Deng Xiaoping theory and the important thought of the 'Three Represents' and keeps pace with the times, an important guiding principle for China's economic and social development, and a major strategic idea that must be adhered to and implemented for the development of socialism with Chinese characteristics."[51] The Congress unanimously agreed to include the scientific outlook on development as a major strategic thought in the constitution of the CPC. The Congress called on the whole party to comprehensively grasp the scientific connotation and spiritual essence of the scientific outlook on development, enhance the consciousness and firmness of implementing the scientific outlook on development, strive to change the ideological concepts that do not adapt to and are not in line with the scientific outlook on development, strive to solve the prominent problems that affect and restrict scientific development, guide the enthusiasm of the whole society to scientific development, and implement the scientific outlook on development in all aspects of economic and social development. The 17th National Congress of the CPC also decided to carry out in-depth study and practice of the scientific outlook on development in the whole party.

After the 17th National Congress of the CPC, the Chinese Communists represented by Hu Jintao formed a series of new expositions, which further enriched and improved the scientific outlook on development. On October 18, 2010, the *suggestions of the CCCPC on formulating the 12th Five-Year Plan for national economic and social development* adopted by the Fifth Plenary Session of the 17th CCCPC further explained the basic connotation of the scientific outlook on development. In March, 2011, the Fourth Session of the 11th NPC passed the *outline of the 12th Five-Year Plan for national economic and social development*, which pointed out that taking scientific development as the theme is the requirement of the times and has a bearing on the overall situation of reform, opening up and modernization; taking accelerating the transformation of the economic growth pattern as the main line is the only way to promote scientific development. It is a profound change in China's economic and social fields. It is a comprehensive, systematic and strategic change. It must run through the whole process and all fields of economic and social development, promote transformation in development and seek development in transformation. On July 23, 2012, Hu Jintao delivered an important speech at the opening ceremony of the special seminar for major leading cadres at the provincial and ministerial levels, which highly summarized the theoretical exploration value and important position of the scientific outlook on development. He pointed out: since the 16th National Congress of the CPC, we have firmly grasped and made good use of important period of strategic opportunity for China's development, overcome a series of severe challenges, and strive to promote the cause of socialism with Chinese characteristics to a new development stage. The most important reason why we can achieve such historic achievements and progress is to adhere to the guidance of Marxism Leninism, Mao Zedong thought, Deng Xiaoping theory and the important thought of Three Represents, have the courage to promote theoretical innovation on the basis of practice, form and implement the scientific outlook on development, and provide strong theoretical guidance for building an overall well-off society and accelerating socialist modernization.

(3) The Proposal of the Theoretical System of Socialism with Chinese Characteristics
With the gradual deepening of the practice of socialism with Chinese charac-teristics, the Sinicization of Marxism continues to bear fruitful theoretical fruits.

While major theories have been produced one after another, people are also thinking: what is the relationship between the theoretical achievements in the past 30 years of reform and opening-up, and what is their common theme? In order to better guide the development of socialism with Chinese characteristics at the new stage of the new century, the Chinese Communists with Comrade Hu Jintao as the main representative made a profound summary and comprehensive answer.

On June 25, 2007, Hu Jintao delivered an important speech at the Party School of the CCCPC, reviewing the development process of China's socialist cause and making a new summary and discussion on the theory of socialism with Chinese characteristics formed and developed in the past 30 years. He stressed that socialism with Chinese characteristics is the banner of the development and progress of contemporary China and the unity and struggle of the whole Party and the people of all ethnic groups. We must unswervingly adhere to the guidance of Deng Xiaoping Theory and the important thought of "Three Represents," thoroughly implement the scientific outlook on development, and unswervingly adhere to and develop socialism with Chinese characteristics. The report of the 17th National Congress of the CPC took a step further. On the basis of summarizing the historical process and valuable experience of reform and opening-up in the past 30 years, it integrated the major strategic ideas such as Deng Xiaoping Theory, the important thought of Three Represents, and the scientific outlook on development, which have been successively formed in the innovative practice of the CPC in building and developing socialism with Chinese characteristics since the new era, into a unified whole and is collectively referred to as the "theoretical system of socialism with Chinese characteristics" and scientifically explained. The report points out: "the theoretical system of socialism with Chinese characteristics is a scientific theoretical system including Deng Xiaoping Theory, the important thought of 'Three Represents' and the scientific outlook on development. This theoretical system adheres to and develops Marxism Leninism and Mao Zedong Thought, and condenses the wisdom and painstaking efforts of several generations of Chinese Communists to lead the people in unremitting exploration and practice. It is the latest achievement of adapting Marxism to Chinese conditions, the party's most valuable political and spiritual wealth, and the common ideological foundation for the unity and struggle of the people of all ethnic groups across the country. The theoretical system of socialism with Chinese characteristics is an open theoretical system of continuous development.[52] Since the reform and opening-up, the fundamental reason for all our achievements and progress is that we have opened up the road of socialism with Chinese characteristics and formed a theoretical system of socialism with Chinese characteristics. To hold high the great banner of socialism with Chinese characteristics, the most fundamental thing is to adhere to this road and this theoretical system. In contemporary China, adhering to the theoretical system of socialism with Chinese characteristics means truly adhering to Marxism.

On July 1st, 2011, the celebration of the 90th anniversary of the founding of the CPC was held in the Great Hall of the people in Beijing, and Hu Jintao delivered an important speech. He once again stressed that the theoretical system of socialism with Chinese characteristics is a scientific theoretical system including Deng Xiaoping Theory, the important thought of Three Represents, the scientific outlook on development and other major strategic ideas, which systematically answers a series of major issues such as what kind of socialism to build, how to build socialism, what kind of party to build, how to build the Party, and what kind of development to achieve in a developing country with a population of more than one billion and how to develop. The scientific outlook on development is a scientific theory that comes down in one continuous line with Marxism Leninism, Mao Zedong Thought, Deng Xiaoping Theory and the important thought of "Three Represents" and keeps pace with the times. It is the concentrated embodiment of the Marxist world outlook and methodology on development. It is the major achievement of adapting Marxism to Chinese conditions, the crystallization of the collective wisdom of the CPC, and the guiding ideology that must be adhered to for a long time in the development of socialism with Chinese characteristics.

3.1.2 The Establishment of the Goal of Building a Moderately Prosperous Society in All Respects

The establishment of the goal of building a moderately prosperous society in all respects has undergone a process of development. On December 6, 1979, Deng Xiaoping first proposed that the goal of China's modernization in the 20th century is to achieve moderately prosperous society. After more than 20 years of active exploration and hard work by the people of all ethnic groups across the country, China successfully achieved the goals of the first and second steps of the "three-step" strategy for modernization at the end of the 20th century, and the people's lives have generally reached a well-off level. However, the well-off society achieved at this point is still a low-level, incomplete and unbalanced one. In order to consolidate and improve the well-off level, in October 2000, the Fifth Plenary Session of the 15th CCCPC clearly announced that "from the beginning of the new century, China will enter a new development stage of building moderately prosperous society in an all-round way and accelerating socialist modernization."[53]

In 2002, the 16th National Congress of the CPC clearly put forward the task of building moderately prosperous society in an all-round way in the first 20 years of the new century on the basis of a profound analysis of the new situation and new tasks faced by the CPC and the Republic, and a summary of the experience since the reform and opening-up, especially since the Fourth Plenary Session of the 13th CCCPC: we should concentrate our efforts on building a higher-level well-off society benefiting more than 1 billion people in an all-round way in the first 20 years of the century, in which the economy is more developed, the democracy is more sound, science and education are more advanced, culture is more prosperous, society is more harmonious, and people's lives are more prosperous. The specific goal of building a moderately prosperous society in an all-round way is set.

(1) On the basis of optimizing the structure and improving efficiency, we will strive to quadruple the GDP to that of 2000 that of 2000 by 2020, and the comprehensive national strength and international competitiveness will be significantly enhanced. We will basically realize industrialization and build a sound socialist market economic system and a more dynamic and open economic system. The proportion of urban population will be increased significantly, and the trend of widening differences between industry and agriculture, between urban and rural areas, and between regions will be gradually reversed. The social security system will be relatively sound, social employment will be relatively sufficient, family property will be generally increased, and the people will live a more prosperous life.

(2) Socialist democracy will be further improved, the socialist legal system will be more complete, the basic strategy of rule of law has been fully implemented, and the political, economic and cultural rights and interests of the people will be respected and effectively protected. Democracy at the grassroots level will be more sound, social order will be good, and the people will live and work in peace and contentment.

(3) The ideological and moral quality, scientific and cultural quality and health quality of the whole nation will be significantly improved, and a relatively perfect modern national education system, scientific, technological and cultural

innovation system, national fitness and medical and health system will be formed. The people will have the opportunity to receive a good education, high school education will be basically popularized and illiteracy will be eliminated. A society of learners in which all people learn and lifelong learn will be formed, and promote well-rounded human development.

(4) The ability of sustainable development will be continuously enhanced, the ecological environment will be improved, and the efficiency of resource utilization will be significantly improved, so as to promote the harmony between man and nature, and promote the whole society to embark on the civilized development path of production development, well-off life and good ecology.

In October, 2005, the Fifth Plenary Session of the 16th CCCPC, in accordance with the overall deployment of the 16th National Congress of the CPC for building moderately prosperous society in an all-round way in the first 20 years of the 21st century, put forward the main objectives of economic and social development during the 11th Five-Year Plan Period: on the basis of optimizing the structure, improving efficiency and reducing consumption, to double the per capita GDP of 2000 in 2010; The efficiency of resource utilization will be significantly improved, and the energy consumption per unit of GDP will be reduced by about 20% compared with the end of the 10th Five-Year Plan; Form a group of advantageous enterprises with independent intellectual property rights, well-known brands and strong international competitiveness; The socialist market economic system is relatively complete, the open economy will reach a new level, and the international balance of payments is basically met; Popularize and consolidate nine-year compulsory education, continuously increase urban employment, improve the social security system, and continue to reduce the number of poor people; The income level and quality of life of urban and rural residents will be generally improved, the overall price level will be basically stable, and the living, transportation, education, culture, health and environmental conditions will be greatly improved; New progress will be made in the construction of the democratic legal system and spiritual civilization, social security and production safety will be further improved, and new progress will be made in building a harmonious society.

In 2007, the report of the 17th National Congress of the CPC once again stressed that building a moderately prosperous society in all respects is the goal of the CPC and the Republic by 2020 and the fundamental interests of the people of all ethnic groups in China; On the basis of the goal of building a moderately prosperous society in all respects set by the 16th National Congress of the CPC, it puts forward new and higher requirements for China's development from five aspects: economy, politics, culture, society and ecological civilization.

(1) We will enhance the Coordination of Development and Strive to Achieve Sound and Rapid Economic Development. Major progress will be achieved in the transformation of the development mode. On the basis of optimizing the structure, improving efficiency, we will strive to quadruple the GDP of 2000 by 2020. The socialist market economic system will be further improved. The ability of self-dependent innovation will be significantly improved, and the contribution of scientific and technological progress to economic growth will be increased significantly, making China an innovative country. The consumption rate of residents will be increased steadily, forming a growth pattern driven by coordinated consumption, investment and export. The coordinated and interactive development mechanism between urban and rural areas and regions and the layout of development priority zones will be basically formed. Significant progress will be made in building a new socialist countryside. The proportion of urban population will be increased significantly.

(2) Expanding socialist democracy and better safeguard the people's rights and interests as well as social equity and justice. Citizens' political participation will expanded in an orderly manner. The basic strategy of the rule of law will be thoroughly implemented, the concept of legal system in the whole society will be further strengthened, and new achievements wil be made in the construction of a government ruled by law. The system of democracy at the grass-roots level will be further improved. The government's ability to provide basic public services will be significantly enhanced.

(3) We will strengthen cultural development and significantly improve the overall quality of the whole population. The system of core socialist values will be deeply rooted in the hearts of the people, and good ideological and moral trends will be further promoted. A public cultural service system covering the whole society will be basically established, the proportion of the cultural industry in the national economy will be significantly increased, the international competitiveness will be significantly enhanced, and cultural products that meet the needs of the people will be more abundant.

(4) We will accelerate the development of social undertakings and comprehensively improve people's lives. The modern national education system will be

more perfect, the lifelong education system will be basically formed, and the education level of the whole people and the training level of innovative talents will be significantly improved. Social employment will be relatively more sufficient. A social security system that covers the urban and rural residents will be basically established, and everyone will be entitled to the basic living guarantee. A reasonable and orderly income distribution pattern will basically take shape, with middle-income people accounting for the majority, and absolute poverty will basically be eliminated. Everyone will enjoy basic medical and health services. The social management system will be sounder.

(5) We will build an ecological civilization and basically form an industrial structure, growth and consumption pattern that saves energy and resources and protects the ecological environment. The circular economy will form a large scale, and the proportion of renewable energy will be increased significantly. The discharge of major pollutants will be effectively controlled, and the quality of the ecological environment will be significantly improved. The concept of the philosophy of ecological civilization will be firmly established in the whole society.

Based on the in-depth summary of the experience of building moderately prosperous society, the report of the 17th National Congress of the CPC further puts forward a new goal of building a moderately prosperous society in all respects: by 2020, when the goal is achieved, our ancient civilization and developing socialist country with a long history will become a country with industrialization basically realized, comprehensive national strength significantly enhanced, and the overall scale of the domestic market ranking in the forefront of the world. We will become a country where the people are generally richer, the quality of life is significantly improved, and the ecological environment is good. We will become a country where the people enjoy fuller democratic rights, have higher overall quality and spiritual pursuit, become a country with more perfect systems in all aspects, a more vibrant society with stability and unity, and become a country that is more open to the outside world, more friendly, and makes greater contributions to human civilization.

The objective of building moderately prosperous society in an all-round way are objectives of comprehensive economic, political and cultural development of socialism with Chinese characteristics, objectives well geared to the efforts to speed up modernization. According to the 2011 "statistical monitoring report on the process of building a moderately prosperous society in all respects in China" issued by the National Bureau of statistics, the results of statistical monitoring of the process of building a moderately prosperous society in all respects throughout the country from 2000 to 2010 show that under the correct leadership of the CCCPC and the State Council, China has worked hard to overcome the impact of the serious international financial crisis, rising production costs, "SARS" epidemic, rare ice and snow disasters, major earthquakes, and debris flows, and the European sovereign debt crisis and many other adverse factors, economic construction has made great achievements, various social undertakings have accelerated development, people's living standards have been continuously improved, and the situation of ecological progress and natural environment protection is good. The whole country and all regions have made great progress in building moderately prosperous society in an all-round way. In 2010, the process of building moderately prosperous society in an all-round way in China has reached 80.1%, 88% in the eastern part of China, 77.7% in the central part of China, 71.4% in the western part of China and 82.3% in the northeast part of China.

3.1.3 Development and Improvement of Democratic Political System

(1) Consolidate and Improve the People's Congress System
Upholding and improving the system of people's congresses is an important part of developing socialist democracy and establishing a socialist political civilization. At the new stage in the new century, the continuous development and improvement of the people's Congress system has led to the continuous strengthening of China's socialist political civilization.

The 16th National Congress of the CPC pointed out that we must continue to actively and steadily promote the reform of the political system on the premise of adhering to the four basic principles, uphold and improve the system of people's congresses and ensure that the congresses and their standing committees exercise their functions according to law and that their legislation and policy decisions better embody the people's will. The Congress also stressed that we should optimize the composition of the standing committees. The proposal was initially implemented at the First Session of the 10th CPC NPC held in March 2003. A group of young and knowledgeable professionals were elected to the Standing Committee of the NPC, which has brought about major changes in the personnel structure of the Standing Committee of the NPC. The meeting also adopted a decision: the NPC set up nine special committees, including the Ethnic Affairs

Committee and the Constitution and Law Committee. In March, 2004, the Second Session of the 10th NPC deliberated and adopted the amendment to *the Constitution of the PRC*, adding "special administrative regions" to the original provision that "the NPC is composed of representatives elected by provinces, autonomous regions, municipalities directly under the central government and the army," and revising the original provision that the term of office of the people's congresses of townships, nationality townships and towns is three years to "the term of office of local people's congresses at all levels is five years"; It is stipulated that the election committee can organize representative candidates to meet with voters, answer voters' questions, and intensify sanctions against election sabotage.

In September, 2004, at the celebration of the 50th anniversary of the founding of the NPC in the capital, Hu Jintao clearly pointed out: "for a long time, the people of all ethnic groups have firmly bore on the future and destiny of the country and the nation in their own hands through the people's Congress system. This is a reliable institutional guarantee that our country and people can withstand all kinds of storms, overcome all kinds of difficulties, and move forward along the socialist road. It is also a reliable institutional guarantee for us to build a moderately prosperous society in an all-round way and achieve the national rejuvenation."[54] In March, 2007, the Fifth session of the 10th CPC NPC passed the decision on the number of deputies and election of the 11th CPC NPC, which made it clear for the first time that rural migrant workers should be represented in provinces and municipalities directly under the central government where rural migrant workers are relatively concentrated. The 17th National Congress of the CPC held in the same year clearly proposed that we must support people's congresses in performing their functions pursuant to law and effectively turn the Party's propositions into the will of the state through legal procedures. We must ensure that deputies to people's congresses exercise their functions and powers in accordance with the law and maintain close ties with the general public. Urban and rural deputies to people's congresses are now elected on the basis of the same population ratio. We must strengthen the institutions of standing committees of people's congresses and improve their membership composition in terms of intellectual background and age. In addition, the report of the 17th National Congress of the CPC also raised for the first time the issue of strengthening the foreign exchanges of the NPC, that is, strengthening the external exchanges of people's congresses, CPPCC committees, the armed forces, localities and people's organizations to enhance mutual understanding and friendship between the Chinese people and the people of other countries. In order to implement the spirit of the report of the 17th National Congress of the CPC, among the deputies of the 11th NPC held in 2008, the proportion of leading cadre representatives of provincial government departments has decreased significantly; Among all the delegates, the number of leading cadre representatives from the constituent departments of the provincial government decreased by one third compared with the previous session. It is worth mentioning that three rural migrant worker representatives of the NPC from Shanghai, Guangdong and Chongqing attended the meeting. In March, 2010, the Third session of the 11th NPC voted and passed the draft decision of the NPC on *Amending the election law of the NPC of the PRC and local people's congresses at all levels*, which stipulates that urban and rural deputies to people's congresses are now elected on the basis of the same population ratio. Deputies to the NPC have broader representativeness. The system of elections is further improved, and better reflects the equality of all people, regions and nationalities.

China's legislature ensures the wide participation of the public in legislation by publishing draft law, hearing, argumentation, symposium and other forms. From 2010 to 2012, the NPC and its Standing Committee enacted and amended 45 laws, including the criminal law, the criminal procedure law, the election law of the NPC and local people's congresses at all levels, the *Law of the PRC on Deputies to the National People's Congress and Local People's Congress at All Levels*, the *State Compensation Law of the PRC*, the organic law of villagers' committees, the administrative enforcement law, and other laws, further improving the legal system for the protection of all human rights. The NPC and its Standing Committee have strengthened supervision in accordance with the law, and the pertinence and effectiveness of supervision have been enhanced.

The people's Congress system has been constantly consolidated and improved, reflecting the common interests and aspirations of the people of all ethnic groups across the country, ensuring that the people are the masters of the country, mobilizing all the people to devote themselves to socialist construction as the masters of the country, and ensuring the coordinated and highly efficient operation of state organs. Over the years, the number of people who enjoy the right to vote and stand for election has accounted for more than 99% of the number of citizens over the age of 18, and the participation rate is about 90%. Deputies to the people's Congress at all levels come from all ethnic groups, industries, strata and parties, and are widely representative. Practice has fully proved that the people's Congress system is rooted in the people and has strong vitality and superiority.

(2) We Shall Uphold and Improve the System of Multi-Party Cooperation and Political Consultation Led by the Communist Party

The system of multi-party cooperation and political consultation led by the CPC is a socialist system of political parties with Chinese characteristics. The 16th National Congress of the CPC pointed out that we should adhere to and improve the system of multi-party cooperation and political consultation led by the CPC, uphold the principle of "long-term coexistence, mutual supervision, treating each other with all sincerity and sharing weal and woe," step up our cooperation with the democratic parties and better display the features and advantages of the Chinese socialist system of political parties. In September, 2004, Hu Jintao stressed at the celebration of the 55th anniversary of the founding of the CPPCC that "we must adhere to and improve the system of multi-party cooperation and political consultation led by the CPC, and rally all the forces to work together to build a moderately prosperous society in an all-round way and realize the great national rejuvenation."[55]

In February, 2005, Hu Jintao put forward five requirements on Further Strengthening the construction of multi-party cooperation and political consultation system led by the CPC at the Spring Festival Symposium of non-party personages: we should adhere to the political development under socialism with Chinese characteristics; We should adhere to the leadership of the CPC and give full play to socialist democracy; We should take development as the fundamental task of multi-party cooperation and political consultation; We should persist in promoting the institutionalization, standardization and procedure of multi-party cooperation and political consultation; We should adhere to the mutual promotion between the construction of the ruling party and the construction of the participating parties. Since then, from the perspective of building a socialist political civilization, the CCCPC has successively promulgated three important documents, namely, the *opinions on Further Strengthening the construction of the multi-party cooperation and political consultation system led by the CPC*, the *opinions on strengthening the work of the CPPCC*, and the opinions on consolidating and strengthening the United Front in the new stage of the new century. On the basis of systematically summarizing the historical experience of multi-party cooperation and political consultation since the founding of new China for more than 50 years, it further clarified the status, principles, contents, methods and procedures of multi-party cooperation and political consultation, providing theoretical guidance, policy basis and institutional guarantee for adhering to and improving the work of multi-party cooperation and political consultation led by the CPC in the new century. On this basis, the 17th National Congress of the CPC in 2007 further stressed the need to implement the policy of "long-term coexistence, mutual supervision, treating each other with sincerity, sharing weal and woe," the need to strengthen our cooperation with the democratic parties, support them and personages without party affiliation in better performing their functions of participation in the deliberation and administration of state affairs and democratic oversight, and select and recommend a greater number of outstanding non-CPC persons for leading positions.

At this stage, our country should adhere to and improve the system of multi-party cooperation and political consultation under the leadership of the CPC, make the Chinese CCCPC serve as a major channel for conducting consultative democracy make political consultation a part of the policymaking process, and conduct consultations before and when policy decisions are made, and make democratic consultation more effective. From 2008 to 2012, the 11th National Committee of the Chinese CCCPC held more than 420 consultations of various kinds.

(3) Develop and Improve Community-Level Democracy

Community-level democracy is an effective form of people's rule of the country. It ensures the extensive and direct participation of all citizens in all affairs of social life through rural community-level democracy with villagers' autonomy as the core, urban community-level democracy with community residents' autonomy as the core, and community-level democracy in enterprises and institutions with workers' conferences as the core. Extending democracy at the community level is an inevitable trend and the groundwork for developing socialist democracy.

The CPC and the Chinese government have attached great importance to and deeply elaborated on the construction of community-level democracy in China. With the development of urban community construction, in order to further expand the construction of urban community-level democracy, in 2000, the general office of the CCCPC and the general office of the State Council forwarded the *opinions of the Ministry of Civil Affairs on promoting urban community construction throughout the country*, opening a new stage of the development of urban community residents' autonomy. In 2002, the general office of the CCCPC and the general office of the State Council issued the *notice on further improving the election of villagers' committees*, promoting the institutionalization and standardization of the work of rural villagers' committees. Subsequently, the CCCPC and the state council issued the "notice on further implementing the openness of factory affairs in SOEs, collective enterprises and their holding enterprises," which effectively promoted the improvement of the enterprise democratic management system with the workers' conferences as the carrier. In the same year, the 16th National Congress of the CPC clearly proposed that extending democracy at the community level is the groundwork for developing socialist democracy, and clearly summarized community-level democracy into three aspects: rural villagers' autonomy, urban residents' autonomy, workers' conferences and other forms of democratic management system of enterprises and institutions.

In September, 2004, the Fourth Plenary Session of the 16th CCCPC proposed to extend community-level democracy, improve the management system of government authorities, community-level self-governance, enterprises and institutions, adhere to and improve the system of making government affairs, factory affairs, village affairs and other public affairs known to the public, and ensure that the grass-roots people exercise their democratic rights such as the right to vote, the right to stay informed, the right to participate, and the right to oversee in accordance with the law. In October, 2007, the 17th National Congress of the CPC listed the community-level self-governance system as one of the four important systems of China's socialist democratic political construction for the first time, and further emphasized that the most effective and extensive way for the people to be masters of the country is that they directly exercise their democratic rights in accordance with the law to manage public affairs and public service programs at the primary level, practice self-management, self-service, self-education and self-oversight, and exercise democratic oversight over cadres. Such practices must be emphasized and promoted as the groundwork for developing socialist democracy. In October 2010, the Standing Committee of the NPC revised the organic law of villagers' committees to further improve and standardize the procedures for the election and dismissal of members of village committees. In order to thoroughly implement the spirit of the 17th National Congress of the CPC, meet the needs of the new situation and new tasks, further improve the community-level self-governance system, and improve the urban community-level management and service system, in November 2010, the general office of the CCCPC and the general office of the State Council issued the opinions on strengthening and improving the construction of urban community residents committees, which not only defined the legal basis and important principles that should be followed to strengthen and improve the construction of community residents committees, it also defines the goals and tasks of the construction of China's urban community residents' committees in the next five years and by 2020, and emphasizes the need to build community residents' committees into community-level self-governance organizations with a full range of functions, vitality, obvious roles and people's satisfaction, which provides guide to action for us to strengthen and improve the construction of community residents' committees in the future.

With the development and progress of China, the scope of community-level democracy in urban and rural areas throughout the country has been extended continuously, the channels for citizens' orderly political participation have increased, the forms of democracy have become increasingly rich, and the construction of community-level democracy has made great achievements. The general election of rural villagers' committees and urban community residents' committees has been institutionalized, standardized and has its own procedures. By the end of 2012, the vast majority of provinces across the country had carried out 8–9 rounds of villagers' committee elections. More than 98% of the villager's committees nationwide have implemented direct elections, and the average participation rate of villagers has reached 95%. The proportion of female members of villager' committees has increased. 95% of the villages in the country have made village affairs public, more than 90% of the counties have formulated a catalogue to make village affairs public, and 91% of the villages have established a column to make village affairs public. Every year, about 1.7 million village cadres report on their work and their efforts to perform their duties honestly, the economic responsibility of more than 230,000 village cadres would be audited, and the villagers assess nearly 2.09 million village cadres. From 2010 to 2012, a new round of elections was held in most urban communities across the country, with a direct election rate of more than 30%. Female members of urban community residents' committees reached 49.42%. All kinds of subjects in the community can equally participate in community public affairs and democratic decision-making through the forms of deliberation and consultation on public affairs of residents' meetings and democratic hearings.

In addition, some new social organizations have emerged at the community-level in urban and rural areas, which have played an important role in managing community-level public affairs, serving the residents and safeguarding the legitimate rights and interests of residents. In rural areas, a large number of specialized farmers' cooperatives have emerged. In cities, various types of community non-governmental organizations have been fostered and developed. All over the country, there have also been various attempts and innovations in democratic reform in the management system of the community-level government authorities. Since 2005, neighborhood committees in Shenzhen, Beijing, Xiamen and other places have carried out an attempt to "separating decision-making from executing." After the "separation of decision-making and execution," the neighborhood committees implemented the mode of "one meeting and one station." The "meeting" is the neighborhood committee, and the "station" is the community affairs workstation. In September, 2011, Tongling City, Anhui Province began to implement the pilot work of canceling streets, "establishing large communities," and implementing "flat" and "grid" management.

3.1.4 The Struggle against Ethnic Separatist Forces and New Progress in the Construction of the System of Regional Ethnic Autonomy

(1) Consolidate and Develop the Great Unity of the People of All Ethnic Groups across the Country and Resolutely Crack down on Ethnic Separatist Activities
Ethnic unity is the fundamental principle for China to deal with ethnic issues, and it is also the core content of China's ethnic policy. China is a united multi-ethnic country. According to the sixth national census, the population of ethnic minorities is 137.9 million, accounting for 8.49% of the total population. In a multi-ethnic country like China, it is of great significance to maintain ethnic unity.

After the "September 11" incident, the "three Evils" at home and abroad were eager to adjust their strategies in order to get rid of the bad name of "terrorism." They once excused and purged themselves in public. Their destructive activities have converged, but they are still accumulating forces, integrating organizations, and waiting for opportunities to carry out violent terrorist activities. Around 2008, the "three Evils" at home and abroad took the Beijing Olympic Games as an opportunity to collude with each other and try their best to incite various interference, destruction, division and subversion activities. In 2008, the "March

14" incident in Xizang was a serious violent criminal incident caused by the organized, premeditated and carefully planned incitement of the Dalai clique and the collusion of the separatist forces of "Xizang independence" at home and abroad. Before and after the Beijing Olympic Games, under the stimulation and specific command of hostile forces at home and abroad, many violent terrorist activities such as the "3.7" aircraft bombing attempt and the "8.4" police attack occurred in Xinjiang. On July 5, 2009, ethnic separatist forces at home and abroad colluded with each other, plotted and incited abroad, organized and implemented in China, and deliberately and systematically committed the "July 5" incident of serious violent crimes of beating, smashing, looting and burning in Urumqi, the capital of Xinjiang Uygur Autonomous Region.

In the face of the rampant acts of ethnic separatists, the CPC and the Chinese government have taken various measures to eliminate all factors detrimental to ethnic unity, take a clear-cut stand against ethnic separatist activities, unswervingly maintain social stability and ethnic unity, and promote the common prosperity and development of all ethnic groups.

First, the state guarantees the legitimate rights and interests of all ethnic minorities. In order to fully ensure that ethnic autonomous areas exercise autonomy pursuant to law and ensure that ethnic minorities are masters of the country, China, proceeding from its own national conditions and realities, has constantly adhered to and improved the system of regional ethnic autonomy, made efforts to eliminate ethnic discrimination and ethnic estrangement left by history, and promoted the unity and development of all ethnic groups. In order to protect the legitimate rights and interests of ethnic minorities in cities and scattered areas, the State formulates and implements laws and regulations such as the regulations on urban ethnic work and the regulations on administrative work in ethnic townships, effectively strengthens services and management, focuses on helping them develop production, improve their lives, and meet their special needs in festivals, meals, funerals, etc.

Second, the state insists on accelerating the economic and social development of ethnic minorities and ethnic areas as the fundamental way to solve China's ethnic problems. In the final analysis, the solution to the difficulties and problems in ethnic areas depends on development. Over the years, the state has strategically attached great importance to the development of ethnic minorities and ethnic regions. In view of the actual development of ethnic minorities and ethnic regions in different periods, the state has put forward working principles and made strategic arrangements to support the development of ethnic minorities and ethnic regions in terms of policies, funds, talents, technology and other aspects. The state has always taken improving the living standards of the people of all ethnic groups as the fundamental starting point and purpose of all work, and has done everything possible to accelerate development, earnestly grasp the first priority of development, and strive to achieve common prosperity and development of all ethnic groups. Through unremitting efforts, the production and living conditions of the people of ethnic minorities and ethnic areas have been significantly improved, and their ideological and ethical standards and scientific and educational levels and health have been greatly improved.

Third, the state continues to strengthen the publicity and education of ethnic unity. The state has incorporated the education of ethnic unity into the whole process of moral education and the development of socialist spiritual civilization, unremittingly carried out the education of ethnic theory, policies toward ethnic minorities, laws concerning ethnic minorities and regulations and knowledge concerning ethnic minorities among the cadres and the masses of all ethnic groups, and paid attention to enhancing the pertinence and effectiveness of education. The state attaches special importance to the education of ethnic unity among teenagers, and requires that ethnic unity education be introduced into schools, classrooms and textbooks, so that the fine tradition of ethnic unity can be passed on from generation to generation. In 2008, the state issued the guiding outline for ethnic unity education in schools (Trial). In 2009, the state included ethnic unity education in the national primary school examination, the middle school examination, the college entrance examination and the graduation examination of secondary vocational education. The state pays attention to the relevant training of news media and publishing practitioners, guides and encourages them to accurately understand and actively publicize policies toward ethnic minorities, laws and regulations concerning ethnic minorities, and basic knowledge concerning ethnic minorities, and launch more works to publicize ethnic unity and national unity. At the same time, attention should be paid to strengthening the management of publications, radio, film and television works and the Internet to prevent contents that hurt the feelings of any ethnic group and harm the ethnic unity. In 2005 and 2009, the State Council held two national commendation conferences for ethnic unity and progress to commend the models of ethnic unity and progress emerging on all fronts, vigorously publicize their advanced deeds, and create a good social atmosphere to cherish and maintain ethnic unity and achieve common progress.

In February, 2010, the Propaganda Department of the CCCPC, the United Front Work Department and the State Ethnic Affairs Commission jointly issued the "opinions on further carrying out activities to create ethnic unity and progress," in order to promote the implementation of the policies toward ethnic minorities of the CPC and the Chinese government, maintain ethnic unity, social stability and national unity, promote the economic and social development of ethnic areas, and maintain ethnic unity, social stability and national unity. In December, 2011, in order to fully implement the policies toward ethnic minorities of the CPC and the Chinese government, effectively do a good job in the ethnic work of state-owned and state-owned holding enterprises under the new situation, and promote the common unity and struggle, common prosperity and development of all ethnic groups, the State Ethnic Affairs Commission and the state owned assets supervision and Administration Commission of the State Council jointly issued the guiding opinions on further doing a good job in the ethnic work of SOEs under the new situation.

Fourth, the state should properly handle contradictions and problems that affect ethnic unity. The state adheres to the principle of unity, education, persuasion and resolution, analyzes specific problems, and solves whatever problems are, so as to avoid the expansion of the situation and the intensification of contradictions. The central and local governments at all levels have established long-term mechanisms and emergency plans to deal with problems affecting ethnic unity, timely and properly handled various contradictions, disputes and events affecting ethnic unity, and maintained ethnic unity and social stability.

China's ethnic problems are China's internal affairs. The Chinese government firmly opposes and resists all external forces' interference in China's ethnic problems under the banner of "ethnicity," "religion" and "human rights," and strictly prevents and combats the infiltration, destruction and subversion of various terrorist forces, separatist forces and extreme religious forces at home and abroad. History and reality show that ethnic unity and fraternity lead to political harmony and prosperity; Ethnic conflicts and disputes will lead to social unrest and people suffering.

(2) New Progress in the Construction of the System of Regional Ethnic Autonomy
The system of regional ethnic autonomy is a basic policy of the CPC to solve China's domestic ethnic problems and a basic political system of China. Regional

ethnic autonomy means that under the unified leadership of the state, autonomous organs are set up in places where ethnic minorities live in compact communities to exercise autonomy and implement regional autonomy. Since the 16th National Congress of the CPC, the Chinese government has consistently adhered to regionalethnic autonomy, improved regionalethnic autonomy with the times, and made remarkable achievements.

Ethnic autonomous areas have generally established. In China, ethnic minority inhabited areas suitable for the establishment of ethnic autonomous areas have basically established ethnic autonomous areas. As of 2011, a total of 155 ethnic autonomous areas have been established across the country, including 5 autonomous regions, 30 autonomous prefectures, 120 autonomous counties (banners), and 1,173 ethnic townships. Among the 55 ethnic minorities, 44 have established autonomous areas. The population of ethnic minorities implementing regional autonomy accounts for 71% of the total population of ethnic minorities, and the area of ethnic autonomous areas accounts for 64% of the national territory. In 2012, 55 ethnic minorities had their own deputies to the NPC and members of the National Committee of the Chinese CCCPC, and ethnic minorities with a population of more than one million had their own members of the Standing Committee of the NPC. At the same time, we should actively train and employ ethnic minority cadres. There are a certain proportion of ethnic minority cadres in the central and local organs of state power, administrative organs, judicial organs and procuratorial organs. Among the standing committees of the people's congresses of 155 ethnic autonomous areas, citizens of the ethnic groups exercising regional autonomy serve as directors or deputy directors, and the chairmen, governors, county heads or flag heads of the governments of ethnic autonomous areas are all citizens of the ethnic groups exercising regional autonomy.

The system of regional ethnic autonomy has continued to develop and improve. In November, 2002, the 16th National Congress of the CPC clearly included upholding and improving the system of regional ethnic autonomy in the overall requirements and process of building a socialist political civilization, and stressed that upholding and improving the system of regional ethnic autonomy is an important part of developing socialist democracy and the basic experience that the CPC must adhere to for a long time in leading the Chinese people to build socialism with Chinese characteristics. In May, 2005, the first central working conference on ethnicities in the new stage of the new century was held. The conference issued several provisions on the implementation of the *law of the PRC on Regional Ethnic Autonomy* by the State Council. This is the first administrative regulation with milestone significance to adhere to and improve the system of regionalethnic autonomy. It is an important measure to adhere to and improve the system of regional ethnic autonomy. It has made new breakthroughs in promoting the economic and social, educational and cultural undertakings of ethnic autonomous areas and the training of ethnic minority cadres and all kinds of talents. In 2007, the 17th National Congress of the CPC further emphasized that to adhere to the path of socialist political development with Chinese characteristics and continuously promote the self-improvement and development of the socialist political system, we must adhere to and improve the system of regional ethnic autonomy.

During this period, the CPC and the Chinese government adhered to the guidance of the scientific outlook on development and further increased support for ethnic minorities and ethnic areas. In 2005, the CCCPC and the State Council made the decision on further strengthening ethnic work and accelerating the economic and social development of ethnic minorities and ethnic areas, which clearly regards development as the key to solving the difficulties and problems in ethnic areas. In 2007, the State Council examined and approved the "11th Five-Year Plan" for the cause of ethnic minorities and the "11th Five-Year Plan" for the action to revitalize the border areas and enrich the people, and vigorously supported the development of the cause of ethnic minorities. In the same year, the State Council issued several opinions on further promoting the economic and social development of Xinjiang, which put forward requirements and made arrangements for accelerating the economic and social development of Xinjiang and further improving the living standards of the people of all ethnic groups in Xinjiang. Since 2008, the state has successively formulated and promulgated a series of preferential policies and measures to promote the economic and social development of Xizang and Yunnan border areas in Ningxia, Qinghai and other provinces (autonomous regions), increased investment, improved infrastructure, developed industries with local advantages, promoted the development of social undertakings, and accelerated the economic and social development of ethnic minorities and ethnic minority areas. On February 18, 2009, the 50th executive meeting of the State Council deliberated and adopted the *Plan for the Protection and Construction of Tibet's Ecological Security Barrier (2008–2030)*, proposing an investment of 15.5 billion yuan to basically build Xizang's shields for ecological security by 2030. In September 2009, Hu Jintao emphasized at the Fourth Plenary Session of the 17th CCCPC that development is the main task of ethnic work at this stage. Supporting the accelerated development of ethnic minorities and ethnic areas is a basic policy of the Central Committee, and it is also the primary task of promoting the large-scale development of China's western region. In January and May 2010, the CCCPC and the State Council held a symposium on work in Xizang and a symposium on work in Xinjiang. The meeting comprehensively summarized the achievements and experience of the development and stability of Xizang and Xinjiang, thoroughly analyzed the situation and tasks faced by Xizang and Xinjiang, clarified the guiding ideology, main tasks and work requirements for doing a good job in Xizang and Xinjiang at present and in the future, and made a strategic deployment for promoting the leapfrog development and long-term stability of Xizang and Xinjiang. The meeting stressed the need to focus on economic development, take ethnic unity as the guarantee, and take improving people's livelihood as the starting point and purpose, and strive to promote the leapfrog development and long-term stability of Xizang and Xinjiang.

With the great help and support of the state and developed regions, and through the hard work and unity of the people of all ethnic groups in ethnic areas, great achievements were made in the economic and social development of ethnic areas, and the people's living standards rose notably. In 2008, the total economic aggregate of ethnic minority areas increased from 5.79 billion yuan in 1952 to 3.06262 trillion yuan, an increase of more than 500 times at comparable prices; The per capita disposable income of urban residents increased from 307 yuan in 1978 to 13.17 thousand yuan, an increase of more than 40 times; The per capita net income of farmers and herdsmen increased from 138 yuan in 1978 to 3,389 yuan, an increase of more than 20 times. A number of key projects such as the "West to East Gas Transmission" and "West to East Power Transmission" have been completed, and a number of infrastructure projects such as airports, expressways and water conservancy hubs have been built. In 2007, the Qinghai-Xizang railway was laid to Lhasa, ending Xizang's history of no railway, providing an economic, fast, all-weather and high-capacity transportation channel between Xizang and the mainland, and providing wings for Xizang's economic take-off. There are 72,711 schools of all kinds in ethnic areas, with 34.503 million students. Nine-year compulsory education has been basically popularized and illiteracy among young and middle-aged people has been eradicated. The medical and health undertakings in ethnic areas have made great progress, and the health of the people of all ethnic groups has been continuously improved. Among them, the GDP of Xizang increased from 129 million yuan in 1951 to 70.1 billion yuan in 2012, with an average annual growth of 8.5%, and the per capita GDP reached 22,900 yuan. In 2012, the per capita net income of farmers and herdsmen in the region reached 5,719 yuan, maintaining a double-digit growth for 10 consecutive years, and the per capita disposable income of urban residents reached 18,028 yuan. Since 2006, the building of a new socialist countryside with the housing project as a breakthrough has benefited the majority of farmers and herdsmen. By the end of 2012, 408,300 households of secure housing had been built in the region, accounting for 88.7% of the total number of farmers and herdsmen. At the same time, Xizang has increasingly close economic ties with the world. In 2012, the total import and export volume of the region was 3.424 billion U.S. dollars, more than 850 times that of 4 million U.S. dollars in 1953, with an average annual growth of 12.1%. By the end of 2012, Xizang had actually utilized 470 million U.S. dollars of foreign capital.

The Chinese government protects the cultural rights and interests of ethnic minorities in earnest. 515 representative projects of 55 ethnic minorities in China have been included in the national intangible cultural heritage protection list, 524 ethnic minorities have become the representative inheritors of national intangible cultural heritage projects, five experimental areas for cultural and ecological protection of ethnic minorities have been established successively, and 18 ethnic minority projects have been selected into the United Nations "list of representative works of human intangible cultural heritage" and "list of intangible cultural heritage in urgent need of protection." By may 2012, there were 73 radio stations, 441 programs and 105 ethnic language programs in ethnic autonomous areas; There are 90 TV stations, 489 programs and 100 ethnic language programs. By the end of 2011, books in minority languages in 23 languages had been published. There are 84 ethnic newspapers and 223 ethnic periodicals. There are 50,834 cultural institutions of all kinds in the ethnic autonomous areas, including 653 libraries, 784 cultural centers, 8,153 cultural stations and 385 museums. The state holds an ethnic minority art show and an ethnic minority traditional sports meet. From 2009 to 2012, the central government has invested 510 million yuan to implement the protection and development project of ethnic minority villages, and carried out pilot projects in 600 villages in 28 provinces (autonomous regions and municipalities directly under the central government). Minority languages are specially protected. The Central People's Radio and local radio stations broadcast in 21 minority languages every day. More than 10,000 schools across the country use 29 languages from 21 ethnic groups to carry out bilingual teaching, with more than 6 million students in schools. In 2011, 3,665 ethnic language textbooks were compiled and published, with a total of more than 47.03 million copies.

However, restricted and influenced by many factors such as historical basis and geographical conditions, the economic and social development of the western part of China, where ethnic minorities are concentrated, is still lower than that of the eastern developed part of China, especially some remote areas. Adhering to and improving regionalethnic autonomy, giving full play to institutional advantages, and constantly improving the level of economic and social development in ethnic areas are the problems that China should strive to solve in building moderately prosperous society in an all-round way in the new century.

3.1.5 The Fourth "Constitutional Amendment" and the Construction of Socialist Rule of Law with Chinese Characteristics

(1) The Fourth "Constitutional Amendment" in the New Era
The *Constitution of the PRC* is the fundamental law of new China, and the provisions have the highest legal effect. New China has formulated four constitutions, and the current fourth constitution was adopted by the Fifth NPC in 1982. Since the promulgation and implementation of the *Constitution of the PRC* in 1982, amendments have been adopted to amend and adjust the constitution, resulting in three constitutional amendments in 1988, 1993 and 1999. Practice has proved that the current constitution provides the most fundamental legal guarantee for the smooth progress of China's reform and opening-up and socialist modernization. At the same time, we should also see that with the continuous promotion and deepening of the great practice of socialism with Chinese characteristics, the constitution is required to make corresponding amendments and adjustments in a timely manner in accordance with the development and changes of social reality. In 2004, according to the proposal of the CCCPC, the Second Session of the 10th NPC revised China's current constitution again, resulting in the fourth amendment to China's current constitution.

Shortly after the conclusion of the 16th National Congress of the CPC, the New Political Bureau of the CCCPC put the revision of some parts of the Constitution on the agenda. In March, 2003, the Standing Committee of the Political Bureau of the CCCPC held a meeting to study and deploy the constitutional amendment.

The general principle of this constitutional amendment was to adhere to the guidance of Marxism-Leninism, Mao Zedong Thought, Deng Xiaoping Theory and the important thought of "Three Represents," implement the spirit of the 16th National Congress of the CPC, reflect the basic experience since the Fourth Plenary Session of the 13th CCCPC, and write the major theoretical views and major principles and policies determined by the 16th National Congress of the CPC into the constitution. The meeting decided to establish a central constitutional amendment group headed by Wu Bangguo to carry out work under the leadership of the Standing Committee of the Political Bureau of the CCCPC. The work of amending the constitution was officially launched.

In October, 2003, the Third Plenary Session of the 16th CCCPC deliberated and adopted the "proposal of the CCCPC on amending some parts of the constitution" and decided to submit it to the Standing Committee of the 10th NPC. In December, the Sixth Session of the Standing Committee of the 10th NPC was held. An important agenda of this meeting is to discuss the "proposal of the CCCPC on amending some parts of the constitution," and decide to submit for deliberation the proposal of the Standing Committee of the NPC on submitting the draft amendment to the constitution to the Second Session of the 10th NPC. At this point, the constitutional amendment officially entered the legal procedures. Finally, in March, 2004, the Second Session of the 10th NPC passed the amendment to the constitution.

This amendment to the current constitution involves 13 aspects. It not only establishes the guiding position of the important thought of "Three Represents" in the country's political and social life, but also increases the content of promoting the coordinated development of material civilization, political civilization and spiritual civilization. It also includes improving the land requisition system, adding "builders of the socialist cause" to the expression of the United Front, and adding provisions for establishing and perfecting the social security system, improving the provisions on the composition of the NPC, amend the "martial law" to "enter a state of emergency," add provisions on the functions and powers of the president of the state, amend the term of office of township governments, add provisions on the national anthem, further clarify the state's policy on the development of the non-public economy, and write "the state respects and protects human rights" and "citizens' legitimate private property is inviolable" into the constitution for the first time. The revised constitution, which is further embodied in the valuable experience gained in the new practice of reform and opening-up and socialist modernization and proved to be mature by practice, will provide a more powerful legal guarantee for the people of all ethnic groups across the country to continue to prosper along the path of socialism with Chinese characteristics.

(2) The Construction of the Rule of Law

Developing socialist democracy and perfecting the socialist legal system is an important strategic task of building socialism with Chinese characteristics. In the new century, China's legal construction continues to move forward. The 16th National Congress of the CPC held in 2002 took the improvement of socialist democracy, the improvement of socialist legal system and the complete implementation of ruling the country by law as the important goals of building a moderately prosperous society in an all-round way. In 2007, the report of the 17th National Congress of the CPC emphasized the need to "comprehensively implement the rule of law as a fundamental principle and speed up the building of a socialist country under the rule of law" from the strategic height of upholding and developing socialism with Chinese characteristics, and made a comprehensive deployment for strengthening the construction of the socialist rule of law.

Under the leadership of the CPC and in the great practice of building socialism with Chinese characteristics, China has made great achievements in the construction of the rule of law.

The socialist law system with Chinese characteristics with the constitution as the core was basically in place. By the end of August 2011, China had formulated 240 current constitutions and effective laws, 706 administrative regulations and more than 8,600 local regulations. The legal departments covering all aspects of social relations have been completed, the basic and main laws in each legal department have been formulated, the corresponding administrative regulations and local regulations are relatively complete, the internal legal system is generally scientific, harmonious and unified, and the socialist legal system with Chinese characteristics has been formed.

We should actively, steadily and pragmatically promote the reform of the judicial system and working mechanism. Since 2004, China has launched a large-scale judicial reform with unified planning, deployment, organization and implementation. Starting with the prominent problems strongly reflected by the public and the key links affecting judicial justice, in accordance with the requirements of judicial justice and strict law enforcement, and proceeding from the laws and characteristics of justice, China has improved the judicial organs, the delimitation of their functions and powers and their management systems so as to form a sound judicial system featuring clearly specified powers and responsibilities, mutual coordination and restraint and highly efficient operation. China's judicial reform is moving towards a stage of overall planning and orderly promotion. Since 2008, China has launched a new round of judicial reform, which has entered a new stage of focusing on key areas and systematic promotion. The reform starts from the judicial needs of the people, takes safeguarding the common interests of the people as the fundamental, takes promoting social harmony as the main line, focuses on strengthening the supervision and restriction of power, seizes the key links that affect judicial justice and restrict judicial ability, solves systematic, institutional and security obstacles. Reform tasks are put forward from four aspects including optimizing the allocation of judicial powers, implementing the criminal policy of tempering justice with mercy, strengthening the construction of the judicial team, strengthening the guarantee of judicial funds. As of October 2012, the task of this round of judicial reform has been basically completed.

The level of administration by law has been continuously improved. The administrative power of people's governments at all levels in China has been gradually on the path of rule of law, a law system regulating the acquisition and operation of government power has basically taken shape, and important progress has been made in administration by law. In 2003, the Fourth Session of the Standing Committee of the 10th NPC passed the administrative license law of the PRC, which further deepened the reform of the administrative examination and approval system and ensured and supervised the effective implementation of administrative management by administrative organs. In March, 2004, the State Council issued the "implementation outline for comprehensively promoting administration according to law," which made an overall layout of administration by law and building a government under the rule of law, and clearly put forward for the first time the goal of building a government under the rule of law after about ten years of unremitting efforts. In June, 2008, the State Council issued the decision on strengthening the administration of municipal and county governments according to law to further promote the implementation of the goal of building a government under the rule of law. In March, 2011, the Political Bureau of the CCCPC conducted the 27th collective study on promoting administration according to law and carrying forward the socialist spirit of the rule of law. When presiding over the study, Hu Jintao, general secretary of the CCCPC, stressed that comprehensively promoting administration according to law and carrying forward the socialist spirit of rule of law is an inevitable requirement for adhering to the principle of building the party for the public and it exercises power for the people, and for promoting scientific development and promoting social harmony. We must strengthen our consciousness and initiative to comprehensively promote administration according to law and carry forward the spirit of socialist rule of law, and speed up the building of a socialist country under the rule of law.

Human rights are protected by reliable laws. With the continuous improvement of legal provisions, judicial system and mechanism for safeguarding rights and interests, human rights have been more fully protected in all links of legislation, law enforcement and justice, and citizens' political, economic, social and cultural rights have been effectively respected and comprehensively guaranteed. In March, 2003, the "Sunzhigang incident" gave birth to the *measures for the relief and management of vagrants and beggars who have no means of living in the city*, and abolished the *measures for the reception and repatriation of Urban Vagrants and beggars*, which has been implemented for 20 years, reflecting the ruling concept of "putting people first" and the government's respect for civil rights. In 2004, "human rights" was written into the Constitution for the first time. At the same time, the amendment to the Constitution also established citizens' private property rights. From the second half of 2006, the second instance of all death penalty cases must be heard; In 2007, all death penalty reviews were transferred to the Supreme People's court. All these reflect the law's cherishing of life and the protection of human rights. *The property law* promulgated in 2007 further clarifies citizens' property rights and adds differentiated ownership of commercial housing. In April, 2010, the 14th Session of the Standing Committee of the 11th NPC passed a decision on *Amending the State Compensation Law of the PRC*, which defined the right of citizens to claim compensation from the state when they were infringed by public power. In January, 2011, the 141st executive meeting of the State Council passed the regulations on the expropriation and compensation of houses on state-owned land, which is the so-called "new demolition regulations." The "new demolition regulation" is mainly aimed at the situation that in recent years, with the acceleration of urbanization, it is difficult to reach an agreement on demolition compensation, violent demolition, extreme confrontation and other extreme events and extreme phenomena continue to occur, which cannot be effectively curbed. The main purpose of its promulgation is to further regulate the housing expropriation and compensation activities of state-owned land, safeguard public interests, and protect the legitimate rights and interests of the expropriated. In February, 2011, the 19th Session of the Standing Committee of the 11th NPC passed the criminal law amendment (VIII), which further implemented the criminal policy of tempering justice with mercy and abolished the death penalty for 13 economic non-violent crimes. The revised criminal law has also added provisions on lenient punishment for crimes committed by the elderly, and the lenient punishment for crimes committed by minors has also been further strengthened, which has further provided more reliable legal protection for human rights. At the same time, it has made China's penalty structure more reasonable and the socialist legal system with Chinese characteristics more perfect. The newly revised criminal procedure law in 2012 includes the content of "respecting and safeguarding human rights," and implements the spirit of respecting and safeguarding human rights in the modification and improvement of the evidence system, defense system, coercive measures, investigation measures, examination and prosecution, trial procedures, execution procedures and the addition of special procedures. This is a major progress in the cause of human rights in China, and is of great significance for punishing crimes, protecting the people, and protecting citizens' litigation rights and other legitimate rights. The *Civil Procedure Law of the PRC* revised in 2012 further guarantees the litigation rights of the parties, improves the prosecution and acceptance procedures, pre-trial preparation procedures, summary procedures, trial supervision procedures and execution procedures, improves the preservation system, evidence system and judicial document disclosure system, and increases the public interest litigation system and the relief procedures for the infringed outside the case.

Summary

In the new century, the establishment of the guiding position of the important thought of "Three Represents," the scientific outlook on development written into the constitution of the CPC, and the proposal of the theoretical system of socialism with Chinese characteristics continue to promote the theoretical innovation of adapting Marxism to Chinese conditions. Constant improvement was made in the system of people's congresses, the system of multiparty cooperation and political consultation under the leadership of the CPC and the system of regional ethnic autonomy and led to the continuous strengthening of China's socialist political civilization. In the face of the rampant acts of ethnic separatists, the CPC and the Chinese government have taken various measures to eliminate all factors detrimental to ethnic unity, take a clear-cut stand against ethnic separatist activities, unswervingly maintain social stability and ethnic unity, promote the common prosperity and development of all ethnic groups, and make new progress in the construction of the system of regional ethnic autonomy. At the same time, in the great practice of building socialism with Chinese characteristics, China has made great achievements in the construction of the rule of law.

SECTION 2

Developing Socialist Economy with Chinese Characteristics

3.2.1 Improving the Socialist Market Economic System and Promoting Sound and Rapid Development of the National Economy

(1) Improve the Socialist Market Economic System
It is an unprecedented great pioneering to introduce a reform and opening-up and establish the socialist market economy. By the end of 2000, the socialist market economy has taken shape initially in China. However, it must be noted at the same time that the initially established socialist market economic is still far from perfect, and there are still many arduous tasks to be completed and many deep-seated contradictions to be solved. Therefore, the 16th National Congress of the CPC in 2002 clearly stated that improving the socialist market economic is still one of the main tasks of economic development and reform in the first 20 years of this century.

In order to implement the strategic deployment of building a sound socialist market economic and a more dynamic and open economic system proposed by the 16th National Congress of the CPC, deepen the reform of the economic system and promote the all-round development of economy and society, in October 2003, the Third Plenary Session of the 16th CCCPC deliberated and adopted the decision of the CCCPC on Several Issues concerning the improvement of the socialist market economic system. The decision is a programmatic document for improving the socialist market economic in the new century. It summed up the experience of reform and opening-up over the past 20 years, profoundly expounded the importance and urgency of deepening economic system reform, the goals and tasks of improving the socialist market economic, and the guiding ideology and principles of deepening the reform of the economic system, and emphasized that we should coordinate urban and rural development, regional development, economic and social development, harmonious development between man and nature, domestic development and opening up, and we should give greater play to the fundamental role of the market in resource allocation and provide a strong institutional guarantee for building moderately prosperous society in an all-round way.

In 2005, on the basis of in-depth analysis of the international and domestic situation facing China's economic and social development in the coming period, the Fifth Plenary Session of the 16th CCCPC clearly pointed out that reform is a powerful driving force to promote economic and social development. At present, China is at the critical stage of reform, and it is necessary to accelerate the reform with greater determination, so as to make breakthroughs in the major system reform related to the overall economic and social development. We should adhere to and improve the basic economic system, promote the reform of the fiscal and tax system, speed up the reform of the financial system, strengthen the construction of a modern market system, form a mechanism conducive to changing the mode of economic growth and promoting comprehensive, coordinated and sustainable development, and improve the institutional guarantee for the implementation of the scientific outlook on development.

In 2007, the 17th National Congress of the CPC held high the great banner of socialism with Chinese characteristics and systematically expounded the profound connotation and basic content of the scientific outlook on development. The scientific outlook on development has become the guiding ideology for China to establish and improve the socialist market economic, marking that China's economic system reform, especially the development of the socialist market economy, has entered a new stage. The Congress clearly put forward one of the new requirements of taking improving the socialist market economic as the goal of building a moderately prosperous society in an all-round way. The Congress emphasized that the key to achieving the goals of future economic development is to make significant progress in transforming the economic growth pattern and improving the socialist market economy, and highlighted the need to accelerate the improvement of the socialist market economy, give better play to the fundamental role of the market in resource allocation, form a macro-control system conducive to scientific development, and accelerate the formation of a unified, open, competitive and orderly modern market system, and further improve the basic economic system.

In October, 2010, the Fifth Plenary Session of the 17th CCCPC pointed out that reform is a powerful driving force to accelerate the transformation of the economic growth pattern. We must comprehensively promote the reform in all fields with greater determination and courage, vigorously promote the reform of the economic system, actively and steadily promote the reform of the political system, accelerate cultural and social restructuring, make the superstructure more adapt to the development and changes of the economic foundation, and provide a strong guarantee for scientific development.

In March, 2011, the Fourth Session of the 11th NPC pointed out that a sound market mechanism and effective macro-control are indispensable components of the socialist market economic. In response to the impact of the international financial crisis, we have strengthened and improved macro-control, corrected market distortions in a timely manner, made up for market failures, and prevented major economic ups and downs. Our Practice has proved to be completely correct. We must constantly improve the socialist market economic, give full play to the fundamental role of the market in the allocation of resources, stimulate the internal vitality of the economy, and at the same time, scientifically use macro-control means to promote long-term, stable and rapid economic development.

(2) Promoting Sound and Rapid Development of the National Economy
Since entering the new era, China's socialist modernization has made remarkable achievements, and the national economy has maintained a sustained and rapid development. But we should also be soberly aware that the resource and environmental costs of economic growth are too high, there remains an imbalance in development between urban and rural areas, among regions, and between the economy and society, and it has become more difficult to bring about a steady growth of agriculture and continued increase in farmers' incomes remains a big problem. Therefore, in the new century, the CPC and the Chinese government put forward the strategic idea of transforming the economic growth pattern and promoting the sound and rapid development of the national economy.

In November, 2002, the 16th National Congress of the CPC proposed to build a higher-level well-off society benefiting more than one billion people in an all-round way in the first 20 years of this century. On the basis of optimizing the structure and improving efficiency, the GDP will strive to quadruple that of 2000 by 2020; It also proposes to take a new road to industrialization, that is, a new road with high scientific and technological content, good economic benefits, low resource consumption, less environmental pollution, and full play to the advantages of human resources. In March, 2003, Hu Jintao pointed out at the central Symposium on population, resources and environment that we should accelerate the transformation the economic growth pattern, and apply the development concept of circular economy to regional economic development, urban and rural construction and product production, so as to make the most effective use of resources, minimize exhaust emissions, and gradually make the ecosystem enter a virtuous cycle. In October, 2003, the Third Plenary Session of the 16th CCCPC stressed that we should adhere to putting people first, establish a comprehensive, coordinated and sustainable development concept, and promote the all-round development of economy, society and people. In October, 2005, the Fifth Plenary Session of the 16th CCCPC adopted the proposal of the CCCPC on formulating the *11th Five-Year Plan for National Economic and Social Development.* When proposing to avoid ups and downs in the economy and achieve rapid and sound development, the proposal stressed that development should not only have a faster growth rate, but also pay attention to improving the quality and efficiency of growth. Here, we should pay more attention to improving the quality and efficiency of growth, that is to say, it is sound and rapid, and the word "sound" is put before the word "rapid."

In December, 2006, the central economic work conference was held. The meeting clearly emphasized that sound and rapid development is the essential requirement for the full implementation of the scientific outlook on development. The meeting pointed out that, based on the experience of recent years and in combination with the new situation faced by the current economic and social development, we should continue to strengthen and improve macro-control, focus on adjusting the economic structure and transforming the economic growth pattern, strengthen resource conservation and environmental protection, promote reform and opening-up and self-dependent innovation, strive to promote social development and solve people's livelihood problems, promote economic and social development into the track of scientific development, and strive to achieve sound and rapid development of the national economy, and create a good environment for the convening of the 17th National Congress of the CPC. In March, 2007, the

Fifth Session of the 10th NPC once again emphasized the full implementation of the scientific outlook on development to achieve sound and rapid economic development.

In 2007, the 17th National Congress of the CPC was held. On the basis of the goal of building a moderately prosperous society in an all-round way set by the 16th National Congress of the CPC, the report of the 17th National Congress of the CPC puts forward new and higher requirements for China's economic and social development: the development pattern will be significantly transformed, and on the basis of optimizing the structure, improving efficiency, reducing consumption and protecting the environment, the per capita GDP will quadruple that of 2000 by 2020. Focusing on promoting the sound and rapid development of the national economy, the report made key arrangements for the strategic tasks of economic development from eight aspects: improving the ability of self-dependent innovation and building an innovative country; Accelerating the transformation of economic growth pattern and promote the optimization and upgrading of industrial structure; Coordinating urban and rural development and promoting the construction of a new socialist countryside; Strengthening energy and resource conservation and ecological environment protection, and enhancing the ability of sustainable development; Promoting coordinated regional development and optimizing the pattern of land development; Improving the basic economic system and the modern market system; Deepening the reform of fiscal, tax, financial and other systems, and improving the macro-control system; Expanding the breadth and depth of opening-up and further liberalize our economy.

Transforming the economic growth pattern and promoting the sound and rapid development of economy is a pressing strategic task vital to the national economy as a whole. By ensuring sound and rapid growth of the national economy, we will further enhance China's economic strength, and enable our socialist market economy to exhibit its great vitality.

3.2.2 Formulate and Implement the 11th Five-Year Plan and the 12th Five-Year Plan

(1) Formulation and Implementation of the 11th Five-Year Plan
As early as 2003, the preparation of the 11th Five-Year Plan had begun. On July 8, 2003, the executive meeting of the State Council discussed and approved the

request for instructions on issues related to the preliminary work of the 11th Five-Year Plan issued by the National Development and Reform Commission (NDRC), and the preparatory work for the plan was officially launched. In October, 2005, the Fifth Plenary Session of the 16th CCCPC was held. The meeting reviewed and adopted the proposal of the CCCPC on formulating the *11th Five-Year Plan for National Economic and Social Development*, put forward the goals, guidelines and main tasks for national economic and social development in the next five years, and put forward guiding opinions on the 11th Five-Year Plan drafted by the State Council. The plenary session pointed out that the formulation of the 11th Five-Year Plan should be guided by Deng Xiaoping Theory and the important thought of "Three Represents" and fully implement the scientific outlook on development. In order to further improve the scientific, democratic and standardized decision-making procedures for major decisions, and further improve the social participation and transparency of the planning process, so as to better prepare the outline of the 11th Five-Year Plan that conforms to China's national conditions, conforms to the requirements of the times, and condenses the will of the people.

After the Fifth Plenary Session of the 16th CCCPC, the outline of the 11th Five-Year Plan officially entered the drafting stage. On February 21, 2006, Hu Jintao, general secretary of the CCCPC, presided over a meeting of the Political Bureau of the CCCPC to discuss the draft of the planning outline. The meeting held that the following five years of the 11th Five-Year Plan will be a crucial period for building a moderately prosperous society in all respects. The scientific compilation of the outline of the 11th Five-Year Plan is of great significance for grasping the important period of strategic opportunity and promoting the rapid and sound development of China's economy and society. The meeting called for democracy and brainstorming in the process of submitting the draft outline of the 11th Five-Year Plan to the Fourth Session of the 10th NPC for review and the Fourth Session of the 10th CPPCC National Committee for discussion, so as to facilitate the formulation and implementation of the outline of the plan. In March, 2006, the Fourth Session of the 10th NPC was held in Beijing, and the outline of the 11th Five-Year Plan was adopted by a high vote.

The implementation period of the 11th Five-Year Plan (2006–2010) is an extraordinary five years in the history of the construction and development of socialism with Chinese characteristics. In the face of complex changes and major risks and challenges in the domestic and international environment, the CCCPC and the State Council have sized up the situation, united and led the people of all ethnic groups across the country, adhered to the development, which is the first priority for the CPC to govern and revitalize the country, implemented the CPC's theories, lines, principles and policies, implemented correct and effective macro-control, gave full play to the political advantages of China's socialist system, and the fundamental role of the market in resource allocation, and bring about new historic changes in the face of the country. China has effectively responded to the huge impact of the international financial crisis, maintained a good momentum of steady and rapid economic development, defeated major natural disasters such as the Wenchuan earthquake in Sichuan, the Yushu earthquake in Qinghai, and the massive mountain torrents and mudslides in Zhouqu, Gansu, successfully hosted the Beijing Olympic Games, the Shanghai World Expo, and the Guangzhou Asia Games, and successfully completed the main goals and tasks defined in the 11th Five-Year Plan. The overall national strength has increased significantly. In 2010, the GDP reached 40 trillion yuan, ranking second in the world, and the national fiscal revenue reached 8.3 trillion yuan; Major leaps have been made in cutting-edge scientific and technological fields such as manned spaceflight, lunar exploration program and supercomputer. The pace of economic restructuring has accelerated, agriculture, especially grain production, has achieved good harvests year after year, positive progress has been made in the optimization and upgrading of industrial structure, solid progress has been made in energy conservation and emission reduction and ecological environment protection, positive results have been achieved in controlling greenhouse gas emissions, and a distinctive regional development pattern has initially taken shape. People's lives have been improved significantly, more job oppurtunities are created, and the income growth of urban and rural residents has been one of the fastest periods since the reform and opening-up. Education of various kinds and at different levels developed rapidly, and the social security system has been steadily improved. System reform has been carried out in an orderly manner. New breakthroughs have been made in the comprehensive reform in rural areas, medicine and public health, finance and taxation, and cultural systems, and the vitality of development continues to emerge. Opening up has reached a new level. In 2010, the total import and export volume reached 2.97 trillion U.S. dollars, ranking second in the world. Foreign capital has been used more effectively, overseas investment has been significantly accelerated, and China's international status and influence have been significantly improved. Significant progress has been made in socialist economic, political, cultural, social and ecological civilization, and a new chapter in the cause of socialism with Chinese characteristics has been written. The achievements made in the past five years have not come easily, the accumulated experience is precious, and the spiritual wealth created has a far-reaching impact.

(2) Formulation of the 12th Five-Year Plan

In June 2008, more than half of the 11th Five-Year Plan was implemented, and the NDRC organized the mid-term evaluation of the 11th Five-Year Plan; In December of the same year, he reported to the Standing Committee of the NPC on the mid-term implementation of the 11th Five-Year Plan and put forward suggestions on some key issues that may be faced during the 12th Five-Year Plan period, so as to find outstanding problems in time, put forward solutions in time, improve the preparation of the "Outline" in time, and pave the way for the formulation of the next Five-Year Plan.[56]

In early February, 2010, the provincial and ministerial level leading cadres of the Party School of the CCCPC held a special seminar on thoroughly implementing the scientific outlook on development and accelerating the transformation of economic growth pattern. Hu Jintao and Wen Jiabao delivered important speeches, systematically reviewed the decision-making process and practical process of China's response to the impact of the international financial crisis and maintaining steady and rapid economic development in the previous period, and profoundly expounded the importance and urgency of accelerating the transformation of the economic growth pattern, further put forward the work requirements of accelerating the transformation, and set the tone for the basic idea of the 12th Five-Year Plan.

In July, 2010, Hu Jintao, general secretary of the CCCPC, presided over a meeting of the Political Bureau of the CCCPC. He stressed that the formulation of the 12th Five-Year Plan must adapt to the new changes in the situation at home and abroad, comply with the new expectations of people of all ethnic groups to live a better life, adhere to scientific development, accelerate the transformation of the economic growth pattern, constantly deepen reform and opening-up, effectively ensure and improve people's livelihood, consolidate and expand the achievements of coping with the impact of the international financial crisis, promote long-term stable and rapid economic development, and lay a decisive foundation for building a moderately prosperous society in all respects. This important speech has become an important guiding principle for the preparation of the compilation of the outline of the 12th Five-Year Plan.

In October, 2010, the Fifth Plenary Session of the 17th CCCPC adopted the "suggestions of the CCCPC on formulating the 12th Five-Year Plan for national economic and social development," which analyzed the domestic and international situation, and clearly put forward the economic and social development path and prospects that conform to China's national conditions, conform to the requirements of the times and unite the will of the people in the next five years according to China's basic national conditions and development stages. The meeting pointed out that the 12th Five-Year Plan should take scientific development as the theme and accelerate the transformation of the economic growth pattern as the main line. This points out the direction for the preparation of the outline of the 12th Five-Year Plan.

After the Fifth Plenary Session of the 17th CCCPC, the outline of the 12th Five-Year Plan officially entered the drafting stage. Hu Jintao has presided over many meetings of the Political Bureau of the CCCPC and the Standing Committee of the Political Bureau of the CCCPC to discuss and study major issues of development during the 12th Five-Year Plan period, and made a series of important instructions to give strong guidance to the preparation of the compilation of the outline of the 12th Five-Year Plan.

In March, 2011, the Fourth Session of the 11th NPC was held in Beijing, and adopted the *outline of the 12th Five-Year Plan for the national economic and social development of the PRC*, which is a program of action to promote China's scientific development in the next five years. The outline emphasizes that the period of the 12th Five-Year Plan (2011–2015) is a critical period for building a moderately prosperous society in an all-round way and for deepening reform and opening-up and accelerating the transformation of the economic growth pattern. In accordance with the requirements of closely connecting with the major deployment to deal with the impact of the international financial crisis and the goal of building a moderately prosperous society in an all-round way by 2020, and taking into account the future development trends and conditions, the main goal of economic and social development in the next five years is: steady and rapid economic development. The average annual growth of GDP is 7%, 45 million new urban jobs are created, the urban registered unemployment rate is controlled within 5%, the overall price level is basically stable, the international balance of payments tends to be basically balanced, and the quality and efficiency of economic growth are significantly improved. Notable headway will be made in economic restructuring. The ratio of consumption to GDP of residents was up. The agricultural as the foundation of the economy was further consolidated, the industrial structure continued to be optimized, breakthroughs were made in the development of strategic emerging industries, and the proportion of the added value of the service industry in the GDP increased by 4 percentage points. The level of urbanization has risen by 4%, and development between urban and rural areas and between regions has become better balanced. The scientific, technological and education level have been significantly improved. The quality of nine-year compulsory education has been significantly improved. The consolidation rate of nine-year compulsory education has reached 93%, and the gross enrollment rate of high school education has increased to 87%. Research and experimental development expenditure accounted for 2.2% of GDP, and the number of invention patents per 10,000 people increased to 3.3. Remarkable achievements have been made in resource conservation and environmental protection. The area of arable land remained at 1.818 billion mu. The water consumption per unit of industrial added value will be reduced by 30%, and the effective utilization coefficient of agricultural irrigation water will be increased to 0.53. Non-fossil energy will account for 11.4% of primary energy consumption. Energy consumption per unit of GDP will be reduced by 16%, and carbon dioxide emissions per unit of GDP will be reduced by 17%. The total emission of major pollutants will be significantly reduced, with chemical oxygen demand and sulfur dioxide emissions reduced by 8% and ammonia nitrogen and nitrogen oxide emissions reduced by 10% respectively. The forest coverage rate will be increased to 21.66%, and the forest volume will be increased by 600million cubic meters. People's living standards will be improved significantly. The total population of the country will be controlled within 1.39 billion. The average life expectancy will be increased by one year to 74.5 years. The per capita disposable income of urban residents and the per capita net income of rural residents will be increased by more than 7% annually respectively. The new rural social endowment insurance system will achieve full coverage, with 357 million people participating in basic endowment insurance in cities and towns, and the participation rate of the three basic urban and rural healthcare systems has increased by 3 percentage points. 36 million sets of affordable housing projects will be built in cities and towns. The number of poor people will be decreased significantly. Social construction has been significantly strengthened. The basic public service system covering both urban and rural residents will be gradually improved. The ideological and ethical standards, the scientific and cultural qualities, and the health of the whole people will be enhanced notably. Socialist democracy and the law system will become sounder, and the rights and interests of the people will be effectively protected. The development of cultural programs will be accelerated, and the proportion of cultural industries in the national economy will be increased significantly. The social management system tends to be improved, and the society is more harmonious and stable. Reform and opening-up will be deepened. Significant progress will be made in the reform of important areas and key links such as finance, taxation, factor prices, and monopoly industries. The change of government functions will be accelerated, and the public trust in the government and administrative efficiency will be further improved. The breadth and depth of opening-up will be continuously expanded, and the pattern of mutually beneficial and win-win opening-up will be further formed. The outline also defines major policy directions from ten aspects: strengthen and improve macro-control, establish a long-term mechanism to expand consumption demand, adjust and optimize the investment structure, synchronously promote industrialization, urbanization and agricultural modernization, rely on scientific and technological innovation to promote industrial upgrading, promote regional coordinated and interactive development, improve the incentive and restraint mechanism for energy conservation and emission reduction, promote the equalization of basic public services, and accelerate the income growth of urban and rural residents, strengthen and make innovations in social administration.

3.2.3 The Nine "No. 1 Documents" of the Central Committee and the Construction of a New Socialist Countryside

(1) Nine Central "No. 1 Documents" on the "Issues Relating to Agriculture"
The problems of agriculture, rural areas and farmers have a direct bearing on the overall development of the great cause of the socialist construction of the CPC and the Republic. In the 1980s, the CCCPC and the State Council issued the central "No. 1 document" on rural policy for five consecutive years. In the new century, facing the weak agricultural foundation, low-level farmers' income and lagging rural development, since 2004, the CCCPC and the State Council have issued nine central "No. 1 documents" to guide agricultural and rural development,

and issued a series of special policies to support and benefit agriculture, rural areas and farmers.

In December, 2003, the CCCPC and the State Council issued the first central "No. 1 document" on "agriculture, rural areas and farmers" since the 21st century—the opinions of the CCCPC and the State Council on several policies to promote farmers' income increase. The document requires that we should adjust the agricultural structure, create more job opportunities for farmers, accelerate scientific and technological progress, deepen rural reform, increase agricultural investment, strengthen support and protection, strive to achieve rapid growth in farmers' income, and reverse the widening trend of the income gap between urban and rural residents as soon as possible. In December, 2004, the CCCPC and the State Council issued the *opinions on several policies to further strengthen rural work and improve the comprehensive agricultural production capacity*, namely the second central "No. 1 document." The document points out that it is necessary to stabilize, improve and strengthen various agricultural support policies, effectively strengthen the construction of comprehensive agricultural production capacity, continue to adjust the agricultural and rural economic structure, further deepen rural reform, strive to achieve a stable increase in grain production and sustained increase in farmers' income, and promote the all-round development of rural economy and society. In December, 2005, the CCCPC and the State Council issued the *several opinions on promoting the construction of a new socialist countryside*, which is the third central "No. 1 document." The document requires that we should improve and strengthen the policy of supporting agriculture, build modern agriculture, stably develop grain production, actively adjust the agricultural structure, strengthen infrastructure construction, strengthen the construction of rural democracy and spiritual civilization, speed up the development of social undertakings, promote comprehensive rural reform, promote the continuous increase of farmers' income, and ensure a good start in the construction of a new socialist countryside. In December, 2006, the CCCPC and the State Council issued the *several opinions on actively developing modern agriculture and solidly promoting the construction of a new socialist countryside*, namely the fourth central "No. 1 document." The document emphasizes that developing modern agriculture is the primary task of building a new socialist countryside. We should equip agriculture with modern material conditions, transform agriculture with modern science and technology, improve agriculture with modern industrial system, promote agriculture with modern forms of management, guide agriculture with modern development concepts, develop agriculture with the cultivation of new farmers, improve the level of agricultural water conservancy, mechanization and informatization, and improve the rate of land output, resource utilization and agricultural labor productivity, improve agricultural quality, efficiency and competitiveness. In December, 2007, the CCCPC and the State Council issued the "several opinions on strengthening agricultural infrastructure construction and further promoting agricultural development and increasing farmers' income," which is the Fifth Central "No. 1 document." The document proposed that we should take the path of agricultural modernization with Chinese characteristics, establish a long-term mechanism of promoting agriculture with industry and leading villages with cities, and form a new pattern that integrates economic and social development in urban and rural areas. In February, 2009, the CCCPC and the State Council issued the "several opinions on promoting the stable development of agriculture and the continuous increase of farmers' income," which is the Sixth Central "No. 1 document." The document points out that it is necessary to strengthen the crisis awareness, fully estimate the difficulties, firmly grasp the opportunities, resolutely take measures to prevent the decline of grain production, resolutely prevent farmers' income from wandering, ensure the stable development of agriculture and ensure the stability of rural society. In December, 2009, the CCCPC and the State Council issued the "several opinions on strengthening the overall planning of urban and rural development and further consolidating the foundation of agricultural and rural development," namely the Seventh Central "No. 1 document." The document emphasizes that at present, China's agriculture is more open, the correlation between urban and rural economies is significantly enhanced, the impact of climate change on agricultural production is increasing, the favorable conditions and positive factors for agricultural and rural development are accumulating, and various traditional and non-traditional challenges are also superimposed and highlighted. In the face of the complicated and volatile development environment, there are more and more constraints to promote agricultural production to a new high, it is more and more difficult to maintain the rapid growth of farmers' income, the requirements for transforming the agricultural development pattern are higher and higher, and the burden of breaking the urban-rural dual structure is growing. In December, 2010, the CCCPC and the State Council issued the decision on accelerating the reform and development of water conservancy, which is the eighth "No. 1 document" of the CCCPC. This is the decision of the CCCPC and the State Council to systematically deploy the comprehensive work of water conservancy reform and development for the first time in the 62 years since the founding of new China. The document emphasizes that: take water conservancy as a priority area of national infrastructure construction, take farmland water conservancy as a key task of rural infrastructure construction, take strict water resource management as a strategic measure to accelerate the transformation of economic growth pattern, and vigorously develop water conservancy for people's livelihood, strive to blaze a path of water conservancy modernization with Chinese characteristics. In December, 2011, the CCCPC and the State Council issued several opinions on accelerating the promotion of agricultural scientific and technological innovation and continuously enhancing the supply guarantee capacity of agricultural products, which is the nineth "No. 1 document" of the Central Committee. The document stressed that the fundamental way to achieve sustainable and stable agricultural development and ensure the effective supply of agricultural products in the long term lies in science and technology. We must firmly grasp the historical opportunity of the world's scientific and technological revolution in full swing, adhere to the strategy of developing agriculture relying on science and education, place agricultural science and technology in a more prominent position, and be determined to break through systematic and institutional barriers, substantially increase investment in agricultural science and technology, promote the leapfrog development of agricultural science and technology, and inject strong impetus into agricultural production, farmers' income, and rural prosperity. So far in the new stage of the new century, the nine central "No. 1 documents" focusing on the work of "agriculture, rural areas and farmers" have complied with and guided the rural reform, effectively promoted the rural reform and agricultural production, and brought great changes to China's rural areas.

Although the themes of the nine central "No. 1 documents" at this stage are different every year, they all focus on the main line of strengthening the work of "agriculture, rural areas and farmers," issue a series of policies to strengthen agriculture and benefit agriculture, clarify the basic strategy of coordinating urban and rural economic and social development, jointly form the strategic thinking and guiding principles of strengthening the work of "agriculture, rural areas and farmers" in the new century, and preliminarily build the basic policy framework for the agriculture, rural areas, farmers and the coordinated development of urban and rural areas in the new stage of the new century, point out the direction of the work of "agriculture, rural areas and farmers" in the new period and new stage, and reflects the common aspiration of hundreds of millions of farmers.

(2) Building a New Socialist Countryside

At the new stage of the new century, China's agricultural foundation is still weak, rural development is still lagging behind, and it is still difficult for farmers to increase their income. Building a new socialist countryside is proposed under this background.

The formation of the concept of "building a new socialist countryside" began at the 16th National Congress of the CPC. In 2002, the 16th National Congress of the CPC made "building moderately prosperous society in an all-round way is to make overall planning for urban and rural economic and social development, build modern agriculture, develop the rural economy and increase the income of farmers "one of the major tasks. In October, 2003, the Third Plenary Session of the 16th CCCPC passed the decision of the CCCPC on Several Issues concerning the Improvement of the Socialist Market Economic system, which made specific arrangements for the work of "agriculture, rural areas and farmers" from the perspective of system reform: (1) improve the rural land system. (2) We will improve agricultural socialized services, agricultural product markets, and the support and protection system for agriculture. (3) Deepen the reform of taxes and fees in rural areas. (4) Improve the environment for the transfer and employment of surplus rural labor. In October, 2005, the *proposal of the CCCPC on formulating the 11th Five-Year Plan for national economic and social development* adopted at the Fifth Plenary Session of the 16th CCCPC pointed out that building a new socialist countryside is a major historical task in the process of China's modernization. It should be promoted actively and steadily in accordance with the requirements of production development, affluent life, civilized rural style, clean and tidy village appearance, and democratic management, which fully reflects the development requirements of rural economy, politics cultural and social development. In December of the same year, the central rural work conference was held in Beijing to study the task of promoting the construction of a new socialist countryside during the 11th Five-Year Plan period, and discussed the *several opinions on promoting the construction of a new socialist countryside (discussion draft)*. The revised document was issued as the "No. 1 Document" of the Central Committee in 2006. It is a programmatic document to comprehensively promote the construction of a new socialist countryside.

In February, 2006, the CCCPC held a special seminar for major leading cadres at the provincial and ministerial levels to build a new socialist countryside. Wen Jiabao delivered an important speech, pointing out that in accordance with the requirements of the scientific outlook on development and the idea of overall planning of urban and rural areas, we should take the fundamental interests of the broad masses of farmers as the starting point and purpose, comprehensively promote the construction of a new socialist countryside, and make a big change in the rural appearance after long-term unremitting efforts. In December, 2006, the *several opinions on actively developing modern agriculture and solidly promoting the construction of a new socialist countryside* was issued. The document once again emphasized that we should take solving the issues relating to agriculture as the top priority of the work of the whole Party, coordinate the economic and social development of urban and rural areas, implement the policies of industry supporting agriculture in return, cities supporting rural areas, and "giving more, taking less, and letting go," and put forward the need to effectively increase agricultural investment, actively promote the construction of modern agriculture, strengthen rural public services, and deepen comprehensive rural reform.

In order to further strengthen the basic position of agriculture, ensure the stable development of agriculture, the continuous increase of farmers' income and the all-round development of rural areas, the 17th National Congress of the CPC in 2007 proposed to take the path of agricultural modernization with Chinese characteristics, and took it as one of the five specific paths under the general path of socialism with Chinese characteristics. This points out the direction for future agricultural development. In October, 2008, the Third Plenary Session of the 17th CCCPC was held. The plenary session studied several major issues in promoting rural reform and development under the new situation, and pointed out that only by persisting in solving the problems of agriculture, rural areas and farmers as the top priority of the work of the whole Party, adhering to the basic position of agriculture, adhering to the direction of socialist market economy reform, adhering to the path of agricultural modernization with Chinese characteristics, and adhering to ensuring the material interests and democratic rights of farmers, can we continuously liberate and develop rural social productive forces, promote the all-round development of rural economy and society. In October, 2010, the Fifth Plenary Session of the 17th CCCPC further emphasized the need to promote agricultural modernization, accelerate the construction of a new socialist countryside, coordinate urban and rural development, accelerate the development of modern agriculture, strengthen infrastructure and public services in rural areas, open up more channels to increase rural income, improve rural development systems and mechanisms, and build a beautiful home for farmers to live a happy life. In order to continuously improve the living standards of the rural poor population, in 2011, the Chinese government issued the *outline of China's rural poverty alleviation and development (2011–2020)*, which clearly stated that by 2020, the poverty alleviation targets will steadily achieve the general goals of not worrying about food and clothing, as well as ensuring their compulsory education, basic medical treatment and housing.

Since the construction of a new socialist countryside has been promoted at the new stage of the new century, remarkable achievements have been made in the construction of a new countryside, and the outlook of rural life has been significantly improved. The State implements the general plan of coordinating urban and rural economic and social development and the policy of industry to support agriculture in return for agriculture's earlier contribution to its development and cities support rural areas by "giving more, taking less, and letting go," so as to comprehensively promote the development of rural economy and society and benefit poor areas and rural poor people. By the end of 2012, the central government had invested nearly 4.47 trillion yuan in "agriculture, rural areas and farmers," completely abolished agricultural taxes and various fees, ended the history of farmers paying taxes on farming, and reduced farmers' burden by more than 133.5 billion yuan every year; had established the subsidy system for grain farmers and the benefit compensation mechanism for main production areas, and the production subsidy funds for farmers had reached 192.3 billion yuan in 2012; strengthened rural financial services, and the balance of agricultural loans had increased from 6.12 trillion yuan at the end of 2007 to 17.63 trillion yuan at the end of 2012; the minimum purchase price policy of grain was implemented, and the minimum purchase price of wheat and rice had increased by 41.7% to 86.7%. The central government had strictly protected arable land, and maintain the arable land area at more than 1.82 billion mu; had promoted the progress of agricultural science and technology and the construction of modern agriculture, and increase support for improved seed breeding, animal and plant disease prevention and control, and grass-roots agricultural technology promotion. Grain output had repeatedly hit record highs, with the total national grain output reaching 571.21 million tons in 2011. In 2012, the per capita net income of farmers reached 7917 yuan, achieving sustained and rapid growth, and the relative income gap between urban and rural residents gradually narrowed. The comprehensive rural reform has been steadily promoted, and the reform of the collective forest ownership system and the reform of the management system of state-owned farms had been carried out in an all-round way. The construction of agricultural and rural infrastructure had been accelerated, 1.465 million kilometers of rural roads were newly built and reconstructed, 10.33 million dilapidated houses in rural areas were renovated, the drinking water safety of more than 300 million rural people and the electricity consumption of 4.45 million people in non-electricity areas were solved, and the rural production and living conditions had been continuously improved. The reform of the main body in tenure of collective forests system had been basically completed, the confirmation and certification of rural collective land rights have been comprehensively promoted, and pilot projects for the registration of management rights of land contracted by peasants have been carried out. The promising situation of agricultural and rural development has provided important support for coping with the serious impact of the international financial crisis and various natural disasters and stabilizing the overall economic and social development.

3.2.4 Facing the International Financial Crisis

In the second half of 2007, the global financial crisis triggered by the U.S. subprime mortgage crisis brought great disasters to countries all over the world, and also brought great impact to China's economy. In the face of the severe situation, the CCCPC and the State Council made decisions decisively, calmly responded to challenges, turned challenges into opportunities, and continuously launched and enriched and improved the package plan and relevant policies and measures to deal with the international financial crisis.

As early as August 2007, in the collective study in the Political Bureau of the CCCPC, Hu Jintao pointed out that in the face of economic globalization and the continuous expansion of the scope of China's opening-up to the outside world, it is necessary to strengthen the national economic security monitoring and early warning, crisis response and response capabilities, and enhance ability of the financial industry to withstand risks.

In June, 2008, the CCCPC and the State Council held a meeting of major heads of provinces, municipalities and central departments. The meeting pointed out that we should be on full alert against economic risks, fully understand the sudden nature of the financial crisis, properly grasp the rhythm and range of financial opening-up, and effectively ensure financial security. On the basis of a series of symposiums and seminars held by the CCCPC and the State Council, Hu Jintao chaired a meeting of the Political Bureau of the CCCPC on July 25 to study the current economic situation and economic work. On the basis of in-depth analysis of challenges and difficulties, this meeting stressed the need to enhance the predictability, pertinence and flexibility of macro-control, and grasp the key points, pace and intensity of regulation. The meeting proposed that maintaining steady and rapid economic development and controlling the excessive rise of prices should be the primary task of macro-control in the second half of the year, and the suppression of inflation should be given a prominent position.

Since September, 2008, the international economic situation has turned sharply downward, and the adverse impact on China's development has increased significantly. On October 7, Hu Jintao presided over a Meeting of the Standing Committee of the Political Bureau of the CCCPC to analyze the situation of the international financial crisis and study countermeasures. The meeting decided to hold an economic briefing of the international financial crisis and related work to inform the main heads of provinces, autonomous regions and municipalities, central departments and major military units. The meeting also decided to establish a team to deal with the international financial crisis. The subsequent Third Plenary Session of the 17th CCCPC specially analyzed the economic situation and stressed that China's success in running its own affairs is not only the fundamental purpose for coping with the impact of the financial tsunami, but also the greatest support for the world to overcome the financial crisis. We should boost confidence, observe and cope with the situation cool-headedly, in a multi-pronged manner, adopt flexible and prudent macroeconomic policies, strive to expand domestic demand, especially consumer demand, and maintain economic stability, financial stability, and capital market stability. On November 5, the executive meeting of the State Council decided to take 10 measures to further expand domestic demand and promote economic growth, including accelerating the construction of affordable housing projects, rural infrastructure, railways, highways, airports and other major infrastructure. It is preliminarily estimated that the implementation of these projects will require an investment of about 4 trillion yuan by the end of 2010. On November 10, the State Council held a meeting of major heads of provinces, autonomous regions and municipalities and departments of the State Council to make comprehensive arrangements for the implementation of the major decisions of the central government to deal with the crisis. In December, the central economic work conference held that the fundamentals and long-term trends of China's economic development have not changed, and important strategic opportunities for China's development still exist.

In 2009, the primary task of economic work must be to maintain steady and rapid economic development. We should work hard to maintain growth, take expanding domestic demand as the fundamental way to maintain growth, take accelerating the transformation of development pattern and structural adjustment as the main direction to maintain growth, take deepening the reform of key areas and key links and improving the level of opening up as a strong driving force to maintain growth, and take improving people's livelihood as the starting point and purpose to maintain growth.

Entering 2009, the international financial crisis still spreading, the world economy is in a deep recession, China's economy has been seriously impacted, exports have fallen sharply, many enterprises have difficulties in operation, some are even shut down, a large number of unemployed people have increased, a large number of rural migrant workers have returned home, and the economic growth rate has fallen sharply. The CCCPC and the State Council have continuously strengthened their policies and enriched and improved the package plan.

In the more than 40 days from January 14 to February 25, 2009, the State Council held six executive meetings in succession to consider and adopt the adjustment and reinvigorating plans for ten key industries, including automobile, steel, textile, equipment manufacturing, shipbuilding, electronic information, light industry, petrochemical, non-ferrous metals, logistics, etc. Around this period, the State Council issued the outline of the reform and development plan for the Pearl River Delta region (2008–2020), and successively approved the reinvigorating plans for Chongqing to coordinate urban and rural reform and development, Shanghai to accelerate the development of modern service industry and advanced manufacturing industry, build an international financial center and international shipping center, and Fujian to accelerate the construction of the Economic Zone on the West Coast of the Strait. In the early and middle of March, the Second Session of the 11th NPC approved a package plan to deal with the crisis. Taking into account the needs and possibilities of China's development, it took "maintaining GDP growth of about 8%" as the main goal of economic work in 2009. In July, 2009, the Political Bureau of the CCCPC discussed and studied the current economic situation and economic work, and clarified China's ideas and plans for coping with the impact of the international financial crisis in the second half of 2009. The meeting pointed out that at present, China's economic development was in a critical period of stabilization and recovery, China's economic development still faced many difficulties and challenges, the foundation of economic recovery was not stable, and there were still many unstable and uncertain factors at home and abroad. We should continue to take promoting steady and rapid economic development as the primary task of economic work and maintain the continuity and stability of macroeconomic policies.

In September, 2009, the Fourth Plenary Session of the 17th CCCPC pointed out that we should work with one heart and one mind, rise to the challenges, be determined to reform, overcome difficulties, make every effort to ensure growth, people's livelihood and stability, increase efforts to transform the economic growth pattern and adjust the economic structure, and achieve remarkable results in coping with the impact of the international financial crisis and maintaining steady and rapid economic development. On November 27, 2009, the Political Bureau of the CCCPC held a meeting and pointed out that this year was the most difficult year for China's economic and social development since the new century, and it was also a year for us to forge ahead and withstand severe tests. China's economic rebound has been continuously consolidated, and remarkable achievements have been made in economic and social development. It is extremely difficult to achieve such a result. At the end of 2009, the central economic work conference comprehensively analyzed the current international and domestic economic situation, profoundly expounded the importance and urgency of accelerating the transformation of economic growth pattern, and pointed out that we should focus on optimizing the economic structure and improving the ability of self-dependent innovation, and focus on improving the performance assessment mechanism to enhance the consciousness and initiative of accelerating the transformation of economic growth pattern. By the second half of 2009, the downward trend of China's economic growth had been effectively contained.

In the face of the sweeping international financial crisis, China has actively participated in the international cooperation to deal with the crisis, despite its great difficulties and severe challenges. China has actively participated in the construction of the G20 and other global economic governance mechanisms, promoted the reform of the international financial system, participated in the coordination of macroeconomic policies of various countries, participated in international trade financing plans and financial cooperation, organized large procurement missions to purchase overseas, extended assistance to troubled countries, and fully demonstrated China's image as a "responsible" big country.

Under the strong leadership of the CPC, the people of all ethnic groups across the country have strengthened their confidence, risen to challenges, worked with fortitude, calmly responded to the impact of the international financial crisis, took the lead in the world to achieve economic recovery, made new major achievements in reform and opening-up and socialist modernization, and the national economy has stepped up to a new level.

3.2.5 Building an Innovative Country

As early as 2002, the 16th National Congress of the CPC had pointed out that innovation sustains the progress of a nation, it is an inexhaustible motive force for the prosperity of a country and the source of the eternal vitality of a political party. In October, 2003, the Third Plenary Session of the 16th CCCPC once again emphasized the need to deepen the reform of the systems of science, technology, education, culture and health, innovate the working mechanism, create an institutional environment for implementing the strategy to make China a talent-strong country, and speed up the construction of the national innovation system. In September, 2004, the Fourth Plenary Session of the 16th CCCPC pointed out that we should vigorously implement the strategy for invigorating China through science and education, speed up the construction of the national innovation system, and give full play to the role of science and technology as the primary productive force. In October, 2005, the Fifth Plenary Session of the 16th CCCPC took improving the ability of self-dependent innovation and building an innovative country as one of the main tasks during the 11th Five-Year Plan period. The meeting deliberated and adopted the proposal of the CCCPC on formulating the *11th Five-Year Plan for National Economic and Social Development*, which takes strengthening the ability of self-dependent innovation as an important content of the proposal, and takes strengthening the ability of self-dependent innovation as the strategic base point of scientific and technological development and the central link of adjusting the industrial structure and transforming the growth pattern.

In order to mobilize the whole society to adhere to the path of self-dependent innovation with Chinese characteristics, strive to build an innovative country, further create a new situation of building a moderately prosperous society in an all-round way and accelerating socialist modernization, in January 2006, the first national science and technology conference of the new century was held. Hu Jintao delivered an important speech entitled "adhering to the path of self-dependent innovation with Chinese characteristics and striving to build an innovative country." For the first time, it systematically expounds the strategic significance of improving the ability of self-dependent innovation and building an innovative country, and makes important arrangements on how to improve the ability of self-dependent innovation and build an innovative country. He stressed the macro goal of building China into an innovative country in 15 years: by 2020, China's capacity for self-dependent innovation, the ability of science and technology to promote economic and social development and ensure national security will be significantly enhanced, the comprehensive strength of basic science and cutting-edge technology research will be significantly enhanced, a number of scientific and technological achievements with great impact in the world will be achieved, and China will enter the ranks of innovative countries, and provide strong support for building moderately prosperous society in an all-round way.

In February, 2006, the outline of the national medium- and long-term science and technology development plan (2006–2020) was officially announced. Based on the national conditions and facing the world, this "planning outline" takes Deng Xiaoping Theory and the important thought of "Three Represents" as the guidance, thoroughly implements the scientific outlook on development, takes enhancing the ability of self-dependent innovation as the main line, and takes building an innovative country as the goal, and makes a comprehensive plan and deployment for the development of science and technology in China in the next 15 years. It is a programmatic document guiding the development of science and technology in China in the new era. In October of the same year, the Sixth Plenary Session of the 16th CCCPC was held. The meeting once again clearly stated that by 2020, we should basically build an innovative country.

In February, 2007, the NDRC released the *"11th Five-Year Plan" (2006–2010)* for the construction of national self-dependent innovation infrastructure. The plan points out that we should adhere to the guidance of the scientific outlook on development, implement the scientific and technological development policy of "self-dependent innovation, key leaps, supporting development, and leading the future," follow the general principle of "focusing on long-term development, optimizing the overall layout, improving systems and mechanisms, and improving innovation capabilities," reflect the requirements of high-level, non-duplication, promoting resource sharing, and military civilian integration, and plan the construction of national self-dependent innovation infrastructure as a whole, and provide the necessary material and technological foundation for building China into an innovative country. In October, 2007, the 17th National Congress of the CPC further clearly pointed out to improve the ability of self-dependent innovation and build an innovative country. This is the core of our national development strategy and a crucial link in enhancing the overall national strength. We need to keep to the path of independent innovation with Chinese characteristics and improve our capacity for independent innovation in all areas of modernization.

In June, 2008, the 14th academician conference of the Chinese Academy of Sciences and the Nineth Academician Conference of the Chinese Academy of Engineering were held in Beijing. Hu Jintao attended the meeting and delivered an important speech. Hu Jintao stressed that we should adhere to the guiding principles of "self-dependent innovation, key leaps, supporting development and leading the future," take enhancing the ability of self-dependent innovation as the strategic base point for the development of science and technology, as the central link for the adjustment of industrial structure and the transformation of development mode, take the construction of an innovative country as a major strategic choice for the future, and take the path of self-dependent innovation with Chinese characteristics more consciously and firmly."

In January, 2010, the NDRC decided to expand the pilot scope on the basis of promoting the pilot work of creating a national innovative city in Shenzhen, focus on improving the regional innovation system, enhancing the capacity of sustainable development, accelerating the realization of innovation driven development, continuing to guide and promote a number of cities to carry out the pilot work of creating a national innovative city, and striving to give full play to the leading, demonstration and driving role of cities, especially innovative cities, gathering to form a number of innovative urban agglomerations, taking the lead in breaking through the bottleneck that restricts innovation and development, and speeding up the process of building an innovative country. This major measure marks that China's construction of an innovative country has entered a critical stage.

In June, 2010, the 15th academician conference of the Chinese Academy of Sciences and the 10th academician conference of the Chinese Academy of engineering were open. At the conference, Hu Jintao emphasized that to build an innovative country, accelerate the transformation of the economic growth pattern, and win the development opportunity and initiative, the most fundamental thing was to rely on the power of science and technology, and the most critical thing was to significantly improve the ability of self-dependent innovation. In October, 2010, the Fifth Plenary Session of the 17th CCCPC clearly proposed to take scientific development as the theme and change the economic growth pattern as the main line, and proposed to adhere to scientific and technological progress and innovation as an important support to accelerate the transformation of the economic growth pattern. This further pointed out the direction and important focus of China's current scientific and technological development that is to give full play to the leading and fundamental role of scientific and technological innovation, and provide strong scientific and technological support for accelerating the transformation of economic growth pattern and achieving the goals and tasks of the 12th Five-Year Plan. In March, 2011, the Fourth Session of the 11th NPC passed the outline of the 12th Five-Year Plan for the national economic and social development of the PRC. The outline clearly requires the in-depth implementation of the strategy of rejuvenating the country through science and education and the strategy for invigorating China through science and education, and speed up the construction of an innovative country.

Under the guidance of the major strategic decision of building an innovative country, China has made great achievements in science and technology. China has become a major scientific and technological country with a relatively complete scientific and technological system, the world's first scientific and technological human resources, and the continuous emergence of scientific and technological achievements. Specifically:

First, a relatively complete system of modern science and technology had been established. China has become one of the few countries in the world with relatively comprehensive discipline construction. In terms of basic research, cutting-edge technology research, social welfare research, application development and industrialization, China has formed a more reasonable and multi-level layout of scientific and technological forces, including national scientific research institutions, colleges and universities, local scientific research institutions and various types of enterprises.

Second, in terms of R&D team and scale, China's total scientific and technological human resources reached 42 million in 2009, ranking first in the world. In 2010, China's scientific and technological R&D expenditure reached 1.75% of GDP, a record high.

Third, scientific and technological strength has been significantly enhanced. Since the beginning of the new century, the CCCPC and the State Council have adopted a series of major strategic measures to accelerate the development of China's science and technology undertakings. Through the tenacious efforts of the vast number of scientific and technological personnel, China has made a number of major scientific and technological achievements marked by manned spaceflight, the lunar exploration project, the application of hybrid rice, high-performance computers, genome research, etc., has a number of independent intellectual property rights that play an important role in agriculture and industry, has broken through the scientific and technological difficulties of a number of major projects, such as the Three Gorges Hydro-Power Project, the Qinghai-Xizang railway, etc., and has promoted the rapid rise of a number of high-tech industrial clusters. It has created a number of excellent enterprises with independent well-known brands, and the scientific and technological level of the whole society has been significantly improved.

Fourth, international scientific and technological cooperation has presented a new situation. As of February 2011, China has joined more than 1,000 international scientific and technological cooperation organizations, and international scientific and technological cooperation has been promoted from the personnel exchange level to the deep-seated cooperation level of joint research and development and joint key technology research. China has actively participated in the international nuclear fusion energy program, Galileo program, International Earth Observation and other major international scientific projects. As of 2009, China has established scientific and technological cooperation relations with 152 countries and regions, and has signed 104 intergovernmental scientific and technological cooperation agreements with 97 of them.

3.2.6 Promote Coordinated Regional Development

(1) "Revitalizing the Old Industrial Bases in the Northeast" Strategy
At the early stage of socialist industrialization, the old industrial bases in the northeast have made historic and significant contributions to the establishment of an independent and complete national economic system, the promotion of China's industrialization and urbanization. Since the 1990s, due to various reasons such as system and mechanism, the old industrial bases in the northeast have begun to face many obstacles in the process of fully integrating into the market economy.

In 2002, the 16th National Congress of the CPC emphasized "supporting the old industrial bases in the northeast and other parts of China to speed up the adjustment and transformation" as an important measure to realize the "gradual reversal of the trend of expanding regional differences." In June, 2003, Premier Wen Jiabao made a personal visit to the northeast and held a symposium, putting forward the basic ideas for revitalizing the old industrial bases in the northeast and other parts of China. In September, 2003, the Political Bureau of the CCCPC held a meeting to discuss the implementation of the revitalization strategy of old industrial bases such as the northeast region. The meeting pointed out: "supporting the revitalization of old industrial bases such as the northeast region is a major strategic task put forward by the 16th National Congress of the CPC from the overall perspective of building moderately prosperous society in an all-round way. All regions and departments should have a deep understanding of the great significance of implementing the revitalization strategy of old industrial bases such as the northeast region from the perspective of the long-term development of China's reform and opening-up and socialist modernization at the new stage of the new century.[57] "The implementation of the strategy of revitalizing the northeast region and other old industrial bases was officially announced. In October, 2003, several opinions of the CCCPC and the State Council on implementing the revitalization strategy of old industrial bases in the northeast and other regions were officially issued, pointing out the guiding ideology and basic principles for revitalizing old industrial bases in the northeast and other regions, emphasizing that we should further deepen system reform, strive to promote system and mechanism innovation, eliminate institutional obstacles that are not conducive to economic development and adjustment and transformation, and enhance the internal driving force for the adjustment and transformation of old industrial bases, which is the key and premise to realize the revitalization of the old industrial bases. In April, 2004, the State Council established the office of revitalizing the old industrial bases in the northeast and other regions to comprehensively launch this strategic initiative.

The guiding ideology of revitalizing the old industrial bases in the northeast is: take the important thought of "Three Represents" as the guidance, fully implement the spirit of the 16th National Congress of the CPC, further emancipate the mind, deepen reform, expand the scope of opening-up, strive to promote system innovation and mechanism innovation, and form a new economic growth mechanism; according to the requirements of taking the new road of industrialization, adhere to the market-oriented, promote the optimization and upgrading of industrial structure, and improve the overall quality and competitiveness of enterprises; adhere to overall planning, achieve comprehensive, coordinated and sustainable economic and social development in old industrial bases in the northeast and other parts of China, and make new contributions to building moderately prosperous society in an all-round way and realizing socialist modernization. The basic principles are: first, we should adhere to deepening reform and opening-up, and promote adjustment and transformation with reform and opening-up. Second, we should adhere to the principle of relying mainly on market mechanisms and give full play to the role of the government. Third, we should persist in trying to do certain things and refrain from doing other things, and give full play to our comparative advantages. Fourth, we should adhere to overall planning and pay attention to coordinated development. Fifth, the state should give necessary support to self-reliance. Sixth, we should proceed from reality and strive for practical results.

After 2004, the national policy of supporting the revitalization of the old industrial bases in Northeast China has been implemented successively: first, it took the lead in implementing the policy of full exemption of agricultural tax in Heilongjiang and Jilin provinces; second, on the basis of summarizing the pilot experience of improving the urban social security system in Liaoning Province, the pilot scope was be expanded to Heilongjiang and Jilin provinces; third, some old industrial base cities were selected to carry out the pilot of separating social functions, to properly solve the problem of "large collectives" run by factories, and give priority to the enterprises in the old industrial bases that meet the bankruptcy conditions into the national enterprise merger and bankruptcy work plan; fourth, commercial banks were allowed to take further measures to dispose of non-performing assets and reduce the off-balance sheet interest of loan enterprises independently, so as to help reduce the debt burden of relevant enterprises; fifth, it took the lead in piloting fiscal and tax policies such as value-added tax transformation pilot and enterprise income tax reform in the three northeastern provinces; sixth, it simplified the approval procedures for the adjustment and transformation projects of old industrial bases, and increased the support of national debt or special funds for old industrial bases; seventh, it implemented the policy of exempting enterprises in the northeast old industrial bases from historical tax arrears.

In 2005, the leading group office for revitalizing the old industrial bases in the northeast and other parts of China proposed to focus on eight aspects: further strengthening agriculture; promoting the optimization and upgrading of industrial structure; accelerating the innovation of systems and mechanisms; continuing to expand opening up to the outside world; coordinating the harmonious development between man and nature; vigorously strengthening the construction of talent team in Northeast China; effectively solving the affairs of immediate concern for the people; strengthening coordination and cooperation, and carrying out in-depth investigation and research. In March, 2006, the Fourth Session of the 10th NPC voted and passed a resolution on the outline of the 11th Five-Year Plan for national economic and social development, emphasizing that the northeast region should accelerate the adjustment of industrial structure and the reform, reorganization and transformation of SOEs, so as to achieve revitalization in the reform and opening-up.

In order to promote the comprehensive revitalization of old industrial bases in Northeast China, cope with the international financial crisis, and promote the steady and rapid development of the national economy, the State Council issued several opinions on further implementing the Revitalization Strategy of old industrial bases in the northeast and other parts of China in 2009. The opinions put forward 28 suggestions in 9 aspects, including: optimizing the economic structure and establishing a modern industrial system; accelerating the technological progress of enterprises and comprehensively improving the ability of self-dependent innovation; accelerating the development of modern agriculture and consolidating the basic position of agriculture; Strengthening infrastructure construction and creating conditions for comprehensive revitalization; actively promoting the transformation of resource-based cities and promote sustainable development; effectively protecting the ecological environment and vigorously developing the green economy; focusing on solving people's livelihood problems and accelerate the development of social undertakings; deepening provincial and regional cooperation and promoting the development of regional economic integration; continuing to deepen reform and opening-up and invigorating economic and social growth. In October, 2010, the Fifth Plenary Session of the 17th CCCPC passed the "suggestions of the CCCPC on formulating the 12th Five-Year Plan for national economic and social development," emphasizing the comprehensive revitalization of old industrial bases such as the northeast region, giving play to the advantages of a strong industrial and technological foundation, improving the modern industrial system, and promoting the transformation the economies of areas where natural resources are exhausted.

Implementing the Revitalization Strategy of old industrial bases such as the northeast region is a major strategic decision made by the CPC and the Chinese government under the new historical conditions after sizing up and planning the overall situation, and focusing on the overall situation of building moderately prosperous society in an all-round way and speeding up the modernization drive. Since the implementation of the Revitalization Strategy of old industrial bases such as the northeast region, major breakthroughs have been made in the innovation of systems and mechanisms focusing on the reform of SOEs. The economy of various forms of ownership has flourished, the economic structure has been further optimized, the ability of self-dependent innovation has been significantly improved, the level of opening to the outside world has been significantly improved, infrastructure conditions have been improved, key livelihood issues have been gradually solved, and great changes have taken place in the face of urban and rural areas. In 2008, the proportion of the GDP of the three northeastern provinces in the country rose to 8.62%, 0.14 percent higher than that in 2007. This is the first time that the proportion of the GDP of the three northeastern provinces in the country had stopped falling and rebounded after entering the new century. In 2012, the GDP of the three northeastern provinces exceeded 5 trillion yuan, reaching 5.04 trillion yuan. Since the implementation of the strategy of revitalizing the old industrial bases in the northeast and other parts of China for ten years (2003–2012), the regional GDP of the three northeastern provinces has more than quadrupled from 1.14 trillion yuan in 2002, with an average annual growth rate of 12.7%. Practice has proved that the central government's decision to implement the strategy of revitalizing the old industrial bases in the northeast and other parts of China is timely and correct.

(2) The Rise of the Central Area Strategy
After more than 20 years of reform and opening-up, the eastern coastal area, which has achieved the first mover effect of reform and opening-up, has always been the most important force for rapid economic growth. With the implementation of the large-scale development of China's western region in 2000, the economy of western provinces has also maintained a high growth rate. However, the overall development of the central economy has shown an obvious slowdown, which restricts the development of the entire national economy. Under this background, the CCCPC proposed to implement the strategy of the rise of the central area.

Hubei, Henan, Hunan, Anhui, Jiangxi and Shanxi are six important provinces connected by the central border. As a bridge and linkage connecting the East and the West, the rise of the central area is the interaction between the East and the West, North-South cooperation, and a solid support for the balanced and coordinated development of China's economic layout. Promoting the rise of the central area is an important part of comprehensively implementing the scientific outlook on development and realizing the coordinated development of regional economy. It is also a major strategic issue in China's modernization.

In October, 2003, the *Decision of the CCCPC on Several Issues concerning the improvement of the socialist market economic system* adopted at the Third Plenary Session of the 16th CCCPC stressed the need to "strengthen the coordination and guidance of regional development ... Effectively give play to the comprehensive advantages of the central area and support the accelerated reform and development of the central and western regions."[58]

On March 5, 2004, the Second Session of the 10th NPC proposed to promote the rise of the central area and form a new pattern of interaction between the East and the West, complementary advantages, mutual promotion and common development. In September, 2004, the Fourth Plenary Session of the 16th CCCPC once again clearly proposed to promote the rise of the central area. At the central economic work conference, which ended on December 5, 2004, the term the rise of the central area first appeared in the six tasks of economic work in 2005. On March 5, 2005, Wen Jiabao outlined the strategic thinking of the central area in his Report on the Work of the Government: paying close attention to studying and formulating plans and measures to promote the rise of the central area. Giving full play to the regional and comprehensive economic advantages of the central area, strengthening the construction of modern agriculture, especially the main grain producing areas, strengthening the construction of comprehensive transportation system and energy and important raw material bases, and accelerating the development of competitive manufacturing and high-tech industries; expanding the large market in the central area and developing large circulation. The state should provide support in terms of policies, funds and major construction layout. Subsequently, Hu Jintao and other central leaders inspected and spoke in the central provinces, and basically established the general idea of the rise of the central area: adhering to the principles of highlighting characteristics, integrating resources, overall optimization and linkage promotion, and focusing on the implementation of industrial chain strategy, urban agglomeration strategy, logistics network strategy and big market strategy around the overall layout of "one urban agglomeration, two economic belts, three plains agriculture, four high-tech industries and five pillar industries," to realize the innovative development of the central area finally.

On August 14, 2005, when Wen Jiabao presided over the Symposium on promoting the rise of the central area in Changsha, he proposed that the most important thing to implement the strategy of promoting the rise of the central area was to adhere to the overall situation of economic and social development under the guidance of the scientific outlook on development, further emancipate the mind, further update the concept of development, further enhance the awareness of innovation, accelerate reform and opening-up, and accelerate institutional innovation, mechanism innovation, and scientific and technological innovation, accelerate the adjustment of the economic structure and the transformation of the growth pattern, strive to develop a conservation oriented economy, an environmental friendly economy, and a high-quality economy, and strive to promote the common progress of economical, political, cultural development and in building a harmonious society. At this meeting, Wen Jiabao also put forward specific measures for the rise of the central area: first, strengthen the important position of agriculture, especially the main grain producing areas, and build a new socialist countryside; second, promote the adjustment and upgrading of industrial structure and take a new road to industrialization; third, strengthen the construction of comprehensive transportation system and develop modern market and circulation; fourth, actively and steadily promote urbanization and coordinate urban and rural development; fifth, actively promote reform and speed up innovation in systems and mechanisms; sixth, expand the scope of opening-up to the outside world and comprehensively improve the level of opening-up; Seventh, strengthen ecological progress and environmental protection, and promote the harmonious development between man and nature.

On April 15, 2006, the guiding document of the rise of the central area, *several opinions of the CCCPC and the State Council on promoting the rise of the central area*, was officially issued. The opinions proposed to build the central area into an important national grain production base, energy raw material base, modern equipment manufacturing and high-tech industry base and comprehensive transport hub, namely "three bases and one hub." Since then, the relevant departments of the State Council have put forward corresponding supporting measures successively. In May, 2006, the general office of the State Council issued the notice on implementing the relevant policies and measures of the CCCPC and the State Council on promoting the rise of the central area, and put forward 56 detailed implementation opinions. In January, 2007, the general office of the State Council also issued the notice on the scope of policies related to the revitalization of old industrial bases in the northeast and other regions and the large-scale development of China's western region in the six provinces in Central China, which defined the relevant policies related to the revitalization of old industrial bases in the northeast and other regions in 26 cities in the six provinces in Central China, and the relevant policies related to the large-scale development of China's western region in 243 counties (cities, districts). In April, 2007, the national office for promoting the rise of the central area was officially listed in the NDRC, marking the establishment of the coordinating organization for the rise of the central area. On September 23, 2009, the executive meeting of the State Council discussed and approved in principle the plan for promoting the rise of the central area. The plan is a programmatic document guiding the economic and social development of the central area. It defines the 12 main quantitative goals and a series of qualitative task requirements for the rise of the central area in 2015, and puts forward the overall goal of promoting the rise of the central area in 2020. In order to implement this plan, the NDRC issued the opinions on the implementation of the plan for promoting the rise of the central area in August 2010.

In order to vigorously implement the strategy of promoting the rise of the central area and promote the sound and rapid economic and social development of the central area, in August 2012, the State Council issued several opinions on vigorously implementing the strategy of promoting the rise of the central area, and put forward new requirements for promoting the rise of the central area under the new situation: to vigorously implement the strategy of promoting the rise of the central area, we must thoroughly implement the scientific outlook on development, adhere to the theme of scientific development, and take accelerating the transformation of the development pattern as the main line, with expanding domestic demand as the strategic starting point and deepening reform and opening-up as the driving force, we should pay more attention to transformation and development, accelerate the optimization and upgrading of economic structure, and improve the quality and level of development; we should pay more attention to innovative development, strengthen the construction of regional innovation system, and rely more on scientific and technological innovation to drive economic and social development; we should pay more attention to coordinated development, synchronously promote agricultural modernization in the in-depth development of industrialization and urbanization, and accelerate the formation of a new pattern of urban and rural economic and social integration development; we should pay more attention to sustainable development, accelerate the construction of a resource-conserving and environment-friendly society, and promote the coordination between economic development and population, resources and environment; we should pay more attention to harmonious development, vigorously ensure and improve people's livelihood, and enable the broad masses of the people to further share the fruits of reform and development.

With the promotion of the strategy of the rise of the central area, great achievements have been made in the reform and development of the central area, and the regional advantage of connecting the East and opening the West has been further highlighted. Wuhan city circle, Zhongyuan city group, Chang (Sha) Zhu (Zhou) (Xiang) Tan city group, Wanjiang City belt, Poyang Lake Ecological Economic Zone, Taiyuan city circle and other key economic zones have accelerated their development and become important growth poles to drive economic development. With the rapid economic and social development, the income level of urban and rural residents in the central area has increased significantly, the growth rate is significantly higher than that in the eastern region, and the gap with the national average has gradually narrowed. In 2012, the per capita disposable income of urban residents in the central area reached 20,697 yuan. The construction of major infrastructure and public service facilities in the central area has been accelerated, and the basic support capacity has been significantly enhanced. By the end of 2012, the railway operating mileage in the central area had reached 22,400 kilometers, an increase of 29.1% over 2004; the highway mileage reached 1,155,400 kilometers, an increase of 151.3% over 2004.

Summary

Improving the socialist market economic is still one of the main tasks of economic development and reform in the first 20 years of this century. The promotion of relevant reforms has provided an important guarantee for the sound and rapid development of the national economy. The formulation and implementation of the 11th Five-Year Plan and the 12th Five-Year Plan, the successful response to the international financial crisis, the implementation of regional coordinated development strategies such as "revitalizing the old industrial base in Northeast China" and the rise of the central area have promoted the steady and rapid development of China's economy, with China's GDP reaching 51.9 trillion yuan, jumping to the second place in the world. The promulgation of the nine central "No. 1 documents" on agriculture, rural areas and farmers and the construction of a new socialist countryside have accelerated the development of China's agricultural and rural areas, and the grain output has achieved "nine consecutive increases." The steady progress of the construction of an innovative country has greatly improved China's ability of self-dependent innovation, and major breakthroughs have been made in manned space flight, lunar exploration project, manned deep-sea submerible, Beidou Navigation Satellite System, supercomputer, high-speed railway, etc.

SECTION 3

Advancement of Socialist Culture with Chinese Characteristics

3.3.1 Strengthening the System of Socialist Core Value System

(1) Establishing a Socialist Concept of Honor and Disgrace
The current social conduct is an important symbol of the degree of social civilization and the concentrated embodiment of social value base. With the development of socialist market economy, it has become an urgent task for us to guide people to establish a correct outlook on the world and life and correct values, constantly improve moral sentiment, build an ideological and moral defense line against bad habits, and improve the ideological and moral standards of the whole nation.

On March 4, 2006, when visiting members attending the Fourth Session of the 10th CPPCC, Hu Jintao pointed out: "we should educate the cadres and the masses, especially the young people, to establish a socialist concept of honor and disgrace, and adhere to the principles of honor to those who love the motherland, shame on those who harm the motherland; honor to those who serve the people, shame on those who betray the people; honor to those who believe in science, shame on those who choose to remain ignorant; honor to those who are hardworking, shame on those who are lazy and avoid work; honor to those who uphold unity and help one another, shame on those who seek personal gain at other's expense; honor to those who are honest and trustworthy, shame on those who trade principle for profits; honor to those who are disciplined and law-abiding, shame on those who are undisciplined and break the laws; honor to those who practice plain living and defy adversity, shame on those who indulge in extravagance and pleasures-seeking."[59] Hu Jintao stressed that we should promote patriotism, collectivism and socialist ideology in the whole society, advocate the basic socialist ethics, uphold the right and eliminate evil, promote the good and punish the evil, and promote the formation and development of a good social conduct.

The "Eight Honors and Eight Disgraces" raised by Hu Jintao is a systematic elaboration of the socialist concept of honor and disgrace, which immediately generated a warm response among the representatives, members of the "two sessions" and the broad masses of cadres and the masses. Party committees at all levels of the CPC and Chinese governments at all levels attach great importance to it. All localities and departments have acted quickly, and the broad masses of cadres and masses have actively participated in it. A climax of discussion and study of the socialist concept of honor and disgrace has been set off in succession, forming a strong atmosphere for learning, publicizing and practicing the socialist concept of honor and disgrace. On March 17, 2006, in order to seriously study and implement General Secretary Hu Jintao's important exposition on the socialist concept of honor and disgrace, the Propaganda Department of the CCCPC and the office of the Central Steering Committee for the construction of spiritual civilization issued a notice on organizing publicity and education nationwide and making arrangements. The notice requires that under the guidance of Deng Xiaoping Theory and the important thought of "Three Represents" and under the guidance of the scientific outlook on development, we should vigorously publicize the great significance and essence of General Secretary Hu Jintao's important exposition on the socialist concept of honor and disgrace, publicize the scientific connotation and basic requirements of the socialist concept of honor and disgrace, publicize the specific measures and progress results implemented by various departments in various regions, and publicize the advanced models and fresh experience emerging in various regions. Through solid and effective publicity and education, the socialist concept of honor and disgrace is well known and deeply rooted in the hearts of the people. In October, 2006, the Sixth Plenary Session of the 16th CCCPC further emphasized the need to adhere to the combination of rule of law and rule of virtue, establish a socialist concept of honor and disgrace with "Eight Honors and Eight Disgraces" as the main content, advocate patriotism, professionalism, integrity, friendship and other moral norms, carry out social ethics, professional ethics, family virtue education, strengthen the ideological and moral progress of teenagers, form a trend of knowing honor and disgrace, stressing righteousness, promoting harmony in the whole society, and form gender equality, respect the old and love the young, help the poor, be courteous and tolerant.

The socialist concept of honor and disgrace with "Eight Honors and Eight Disgraces" as its main content is an important thought put forward by the ruling CPC from the height of building moderately prosperous society in an all-round way and accelerating the socialist modernization, putting the development of the advanced culture in a prominent position to improve people's quality and promote people's all-round development, strengthen ideological and moral construction, and train citizens so that they have high ideals, moral integrity, a good education and a strong sense of discipline. The socialist concept of honor and disgrace is closely linked and organically unified with the scientific outlook on development, building a socialist harmonious society, and strengthening the advanced nature of the party. It is an incisive summary of Marxist morality, a systematic summary of socialist morality, and a powerful ideological weapon and important guiding principle for strengthening ideological and moral construction under the condition of socialist market economy.

The socialist concept of honor and disgrace, with "Eight Honors and Eight Disgraces" as its main content, is concise, incisive, profound and rich in connotation. It organically integrates the socialist ideological and moral concepts that are compatible with the socialist market economy, coordinated with the socialist legal norms, and inherited with the traditional virtues of the Chinese nation, and organically integrates the progressiveness and the extensiveness of ideological and moral construction, providing a basis to judge the gains and losses of behavior, determine value orientation, and make moral choices for all ethnic groups, people of all social strata and different interest groups under the conditions of socialist market economy. Firmly establishing the socialist concept of honor and disgrace has great practical and far-reaching historical significance for strengthening the socialist ideology and morality, forming good social customs, and improving the quality of citizens' civilization and the degree of social civilization under the new historical conditions.

(2) Strengthening the Construction of Socialist Core Value System

The socialist core value system is the foundation of building a harmonious culture, the spiritual force for the whole nation to work hard and the spiritual bond of unity and harmony.

In October, 2006, the Sixth Plenary Session of the 16th CCCPC first put forward the scientific proposition of "socialist core value system," which profoundly revealed the connotation of the socialist core value system and clearly put forward the basic content of the socialist core value system. The meeting pointed out that the guiding ideology of Marxism, the common ideal of socialism with Chinese characteristics, the national spirit with patriotism as the core and the spirit of the times with reform and innovation as the core, and the socialist concept of honor and disgrace constitute the basic contents of the socialist core value system. The meeting stressed that we should incorporate the socialist core value system into the whole process of national education and ethical progress and run through all aspects of modernization. We should adhere to arming the whole Party and educating the people with the latest achievements of in adapting Marxism to Chinese conditions, condensing strength and stimulating vitality with the national spirit and the spirit of the times, advocating patriotism, collectivism and socialism, strengthening education in ideals and beliefs, strengthening education in national conditions and situations and policies, and constantly enhancing faith and confidence in the leadership of the CPC, the socialist system, the cause of reform and opening-up, and the goal of building a moderately prosperous society in all respects. We should work harder to study and develop Marxist theory, and enhance the creativity, persuasion and appeal of the party's ideological and theoretical work. We should adhere to the socialist core value system to lead social trends of thought, respect differences, tolerate diversity, and form a consensus of social thought to the greatest extent.

In October, 2007, the 17th National Congress of the CPC pointed out that the socialist core value system represents the essence of the socialist ideology. The meeting put forward new requirements for the construction of the socialist core value system: we must consolidate the guiding position of Marxism, persistently arm the whole Party with and educate the people in the latest achievements in adapting Marxism to Chinese conditions, rally the people with our common ideal of socialism with Chinese characteristics, inspire the people with patriotism-centered national spirit and with the spirit of the times centering on reform and innovation, guide social ethos with the socialist maxims of honor and disgrace, and solidify the common ideological basis of the joint endeavor of the whole Party and the people of all ethnic groups. We must make every effort to carry out theoretical innovation and give Marxism of contemporary China distinct characters of practice, of the Chinese nation and of the times. We must publicize the theories of socialism with Chinese characteristics, and take Marxism of contemporary China to the general public. We must carry on the Project to Study and Develop Marxist Theory to provide in-depth answers to major theoretical and practical questions and to bring up a group of Marxist theoreticians, especially young and middle-aged ones. We must incorporate the socialist core values into all stages of national education and the entire process of cultural and ethical progress to make them the targets pursued by the people of their own accord. We must explore effective ways of letting the system of socialist core values guide trends of thought and take the initiative in ideological work, respecting divergence and allowing diversity while effectively resisting the influence of erroneous and decadent ideas. We should promote the prosperity and development of philosophy and social sciences, promote the innovation of discipline system, academic views and scientific research methods, encourage the philosophy and social sciences community to play a think tank role for the cause of the Party and the people, and introduce the excellent achievements and talents of Chinese philosophy and social sciences to the world arena.

On September 18, 2009, the decision of the CCCPC on several major issues of strengthening and improving Party building under the new situation, adopted at the Fourth Plenary Session of the 17th CCCPC, stressed that we should take the study and education of the socialist core values as an important task of building a learning-oriented Marxist party and pay close attention to it. In October, 2010, the Fifth Plenary Session of the 17th CCCPC further regarded the construction of a socialist core value system as an important part of improving the culture and ethical quality of the whole nation. In March, 2011, the outline of the 12th Five-Year Plan was publicly released. The outline points out that during the 12th Five-Year Plan period, we should continue to strengthen the education of ideals and beliefs in taking the road of socialism with Chinese characteristics and realizing the great national rejuvenation, vigorously carry forward the national spirit with patriotism as the core and the spirit of the times with reform and innovation as the core, and strive to practice the socialist concept of honor and disgrace. We should advocate patriotism, law-abiding, dedication, honesty, diligence and frugality, and build a code of ethics and conduct that inherits traditional Chinese virtues, meets the requirements of socialist spiritual civilization, and adapts to the socialist market economy. We should launch a civic morality campaign to raise public ethical standards, and enhance work ethics, family virtues, and personal integrity. In October, 2011, the Sixth Plenary Session of the 17th CCCPC stressed that the socialist core values are the soul of the Chinese nation, the essence of socialist advanced culture, and serve as the guide for building socialism with Chinese characteristics. We must integrate the socialist core value system into the whole process of national education, culture and ethical progress and Party building, run through all fields of reform and opening-up and socialist modernization, reflect all aspects of the creation, production and dissemination of spiritual and cultural products, and adhere to the socialist core value system to lead social trends of thought, and form a unified guiding ideology, common ideals and beliefs, strong spiritual force, and basic moral norms in the whole Party and society. We should adhere to the guiding position of Marxism, strengthen the common ideal of socialism with Chinese characteristics, carry forward the national spirit with patriotism as the core and the spirit of the times with reform and innovation as the core, and establish and practice the socialist concept of honor and disgrace.

The proposal of building a socialist core value system shows the distinctive banner of socialist China to the contemporary world in ideology and spirit. Some scholars in the theoretical circle pointed out that the socialist core value system, as a social value system that occupies a dominant and guiding position in social life, can effectively restrict the role of non-core and non-dominant social value system, and ensure the stability and development of social economic system, political system and cultural system.

3.3.2 Deepening the Reform of the Cultural System and the Development of Cultural Undertakings and Industries

Since the new stage of the new century, the CPC and the Chinese government have attached great importance to cultural restructuring and clearly put forward the task of deepening structural reform of the culture sector. In October, 2002, the 16th National Congress of the CPC clearly proposed to promote cultural restructuring according to the characteristics and laws of the culture and ethical progress and the requirements of the development of the socialist market economy, accelerate cultural restructuring and stressed the need to speed up the formulation of the overall plan for cultural restructuring. In June, 2003, the State Council held a national conference on the pilot work of cultural restructuring, and deployed the pilot work in 9 provinces and cities including Beijing and Shanghai and a number of cultural units. On this basis, in September 2003, the Third Plenary Session of the 16th CCCPC stressed the need to gradually establish a cultural management system under the leadership of the Party committee with government management, industry self-discipline, and enterprises and institutions operating in accordance with the law. In September, 2004, the decision of the CCCPC on building up the Party's governing capacity, adopted by the Fourth Plenary Session of the 16th CCCPC, made a comprehensive deployment for cultural restructuring to further remove the institutional barriers that restrict cultural development. In October, 2005, the Fifth Plenary Session of the 16th CCCPC once again stressed the need to deepen structural reform of the culture sector, actively develop cultural undertakings and cultural industries, and create more excellent cultural products that better meet the needs of the people. In December, 2005, on the basis of summarizing the successful experience of the pilot work, the CCCPC and the State Council issued the *several opinions on deepening structural reform of the culture sector*, which determined the guiding ideology, principle requirements, objectives and tasks of cultural restructuring. The restructuring was carried out steadily throughout the country in accordance with the principle of "treating differently, working in accordance with different requirements, advancing by steps."

In March, 2006, the CCCPC and the State Council clearly extended the pilot work of reform of the culture system to all provinces (autonomous regions and municipalities directly under the central government) except Xizang and Xinjiang, and newly identified 89 regions and 170 units across the country as the pilot work of cultural restructuring. In the same month, the National Conference on cultural restructuring summarized the pilot work of cultural restructuring and made specific arrangements for promoting the cultural restructuring. In September, 2006, the outline of the national cultural development plan for the 11th Five-Year Plan period was promulgated, which made specific arrangements for cultural restructuring and the development of cultural undertakings during the 11th Five-Year Plan period. In October, 2006, the Sixth Plenary Session of the 16th CCCPC continued to emphasize the need to promote cultural restructuring and form a dynamic cultural management system and a mechanism for the production and operation of cultural products. In October, 2007, the 17th National Congress of the CPC was held, which put forward new requirements for further deepening the reform from the strategic height of rising a new upsurge of socialist cultural development and promoting vigorous development and prosperity of socialist culture. On the basis of affirming the important progress made in cultural restructuring, the meeting stressed the need to promote the innovation of cultural content forms, systems and mechanisms, and means of communication at the high starting point of the times, further deepen structural reform of the culture sector, improve the policies to support public welfare cultural undertakings, develop cultural industries, and encourage cultural innovation, and create an environment conducive to the production of high-quality products, talents, and benefits. In December, 2008, Hu Jintao once again stressed at the meeting commemorating the 30th anniversary of the Third Plenary Session of the 11th CCCPC that we should deepen structural reform of the culture sector, vigorously promote cultural innovation, stimulate the cultural creativity of the whole nation, enhance culture as part of the soft power of our country, promote the continuous development of cultural undertakings and cultural industries, and make the cultural market more prosperous, to better guarantee the people's basic cultural rights and interests In July, 2009, the executive meeting of the State Council approved the plan for the revitalization of the cultural industry. This is the first time that China has made a plan for the development of the cultural industry, marking that the cultural industry has risen to a national strategic industry.

In 2010, cultural restructuring was carried out in an orderly manner, and new breakthroughs were made in key areas, laying a solid foundation for a good start in cultural deveopment during the 12th Five-Year Plan period. The transformation of state-owned academies and regiments into enterprises extended to the grass-roots level, the reform of the press and publication system was imminent, and the pilot of "the integration of telecommunications networks, radio and television networks, and the Internet" of radio and television was accelerated. In July, the Political Bureau of the CCCPC held the 22nd collective study on deepening the research on China's cultural restructuring. Hu Jintao once again emphasized the important position of culture in social development, elaborated on the great significance of deepening structural reform of the culture sector, and further clarified the guiding ideology and key work that must be adhered to in deepening structural reform of the culture sector. In August, the National Working Conference on cultural restructuring was held. The meeting stressed the need to take more solid and effective measures to further promote cultural restructuring and promote the great development and prosperity of socialist culture. In October, the Fifth Plenary

Session of the 17th CCCPC was held. The meeting once again emphasized the need to deepen structural reform of the culture sector, innovate the ways of cultural production and dissemination, liberate and develop cultural productive forces, and enhance the vitality of cultural development. In the "suggestions of the CCCPC on formulating the 12th Five-Year Plan for national economic and social development" adopted at the plenary session, a chapter was devoted for the first time to the deployment of China's structural reform and development of the culture sector during the 12th Five-Year Plan period, and clearly put forward the strategic goal of basically building a public cultural service system and promoting the cultural industry to become a pillar industry of the national economy. It reflects that cultural development plays an increasingly prominent role in the development of China's economic and social sciences, and reflects that the CPC and the Chinese government have raised their understanding and grasp of the law of cultural development to a new height.

2011 was the first year of China's 12th Five-Year Plan. The CCCPC and the State Council have put forward the "twenty-character General requirements" for deepening structural reform of the culture sector, which are to strengthen efforts, accelerate progress, consolidate and improve, make breakthroughs in key areas and comprehensively promote, and strive to make breakthroughs in the two key areas of literary and art troupes and non-current political newspapers and periodicals. At the end of April, the National Working Conference on cultural restructuring was held. The meeting stressed that we should thoroughly implement the spirit of Hu Jintao's important speech at the 22nd collective study of the Political Bureau of the CCCPC and the spirit of the Fifth Plenary Session of the 17th CCCPC, firmly grasp the theme of scientific development and speed up the transformation of the economic growth pattern in accordance with the overall deployment of the national "12th Five-Year Plan" for economic and social development, strive to remove institutional barriers restricting cultural development, and change the pattern of cultural development, to make a good start in structural reform and development of the culture sector during the 12th Five-Year Plan period. On July 1, Hu Jintao stressed at the celebration of the 90th anniversary of the founding of the CPC: "we must be highly cultural conscious and confident, focus on improving national quality and shaping noble personality, promote structural reform and development of the culture sector with greater efforts, create culture in the great practice of socialism with Chinese characteristics, and let the people share the fruits of cultural development."[60] On October 15, the Sixth Plenary

Session of the 17th CCCPC was held. The plenary session deliberated and adopted the decision of the CCCPC on several major issues concerning deepening structural reform of the culture sector and promoting vigorous development and prosperity of socialist culture. On the basis of summing up historical experience and scientifically analyzing the situation, and from the height of the overall layout of the cause of socialism with Chinese characteristics, the plenary session clarified the development path of socialist culture with Chinese characteristics, established the grand goal of building a socialist cultural power, and put forward the guiding ideology, important guidelines, objectives, tasks, policies and measures for promoting structural reform of the culture sector under the new situation. The plenary session stressed that to adhere to cultural development under socialism with Chinese characteristics, deepen structural reform of the culture sector, and promote vigorous development and prosperity of socialist culture, we must fully implement the spirit of the 17th CPC, hold high the great banner of socialism with Chinese characteristics, take Marxism-Leninism, Mao Zedong Thought, Deng Xiaoping Theory, and the important thought of the "Three Represents" as the guidance, thoroughly implement the scientific outlook on development, and adhere to the direction of advanced socialist culture. With scientific development as the theme, building a socialist core value system as the fundamental task, meeting the people's spiritual and cultural needs as the starting point and purpose, and reform and innovation as the driving force, we must develop a national, scientific and popular socialist culture oriented to modernization, the world and the future, cultivate a high degree of cultural consciousness and cultural confidence, improve the cultural and ethical quality of the whole nation, enhance culture as part of the soft power of our country, carry forward Chinese culture, Strive to build a socialist culture power.

With the promotion of cultural restructuring, cultural productivity has been further released, and cultural undertakings and cultural industries have achieved great development. The role of public welfare cultural undertakings in safeguarding the basic cultural rights and interests of the people has become increasingly prominent. The proportion of commercial cultural industries in the national economy has significantly increased, the international competitiveness has gradually increased, the cultural market has become increasingly prosperous, and excellent works have been emerging, creating a new situation in the development of socialist culture with Chinese characteristics. It is mainly reflected in the following four aspects:

First, the framework of a public cultural service system covering urban and rural areas has been basically established, and the basic cultural rights and interests of the people have been better protected. The state has gradually improved the network of public cultural facilities and basically achieved the goal of "there should be cultural center and library in every county and comprehensive cultural station in every township." By the end of 2012, the national cultural system had 2,089 art performance groups, 2,838 museums, 2,975 public libraries, 3,286 cultural museums, and 34,139 township comprehensive cultural stations. The cultural information resource sharing project has basically completed the service network covering urban and rural areas. As of May 2012, one national center, 33 provincial sub-centers, 2,840 county-level sub-centers, 28,595 township grass-roots service points and 602,000 administrative village grass-roots service points have been built. The total amount of digital resources construction had reached 136.4 trillion bytes, and the cumulative number of service people has exceeded 1.2 billion. The state has continuously met the cultural needs of people living in rural and remote areas through the radio and television "village to village" project and the rural bookstore project. By the end of 2012, 100% of administrative villages and 95% of natural villages with more than 20 households had access to the telephone, 100% of towns and townships basically had Internet access capability, and 100% of towns and townships and 88% of administrative villages had broadband access. As of August 2012, the state had invested more than 18 billion yuan to build more than 600,000 rural bookstores that meet the unified standards, equipped with 940 million books, 540 million newspapers and periodicals, 120 million audio-visual products and electronic publications, and more than 600,000 sets of film and television projection equipment and reading facilities. Fresh progress was made in public fitness programs. In February, 2011, the State Council promulgated the National Fitness Plan (2011–2015). By the end of 2012, there had been more than 1 million sports venues across the country, 348,000 "farmers' sports fitness projects" and 261,000 "national fitness paths."

Second, the cultural industry was booming, and its overall scale and strength were rapidly improving. The cultural industry had increasingly become a new growth point of China's economic development. The cultural market was unprecedentedly prosperous, the international cultural trade deficit had significantly improved, the investment and financing system of the cultural industry had been improved, and special policies had been issued to support the revitalization, development and prosperity of the cultural industry, so as to promote cultural enterprises to make use of the capital market to become bigger and stronger. In 2011, the added value of China's cultural and related industries was 1,347.9-billion-yuan, accounting for 2.85% of GDP in the same period. In 2012, 47.6 billion newspapers, 3.4 billion periodicals and 8.1 billion books were published. The total volume of electronic publications and the total output value of the printing industry ranked second and third in the world, respectively. In 2012, 745 feature films and 148 science and education, recording, animation and special films were produced. As of 2011, there were 1.5404 million performances by various art performance groups across the country, with the size of the national entertainment market reaching 56.618 billion yuan, and the total transaction volume of the art market reaching 195.9 billion yuan; There were 146,000 Internet cafes, 452 online music related enterprises, and the online game market size was 46.85 billion yuan. Since the national implementation of the stage art boutique project in 2002, a total of 100 excellent plays and more than 200 good plays have been launched. The national major historical theme art creation project launched 104 excellent art works. The national Kunqu Opera Art rescue, protection and support project, the national key Peking Opera Troupe protection and support plan, and the Chinese national music development and support project had been implemented successively, and the excellent national culture and art had been protected and promoted. Art activities such as the China Art Festival, the selection of excellent reserved plays, the exhibition of excellent plays by national private art troupes, and the exhibition of excellent plays of national modern drama were successfully held. The activities of "bringing culture to the countryside" and "bringing elegant art to campus" continued to be carried out in depth.

Third, promoting the equal access to public cultural services. We should extensively carry out public cultural services for special groups, and strengthen the protection of the cultural rights and interests of rural migrant workers, the elderly, minors, low-income people, and people with disabilities. We should implement the Chinese children's song promotion plan and hold activities such as the Chinese Children's Chorus Festival and the Chinese Elderly Chorus Festival. In May, 2010, the children's Library, namely the children's Digital Library, of the national library was officially opened. In 2012, "China Digital Library for the blind" and "China Digital Library for the disabled" provided barrier free books, lectures, music and other cultural services to more than one million disabled people. We had implemented the construction plan of public electronic reading rooms, and had built 28,612 stations at all levels, including towns, streets and communities, focusing on providing services to minors, the elderly, rural migrant workers and other groups. In 2011, the relevant departments of the state jointly issued the "opinions on Further Strengthening the cultural work of rural migrant workers," which put forward the general idea of gradually forming a cultural work mechanism of rural migrant workers "led by the government, jointly built by enterprises and participated by society" supported by the public cultural service system. Since 2010, the Ministry of Culture has actively carried out the national cultural volunteer frontier activities. Over the past three years, more than 20 inland provinces (cities) and units have formed more than 50 volunteer groups, recruited more than 2,000 cultural volunteers, and successively organized more than 450 cultural performances, more than 2,000 class hours of business training, and more than 600 days of cultural exhibitions for 12 frontier ethnic provinces, regions, and Xinjiang Production and Construction Corps, benefiting hundreds of thousands of people. It promoted the addition of subtitles and sign language to TV programs, and use the Internet to carry out barrier free online live broadcasting services for major events, benefiting more than 70,000 people with hearing disabilities. In 2012, the Ministry of culture, together with the central civilization office, issued the "opinions on the extensive development of grassroots cultural volunteer service activities," which proposed to widely carry out cultural volunteer service activities by relying on public cultural facilities, cultural programs in the public interest, important festivals and anniversaries, and pairing assistance of the mainland counterpart support.

Fourth, important progress had been made in the protection and inheritance of cultural heritage. In 2011, the Standing Committee of the NPC enacted the intangible cultural heritage law, which placed the protection, preservation, inheritance and dissemination of intangible cultural heritage on the legal track, providing a legal guarantee for inheriting and carrying forward the excellent traditional culture of the Chinese nation. In 2011, the state completed the third national census of cultural relics, investigating and registering nearly 770,000 immovable cultural relics. The State Council announced six batches of 2,352 national key cultural relics protection units, including 119 historic cities, 350 historic and cultural towns and villages and three batches of 1,219 national intangible cultural heritage list projects. The Ministry of Culture named four batches of representative inheritors of 1986 national projects and set up 15 national experimental areas for cultural and ecological protection. By the end of 2012, China had 41 world heritage sites, ranking third in the world in total; 29 intangible cultural heritage projects were selected into the UNESCO "representative list of human intangible cultural heritage," 7 were selected into the "list of intangible cultural heritage in urgent need of protection," and 1 was selected into the "list of excellent practices."

3.3.3 The Formulation of the *Outline of China's National Plan for Medium and Long-Term Educational Reform and Development* and the Development of Education Cause

(1) Formulation of the "Outline of China's National Plan for Medium and Long-Term Educational Reform and Development"

Education is the foundation of a long-term plan. Giving priority to education and modernizing the education system is of decisive significance for achieving the goal of building a moderately prosperous society in an all-round way and making China a prosperous, strong, democratic, culturally advanced and harmonious modern socialist country.

In order to meet the new requirements of building a moderately prosperous society in an all-round way, the new situation of development at home and abroad, and the new expectations of the people for education, Wen Jiabao chaired the first meeting of the national leading group for science, technology and education on August 29, 2008, reviewed and approved in principle the work plan for the formulation of the *Outline of China's National Plan for Medium and Long-Term Educational Reform and Development*, and officially launched the research and formulation of the outline of the plan, A leading group headed by Wen Jiabao and a working group headed by State Councilor Liu Yandong were established.

On October 14th, 2008, Liu Yandong chaired a working group meeting to review the research work plan and deploy the formulation of the outline. According to the arrangement of the work plan and after asking for the opinions of the leading comrades of the State Council, the office of the working group on the outline of the plan had carried out two rounds of public consultation with all sectors of society from January to February 2009 and from February to March 2010. It had widely solicited opinions and wisdom, and had made several rounds of amendments to the text of the outline of the plan, forming the draft of the outline of the plan for examination. During the review, the central leaders put forward a series of important guiding opinions. On June 21, 2010, Hu Jintao presided over a meeting of the Political Bureau of the CCCPC, which reviewed and adopted the

Outline of China's National Plan for Medium and Long-Term Educational Reform and Development (2010–2020). In July, 2010, the CCCPC and the State Council held the first national education work conference in the new century. Hu Jintao and Wen Jiabao made important speeches at the meeting, profoundly summarized the achievements of new China in education sector, systematically analyzed the new requirements of the new international and domestic situation for education reform and development. By closely integrating the implementation of the national medium- and long-term education reform and development plan outline (2010–2020), a comprehensive deployment was made around the strategic goal of "basically achieving the modernization of education, basically forming a learning society and entering the ranks of powerful countries in human resources by 2020." On July 29, the CCCPC and the State Council announced the *Outline of China's National Plan for Medium and Long-Term Educational Reform and Development (2010–2020)*, and issued a notice requiring all regions and departments to earnestly implement it in combination with reality.

The *Outline of China's National Plan for Medium and Long-Term Educational Reform and Development (2010–2020)* is composed of "preamble," four parts and "implementation," with a total of 22 chapters, 70 articles and about 27,000 words. It is China's first education development plan since the beginning of the new century and a programmatic document guiding the national education reform and development in the coming period. It not only puts forward the goals and tasks of education reform and development in 2020, but also focuses on promoting education equality, improving education quality, and enhancing the capacity of sustainable development. Focusing on strengthening weak links and key areas, it designs ten major projects and ten pilot works of reform to be launched and implemented in the near future. Its promulgation is a new milestone in the history of China's education reform and development. It responds to the widespread hot and difficult issues of education that the masses are concerned about, and provides a scientific direction for all regions to formulate specific measures. It is of great strategic significance for building a country rich in human resources, meeting the needs of the people to receive a good education, and building moderately prosperous society that benefits more than a billion people in an all-round way.

(2) Development of Education Cause

Since the new stage of the new century, the CCCPC and the State Council have always attached great importance to education. Through unremitting efforts,

China's education has made great achievements that have attracted worldwide attention and opened up the educational development under socialism with Chinese characteristics. At present, the world's largest education system has been established in China, ensuring the right of hundreds of millions of people to receive education. In 2009, there were 260 million students, 13.962 million full-time teachers, and 552,000 schools of various kinds and at different levels across the country, both in urban and rural areas. Its remarkable achievements are as follows:

First, preschool education has developed rapidly. The *Outline of China's National Plan for Medium and Long-Term Educational Reform and Development (2010–2020)*, issued at the end of July 2010, clearly stated that the goal of achieving popularization of preschool education by 2020, and for the first time stated that preschool education was the responsibility of the government. In 2011, there were 166,800 kindergartens nationwide, with 34.2445 million children in kindergartens (including affiliated classes), and the gross enrollment rate of preschool education reached 62.3%. There are 1.496 million kindergarten principals and teachers.

Second, the century dream of basically popularizing nine-year compulsory education has been realized, and free education has been realized completely. By the end of 2010, all 2856 counties (cities and districts) in China had achieved "Two Basics," and the national "Two Basics" population coverage rate was nearly 100%.

Third, the scale of high school education had grown rapidly, and the level of popularization had increased significantly. In 2011, there were 27,638 high schools (including general high schools, adult high schools and secondary vocational schools) in China, with 46.8661 million students, and the gross enrollment rate in high school reached 84%.

Fourth, a major breakthrough had been made in the development of vocational education. Tertiary vocational education and secondary vocational education account for half of higher education and high school education, respectively. In 2010, the enrollment of secondary vocational education was 8.7042 million, accounting for 50.94% of the total enrollment of high school education, which had exceeded the enrollment scale of high schools. China's tertiary vocational education had also achieved remarkable development. In the past 10 years, tertiary vocational colleges had trained nearly 13 million graduates, making positive contributions to national economic and social development.

Fifth, we have reformed the management system of higher education, formed a development pattern that highlights the key areas and drives the overall development, and completed a great leap forward in the popularization of higher education. Higher education enrollment opportunities had further increased, with the gross enrollment rate reaching 26.9% in 2011, entering the stage of popularization. In August, 2011, the total number of students in institutions of higher learning at all levels and of all types in China reached 31.05 million, ranking first in the world.

Sixth, reform the school running system, and a pattern of common development of public schools and private schools has been formed. In 2011, there were 130,800 private schools (educational institutions) at all levels and of all kinds, with 37.1399 million students in all kinds of education.

While China's education at all levels and of all types continues to develop in a coordinated and rapid manner, educational equality has also been constantly promoted. In the central and western regions and rural areas, the state has implemented a series of major projects, such as the rural boarding school program, the modern distance education program for rural primary and secondary schools, the rural junior middle school construction project, and the "special post plan," which have improved the basic school running conditions of schools in the stage of compulsory education in rural areas and narrowed the gap in education development between regions. The national funding system has wider coverage, larger proportion, higher standards and better effects. In 2009, the central government allocated 2 billion yuan to solve the problem of equal access to education for rural migrant workers' children. The proportion of rural migrant workers' children studying in urban public schools reached 80% in 2009. As of 2012, 12.6 million children with rural registered residence have received compulsory education in cities, which had initially solved the problem of the access to urban compulsory education of rural migrant workers' accompanying children. As of 2012, the financial aid system for students from economically disadvantaged families had achieved full coverage from preschool education to graduate education, with an annual subsidy of nearly 100 billion yuan and covering nearly 80 million students.

Entering the new stage of the new century, after more than 10 years of unremitting efforts, China's national quality had been greatly improved, and the transformation from a country with a large population to a country rich in human resources had been realized. Due to the popularization and development of education for all, the average length of education of China's population over the age of 15 had exceeded 9.5 years, and the average length of education of the new labor force was close to 12.4 years, both exceeding the world average. The number of people with advanced education had reached 82 million, and the number of employees with advanced education qualifications had ranked among the top in the world. China is striding forward to become a country rich in human resources, providing strong human resources guarantee for building moderately prosperous society in an all-round way and socialist modernization.

3.3.4 New Achievements in the 2008 Beijing Olympic Games in National Fitness and Competitive Sports

(1) 2008 Beijing Olympic Games

As early as the beginning of the new era, Deng Xiaoping had made it clear that China should not only participate in the Olympic Games, but also undertake the obligation of hosting the Olympic Games. In 1991, the CPC and the Chinese government made a decision to support Beijing's bid to host the 27th Olympic Games in 2000. Although the Chinese people failed to obtain the right to host the Olympic Games at that time, they expressed their strong desire to host the Olympic Games to the international community. Entering the new stage of the new century, the CPC and the Chinese government had once again made a decision to support Beijing's bid to host the 2008 Olympic Games. On June 20, 2000, Beijing formally submitted its application to the IOC. On July 13, 2001, at the 112nd plenary session of the IOC held in Moscow, Beijing won the right to host the 29th Summer Olympic Games in 2008 and the 13th Paralympic Games. The Chinese nation has finally realized the Olympic dream that it has been looking forward to for a hundred years.

To host a distinctive and high-level Olympic and Paralympic Games was a solemn commitment made by China to the world. The Chinese government repeatedly expressed its full support to Beijing in hosting the 2008 Olympic and Paralympic Games, so as to achieve "two games with equal splendour." On December 13, 2001, the Organizing Committee of the 29th Olympic Games was established, marking the official launch of the preparations for the Beijing 2008 Olympic Games. On July 13, 2002, the Beijing Olympic Action Plan jointly formulated by the Beijing municipal government and the Beijing Organizing Committee of Olympic Games (BOCOG) was officially announced and implemented, putting forward two themes of "New Beijing and New Olympics" and three concepts of "Green Olympics, High-tech Olympics and People's Olympics." On December 24, 2003, the construction of the National Stadium and National Swimming Center of China began, marking the prelude to the construction of sports venues for the 2008 Beijing Olympic Games.

On June 26, 2005, at the release ceremony held at Beijing Workers' Stadium, BOCOG announced that the theme slogan of the 29th Olympic Games was "One World, One Dream." On November 11, 2005, the mascots of the 29th Olympic Games were announced in Beijing. Five Fuwa with the images of fish, panda, Olympic flame, Xizang antelope and Jingyan are named Beibei, Jingjing, Huanhuan, Yingying and Nini, respectively, that is, "Welcome to Beijing." On March 31, 2008, the torch relay of the Beijing Olympic Games was launched. In the following four months, it traveled all over the world and all over the country.

On August 8, 2008, the 29th Summer Olympic Games officially opened. In addition to most of the competitions held in Beijing, sailing competitions are held in Qingdao, equestrian competitions are held in Hong Kong, and some football preliminaries are held in Tianjin, Shanghai, Shenyang and Qinhuangdao. It closed on August 24. There are 204 participating countries and regions, 11,438 athletes, and 302 (28 sports) events. The host Chinese sports delegation had a total of 1,099 people, including 639 contestants, which was not only the largest number of contestants in China's previous Olympic Games, but also the largest delegation in this Olympic Games, winning a total of 51 gold medals, ranking first. Subsequently, on September 6, the 13th Paralympic Games was held in Beijing. The Paralympic Games was the largest Paralympic Games. A total of 20 major events were held, resulting in 471 gold medals. More than 4,000 disabled athletes from 147 countries and regions gathered in Beijing. The Chinese delegation finally ranked first in the Paralympic gold medal list and medal list with 89 gold, 70 silver and 52 bronze. On September 17, with the flame of the Paralympic Games extinguished, the two equally wonderful Olympic Games in Beijing in 2008 came to a successful conclusion.

The Beijing Olympic Games and Paralympic Games have set 38 world records, 85 Olympic records, 279 disabled world records and 339 Paralympic records respectively, and many countries and regions have achieved breakthroughs in Olympic and Paralympic gold medals and medals. During the Beijing Olympic Games, more than 100 foreign dignitaries, more than 10,000 athletes from 204 countries and regions, and hundreds of thousands of tourists from all over the world came to Beijing. More than 30,000 foreign reporters interviewed and reported, and more than 4 billion TV viewers worldwide watched the Olympic Games. During the Beijing Paralympic Games, more than 4,000 disabled athletes from 147 countries and regions gathered in Beijing, and more than 6,000 Chinese and foreign journalists conducted interviews and reports. The global media delivered the Olympic Games and China to all corners of the world in various languages.

(2) Fresh Progress Was Made in Public Fitness Programs and Competitive Sports

With economic development, social progress and the continuous improvement of people's living standards, under the correct leadership of the CPC and the Chinese government, with the active support and broad participation of all sectors of society and the people of the whole country, the national sports front was guided by the scientific outlook on development, united as one, worked hard and enterprising, and took the opportunity of seriously preparing for and successfully hosting the Beijing Olympic Games to promote the all-round progress of all sports work. The development of sports has made brilliant achievements and reached a new historical height.

On the one hand, the cause of national fitness in China had made remarkable achievements, and national fitness had become a household name and was deeply rooted in the hearts of the people. First, the CCCPC and the State Council had vigorously advocated "national fitness goes hand in hand with the Olympic Games." The sports awareness of the people had been further enhanced, and the number of people who often participated in physical exercise had increased significantly. The physical levels and health of the people had been continuously improved. Second, mass fitness venues and facilities were all over urban and rural areas, with more than 1 million sports venues of all kinds. Among the schools with opening conditions in the country, 1/3 had opened stadiums and gymnasiums to the public. Third, Fitness for All Programs had been vigorously carried out, and colorful mass sports competitions, performances and special activities in various forms and adapted to local conditions had become increasingly dynamic. Fourth, the construction of national fitness organizations had been strengthened day by day, the leading institutions of national fitness of governments at all levels had become more sound, various sports associations had increased, fitness activity sites had been widely covered, and the number of social sports instructors had grown to 650,000. Fifth, the sports fitness service industry had developed steadily, explored effective ways to develop the sports fitness industry under the condition of market economy, and had become a growth point with vigorous vitality in the sports industry. Sixth, the system of policies and regulations for the cause of national fitness had been further improved. The promulgation and implementation of a series of important sports policies and regulations, such as the regulations on public cultural and sports facilities, the opinions of the CCCPC and the State Council on strengthening youth sports and enhancing youth physique, and the regulations on national fitness, provide an important guarantee for the cause of national fitness. In February, 2011, the State Council issued the national fitness plan (2011–2015) to further mobilize and deploy the national fitness cause in the whole society. The goal is to form a relatively sound national fitness public service system covering urban and rural areas by 2015. Seventh, the field of foreign exchange of mass sports has been constantly expanding, and the development mode of mass sports in China has been widely given a lot of attention by the international mass sports community.

On the other hand, China's comprehensive strength and international competitiveness of competitive sports have been continuously improved, and gradually formed a competitive sports development strategy with the "Olympic Games" as the highest level and a national competitive sports system with Chinese characteristics. China has become an important force with strong competitiveness on the international sports stage. During the 11th Five-Year Plan period alone, Chinese athletes won 634 World Championships, setting and breaking the world record 88 times. In 2008, the Beijing Olympic and Paralympic Games, which attracted worldwide attention, were a complete success, realizing the Centennial expectation of the Chinese nation, becoming an unparalleled wonderful event in the history of the Olympic Games, and greatly stimulating the patriotic enthusiasm and national pride of the Chinese people. The 2010 Guangzhou Asiad is a major international sports event hosted by China after the 2008 Beijing Olympic Games, and it is also the largest Asia Games. It has won high praise and extensive praise from participants from all countries and regions in Asia.

The development and progress of sports have made due contributions to the national economic and social development, and laid a good foundation for the development of sports in the future. The rapid development of sports industry has become a new highlight of the national economy. Residents' sports consumption has increased rapidly, and the number of employees has continued to increase. In 2011, the number of employees in the sports industry nationwide was 3.37 million, with an added value of 222 billion yuan, accounting for 0.55% of GDP that year. The construction of sports talent team has been continuously strengthened, sports science and technology, sports education, sports publicity and other undertakings have made great progress, sports foreign exchanges have been expanding and deepening, and China's influence in international sports affairs has been increasing. At the end of 2009, a total of 259 people in China held 409 positions in world and Asian sports organizations, 230 held posts above the secretary general level, and 34 won the Olympic medals successively.

Summary

In the present era, culture has become a more and more important source of national cohesion and creativity and a factor of growing significance in the competition in overall national strength, and the Chinese people have an increasingly ardent desire for a richer cultural life. In this context, the CPC and the Chinese government have strengthened the system of core socialist values and firmly grasped the leadership and discourse power in the ideological field. Comprehensive progress has been made in cultural restructuring; important headway has been made in providing public cultural services; We will accelerate the development of the cultural industry and make cultural creation and production more prosperous. We formulated the *Outline of China's National Plan for Medium and Long-Term Educational Reform and Development* to respond to the hot and difficult issues of education that the people are generally concerned about. The 2008 Beijing Olympic Games was successfully held, and new achievements were made in national fitness and competitive sports. During this period, remarkable achievements were made in the development of socialist culture with Chinese characteristics.

Building a Harmonious Socialist Society with Chinese Characteristics

3.4.1 Put Forward the Strategic Task of Building a Socialist Harmonious Society

Realizing social harmony and building a better society has always been the social ideal that human beings have been striving for, and it is also the social ideal that Marxist political parties untiringly pursue, including the CPC. Since the 16th National Congress of the CPC, the Chinese Communists represented by Comrade Hu Jintao have comprehensively analyzed the situation and tasks in the new stage of the new century from the overall layout of the cause of socialism with Chinese characteristics and the overall situation of building moderately prosperous society in an all-round way, deeply understood the phased characteristics of China's development, and clearly put forward major strategic ideas and major strategic tasks for building a socialist harmonious society.

In November, 2002, when the 16th National Congress of the CPC elaborated the goal of building a moderately prosperous society in an all-round way, it clearly put forward the development requirements of "a more harmonious society." In September, 2004, the Fourth Plenary Session of the 16th CCCPC clearly put forward the strategic task of building a socialist harmonious society and clarified the main contents of building a socialist harmonious society: comprehensively implement the policy of respecting labor, knowledge, trained personnel and creativity, and enhance the creativity of the entire society; properly coordinate the interests of all parties and correctly handle the contradictions among the people; strengthen social construction and management, and promote the innovation of social management system; improve the working mechanism and maintain social stability. In February, 2005, Hu Jintao delivered an important speech at the special seminar for major leading cadres at the provincial and ministerial levels, proposing that a socialist harmonious society should be a society of democracy and the rule of law, equity and justice, honesty and fraternity, vigor and vitality, stability and order, and harmony between humankind and nature.

In October, 2006, the Sixth Plenary Session of the 16th CCCPC comprehensively analyzed the current situation and tasks, and adopted the Resolution of the CCCPC on the Development of Socialist Harmonious Society. This is a outline document of great significance in guiding the construction of a socialist harmonious society, reflects the internal requirements of building China into a prosperous, democratic, culturally advanced, harmonious, modern socialist country, and embodies the common aspirations of the whole Party and the people of all ethnic groups. The "Resolution" profoundly expounds the nature of a harmonious society: the socialist harmonious society we want to build is a harmonious society jointly built and enjoyed by all the people under the leadership of the CPC on the road of socialism with Chinese characteristics. The Resolution also clearly puts forward the guiding ideology, objectives, tasks and working principles of building a socialist harmonious society. To build a socialist harmonious society, we must adhere to the guidance of Marxism-Leninism, Mao Zedong Thought, Deng Xiaoping Theory and the important thought of "Three Represents," adhere to the Party's basic guidelines, programs and experience, adhere to the Scientific Outlook on Development to guide the overall economic and social development, and follow the general requirements of a society of democracy and the rule of law, equity and justice, honesty and fraternity, vigor and vitality, stability and order, and harmony between humankind and nature. With the focus on solving the most concerned, direct and realistic interests of the people, we should strive to develop social undertakings, promote social equality and justice, build a harmonious culture, improve social management, enhance social creativity, take the road of common prosperity, and promote the coordinated social, economic, political and cultural development. By 2020, the goals and main tasks of building a socialist harmonious society are: the socialist democracy and legal system will be further improved, the basic strategy of ruling the country by law will be fully implemented, and the rights and interests of the people will be effectively respected and guaranteed; the trend of widening the development gap between urban and rural areas and between regions has been gradually reversed, a reasonable and orderly income distribution pattern has basically taken shape, people have more family property, and a more prosperous life; there is a higher rate of employment, and a social security system covering urban and rural residents is basically established; the basic public service system is more complete, and the government management and service have been greatly improved; the ideological and moral quality, scientific and cultural quality and health quality of the whole nation have been significantly improved, and good moral habits and harmonious interpersonal relationships have been further formed; the creativity of the entire society has been significantly enhanced, and an innovative country has been basically completed; the system of social management is further improved and the social order is good; the efficiency of resource utilization has been significantly improved, and the ecological environment has been improved significantly; and we will realize the goal of building a moderately prosperous society at a higher level that benefits more than a billion people in an all-round way, and work to create a state of harmony in which all people can give rein to their talents and find their proper place. To build a socialist harmonious society, we must adhere to the principles of putting people first, scientific development, reform and opening-up, correctly handling the relationship between reform, development and stability, and adhering to the joint construction of the whole society under the leadership of the CPC.

At the same time, the Resolution made a comprehensive deployment for the construction of a socialist harmonious society at present and in the future, emphasizing the need to adhere to coordinated development and strengthen the construction of social undertakings; we should strengthen system construction and ensure social fairness and justice; we should build a harmonious culture and consolidate the ideological and moral foundation of social harmony; we should improve social management and maintain social stability and order; we should stimulate social vitality and enhance social unity and harmony; we should strengthen the leadership of the CPC in building a socialist harmonious society.

In order to further promote the construction of a socialist harmonious society, in March 2007, Hu Jintao stated that the construction of a socialist harmonious society must adhere to the major principle of "sharing in joint construction and joint construction in sharing." In June, 2007, Hu Jintao delivered an important speech at the Party School of the CCCPC, clearly proposing that scientific development and social harmony are the basic requirements for the development of socialism with Chinese characteristics and the internal needs for achieving sound and rapid economic and social development, which must be unswervingly implemented. In October of the same year, the 17th National Congress of the CPC further pointed out that scientific development and social harmony are integral to each other. Neither is possible without the other. Building a harmonious socialist society is a historical mission throughout the cause of socialism with Chinese characteristics, as well as a historical process and the social outcome of correctly handling various social problems on the basis of development.

Social harmony is an essential attribute of socialism with Chinese characteristics and constitutes an important guarantee for making China prosperous and strong, rejuvenating the Chinese nation, and bringing happiness to the people. The proposal of the strategic goal of building a socialist harmonious society has made the overall layout of the cause of socialism with Chinese characteristics develop from the "Trinity" of economic, political and cultural development to the "four in one" of economic, political, cultural and social development, which meets the new requirements of the Party and the country to continue to deepen reform and opening-up in the new era and enriches the connotation of reform and opening-up and socialist modernization.

3.4.2 The Reform of Social Security System and the New Development of Social Security Undertakings

Social security is closely related to the well-being of the people. Social security work is related to the overall situation of reform and opening-up and socialist modernization. At the new stage of the new century, the reform of the social security system has been further deepened, which has promoted the great development of social security.

As early as 2002, the 16th National Congress of the CPC took "a fairly sound social security system" as one of the goals of building a moderately prosperous society in an all-round way. In 2003, the Third Plenary Session of the 16th CCCPC proposed to "accelerate the construction of a social security network suited with the level of economic development," and determined the basic ideas of reform. On this basis, in March, 2004, the Second Session of the 10th NPC adopted the Amendment to the Constitution of the PRC, which clearly stipulated that the state should establish and improve a social security system suited with the level of economic development, pointed out the direction for the development of China's future social security network, and the social security network began to rise to the level of legislative norms. In 2005, the Fifth Plenary Session of the 16th CCCPC proposed to improve the basic old-age insurance and basic medical insurance, unemployment, workers' compensation and maternity insurance systems for urban workers, and seriously solve the social security problems of rural migrant workers. In 2006, the Sixth Plenary Session of the 16th CCCPC clearly proposed to adapt to the aging population, urbanization and diversification of employment methods, gradually establish a social security network covering urban and rural residents that integrates social insurance, assistance and welfare and philanthropy, and take the basic establishment of a social security network covering urban and rural residents as one of the goals and main tasks of building a socialist harmonious society in 2020. In 2007, the 17th National Congress of the CPC took the social security system as one of the "six tasks" of "accelerating social construction focusing on improving people's livelihood," emphasizing the need to speed up the improvement of the social security system based on social insurance, social assistance and welfare, with basic old-age pension, basic medical care and subsistence allowances as its backbone, and supplemented by charity and commercial insurance. In order to further promote the construction of a new socialist countryside, the Third Plenary Session of the 17th CCCPC in 2008 highlighted the need to improve the rural social security system. In order to effectively maintain social harmony and stability, the Fifth Plenary Session of the 17th CCCPC in 2010 once again proposed to improve the social security system covering urban and rural residents, making great efforts to ensure and improve public wellbeing.

Under the guidance of the relevant principles and policies of the CPC and the Chinese government, China's social security system reform has made considerable progress. In October, 2002, the Decision of the CCCPC and the State Council on Further Strengthening Rural Health Work was issued. The "Decision" proposes that by 2010, a rural health care system and a rural cooperative medical system that meet the requirements of the socialist market economy and the rural economic and social development will be basically established in rural areas across the country. In 2003, the State Council issued the Regulations on Work-related Injury Insurance, which further improved insurance against workplace injury. In the same year, the new rural cooperative medical system was piloted in some counties (cities) across the country. In December, 2005, the State Council issued the Decision on Improving the Basic old-age Insurance for Enterprise Employees, expanding the coverage of basic old-age insurance to all kinds of enterprise employees, individual industrial and commercial households and flexible employment personnel in cities and towns, reforming the calculation and payment methods of basic old-age pensions, improving the incentive mechanism to encourage employees to participate in insurance and pay contributions, and improving the level of overall planning. In 2006, the State Council issued Several Opinions on Solving the Problems of Rural Migrant Workers, proposing to actively and steadily solve the problem of social security for migrant workers. In August 2007, the State Council issued the Notice on Establishing a Rural Basic Minimum Living Allowance

System nationwide, requiring that a standardized rural minimum living security system be established nationwide in 2007. In the same year, the Guiding Opinions of the State Council on Carrying out the Pilot of Basic Medical Insurance for Urban Residents was issued. It is planned to launch the pilot of basic medical insurance for urban residents nationwide in three years to make the basic medical insurance system cover all urban residents. In 2008, the central government decided to reform the basic old-age insurance system for employees of government-affiliated institutions in some provinces and cities. In the same year, a rural medical care system based on mutual assistance of the participants basically achieved full coverage. In February, 2009, the Ministry of Human Resources and Social Security (MHRSS) formulated the Measures for Rural Migrant Workers to Participate the Basic old-age Pension Program. The Measures clarify the policies for the transfer of old-age pension relationships and the accumulation and continuation of rights and interests of rural migrant workers. In September, the Guiding Opinions of the State Council on Carrying out the Pilot of New Rural Social old-age Insurance, requiring the establishment of a "new rural social pension insurance" system combining individual contributions, collective subsidies and government subsidies, the combination of social planning and individual accounts, and the matching of family pension, land security, social assistance and other social security policies and measures to ensure the basic living standards of rural residents for the elderly. It is decided that the pilot will cover 10% of the counties in the country in 2009, and will be gradually expanded and widely implemented throughout the country. By 2020, the full coverage of rural residents of the right age will be basically achieved. At present, in some economically developed provinces and cities, the "new rural social pension insurance" system has taken the lead in popularizing. On January 1, 2010, the Provisional Measures for the Transfer and Continuation of the Basic Old-age Pension relationship of Urban Enterprise Employees came into force. All personnel participating in the basic old-age pension scheme of urban enterprise employees, including rural migrant workers, can transfer their pension when they are employed across provinces. A key step has been taken in the reform of the basic old-age insurance system. In October 2010, the 17th Meeting of the Standing Committee of the 11th NPC adopted the Social Insurance Law, which came into force on July 1, 2011. This is the first comprehensive law of the social security system in China, which is of great significance for establishing a social security system covering urban and rural residents, safeguarding the legitimate rights and interests of citizens to participate in social insurance and enjoy social insurance benefits, and promoting the construction of a socialist harmonious society. On December 20, 2010, Wen Jiabao signed Decree No. 586 of the State Council, amending the Regulations on Work-related Injury Insurance, which further improved insurance against workplace injury again. In 2012, the NDRC and other six departments jointly issued the Guiding Opinions on the Implementation of Serious Illness Insurance for Urban and Rural Residents. 28 provinces across the country have launched the pilot work of serious illness insurance, and 8 provinces have fully launched it.

Through arduous efforts, China's social security has been continuously improved. Despite a relatively underdeveloped economy, China has initially established the world's largest social security system in line with the current social reality of China.

First, the coverage of social security programs continued to expand. The state has formulated the Social Insurance Law and revised the Regulations on Work-related Injury Insurance. China has systematically achieved full coverage of basic old-age pension and basic medical insurance for urban and rural residents. In 2012, 790 million people participated in various old-age insurances, 130.75 million urban and rural elderly residents received pensions on a monthly basis, and the basic pension of enterprise retirees increased from 700 yuan per capita per month in 2004 to 1,721 yuan; More than 1.3 billion people participated in various medical insurance, including more than 800 million people who participated in the new rural cooperative medical insurance; the number of people participating in national work-related injury insurance reached 189.93 million, including 71.73 million rural migrant workers; the number of people participating in unemployment insurance reached 152.25 million; the number of people participating in maternity insurance reached 154.45 million. China has comprehensively established a provincial-level overall planning system for old-age insurance, implemented the method of transferring and connecting the basic old-age insurance relationship across provinces, and generally realized the orderly transfer of the old-age insurance relationship of insured workers, including rural migrant workers. A linkage mechanism has also been established between the unemployment insurance standard and the rise in prices. The government subsidy standards of the new rural cooperative medical system and the basic medical insurance for urban residents were increased from the initial annual per capita of

20 yuan and 40 yuan to 240 yuan in 2012. Within the scope of the basic medical insurance for urban workers, the basic medical insurance for urban residents and the new rural cooperative medical care policy, the reimbursement proportion of hospitalization expenses is increased to more than 75%, more than 70% and about 75% respectively, and the maximum payment limit is increased to more than 6 times of the annual average salary of local workers, more than 6 times of the annual disposable income of local residents, and more than 8 times of the per capita net income of farmers in the country, all of which are not less than 60,000 yuan, and the coverage is extended from inpatient to outpatient. In 2012, on the basis of comprehensively launching the pilot of eight major diseases such as uremia and childhood leukemia, 12 major diseases such as lung cancer, esophageal cancer and gastric cancer were included in the pilot scope of major disease protection, and the reimbursement ratio is up to 90%.

Second, citizens' right to social assistance has been further guaranteed. In terms of subsistence allowances, the state has successively issued a series of normative documents, such as the Opinions of the State Council on Further Strengthening and Improving the Work of Minimum Living Security, and the Measures for the Examination and Approval of Minimum Living Security (Trial). In terms of natural disaster relief, the national Regulations on Natural Disaster Relief and the National Emergency Plan for Natural Disaster Relief were fully implemented, and the Guiding Opinions on Strengthening Social and Psychological Assistance for Natural Disasters were issued. In terms of medical assistance, the state formulated the "Opinions on Carrying out Pilot Work of Medical Assistance for Major Diseases," and carried out pilot work in 273 pilot areas across the country. In terms of relief for vagrants and beggars, the government has implemented the Opinions of the General Office of the State Council on Strengthening Rescue and Protection of Homeless Minors, launching special campaigns to "send street children home" and "help street children back to school." As of 2012, there were 1,788 relief agencies (assistance and management stations, relief and protection centers for homeless minors) across the country. From 2010 to 2011, 4,128,709 vagrants and beggars were rescued nationwide.

Third, the social security and service for persons with disabilities was improving. In March, 2010, the general office of the State Council forwarded the Guiding Opinions on Accelerating the Construction of the Social Security System and Service System for the disabled. The total amount of funds allocated by the central government for the development of undertakings for the disabled during the 12th Five-Year Plan period increased by nearly four times compared with the 11th Five-Year Plan period. In 2012, 2,794 districts and counties across the country carried out community rehabilitation. Through the implementation of a number of key rehabilitation projects, 7.602 million disabled people were rehabilitated to varying degrees, and 15,000 disabled children received pre-school education grants at national and local levels; 299,000 urban disabled people received vocational training, 141,000 families of poor disabled people were subsidized for adapting their houses, legal aid and relief institutions at all levels provided legal services for the disabled nearly 100,000 people, 2,391,000 and 363,000 eligible urban and rural disabled people enjoyed stable living subsidies and nursing subsidies respectively, and 554,000 disabled people received fuel subsidies for motor wheelchairs. By the end of 2012, 10.705 million disabled people in urban and rural areas had been included in the scope of minimum living allowance, the level of family assistance for the disabled had been improved, and 2.809 million urban disabled workers had participated in various social insurances; Nationwide, 7275 boarding care service institutions and day-care institutions for the disabled have been established, providing care services to 747,000 disabled people in various forms such as institutional and home care; various activities such as disabled people's culture week, fitness week and "disabled people's culture into the community" were carried out, so that the cultural and sports life of disabled people were richer and more active; social resources were collected and information accessibility standards were formulated; the "China disabled service network" was launched to provide accessible on-line services in the fields of information, employment, rehabilitation, assistance and so on.

3.4.3 The Fight against SARS in 2003 and Wenchuan Earthquake in 2008

(1) Fight against SARS in 2003
On November 16, 2002, the first SARS case was found in Foshan, Guangdong Province. Since then, imported cases were found in Guangxi, Hunan, Sichuan, Shanxi and other places. In March, 2003, the epidemic spread to Beijing and gradually spread to the whole country. SARS occurred in 24 provinces (autonomous regions and municipalities directly under the central government) in the mainland, affecting a total of 266 counties and cities (districts). As of August 7 of that year, a total of 5,327 cases (including 969 medical personnel) had been reported in mainland China, with 349 deaths; A total of 1,755 cases and

300 deaths were reported in Hong Kong, China; 665 cases and 180 deaths were reported in Chinese Taiwan. According to the statistics of the Asian Development Bank (ADB), due to the impact of SARS, the total economic loss of mainland China was 17.9 billion U.S. dollars, accounting for 1.3% of China's GDP that year.

After the sudden outbreak of the epidemic, the CCCPC and the State Council put the protection of people's health and life safety in the first place, accurately judged the severe situation of the spread of the SARS epidemic, and resolutely took a series of major measures. On April 2, Wen Jiabao chaired the executive meeting of the State Council to study the prevention and control of SARS. On April 17, the Standing Committee of the Political Bureau of the CCCPC held a meeting to listen to the reports of relevant departments on the prevention and treatment of SARS, and made research and deployment for further doing this work well. On April 18, the general office of the CCCPC and the general office of the State Council issued a notice requiring further efforts to prevent and control SARS. The notice stressed that strengthening the prevention, treatment and control of SARS was related to the health and life safety of the broad masses of the people, the overall situation of reform, development and stability, national interests and international image. We must respond calmly, take decisive measures, rely on science and effective prevention and control, strengthen cooperation and improve the mechanism. The notice defined five basic tasks: further clarify the responsibilities of leaders at all levels, establish a unified leadership mechanism for epidemic prevention, do everything possible to control the spread of the epidemic as soon as possible, strictly enforce the epidemic reporting system, and make overall arrangements in all areas of work.

On April 20, the CCCPC and the State Council made it clear that the epidemic situation should be detected, reported and announced in a timely manner with a high sense of responsibility to the people, and delayed reporting, under-reporting and covered-up reporting should never be allowed. On the same day, "SARS" was listed as a notifiable epidemic in China. From April 21, the country implemented a daily reporting and publishing system for newly confirmed and suspected cases of SARS. On April 23 Wen Jiabao chaired the executive meeting of the State Council. The meeting decided that in order to further strengthen the prevention and control of SARS, an anti-SARS headquarter of the State Council, with Vice Premier Wu Yi as the General Commander, was established to uniformly command and coordinate the prevention and control of SARS throughout the country; the central government set up a SARS prevention and control fund with a total amount of 2 billion yuan, which was mainly used for the treatment of SARS patients among farmers and urban poor people, the emergency transformation of county-level hospitals in difficult areas in the central and western regions, the purchase of medical equipment for the treatment of SARS, and the support of scientific and technological breakthroughs in the prevention and control of SARS. On April 28, the Political Bureau of the CCCPC held a meeting to emphasize that all regions and departments should stand at the height of the overall situation, deal with the relationship between the prevention and control of SARS and economic work, pay attention to the major event of the prevention and control of SARS on the one hand, and pay attention to the center of economic development on the other hand. At the meeting, Hu Jintao pointed out that in the current fight against SARS, we should vigorously carry forward the spirit of unity, overcoming difficulties and daring to win.

On May 9, Wen Jiabao signed Decree No. 376 of the State Council, promulgating and implementing the Regulations on Public Health Emergency Response, which marks the legalization of China's emergency response to public health emergencies. On May 12, the Ministry of Health issued the Administrative Measures for the Prevention and Control of SARS in the form of an order of the Ministry of Health, aiming at the urgent problems to be solved in the prevention and control of SARS, and improved the epidemic information reporting system and prevention and control measures.

Due to the right policies and effective measures, the Chinese people, Chinese society and Chinese government withstood the test, and the epidemic was quickly and effectively controlled. On May 23, the World Health Organization (WHO) made a decision to cancel the travel warning imposed on Hong Kong and Guangdong in China due to SARS. On June 24, the WHO announced the lifting of the travel warning for Beijing and the deletion of Beijing from the list of "SARS" epidemic areas, with immediate effect. So far, the Chinese mainland had won a decisive victory in the fight against SARS, which also meant that China's achievements in the prevention and control of SARS had been affirmed by the international community.

On July 17, the national SARS prevention and control headquarters held a phased summary meeting in accordance with the overall deployment and requirements of the CCCPC and the State Council after the national SARS prevention and control work achieved a major victory. The meeting proposed that the prevention and control work should be switch from emergency response to normalized management, and the constituent departments of the headquarters should implement regular prevention and control measures in accordance with the unified deployment and requirements. On July 28, the CCCPC and the State Council held a national working conference on the prevention and control of SARS, while the Ministry of Health held a national health working conference at the same time, summarizing the experience and lessons of the prevention and control of SARS, and making arrangements for doing a good job in the prevention and control work in the future and strengthening public health construction. On August 16, the last two SARS patients in mainland China recovered and were discharged from hospital. The battle against SARS came to a great victory.

Through the fight against SARS, the CPC and the Chinese government have deeply realized that China's economic development and social development, urban development and rural development are not coordinated enough; the development of public health lags behind, and the public health system has defects; the emergency mechanism for emergencies is not complete, and the ability to deal with and manage crises is not strong; some localities and departments lack the preparation and ability to deal with emergencies. Taking this opportunity, the CPC and the Chinese government attach great importance to the existing problems and take practical measures to solve them. The emergency early warning and handling mechanism for public health events has initially taken shape, and has withstood the test of the prevention and control of influenza A/H1N1 flu in 2009, which truly makes this fight against SARS an important opportunity to improve public health work and better promote the development of public health.

(2) Fight against Wenchuan Earthquake in 2008

At 14:28:04 on May 12, 2008, a magnitude 8.0 earthquake struck Wenchuan, Sichuan Province, China. It was the most destructive earthquake since the founding of the PRC, with the widest scope and the greatest difficulty in disaster relief. It affected more than 10 provinces (autonomous regions and municipalities directly under the central government) including Sichuan, Gansu, Shaanxi and Chongqing. The total area of the disaster area was about 500,000 square kilometers. 46.25 million people were affected, 692,270 people were killed, 374,643 people were injured and 17,923 people were missing, and the direct economic losses reached 845.2 billion yuan.

After the earthquake, the CCCPC and the State Council quickly made decisions and launched an earthquake rescue and relief operation that accomplished its work faster, mobilized more personnel and committed more resources than ever before in China's history. Less than an hour after the earthquake, Hu Jintao made important instructions: rescue the wounded as soon as possible to ensure the safety of people in the disaster areas. Wen Jiabao arrived in Dujiangyan, Sichuan by charter airplane that afternoon to command the earthquake relief work. On the evening of the 12th, the Standing Committee of the Political Bureau of the CCCPC held a meeting to comprehensively deploy the earthquake relief work. The meeting decided to a headquarter for resisting the earthquake and providing disaster relief, with Wen Jiabao as the commander-in-chief, fully responsible for the current earthquake relief work. That night, the headquarter held its first meeting in the front line of Sichuan disaster area to analyze the situation of earthquake relief and deploy the next step of earthquake relief work. Within 72 hours after the earthquake, a total of 6 meetings of the general headquarter for earthquake rescue and relief under the State Concil were held.

On May 14, the Standing Committee of the Political Bureau of the CCCPC held another meeting to further study and deploy the earthquake relief work. On the morning of May 16, Hu Jintao flew to the earthquake-stricken areas in Sichuan Province to guide the earthquake relief work on the spot. Other leading comrades of the Central Committee also came to the front line of disaster relief to make specific arrangements for earthquake relief. On May 18, in order to express the deep sorrow and sincere condolences of the people of all ethnic groups for the victims of the Wenchuan earthquake in Sichuan, and the State Council decided that May 19–21, 2008 would be the National Day of Mourning.

On May 21, Wen Jiabao chaired an executive meeting of the State Council to study and deploy earthquake relief and economic work. The meeting stressed that on the one hand, we should not relent our efforts in earthquake relief and on the other hand, we should unswervingly focus on economic development. The meeting decided that the central government would first allocate 70 billion yuan to establish a post-disaster recovery and reconstruction fund in 2008, and continue to make corresponding arrangements in 2009 and 2010. On May 26, the Standing Committee of the Political Bureau of the CCCPC held a meeting to further study and deploy the earthquake relief work. The meeting pointed out that we should speed up the formulation of post-disaster reconstruction plans and specific implementation plans, establish a counterpart support mechanism, and use the strength of the whole country to speed up the recovery and reconstruction. On June 5, Hu Jintao presided over a Meeting of the Standing Committee of the Political Bureau of the CCCPC and made a major decision of "one province to help one severely affected county." On June 8, the State Council promulgated the Regulations on Post Wenchuan Earthquake Recovery and Reconstruction, which is China's first local regulation specifically for the post-earthquake recovery and reconstruction of a earthquake. It provides action guidelines and legal basis for different stages of post disaster transitional resettlement, investigation and evaluation, recovery and reconstruction planning, recovery and reconstruction and so on. On June 11, the State Council issued the "Wenchuan Earthquake Recovery and Reconstruction Counterpart Support Plan," which determined that 19 provinces and cities including Guangdong, Jiangsu, Shanghai, Shandong, Zhejiang, Beijing, Liaoning, Henan, Hebei, Shanxi, Fujian, Hunan, Hubei, Anhui, Tianjin, Heilongjiang, Chongqing, Jiangxi and Jilin should immediately organize and carry out the post disaster recovery and reconstruction counterpart support work. Each supporting province and city should arrange the implementation of counterpart support according to 1% of the local fiscal revenue of the province and city last year. On the afternoon of June 30, the CCCPC held a symposium on representatives of advanced grassroots party organizations and outstanding communist party members in Huairen Hall, Zhongnanhai. Hu Jintao attended the Symposium and delivered an important speech. He summarized the great earthquake relief spirit of "unite as one for the victory, be dauntless, indomitable, people-oriented and respect science," and pointed out that the earthquake relief work was entering the stage of resettlement of the affected people and recovery and reconstruction. So far, the earthquake relief struggle had achieved a major phased victory. On July 4, the Guiding Opinions of the State Council on Doing a Good Job in the post Wenchuan Earthquake Recovery and Reconstruction was issued. The Opinion pointed out that China would strive to complete the main task of post-disaster recovery and reconstruction in about three years, so that the basic living and production conditions of the people in the disaster areas can reach or exceed the pre-disaster level, and lay a solid foundation for sustainable development. In August, the State Council issued the *Overall Plan for Post-Wenchuan Earthquake Recovery and Reconstruction (Draft for public comment)*.

In the arduous struggle against the catastrophic earthquake disaster, under the effective command and leadership of the CCCPC and the State Council, the whole society was mobilized. The Chinese government released information accurately, timely and objectively, and major media informed the public of the disaster and the progress of disaster relief in a timely manner. The China Earthquake Administration, the National Disaster Reduction Commission, the Ministry of Civil Affairs, the Ministry of Public Security, the Ministry of Health, the State Food Administration and other departments quickly launched emergency plans, dispatched rescue teams and allocated relief materials. At the same time, Great importance was attached to health and epidemic prevention and monitoring to ensure that there was no major epidemic in the affected areas after a major disaster. Within two days of the earthquake, 100,000 officers and soldiers of the PLA and the armed police force went to the severely affected areas to carry out rescue. As of June 9, 2008, 83,988 people had been rescued from the ruins in the disaster areas in Sichuan alone, rescuing and transferring 1.486 million people. As of 12:00 on June 10, 2008, more than 1 million disaster relief tents, more than 4.7 million quilts and nearly 14 million pieces of clothing had been dispatched to the disaster areas.

In the post disaster recovery and reconstruction, the Chinese government, in accordance with the principles of people-oriented, respect for nature, overall planning and scientific reconstruction, scientifically formulated the post-disaster recovery and reconstruction plan, promptly issued a series of policies and measures to support the disaster areas, actively carried out counterpart support, and quickly organized the post-disaster recovery and reconstruction work. With the strong support of the people of the whole country, the affected areas made remarkable achievements in the reconstruction of urban and rural residents' houses, the reconstruction of public service facilities such as schools and hospitals, the restoration and reconstruction of infrastructure, industrial reconstruction and structural adjustment, historical and cultural protection, and ecological restoration. All these laid a solid foundation for the overall victory of the earthquake relief struggle. As of May 9, 2011, a total of 1,020.5 billion yuan had been invested in recovery and reconstruction, of which 302.6 billion yuan was allocated by the central government for post disaster recovery and reconstruction; all the projects included in the national reconstruction plan in the disaster areas of Sichuan, Shaanxi and Gansu started reconstruction, with the completed projects accounting for 95% of the planned projects and the completed investment accounting for 95% of the total planned investment; the main tasks of post-disaster recovery and reconstruction was completed. The economic and social development and the basic production and living conditions of the people in the disaster areas significantly exceeded the pre-disaster level, and the reconstruction goals of "every family has housing, every household has employment, everyone has security, facilities have been improved, economy has developed, and ecology has improved" have been basically achieved. The post disaster recovery and reconstruction has achieved a decisive victory.

3.4.4 Social Fashion in the Internet Era

The Internet is the crystallization of human wisdom, a major scientific and technological invention in the 20th century, and an important symbol of contemporary advanced productive forces. It has a profound impact on the development of world economy, politics, culture and society, and promotes the transformation of social production and life and information dissemination. At present, China has become the country with the largest population of Internet users in the world. By the end of June 2011, the number of Chinese Internet users had reached 485 million.

The CPC and the Chinese government welcome the arrival of the Internet era with a positive attitude, strive to give full play to the important role of the Internet in China's socialist cultural construction, and actively create a good cultural atmosphere and social fashion. In November, 2002, the 16th National Congress of the CPC clearly announced that Internet websites should become an important arena for the dissemination of advanced culture. In September, 2004, the Fourth Plenary Session of the 16th CCCPC stressed that we should attach great importance to the impact of new media such as the Internet on public opinion, accelerate the establishment of a management system combining legal norms, administrative supervision, industry self-discipline and technical support, strengthen the construction of the Internet publicity team, and form a strong online positive public opinion. In October, 2006, the Sixth Plenary Session of the 16th CCCPC pointed out that we should strengthen the application and management of the Internet, straighten out the management system, advocate civilized Internet management and Internet access, and make all kinds of emerging media an important arena to promote social harmony. In January, 2007, in his speech at the 38th collective study of the Political Bureau of the CCCPC, Hu Jintao put forward five requirements for strengthening the construction and management of network culture: first, we should adhere to the development direction of socialist advanced culture and advocate the main theme of online ideology and culture; second, we should improve the supply capacity of network cultural products and services, and improve the scale and specialization of network cultural industry; third, we should strengthen the construction of on-line ideological and public opinion arena and grasp the dominant power of on-line public opinion; fourth, we should advocate civilized Internet management and civilized Internet access, and purify the network environment; fifth, we should adhere to legal, scientific and effective management. In October, 2007, the 17th National Congress of the CPC once again stressed the need to strengthen efforts to develop and manage Internet culture and foster a good cyber environment. On June 20, 2008, Hu Jintao pointed out during his inspection at the People's Daily that the Internet had become a distribution center of ideological and cultural information and an amplifier of public opinion. We should fully understand the social influence of emerging media represented by the Internet, attach great importance to the construction, application and management of the Internet, and strive to make the Internet a forward arena for the dissemination of advanced socialist culture and an effective platform for providing public cultural services and a broad space for promoting the healthy development of people's spiritual life. On July 23, 2010, in the collective study of the Political Bureau of the CCCPC, Hu Jintao once again clearly emphasized the need to consciously resist vulgarity and kitsch in the Internet and establish a good social fashion. In February, 2011, Hu Jintao delivered an important speech at the opening ceremony of the symposium on social management and innovation for major leading cadres at the provincial and ministerial levels. He pointed out that we should further strengthen and improve information network management, improve the management level of virtual society, and improve the on-line public opinion guidance mechanism.

With the active efforts of the Chinese government, at present, the Internet has become an important public platform for citizens to discuss public affairs, express opinions, supervise by public opinion, and study, work, communication, political and economic activities.

The Internet has become an important way for people to obtain news information. Since the Internet came into China, people have made full use of the Internet to spread news and information. China's news agencies, newspapers, radio stations, television stations, etc. have used their resource and brand advantages to carry out online news dissemination to meet people's news and information needs. A number of comprehensive news and information service websites have been formed, such as People's Daily Online, Xinhuanet, China International Television (CCTV), China National Radio's affiliated website, etc., which not only expand the scope of authoritative news and information dissemination, but also expand new space for the development of traditional media. The Internet has become an important way for people to obtain news information. According to statistics, more than 80% of Internet users mainly rely on the Internet to obtain news information. The development of network media not only enhances the timeliness and effectiveness of news communication, but also plays a unique role in reporting important news events, which fully meets people's information needs. It has become a practice for on-line media to broadcast live the National Congress of the CPC, the NPC and the Chinese CCCPC.

Chinese citizens are fully entitled to freedom of speech in accordance with the law. The Constitution of the PRC provides that all citizens have the right of freedom of speech. Chinese citizens' freedom of speech on the Internet is protected by law and can express their opinions online in various forms. Active online communication is a major feature of China's Internet development. The huge number of forum posts and blog posts is unimaginable for other countries in the world. Chinese websites attach great importance to providing Internet users with speech services, and about 80% of them provide on-line bulletin board services. According to the white paper "the Internet in China" issued by the Information Office of the State Council of China on June 8, 2010, there were millions of forums and 220 million blog users in China at that time. According to sample statistics, people made more than 3 million comments through forums, news comments, blogs and other channels every day; more than 66% of Chinese netizens often make comments on the Internet, discuss various topics, and fully express their ideas and interests. New applications and services of the Internet provide a broader space for people to express their opinions. Blog, microblog, video sharing, social networking sites and other emerging network services have developed rapidly in China, providing more convenience for Chinese citizens to communicate through the Internet. Netizens actively participate in on-line information dissemination and on-line content creation, which greatly enriches the information content on the Internet.

The Chinese government gives full play to the supervisory role of the Internet. The Chinese government actively creates conditions for the people to supervise the government, attaches great importance to the supervisory role of the Internet, and requires governments at all levels to investigate and solve problems reported by people through the Internet in a timely manner, and feedback the handling results to the public. The vast majority of government websites have published e-mail addresses and phone numbers, so that the public can reflect the problems existing in the work of the government. In recent years, a large number of problems reflected through the Internet have been solved. In order to facilitate the public to report corruption and other issues, the central discipline inspection and supervision institution, the Supreme People's Court and the Supreme People's Procuratorate have set up reporting websites. After the opening of the reporting website of the CCDI of the Party and the Ministry of Supervision and the website of the National Bureau of Corruption Prevention, they have played an important role in punishing and preventing corruption. According to a sample survey, more than 60% of netizens gave a positive evaluation of the government's role in supervising the Internet, believing that this is the embodiment of China's social democracy and progress.

The Chinese government attaches great importance to the public opinion reflected on the Internet. The Internet has built a direct communication bridge between the government and the public. Understanding people's feelings and gathering people's wisdom through the Internet has become a new channel for the Chinese government to govern for the people and improve its work. Public comments on the Internet are receiving unprecedented attention. Chinese leaders often go on-line to hear the public voice, and sometimes directly communicate with netizens on-line to discuss national affairs and answer netizens' questions. It has become a common practice for governments at all levels to solicit opinions through the Internet before introducing major policies. During the NPC and the Chinese CCCPC, public opinions are solicited through the Internet every year. From 2009 to 2012, millions of suggestions were solicited through the Internet every year, providing a useful reference for improving government work.

However, at the same time, it should be pointed out that the Internet has not only provided unprecedented convenience for people, but also produced a large number of immoral and uncivilized behaviors and phenomena. Such as spreading rumors, spreading false information, snooping and spreading others' privacy, making and spreading network viruses, "hackers" malicious attacks, abuse, spreading junk mails, etc. Therefore, the Chinese government is actively using, managing in accordance with law, scientifically and effectively managing the Internet, and striving to improve the Internet management system integrated with legal norms, administrative supervision, industry self-discipline, technical support, public supervision and social education.

3.4.5 Traditional Festivals Are Made Statutory Festival and Holidays

In 1999, the State Council revised the Measures for the National Annual Festival and Memorial Day Holiday and began to implement the "Golden Week" long holiday system. This vacation arrangement has made a positive contribution to stimulating domestic demand and promoting economic growth. However, with the passage of time and the further development of economy and society, many social problems have emerged one after another. On the one hand, the arrangement of statutory holidays is too centralized, resulting in "overload" of transportation, scenic spots and services, causing great damage to the environment and ecology. On the other hand, there is a lack of traditional cultural characteristics, and there is a tendency to replace personal holidays with statutory holidays.

In the following years, some deputies to the NPC and CPPCC members have repeatedly called for attention to the problems existing in China's current statutory holiday arrangements, suggesting that the current holiday arrangements be adjusted, adding traditional festivals to statutory holidays and dispersing holiday arrangements. The CCCPC and the State Council attach great importance to this, and require the NDRC and relevant departments to put forward a scientific, reasonable and feasible adjustment plan based on the overall situation of the national economy and society on the basis of in-depth investigation and research and full consideration to the opinions of all parties involved.

From the second half of 2005, holiday adjustment began to be put on the agenda. In June, 2005, relevant central departments issued documents detailing the importance of adding New Year's Eve, Lantern Festival, Tomb Sweeping Day, Dragon Boat Festival and Mid-Autumn Festival. In 2006, the NDRC set up a special research group to comprehensively study the evolution and current situation of China's holiday system and leave system, and to study in more detail the statutory holiday and paid vacation system in HKSAR, MSAR, Chinese Taiwan and other countries. From November 2006 to July 2007, the NDRC held six symposiums to listen to the opinions of all parties, and on this basis, a preliminary plan for the adjustment of national statutory holidays was formed.

After the formation of the preliminary plan, the NDRC solicited the opinions of 16 departments and units, including the Ministry of Public Security, the Ministry of Labor and Social Security, on the general idea and preliminary plan for the adjustment of national statutory holidays three times successively in December 2006, April 2007 and June 2007 respectively. On the basis of fully absorbing the opinions and suggestions of all parties, the administration has made many modifications and adjustments to the holiday adjustment plan, forming the national statutory holiday adjustment plan (Draft).

After the formation of the national statutory holiday adjustment plan (Draft), with the consent of the CCCPC and the State Council, the NDRC further solicited opinions from all sides on the content of the plan through various ways and channels. On November 5, 2007, the general office of the CCCPC and the general office of the State Council sent a message, requiring the Party committees and people's governments of all provinces (autonomous regions and municipalities directly under the central government), ministries and commissions of central and state organs, headquarters and major units of the PLA, democratic parties and people's organizations to solicit opinions on the relevant contents of the national statutory holiday adjustment plan within their respective jurisdictions and units. From November 9 to 15, 2007, the NDRC conducted an on-line questionnaire survey on the relevant contents of the national statutory holiday adjustment plan. The survey showed that more than 80% of netizens agreed to adjust the national statutory holidays. On December 7, 2007, Premier Wen Jiabao of the State Council presided over the executive meeting of the State Council, which adopted in principle the "Decision of the State Council on Amending the Measures for the National Annual festival and Memorial Day holidays" (Draft) and the "Regulations on Paid Annual Vacation of Employees (Draft)." On December 14, 2007, the State Council officially promulgated the revised Measures for the National Annual Festival and Commemorative Day Holiday, and decided that the Measures will be implemented from January 1, 2008. The Measures stipulates that the total number of national statutory holidays is increased from 10 days to 11 days; three traditional festivals are added: Tomb Sweeping Day, Dragon Boat Festival and Mid-Autumn Festival, and adjust the starting time of the Spring Festival holiday to New Year's Eve; Weekends are allowed to be adjusted, forming two seven day "golden weeks" (Spring Festival and National Day) and five three-day "national holidays" (New Year's Day, Tomb Sweeping Day, international Labor Day, Dragon Boat Festival and Mid-Autumn Festival), which increases the number of holidays and makes the distribution of holidays more reasonable.

The adjustment of national statutory holidays is mainly considered from the national perspective. Taking into account the certain regional nature of the traditional festivals of ethnic minorities, the Measures for the National Annual Festival and Commemorative Day Holiday before and after the revision have made special provisions: "the local people's governments in areas inhabited by ethnic minorities, according to the habits of each ethnic group, set the holiday date."[61] In addition to the statutory holidays uniformly stipulated by the state, at present, about 38 national minority festivals in the country have been stipulated by the local governments or the NPCes.

The adjustment of national statutory holidays implements the general idea of "enriching connotation, optimizing structure, improving system, improving quality, benefiting development and promoting harmony," and follows the four principles of holiday adjustment that should be compatible with the stage of economic and social development, conducive to the inheritance of national traditional culture, relatively dispersed time distribution and combined with the improvement of the paid annual leave system for employees, which are related to the vital interests of the broad masses of the people. It is the need to carry forward Chinese traditional culture and enhance national cohesion, reflects the ruling concept of "people-oriented" of the CPC and the Chinese government, and is conducive to ensuring that the people share the fruits of economic prosperity, in line with the requirements of the Scientific Outlook on Development.

Summary

At the new stage of the new century, unprecedented social changes have brought great vitality to China's development and progress, as well as contradictions and problems. In this context, the CPC and the Chinese government have always kept a clear head, prepared for danger in times of peace, deeply understood the phased characteristics of China's development, scientifically analyzed the contradictions and problems affecting social harmony, more actively faced up to and resolved the contradictions, maximized the factors of harmony and reduced the factors of disharmony. The Party continued to strengthen social development, took the construction of a socialist harmonious society as a long-term historical task throughout the whole process of the cause of socialism with Chinese characteristics and a major practical task of building moderately prosperous society in an all-round way, paid close attention to it, solved the problems related to the most direct and realistic interests of the people, and safeguarded the fundamental interests of the overwhelming majority of the people. The Party further deepened the reform of the social security system and accelerated the construction of the social security system, and basically maintained social harmony and stability. The Party overcame the sudden "SARS" epidemic and won a major victory in the fight against serious natural disasters such as the Wenchuan earthquake and post-disaster recovery and reconstruction. The Party actively welcome the arrival of the Internet era and created a good cultural atmosphere and social fashion. During this period, the construction of a socialist harmonious society achieved remarkable results.

SECTION 5

Peaceful Development Path of Socialism with Chinese Characteristics

3.5.1 Taking the Path of Peaceful Development and Building a Harmonious World

(1) Take the Path of Peaceful Development

As a specific political concept, the path of peaceful development was put forward at the new stage of the new century.

On April 24, 2004, Hu Jintao delivered a speech at the opening ceremony of the Boao Forum for Asia Annual Conference, pointing out that "China will adhere to the path of peaceful development, hold high the banner of peace, development and cooperation, create a new situation for the revitalization of Asia with Asian countries, and strive to make greater contributions to the lofty cause of human peace and development."[62] Since then, Chinese leaders have repeatedly expounded China's position of adhering to the path of peaceful development in various domestic and foreign meetings.

In December, 2005, the Information Office of the State Council issued a 12,000 word white paper entitled *China's Peaceful Development*, which comprehensively and systematically expounded for the first time the inevitability and firm determination of China to take the path of peaceful development, as well as the strategic principles and policy measures it has taken to achieve this goal. The white paper clearly points out that China will unswervingly follow the path of peaceful development, which is an inevitable choice based on China's national conditions, China's historical and cultural traditions, and the development trend of the world today. As for the connotation of China's peaceful development path, the white paper points out that China will strive for a peaceful international environment to develop itself and promote world peace with its own development; China will rely on its own strength to reform and innovate to achieve development, while adhering to the implementation of opening up; China will comply with the development trend of economic globalization and strive to achieve mutual benefit, win-win results and common development with all countries; China will adhere to peace, development and cooperation, and work with all countries to build a harmonious world of lasting peace and common prosperity. The white paper emphasizes that peace, openness, cooperation, harmony and win-win are our proposition, our philosophy, our principles and our pursuit. In this way, we can both promote China's domestic development and open the country to the outside world and advance both China's development and the development of the world as a whole, as well as the interests of both the Chinese people and other peoples. China adheres to harmonious development internally and peaceful development externally. These two aspects are closely linked and organically unified, which are conducive to building a harmonious world of lasting peace and common prosperity. The white paper puts forward that taking the path of peaceful development is in line with the fundamental interests of the Chinese people and the objective requirements of the development and progress of human society. China is committed to peaceful development now and it will not change this when it is stronger in the future. The Chinese government and people are resolute in taking the path off peaceful development.

In October, 2006, the Sixth Plenary Session of the 16th CCCPC made a clear discussion on the path of peaceful development in the resolution document of the CCCPC for the first time. In October, 2007, the 17th National Congress of the CPC once again announced to the world that China will unswervingly follow the path of peaceful development. This is a strategic choice the Chinese government and people have made in light of the development trend of the times and their own fundamental interests.

In September, 2011, the Information Office of the State Council issued the white paper *China's Peaceful Development*, which once again focused on responding to world concerns and elaborated on the development path China has chosen. This 13,000-word white paper is divided into five chapters: 1) The Path of China's Peaceful Development: What It Is About; 2) What China Aims to Achieve by Pursuing Peaceful Development; 3) China's Foreign Policies for Pursuing Peaceful Development; 4) China's Path of Peaceful Development Is a Choice Necessitated by History; 5) What China's Peaceful Development Means to the Rest of the

World , which answers in detail the issue that the world focuses on-"what kind of development path China has chosen and what does China's development mean to the world?" This is the second white paper on peaceful development issued by the Chinese government after a lapse of six years.

As for the summary of China's peaceful development path, the white paper points out that China will strive for a peaceful international environment to develop itself and promote world peace with its own development; China will rely on its own strength to reform and innovate to achieve development, while adhering to the implementation of opening up; China will comply with the development trend of economic globalization and strive to achieve mutual benefit, win-win results and common development with all countries; China will adhere to peace, development and cooperation, and work with all countries to build a harmonious world of lasting peace and common prosperity. The most distinctive features of this road are scientific development, independent development, open development, peaceful development, cooperative development and common development.

The white paper emphasizes that China's unremitting pursuit of peaceful development is to seek development and harmony at home and seek cooperation and peace abroad. Specifically, through the hard work and reform and innovation of the Chinese people, and through long-term friendly coexistence, equality and mutually beneficial cooperation with other countries in the world, the Chinese people can live a better life and make due contributions to the development and progress of all mankind. This has become China's national will, translated into national development plans and major policies, and implemented in the extensive practice of China's development process.

The white paper points out that as a member of the international community, China has good expectations for the future world and adheres to the concept of international relations and foreign policies that are compatible with peaceful development. Taking the path of peaceful development is a strategic choice made by the Chinese government and people to inherit the excellent tradition of Chinese culture and in accordance with the development trend of the times, China's fundamental interests and the internal need of China's development. The path of peaceful development is a new development path explored by China, the world's largest developing country. With the passage of time, this path has shown and will further show its world significance. The success of this path requires both the unremitting efforts of the Chinese people and the understanding and support of the outside world.[63]

Along the path of peaceful development, China has experienced extensive and profound changes, achieved remarkable development achievements, made major contributions to world prosperity and stability, and is more closely linked with the world. Practice has proved that China is an important member of the international community, and China's path of peaceful development is promoting the international political and economic order towards a more equitable and reasonable direction.

(2) Building a Harmonious World of Lasting Peace and Common Prosperity

After entering the new century, "on the road of maintaining world peace and promoting common development, we are facing both rare opportunities and severe challenges. Peace, development and cooperation are the theme of our great times. The trend of world multiploidization and economic globalization is developing in depth, scientific and technological progress is changing with each passing day, world productivity has increased significantly, the global economy has maintained overall growth, all kinds of global and regional cooperation are vibrant, and the democratization of international relations is constantly advancing. Mankind is developing at an unprecedented speed. At the same time, Peace and development are the two major issues in the world, and neither one has been resolved. Local wars and conflicts caused by various reasons rise and fall from time to time, regional hot spot issues are complex, the gap between the north and the south is further widened, the basic survival and even life safety of the people in many countries are not guaranteed, international terrorist forces, national separatist forces and extreme religious forces are still quite active in some regions, and transnational problems such as environmental pollution, drug smuggling, transnational crime and serious infectious diseases are becoming increasingly prominent. Mankind still has a long way to go to realize the ideal of universal peace and common development."[64] In the face of such a complex world, building a harmonious world of lasting peace and common prosperity is the common aspiration of the people of all countries in the world, the inevitable requirement of human social development, and China's noble goal of taking the path of peaceful development.

On April 22, 2005, Hu Jintao delivered a speech entitled *Keep Pace with the Times, Carry forward the Past and Forge ahead into the Future, and Build a New Type of Strategic Partnership between Asia and Africa* at the Asia Africa summit, which expounded the idea of building a harmonious world from the perspective of the diversity of civilizations. In September, 2005, Hu Jintao delivered a speech entitled "Build Towards a Harmonious World of Lasting Peace and Common Prosperity" at the high-level meeting to commemorate the 60th anniversary of the founding of the United Nations, comprehensively expounded the concept of building a harmonious world, and incisively discussed the opportunities and challenges faced by building a harmonious world at present and how to build a harmonious world. In 2007, the report of the 17th National Congress of the CPC described the bright prospects for a harmonious world in the future, pointing out that we maintain that the people of all countries should join hands and strive to build a harmonious world of lasting peace and common prosperity. To this end, all countries should uphold the purposes and principles of the *UN Charter*, observe international law and universally recognized norms of international relations, and promote democracy, harmony, collaboration and win-win solutions in international relations. Politically, all countries should respect each other and conduct consultations on an equal footing in a common endeavor to promote democracy in international relations. Economically, they should cooperate with each other, draw on each other's strengths and work together to advance economic globalization in the direction of balanced development, shared benefits and win-win progress. Culturally, they should learn from each other in the spirit of seeking common ground while shelving differences, respect the diversity of the world, and make joint efforts to advance human civilization. In the area of security, they should trust each other, strengthen cooperation, settle international disputes by peaceful means rather than by war, and work together to safeguard peace and stability in the world. On environmental issues, they should assist and cooperate with each other in conservation efforts to take good care of the Earth, the only home of human beings.

In September 2009, Hu Jintao delivered an important speech entitled "Pulling Together Through Adversity and Toward a Shared Future for All" at the 64th Session of the UNGA, stressing that in the face of unprecedented opportunities and challenges, the international community should continue to work together, uphold the concepts of peace, development, cooperation, win-win results and inclusiveness, promote the construction of a harmonious world with lasting peace and common prosperity, and make unremitting efforts for the noble cause of human peace and development. In September, 2011, the Information Office of the State Council of China issued the white paper "China's Peaceful Development," which further elaborated China's important idea of "building a harmonious world of lasting peace and common prosperity." The white paper points out that maintaining world peace and promoting common development are the purposes of China's foreign policy. China advocates and is committed to working with other countries in the world to build a harmonious world with lasting peace and common prosperity. It is both a long-term goal and a practical task. In order to build a harmonious world, all countries should strive to achieve: politically, they should respect each other and conduct consultations on an equal footing in a common endeavor to promote democracy in international relations. Economically, they should cooperate with each other, draw on each other's strengths and work together to advance economic globalization in the direction of balanced development, shared benefits and win-win progress. Culturally, they should learn from each other in the spirit of seeking common ground while shelving differences, respect the diversity of the world, and make joint efforts to advance human civilization. In the area of security, they should trust each other, strengthen cooperation, settle international disputes by peaceful means rather than by war, and work together to safeguard peace and stability in the world. On environmental issues, they should assist and cooperate with each other in conservation efforts to take good care of the Earth, the only home of human beings.

It is precisely under the guidance of the above-mentioned new diplomatic concepts, diplomatic strategies and diplomatic thoughts that in the early decade of the 21st century, that is, the third important historical development stage after new China's diplomacy entered the new period of reform and opening-up and socialist modernization, new China's independent peace diplomacy has made remarkable achievements and made major breakthroughs and progress in all fields.

3.5.2 Big Country Is the Key

(1) China-US Relations
Developing relations with world and regional powers is the focus of China's diplomatic strategy. In the new century, China will actively strengthen strategic dialogue with major countries, enhance strategic mutual trust, deepen mutually beneficial cooperation, properly handle differences, explore the establishment and development of a new type of major country relations, and promote the long-term, stable and healthy development of mutual relations.

China-US relations are the top priority of China's major country diplomacy. At the beginning of the new century, in 2001, US President George W. Bush's positioning of the "strategic competitive partner" of China-US relations and the "China-US aircraft collision incident" in April of the same year made China-US relations once face a severe test. After the September 11 attacks, the Chinese government took the initiative to express condolences to the U.S. government and people, and reached many unanimous views on major issues such as combating terrorism and maintaining world peace and stability. In the same year, the informal meeting of the leaders of the APEC Organization was held in Shanghai, during which George W. Bush and Jiang Zemin met, and the two countries re established "building a constructive strategic partnership." China-US relations began to warm up.

During his visit to the United States in December 2003, Wen Jiabao put forward five principles to ensure the sustained and healthy development of Sino-US economic and trade relations: mutual benefit and win–win results, putting development first, giving play to the role of the bilateral economic and trade coordination mechanism, negotiating on an equal footing, and not politicizing economic and trade issues. George W. Bush agreed. In November, 2005, George W. Bush visited China. The two countries agreed to enhance understanding, expand consensus, deepen mutual trust and comprehensively promote Sino-US constructive cooperative relations in the 21st century. In April, 2006, Hu Jintao visited the United States and put forward six constructive suggestions on comprehensively promoting the constructive and cooperative relationship between China and the United States. China and the United States agreed that China and the United States have broad and important common strategic interests. They should not only be stakeholders, but also constructive collaborators. Good Sino-US relations are of strategic significance to maintaining and promoting peace, stability and prosperity in the Asia and the Pacific region and the world. On September 23, 2008, Wen Jiabao delivered a speech entitled "Carry forward the Past and Forge ahead into the Future, and jointly Create a Better Tomorrow for China-US Relations" in New York. He pointed out that China-US relations should move forward. China and the United States are not competitors, but partners, and can also become friends.

In April, 2009, Hu Jintao and the new US President Barack Obama held their first meeting in London. They decided to "work together to build a positive, cooperative and comprehensive China-US relationship in the 21st century," and decided to establish a China-US strategic and economic dialogue mechanism to reach important consensus on jointly responding to the international financial crisis, expanding bilateral areas and coordinating and cooperating on major international and regional issues. In November of the same year, Obama visited China. Hu Jintao put forward five important propositions on further promoting the development of China-US relations. The two countries agreed to work together to build a positive, cooperative and comprehensive China-US relationship in the 21st century, and will take practical actions to steadily establish a partnership to address common challenges. In April, 2010, Hu Jintao met with Obama in Washington. The two sides exchanged views and reached important consensus on China-US relations and major international and regional issues of common concern. Hu Jintao put forward five important propositions on next stage of the development of China-US relations. In January, 2011, Hu Jintao held talks with Obama in Washington. The two countries issued a joint statement, saying that "China and the United States are committed to working together to build a cooperative partnership of mutual respect, mutual benefit and win-win results."[65] From May 3 to 4, 2012, the fourth round of China-US strategic and economic dialogue was held in Beijing. Dai Bingguo, special representative of Chinese President Hu Jintao and state councilor, and Hillary Clinton, special representative of U.S. President Barack Obama and Secretary of state, CO-chaired the strategic dialogue, with the participation of heads of relevant departments of the two governments. The two sides exchanged in-depth views on major bilateral, regional and global issues, and reviewed the progress made by the four rounds of dialogue in deepening strategic mutual trust and promoting the consensus reached between President Hu Jintao and President Obama on building a mutually respectful and beneficial, and win-win China-US cooperative partnership. Under the framework of the economic dialogue, China and the United States conducted in-depth communication on strategic, long-term and overall issues related to China and the United States and the international economic field, focusing on the theme of "deepening strategic communication and practical cooperation and promoting lasting and mutually beneficial China-US economic relations," and achieved 67 specific results. In terms of trade and investment, the two sides agreed to build a more open global trading system and create an open and convenient investment environment. The United States promised to fully consider China's concerns in the reform of the export control system and strive to promote the export of civilian high-tech products to China. The US side promised to provide a sound convenience for Chinese enterprises to invest and start business in the US. China promised to treat foreign enterprises' investment in China fairly and to continue to simplify the examination and approval procedures for foreign investment. Since the establishment of the China-US strategic and economic dialogue mechanism in 2009, 218 economic achievements have been made. On the day of the opening ceremony, Hu Jintao delivered an important speech, pointing out that the strategic and economic dialogue between China and the United States has promoted high-level strategic communication between the two countries, deepened the understanding of each other's strategic intentions and policies, and expanded the consensus on the growing of China-US relations; it has vigorously promoted mutually beneficial cooperation and enhanced mutual understanding and friendship between the two peoples; it has enriched exchanges between the two countries in various fields and at all levels. Hu Jintao stressed that China and the US are the world's largest developing country and largest developed country respectively. The sustained, healthy and stable development of China-US relations will not only bring tangible benefits to the people of the two countries, but also make valuable contributions to promoting world peace, stability and prosperity. No matter how the international situation evolves, no matter how the domestic situation of China and the United States develops, both sides should firmly promote the construction of cooperative partnership and strive to develop a new type of major country relationship that reassures the people of both countries and the people of all countries. Hu Jintao pointed out that the development of the new model of major country relations between China and the United States requires innovative thinking and practical action to explore a new path for the development of major country relations in the era of economic globalization; second, we need mutual trust. Our planet has enough space to accommodate the common development of China, the United States and other countries; third, we need equality and mutual understanding, respect and take care of each other's interests and concerns, and properly handle differences; fourth, we need to take positive actions to implement all consensus, promote practical cooperation in a wide range of areas, and let the people of the two countries and all countries enjoy the benefits of China-US cooperation; fifth, we need to cultivate friendship, actively promote exchanges between all sectors of society between the two countries, and let more people become participants and supporters of China-US friendly cooperation. Hu Jintao finally said: over the past 40 years, the breadth and depth of the development of China-US relations have far exceeded people's imagination at that time. The sustained, healthy and stable development of China-US relations will not only bring tangible benefits to the people of the two countries, but also make valuable contributions to promoting world peace, stability and prosperity. People believe that when China and the United States cooperate, the two countries and the world will benefit; when China and the United States are in confrontation, the two countries and the world will suffer severely. Both sides should firmly promote the construction of cooperative partnership and strive to develop a new type of major country relationship that reassures the people of both countries and the people of all countries. At present, mankind has entered the second decade of the 21st century. Our thoughts, policies and actions should keep pace with the times, break the traditional logic of confrontation and conflict among major countries in history with innovative thinking and practical actions, and explore a new path to develop major country relations in the era of economic globalization.

In February 2012, Chinese Vice President Xi Jinping made an official visit to the United States, and after meeting with President Obama in Washington, D.C., as agreed, China and the United States released the Joint Information Note on Strengthening US-China Economic Relations agreed upon in the framework of the China-US strategic and economic dialogue. China and the United States agreed to promote the healthy and stable development of China-US cooperative partnership based on the principles of mutual respect, mutual benefit and win-win results.

In June 2012, Hu Jintao held a meeting with Obama during his visit to Mexico to attend the seventh G20 Leaders' summit. The two Presidents had in-depth exchange of views on bilateral relations and international and regional issues of mutual interest. Hu Jintao said, the two sides maintained generally steady development in relations during the past three years or so. The two sides jointly made a strategic decision to build a mutually respectful, mutually beneficial and win-win cooperative partnership between China and the United States, pointing out the direction for the development of bilateral relations. New progress has been made in bilateral cooperation in various fields, and the global impact and strategic significance of China-US relations have become increasingly prominent. China is willing to work with the United States to firmly grasp the general direction of building a cooperative partnership, continuously enhance mutual trust and cooperation, properly handle differences and sensitive issues, and promote the sustained, healthy and stable development of China-US relations. Hu Jintao put forward four suggestions on the development of a new model of major country relations between China and the United States. First, adhere to dialogue, enhance mutual trust, continue to maintain high-level strategic communication through visits, meetings, phone calls, communications and other forms, and give full play to the important guiding and promoting role of high-level exchanges in China-US relations. Second, deepen cooperation, achieve mutual benefit and win-win results, solidly promote cooperation in traditional fields such as economy and trade, investment, law enforcement, education, science and technology, expand cooperation highlights in emerging fields such as energy, environment, infrastructure construction, and promote local exchanges and cooperation, and consolidate and expand exchanges in politics, economy, security, humanities, education, youth and other fields. Third, properly handle differences and eliminate interference. It is hoped that the United States will firmly pursue an active and pragmatic policy towards China, eliminate domestic political interference, strengthen the guidance of public opinion, support the peaceful development of cross-strait relations with practical actions, and ensure the stability of China-US relations in the US election year. Fourth, share responsibilities and meet challenges together. China is willing to continue frank dialogue, increase trust and resolve doubts, and pragmatic cooperation with the United States to achieve benign interaction in the Asia and the Pacific region. It is hoped that the US side will respect China's major interests and reasonable concerns. China is willing to continue to communicate and coordinate with the United States on regional hot spot issues and promote the proper resolution of the issues. Obama said he was glad to meet with President Hu Jintao again. Over the past three years, the Presidents of the United States and China have held 12 meetings, which is a record. Over the past year, China-US relations have made new and important progress. The new round of strategic and economic dialogue has been successful, and the economic and trade relations between the United States and China have been further expanded. The two sides have enjoyed good cooperation in mechanisms including the G20, and have played a positive role in promoting world economic growth. The United States and China have carried out constructive dialogue on East Asian and Pacific Affairs and conducted fruitful cooperation on some regional hot spot issues. Both sides should properly handle some sensitive issues in bilateral relations. All these fully demonstrate that the China-US relations are constantly maturing. I sincerely thank President Hu for his leadership in developing the China-US cooperative partnership and within the G20. Obama said he agreed with President Hu Jintao's outlook for the next stage of bilateral relations. The United States reiterated that a prosperous and stable China is in the interests of the United States and the world, and a prosperous and growing United States is also in the interests of China and the world.

Generally speaking, the general trend of China-US relations is to move forward, but it can not be ignored that China-US relations also have twists and turns from time to time. The United States often makes a big fuss on issues such as trade deficit and RMB exchange rate, and takes some wrong actions on issues such as Chinese Taiwan, Xizang and the South China Sea, which constantly disturbs and damages China-US relations. The Obama administration put forward the "return to Asia" strategy in 2010, aiming to curb the rise of China.

(2) China-Russian Relations

After entering the new century, the China-Russian strategic partnership of coordination has been continuously strengthened, and the relations between the two countries have achieved unprecedented development. In July, 2001, China and Russia signed the *Treaty of Good-Neighborliness and Friendly Cooperation between the PRC and the Russian Federation*, which established the peaceful thought of "ever-lasting friendship and never becoming enemies," and laid a solid legal foundation for the long-term, healthy and stable development of bilateral relations. In June, 2005, China and Russia exchanged the instrument of ratification of the Supplementary Agreement on the Eastern Section of the China-Russian border. On July 1st, 2005, President Hu Jintao and President Putin signed the Joint Statement of the PRC and the Russian Federation on the International Order in the 21st Century in Moscow, further deepening the strategic cooperation between China and Russia in the international field. In 2006 and 2007, the "national year" activities jointly held by China and Russia achieved great success, which had a positive and far-reaching impact on deepening mutual understanding between the two countries, enhancing the friendship between the two peoples, and improving the level of the strategic partnership of coordination between the two countries. On June 17, 2009, Hu Jintao and Russian President Dmitry Medvedev proposed three guiding principles for the future development of bilateral relations: first, mutual trust, second, the overall situation, and third, the long term. In September, 2010, Medvedev visited China. The Presidents signed the China Russia Joint Statement on comprehensively Deepening the Strategic Partnership of Coordination, further promoting the sustained, healthy and stable development of China Russia relations. On June 16, 2011, Hu Jintao held talks with Medvedev in Moscow. The two Presidents comprehensively summarized the development achievements of China-Russia relations in the past decade and exchanged in-depth views on the development plan of bilateral relations in the next decade. The two sides signed the China Russian Joint Statement on the Current International Situation and Major International Issues, and issued the Joint Statement of the Heads of State of China and Russia on the 10th anniversary of the signing of the Treaty of Good-neighborliness and Friendly Cooperation between China and Russia. On the same day, Hu Jintao met with Russian Prime Minister Putin in Moscow to have a frank and in-depth exchange of views on China-Russian relations and deepening cooperation between the two countries in various fields.

With the increasing political exchanges between China and Russia, the two countries have established mechanisms such as annual mutual visits of heads of state, regular meetings of prime ministers and regular consultations of foreign ministers, and high-level leaders have visited each other continuously. From July 2000 to June 2011, there were 35 China-Russian summit meetings. From November 2000 to November 2011, the prime ministers of the two countries have held 16 regular meetings. The two countries firmly support each other on issues related to their respective core interests, and have conducted fruitful cooperation with the G20 Summit, the SCO, the BRICs and other organizations on the regional hot spot issues. The cooperation between the two sides in science and technology, culture, economy and other fields has also been expanding. The trade between China and Russia has maintained rapid growth year after year, reaching a new record of 88.16 billion U.S. dollars in 2012.

From June 5 to 7, 2012, at the invitation of President Hu Jintao, President Putin of the Russian Federation paid a state visit to China. This is Putin's first visit to China since he took office as president of Russia again. On June 5, Hu Jintao and Putin held small-scale and large-scale talks successively. The Presidents from the two countries had an in-depth exchange of views on bilateral ties and international and regional issues of mutual interest and reached important consensus. Both sides agreed to further deepen the China Russia comprehensive strategic partnership of coordination based on equality and trust, promote common development and maintain world peace, security and stability. After the talks, the two heads of state jointly signed the Joint Statement of the PRC and the Russian Federation on Further Deepening the China-Russia Comprehensive Strategic Partnership of Coordination based on equality and trust. The joint statement stressed that the two sides will work to further strengthen the China Russia comprehensive strategic partnership of coordination based on equality, trust, mutual support, common prosperity and friendship from generation to generation, abide by the principles of respecting each other's interests and the right to independently choose social systems and development paths, non-interference in each other's internal affairs, mutual support, mutual benefit and win-win results, and non-confrontation on issues of sovereignty, territorial integrity, security and other core interests. The two heads of state pointed out that this policy was one of the most important priorities of bilateral diplomacy, which was in line with the fundamental national interests of the two countries, was conducive to the development and prosperity of the two countries, and was conducive to the maintenance of regional and world peace, security and stability.

(3) China-EU Relations

After entering the new century, through the unremitting efforts of both sides for many years, the relationship between China and the EU has made great progress, and has formed an all-dimensional, wide-ranging and multi-level cooperation situation.

In 2001, a comprehensive partnership was established between China and EU. In October, 2003, after the Sixth China-EU Summit, the two sides decided to develop a comprehensive strategic partnership. In the same month, the Chinese government issued the "China's Policy Paper on the EU," which comprehensively planned the cooperation between the two sides. In 2005, Hu Jintao and Wen Jiabao visited Europe in October and December respectively. In November, 2007, the 10th China-EU Summit was held in Beijing. The two sides agreed to establish a China-EU High-level Economic and Trade Dialogue Mechanism at the vice premier level. In January, 2009, Wen Jiabao paid an official visit to the EU headquarters. The two sides said that they should attach great importance to China-EU relations globally and strategically, and decided to hold the 11th China-EU Summit as soon as possible within the year. In 2010, China-EU relations continued to heat up. In September, 2010, the first round of China-EU High Level Strategic Dialogue Mechanism was successfully launched; from October to November, Chinese leaders visited Greece, Germany, France, Portugal and other countries, and repeatedly made oral commitments and expressed China's willingness to take practical measures to support Europe in coping with the debt crisis. In May, 2011, the second round of China-EU High Level

Strategic Dialogue was held in Hungary. China and the EU exchanged views on the new development of the international situation, China's development path and China-EU relations, so as to further enhance understanding and mutual trust.

Good political relations have also effectively promoted the rapid development of bilateral economic and trade cooperation. From 2003 to 2011, the trade volume between China and Europe increased from 100 billion U.S. dollars to 567.2 billion U.S. dollars, with an average annual growth of 20.8%; the EU has maintained the status of China's largest trading partner for eight consecutive years, while China is the second largest trading partner of the EU; EU enterprises' investment in China has developed rapidly, accumulating more than 80 billion U.S. dollars, and Chinese enterprises' investment in Europe has also increased from more than 100 million U.S. dollars in 2003 to 4.3 billion U.S. dollars in 2011; the EU is also China's largest source of technology introduction, and the two sides have signed technology introduction contracts totaling 150 billion U.S. dollars. Personnel exchanges between the two sides have become increasingly frequent. In 2011 alone, nearly 2 million Chinese citizens traveled and studied in Europe, five times as many as in 2003.

Since 2012, China-EU economic and trade cooperation has encountered great difficulties due to the weak recovery of the world economy, especially the continuous fermentation of the eurozone sovereign debt crisis. Bilateral trade has declined, and EU investment in China has shrunk. But in general, China-EU relations rose steadily and made progress in changes in 2012, making a positive contribution to world peace, stability and development. Hu Jintao, Wu Bangguo, Wen Jiabao, Xi Jinping, Li Keqiang and other Party and State leaders visited Europe, covering large, medium and small European countries, regions and EU institutions. The 14th and 15th China-EU summit have been successful. The two sides have established the China-EU urbanization partnership and put forward a package plan for future cooperation to promote China-EU cooperation to a new stage. The second China-German government consultation and the "China-Committee of European Economic Cooperation (CEEC) 16 leaders' meeting" were successfully held. China has put forward and actively implemented 12 measures to strengthen cooperation with CEEC, and established the China-CEEC Secretariat for Cooperation, which provides a useful reference for China's cooperation with other parts of Europe. High level exchanges have promoted the development of China-EU comprehensive strategic partnership.

In 2012, the Chinese government also actively increased 43 billion U.S. dollars to the International Monetary Fund to support Europe in dealing with the European debt issue. From January to October 2012, China-EU trade volume reached 452.83 billion U.S. dollars. China-EU cooperation in education, science and technology, culture, youth and other fields is also booming. In 2012, the China-EU, China-UK High-level People-to-People Dialogue Mechanism was successfully launched, and large-scale activities such as the "the China-EU Year of Intercultural Dialogue," the "Year of Chinese Culture "and the "China-French language year" in Germany were successfully held. Chinese writer Mo Yan won the Nobel Prize for literature, and Chinese cultural works were widely praised at well-known European art festivals such as the Avignon Drama Festival in France and the Edinburgh Art Festival in Britain.

In general, China and Europe share the same or similar views on many international issues, share many common interests, advocate the path of peaceful development, are both rising forces on the international stage, and are both willing to play a more important role in international affairs. However, the differences in historical background, cultural tradition and ideology, coupled with the different levels of development, have also led to disharmonious noises in China-EU relations. For example, EU member states continue to put pressure on China on issues such as Xizang, human rights and Internet freedom, and the EU does not recognize China as a full market economy, etc.

(4) China-Japanese Relations

Japan is an important neighbour for China. After entering the new century, China has always viewed and developed China-Japanese relations from a strategic and long-term perspective. However, on historical issues, Taiwan questions, Diaoyu Islands and other issues, the right-wing forces in Japan have repeatedly violated the principles set forth in the *Sino-Japan Joint Declaration (1998)*, the *Sino-Japan Joint Declaration (1972)* and the *Treaty of Peace and Friendship (1978)*, and have made various provocative acts that hurt the feelings of the Chinese people, resulting in the most difficult period since the resumption of diplomatic relations between the two countries. The exchange of high-level visits between the two sides was interrupted, and exchanges in all aspects were seriously affected.

China has made considerable efforts to overcome this temporary difficult situation in China-Japanese relations. In April, 2005, Hu Jintao met with Japanese Prime Minister Junichiro Koizumi during the Asia Africa Summit held in

Indonesia and put forward five proposals on the development of China-Japanese relations: first, we should strictly abide by the three political documents of the Sino-Japan Joint Declaration, the China Japan Joint Statement and the Treaty of Peace and Friendship, and commit ourselves to developing the 21st century China Japan friendly and cooperative relations with practical actions. Second, we should take history as a mirror and face the future. The war of aggression waged by the Japanese militarism untold sufferings to people in China and also made Japan people suffer a lot. To correctly understand and treat history is to put the introspection on that aggressive war into action, and never do anything to hurt the feelings of the people of China and the relevant countries in Asia. It is hoped that Japan can handle historical issues in a serious and prudent manner. Third, we should correctly handle the Taiwan question. The Taiwan question is China's core interest and involves the national feelings of the 1.3 billion Chinese people. The Japanese government has repeatedly stated that it adheres to the one China policy and does not support "Taiwan independence." It is hoped that Japan will take concrete actions to meet the above commitments. Fourth, we should adhere to dialogue and equal consultation, properly handle differences between China and Japan, and actively explore ways to resolve differences, so as to avoid new interference and impact on the overall situation of China Japan friendship. Fifth, we should further strengthen exchanges and cooperation between the two sides in a wide range of fields, and further strengthen non-governmental friendly exchanges, so as to enhance mutual understanding, expand common interests, and promote the healthy and stable development of China Japan relations.

In October, 2006, Japanese Prime Minister Shinzo Abe paid an official visit to China and launched an "ice-breaking visit." The two countries issued a joint press communique and agreed to work hard to build a mutually beneficial relationship based on common strategic interests. China Japan relations began to break the political deadlock.

In April, 2007, Premier Wen Jiabao visited Japan to start the "ice melting journey." The two sides issued the *China Japan Joint Press Communique* and reached a consensus on building a "mutually beneficial relationship based on common strategic interests." In December of the same year, Japanese Prime Minister Yasuo Fukuda visited China, embarking China-Japanese relations on a "trip of spring." In 2007, China became the biggest trading partner of Japan, exceeding the US for the first time. In May, 2008, President Hu Jintao successfully made a "warm spring" trip to Japan. During his visit, Hu Jintao pointed out that with the continuous development of China Japan relations and the profound changes in Asia and the international situation, the common interests of the two countries are constantly expanding and their common responsibilities are also constantly increasing. Looking at the overall situation, China Japan relations are standing at a new historical starting point and facing new opportunities for further development. Both sides should work together to seize the opportunity to advance China Japan relations to a higher stage. Hu Jintao put forward the following suggestions: 1) consolidate the political foundation of China Japan relations. The two sides should abide by all principles embedded in the three China-Japan political documents including the China Japan Joint Statement, properly handle the issue of history and the Taiwan question, and maintain the political foundation of our bilateral relations. 2) Strengthen Strategic Mutual Trust. Both sides should regard each other as long-term partners, support each other's peaceful development, take care of each other's major concerns, and adhere to properly handling their differences through dialogue and consultation. 3) Deepen Mutually Beneficial Cooperation. The two sides should give full play to their complementary economic advantages, create new key areas and highlights of cooperation, achieve a leap from quantity to quality in China Japan economic and trade cooperation, and consolidate the material foundation for the development of China Japan relations. 4) Enhance the Feelings between the Two Peoples. Both sides should focus on the long-term development of China Japan relations, constantly promote people to people and cultural exchanges at multiple levels, channels and fields, deepen the mutual understanding and friendly feelings between the two peoples, especially teenagers, and consolidate the social foundation of China Japan friendship. 5) Establish and Improve Cooperation Mechanisms in Various Fields. The two sides should constantly improve the exchange and cooperation mechanisms in the fields of government, political parties, legislative bodies, economy, culture, defense and so on, build a framework for the long-term healthy and stable development of bilateral relations, and provide a strong mechanism guarantee for the development of China Japan relations. 6) Expand Cooperation in International and Regional Affairs. The two sides should focus on Asia, strengthen strategic coordination and cooperation, work together to promote the establishment of a peace mechanism in Northeast Asia and regional cooperation in Asia, work together to revitalize Asia and jointly address global challenges. China and Japan issued the fourth political document, the China Japan Joint Statement on Comprehensively Promoting Strategic and Mutually Beneficial Relations, which defined the guiding principles for the long-term development of bilateral relations, mapped out the blueprint for the future development of China Japan relations, and pointed out the development direction of bilateral relations in the 21st century. In September 2009, Hu Jintao met with Japanese Prime Minister Yukio Hatoyama and put forward five suggestions on the development of China Japan Relations: 1) strengthen high-level exchanges and enhance political mutual trust. The leaders of the two countries can continue to maintain contact and inject political impetus into the development of bilateral relations. 2) Strengthen economic and trade cooperation and strengthen the ties of interests. Both China and Japan are major economies in the world and each other's most important economic and trade partners. Strengthening economic and trade cooperation will help the two countries overcome the impact of the international financial crisis as soon as possible and promote the recovery of their respective economies and the world economy. In June this year, the second China Japan high level economic dialogue was successfully held in Japan, setting the goals of economic and trade cooperation between the two countries at present and in the future. The relevant departments of both sides should take practical measures to fully implement the results of the dialogue and promote the economic and trade cooperation between the two countries to a higher level. 3) Enhance the emotional bond and consolidate the foundation of public support. The two sides should focus on the trend of the times of China Japan friendship, and continue to carry out exchanges between teenagers, young and middle-aged cadres, culture and media, so as to promote the continuous improvement of emotional bond between the two countries. 4) Strengthen cooperation in Asian Affairs and promote coordination in international affairs. As important countries in the region, China and Japan should work together to promote the denuclearization of the Korean Peninsula and maintain peace and stability in Northeast Asia. The two sides can also conduct dialogue, coordination and cooperation on jointly addressing global challenges such as the international financial crisis, climate change, environment and energy. 5) Properly handle differences and maintain the overall situation of friendship. As close neighbors, China and Japan will inevitably encounter some problems and differences in their relations. For this, both sides should focus on the overall situation, accurately grasp the positioning, carefully and properly handle it, so as to prevent affecting the overall situation of the stable development of bilateral relations.

Since then, high-level interactions between the two countries have been frequent, economic and trade exchanges have continued, and personnel exchanges have heated up. China Japan relations continue to improve and develop. The two sides have maintained close communication and coordination in international and regional affairs. However, in September 2010, the "Diaoyu Island collision incident" occurred, and China Japan relations experienced twists and turns again. China has repeatedly expressed its solemn position, affirming that the Diaoyu Island and its affiliated islands are China's inherent territory, but China also said that maintaining and promoting China Japan strategic and mutually beneficial relations is in the fundamental interests of the two countries and their peoples. Since then, the leaders of China and Japan have held many meetings and contacts on multilateral occasions, reached important consensus, and promoted the improvement and development of China Japan relations. On March 11, 2011, after the great earthquake in Japan, China publicly expressed its concern about the devastating earthquake in Japan and promised to continue to provide necessary assistance according to Japan's needs. On August 30 of the same year, yoshihihiko Noda was elected the new Prime Minister of Japan. China hopes that China and Japan will work together to strengthen exchanges and cooperation and comprehensively promote the healthy and stable development of China Japan strategic mutually beneficial relations.

Regrettably, China Japan relations, which had gradually warmed up and improved since 2006, have fallen into the most serious situation since the normalization of diplomatic relations because the Japanese government unilaterally changed the status quo of the Diaoyu Islands issue, a historical territorial dispute between China and Japan (announced the so-called "nationalization" policy) in September 2012. As a result, a series of activities originally scheduled to commemorate the 40th anniversary of the normalization of diplomatic relations between China and Japan had to be cancelled or postponed. In September 2012, the Japanese government announced the "purchase" of the Diaoyu Island and its affiliated islands and the implementation of the so-called "nationalization." The Chinese government fought resolutely with Japan, issued the Statement of the Government of the PRC on the Baselines of the Territorial Sea of Diaoyu Dao and its Affiliated Islands and the "Diaoyu Dao, an Inherent Territory of China" white paper, and implemented the management of the Diaoyu Island and its adjacent waters through normalized law enforcement cruises and other measures to safeguard national sovereignty.

Generally speaking, China Japan relations in this period are facing development opportunities. The two countries have extensive cooperation space in dealing with climate change, environmental protection and energy conservation, development assistance to Africa, solving the North Korea nuclear issue and regional cooperation in East Asia, but there are also many risks and challenges.

3.5.3 The Neighbourhood as the Priority

For neighboring countries, China continued to follow the foreign policy of building friendship and partnership with them, implement amity, sincerity, mutual benefit and inclusiveness and practical cooperation with them, vigorously develop friendly relations with neighboring and other countries and energetically engage in regional cooperation in order to jointly create a peaceful, stable regional environment featuring equality, mutual trust and win-win cooperation.

In November, 2002, the report of the 16th National Congress of the CPC clearly pointed out: "we will continue to strengthen good neighbourliness and friendship, adhere to promoting friendship and partnership with our neighbors, strengthen regional cooperation, and promote exchanges and cooperation with surrounding countries to a new level." Subsequently, China put forward a new proposition of "implementing amity, sincerity, mutual benefit." Under the guidance of the good neighborly thought and policy of "promoting friendship and partnership with our neighbors" and "implementing amity, sincerity, mutual benefit," the CPC and the Chinese government promoted good neighborly diplomacy to a new stage of historical development during this period.

In the political field, high-level visits and frequent exchanges have further developed good-neighborly, friendly, cooperative relations. In East Asia, from 2008 to may 2012, the leaders' meetings of China, Japan and the Republic of Korea have been held for five times, establishing partnerships and a mechanism for regular leaders' meetings, which have helped East Asia withstand the international financial crisis, major natural disasters and the complex regional and international situation, strengthened mutual communication and coordination, and continuously expanded areas of cooperation, promoted the economic and social development of the three countries and maintained regional peace and stability. In South Asia, new progress has been made in the relations between China and South Asian countries. In April, 2005, Premier Wen Jiabao visited India and Pakistan. China and India announced the establishment of a strategic partnership for peace and prosperity. China and Pakistan signed the Treaty of Good-neighborliness and Friendly Cooperation between China and Pakistan, announcing the development of a closer strategic partnership. In November, 2006, President Hu Jintao paid a state visit to India and Pakistan, which further consolidated the good neighborly and friendly relations between China and the two countries. In 2008, Indian Prime Minister Manmohan Singh visited China successfully, and the two sides signed the *Common Vision for the 21st Century* between China and India. In December 2010, Premier Wen Jiabao visited India and Pakistan again. China and India have established a mechanism for regular exchange of visits between state leaders, opened a hotline between the prime ministers of the two countries, and established an annual mutual visit mechanism between the foreign ministers of the two countries. China and Pakistan have established the annual leaders' meeting mechanism and the foreign ministers' dialogue mechanism. This visit has promoted the development of China-India and China-Pakistan strategic partnership of cooperation, enhanced political mutual trust between China and India, consolidated the traditional friendship between China and Pakistan, and expanded practical cooperation and friendly exchanges between China and the two countries.

In the economic field, China has actively promoted regional cooperation with neighboring countries, and economic and trade exchanges have become increasingly active. In Southeast Asia, in November 2002, the leaders of China and the ten ASEAN countries signed the *Framework Agreement on Comprehensive Economic Cooperation between the PRC and the Association of Southeast Asian Nations*, decided to build the China-ASEAN Free Trade Area by 2010, and officially launched the construction of the China-ASEAN FTA. In 2004, Premier Wen Jiabao attended the Eighth China-ASEAN Summit. During the meeting, the two sides signed the Agreement on Trade in Goods of the *Framework Agreement on Comprehensive Economic Co-operation between the PRC and the Association of Southeast Asian Nations* and the *Agreement on the Dispute Settlement Mechanism of the Framework Agreement on Comprehensive Economic Co-operation between the PRC and the Association of Southeast Asian Nations*, and the China-ASEAN FTA entered the substantive construction stage. In 2010, the China-ASEAN FTA was fully completed, becoming the largest free trade area among developing countries, significantly improving the flow efficiency of production factors such as capital, resources, technology and talents, and providing an unprecedented good environment for expanding trade and investment cooperation. In East Asia, China cooperated closely with other countries in various regional, subregional and cross regional mechanisms such as ASEAN, China, Japan and South Korea (ASEAN Plus Three countries or 10 + 3), the East Asia Summit, China, South Korea and

Japan cooperation, APEC, the Asia-Europe Meeting (ASEM), the Asia Latin America and the Caribbean Forum, advocated active free trade arrangements, comprehensively promoted the research and construction of free trade areas in the region, and promoted the process of regional cooperation. In 2004, China proposed that China, Japan and South Korea study the establishment of a free trade area in Northeast Asia. In 2010, China, Japan and South Korea set the goal of completing the joint study of government, industry and universities in the three countries' free trade zones in 2012. With the joint efforts of the three countries, the trade volume between China and its neighboring countries has continued to grow. Among the 10 ASEAN countries, Malaysia, Thailand, Indonesia and Singapore were the top four import sources in the trade between China and ASEAN. In addition, China has also become the largest trading partner of North Korea, Mongolia, Japan, South Korea, Vietnam, Indonesia, India and other maritime and land neighbors.

In the field of security, China adhered to the new security concept with mutual trust, mutual benefit, equality and cooperation as the core, actively promoted friendly exchanges and cooperation with neighboring countries, and maintained regional peace and stability. On the one hand, China actively promoted regional security dialogue and cooperation and played an active and constructive role in regional mechanisms such as China-ASEAN, ASEAN and China, Japan and the Republic of Korea, the SCO, APEC, the ASEAN Regional Forum, and the Asia Cooperation Dialogue. In Central Asia, the Shanghai Convention on Combating Terrorism, Separatism and Extremism was signed when the SCO was established in 2001. After the "9.11" incident, the SCO Member States strengthened anti-terrorism cooperation centered on combating the "three forces" of terrorism, extremism and separatism in the region. In June, 2004, the SCO Regional Counter-Terrorism Structure was officially launched in Tashkent. In June, 2009, the heads of state of the member states signed the Convention on Combating Terrorism and other documents in Yekaterinburg, Russia, which consolidated the legal basis of anti-terrorism cooperation among the member states. On the nuclear issue on the Korean Peninsula, China adhered to the peaceful settlement of the issue through consultation and dialogue, maintained close communication and coordination with all parties concerned, actively promoted peace and talks, mediated coordination, and promoted all parties concerned to fulfill their commitments. After the "Tian'an" incident and the artillery attack on Yeonpyeong island in 2010, China called for the convening of an emergency meeting of the heads of the Six-Party Talks to persuade the parties concerned not to add fuel to the fire. China's efforts to maintain peace and stability in Northeast Asia are obvious to all. On the other hand, in the spirit of universally recognized norms of international law and equal consultation, mutual understanding and mutual accommodation, China has properly resolved border issues with its neighbors, resolved disputes and promoted stability. In 2003, China and India established the mechanism of special representatives on border issues. In April, 2005, China and India signed the Protocol on the Implementation of Confidence Building Measures in the Military Field in the Area of the Line of Actual Control along the China India Border, and reached a consensus on the political guiding principles for solving the border issue. The China Indian border negotiations were moving forward, and the border areas generally maintained peace and tranquility.

While most of the land boundary issues had been properly resolved, negotiations on the maritime boundary were under way. In 2000, China and Vietnam signed the *Agreement on the Delimitation of the Beibu Gulf*, which is the first maritime boundary between China and its neighbors. "Shelving disputes and jointly developing" is a vivid embodiment of the combination of the firmness of principles and the flexibility of strategies in China's diplomacy. Due to historical reasons, China and its surrounding countries have border disputes, territorial disputes and other issues, and the two sides have great differences in understanding these issues, so it is difficult to find common ground in a short time. In 1984, Deng Xiaoping pointed out "there were many disputes in the world, and we must find ways to solve them. Over the years I had been considering how those disputes could be solved by peaceful means, rather than by war." In dealing with territorial disputes with neighboring countries, he put forward the idea of "shelving disputes and jointly developing." In accordance with the principled position of "shelving disputes and jointly developing," China has gradually normalized its relations with Southeast Asian countries since 1990. Chinese leaders also held many multilateral talks with the leaders of relevant ASEAN countries. The two sides specially sent delegations to conduct specific consultations on marine environmental protection, meteorology, fisheries and other issues in the South China Sea, creating the best and most stable period of relations between China and its surrounding countries since the founding of new China, and striving for a peaceful surrounding environment for China's economic development. At the same time, it has also had a positive impact on the peace and development of the Asia-Pacific region and even the entire international community. China has been committed to peacefully resolving differences with its neighbors on the Yellow Sea, the East China Sea, the South China Sea and other issues through dialogue and consultation. In 2002, China and ASEAN countries signed the Declaration on the Conduct of Parties in the South China Sea (DOC), emphasizing the peaceful settlement of disputes in the South China Sea through friendly consultations and negotiations. In December 2004, China and ASEAN held a senior officials' meeting on the follow-up to the implementation of the DOC. At the meeting, important consensus was reached on the initiation of cooperation in the South China Sea, and it was decided to establish a joint working group on the follow-up to the implementation of the DOC. In March, 2005, China, the Philippines and Vietnam signed the agreement on Joint Marine Seismic Work in the South China Sea Agreement Area, which became the first practice of the principle of "shelving disputes and joint development." In October, 2006, China and ASEAN countries renewed their joint commitment to effectively implement the DOC and make efforts to finally reach a code of conduct for parties in the South China Sea on the basis of existing consensus. On July 20, 2011, in response to the escalating tensions between China and the relevant South China Sea claimants over the sovereignty of the Nansha Islands and Reefs in recent years (China's maritime neighbors such as Vietnam and the Philippines took practical actions to once again declare their sovereignty over the Nansha Islands, and jointly held a series of military exercises with the United States). At the senior officials' meeting on the implementation of the DOC held in Bali, Indonesia, China and ASEAN countries reached an agreement on the guidelines for the implementation of DOC, agreed to resolve the relevant disputes in the South China Sea by peaceful means, and adopted by the China-ASEAN foreign ministers' meeting held on July 21, which paved the way for promoting the implementation of the DOC and promoting practical cooperation in the South China Sea. Since then, the once heated dispute over the South China Sea had subsided.

However, since 2012, with the involvement of the United States and other countries, the South China Sea issue has become more variable. In this regard, the Chinese government, proceeding from the overall situation of maintaining regional peace and stability, pointed outed that China had always insisted on handling disputes over territorial and maritime rights and interests with its neighbors through dialogue and negotiation, and had done its utmost to maintain peace and stability in the South China Sea, the East China sea, the Yellow Sea and surrounding areas.

In 2012, infringement events in the South China Sea continued, and the situation of maritime struggle was grim. On April 10, 2012, the Philippines used warships to harass Chinese fishermen working in the waters of Huangyan Dao, China, causing the Huangyan Dao incident. On June 21, Vietnam's National Assembly adopted the "Law of the Sea," which contains provisions that damage China's territorial sovereignty. In order to counter the infringement of relevant countries and better safeguard China's territorial sovereignty and maritime rights and interests, on June 21, 2012, China's Ministry of Civil Affairs issued a notice—"Notice of the Ministry of Civil Affairs on the Approval of the State Council for the Establishment of Prefecture-level Sansha city": "the State Council recently approved the cancellation of the offices of the Xisha Islands, the Nansha Islands and the Zhongsha Islands in Hainan Province, and the establishment of prefecture-level Sansha city to govern the islands and reefs of the Xisha Islands, the Zhongsha Islands and the Nansha Islands and their sea areas. Sansha Municipal People's government is located in Yongxing Island, Xisha." The establishment of Sansha city marks the emergence of the second prefecture-level city in China with islands as its administrative division after Zhoushan City in Zhejiang Province. It is also the southernmost city in China's geographical latitude.

3.5.4 Developing Countries Are the Foundation

Strengthening solidarity and cooperation with other developing countries in Asia, Africa and Latin America has always been the foothold of China's foreign policy. Since entering the new stage of the new century, as the largest developing country in the world, China has strengthened its solidarity with developing countries, deepened traditional friendship, expanded mutually beneficial cooperation, and sincerely helped developing countries achieve independent development and safeguarded the legitimate rights and common interests of developing countries through assistance and investment.

The Chinese government has always valued developing and strengthening friendly and cooperative relations with Latin American countries. Since the beginning of the 21st century, China and Latin American countries have continuously deepened political mutual trust, deepened cooperation in economy and trade, science and technology, culture and education, and maintained close communication and coordination in international affairs. The bilateral relations have shown a new situation of all-round, multi-level and wide-ranging development. In November, 2004, Hu Jintao visited Brazil, Argentina, Chile, Cuba and other countries for the first time as Chinese president. Meanwhile, Hu Jintao pointed out that China-Latin America Cooperation was facing unprecedented historic opportunities. He also looked forward to the development goals that China Latin America relations can achieve in the near future: to support each other politically and become reliable all-weather friends; to complement each other economically and become a mutually beneficial and win-win partner at a new starting point; to make close cultural exchanges become a model of active dialogue among civilizations.

In November, 2008, the Chinese government issued the *China's Policy Paper on Latin America and the Caribbean*, which elaborated the overall objectives of China's policy on Latin America and comprehensively planned the friendly cooperation between China and Latin America in various fields in the coming period. The document pointed out that though geographically far apart, China and Latin America and the Caribbean enjoy a friendship that dates back to antiquity. At present, both sides are at a similar stage of development and face the same development tasks. Both sides have a common desire to enhance understanding and strengthen cooperation. Latin America and the Caribbean is an important part of developing countries and an important force on the international stage today. Under the new circumstances, China-Latin America relations are facing new opportunities for development. The Chinese government has formulated a policy document for Latin America and the Caribbean, which aims to further clarify China's policy objectives for the region, put forward guiding principles for China-Latin America cooperation in various fields in the coming period, and promote the continuous healthy, stable and comprehensive development of China-Latin America relations. China always views its relations with Latin American and the Caribbean states from a strategic height and long-term perspective, and stands ready to work together with them to advance the comprehensive and cooperative partnership featuring equality, mutual benefit and common development. The overall objectives of China's Latin American policy are: (1) mutual respect and trust, and expand consensus. Adhere to the Five Principles of Peaceful Coexistence, treat each other as equals and respect each other with Latin American countries. Dialogue and communication with Latin American countries should continue to be strengthened, political mutual trust and strategic consensus should be expanded, and the two should understand and support each other on issues related to each other's core interests and major concerns. (2) Mutual Benefit and Win-win Results and Deepen Cooperation. Full play should be given to their respective advantages, the potential of cooperation should be tapped continuously, and China should become mutually beneficial economic and trade partners with Latin American countries, and promote the common development of both sides. (3) Learn from each other, Make Progress and have Close Exchanges. People to people and cultural exchanges should be actively carried out, and the two should learn from each other's useful experience, and jointly promote the development and progress of human civilization. The document stressed that the one-China principle is the political precondition and foundation for the establishment and development of China's relations with African countries and regional organizations. The Chinese government appreciates the fact that most countries abide by the one-China principle, support China's reunification, and refuse to have official relations and contacts with Chinese Taiwan. The Chinese government stands ready to develop friendly and cooperative relations with Latin American countries on the basis of the one-China principle. The document also expounded how China can strengthen all-round cooperation with Latin America and the Caribbean from the aspects of politics, economy, humanities and society, peace and security, and justice. This is the first time that the Chinese government has issued a policy document on Latin America and the Caribbean.

In the same month, Hu Jintao visited Costa Rica, Cuba, Peru and other Latin American countries, and put forward important guidelines for developing China Latin America relations in the process: First, continue to maintain close political relations, maintain high-level exchanges and contacts, improve multi-level bilateral and multilateral political consultation and dialogue mechanisms, and constantly enhance political mutual trust. Second, deepen mutually beneficial economic and trade cooperation, strive to optimize the trade structure, strive to increase mutual investment, focus on strengthening investment cooperation in manufacturing, infrastructure construction, energy and minerals, agriculture, high-tech industries and other fields, and encourage enterprises of both sides to strengthen strategic cooperation on trade and investment. China stands ready to provide support in the development of social economy to Latin American and Caribbean countries to the best of its capacity. Third, strengthen coordination and cooperation in international affairs, coordinate positions on global issues such as climate change, food security, energy security, financial security, the multilateral trading system, the UN Millennium Development Goals, and jointly participate in the formulation of international economic, financial, and trade rules, so as to promote the development of the international economic order in a more just and reasonable direction. Fourth, attach importance to mutual learning and progress in the social field, actively explore substantive cooperation in specific areas such as poverty alleviation, education, social security, health care, environmental protection, disaster reduction and relief, and encourage domestic enterprises to assume corresponding social responsibilities in the process of each other's investment and development, so as to contribute to local social development. Fifth, enrich people to people dialogue and cultural exchanges, deepen and expand exchanges and cooperation in culture, sports, journalism, tourism and other fields, give full play to the role of local and non-governmental friendly exchanges and mechanisms, and enhance mutual understanding. In April, 2010, Hu Jintao visited Brazil. The purpose of this visit was to deepen friendship, enhance mutual trust, expand cooperation and seek common development. In February 2009, Vice President Xi Jinping visited five countries: Mexico, Jamaica, Colombia, Venezuela and Brazil. In June 2011, Vice President Xi Jinping visited three Latin American countries, including Cuba, Uruguay and Chile. In December, 2011, the community of Latin American and Caribbean States (CELAC) was officially established. In June 2012, Chinese leaders put forward a series of initiatives on the overall cooperation between China and Latin America. In August of the same year, China established a regular dialogue system with the foreign ministers of the "troika" of CELAC (the predecessor of the "quartet" now). At the same time, leaders of Latin American countries have also visited China frequently. China has established strategic partnerships with Argentina, Chile, Mexico, Peru, Venezuela and other countries, and has established a comprehensive strategic partnership with Brazil. China and Latin America have always understood and supported each other on issues involving their respective core interests and major interests, maintained good communication and cooperation on major international and global issues, and deepened political mutual trust. With the continuous strengthening of political relations between China and Latin America, the cooperation between China and Latin America in the fields of trade, investment, project contracting and so on has been deepened. At the same time, the cooperation fields have also been expanded to the fields of finance, infrastructure construction, agriculture, high-tech industries and so on. Especially in the process of coping with the international financial crisis, China and Latin America have worked together to overcome difficulties and achieved fruitful results, which fully shows the great complementarity of the two economies. In April, 2009, China and Peru signed the China Peru Free Trade Agreement, which is the first package of free trade agreements signed between China and Latin American countries. As the second largest economy in Latin America, Mexico has a homogeneous trade relationship with China, but with the development of China-Mexican economy and trade, by the end of 2011, Mexico had cancelled the last batch of 204 anti-dumping tariff lines against China. In 2012, China-Latin America trade exceeded 250 billion U.S. dollars, and China has become the third largest source of foreign investment in Latin America. Among them, the trade between Brazil and China continued to expand, reaching nearly 100 billion U.S. dollars.

The Chinese government and leaders have always attached great importance to Africa and its relations with Africa, and have always taken the development of China-Africa traditional friendship and cooperative relations as a priority in China's diplomacy. In October, 2000, the first Ministerial Conference of the Forum on China-Africa Cooperation (FOCAC), jointly founded by China and Africa, announced that China and Africa would establish a new type of partnership featuring long-term stability, equality and mutual benefit. At the second ministerial conference in 2003, China and Africa proposed to further consolidate and develop "a new type of partnership featuring long-term stability, equality and mutual benefit." On January 12, 2006, the Chinese government issued the *China's Africa Policy Papaer*. The document reviewed the course of China-Africa friendship over the past half century and puts forward the general principles and objectives of China's policy towards Africa as follows: (1) Sincere friendship and equality. Adhere to the Five Principles of Peaceful Coexistence, respect African countries' independent choice of development path, and support African countries' self-strengthening through unity. (2) Mutual Benefit and Common Prosperity. Support African countries in developing their economies and building their countries, and carry out various forms of cooperation with African countries in the fields of economic, trade and social development to promote common development. (3) Mutual Support and Close Cooperation. Strengthen cooperation with Africa in multilateral mechanisms such as the United Nations and support each other's legitimate demands and reasonable propositions; Continue to promote the international community to attach importance to peace and development in Africa. (4) Learn from each other and Seek Common Development. Learn from each other's experience in governance and development, strengthen exchanges and cooperation in the field of science, education, culture and health, support African countries to strengthen capacity-building and jointly explore the path of sustainable development.

In April, 2006, Chinese President Hu Jintao paid a state visit to Morocco, Nigeria and Kenya at invitation, and delivered an important speech on developing relations between China and African countries under the new situation, clearly proposing to comprehensively promote a new strategic partnership of mutual trust in politics, mutual benefit in economy and mutual assistance in international affairs. At the FOCAC Beijing Summit held in November 2006, Hu Jintao said that in order to promote the development of the new type of strategic partnership between China and Africa and promote China-Africa cooperation in a wider range, in a wider range of fields and at a higher level, the Chinese government will adopt eight policy measures, including expanding the scale of aid to Africa, providing preferential loans, and encouraging Chinese enterprises to invest in Africa. In February, 2007, when Hu Jintao visited South Africa, he delivered an important speech entitled "Strengthening China Africa Solidarity and Cooperation to Promote the Construction of a Harmonious World." Hu Jintao stressed that inheriting traditional friendship, deepening practical cooperation and comprehensively developing the new type of strategic partnership between China and Africa were the aspirations of the people and the requirements of the times. We should conform to this general trend of development, and strive to raise China Africa friendly cooperation, which features friendship and equality, unity and common development, to a new level. During his visit to Tanzania in February 2009, Hu Jintao stressed that China was willing to work with African countries to focus on the following aspects: first, unity and mutual assistance, and work together to meet the challenges of the international financial crisis. Second, enhance mutual trust and consolidate the political foundation of China-Africa traditional friendship. Third, enhance the practical economic and trade cooperation between China and Africa through mutual benefit. Fourth, expand exchanges and deepen China-Africa cooperation in the people-to-people and cultural field. Fifth, closely cooperate and strengthen coordination in international affairs. Sixth, strengthen cooperation and jointly promote the construction of the FOCAC. The fourth FOCAC Ministerial Conference was held in Egypt in November, 2009. The meeting adopted the Forum on China-Africa Cooperation Sharm El Sheikh Declaration and the Forum on China-Africa Cooperation

Sharm El Sheikh Action Plan (2010–2012). In July, 2012, The Fifth Ministerial Conference of the FOCAC was held in Beijing. China and 51 African members of the forum attended the meeting. At the opening ceremony, Chinese President Hu Jintao announced, on behalf of the Chinese government, five measures for the Chinese government to "support the cause of peace and development in Africa and promote the new type of strategic partnership between China and Africa" in the next three years: first, expand cooperation in investment and financing to provide assistance for the sustainable development of Africa; second, continue to expand aid to Africa so that the fruits of development can benefit the African people; third, support the construction of African integration and help Africa improve its overall development capacity; fourth, enhance China Africa non-governmental friendship and lay a solid public opinion foundation for the common development of China and Africa; fifth, promote peace and stability in Africa and create a secure environment for its development. At the end of the meeting, two outcome documents, the Beijing Declaration of the Fifth Ministerial Conference of the FOCAC and the FOCAC Beijing Action Plan (2013–2015), were adopted, drawing a beautiful blueprint for China Africa cooperation in all fields in the next three years. Good political relations have also effectively promoted the development of China-Africa economic and trade relations. Against the backdrop of sluggish global economic recovery, China-Africa trade had maintained a rapid development trend. China has been Africa's largest trading partner since 2009. In 2012, the total trade volume between China and Africa reached 19.49 billion U.S. dollars. By the end of 2012, China had signed bilateral investment protection agreements with 32 African countries, and established Joint Economic Committees with 45 countries. As one of the eight measures launched by the Beijing Summit of the FOCAC, by the end of 2012, the China-Africa Development Fund had invested 61 projects in 30 African countries, with a decision-making investment of 2.385 billion U.S. dollars, and has actually invested 1.806 billion U.S. dollars in 53 projects. China's assistance to Africa has also been increasing. From 2009 to 2012, China's total aid to Africa nearly doubled, further tilted towards people's livelihood development, poverty reduction and poverty alleviation, disaster prevention and mitigation, and capacity-building, and built new schools, hospitals, roads and bridges, and water supply projects for Africa; a large number of agricultural technical experts and medical team members had been sent to train 21,000 personnel of all kinds for African countries. China has repeatedly provided emergency food aid to famine-stricken countries in Africa such as the Horn of Africa, and has assisted African countries in implementing a number of agricultural demonstration center projects and nearly 100 clean energy projects, which has played a positive role in Africa's response to challenges such as food security and climate change.

Entering the new stage of the new century, despite the changing international situation and the continuous conflicts in the Middle East, the friendship and cooperative relations between China and Arab countries have not been affected, but have continued to develop steadily. In January, 2004, when visiting the headquarters of the Arab League in Egypt, Chinese President Hu Jintao put forward four suggestions for establishing a new type of partnership between China and Afghanistan: enhancing political relations on the basis of mutual respect; close economic and trade exchanges with common development as the goal; expanding cultural exchanges with mutual reference as the content; with the purpose of maintaining world peace and promoting common development, strengthening cooperation in international affairs. China and the Arab League also jointly announced the establishment of China-Arab States Cooperation Forum (CASCF), which has built a new platform for collective dialogue, exchanges and cooperation on the basis of equality and mutual benefit. September 14th, 2004, the first Ministerial Meeting of the CASCF opened up in Egypt. The conference issued the Declaration of the CASCF and the execution plan of the China-Arab Cooperation Forum, saying that the forum is a framework for collective dialogue and cooperation between the two sides on the basis of equality and mutual benefit, with the purpose of enriching the connotation of China-Arab relations, expanding and consolidating China-Arab cooperation at all levels and in all fields, and establishing a new type of partnership of equal and comprehensive cooperation. In May, 2006, the second Ministerial Meeting of the CASCF was held in Beijing. During this period, when meeting with the heads of Arab delegations attending the meeting, Hu Jintao stressed that he was willing to promote the development of China-Arab relations from four aspects: (1) Strengthen political cooperation and consolidate and enrich the political foundation of China-Arab relations. Both sides should continue to firmly support the other side in safeguarding national sovereignty, independence and national dignity, and respect and support the other side in choosing its own development path according to its national conditions. China thanks Arab countries for their valuable support to China on Chinese Taiwan region, human rights and other issues. No matter how the international situation changes, the Chinese government and people will always firmly support the just cause of Arab countries and peoples.

(2) Strengthen economic cooperation, strive to explore and innovate, and achieve mutual benefit and win-win results. The two sides should focus on the central task of promoting common development, further expand cooperation in trade, investment, energy, infrastructure construction, human resource development, science and technology, environmental protection and other fields, actively explore new mechanisms, new ways of cooperation, and jointly raise China-Arab practical cooperation to a new height. (3) Strengthen cultural cooperation, expand dialogue and exchanges, and carry forward traditional friendship. The two sides should continue to deepen exchanges and cooperation in culture, education, journalism, health, tourism and other fields, fully rely on the profound historical and cultural heritage of China-Arab relations and take various forms to carry out in-depth dialogue among civilizations, learn from each other, and promote the harmonious development of different civilizations. (4) Strengthen international cooperation, close coordination and cooperation, and promote peace and stability. Both sides should jointly address global challenges through bilateral and multilateral cooperation, advocate the peaceful settlement of regional disputes through consultation and dialogue, promote multilateralism and the democratization and rule of law of international relations, and jointly build a harmonious world. In May, 2008, the Third Ministerial Meeting of the CASCF was held in Bahrain. The meeting adopted and signed the conference communiqué and the execution plan for 2008–2010 of the China-Arab Cooperation Forum. The two sides agreed to further establish a "new China-Arab partnership for peace and sustainable development." In November, 2009, Premier Wen Jiabao visited the headquarters of the Arab League. In May, 2010, Wen Jiabao attended the opening ceremony of the fourth Ministerial Feeting of the CASCF. At the beginning of 2012, Premier Wen Jiabao visited Saudi Arabia, the United Arab Emirates and Qatar, which promoted the development of strategic cooperative relations with Gulf countries. At the end of May 2012, the fifth Ministerial Meeting of the CASCF was held in Tunisia. The meeting reconfirmed the strategic cooperative relationship between China and Afghanistan and mapped out a blueprint for the development of bilateral relations in the future. Driven by the high-level exchange visits and the multi-level cooperation and exchange mechanism, China and Argentina have closely cooperated in the fields of economy, trade, humanities and so on. From January to September 2012, China-Arab trade volume reached 165 billion U.S. dollars. Remarkable achievements have been reaped in the cooperation covering such areas as energy, finance, investment, and infrastructure building. China-Arab

Cooperation in culture, education, scientific research, journalism, environmental protection, human resources and non-governmental exchanges has also deepened.

3.5.5 Multilateral Fora Is an Important Stage

Entering the new stage of the new century, the CPC and the Chinese government have always valued multilateral diplomacy. In 2002, the 16th National Congress of the CPC clearly regarded multilateral diplomacy as an important part of its foreign exchange strategy. In 2005, the Fifth Plenary Session of the 16th CCCPC clearly put forward the diplomatic policy of "major countries as the key, the neighborhood as the priority, developing countries as the foundation, and multilateral fora as an important stage." In 2007, the 17th National Congress of the CPC once again stressed that we would continue to take an active part in multilateral affairs, assume our due international obligations, play a constructive role, and work to make the international order fairer and more equitable. In 2011, the white paper *China's Peaceful Development* issued by the Chinese government further pointed out that we will continue to "actively participate in multilateral affairs and the governance of global issues, assume our due international obligations, play a constructive role, and work to make the international political and economic order fairer and more equitable."[66]

According to this guiding ideology, China has actively expanded multilateral diplomacy, further integrated into the international community, and increasingly become a constructive power in the international community. China succeeded in transforming a closed and semi-closed economy into a fully open economy. As of 2011, the Chinese government had participated in more than 80 major global and regional intergovernmental multilateral organizations. The CPC has also established contacts and carried out exchanges with international and regional political parties and organizations, such as the Socialist International, the International Conference of Asian Political Parties (ICAPP), the European Socialist Parties, the Green Party in European Parliament, the Group of the European Peoples Party, Sao Paulo Forum, etc., and has incorporated the multilateral exchanges of political parties into the country's overall diplomacy and multilateral diplomacy.

After entering the new century, China continues to attach great importance to the important role of the United Nations as the core of international multilateral mechanisms in international affairs, and is more actively engaged in the multilateral diplomacy of the United Nations. China adheres to the new security concept with mutual trust, mutual benefit, equality and cooperation as the core, actively participates in the cooperation of the United Nations on issues such as counter-terrorism, arms control, disarmament and non-proliferation, as well as the activities of the specialized agencies of the United Nations, actively promotes the peaceful settlement of regional hotspot issues through consultation, dialogue and negotiation within the framework of the United Nations, and highlights the good image of a responsible power. China has actively and constructively participated in the settlement process of international hotspot issues such as the North Korean nuclear issue, the Iranian nuclear issue, the Palestine-Israel conflict, the Lebanon-Israel conflict, the East Timor issue, the Iraq issue, the Afghanistan issue, the Sudan's Darfur issue, and has made important contributions to jointly addressing new threats and challenges. China has vigorously participated in UN peacekeeping operations. By the end of 2010, China had sent about 21,000 personnel of all kinds to 30 United Nations peacekeeping missions, making it the permanent member of the United Nations Security Council with the largest number of peacekeepers. China has actively participated in international cooperation in the field of counter-terrorism and non-proliferation, providing humanitarian assistance to countries suffering from serious natural disasters and sending rescue teams; in order to combat piracy, naval convoys were dispatched to the Gulf of Aden and the waters off the Somalia coast.

In September, 2005, he high-level meeting to commemorate the 60th anniversary of the founding of the United Nations, Hu Jintao announced that China would grant zero tariff treatment to some commodities of 39 least developed countries that have established diplomatic relations with China, expand the scale of assistance to heavily indebted poor countries and least developed countries, help developing countries strengthen infrastructure construction, and help relevant countries speed up talent training. By the end of 2009, China had provided a total of 256.3 billion yuan of assistance to 161 countries and more than 30 international and regional organizations, reduced 380 debts of 50 heavily indebted poor countries and least developed countries, trained 120,000 personnel for developing countries, and sent 21,000 medical team members and nearly 10,000 teachers for foreign aid. China has vigorously participated in UN activities in the field of human rights. By the end of 2008, China had acceded to 25 international human rights conventions and earnestly fulfilled its obligations under the conventions. China has actively promoted the least developed countries to expand exports to China, and has promised to give zero tariff treatment to 95% of the products exported to China from all the least developed countries that have established diplomatic ties with China.

China has actively carried out UN climate diplomacy, actively participated in UN climate change negotiations, and worked with developing countries to strive for a fair and reasonable "new climate order." In September, 2009, Hu Jintao went to the United States to attend the United Nations climate change summit and delivered an important speech entitled "Work Hand in Hand with to Tackle the Climate Challenge." In December, 2009, N Climate Change Conference was held in Copenhagen, the capital of Denmark, and Wen Jiabao attended the conference.

China attaches importance to the role of the United Nations in international affairs, firmly supports the reform of the United Nations, and supports developing countries to play a greater role in the United Nations, including the Security Council. On June 7, 2005, the Chinese government issued the "China's Position Paper on the Reform of the United Nations," which comprehensively and systematically expounded China's views and propositions on the reform of the United Nations in various fields in the form of an official document for the first time. The document pointed out that the role of the United Nations in international affairs was indispensable. As the most universal, representative and authoritative intergovernmental international organization, the United Nations is the best place to practice multilateralism and an effective platform to collectively respond to various threats and challenges. It should continue to be an ambassador for maintaining peace and a pioneer in promoting development. Strengthening the role of the United Nations through reform is in the common interest of all mankind. China believes that the reform of the United Nations should follow the following principles: (1) The reform should be conducive to promoting multilateralism, improving the authority and efficiency of the United Nations, and the ability to respond to new threats and challenges. (2) Reform should uphold the purposes and principles of the *UN Charter*, especially sovereign equality, non-interference in internal affairs, the peaceful settlement of disputes, and the strengthening of international cooperation. (3) Reform is all-round and multidisciplinary, and we should make achievements in both security and development. In particular, we should reverse the trend of "emphasizing security and neglecting development" in the work of the United Nations, increase investment in the field of development, and promote the implementation of the millennium development goals. (4) The reform should meet the requirements and concerns of all member states, especially developing countries, to the greatest extent. We should promote democracy, fully consult and strive to seek the broadest possible agreement. (5) Reform should be carried out in an orderly and gradual manner by addressing the easier issues before tackling the more difficult ones, which will help maintain and enhance the unity of the United Nations member states. Decisions can be made and implemented as soon as possible on the agreed recommendations; we should take a cautious attitude towards major issues that still have differences, continue consultations, strive for broad agreement, and do not artificially set a time limit or force decisions. On September 15, 2005, Hu Jintao attended the round table meeting of the high-level meeting to commemorate the 60th anniversary of the founding of the United Nations and delivered an important speech entitled "Upholding Democratic Consultation and Promoting the Reform Process." In his speech, Hu Jintao put forward four views on the reform of the United Nations: we should focus on the overall situation and adhere to principles; we should promote democracy and extensive consultation; we should be positive and steady, step by step; we should grasp the key points and promote them in an all-round way.

In addition to actively participating in the multilateral activities of the United Nations, China also attaches importance to other international multilateral mechanisms. China actively participates in and vigorously promotes the holding of major multilateral diplomatic activities from time to time with regional and cross-regional intergovernmental organizations and international conferences as the carrier, and carries out multilateral practical cooperation in security, development, humanitarian assistance, environment and climate, prevention and control of avian influenza, earthquake disasters, and combating transnational crime. The SCO and the Boao Forum for Asia Annual Conference initiated or founded by China are gradually becoming an important platform for China to carry out multilateral diplomacy. Among them, the Boao Forum for Asia Annual Conference, as the only non-governmental and non-profit international conference organization located in China, plays a unique role in China's multilateral diplomacy. China's extensive participation in the series of leaders' meetings on East Asia cooperation, the China-EU summit, the APEC, the ASEM and other regional and cross-regional multilateral cooperations and dialogues has promoted the formation and operation of the Six-Party Talks mechanism on the Korean nuclear issue. Among them, APEC is the economic cooperation forum with the most complete mechanism and the greatest influence, which is the most highly represented in the Asia Pacific region. The Chinese president has attended all the informal APEC leaders' meetings, and APEC has become an important international stage for China to play its role as a major power. In October, 2008, China successfully hosted the seventh ASEM Summit, and leaders and representatives of 45 ASEM members from both Asia and Europe gathered in Beijing. The meeting was held against the backdrop of major challenges such as the financial crisis facing the world. Chinese President Hu Jintao attended the opening ceremony and delivered an important speech. Focusing on the theme of "dialogue and cooperation, and win-win cooperation," leaders of all countries exchanged in-depth views on major and urgent issues such as the current international financial crisis and deepening Asia-Europe regional cooperation, and reached many important consensus, which effectively promoted the cooperation between Asian and European countries.

China is also an important member of the G20, BRICs countries, China, Russia and India and other multilateral cooperation mechanisms. China advocates that developed and developing countries establish equal partnerships for cooperation to achieve mutual benefit and win-win results. In November, 2008, Chinese President Hu Jintao attended the G20 financial markets and world economic summit (the first summit) held in Washington, D.C., and delivered an important speech entitled "Stand together in Face of Difficulties to Tide over Difficulties." What is worth mentioning is the BRICs cooperation mechanism. In June, 2009, the leaders of the BRICs held their first meeting in Russia and issued the Joint Statement on the Meeting of the Leaders of the "BRICs" in Yekaterinburg, Russia. In April, 2010, the second BRICs leaders' meeting was held in Brazil. After the meeting, the leaders of the four countries issued a "Joint Statement," elaborated their views and positions on the world economic situation and other issues, and agreed on specific measures to promote cooperation and coordination among the BRICs countries. In December, 2010, the BRICs countries absorbed South Africa as an official member, and the BRICs countries became the "BRICs five" and changed their name to BRICs countries. In April, 2011, the third BRICs leaders' meeting was held in Sanya, China. The summit adopted the Sanya Declaration, reached consensus on major issues in the fields of international finance and development, and planned future cooperation. In March, 2012, the fourth BRICs leaders' meeting was held in New Delhi, India. The theme of this meeting is "BRICs countries are committed to a partnership of stability, security and prosperity," and the two topics discussed are global governance and BRICs countries and sustainable development. Chinese President Hu Jintao delivered an important speech entitled "Strengthening Mutually Beneficial Cooperation and for a Better fFuture" at the meeting. Hu Jintao pointed out that the BRICs countries were an important part of the family of emerging market countries and developing countries and a positive force for maintaining world peace and promoting common development. At present, the BRICs cooperation is at a new starting point. We should carry forward the past, forge ahead, and move towards a new height. Hu Jintao put forward four suggestions on strengthening BRICs cooperation: first, adhere to common development and promote common prosperity; second, adhere to equal consultation and deepen political mutual trust; third, adhere to pragmatic cooperation and consolidate the foundation of cooperation; fourth, adhere to international cooperation and promote world development. In addition, China has also established cooperation forum mechanisms with relevant countries and international organizations, such as China-Africa, China-Arab, China-South Pacific Island countries, and China-Caribbean economic and trade cooperation forums, further strengthening solidarity and cooperation with developing countries. In addition, China has successfully conducted multilateral diplomacy through the Olympic Games, World Expo, Asian Games, Universiade and other platforms. During the 2008 Beijing Olympic Games, leaders of the CPC and the Chinese government held more than 100 meetings with dignitaries from various countries.

Summary

Against the backdrop of economic globalization and world multipolarization, China has adhered to the path of peaceful development. China advocates and is committed to working with other countries in the world to build a harmonious world with lasting peace and common prosperity. China has strengthened strategic dialogue with major countries, expanded the basis of common interests and cooperation, and promoted the long-term, stable and healthy development of mutual relations. China has adhered to the policy of friendship and partnership with neighboring countries, strengthened friendly relations and cooperation with them and deepened regional and sub-regional cooperations with them. China has enhanced its traditional friendships and cooperation with other developing countries, further made use of and build on its achievements in cooperation, and given impetus to innovations in cooperation and the development of related mechanisms. China has actively carried out multilateral diplomacy, played a constructive role in promoting the resolution of hotspot issues and global issues, and fulfilled its due international responsibilities and obligations. China has secured more representation and a greater say in international affairs, and created favorable international conditions for China's reform and development.

SECTION 6

The Successful Practice of "One Country, Two Systems" and the New Path of Peaceful Development of Cross-Strait Relations

3.6.1 The Successful Practice of "One Country, Two Systems" in Hong Kong and Macao Special Administrative Regions

As early as 1985, when the *Sino-British Joint* Declaration was signed and an exchange of letters took effect, and Hong Kong had just entered the "12-year transition period," Deng Xiaoping had put forward and repeatedly emphasized two "simple" judgment criteria on whether the practice of "One Country, Two Systems" in Hong Kong and Macao was really successful: one was whether the "smooth transition" and "smooth handover" could be achieved before "1997" and "1999," and the other is whether we can "continue to maintain long-term stability and prosperity" after "1997" and "1999." Academic circles call it "Two Articles of Deng" for short. For the previous test, after overcoming all kinds of "expected difficulties" from inside and outside Hong Kong and Macao society, and through the joint efforts of the central government, the government of the Hong Kong and MSAR and the compatriots in Hong Kong and Macao, an "excellent answer sheet" with "unexpected satisfaction of the world" was finally submitted—because there was "no major accident" at the "handover ceremony" in Hong Kong and Macao. For the latter test, under the background of economic globalization and the peaceful rise of mainland China, the "new" Hong Kong and Macao, after overcoming various "unexpected difficulties" from both inside and outside Hong Kong and Macao society, and through the joint efforts of the central government, the government of the HKSAR and MSAR and Hong Kong and Macao compatriots, also submitted an answer sheet "the world is relatively satisfied."

At the beginning of the construction of "One Country, Two Systems" in the HKSAR and MSAR, Jiang Zemin also prospectively put forward "four basic bases" on how to "observe and evaluate the situation in Hong Kong and Macao": Deng Xiaoping's great idea of "One Country, Two Systems" and the policy of "Hong Kong people governing Hong Kong," "Macao people governing Macao" and a high degree of autonomy are completely correct. Hong Kong and Macao compatriots are fully capable of and able to manage Hong Kong and Macao well, The wisdom and experience of the governments of the SARs can control complex situations. The great socialist motherland is a strong backing for Hong Kong and Macao to maintain prosperity and stability and overcome difficulties and risks in their progress. Academic circles call it "Four Articles of Jiang" for short. It expresses the ardent hope and firm confidence of the central government and the people of all ethnic groups in China in "opening a new era in the history of Hong Kong and Macao" and "Hong Kong and Macao will have a better tomorrow." Since the return of Hong Kong and Macao, the construction practice of "One Country, Two Systems" in HKSAR and MSAR has fully proved the correctness of this scientific conclusion. We believe that the "Two Articles of Deng" and "Four Articles of Jiang" should be and must be the basic "observation points" and measurement standards for the international community, Chinese people at home and abroad, including Hong Kong and Macao compatriots, to correctly understand and evaluate the "new" general trend of political and economic development in Hong Kong and Macao.

The return of Hong Kong and Macao and the practice of "One Country, Two Systems" in the HKSAR and MSAR are two pilot fields for the "peaceful reunification" project of "One Country, Two Systems" in contemporary China. The Hong Kong and Macao SARs have been facing the negative impact of the Asian financial turmoil, the SARS and the international financial crisis, and the positive impact of Mainland China's accession to the WTO, the signing of the Closer Economic Partnership Arrangement with Hong Kong and Macao, and the opening of the Individual Visit Scheme to Hong Kong and Macao in some provinces and cities. In building a material, spiritual and political civilization and a "harmonious society" in Hong Kong and Macao, we have made a way to remain the "tradition" and "location advantage" of a "free port," a "separate customs territory" and an "international economic center," "center of cultural exchange between East and West." China has continued to maintain the "tradition" and "core values" of "freedom, democracy, human rights and the rule of law," that is, "to continue to maintain long-term stability and prosperity" of the "One Country, Two Systems" of the "Hong Kong and Macao model" construction of the new road.

As for the general trend of political and economic development since the return of Hong Kong and Macao, the central government, the government of the SAR, Hong Kong and Macao compatriots and the international community have a basic evaluation: in Hong Kong and Macao SARs, "One Country, Two Systems" has changed from a scientific concept to a vivid reality; "One Country, Two Systems" has been integrated into the lives of Hong Kong and Macao SARs. On July 1, 2012, on the occasion of the celebration of the 15th anniversary of the return of Hong Kong, Chinese President Hu Jintao delivered a speech, comprehensively summarizing the great achievements of the practice of "One Country, Two Systems" in the HKSAR. He pointed out that "over the past 15 years, the principles of 'One Country, Two Systems,' Hong Kong people governing Hong Kong 'and a high degree of autonomy have been fully implemented. The people of Hong Kong, now masters of their own house, run their local affairs within the purview of autonomy of the HKSAR. The people of Hong Kong enjoy more extensive democratic rights and freedoms than at any other time in its history. After experiencing the impact of the international financial crisis, Hong Kong's economy has developed steadily and continues to maintain its status as an international financial, trade and shipping center. It has been recognized as the world's most free, open and competitive economy and one of the most dynamic regions. Hong Kong's social undertakings have made comprehensive progress, the level of employment has continued to improve, and social security has improved significantly. Exchanges between Hong Kong and the mainland of the motherland have expanded in an all-round way, economic and trade relations have become closer, and cooperation in various fields has been deepened. Hong Kong continues to make unique contributions to the country's reform, opening up and modernization drive, and has received more and more development opportunities and continuous development impetus from the mainland of the motherland. Hong Kong compatriots' recognition and feelings for the country and nation are growing day by day. In the face of all kinds of serious disasters, they are in the same boat and help each other with the people of the mainland of the motherland, which fully reflects the kinship of compatriots who shared the same ethnic origin. Hong Kong has increased its external interactions, and raised its international profile. What has happened fully demonstrates that the concept of "One Country, Two Systems" provides the best solution to the historical question of Hong Kong and the best institutional arrangement to ensure Hong Kong's long-term prosperity and stability after its return. Promoting the cause of 'One Country, Two Systems,' is not only in line with the interests and aspirations of our compatriots in Hong Kong, but also in line with the fundamental interests of the state and the nation. In the great practice of "One Country, Two Systems,"

Hong Kong, a bright pearl, radiates more brilliant colors.[67] On December 20, 2009, on the occasion of the 10th anniversary of Macao's return to China, Hu Jintao delivered a speech comprehensively summarizing the great achievements of the MSAR in the practice of "One Country, Two Systems," Mr. Edmund Ho Hau Wah, Chief Executive of the MSAR, and the SAR Government have led all sectors of the community to be united, pragmatic and enterprising, actively responding to the severe challenges brought about by the Asian financial crisis, the SARS epidemic and the international financial crisis, and striving to overcome the difficulties encountered in the development process of Macao. The city's long history as a merchant city has been brought to life with unprecedented vitality. The successful practice of "One Country, Two Systems" in Macao has written a new brilliant chapter for the development of Macao and added dazzling luster to the national development! The 10 years since Macao's return to the motherland have been the 10 years of the successful implementation of "One Country, Two Systems" in Macao, the 10 years of the smooth implementation of Macao's basic law, and the 10 years of people from all walks of life in Macao actively exploring a development path in line with Macao's reality and constantly making progress."[68]

On October 15, 2007, in the report of the 17th National Congress of the CPC, Hu Jintao raised the issue of "maintaining the long-term prosperity and stability of Hong Kong and Macao" to the strategic height of "major issues facing the Party in governing the country under the new situation." He stressed that since the return of Hong Kong and Macao to the motherland, more and more experience has been gained in putting into practice the principle of "One Country, Two Systems." The principle is perfectly correct and full of vigor. A major task the Party faces in running the country in the new circumstances is to ensure long-term prosperity and stability in Hong Kong and Macao. We will unswervingly implement the principles of "One Country, Two Systems," "Hong Kong people governing Hong Kong," "Macao people governing Macao," and a high degree of autonomy, and act in strict accordance with the basic law of the Special Administrative Region; we will fully support the government of the Special Administrative Region in administering affairs in accordance with the law, and strive to develop the economy, improve people's livelihood, and promote democracy; we will encourage people from all walks of life in Hong Kong and Macao to work together under the banner of patriotism and love for Hong Kong and Macao to promote social harmony; we will strengthen exchanges and cooperation between the mainland and Hong Kong and Macao to achieve complementary advantages and common development; we will actively support Hong Kong and Macao in carrying out foreign exchanges and resolutely oppose external forces' interference in Hong Kong and Macao Affairs. Our compatriots in Hong Kong and Macao are wise enough and capable of managing and building Hong Kong and Macao well. Hong Kong and Macao have played and will continue to play an important role in national modernization. The great motherland will always be the strong backing for the prosperity and stability of Hong Kong and Macao.

As the practice of "One Country, Two Systems" in Hong Kong and Macao is an innovative experiment and exploration with no precedent to follow and no experience to learn from, there have also been some problems in the practice of "One Country, Two Systems" in HKSAR and MSAR, such as the economic development of Hong Kong SAR has not found a suitable breakthrough and new growth point, and a series of disharmonious sounds have appeared in the political development of HKSAR, etc. However, in general, the governments of the Hong Kong and Macao SARs and their compatriots, who "love Hong Kong and the motherland" and "love Macau and the motherland," with the support of the Central People's government and the mainland of the motherland, have all faced the challenges directly, made concerted efforts, constantly "changing danger into safety" and "turned danger into opportunity," constantly overcome various difficulties in the political and economic development path of Hong Kong and Macao, and accumulated successful experience in the political and economic integration process of "seeking the common ground of one country and preserving the great differences between the two systems." It has not only maintained the overall situation of political stability and economic prosperity in Hong Kong and Macao, but also gradually shaped and matured the "Hong Kong and Macao model" of "One Country, Two Systems." Practice has proved that the practice of "One Country, Two Systems" in Hong Kong and Macao is successful, and the "Hong Kong and Macao model" of "One Country, Two Systems" has strong vitality.

3.6.2 Opening Up a New Path for the Peaceful Development of Cross-Strait Relations

(1) New Policy under the New Situation
After entering the new stage of the new century, the Chinese Communists, mainly represented by Comrade Hu Jintao, continued to hold high the banner of "adhering to the one China principle" in solving the Taiwan question and developing cross-

strait relations. Hu Jintao stressed that adherence to the one-China principle is the basis for the development of cross-straits relations and the realization of peaceful reunification. After the 16th National Congress of the CPC in 2002, the CPC and the Chinese government have made it clear that: adherence to the one-China principle is the basis for the development of cross-straits relations and the realization of peaceful reunification. On this issue of right and wrong, which concerns the fundamental interests of the Chinese nation, China's position is clear-cut, firm and consistent."[69] and repeatedly stressed: "we will never compromise our position of adhering to the one China principle." We must continue to adhere to the one-China principle." On March 14, 2005, the *Anti-Secession Law* passed at the Third Session of the 10th NPC clearly stipulates for the first time in a legal language that reflects the will of the state: "adhering to the one China principle is the basis for the peaceful reunification of the motherland."

After entering the new stage of the new century, in order to reflect the sincerity, goodwill and novelty of the CPC and the Chinese government in "adhering to the one China principle," the Chinese Communists, mainly represented by Comrade Hu Jintao, also "keep pace with the times" to adjust the "specific connotation" of the "one China principle": from the old "syllogism" that "there is only one China in the world, Chinese Taiwan is a part of China, and the only legal government representing China in the international community is the government of the PRC," into a new "syllogism" that "there is only one China in the world, the mainland and Chinese Taiwan region belong to one China, and China's sovereignty and territorial integrity are indivisible." On December 31, 2008, in an important speech at the symposium to the 40th anniversary of issuing *Message to Compatriots in Chinese Taiwan*, Hu Jintao put forward the "six points of view" (the famous "Six Points of View of Hu") of "firmly grasp the theme of the peaceful development of cross-strait relations and actively promote the peaceful development of cross-strait relations," and put forward that "there is only one China in the world, and China's sovereignty and territorial integrity cannot be divided." Since 1949, although the mainland and Chinese Taiwan have not been reunified, it is not the division of China's territory and sovereignty, but the political confrontation left over and continued by China's civil war in the mid and late 1940s, which has not changed the fact that the mainland and Chinese Taiwan belong to one China. The reunification of the two sides of the Strait is not a rebuilding of sovereignty and territory, but an end to political confrontation,"[70] which is the latest interpretation of the nature of the Taiwan question and the status quo of cross-strait relations.

The peaceful reunification of contemporary China through equal negotiations between the ruling CPC and the KMT of China on both sides of the Taiwan Strait is a basic political proposition for the successive CPC leaders and the Chinese government to solve the Taiwan question since the second half of the 20th century. After entering the new stage of the new century, the Chinese Communists, mainly represented by Comrade Hu Jintao, have never given up on the basis of "adhering to the one China principle," whether in 2000, when the Chinese KMT lost its ruling power in Chinese Taiwan, or in 2008, when the Chinese KMT restored its ruling power in Chinese Taiwan, and has continued to adhere to the basic position of realizing the peaceful reunification of contemporary China by promoting cross-strait political dialogue and negotiation.

As for the specific content of cross-strait political negotiations, after entering the new stage of the new century, the basic open position of the Chinese Communists, mainly represented by Comrade Hu Jintao, is consistent, that is, "On the premise of the one-China principle, all issues can be discussed." On March 4, 2005, when visiting some members of the Third Session of the 10th CPPCC National Committee, Hu Jintao put forward four points on the development of cross-strait relations under the new situation (the famous "Four Points of Views of Hu"), pointing out: "as long as the Chinese Taiwan authorities recognize the '1992 Consensus,' cross-strait dialogue and negotiations can be resumed, and any issue can be discussed. We can not only talk about the issues we have raised, such as formally ending the state of hostility between the two sides of the Strait and establishing military mutual trust, the space for Chinese Taiwan to move in the international community in line with its identity, the political status of the Chinese Taiwan authorities, and the framework for the peaceful and stable development of cross-strait relations, but also talk about all the issues that need to be solved in the process of achieving peaceful reunification. We welcome the efforts made by anyone and any political party in China's Chinese Taiwan towards recognizing the one China principle. As long as we recognize the one China principle and the 1992 Consensus, no matter who or what political parties they are, or what they have said or done in the past, we are willing to talk with them about developing cross-strait relations and promoting peaceful reunification."[71] On March 14, 2005, the Third Session of the 10th NPC passed the Anti-Secession Law, which is the first time to further "concretize" the "three 'negotiables'" at the policy level of the ruling party of the "cross-strait political negotiation" and upgrade it to the "six 'negotiables'" at the national legal level.

On March 4, 2008, when visiting some members of the First Session of the 11th CPPCC National Committee, Hu Jintao put forward important opinions on the development of cross-strait relations, pointing out: "we are ready to conduct exchanges, dialogue, consultations and negotiations with any political party in Chinese Taiwan on any issue as long as it recognizes that both sides of the Straits belong to one and the same China. The status of negotiations is equal, the topics are open, and any issue can be discussed. Through negotiations, we should seek solutions to important issues such as politics, economy, military affairs, culture and foreign exchanges across the Straits, and plan for the future development of cross-strait relations. We expect that with the joint efforts of the two sides: on the basis of the one-China principle, let us discuss a formal end to the state of hostility between the two sides, reach a peace agreement, construct a framework for peaceful development of cross-strait relations, and thus usher in a new phase of peaceful development." "For those who once had illusions about 'Taiwan independence,' advocated 'Taiwan independence' and even engaged in 'Taiwan independence' activities, we should also strive for unity. As long as they return to the right path to promote the peaceful development of cross-strait relations, we will warmly welcome them and treat each other sincerely."[72]

On December 31, 2008, in an important speech at the symposium to the 30th anniversary of issuing *Message to Compatriots in Chinese Taiwan*, Hu Jintao further released his sincerity, goodwill and new ideas for promoting cross-strait political negotiations, and released his confidence, tolerance and breadth of mind for promoting cross-strait political negotiations. It is proposed that "in order to facilitate the negotiation between the two sides of the Strait and make arrangements for their exchanges, the two sides of the Strait can carry out pragmatic discussions on political relations under the special circumstances of the reunification of the country. In order to help stabilize the situation in the Taiwan Strait and alleviate military security concerns, the two sides of the Strait can conduct contacts and exchanges on military issues in a timely manner and discuss the establishment of a cross-Straits confidence-building mechanism for military security. Here we would like to make a solemn appeal again: on the basis of the one-China principle, let us discuss a formal end to the state of hostility between the two sides, reach a peace agreement, construct a framework for peaceful development of cross-Straits relations, and thus usher in a new phase of peaceful development. "On the issue of Taiwan's participation in the activities of international organizations, under the premise of not creating 'two Chinas' and 'one China, one Taiwan,' reasonable arrangements can be made through pragmatic cross-strait consultations" Hu Jintao once again stressed: "for those who have advocated, engaged in and followed 'Taiwan independence,' we also sincerely welcome them to return to the right direction of promoting the peaceful development of cross-strait relations. We hope that the Democratic Progressive Party (DPP) will recognize the current situation, stop the separatist activities of 'Taiwan independence' and stop running counter to the common will of the whole nation. As long as the DPP changes its separatist stance on 'Taiwan independence,' we are willing to make a positive response."[73]

(2) "Place Hope on the People of Taiwan"

To solve the Taiwan question (including through "cross-strait political negotiations" with the Taiwan authorities) and realize the peaceful reunification of contemporary China, a "prerequisite" and "basic" condition is to solve the "return of the people's hearts" of the Taiwan people, that is, the Chinese Communist Party and the Chinese government have always emphasized "placing hope on the Taiwan people." After entering the new stage of the new century, the Chinese Communists, mainly represented by Comrade Hu Jintao, attach great importance to solving the problem of the "return of the people's hearts" of the Taiwan people, and always regard "doing a good job of the Taiwan people" as one of the most important goals of the CPC and the Chinese government in their work on Taiwan. The CPC and the Chinese government have clearly pointed out that 23 million Taiwan compatriots are our blood brothers with a glorious patriotic tradition. They are the basis and subjective force for the peaceful development of cross-strait relations and the peaceful reunification of the motherland. They are also the basis and subjective force for opposing and curbing the separatist forces and activities of "Taiwan independence" at present. To solve the Taiwan question and realize the peaceful reunification of the motherland, we should not only adhere to "the Chinese do not fight the Chinese," but also adhere to "the Chinese do their things on their own." To solve the Taiwan question "we must put our own needs first," and we must work together with 1.3 billion mainland compatriots and 23million Taiwan compatriots.

After the reform and opening-up, the scientific concept of "peaceful reunification and 'One Country, Two Systems'" and the specific contents of the basic national policy have been constantly adjusted in response to the evolution of the political ecology on Taiwan and the changes in cross-strait relations, and have undergone a transmutation and transformation from the two different "Hopes" approaches of "hope in the people of Taiwan and hope in the Taiwan authorities" and "hope in the Taiwan authorities and more hope in the people of Taiwan" to the one "Hope" approach of "hope in the people of Taiwan," which has become more practical and targeted.

After entering the 1990s and the new century, all the working meetings of the CPC and the Chinese government on Taiwan, all the policy documents and relevant laws issued on Taiwan, and all the talks between leaders and people involved in Taiwan at home and abroad, without exception, regard "doing a good job of the people of Taiwan" and striving for the "return of the people of Taiwan" as the "top priority"; the issue of "doing a good job of the people of Taiwan" and striving for the "return of the people of Taiwan" should be raised to the strategic height of solving the Taiwan question and realizing the peaceful reunification of contemporary China.

After the 16th National Congress of the CPC in 2002, the Chinese Communists, mainly represented by Comrade Hu Jintao, continued to hold high the banner of "placing hope on the people of Taiwan" and "do a solid job in winning the hearts of the people of Taiwan." Hu Jintao clearly stated that "we will never change the principle of placing our hopes on the people of Taiwan." On March 4, 2005, when visiting some members of the Third session of the 10th CPPCC National Committee, Hu Jintao put forward four suggestions on the development of cross-strait relations under the new situation, pointing out: "Taiwan compatriots are our brothers and sisters, an important force in developing cross-strait relations, and an important force in curbing the separatist activities of 'Taiwan independence.' The more the 'Taiwan independence' separatist forces want to separate Taiwan compatriots from us, the closer we need to unite Taiwan compatriots. In any case, we respect them, trust them, rely on them, put ourselves in their shoes, and do everything possible to take care of and safeguard their legitimate rights and interests We will make every effort to achieve anything that serves the interests of our Taiwan compatriots, contributes to the maintenance of peace in the Taiwan Straits region, and facilitates peaceful national reunification. This is our solemn commitment to our Taiwan compatriots." For the first time, it formally put forward the "four 'advantages' of doing a good job of winning the hearts and minds of the people in Taiwan."

Since the 16th National Congress of the CPC, the Chinese Communists, mainly represented by Comrade Hu Jintao, have further put forward new ideas and views that the people on both sides of the Strait are a "community with a shared future" on the basis of adhering to the guiding ideology and basic principles of "we will never change the principle of placing our hopes on the people of Taiwan." Hu Jintao clearly pointed out: whether in the past, now or in the future, the 1.3 billion people on the mainland and the 23 million people in Taiwan are of the same blood and share a common destiny. The compatriots on both sides of the Strait share the same root, nationality and vein. The Chinese nation's 5000 year long history and splendid culture have closely linked us. We are all descendants of the Chinese nation, and we should be proud of our great nation and take the revitalization of our great nation as our own responsibility. China is China with 1.3 billion Chinese people, including 23 million Taiwan compatriots. The mainland is the mainland with 1.3 billion Chinese people, including 23 million Taiwan compatriots. Taiwan is also Taiwan with 1.3 billion Chinese people, including 23 million Taiwan compatriots. Any issue involving China's sovereignty and territorial integrity must be decided jointly by the 1.3 billion people of China. China is the common homeland for the compatriots on both sides of the Straits, who have every reason to join hands to safeguard and develop this homeland.

In October, 2007, Hu Jintao put forward the important idea of "firmly grasping the theme of peaceful development of cross-strait relations" for the first time in the report of the 17th National Congress of the CPC, setting the main tone for the work and policies of the CPC and the Chinese government on Taiwan in the coming period.

On December 31, 2008, in an important speech at the symposium to the 30th anniversary of issuing Message to Compatriots in Taiwan, Hu Jintao put forward the "Six Points of View" to "firmly grasp the theme of the peaceful development of cross-strait relations and actively promote the peaceful development of cross-strait relations:" first, adhere to one China and enhance political mutual trust; second, promote economic cooperation and common development; third, carry forward Chinese culture and strengthen spiritual ties; fourth, strengthen personnel exchanges and expand exchanges from all walks of life; fifth, safeguard national sovereignty and negotiate foreign affairs; sixth, end hostilities and reach a peace agreement. The "Six Points of View of Hu" once again embodies the goodwill, sincerity and new ideas of the CPC and the Chinese government in solving the Taiwan question, and is a new outline document for the CPC and the Chinese government in solving the Taiwan question.

Since March, 2008, with the correct guidance and positive promotion of the CPC and the Chinese government, and the joint efforts of compatriots on both sides of the Strait, significant positive changes have taken place in the political ecology of Taiwan Island and the situation of cross-strait relations, and cross-strait relations have ushered in a rare historical opportunity. The Chinese KMT, which opposed "Taiwan independence" and recognized the "1992 Consensus," showed great enthusiasm for the development of "normalized" cross-strait relations before and after it returned to power in Taiwan, and put forward a new concept of developing cross-strait relations that "face the reality, create the future, shelve disputes, and pursue a win-win situation." We have given a positive response to this. On April 29, 2008, Hu Jintao met with Lien Chan, honorary chairman of the Chinese KMT, and exchanged views on the development of cross-strait relations. Hu Jintao clearly pointed out that the current situation in Taiwan has undergone positive changes, and cross-strait relations have shown a good momentum of development. Both sides of the Strait should work together to "build mutual trust, shelve disputes, seek common ground while reserving differences, and create a win-win situation." On May 28, Hu Jintao met with Wu Boxiong, chairman of the Chinese KMT, and exchanged in-depth views on promoting the improvement and development of cross-strait relations under the new situation. Hu Jintao said sincerely to Wu Boxiong that with the joint efforts of the KMT and the Communist Party and compatriots on both sides of the Strait, the situation in Taiwan region has undergone positive changes, and the development of cross-strait relations is facing a rare historical opportunity. This positive momentum is hard-won and shall be all the more cherished.

Since June 2008, with the joint efforts of both sides of the Strait, the communication channels and mechanisms between the ARATS and the Taiwan Straits Exchange Foundation, which had been suspended for a long time, have been restored, and consultations have been held on the "three direct links" and comprehensive economic exchanges and cooperation between the two sides of the Strait, and a series of important progress and breakthroughs have been made. From June, 2008 to August, 2012, Chen Yunlin, the new chairman of the

ARATS, and Jiang Bingkun, the new chairman of the SEF, held eight regular "Chen Jiang meetings" in succession, and jointly signed the *minutes of the cross strait charter talks, agreement between the two sides of the Taiwan Strait on mainland residents' travel to Taiwan, agreement between the two sides of the Taiwan Strait on air transport, agreement between the two sides of the Taiwan Strait on maritime transport, agreement between the two sides of the Taiwan Strait on postal services, agreement on food safety across the Taiwan Strait The agreement on cross strait financial cooperation, the supplementary agreement on Cross Strait air transport, the agreement on joint fight against crime and mutual legal assistance between the two sides of the Taiwan Strait, the Agreement on labor cooperation between fishing boat crews on both sides of the Taiwan Strait, the Agreement on Quarantine and Inspection of Agricultural Products on both Sides of the Taiwan Strait, the Agreement on Cooperation in Standard Metrology Inspection and Certification on both Sides of the Taiwan Strait, the Economic Cooperation Framework Agreement (ECFA), the Agreement on Cross-straits Cooperation in Intellectual Property Protection Cross-Straits Medical and Health Cooperation Agreement, the Cross-straits Nuclear Power Safety Cooperation Agreement, Cross-Strait Customs Cooperation Agreement,* etc. The signing of these cooperation agreements has not only successfully solved the long-standing outstanding issue of the "three direct links" between the two sides of the Strait, but also gradually institutionalized cross-strait economic exchanges and cooperation, becoming increasingly comprehensive and in-depth.

Since 2008, a gratifying new situation has emerged in cross-strait relations. The two sides have properly handled a series of issues, maintained the momentum of improvement and development of cross-strait relations, and promoted the prospects for peaceful development of cross-strait relations. The frequent exchanges between compatriots on both sides of the Straits, the close economic ties, the active cultural exchanges and the wide range of common interests are unprecedented. The Chinese people's cause of safeguarding peace in the Taiwan Strait, promoting the development of cross-strait relations, and realizing the peaceful reunification of the motherland has increasingly won the understanding and support of the international community. All countries in the world have generally recognized that the pattern of one China has been constantly consolidated and developed. After a special freezing period, cross-strait relations have ushered in a "Spring Festival" of melting ice and snow. Just to illustrate the problem with the relevant statistical data of 2012: from January to December 2012, the trade volume between Chinese Mainland and Taiwan was 168.96 billion U.S. dollars (accounting for 4.4% of the total foreign trade volume of Chinese Mainland), an increase of 5.6% year-on-year. Among them, the export of Chinese Mainland to Taiwan was 36.78 billion U.S. dollars, up 4.8% year-on-year; Imports from Taiwan amounted to 132.18 billion U.S. dollars, up 5.8% year-on-year. From January to December 2012, a total of 2,229 Taiwan investment projects were approved in Chinese Mainland, with a year-on-year decrease of 15.5%. The amount of Taiwan investment actually used was 2.85 billion U.S. dollars (accounting for 3.0% of the amount of foreign investment actually used in Chinese Mainland), with a year-on-year increase of 30.4%. By the end of December 2012, 88,001 Taiwan funded projects had been approved in Chinese Mainland, with an actual utilization of 57.05 billion U.S. dollars. According to the statistics of foreign investment actually used, Taiwan investment accounts for 4.5% of the total overseas investment absorbed by Chinese Mainland. From January to December 2012, 5.3402 million Taiwan residents came to Chinese Mainland, an increase of 1.47% year on year; Chinese Mainland residents visited Taiwan 2.6302 million times, an increase of 42.56% year-on-year. Among them, 1.97 million tourists from Chinese Mainland visited Taiwan, an increase of 57.5% year-on-year; 1.78 million team trips, up 46% year-on-year; more than 190,000 individual tourists visited Taiwan, a year-on-year increase of 553%. From January to December 2012, Chinese Mainland had an increase of 52 tourist group agencies to Taiwan, bringing the total number of group agencies to 216; 10 pilot cities including Tianjin as the second batch for personal tours to Chinese Taiwan have been opened, and the number of cities for personal tours to Jinmapeng region has been expanded from 9 prefectures and cities in Fujian to 20 prefectures and cities in Haixi Area. In terms of Chinese Taiwan residents' travel to and from Chinese Mainland, four new Chinese Taiwan compatriots' endorsement points at ports such as Zhengzhou have been added, bringing the total number of Chinese Taiwan compatriots' endorsement points at ports in Chinese Mainland to 30.

Summary

From 2002 to 2012, the practice of "One Country, Two Systems" in the Hong Kong and Macao SARs experienced a major turning point and a major transformation in the past decade. The Chinese Communists, mainly represented by Comrade Hu Jintao, faced all kinds of opportunities and challenges in the practice of "One Country, Two Systems" in the Hong Kong and Macao SARs, and timely raised the issue of "maintaining long-term prosperity and stability" in the Hong Kong and Macao SARs to the strategic height of the CPC in "new issues facing the governance of the country under the new situation" and even "major issues facing the governance of the country under the new situation." Under the correct leadership of the CPC, with the strong support of the central government and the mainland of the motherland, and through the joint efforts of the government of the Special Administrative Region and the compatriots in Hong Kong and Macao, the practice of "One Country, Two Systems" in the Hong Kong and MSAR has reached a new height. This decade is also a decade when cross-strait relations have undergone major turns and transformations. On the basis of the great achievements made by the CPC and the Chinese government in "opposing 'independence' and promoting reunification," compatriots on both sides of the Strait have jointly opened up a new path and a new situation for the peaceful development of cross-strait relations. The peaceful development of cross-straits relationship is the common aspiration of the people on both sides of the Taiwan Straits.

CHAPTER IV

Deepening the Reform and Opening-Up

Chinese Socialism Has Crossed the Threshold into a New Era
(2012–2021)

I n 2012, The 18th National Congress of the CPC in 2012 heralded a new era in building socialism with Chinese characteristics. This new era is a new historic juncture in China's development and also a new historical stage of the reform and opening-up. The new era of socialism with Chinese characteristics is an era in which we will build on past successes to further advance our cause and continue to strive for the success of socialism with Chinese characteristics under new historical conditions; an era in which we will use the momentum of our decisive victory in building a moderately prosperous society in all respects to fuel all-out efforts to build a great modern socialist country; an era in which Chinese people of all ethnic groups will work together to create a better life for themselves and gradually realize the goal of common prosperity; an era in which all the sons and daughters of the Chinese nation will strive with one heart to realize the Chinese Dream of national rejuvenation; and an era in which China will make even greater contributions to humanity.

Since the 18th National Congress of the CPC, as the world, the country, and the Party undergo profound changes, the CPC, with Comrade Xi Jinping at its core, has followed the guidance of Xi Jinping Thought on Socialism with Chinese

Characteristics for a New Era, and promoted the "five-sphere integrated plan" and coordinated the strategic layout of "the four-pronged comprehensives," leading the people of all nationalities to forge ahead towards the grand goal of achieving the great rejuvenation of the Chinese nation. In terms of political construction, we have worked hard to comprehensively deepen reform, adhered to and improved the socialist system with Chinese characteristics, promoted the modernization of the country's governance system and governance capacity, and achieved historical changes, systematic remolding, and overall reconstruction in many fields. We have put forward and developed the whole-process people's democracy, upheld and improved the system of the people's congresses, promoted the extensive and multi-layered institutionalization of socialist consultative democracy, improved the system of regional ethnic autonomy and the system of grassroots people's autonomy, and consolidated and developed the lively, stable and united political situation. We have comprehensively promoted the rule of law, given prominence to the rule of law, and jointly promoted the rule of law, governance and administration according to law. We have built a country, a government and a society under the rule of law, and constantly improve the socialist system of rule of law with Chinese characteristics. We have put forward the goal of strengthening the military in the new era, established the military strategic principles for the new era, promoted the building of the military through politics, reform, science and technology, talents, and rule by law. The people's army has achieved a revolutionary transformation in its entirety. We have creatively put forward the major proposition of the Party's self-revolution, formed the strategic principle of comprehensively and strictly administering the Party, and successfully explored the "second answer" that jumped out of the historical cycle rate. The Party was stronger in the revolutionary forging, the CCCPC's authority and centralized, unified leadership were effectively guaranteed, and the Party's political leadership, ideological leadership, mass organization and social appeal were significantly enhanced. In terms of economic development, we have clarified that China's economic development has entered a new normal, from the high-speed growth stage to high-quality development, and proposed to enter a new development stage, implemented new development concepts, built a new development pattern, promoted supply-side structural reform, built a modernized economy, formulated and implemented a series of important development strategies such as innovation-driven development strategy, regional coordinated development strategy, and rural revitalization strategy, and China will continue to promote high-level opening-up, and the country's economic strength, scientific and technological strength, and comprehensive national strength will rise to a new level. In terms of cultural development, we have highlighted cultural self-confidence, strengthened ideological work, consolidated the guiding position of Marxism in the ideological field, adhered to the socialist core values to guide cultural development, paid attention to using advanced socialist culture, revolutionary culture and excellent traditional Chinese culture to cultivate the soul, deepened the reform of cultural restructuring, and vigorously developed cultural undertakings and cultural industries. In terms of social development, we have thoroughly implemented the people-centered philosophy of development, focused on ensuring and improving people's livelihood, launched a series of major measures in income distribution, employment, education, social security, medical and health care, housing security, etc., improved the social governance system, built a safe China, solidly promoted common prosperity, fought against the COVID-19 epidemic and made major strategic achievements. The people's sense of gain, happiness and their sense of security was significantly improved. We have put forward and implemented a holistic approach to national security, promoted the building of the national security system and capacity, and comprehensively strengthened national security. In the construction of ecological civilization, we have promoted the construction of ecological civilization with unprecedented efforts, adhered to the concept that clear rivers and green mountains are as valuable as mountains of gold and silver, protected the ecological environment with the strictest system and the strictest rule of law, adhered to the integrated protection and systematic management of mountains, rivers, forests, fields, lakes, grass and sand, and accelerated the formation of a green development mode and lifestyle. China's ecological environment protection has undergone historic, turning and overall changes. In terms of major country diplomacy, we have studied and judged the great changes in the world that have not been seen in a century, planned major country diplomacy with Chinese characteristics, promoted the construction of a community with a shared future for mankind, solidly promoted international cooperation under the "Belt and Road Initiative," worked hard to develop global partnerships, and actively participated in the reform and construction of the global governance system. These efforts have resulted in a marked increase in China's international influence, appeal, and power to shape. In terms of "One Country, Two Systems" and the reunification of the motherland, we have fully and accurately implemented and improved the principle of "One Country, Two Systems," implemented the principle of "patriots administering Hong Kong" and "patriots administering Macao," maintained the long-term prosperity and stability of Hong Kong and Macao, and promoted the development of cross-strait relations in the right direction.

During this period, China successfully achieved the First Centenary Goal of building a moderately prosperous society in all respects, deployed the strategic arrangements for achieving the Second Centenary Goal of building a socialist modern country in all respects, and smoothly embarked on a new journey towards the Second Centenary Goal. Historical achievements and changes were made in various undertakings, and the Chinese nation ushered in a great leap from standing up, and becoming rich to becoming strong. The great rejuvenation of the Chinese nation has entered an irreversible historical process.

SECTION I

From the 18th National Congress of the CPC to the 19th National Congress of the CPC

4.1.1 The 18th National Congress of the CPC and the Proposal of the Chinese Dream

(1) The Convening of the 18th National Congress of the CPC

From November 8 to 14, 2012, the 18th National Congress of the CPC was convened in Beijing. There were 2,268 formal representatives and 57 specially invited representatives. This is a very important congress convened by the CPC at the decisive stage of building moderately prosperous society in an all-round way.

On behalf of the 17th CCCPC, Hu Jintao delivered a report entitled "Firmly March on the Path of Socialism with Chinese Characteristics, and Strive to Complete the Building of a Moderately Prosperous Society in all Respects." The underlying theme of the congress is to hold high the great banner of socialism with Chinese characteristics, follow the guidance of Deng Xiaoping Theory, the important thought of Three Represents and the Scientific Outlook on Development, free up the mind, implement the policy of reform and opening-up, pool our strength, overcome all difficulties, firmly march on the path of socialism with Chinese characteristics, and strive to complete the building of a moderately prosperous society in all respects.

The congress clearly pointed out that the scientific outlook on development is the guiding ideology that the CPC must adhere to for a long time, further elaborated the spiritual essence and connotation of the scientific outlook on development, and put forward new requirements for the implementation of the scientific outlook on development. The congress pointed out that the scientific outlook on development was created by integrating Marxism with the reality of contemporary China and with the underlying features of our times, and it fully embodies the Marxist worldview on and methodology for development. This theory provides new scientific answers to the major questions of what kind of development China should achieve in a new environment and how the country should achieve it. It represents a new level of our understanding of the laws of socialism with Chinese characteristics and reaches a new realm in the development of Marxism in contemporary China. The Scientific Outlook on Development is the latest achievement in developing the system of theories of socialism with Chinese characteristics, and it is the crystallization of the collective wisdom of the CPC and a powerful theoretical weapon for guiding all the work of the Party and country. Together with Marxism-Leninism, Mao Zedong Thought, Deng Xiaoping Theory and the important thought of Three Represents, the Scientific Outlook on Development is the theoretical guidance the Party must adhere to for a long time. The Congress formally established the scientific outlook on development as the guiding ideology of the CPC and included it in the newly revised Party Constitution.

The main theme of the Congress is to uphold and develop socialism with Chinese characteristics. The congress stressed that the path of socialism with Chinese characteristics, the system of theories of socialism with Chinese characteristics and the socialist system with Chinese characteristics are the fundamental accomplishments made by the Party and people in the course of arduous struggle over the past 90-plus years. We must cherish these accomplishments, uphold them all the time and continue to enrich them. Taking the path of socialism with Chinese characteristics means we will, under the leadership of the CPC and in light of China's basic conditions, take economic development as the central task, adhere to the Four Cardinal Principles and persevere in reform and opening-up. It means we must release and develop the productive forces, develop the socialist market economy, socialist democracy, an advanced socialist culture and a harmonious socialist society, and promote socialist ecological progress. It also means we must promote the well-rounded development of the person, achieve prosperity for all over time, and make China a modern socialist country that is prosperous, strong, democratic, culturally advanced and harmonious. The system of theories of socialism with Chinese characteristics is a system of scientific theories that includes Deng Xiaoping Theory, the important thought of Three Represents and the Scientific Outlook on Development, and this system represents the Party's adherence to and development of Marxism-Leninism and Mao Zedong Thought. The system of socialism with Chinese characteristics include: the system of people's congresses as China's fundamental political system and the basic political systems of multi-party cooperation and political consultation under the leadership of the CPC, of regional ethnic autonomy, and of community-level self-governance; socialist legal system with Chinese characteristics, the basic economic system with public ownership as the mainstay and multiple ownership economies developing together, as well as the economic system, political system, cultural system, social system and other specific systems established on the basis of these systems.

The path of socialism with Chinese characteristics is a way to achieve the goal, the theory offers a guide to action, and the system provides a fundamental guarantee. All three serve the great cause of building Chinese socialism. This is the salient feature of the long-term endeavors of the CPC leading the people in building socialism. The basic foundation for building socialism with Chinese characteristics is that China is in the primary stage of socialism, that its overall plan is to seek economic, political, cultural, social, and ecological progress, and that its main objective is to achieve socialist modernization and rejuvenation of the Chinese nation.

The Congress proposed to complete the building of a moderately prosperous society in all respects when the CPC celebrates its centenary in 2021, and turn China into a modern socialist country that is prosperous, strong, democratic, culturally advanced and harmonious when the PRC marks its centennial in 2049. According to the actual situation of China's economic and social development and on the basis of the goal of building moderately prosperous society in an all-round way set by the 16th and 17th National Congress of the CPC, the Congress proposed the goal of building moderately prosperous society in an all-round way: sustained and healthy economic development, continuous expansion of people's democracy, significant enhancement of cultural soft power, comprehensive im-provement of people's living standards, and major progress in building a resource-saving and environment-friendly society. The congress stressed that to complete the building of a moderately prosperous society in all respects, we must, with greater political courage and vision, lose no time in deepening reform in key sectors and resolutely discard all notions and systems that hinder efforts to pursue development in a scientific way. It also pointed out that the Party should set up a well-developed, standardized and effective framework of systems, and ensure that operating institutions in all sectors are fully functioning.

According to the Five-Sphere Integrated Plan and the objective of building a moderately prosperous society in an all-round way, the Congress made comprehensive arrangements for promoting the construction of socialism with Chinese characteristics from nine aspects: (1) Accelerating the Improvement of the Socialist Market Economy and the Change of the Growth Model. We need to comprehensively deepen the reform of the economy, implement the innovation-driven development strategy, promote the strategic adjustment of the economic structure, promote the integration of urban and rural development, and comprehensively raise the level of an open economy. (2) Keeping to the Socialist Path of Making Political Advance with Chinese Characteristics and Promoting Reform of the Political Structure. We need to support and ensure the people's exercise of state power through the people's congresses, improve the socialist consultative democracy system, improve the grass-roots democracy system, comprehensively promote the rule of law, deepen the reform of the administrative system, improve the system of restriction and supervision over the operation of power, and consolidate and develop the patriotic united front. (3) Developing a Strong Socialist Culture in China. We need to strengthen the construction of the socialist core value system, comprehensively improve the moral quality of citizens, enrich the people's spiritual and cultural life, and enhance the overall strength and competitiveness of culture. (4) Strengthening Social Development by Improving the People's Wellbeing and Making Innovations in Management. We should strive to run education to the satisfaction of the people, promote higher quality employment, do everything possible to increase the income of residents, promote the construction of the social security system in urban and rural areas, improve people's health, and strengthen and innovate social management. (5) Devoting Serious Energy to Ecological Conservation. We should optimize the pattern of land and space development, comprehensively promote resource conservation, intensify the protection of natural ecosystems and the environment, and strengthen the construction of an ecological civilization system. (6) Accelerating the Modernization of National Defense and the Armed Forces. We must, responding to China's core security needs and following the three-step development strategy for modernizing national defense and the armed forces, ensure both economic development and development of defense capabilities, intensify efforts to accomplish the dual historic tasks of military mechanization and full IT application, striving to basically complete military mechanization and make major progress in full military IT application by 2020. (7) Enriching the Practice of "One Country, Two Systems" and Advancing China's Reunification. We must adhere to "one country" and respect the differences of the "two systems," uphold the power of the central government and ensure a high degree of autonomy in the HKSAR, give play to the role of the mainland as a staunch supporter of Hong Kong and enhance Hong Kong's own competitiveness. At no time should we focus only on one aspect to the neglect of the other. We must ensure the peaceful development of cross-strait relations, always adhere to the one China principle, continue to promote cross-strait exchanges and cooperation, strive to promote the unity and struggle of compatriots on both sides of the Strait, and resolutely oppose the separatist plot of "Taiwan independence." (8) Continuing to Promote the Noble Cause of Peace and Development of Mankind. We call for promoting equality, mutual trust, inclusiveness, mutual learning and mutually beneficial cooperation in international relations and making joint efforts to uphold international fairness and justice. China will continue to hold high the banner of peace, development, cooperation and mutual benefit and strive to uphold world peace and promote common development. (9) Making Party Building More Scientific in All Respects. All Party members must heighten their sense of urgency and sense of responsibility and focus on strengthening the Party's governance capacity, advanced nature and purity. On this basis, we need to continue freeing our minds, carry out reform and innovation, and uphold the principle that the Party should supervise its own conduct and run itself according to a strict code of discipline. We must adhere to the emancipation of ideas, reform and innovation, adhere to the Party to control the Party, strict governance, and comprehensively strengthen the Party's ideological, organizational, and style construction. At the same time, we must become better at fighting corruption, upholding Party integrity, and improving Party rules and regulations, and enhance our capacity to stay true to ourselves and to improve, develop, and surpass ourselves, so as to turn the Party into an innovative, service-oriented, and learning Marxist governing party. Therefore, we must do a good job in eight important tasks: be firm in our ideal and conviction and remain true to the faith of Communists; put people first, exercise governance for the people and always maintain close ties with them; vigorously promote intra-Party democracy and enhance the Party's creative vitality; deepen reform of the system for the management of officials and personnel and build a contingent of competent key officials for governance; adhere to the principle of the Party exercising leadership over personnel management and attract outstanding individuals from all over for the cause of the Party and country; promote community-level Party building in an innovative way and consolidate the organizational foundation for the exercise of governance by the Party; unswervingly combat corruption and preserve Communists' political character of integrity; strictly enforce Party discipline and willingly uphold centralized leadership of the Party.

The Congress adopted the Constitution of the CPC (Amendment), and elected the new Central Committee and the CCDI.

November 11, 2012, the First Plenary Session of the 18th CCCPC elected Xi Jinping, Li Keqiang, Zhang Dejiang, Yu Zhengsheng, Liu Yunshan, Wang Qishan, and Zhang Gaoli as members of the Standing Committee of the Political Bureau of the CCCPC, and Xi Jinping as general secretary of the Central Committee; and decided that he is chairman of the CMC; and approved Wang Qishan as secretary of the CCDI.

(2) The Proposal of the Chinese Dream
On November 29, 2012, shortly after the conclusion of the 18th National Congress of the CPC, all members of the Standing Committee of the Political Bureau of the CCCPC came to the National Museum to visit the exhibition of "The Road to Rejuvenation." Xi Jinping said during the visit, in the old days, the Chinese people went through hardships as grueling as "storming an iron-wall pass." Today, the Chinese nation is undergoing profound changes, like "seas becoming mulberry fields." In the future, the Chinese nation will "forge ahead like a gigantic ship breaking through strong winds and heavy waves. Today, we are closer than ever to the goal of national rejuvenation, and more confident than ever in our ability to realize this goal." He stressed that everyone has an ideal, ambition and dream. We are now all talking about the Chinese Dream. In my opinion, achieving the rejuvenation of the Chinese nation has been the greatest dream of the Chinese people since the advent of modern times. This dream embodies the long-cherished

hope of several generations of the Chinese people, gives expression to the overall interests of the Chinese nation and the Chinese people, and represents the shared aspiration of all the sons and daughters of the Chinese nation. He pointed out: I firmly believe that the goal of building a moderately prosperous society in an all-round way by the 100th anniversary of the founding of the CPC will be realized, the goal of building a prosperous, strong, democratic, civilized and harmonious socialist modern country by the 100th anniversary of the founding of new China will be realized, and the dream of the great rejuvenation of the Chinese nation will be realized.

In March, 2013, Xi Jinping further pointed out at the First Session of the 12th NPC the connotation of the Chinese Dream, the way to realize it, the spiritual motive and the reliance. He pointed out: the Chinese Dream of the great renewal of the Chinese nation is about the prosperity of the country, rejuvenation of the nation, and happiness of the people. He stressed: to realize the Chinese Dream, we must take our own path, which is the path of building socialism with Chinese characteristics. To realize the Chinese Dream, we must carry forward the Chinese spirit. It is the national spirit with patriotism at its core, and it is the spirit of the times with reform and innovation at its core. To realize the Chinese Dream, we must pool China's strength, that is, the strength of great unity among the people of all ethnic groups,

Later, he pointed out: the Chinese Dream is about making our country prosperous and strong, revitalizing the nation and bringing a happy life to its people. It is about cooperation, development, peace and win-win, and it is connected to the beautiful dreams that people in other countries may have. The Chinese Dream will benefit not only the people of China, but also of other countries.

The proposal of the Chinese Dream reflects the ideals and pursuit of the Chinese nation since modern times, reflects the overall interests of the Chinese nation and the Chinese people, and reveals the historical mission and responsibilities of the CPC. It points out the direction for the development of the CPC and various undertakings in China, and becomes a spiritual banner that encourages the Chinese people to unite and forge ahead and open up the future.

4.1.2 The 19th National Congress of the CPC and the Ruling Party Established a New Guiding Ideology

(1) The Convening of the 19th National Congress of the CPC
From October 8 to 24, 2017, the 19th National Congress of the CPC was convened in Beijing. There were 2,280 formal representatives and 74 specially invited representatives. The congress is a meeting of great importance taking place during the decisive stage in building a moderately prosperous society in all respects and at a critical moment as socialism with Chinese characteristics has entered a new era.

On behalf of the 18th CCCPC, Xi Jinping delivered a report entitled, "Secure a Decisive Victory in Building a Moderately Prosperous Society in All Respects and Strive for the Great Success of Socialism with Chinese Characteristics for a New Era." The theme of the Congress is: Remain true to our original aspiration and keep our mission firmly in mind, hold high the banner of socialism with Chinese characteristics, secure a decisive victory in building a moderately prosperous society in all respects, strive for the great success of socialism with Chinese characteristics for a new era, and work tirelessly to realize the Chinese Dream of national rejuvenation.

The congress pointed out: the original aspiration and the mission of Chinese Communists is to seek happiness for the Chinese people and rejuvenation for the Chinese nation. This original aspiration, this mission, is what inspires Chinese Communists to advance. Today, we are closer, more confident, and more capable than ever of realizing the goal of national rejuvenation. The congress pointed out "Four Greats": this great struggle, great project, great cause, and great dream. The Congress stressed that to realize the great dream, we must carry out great struggles, build great projects, and promote great undertakings. This great struggle, great project, great cause, and great dream are closely connected, flow seamlessly into each other, and are mutually reinforcing. Among them, the great new project of Party building plays the decisive role.

The congress spoke highly of the achievements since the 18th NPC and stressed that the achievements of the past five years have touched every area and broken new ground; the changes in China over the past five years have been profound and fundamental. For five years, our Party has demonstrated tremendous political courage and a powerful sense of mission as it has developed new ideas, new thinking, and new strategies, adopted a raft of major principles and policies, launched a host of major initiatives, and pushed ahead with many major tasks.

We have solved many tough problems that were long on the agenda but never resolved, and accomplished many things that were wanted but never got done. With this, we have prompted historic shifts in the cause of the Party and the country. These historic changes will have a powerful and far-reaching effect on the development of this cause.

The congress pointed out: with decades of hard work, socialism with Chinese characteristics has crossed the threshold into a new era. This marks that what we now face is the contradiction between unbalanced and inadequate development and the people's ever-growing needs for a better life. We must recognize that the evolution of the principal contradiction facing Chinese society represents a historic shift that affects the whole landscape and that creates many new demands for the work of the Party and the country. The changes in China's main social contradictions have not changed our judgment on the historical stage of socialism in China. The basic national conditions of China, which is still in the primary stage of socialism and will remain for a long time, have not changed. China's international status as the world's largest developing country has not changed.

In combination with the Two Centenary goals, the Congress made strategic arrangements for winning a decisive victory in building a moderately prosperous society in all respects and starting the new journey of building a modern socialist country in all respects. The congress pointed out: the period between the 19th and the 20th National Congress is the period in which the timeframes of the Two Centenary Goals converge. In this period, not only must we finish building a moderately prosperous society in all respects and achieve the First Centenary Goal; we must also build on this achievement to embark on a new journey toward the Second Centenary Goal of fully building a modern socialist country. Based on a comprehensive analysis of the international and domestic environments and the conditions for China's development, we have drawn up a two-stage development plan for the period from 2020 to the middle of this century. In the first stage from 2020 to 2035, we will build on the foundation created by the moderately prosperous society with a further 15 years of hard work to see that socialist modernization is basically realized. By that time, China's economic strength and scientific and technological strength will rise by leaps and bounds, and China will be in the forefront of an innovative country; the rights of the people to participate and to develop as equals will be adequately protected. Institutions in all fields are further improved; the modernization of China's system and capacity for governance is basically achieved. Social etiquette and civility are significantly enhanced.

China's cultural soft power has grown much stronger; Chinese culture has greater appeal. People are leading more comfortable lives, and the size of the middle-income group has grown considerably. Disparities in urban-rural development, in development between regions, and in living standards are significantly reduced. Equitable access to basic public services is basically ensured; and solid progress has been made toward prosperity for everyone. A modern social governance system has basically taken shape, and society is full of vitality, harmonious, and orderly. There is a fundamental improvement in the environment; the goal of building a Beautiful China is basically attained. In the second stage from 2035 to the middle of the 21st century, we will, building on having basically achieved modernization, work hard for a further 15 years and develop China into a great modern socialist country that is prosperous, strong, democratic, culturally advanced, harmonious, and beautiful. New heights will be reached in every dimension of material, political, cultural-ethical, social, and ecological advancement; modernization of China's system and capacity for governance will be achieved; china will become a global leader in terms of composite national strength and international influence; common prosperity for all will be largely realized; the chinese people will enjoy happier, safer, and healthier lives; and the chinese nation will stand taller and prouder among the nations of the world.

The congress set out comprehensive plans with regard to the cause of the Party and country in accordance with the five-sphere integrated plan for advancing socialism with Chinese characteristics: (1) Applying a new vision of development and developing a modernized economy. We will further supply-side structural reform, move faster to make China a country of innovators, pursue a rural revitalization strategy, and the strategy for coordinated regional development, accelerate the improvement of the socialist market economy, and make new ground in pursuing opening up on all fronts, (2) Improving the system of institutions through which the people run the country and developing socialist democracy. We will uphold the organic unity of the Party's leadership, the people's ownership of the country, and the rule of law, strengthen the institutional guarantee of the people's ownership of the country, give play to the important role of socialist consultative democracy, deepen the practice of administering the country according to law, deepen institutional and administrative reform, and consolidate and develop the patriotic united front. (3) Building stronger cultural confidence and helping socialist culture to flourish. We will hold firmly the leading position in ideological work, cultivate and practice socialist core values, strengthen ideological and moral construction, support the flourishing development of socialist literature and arts, and promote the development of cultural programs and industries. (4) Growing better at ensuring and improving people's well-being and strengthening and developing new approaches to social governance. We will give priority to developing education, improve the quality of employment and raise people's incomes, strengthen the construction of the social security system, resolutely win the battle against poverty, implement the healthy China initiative, establish a social governance model based on collaboration, participation, and common interests, and effectively safeguard national security. (5) Speeding up reform of the system for building an ecological civilization, and build a beautiful China. We will promote green development, focus on solving prominent environmental problems, strengthen ecosystem protection, and reform the environmental system. (6) Staying committed to the Chinese path of building strong armed forces and fully advancing the modernization of national defense and the military. We will adapt to the trend of a new global military revolution and to national security needs; we will upgrade our military capabilities, and see that, by the year 2020, mechanization is basically achieved, IT application has come a long way, and strategic capabilities have seen a big improvement. To comprehensively advance the modernization of military theory, organizational structure, military personnel, and weaponry and equipment in step with the modernization of the country and basically complete the modernization of national defense and the military by 2035; and to fully transform the people's armed forces into world-class forces by the mid-21st century. (7) Adhere to "One Country, Two Systems" and promote the reunification of the motherland. We will fully and faithfully implement the principle of "One Country, Two Systems" under which the people of Hong Kong administer Hong Kong, the people of Macao administer Macao with a high degree of autonomy, act in strict adherence to the Constitution and the Basic Laws, We will support the integration of Hong Kong and Macao into the development of the country; remain committed to the policy for the Hong Kong people to govern Hong Kong and the Macao people to govern Macao, with patriots playing the principal role; develop and strengthen the ranks of patriots who love both our country and their regions, and foster greater patriotism and a stronger sense of national identity among the people in Hong Kong and Macao. With this, our compatriots in Hong Kong and Macao will share both the historic responsibility of national rejuvenation and the pride of a strong and prosperous China. We must uphold the principles of "peaceful reunification" and "One Country, Two Systems," work for the peaceful development of cross-Straits relations, and advance the process toward the peaceful reunification of China. We stand firm in safeguarding China's sovereignty and territorial integrity, and will never allow the historical tragedy of national division to repeat itself. (8) Remaining committed to peaceful development and endeavoring to build a community with a shared future for mankind. China will always hold high the banner of peace, development, cooperation and mutual benefit, adhered to the purpose of its foreign policy of safeguarding world peace and promoting common development, unswervingly developed friendly cooperation with other countries on the basis of the Five Principles of Peaceful Coexistence, and promoted the building of a new type of international relations featuring mutual respect, fairness, justice and win-win cooperation. (9) Exercising strict governance over the Party and improving the Party's ability to govern and lead. The general requirements for Party building for the new era are: uphold and strengthen overall Party leadership and ensure that the Party exercises effective self-supervision and practices strict self-governance in every respect; Take strengthening the Party's long-term governance capacity and its advanced nature and purity as the main thrust; take enhancing the Party's political building as the overarching principle; take holding dear the Party's ideals, convictions, and purpose as the underpinning; and take harnessing the whole Party's enthusiasm, initiative, and creativity as the focus of efforts; comprehensively promote the party's political, ideological, organizational, style and discipline construction; carry out system building throughout and promote the fight against corruption in depth; keep improving the efficacy of Party building and build the Party into a vibrant Marxist governing party that stays at the forefront of the times, enjoys the wholehearted support of the people, has the courage to reform itself, and is able to withstand all tests. Therefore, we must do a good job in eight important tasks: give top priority to the political work of the Party; arm the whole Party with the thought on socialism with Chinese characteristics for a new era; train a contingent of competent and professional officials; Strengthen the development of grass-roots organizations; work ceaselessly to improve Party conduct and enforce Party discipline; win an overwhelming victory in the anti-corruption struggle; secure a sweeping victory in the fight against corruption; improve Party and state oversight systems; Strengthen every dimension of our ability for governance.

The Congress adopted the *Constitution of the CPC (Amendment)*, and elected the 19th Central Committee and the CCDI.

On October 25, 2017, the First Plenary Session of the 19th CCCPC elected Xi Jinping, Li Keqiang, Li Zhanshu, Wang Yang, Wang Huning, Zhao Leji, and Han Zheng as members of the Standing Committee of the Political Bureau of the CCCPC, and Xi Jinping as general secretary of the Central Committee; and decided that he is chairman of the CMC; and approved Zhao Leji as secretary of the CCDI.

(2) Establishment of Xi Jinping Thought on Socialism with Chinese Characteristics for a New Era as the Guiding Ideology

Chinese communists, with Comrade Xi Jinping as their chief representative, have established Xi Jinping Thought on Socialism with Chinese Characteristics for a New Era on the basis of adapting the basic tenets of Marxism to China's specific realities and its fine traditional culture, upholding Mao Zedong Thought, Deng Xiaoping Theory, the Theory of Three Represents, and the Scientific Outlook on Development. By integrating theory with practice, it has systematically addressed the major tasks of our times: what kind of socialism with Chinese characteristics we should uphold and develop in this new era, what kind of great modern socialist country we should build, and what kind of Marxist party exercising long-term governance we should develop, which has answered fundamental issues like the overarching objectives, tasks, plan, and strategy for upholding and developing socialism with Chinese characteristics in the new era; like the direction, model, and driving force of development, and the strategic steps, external conditions, and political guarantees. As well as this, we undertake theoretical analysis and produce policy guidance on the economy, political affairs, rule of law, science and technology, culture, education, the wellbeing of our people, ethnic and religious affairs, social development, ecological conservation, national security, defense and the armed forces, the principle of "One Country, Two Systems" and national reunification, the united front, foreign affairs, and Party building, and thus giving shape to Xi Jinping Thought on Socialism with Chinese Characteristics for a New Era.

The report to the 19th National Congress of the CPC expounded the scientific connotation and the realistic need of Xi Jinping Thought on Socialism with Chinese Characteristics for a New Era with the "eight clarifications" and "fourteen commitments."

The "eight clarifications" are: it makes clear that the overarching goal of upholding and developing socialism with Chinese characteristics is to realize socialist modernization and national rejuvenation, and, that on the basis of finishing the building of a moderately prosperous society in all respects, a two-step approach should be taken to build China into a great modern socialist country that is prosperous, strong, democratic, culturally advanced, harmonious, and beautiful by the middle of the century; it makes clear the principal contradiction facing Chinese society in the new era is that between unbalanced and inadequate development and the people's ever-growing needs for a better life. We must therefore continue commitment to our people-centered philosophy of development, and work to promote well-rounded human development and common prosperity for everyone; it makes clear that the overall plan for building socialism with Chinese characteristics is the Five-sphere Integrated Plan, and the overall strategy is the four-pronged comprehensive strategy and highlights the importance of fostering stronger confidence in the path, theory, system, and culture of socialism with Chinese characteristics; it makes clear that the overall goal of deepening reform in every field is to improve and develop the system of socialism with Chinese characteristics and modernize China's system and capacity for governance; it makes clear that the overall goal of comprehensively advancing "ruling the country by law" is to establish a system of socialist rule of law with Chinese characteristics and build a country of socialist rule of law; it makes clear that the Party's goal of building a strong military in the new era is to build the people's forces into world-class forces that obey the Party's command, can fight and win, and maintain excellent conduct; it makes clear that major country diplomacy with Chinese characteristics aims to foster a new type of international relations and build a community with a shared future for mankind; it makes clear that the defining feature of socialism with Chinese characteristics is the leadership of the CPC; the greatest strength of the system of socialism with Chinese characteristics is the leadership of the CPC; the Party is the highest force for political leadership. It sets forth the general requirements for Party building in the new era and underlines the importance of political work in Party building.

The "fourteen commitments" are: ensuring Party leadership over all work; committing to a people-centered approach; continuing to comprehensively deepen reform, adopting a new vision for development; seeing that the people run the country; ensuring every dimension of governance is law-based; upholding core socialist values; ensuring and improving living standards through development; ensuring harmony between human and nature; pursuing a holistic approach to national security; upholding absolute Party leadership over the people's armed forces; upholding the principle of "One Country, Two Systems" and promoting national reunification; promoting the building of a community with a shared future for mankind; exercising full and rigorous governance over the Party.

The congress established Xi Jinping Thought on Socialism with Chinese Characteristics for a New Era as the guiding ideology in the newly revised Party Constitution, making the ruling party's guiding ideology keep up with the times. The First Session of the 13th NPC held in March 2018 adopted the *Amendment to the Constitution*, which included Xi Jinping Thought on Socialism with Chinese Characteristics for a New Era, making the ruling party's guiding ideology keep up with the times.

In November 2021, the Sixth Plenary Session of the 19th CCCPC adopted the Resolution of the CCCPC on the Major Achievements and Historical Experience of the Party over the Past Century, which developed the "eight clarifications" into "ten clarifications," that is, it was clear that the most essential feature of socialism with Chinese characteristics was the leadership of the CPC, the greatest advantage of the socialist system with Chinese characteristics was the leadership of the CPC, and the CPC was the highest political leadership force. The whole Party must strengthen our consciousness of the need to maintain political integrity, think in big-picture terms, follow the leadership core and keep in alignment with the central Party leadership, stay confident in the path, theory, system, and culture of socialism with Chinese characteristics, and resolutely uphold the Party Central Committee's authority and its centralized, unified leadership; it makes clear that the overarching goal of upholding and developing socialism with Chinese characteristics is to realize socialist modernization and national rejuvenation, and, that on the basis of finishing the building of a moderately prosperous society in all respects, a two-step approach should be taken to build China into a great modern socialist country that is prosperous, strong, democratic, culturally advanced, harmonious, and beautiful by the middle of the century to promote national rejuvenation through a Chinese path to modernization; it makes clear that the principal contradiction facing Chinese society in the new era is that between unbalanced and inadequate development and the people's ever-growing needs for a better life, and the Party must therefore remain committed to a people-centered philosophy of development, develop whole-process people's democracy, and make more notable and substantive progress toward achieving well-rounded human development and common prosperity for all; it makes clear that the integrated plan for building socialism with Chinese characteristics covers five spheres, namely economic, political, cultural, social, and ecological advancement, and that the comprehensive strategy in this regard includes four prongs, namely building a modern socialist country, deepening reform, advancing "ruling the country by law," and strengthening Party self-governance; it makes clear that the overall goal of deepening reform in every field is to improve and develop the system of socialism with Chinese characteristics and modernize China's system and capacity for governance; it makes clear that the overall goal of comprehensively advancing "ruling the country by law" is to establish a system of socialist rule of law with Chinese characteristics and build a country of socialist rule of law; it makes clear that China must uphold and improve its basic socialist economic system, see that the market plays the decisive role in resource allocation and the government plays its role better, have an accurate understanding of this new stage of development, apply a new philosophy of innovative, coordinated, green, open, and shared development, accelerate efforts to foster a new pattern of development that is focused on the domestic economy but features positive interplay between domestic and international economic flows, promote high-quality development, and balance development and security imperatives; it makes clear that the Party's goal of building a strong military in the new era is to build the people's forces into world-class forces that obey the Party's command, can fight and win, and maintain excellent conduct; it makes clear that major-country diplomacy with Chinese characteristics aims to serve national rejuvenation, promote human progress, and facilitate efforts to foster a new type of international relations and build a human community with a shared future; it makes clear that full and rigorous self-governance is a policy of strategic importance for the Party, and the general requirements for Party building in the new era include making all-around efforts to strengthen the Party in political, ideological, and organizational terms and in terms of conduct and discipline, with institution building incorporated into every aspect of this process, continuing the fight against corruption, and ensuring that the political responsibility for governance over the Party is fulfilled. By engaging in great self-transformation, the Party can steer great social transformation.

Comrade Xi Jinping, through meticulous assessment and deep reflection on a number of major theoretical and practical questions regarding the cause of the Party and the country in the new era, has set forth a series of original new ideas, thoughts, and strategies on national governance revolving around the major questions of our times. He is thus the principal founder of Xi Jinping Thought on Socialism with Chinese Characteristics for a New Era.

This is the Marxism of contemporary China and of the 21st century. It embodies the best of the Chinese culture and ethos in our times and represents a new breakthrough in adapting Marxism to the Chinese context. This thought has a strict system and logic, rich connotation. It broad and profound, and shines with the glory of Marxist truth. This thought penetrates Marxist philosophy, political economy and scientific socialism, penetrates history, reality and future, penetrates reform, development and stability, internal affairs, foreign affairs and national defense, and governs the Party, the country and the army. It embodies firm ideals and convictions, demonstrates people's true feelings, penetrates a high degree of self-awareness and self-confidence, embodies a clear problem orientation, and is full of the spirit of fearlessness and responsibility. They are testimony to the new understanding by our Party of the laws of the development of human society, the laws of building socialism, and the laws of governance by the CPC.

Xi Jinping Thought on Socialism with Chinese Characteristics for a New Era is an original contribution to the development of Marxism. This thought is a continuously developing and open theory. It is a scientific theory that keeps pace with the times on the basis of combining theory with practice. In the historical process of guiding the great social revolution and the great self-revolution in the new era, it continues to develop, enrich and improve with the deepening of the great practice of socialism with Chinese characteristics. Xi Jinping's thinking on strengthening the armed forces, economy, diplomacy, ecological civilization, and the rule of law are the development of the series of theoretical system in the relevant fields. There is no end to practice, to seeking truth, and to theoretical innovation. Xi Jinping Thought on Socialism with Chinese Characteristics for a New Era is the Marxism of contemporary China and of the 21st century, which will innovate with the development of times and practice.

4.1.3 Plan the Overall and Strategic Layout of the Cause of Socialism with Chinese Characteristics

Since the 18th National Congress of the CPC, the socialist cause with Chinese characteristics has sought to make overall economic, political, cultural, social, and environmental progress, known as the Five-Point Strategy, and shaping four prongs, that is, building a modern socialist country (now it is building a modern socialist country in all respects), deepening reform, advancing "ruling the country by law," and strengthening Party self-governance.

Since the reform and opening-up, China has gradually deepened its understanding of socialism with Chinese characteristics, and has gone through a development process from the "two civilizations" of material and spiritual to "Trinity" of economic, political and cultural development, and then to the "four in one" of economic, political, cultural and social development. The 18th National Congress included ecological progress in its overall plan for building Chinese socialism, made it possible to incorporate ecological efforts into those for economic, political, cultural and social progress in all respects and throughout the whole process, and thus the overall layout of socialism with Chinese characteristics has been improved, building the overall layout of "The Five-Sphere Integrated Plan." Subsequently, the Party Central Committee, with Comrade Xi Jinping as the core, put forward the overall layout of "The Five-Sphere Integrated Plan" and further clarified the method and path of building the overall layout of the "Five-Sphere Integrated Plan." All aspects of the "Five-Sphere Integrated Plan" are interconnected, mutually promoted and inseparable, and jointly build the overall situation of the cause of socialism with Chinese characteristics. It is an important strategic deployment made by the CCCPC in accordance with the characteristics of the times, the requirements of development and the expectations of the people.

Reform, opening-up and socialist modernization should not only focus on overall planning, but also on the major tasks. Since the 18th NPC, the Party Central Committee with Comrade Xi Jinping at its core has implemented the national rejuvenation strategy within the wider context of once-in-a-century changes taking place in the world. The Party has planned the Party and the country's undertakings in view of the long history, the times and the global conditions; strategic breakthroughs are achieved in solving outstanding problems, the work is advanced in grasping the overall strategic situation, and the four-pronged comprehensive strategy is gradually formed and actively promoted, namely, the strategic layout of building a moderately prosperous society in all aspects, deepening reform in all aspects, comprehensively following the rule of law, and enforcing strict Party self-governance.

With regard to building a moderately prosperous society in all respects, in November 2012, the 18th National Congress of the CPC included "striving for building a moderately prosperous society in all respects" as the theme of the Congress, and emphasized that the grand goal of "building a moderately prosperous society in all respects" should be realized by 2020. With regard to the comprehensive reform, in November 2012, the report of the 18th National Congress of the CPC proposed "an all-round in-depth reform." In November, 2013, a strategic decision was made at the Third Plenum of the 18th CCCPC to comprehensively deepen China's reforms. With regard to a comprehensive framework for promoting the rule of law, in November 2012, the report of the 18th National Congress of the CPC proposed "Advancing 'Ruling the Country by Law.'" In October 2014, the Fourth Plenary Session of the 18th CCCPC made a strategic deployment for a comprehensive framework for promoting the rule of law. With regard to an all-Out effort to enforce strict party discipline, in October 8, 2014, at a meeting summarizing the campaign to study and practice the Party's guiding principle of serving and relying on the people, Xi Jinping stated for the first time the major topic of enforcing strict Party self-governance.

On the basis of expounding the four-pronged strategy, In December 2014, Xi Jinping in his inspection tour in Jiangsu put "enforcing Strict Party Self-Governance" in company with "Completing the Building of a Moderately Prosperous Society in All Respects," "In-Depth Reform in All Respects," and "the rule of law," and required that we make comprehensive moves to complete a moderately prosperous society in all respects, to further reform, to advance the rule of law, and to strengthen Party discipline. In this way, we can push reform and opening-up and socialist modernization to a higher level. In February, 2015, at the opening ceremony of a study session on implementing the decisions of the Fourth Plenary Session of the 18th CCCPC and advancing the rule of law, Xi Jinping stated that since the 18th National Congress of the CPC in 2012, with a view to upholding and developing Chinese socialism, the CCCPC has formulated the Four-Pronged Strategy that consists of four tasks: to complete a moderately prosperous society in all respects, to further reform, to advance the rule of law, and to strengthen Party discipline. This make it clear the strategic layout of the socialist cause with Chinese characteristics is that we will remain dedicated to the Four-Pronged Strategy of finishing building a moderately prosperous society in all respects, deepening all areas of reform, fully advancing the "ruling the country by law" of China, and strengthening every element of Party self-governance. From 2015 to 2016, on the basis of the strategic deployment made by the Third Plenary Session of the 18th CCCPC for comprehensively deepening reform and the strategic deployment made by the Fourth Plenary Session of the 18th CCCPC for ruling the country by law in all respects, the CCCPC successively convened the Fifth Plenary Session of the 18th CCCPC and the Sixth Plenary Session of the 18th CCCPC to conduct special research and make important arrangements for building a moderately prosperous society in all respects and advancing "ruling the country by law." In October 2020, against the background that the goal of building moderately prosperous society in an all-round way is about to be realized, the Fifth Plenary Session of the 19th CCCPC proposed to "win a new victory in building a socialist modern country in an all-round way" and develop "building moderately prosperous society in an all-round way" in "the Four-Pronged Strategy" into "building a socialist modern country in an all-round way."

The Four-Pronged Comprehensive Strategy, is the new strategy in the national governance of the Party Central Committee with Comrade Xi Jinping at its core in grasping the development features of China standing at a new starting point in history, and is a strategic choice upholding and developing socialism with Chinese characteristics in the new era. The strategic layout of "the Four-Pronged Comprehensive Strategy" has both strategic objectives and strategic measures, which is an orderly deployment of the overall strategic deployment. Every "strategy" is of great strategic significance and is a strategic focus that has a bearing on the overall situation. Securing a Decisive Victory in Building a Moderately Prosperous Society in All Respects and Embarking on a Journey to Fully Build a Modern Socialist China are strategic objectives that is an important pacesetter in the Four-Pronged Strategy. In-depth reform in all respects, a comprehensive framework forpromoting the rule of law, and enforcing strict Party self-governance are three strategic moves that provide important guarantees for finishing building a moderately prosperous society in all respects and ruling the country by law in all respects. To achieve the strategic objectives, the three strategic measures are indispensable.

The overall layout of "The Five-Sphere Integrated Plan" and the strategic layout of "the Four-Pronged Comprehensive Strategy" promote each other, coordinate and link each other, and establish the strategic planning and deployment for upholding and developing socialism with Chinese characteristics in the new era from the overall perspective.

Summary

Since the 18th National Congress of the CPC, China's development has reached a new historical starting point. The main social contradiction has been transformed from the contradiction between the people's growing material and cultural needs and backward social production into the contradiction between the people's growing needs for a better life and unbalanced and inadequate development. On this basis, the CCCPC with Comrade Xi Jinping at its core stated that socialism with Chinese characteristics has entered a new era. Focusing on such major issues of the times as what kind of socialism with Chinese characteristics to uphold and develop in the new era, how to uphold and develop socialism with Chinese characteristics, what kind of socialist modernization power to build, how to build a socialist modernization power, what kind of Marxist party to build for long-term governance and how to build a Marxist Party for long-term governance, the contemporary Chinese Communists have launched a series of explorations. They have established the guiding position of Xi Jinping Thought on Socialism with Chinese Characteristics for a New Era, put forward the Chinese Dream as the spiritual banner for the development and progress of contemporary China, clarified the general task of realizing socialist modernization and the great rejuvenation of the Chinese nation, planned the strategic arrangement of building a socialist modernizing power in two steps on the basis of building a moderately prosperous society in all aspects, and deployed the Five-Sphere Integrated Plan and The Four-Pronged Comprehensive Strategy, which have pointed out the direction and road for the development of China in the new era.

SECTION 2

Further Promote the Political Construction of Socialism with Chinese Characteristics

4.2.1 We Are Determined to Promote Comprehensive and In-Depth Reform

(1) Make Clear the All-Round and Deeper-Level Reform Pbjectives
In the new era, reform has entered a critical period and a deep-water area. Some deep-seated system and mechanism problems and the barriers of interests solidification have become increasingly apparent. Some involve complex departmental interests, some are difficult to unify their thinking and understanding, some want to touch the "cheese" of some people, and some need multi-faceted cooperation and multi measures. We can say that our reform has come to a critical juncture.

The Third Plenary Session of the 18th CCCPC was held in Beijing in November, 2013 and adopted the "Decision of the CCCPC on Some Major Issues Concerning Comprehensively Continuing the Reform." This is a programmatic document for comprehensively deepening reform in the new era. The Decision stressed that the overall objectives of comprehensively deepening reform are to develop and improve the system of socialism with Chinese characteristics and to modernize China's system and capacity for governance. It also set forth that by 2020 decisive results in the Decision would have been achieved in the reform of important areas and crucial segments, and the Party should set up a well-developed, standardized and effective framework of systems, and ensure that operating institutions in all sectors are fully functioning. The Decision made arrangements for reforms of economic, political, cultural, and social systems and those pertaining to ecological conservation, national defense and the armed forces, and Party building. It has put forward 336 major reform measures and defined the overall objectives, key strategic ranking of priorities, focal points, working mechanisms, methods of implementation, timetable, and roadmap for the endeavor of comprehensively deepening reform.

The Third Plenary Session of the 11th Central Committee was an epoch-making event that ushered in the new period of reform and opening-up, and social-ist modernization. In the same way, the Third Plenary Session of the 18th Central Committee was also of epoch-making significance. It enabled the transformation of reform from trials and breakthroughs limited to certain areas into an integrated drive being advanced across the board, and thus marked the beginning of a new stage in China's reform and opening-up. Comprehensively deepening reform is not a single soldier's breakthrough and patchwork in a certain field and a certain aspect. Instead, we should pay more attention to the coordination of reforms in various fields and aspects, and place more emphasis on the systematic integration of various systems and measures.

In January 2014, the first meeting of the central leading group for comprehensively deepening reform deliberated and adopted the division of labor plan for relevant central departments to implement the important measures of the Third Plenary Session of the 18th CCCPC, which resolved 336 reform tasks and identified the coordination units, leading units and participating units. In August of the same year, the fourth meeting adopted "the Implementation Plan on Major Reform Measures of the Third Plenary Session of the 18th CCCPC (2014–2020)," which makes overall arrangements for conducting reform in the coming seven years. It emphasized the path, outcome and schedule of each reform measure, the plan serves as the general blueprint and management chart for the next period of reform.

(2) Deepen the Reform of Party and Government Institutions

The comprehensive deepening of reform has gone through the development process of laying foundations and defining initial structures from 2014 to 2016, making overall progress and building momentum from 2017 to 2018, and achieving systematic integration and efficient coordination since 2019.

From 2014 to 2016, the first three years of comprehensively deepening the reform are the stage of laying foundations and defining initial structures. Reform of the economic system, political system, cultural system, social system, ecological civilization system, and the party building system has been vigorously carried out in an all-round way. Reform in the fields of SOEs, finance, taxation and finance, scientific and technological innovation, land system, opening-up to the outside world, culture and education, judicial openness, environmental protection, old-age employment, medicine and health, Party-building and discipline inspection has been comprehensively carried out. A number of landmark and key reform plans have been introduced and implemented, a number of reform initiatives in important fields and key links have made major breakthroughs, a number of important theoretical, institutional and practical innovations have been gradually formed, and the main framework for comprehensively deepening reform has been basically established.

From 2017 to 2018, the medium-term focus of comprehensively deepening reform is to make overall progress and build momentum. China has launched a series of major institutional reforms, which have effectively solved a number of structural contradictions, and achieved historical changes, systematic remodeling and overall restructuring in many fields.

Since the reform and opening-up, the CCCPC has carried out four reforms and the State Council has carried out seven reforms, gradually establishing a functional system of the Party and state organs with Chinese characteristics. However, at the same time, there are still some deep-seated institutional problems in the functions of the Party and state organs. In addition, with the deepening of reform in an all-round way, some new situations and new problems have emerged. In this regard, the CCCPC decided to carry out the reform of the Party and state institutions.

In February 2018, the Third Plenary Session of the 19th CCCPC was held in Beijing. The plenary session adopted the Decision of the CCCPC on Deepening the Reform of Party and State Institutions and the Plan for Deepening the Reform of Party and State Institutions, and agreed to submit some contents of the Plan to the First Session of the 13th NPC for deliberation in accordance with legal procedures. The goal of deepening the reform of the Party and state organs is to build a systematic, scientific, standardized and efficient functional system of the Party and state organs, to form a Party leadership system that takes the overall situation and coordinates all Parties, a government governance system that has clear responsibilities and rules by law, a world-class armed forces system with Chinese characteristics, and a social group system that has extensive external connections and serves the masses. All these systems would promote the NPC, government, CPPCC, supervisory organs, judicial organs, procuratorial organs, people's organizations, enterprises and institutions, and social organizations to coordinate their actions and enhance their synergy under the unified leadership of the ruling party, so as to comprehensively improve the national governance capacity and level of governance.

On March 17, 2018, the First Session of the 13th NPC voted and adopted the decision on the institutional reform plan of the State Council. On March 23, only two days after the full text of the "Plan for Deepening the Reform of Party and State Institutions" was published, the newly established National Commission of Supervision was officially inaugurated and put into operation. This is seen as a sign that a new round of reform of the Party and state organs has been comprehensively launched. On March 28, the CCCPC for Deepening Overall Reform held its first meeting, which released a strong signal to promote comprehensively deepening reform with greater efforts. This round of reform in China is being pursued with unprecedented intensity. At the level of central and state organs alone, institutional reform involves more than 1.8 million people, and involves more than 80 departments in the management, institutional setup, responsibilities and personnel adjustment. Among them, 21 ministerial level institutions were reduced, 58 leading and deputy positions were reduced, 9 assistant ministerial departments were reduced, and 25 positions were reduced.

In a short period of more than one year, various reform plans have been rapidly implemented. By the end of March 2019, according to the timetable and road map determined by the CCCPC, all tasks of institutional reform were completed. On July 5, the summary meeting on deepening the reform of Party and state institutions was held in Beijing.

Deepening the reform of Party and State institutions is a systematic and overall reconstruction of the organizational structure and management system of the Party and the state. The overall leadership of the ruling party has been effectively strengthened, and the institutional and functional system of maintaining the centralized and unified leadership of the CPC has become more sound; the performance of the Party and state organs is more smooth and efficient, and the setup and function allocation of various institutions are more suitable for the overall layout of "the Five-Sphere Integrated Plan" and the strategic layout of the "the Four-Pronged Comprehensive Strategy;" the main institutional setup and functional allocation of provinces, cities and counties are basically corresponding to that of the central authorities, and a smooth and dynamic working system has been established from the central authorities to the local authorities; the cross military and local reform was smoothly promoted; the reform of relevant institutions was promoted simultaneously, and the overall effect of the reform was further enhanced. On the whole, the main framework of the functional system of the Party and state organs that meets the requirements of the new era has been initially established, which provides a strong organizational guarantee for improving and developing the socialist system with Chinese characteristics and promoting the modernization of the national governance system and governance capacity.

(3) Adhere to and Improve the Socialist System with Chinese Characteristics

In September 2019, on the basis of completing the two-stage reform tasks of laying foundations and defining initial structures, and comprehensively making overall progress and building momentum, the 10th meeting of the CCCPC for Deepening Overall Reform proposed that the focus of comprehensively deepening reform should be on strengthening system integration, coordination and efficiency, consolidating and deepening the reform achievements we have made in solving institutional obstacles, mechanism obstacles and policy innovation in recent years, and promote more mature and well-defined systems in all fields.

In October 2019, the Third Plenary Session of the 19th CCCPC was held in Beijing. The plenary session adopted the Decision on Major Issues Concerning Upholding and Improving the System of Socialism with Chinese Characteristics and Modernizing China's System and Capacity for Governance and deployed major tasks and measures to promote institutional construction, which provided a fundamental basis for comprehensively deepening the reform and systematic integration, coordination and efficiency.

The Decision points out that the socialist system with Chinese characteristics is a scientific system formed by the Party and the people through long-term practice and exploration. All work and activities of China's national governance are carried out in accordance with the socialist system with Chinese characteristics. China's national governance system and governance capacity are the concentrated expression of the socialist system with Chinese characteristics and its implementation capacity. The Decision has systematically analyzed the significant advantages of China's national system and governance system: adhering to the party's centralized and unified leadership, adhering to the party's scientific theory, maintaining political stability, and ensuring that the country always advances along the socialist direction; upholding the people's ownership of the country, developing people's democracy, maintaining close ties with the masses, and relying on the people to promote national development; upholding the rule of law in an all-round way, building a socialist country ruled by law, and effectively safeguarding social fairness, justice, and people's rights; adhering to the principle of bearing in mind the general situation in the country, mobilizing the enthusiasm of all quarters, and concentrating our efforts on major issues; adhering to the principle that all ethnic groups are equal, forging a strong sense of the Chinese nation community, and realizing the remarkable advantages of common unity, struggle and common prosperity and development; adhering to the principle of public ownership as the mainstay, the common development of various ownership economies, and the coexistence of distribution according to work as the mainstay and various distribution methods, organically integrating the socialist system with the market economy, and constantly emancipating and developing the remarkable advantages of social productive forces; adhering to the common ideals and beliefs, values and moral concepts, carrying forward the excellent traditional Chinese culture, revolutionary culture and advanced socialist culture, and promoting the remarkable advantages of the people's ideological and spiritual unity; adhering to the people-centered development concept, constantly guaranteeing and improving people's livelihood, enhancing people's well-being, and taking the remarkable advantage of common prosperity; adhering to reform and innovation, keeping pace with the times, being good at self-improvement and self-development, and making the society full of vitality; adhering to the principle of having both ability and political integrity, selecting and appointing talents, pool talents from all over the world, and cultivating more and more outstanding talents; upholding the Party's command of the gun, ensuring that the people's army is absolutely loyal to the Party and the people, and effectively safeguard the country's sovereignty, security, and development interests; adhering to "One Country, Two Systems," maintain the long-term prosperity and stability of Hong Kong and Macao, and promoting the peaceful reunification of the motherland; adhering to the unity of independence and opening-up, actively participating in global governance, and making continuous contributions to building a community with a shared future for mankind. These remarkable advantages are the basis for our confidence in the path, theory, system and culture of socialism with Chinese characteristics.

On the basis of the goal of comprehensively deepening the reform set by the Third Plenary Session of the 18th CCCPC, the decision sets forth the overall goal of upholding and improving the socialist system with Chinese characteristics and promoting the modernization of the national governance system and governance capacity: by the time our Party is 100 years old, we will have achieved remarkable results in making the system more mature and in full function in all aspects; by 2035, systems in all aspects will be further improved, and the modernization of the national governance system and governance capacity will be basically realized; by the 100th anniversary of the founding of new China, the modernization of the national governance system and governance capacity will be fully realized, and the socialist system with Chinese characteristics will be further consolidated and its advantages fully demonstrated. Focusing on this general objective, the decision has made systematic arrangements to uphold and improve the Party's leadership system, the people's ownership system, the socialist legal system with Chinese characteristics, the socialist administrative system with Chinese characteristics, the socialist basic economic system, the socialist advanced cultural system, the people's livelihood security system, the social governance system, the ecological civilization system, the party's absolute leadership system over the people's army, the "One Country, Two Systems" system, the independent foreign policy of peace and the supervisory system of the Party and the state.

On November 26, the CCCPC for Deepening Overall Reform held its 11th meeting, which adopted the division of labor plan for relevant central departments to implement the important measures of the Fourth Plenary Session of the 19th CCCPC. The meeting emphasized that all reforms should be pushed closer to a fully in function system, so that all reforms can complement each other and produce good results. We should pay attention to benchmarking with the fundamental, basic and important systems of socialism with Chinese characteristics, clarify our work ideas and grasp, and promote and implement the reform tasks as planned by the Fourth Plenary Session of the CCCPC. If the reform has established an institutional framework, it is necessary to continue to consolidate and improve it according to the spirit of the Fourth Plenary Session of the CCCPC and establish a long-term mechanism; it is necessary to vigorously tackle difficulties in what is being explored, necessary to achieve breakthroughs, do a good job in summing up and refining, and form institutional arrangements; for those to be planned and launched, we should boldly reform and innovate, and promptly study and formulate plans. We should make full efforts in accurate planning and implementation, and know what problems the reform will solve, when it will be launched, and what effect it will have on system construction. It is necessary to grasp the characteristics and nature of different reforms and persist in introducing plans, improving mechanisms and promoting implementation. In implementing the reform plan, we should adapt measures to local conditions and have a definite aim. A one-size-fits-all approach must be avoided. We should focus on the effective operation of the system and carry out supervision to see whether the reform has achieved the integration of objectives, policies and effects. We should step up the preparation of the implementation plan for the important measures taken at the Fourth Plenary Session of the CCCPC.

In April 2020, the Central Committee for Deepening Overall Reform held its 13th meeting and reviewed and adopted the Implementation Plan on Major Reform Measures of the Third Plenary Session of the 19th CCCPC (2020–2021). We must uphold and improve the system of socialism with Chinese characteristics and continue to modernize the national governance system and capabilities. On this basis, various reform measures were carried out in an orderly manner.

On December 30, 2020, the 17th Meeting of the Central Committee for Deepening Overall Reform reviewed the summary and evaluation report on comprehensively deepening reform since the Third Plenary Session of the 18th CCCPC. The meeting emphasized that the basic institutional framework in various fields has been basically established, and historic changes, systematic remolding and overall reconstruction have been achieved in many fields. This has laid a solid foundation for promoting the formation of a systematic, scientific, standardized and effective institutional system, making the systems in all aspects more mature, and achieving historic great achievements in comprehensively deepening reform. So far, the reform objectives and tasks proposed by the Third Plenary Session of the 18th CCCPC have been completed on schedule.

In 2021, the 50 key reform tasks and 61 other reform tasks deployed by the CCCPC for Deepening Overall Reform were basically completed. The relevant departments of the central and state organs also completed 105 reform tasks, and

216 reform plans were issued in various aspects, achieving the goal of more mature and stable systems by the time the CPC was founded 100 years ago.

In the new era, broader and deeper reform across the board has been consistently promoted. The system of socialism with Chinese characteristics is now more mature and stable, and the modernization of China's system and capacity for governance has reached a higher level. The cause of the Party and the country now radiates with fresh vitality. The reform is only in progress but not completed. Comprehensively deepening the reform will make greater breakthroughs and show greater achievements in the new era and new journey.

4.2.2 Actively Develop People's Democracy in the Whole Process

(1) Putting Forward the Concept of Whole-Process People's Democracy
Democracy is the common value of all mankind, but different countries have different paths of democratic political development, and different types of societies have different forms of democratic politics. To carry out the political construction of socialism with Chinese characteristics, we must first understand what is the democratic politics of socialism with Chinese characteristics and its development path.

In December, 2012, when Commemorating the 30th Anniversary of the Promulgation and Implementation of the Current Constitution, Xi Jinping summarized the core connotation of the road to political development of socialism with Chinese characteristics and stressed: the key to keeping to the socialist path of making political progress with Chinese characteristics is to ensure the unity of the leadership of the Party, the position of the people as masters of the country and ruling the country by law, so as to guarantee the fundamental position of the people, to reach the goal of enhancing the vitality of the Party and the country and keeping the people fully motivated, to expand socialist democracy and to promote socialist political progress.

At the meeting marking the 60th anniversary of the NPC, September 5, 2014, Xi Jinping further elaborated the historical logic, theoretical logic and practical logic of the road of political development of socialism with Chinese characteristics, profoundly summarized the advantages and characteristics of the political system of socialism with Chinese characteristics, and put forward "8 standards" that the best way to evaluate whether a country's political system is democratic and efficient is to observe whether the succession of its leading body is orderly and in line with the law, whether all people can manage state affairs and social, economic and cultural affairs in conformity with legal provisions, whether the public can express their requirements without hindrance, whether all sectors can efficiently participate in the country's political affair, whether national decisions can be made in a rational, democratic way, whether professionals in all fields can be part of the team of the national leadership and administrative systems through fair competition, whether the ruling party can serve as a leader in state affairs in accordance with the Constitution and laws, and whether the exercise of power can be kept under effective restraint and supervision.

On the road of political development of socialism with Chinese characteristics, China has developed a unique the whole-process people's democracy. In November, 2019, when Xi Jinping was inspecting Shanghai, he had a cordial exchange with the representatives of community residents who were participating in the consultation on legislation, and proposed for the first time that "people's democracy is a whole-process people's democracy." In October, 2021, Xi Jinping attended the Central People's Congress Work Conference and made an important speech. The speech systematically explained the major concepts and practices of the whole-process people's democracy, and makes major plans and clear requirements for the continuous development of the whole-process people's democracy. He pointed out: democracy is not a decorative ornament, but an instrument for addressing the issues that concern the people.[74] Whether a country is democratic depends on whether its people are truly the masters of the country; whether the people have the right to vote, and more importantly, the right to participate extensively; whether they have been given verbal promises in elections, and more importantly, how many of these promises are fulfilled after elections; whether there are set political procedures and rules in state systems and laws, and more importantly, whether these systems and laws are truly enforced; whether the rules and procedures for the exercise of power are democratic, and more importantly, whether the exercise of power is genuinely subject to public scrutiny and checks. If the people of a country are only called upon to vote and then are forgotten once they have cast their votes; if the people only hear high-sounding promises during an election campaign but have no say whatsoever afterwards; or if they are wooed when their votes are wanted but are ignored once the election is over, then such a democracy is not a true democracy. He stressed democracy is the right of the people in every country, rather than the prerogative of a few nations. Whether a country is democratic should be judged by its people, not dictated by a handful of outsiders. Whether a country is democratic should be acknowledged by the international community, not arbitrarily decided by a few self-appointed judges. Democracy takes different forms, and there is no one-size-fits-all model. It would be totally undemocratic to measure the diverse political systems in the world with a single yardstick or examine different political civilizations from a single perspective. He stressed that whole-process people's democracy in China is a complete system with supporting mechanisms and procedures, and has been fully tested through wide participation. China has implemented the basic political systems including the state system which is a socialist state under the people's democratic dictatorship led by the working class and based on the alliance of workers and farmers, the system of people's congresses as the system of government, the system of multi-Party cooperation and political consultation under the leadership of the CPC, the system of regional ethnic autonomy, and the system of community-level self-governance, featuring distinctive Chinese characteristics, consolidating and developing the patriotic united front, and constructing a diverse, smooth and orderly democratic channel. All the people exercise democratic election, democratic consultation, democratic decision-making, democratic management and democratic supervision according by, and manage state affairs, economic and cultural undertakings and social affairs through various channels and forms by law. Whole-process people's democracy integrates process-oriented democracy with results-oriented democracy, procedural democracy with substantive democracy, direct democracy with indirect democracy, and people's democracy with the will of the state. It is a model of socialist democracy that covers all aspects of the democratic process and all sectors of society. It is a true democracy that works. We will promote the development of the whole-process people's democracy. The principle of the people being masters of the country will be manifested in the Party's governance policies and measures, in all aspects of the work of Party and state organs at all levels, and in the efforts to meet the people's expectation for a better life.

Under the guidance of the above ideas, the development of socialist democratic politics in China in the new era has been comprehensively promoted, and the system of the people being the masters of the country has been constantly improved.

(2) Improve the System of People's Congresses

The system of people's congresses is an important institutional carrier to realize the whole-process people's democracy of our country. At the beginning of 2017, the general office of the CCCPC issued the implementation opinions on improving the system of people's congresses' regulations on discussing and deciding major issues and reporting to the people's congresses at the corresponding levels before major decisions are made. This is the first guiding document issued by the CCCPC for the People's Congress to exercise the power to decide major issues, providing an important guarantee for people's congresses at all levels to do a good job in relevant work.

In October 2019, the Fourth Plenary Session of the 19th CCCPC made important arrangements for upholding and improving the system of people's congresses.

In October 2021, the first the Central People's Congress Work Conference in China's history was held in Beijing. Xi Jinping summarized the new concepts, ideas and requirements of the new era in promoting the construction of the system of the people's congresses with "six must insist," namely, we must adhere to the leadership of the CPC, we must adhere to the system of people being the masters of the country, we must adhere to the comprehensive rule of law, we must adhere to the democratic centralism, we must adhere to the road of political development of socialism with Chinese characteristics, and we must adhere to modernizing the national governance system and capabilities. He pointed out that the system of the people's congresses is a good system that conforms to China's national conditions and reality, reflects the nature of a socialist country, ensures that the people are the masters of the country, and ensures the realization of the great rejuvenation of the Chinese nation. It is a great creation of our Party and the people in the history of human political systems, and a brand-new political system of great significance in the history of China's political development and even in the history of world political development. We should adhere to the political development under socialism with Chinese characteristics, adhere to and improve the system of people's congresses, strengthen and improve the work of people's congresses in the new era, constantly develop the whole-process people's democracy, and consolidate and develop a lively, stable and united political situation. On how to strengthen and improve the work of the people's Congress in the new era, he stressed that it is necessary to comprehensively implement the Constitution and safeguard the authority and dignity of the Constitution. We should accelerate the improvement of the socialist legal system with Chinese characteristics, promote development with good laws, and ensure good governance. We should make good use of the power of oversight entrusted to the people's Congress by the Constitution, and exercise appropriate, effective, and law-based oversight. It is necessary to give full play to the role of deputies to the people's Congress and ensure that the people's congress responds to public demand. It is necessary to strengthen the consciousness of political organs and strengthen the self-building of people's congresses. We should strengthen the Party's overall leadership over the work of the people's Congress. The speech clearly put forward the guiding ideology, major principles and major work of strengthening and improving the work of the people's Congress in the new era, profoundly answered a series of major theoretical and practical questions on developing socialist democratic politics with Chinese characteristics and upholding and improving the system of the people's congresses in the new era, and pointed out the way forward for upholding and improving the system of the people's congresses and strengthening and improving the work of the people's Congress in the new era.

In November of the same year, the CCCPC issued the opinions on upholding and improving the system of the people's congresses and strengthening and improving the work of the people's Congress in the new era. The "Opinion" reviewed and summarized the glorious history of the Party leading the people to establish, consolidate, develop and improve the system of people's congresses, valuable experience and the significant advantages and great effectiveness of this system, especially that since 18th National Congress of the CPC, under the strong leadership of the Party Central Committee with Comrade Xi Jinping as the core, the work of the NPC has made historic achievements, and the system of people's congresses has become more mature and more established. The "Opinion" stresses that in the new era, the most fundamental thing to uphold and improve the system of the people's congresses and strengthen and improve the work of the people's congress is to uphold the comprehensive leadership of the CPC and ensure that the CPC leads the people to effectively rule the country by law. On the basis of summing up relevant experiences and practices since the 18th National Congress of the CPC, five requirements are put forward. First, adhere to the highest political principle of the Party's overall leadership. Second, follow the guidance of Xi Jinping Thought on Socialism with Chinese Characteristics for a New Era. Third, uphold the Party's leadership. First, we must uphold the centralized and unified leadership of the Party Central Committee. Fourth, the Party's leadership should be run through the whole process of people's Congress work in all aspects. Fifth, improve and implement the system and mechanism of the party's leadership in the work of the people's congress. The Opinions put forward the general requirements and main tasks of the work of the NPC in the new era: we should hold high the great banner of socialism with Chinese characteristics, follow Xi Jinping Thought on Socialism with Chinese Characteristics for a New Era, in-depth study and implement his ideas on the rule of law, his important ideas on adhering to and improving the system of people's congresses, adhere to the Party's leadership, the people's sovereignty, the organic unity of the rule of law, closely focus on the goal of modernizing the national governance system and capabilities, the overall construction of a modern socialist state. In addition, we must adhere to and improve the socialist rule of law system with Chinese characteristics, improve the social environment for the implementation of laws, strengthen the institutional guarantee of people being the masters of the country, gather the majestic power of the people, and provide a strong guarantee for the realization of the Second Centenary Goal and the Chinese Dream of the great rejuvenation of the Chinese nation. The "Opinion" made clear the work that the NPC and its Standing Committee should focus on, including: accelerating the improvement of the socialist legal system with Chinese characteristics with the constitution as the core, and providing a more complete legal guarantee for the comprehensive construction of a modern socialist country; maintain the unity of the rule of law in the country and promote the operation of all national work on the track of the rule of law; ensure the implementation of the decisions and arrangements of the Party Central Committee in accordance with the law, and ensure that the power entrusted by the people is always used for the happiness of the Chinese people and the rejuvenation of the Chinese nation; improve the system of ensuring that the people are the masters of the country, expand the orderly political participation of the people, ensure that the people exercise state power through the people's Congress, and ensure that the people are the masters of the country; promote the complete reunification of the motherland, consolidate national unity, and maintain social harmony and stability; safeguard national sovereignty, security and development interests. Focusing on strengthening and improving the quality and level of the work of the people's Congress, the Opinion made specific arrangements in eight aspects, including developing and improving the whole-process people's democracy, ensuring the full implementation of the Constitution, promoting high-quality legislation, giving play to the leading role of the people's Congress in legislative work, enhancing the rigidity and effectiveness of supervision, promoting the institutionalization and normalization of discussions and decisions on major issues, deepening and expanding the NPC's external work. With regard to giving full play to the role of deputies to the people's Congress, the "Opinion" put forward requirements in five aspects: ensuring the "entrance gate" of deputies to the people's Congress, maintaining close ties between state organs and deputies to the people's Congress, maintaining close ties between deputies to the people's Congress and the masses, promoting the high quality and handling of proposals of deputies to the people's Congress, and strengthening the service guarantee, management and supervision of deputies to the people's Congress in performing their duties. The Opinion also put forward clear and specific requirements for strengthening the self-building of the people's Congress and its Standing Committees in terms of enhancing its political philosophy, organizational construction, discipline and style construction, system construction, work force, theoretical research on the system of the people's congresses, propaganda and public opinion work, and IT application.

The Opinion is a comprehensive document guiding the work of the NPC, focusing on Xi Jinping's important ideas on adhering to and improving the system of people's congresses, reflecting the theoretical, practical and institutional achievements in the construction of the NPC system and the work of the NPC since the 18th National Congress of the CPC, providing scientific guidance and action programs for adhering to and improving the system of people's congresses and strengthening and improving the work of the NPC in the new era, which is of great importance for modernizing the national governance system and capabilities and gathering the wisdom and strength of all parties to comprehensively build a modern socialist state.

Under the guidance of the above decisions and arrangements, the development of China's system of people's congresses in the new era is mainly reflected in the following aspects: first, closely follow the principle of comprehensively ruling the country by law, grasp the key of improving the quality of legislation, and constantly improve the level of sound, democratic, and law-based legislation. From November 2012 to April 2022, the NPC passed amendments to the constitution. The NPC and its Standing Committee formulated 68 new laws, revised 234 laws, adopted 99 decisions on legal issues and other major issues, and made 9 legislative interpretations. Compared with the previous decade, the number of legislations has increased significantly, and the socialist legal system with Chinese characteristics has been further improved. Second, commit to exercising appropriate, effective oversight, and fulfill our oversight duties of people's congresses in accordance with the law. At the same time, exercise more stringent and effective oversight of the lawful performance of the State Council, the National Commission of Supervision, the Supreme People's Court, and the Supreme People's Procuratorate to ensure the full implementation of the state's major decisions and plans. The mechanism for law enforcement inspection should be completed and special inquiries should be improved and completed. The mechanism for examining and supervising budgets and final accounts should be innovated. We should continue to fight the three critical battles against potential risk, poverty, and pollution. We should strengthen supervision over economic work and promote the implementation of the new development concept. We should comprehensively use various forms of oversight to ensure and improve people's livelihood in the course of development. We should step up oversight of supervisory and judicial work to safeguard judicial justice. We should perform our constitutional and legal duty of supervision. Third, people's congresses at all levels and their standing committees implement the relevant deployment requirements, discuss and decide on major issues in economic construction, political construction, cultural construction, social construction and ecological civilization construction throughout the country and within their respective administrative regions, and better give play to the functions of state organs of power. Fourth, the work of deputies has been continuously deepened and expanded. The proportion of front-line workers, farmers, professional and technical personnel and the number of migrant workers among the deputies to the people's Congress have increased, and the performance of their duties by law has been fully guaranteed. Among them, those at county and township levels accounted for 94.5 percent of the total. The universality and authenticity of the election have been fully demonstrated to better ensure that the people are masters of their own affairs. Making full use of their close connections with the people, these deputies diligently fulfill their duties by soliciting and submitting the people's suggestions and advice through various forms and channels. Representatives attending standing committee meetings as nonvoting delegates, participating in law enforcement inspections, and participating in the activities of special committees and working committees have become more and more regular, further unblocking the channels for expressing and reflecting social conditions and public opinions.

(3) Promote the Extensive and Multi-Layered Institutionalization of Socialist Consultative Democracy

Under the leadership of the CPC, consultative democracy is an important form of democracy in which the people from all walks of life carry out extensive consultations before and during the implementation of policy decisions and strive to form consensus around major issues of reform, development and stability and practical issues involving the vital interests of the masses.

Since the 18th National Congress of the CPC, the system design of socialist consultative democracy has become increasingly perfect. The 18th National Congress of the CPC held in 2012 put forward the important proposition of "improving the socialist consultative democratic system." In November 2013, the Third Plenary Session of the 18th CCCPC proposed to "promote multilevel and institutionalized consultative democracy," emphasizing the establishment of a consultative democracy system with reasonable procedures and complete links, broadening the consultation channels of state power organs, CPPCC organizations, Party organizations, grass-roots organizations and social organizations, and conducting in-depth legislative, administrative, democratic, political and social consultations, giving play to the important role of the United Front in consultative democracy and the role of the CPPCC as an important channel for consultative democracy. In February 2015, the CCCPC issued the opinion on strengthening the construction of socialist consultative democracy. The "opinion" put forward that we should continue to focus on strengthening political party consultation, government consultation and CPPCC consultation, actively carry out people's Congress consultation, people's organizations consultation and grass-roots consultation, and gradually explore social organization consultation. We should give play to the advantages of various consultation channels, do a good job in connection and cooperation, and constantly improve and perfect the socialist consultative democratic system. The contents and methods of various consultations should be reasonably determined according to their own characteristics and actual needs. With regard to political party consultations, the "Opinion" requires that we continue to explore and standardize the forms of political party consultations, improve the system whereby the Central Committee of democratic parties directly submits proposals to the CCCPC, and strengthen the construction of a guarantee mechanism for political party consultations. With regard to people's Congress consultations, the opinion requires that consultations in legislative work be carried out in depth, and the role of people's congress deputies in consultative democracy be brought into full play. With regard to government consultation, the Opinion requires exploring the formulation and publication of a list of consultation matters, enhancing the universality and pertinence of consultation, and improving the government consultation mechanism. With regard to the CPPCC consultation, the "Opinion" requires that the main contents of the CPPCC consultation be clarified, the CPPCC meetings and other forms of consultation be improved, the effective connection between the CPPCC consultation and the work of the Party committee and the government be strengthened, and the construction of the CPPCC system be strengthened. With regard to the consultation of people's organizations, the "Opinion" requires the establishment and improvement of the working mechanism for people's organizations to participate in consultations through various channels, and organize and guide the masses to carry out consultations. With regard to grass-roots consultations, the Opinion requires to promote the consultations of townships and sub-districts, administrative villages and communities, and enterprises and institutions. With regard to the consultation of social organizations, the Opinion requires that the Party's leadership and the government's management by law should be adhered to, the working mechanism and communication channels for contacting relevant social organizations should be improved, and social organizations should be guided to carry out consultations in an orderly manner to better serve the society. The "Opinion" clarifies the essential attribute and basic connotation of socialist consultative democracy, expounds the important significance, guiding ideology, basic principles and channels and procedures of strengthening the construction of socialist consultative democracy, and makes comprehensive arrangements for carrying out political party consultation, people's Congress consultation, government consultation, political association consultation, people's organization consultation, grass-roots consultation, and social organization consultation under the new situation. It is a programmatic document guiding the construction of socialist consultative democracy. In October 2019, the Fourth Plenary Session of the 19th CCCPC made new arrangements for strengthening the construction of consultative democracy at the institutional level. It proposed to adhere to the unique advantages of socialist consultative democracy, comprehensively promote political party consultation, people's Congress consultation, government consultation, CPPCC consultation, people's organization consultation, basic level consultation and social organization consultation, and build a consultative democracy system with reasonable procedures and complete links. It proposed to improve the implementation mechanism of consultation before and during the implementation of decisions, and enrich the institutionalized practice of whenever a problem crops up, we should resort to deliberations first and matters involving many people are discussed by all those involved.

Under the guidance of the above system design, the construction of socialist consultative democracy in China has been advanced in an orderly manner.

CPPCC consultation is the main channel of socialist consultative democracy. In June 2015, in order to implement the Opinion on Strengthening the Construction of Socialist Consultative Democracy, the general office of the CCCPC issued the Implementation Opinion on Strengthening the Construction of Consultative Democracy of the CPPCC. The implementation opinions expounds the important significance, guiding ideology and important principles of strengthening the construction of the consultative democracy of the CPPCC, further standardizes the content and form of the CPPCC consultation, puts forward measures to strengthen the connection between the CPPCC consultation and the work of the Party committee and the government. It clarified the focus of the system building of the CPPCC and the requirements for strengthening the consultation capacity of the CPPCC, and emphasized the need to strengthen the Party's leadership in the construction of consultation and democracy of the CPPCC. It is an important document to guide the construction of consultative democracy of the CPPCC, and is of great significance to better play the role of the CPPCC as an important channel and special consultative institution of socialist consultative democracy. In terms of the contents of the consultation, the "implementation opinion" specifies that the main contents of the CPPCC consultation are: major national and local policies and important issues in political, economic, cultural and social life, as well as the common affairs of all democratic parties participating in the work of the CPPCC, important affairs within the CPPCC, and other important issues related to the patriotic united front. It also made provisions on the annual consultation plan formulated by the Party committee, the government and the CPPCC, and encouraged the CPPCC at all levels to enrich the contents of the consultation in light of the development of the situation and the actual conditions. In terms of the form of consultation, the "implementation opinion" has refined the important forms of consultation such as the plenary session of the CPPCC, the Standing Committee meeting on special political issues, and the special consultation meeting. For the first time, the documents have clearly stipulated the topics selection, meeting organization, pre-meeting investigation, results application and other links of the biweekly consultation forum, and standardized the forms of consultations on particular issues with those working on these issues, with representatives from all sectors of society, and with the relevant government departments on the handling of proposals. In terms of the construction of the consultation system, the implementation opinion require that special provisions for democratic supervision be formulated in a timely manner, and various work systems for participation in and discussion of government affairs be established and improved, so as to promote the institutionalization, standardization and procedural implementation of functions. We should study and formulate guiding opinions on standardizing the performance of members' duties and improve the mechanisms for maintaining contact with them. The Implementation Opinions also put forward requirements for establishing and improving the working mechanism of counterpart contact between the special committees of the CPPCC and relevant departments, the working mechanism and guarantee mechanism of the General Office (Office) of the CPPCC and the consultation system of the service sectors of the special committees, and the proposal handling and consultation system.

Party consultation is an important part of the multi-party cooperation and political consultation system led by the CPC and an important part of the socialist consultative democratic system. In May 2015, the CCCPC held the Central Conference on the United Front and promulgated the Regulations on the United Front Work of the CPC (for Trial Implementation). For the first time, "participating in political consultation led by the CPC" was regarded as one of the basic functions of democratic parties, and the basic functions of democratic parties were expanded to "playing their roles in deliberation and administration of state affairs, political consultation and democratic supervision led by the CPC," making arrangements for strengthening party consultation. In December of the same year, the general office of the CCCPC issued the implementation opinions on strengthening political party consultation, which clarified the profound con-notation and important status of political party consultation, clarified the guiding ideology and important significance of strengthening political party consultation, systematically standardized the content, form, procedure and guarantee mechanism of political party consultation at the central level, put forward clear requirements for party committees at all levels to carry out political party consultation, to ensure that party consultation is carried out on the basis of proper institutions, rules, regulations, and procedures. At the First Session of the 13th CPPCC National Committee held in March 2018, Xi Jinping President Xi elaborated on the unique advantages and distinctive features of China's new political party system and revealed the profound difference between our system and the multiparty system and the two party system. He stressed that a new type of party system is new because it is an extensive and reliable means of representing and fulfilling the interests of the maximum number of people of all ethnic groups and social sectors. It avoids the drawbacks of the old political party system that stood for only a small number of people and interest groups. It has effectively avoided the malpractice of the old type of political party system in representing minority people and minority interest groups; what is new is that it unites all political parties and the non-affiliates towards a common goal, effectively mitigating the risks of inadequate oversight in one-party rule, and the problems of continual transfers of governing parties and destructive competition in multiparty political systems.; through standardized institutional procedures and arrangements, it pools ideas and suggestions to ensure informed and democratic decision-making. It avoids the weakness of Western-style political party systems: When making decisions and exercising governance, political parties act in their own interests or the interests of the classes, regions and groups they represent, provoking division in society. It is not only in line with the reality of contemporary China, but also in line with the excellent traditional culture of the Chinese nation, which has always advocated that all under heaven belongs to the people, mutual learning and inclusiveness, and seeking common ground while putting aside differences. It is a major contribution to human political civilization. Since the 18th National Congress of the CPC, the CCCPC has held or entrusted relevant departments to hold more than 170 political party consultative meetings. It has sincerely consulted and listened to opinions from non-party personages on many major issues to ensure that decision-making is more scientific and democratic. Over the years, the central committees of various democratic parties and personages without party affiliation have conducted in-depth investigation and research on major issues related to the national economy and the people's livelihood, such as the construction of the "Belt and Road," integrated development of the Beijing, Tianjin-Hebei region, the development of the Yangtze River economic belt, the construction of the Guangdong-Hong Kong-Macao Greater Bay Area, the integrated development of the Yangtze River Delta, innovation driven high-quality development, and the promotion of supply side structural reform. Many opinions and suggestions put forward to the CCCPC and the State Council have been adopted.

Grass roots consultation is an important part and effective form of socialist consultative democracy construction. In July 2015, the general office of the CCCPC and the general office of the State Council issued the Opinions on Strengthening Consultations in Urban and Rural Communities. The opinions clarifies the leading position of grass-roots party organizations in consultation, and stresses the basic principles of upholding the party's leadership, the grassroots people's autonomy, the legal consultation, democratic centralism, the consultation before and during the implementation of decision-making, and the adaptation to local conditions. It proposes that by 2020, a new situation of urban and rural community consultation with a wide range of consultation subjects, rich content, diverse forms, scientific procedures, sound systems and remarkable results would be basically formed. The Opinions also stipulates the contents, subjects, forms and procedures of urban and rural community consultation and the application of results. This is a special document for strengthening the construction of grass-roots consultation, which is conducive to promoting the institutionalization of grass-roots consultation and realizing and safeguarding the interests of the grass-roots people.

In the new era, China has made great achievements in the construction of consultative democracy. First, establish a leadership system and working mechanism with unified leadership of the Party committee, division of responsibilities among all parties, and active participation of the public. Second, the channels and methods of consultative democracy have been constantly innovated. All sectors of society have conducted extensive consultations through various channels and methods, and established and improved various consultation methods such as proposals, meetings, symposiums, demonstrations, hearings, publicity, evaluation, consultation, networks and public opinion surveys. On October 22, 2013, the first biweekly forum of the National Committee of the Chinese people's Political Consultative Conference was held in the auditorium of the National Committee of the Chinese people's Political Consultative Conference in Beijing. The "biweekly forum," an important form of consultative democracy that was well-known throughout the country in the 1950s and 1960s after the founding of new China, entered people's vision again with a new name and form, and became an important form of consultative democracy. Since the 18th National Congress of the CPC, the central committees of various democratic parties and personages without party affiliation have made in-depth investigations and studies and put forward more than 730 written opinions and suggestions, many of which have been translated into major national decisions. The local Party committees at all levels of the CPC have consulted with the democratic parties and local organizations at all levels on major local issues in the light of reality, and have actively promoted local economic and social development. Third, the process of consultative democracy is becoming more and more standardized. Different channels of consultation are being classified into system norms and working rules, and their participation scope, discussion principles, basic procedures and communication methods are specified accordingly. China has gradually established a system of consultative democracy with clear rights and responsibilities, standardized procedures, smooth relations and effective operation.

(4) We Will Develop Regional Autonomy of Ethnic Minorities and Community-Level Self-Governance

We will adhere to and improve the system under which ethnic minority groups practice self-government in the regions they inhabit. In 2014, the CCCPC and the State Council issued the Opinions on Strengthening and Improving Ethnic Work under the New Situation, which focused on unswervingly following the correct path of solving ethnic problems with Chinese characteristics, promoting economic and social development in ethnic areas around improving people's livelihood, promoting exchanges and integration among ethnic groups, building a common spiritual home for all ethnic groups, improving the ability to manage ethnic affairs according to law and put forward 25 opinions on strengthening the Party's leadership over ethnic work in six aspects. Subsequently, the relevant departments issued a series of important policy documents such as the opinions on comprehensively, deeply and persistently carrying out the work of building national unity and progress and building the sense of community for the Chinese nation. Guided by this, in the new era, China has highlighted the concepts of the big family of the Chinese nation and the sense of national identity, taken the building of a strong sense of the national identity as the main line of the Party's ethnic work, attached great importance to the economic and social development of ethnic areas, improved differentiated regional policies, mechanisms of optimized transfer payment and providing paired assistance, implemented plans to promote the development of ethnic areas and ethnic groups with small populations, and prospered the border areas and the people, to ensure that ethnic minorities and minority areas work together with the whole country to achieve moderately prosperous society and modernization in an all-round way. All regions and departments earnestly implement the Party's ethnic and religious policies, hold high the banner of national unity, carry out in-depth publicity and education on national unity and progress, promote all ethnic groups to hold together like pomegranate seeds, promote all ethnic groups to firmly identify with the great motherland, the Chinese nation, Chinese culture, the CPC and socialism with Chinese characteristics, and constantly promote the development of forging a strong sense of the Chinese nation community. The construction of supporting laws and regulations for the Law of the PRC on Regional Ethnic Autonomy has been continuously strengthened, and the system of laws and regulations for ethnic work has been continuously improved. The system of regional ethnic autonomy has shown more and more strong vitality and superiority, which has effectively promoted the modernization of the ethnic affairs governance system and Governance capacity, improved the level of rule of law in ethnic affairs governance, and prevented and resolved potential risks in the ethnic field. At present, on all standing committees of people's congresses of the 155 ethnic autonomous areas, there are citizens from the ethnic groups exercising autonomy assuming the office of chair or vice chair; all governors, prefectural commissioners, heads of counties, or banners of ethnic autonomous areas are citizens from the ethnic groups exercising autonomy.

We should improve community-level self-governance and make it full off vitality. The CCCPC and the State Council have successively adopted important documents such as the Opinions on Strengthening and Improving Urban and Rural Community Governance and the Opinions on Strengthening the Modernization of the Grass-roots Governance System and Governance Capacity. On this basis, the community-level self-governance has been continuously developed and improved. The people have widely and directly participated in the management of social affairs through villagers' committees, residents' committees, and workers' congresses. As of the end of 2020, all the 503,000 administrative villages in China had established villagers committees, and all the 112,000 urban communities in the country had established residents committees. Corporate trade union committees are the operating mechanism of employees congresses. At present, there are 2.81 million primary-level trade unions in China, covering 6.55 million enterprises and public institutions. Village rules and regulations or villagers charter of self-government have been formulated in rural areas throughout the country, and residents' conventions or regulations on residents' autonomy have been formulated in urban communities. Grassroots democratic innovation is very active. The Chinese people have explored and initiated numerous popular and pragmatic grassroots practices—residents councils, residents workshops, democratic discussions and hearings, courtyard discussions, neighborhood meetings, offline roundtables and online group chats. They have arranged for representatives of Party committees, deputies to the people's congresses, and CPPCC members to visit rural and urban communities. All these down-to-earth and pragmatic forms of democracy encourage people to voice their opinions and suggestions and conduct extensive consultation on matters related to their vital interests. This helps to coordinate the interests of multiple stakeholders, mitigate conflict, and maintain social stability and harmony at the grassroots level.

In the new era, we have made sweeping progress in improving the institutions, standards, and procedures of China's socialist democracy, and given better play to the strengths of the Chinese socialist political system. As a result, our political stability, unity, and dynamism have been reinforced and grown stronger.

4.2.3 Comprehensively Advancing "Ruling the Country by Law"

(1) Plan the Top-Level Design of a Comprehensive Framework for Promoting the Rule of Law

Since the reform and opening-up, China has made great achievements in promoting the rule of law. At the same time, there are serious problems such as failure to abide by the law, lax law enforcement, unfair justice, and failure to investigate violations of the law, and judicial corruption occurs from time to time. Moreover, a large number of contradictions and problems in China's development are related to the inadequacy of the construction of the rule of law. This requires us to further strengthen the construction of the rule of law.

The Party Central Committee with Comrade Xi Jinping as the core is very much aware of this. Since the 18th CCCPC, Xi Jinping has expounded questions related to advancing "ruling the country by law" in many occasions, and formed Xi Jinping's thinking on the rule of law. He has repeatedly stressed the principle and direction of a comprehensive framework for promoting the rule of law. He said, "we must make it clear that people's democracy in China is fundamentally different from the so-called 'constitutionalism' in the West."[75] He pointed out that the CPC leadership is the defining feature of socialism with Chinese characteristics. At the 15th National Congress, it was already clear that ruling the country by law means that the broad masses of the people, under the leadership of the Party and in accordance with the Constitution and other laws, participate in one way or another and through all possible channels in managing state affairs, economic and cultural undertakings and social affairs, and see to it that all work of the state proceeds in keeping with law, and that socialist democracy is gradually institutionalized and codified so that such institutions and laws will not change with changes in the leadership or changes in the views or focus of attention of any leader. When we talk about ruling the country according to the Constitution and governance the country according to the Constitution, we do not mean to deny or give up the leadership of the party. Instead, we emphasize that as it leads the people in formulating and implementing the Constitution and laws, the Party must act within the limits prescribed by the Constitution and laws. China's Constitution, in the form of a fundamental law, reflects the achievements made by the Party in leading the people in revolution, construction and reform, and reflects the Party's leading position formed in history and the people's choice. In November 2020, the first central work conference on comprehensive rule of law in China's history was held in Beijing. The conference summarized the major contents of Xi Jinping's thinking on the rule of law and clarified its leading position in the rule by law. The top-level design of advancing "ruling the country by law" is gradually completed under the guidance of Xi Jinping's thinking on the rule of law.

In 2012, the 18th National Congress of the CPC proposed "Advancing 'Ruling the Country by Law.'"

The Fourth Plenary Session of the 18th CCCPC was held in Beijing in October, 2014 and adopted the "Decision of the CCCPC on Some Major Issues Concerning Advancing 'Ruling the Country by Law.'" The Decision stated that our overall objective is to establish a system of socialist rule of law with distinctive Chinese features and establish China as a socialist country under the rule of law. This is, under the leadership of the CPC, we should adhere to the socialist system with Chinese characteristics, implement the theory of socialist rule of law with Chinese characteristics, form a complete system of legal norms, an efficient system of rule of law implementation, a strict system of rule of law supervision, a strong system of rule of law protection, form a perfect system of party regulations. We should comprehensively promote the rule of law, the rule of law, and jointly promote the rule of governance and administration according to law. We must ensure that a well-conceived approach is taken to legislation, that the law is strictly enforced, that justice is impartially administered, and that the law is observed by everyone. We must adhere to modernizing the national governance system and capabilities. Proceeding from the basic pattern of the rule of law work, the Decision made comprehensive arrangements for relevant work, requiring that accelerating the improvement of the socialist legal system with Chinese characteristics with the constitution as the core; deepen law-based administration, accelerate the building of a rule of law government; ensure fair justice and improve judicial credibility; enhance the concept of the rule of law for all people and promote the construction of a society based on the rule of law; strive to build a strong contingent of professionals devoted to the rule of law; strengthen and improve the Party's leadership in comprehensively promoting the rule of law. Focusing on the overall goal of a comprehensive framework for promoting the rule of law, the plenary session put forward more than 180 major reform measures, covering all aspects of ruling the country by law in all respects. The 15th National Congress of the CPC put forward the basic strategy of ruling the country by law, which opened the Great Voyage of building a socialist country ruled by law. The Fourth Plenary Session of the 18th CCCPC deepened the understanding of the rule of law, promoted the historic leap in the construction of a socialist country under the rule of law, formed the strategic deployment of the advancing "ruling the country by law," and opened a new journey of advancing "ruling the country by law."

In April 2015 the Central Committee for Deepening Overall Reform held its 11th meeting and reviewed and adopted the Implementation Plan on Major Reform Measures of the Fourth Plenary Session of the 18th CCCPC (2015–2020), to provide the general blueprint and management chart for the next period of promoting a comprehensive rule of law.

In 2018, according to the Plan for Deepening the Reform of Party and State Institutions, the CCCPC established the Commission for Overall Law-based Governance of the CCCPC, and held its first meeting on August 24. It reviewed and adopted the working rules of the Commission for Overall Law-based Governance of the CCCPC and the key points of work of the Commission for Overall Law-based Governance of the CCCPC in 2018 and other important documents, further improving the system and mechanism of the CPC's leadership in comprehensively ruling the country by law, and the top-level design of comprehensively administering the country according to law.

In January 2021, the CCCPC issued the Plan on Developing the Rule of Law in China (2020–2025), which is a programmatic document for advancing "ruling the country by law" in the new era. Taking the "five systems" of the socialist legal system with Chinese characteristics as the main framework, the Plan focuses on the comprehensive implementation of the Constitution, the construction of a complete legal norms system, an efficient legal implementation system, a strict legal supervision system, a strong legal guarantee system, and a perfect inner-party legal system, the maintenance of national sovereignty, security and development interests according to law, and the strengthening of the Party's centralized and unified leadership over the construction of China under the rule of law, and put forward relevant reform and development measures. Under the guidance of the above top-level design, the work of advancing "ruling the country by law" was promoted progressively.

(2) Adhere to the Rule of Law

The constitution is the fundamental law of the country. In a comprehensive framework for promoting the rule of law, we must first adhere to the rule of law. On December 4, 2012, shortly after the closing of the 18th National Congress of the CPC, Xi Jinping stressed when commemorating the 30th anniversary of the promulgation and implementation of the current constitution that in essence, the rule of law is rule by the Constitution; the key to rule the country by law is Constitution-based governance.[76] He stressed that comprehensively implementing the Constitution is the primary task and groundwork for building a law-based socialist country. We must persistently ensure the implementation of the Constitution, and raise the comprehensive implementation of the Constitution to a new level. This was the first commemoration meeting after he was the general scretary, and it declared the firm determination of the Party Central Committee with Comrade Xi Jinping at the core to adhere to the rule of law. Subsequently, the CPC and the Chinese government took a series of important measures to promote the rule of law.

To govern the country according to the constitution, we must first establish the authority of the constitution. In October 2014, the Fourth Plenary Session of the 18th CCCPC proposed that December 4 of each year be designated as the National Constitution Day. We would carry out constitutional education throughout society and carry forward the spirit of the constitution. We have established the system of pledging allegiance to the Constitution. All state functionaries elected or appointed by the people's Congress and its Standing Committee shall publicly swear to the Constitution when they take office. In

November, the 11th Meeting of the Standing Committee of the 12th NPC voted and adopted the decision on the establishment of the national constitution day, which established December 4 as the National Constitution Day in the form of legislation to carry forward the spirit of the Constitution and establish the authority of the Constitution in the form of national festivals. In July 2015, the 15th Meeting of the Standing Committee of the 12th NPC adopted the Decision on the Implementation of the System of Pledging Allegiance to the Constitution, which stipulates that state functionaries perform the pledge of allegiance to the Constitution. On February 26, 2016, the first oath of office ceremonies of the Standing Committee of the NPC was held in Beijing. Six state functionaries, including the vice chairmen of all the special committees of the NPC and the vice chairmen of the Standing Committee working bodies, who were appointed at the 19th Meeting of the Standing Committee of the 12th NPC, solemnly pledge here to be loyal to the Constitution, the motherland and the people. This is an example of safeguarding the authority and dignity of the constitution.

Carrying out constitutional review is the key link of administering the country according to the constitution. In October 2017, following the proposal of the Third Plenary Session of the 18th CCCPC to "improve the review mechanism for the legality of normative documents and major decisions," the Fourth Plenary Session of the 18th CCCPC proposed to "strengthen the filing and review system and capacity-building, bring all normative documents into the scope of filing and review, rescind or correct normative documents that conflicted with the Constitution or the law, and prohibit local governments from making and issuing documents of a legislative nature." The 19th National Congress of the CPC further proposed to strengthen the implementation and supervision of the Constitution, promote constitutional review and safeguard the authority of the Constitution. Subsequently, the Fourth Plenary Session of the 19th CCCPC proposed that we should improve institutions and mechanisms to fully implement the Constitution; boost the implementation of the Constitution and oversight of constitutional compliance, put in place a mechanism for constitutional interpretation, and promote constitutionality review, strengthen the filing review system and capacity building, and rescind or correct normative documents that conflicted with the Constitution or the law. This provides a solid policy basis and institutional basis for ensuring the unity of the rule of law and safeguarding the authority of the Constitution, and clarifies the focus of work for administering the country according to the constitution. In December 2017, the 31st Meeting of the

Standing Committee of the 12th NPC reviewed the report on the work of filing and review since the 12th NPC and in 2017. This is the first time that the Standing Committee of the NPC has deliberated on the work of filing and review. As of early December 2017, the general office of the Standing Committee of the 12th NPC had received 4778 normative documents submitted for the record. The filing and review of normative documents is an important institutional arrangement for safeguarding the dignity of the Constitution and ensuring the implementation of the Constitution, and has laid a solid foundation for promoting the constitutional review.

On March 11, 2018, the First Session of the 13th NPC passed the amendment to the Constitution of the PRC by an overwhelming majority vote, renaming the "the NPC Legislative Affairs Commission" to the "the NPC Constitution and Law Committee." This is a milestone in the history of China's constitutional development.

In January 2021, the Standing Committee of the NPC heard a report on the work of filing and review in 2020. For the first time, the report gives a separate introduction to the constitutionality and constitutionality related issues. At the same time, it has also disclosed the constitutionality review suggestions put forward by three citizens and their handling. One of them, a citizen from Xuancheng, Anhui Province, proposed a constitutional review on the Supreme People's Court's practice of treating urban residents and rural residents differently in its judicial interpretation, and calculating disability compensation and compensation for based on the per capita disposable income of urban residents and the per capita net income of rural residents. After review and study, the Legislative Affairs Commission of the NPC Standing Committee sent a letter to the Supreme People's Court, suggesting that the Supreme People's Court improve the relevant systems in a timely manner and feed back the review and study results to the citizen in a timely manner. In addition, the Supreme People's Court has authorized the higher people's courts of all provinces, autonomous regions and municipalities directly under the central government and the branches of Xinjiang Production and Construction Corps to carry out the pilot work of unifying urban and rural injury compensation. This not only vividly reflects China's emphasis on and protection of citizens' legitimate rights, but also means that the constitutional review has made major breakthroughs and is gradually moving towards openness and normalization.

In addition, the Standing Committee of the NPC has also improved the laws and regulations pertaining to the Constitution, revised the Legislation Law, the

Law on the Oversight by the Standing Committees of People's Congresses at All Levels, the Rules of Procedure of the NPC Standing Committee, the State Council Organic Law, and the Administrative Reconsideration Law and other laws. It has also ensured that the procedures and mechanisms for interpreting the Constitution are well implemented and that concerns about constitutional issues are attended to. It has also enhanced oversight and inspections of the implementation of the Constitution, and expanded channels for constitutional oversight.

(3) Develop a Law-Based Country, Government and Society

The comprehensive advancement of the rule of law in China represents a systematic undertaking, and it needs not only good laws but also good governance.

Good laws are the foundation of sound governance. While promoting the rule of law according to the Constitution, China also pays attention to the legislative work of other laws and is striving to establish a complete legal standard system. In March 2015, the Third Session of the 12th NPC made important amendments to the Legislative Law of the PRC, giving local legislative power to cities divided into districts according to law, clarifying the local legislative authority and scope, to further improve China's legislative system.

On this basis, the state strives to strengthen legislation in key areas and improve the socialist legal system with Chinese characteristics with the Constitution as the core. We have accelerated the building of the rule of law for national security. We have successively promulgated a number of important laws, including the State Security Law of the PRC, the Counter-Espionage Law, the Counter Terrorism Law, the Law on the Administration of Activities of Overseas Non-Governmental Organizations within the Territory of China, the Cyber Security Law, the National Intelligence Law, the Law of the PRC on National Defense Transportation, the Military Facilities Protection Law, and the Nuclear Safety Law, providing a strong legal guarantee for safeguarding national security, core interests, and major interests. We have strengthened legislation on the socialist market economy, formulated the Environmental Protection Tax Law, the Tobacco Leaf Tax Law, and Vessel Tonnage Tax Law, and revised the Vessel Tonnage Tax Law. We have launched the clear-up of the laws on property rights protection. We have revised the Anti-Unfair Competition Law, the Law on Promoting Small and Medium-Sized Enterprises, the Law of the PRC on Specialized Farmers Cooperatives, the Law of the PRC on Promoting the Transformation of Scientific and Technological Achievements, the Standardization Law, the Patent Law, the Advertising Law and promulgated the Tourism Law and the Asset Appraisal Law and other laws. In addition, the legislative work in social, cultural and ecological fields has been continuously strengthened. From 2013 to 2018, the 12th NPC and its Standing Committee formulated 25 laws, revised 127 laws, adopted 46 decisions on legal issues and major issues, and made 9 legal interpretations. From 2018 to September 2021, the 13th NPC and its Standing Committee formulated 36 laws, amended 96 laws, and adopted 40 decisions on legal issues and major issues.

In May 2020, the Third Session of the 13th NPC voted to adopt the *Civil Code of the PRC*. The civil code is the first codified law in the history of new China. It is the "Encyclopedia of Social Life" and occupies a fundamental position in the legal system. According to statistics, the relevant draft laws of the civil code have been deliberated by the NPC Constitution and Law Committee for 34 times, the Standing Committee of the NPC for 10 times, and the NPC for 2 times. From the decision of the Fourth Plenary Session of the 18th CCCPC on the major legislative task of compiling the civil code in 2014, to the start of the civil code compilation in 2015, to the completion of the deliberation of the *General Principles of the Civil Law of the PRC*, the draft of each part of the civil code and the draft of the "complete version" of the civil code from 2017 to 2019, and finally to the adoption of the civil code by voting in 2020, the careful and meticulous compilation process of the civil code is a microcosm and portrayal of the continuous promotion of the comprehensive rule of law and perfecting the socialist legal system with Chinese characteristics. By the end of September 2021, there were 286 laws, more than 600 administrative regulations, 1 supervisory regulation and more than 12,000 local regulations in force in China. A socialist legal system with Chinese characteristics has been formed and constantly improved and developed, with the Constitution as the core, the laws of many legal departments such as the relevant laws of the Constitution, civil law and commercial law, administrative law, economic law, social law, criminal law, procedural laws related to litigation and non-litigation as the backbone, and composed of laws, administrative regulations, supervisory regulations, local regulations and other legal norms at multiple levels.

As for good governance, a prominent feature of socialism with Chinese characteristics entering the new era lies in the integrated construction of a country ruled by law, a government ruled by law and a society ruled by law.

A country ruled by law is the goal of the building of the rule of law. On the basis of the general goal of comprehensively promoting the rule of law put forward by the Fourth Plenary Session of the 18th CCCPC, the CCCPC issued *the Plan on Developing the Rule of Law in China (2020–2025)*. The Plan further details and clarifies the overall goal of building a country ruled by law, and stresses that to achieve this goal, we should achieve scientific, complete and unified legal norms, fair and efficient law enforcement and judicial authority, effectively restrict and supervise the operation of power, fully respect and guarantee the legitimate rights and interests of the people, universally establish the belief in the rule of law, and comprehensively build a country, government and society ruled by law. The plan proposes that by 2025, the system and mechanism of the Party's leadership in comprehensively ruling the country by law will be more perfect, the socialist legal system with Chinese characteristics with the Constitution as the core will be more complete, the government governance system with clear responsibilities and administration according to law will be more perfect, the judicial power operation mechanism with mutual cooperation and mutual restriction will be more scientific and effective, the construction of a society ruled by law will make significant progress, and the system of laws and regulations within the Party will be more perfect, and the socialist legal system with Chinese characteristics will have taken the initial shape. By 2035, The rule of law for the country, the government, and society will be comprehensively in place and the rights of the people to participate and to develop as equals will be adequately protected. We will have modernized the governance system and capacity. This is the first special plan on the building of China under the rule of law since the founding of new China. It is the general blueprint, road map and management chart for comprehensively promoting the building of China under the rule of law during the 14th Five-Year Plan period and is of great significance.

To promote the rule of law in an all-round way, the building of a government ruled by law is the key task and the major project. In December 2015, the CCCPC and the State Council issued the *Implementation Outline for Building a Law-Based Government (2015–2020)*. The outline proposes that, through unremitting efforts, China is committed to building a well-functioning, open and fair, clean and efficient, law-based government with integrity. It is emphasized that to build a government under the rule of law, we must adhere to the leadership of the CPC, adhere to the people's dominant position, adhere to the principle that all are equal before the law, adhere to the integration of the rule of law with the rule of virtue, adhere to basing our work on the prevailing conditions in China, adhere to the principle of exercising governance in accordance with the Constitution and other laws, streamlining administration and delegating power, and bring all government work in line with the rule of law, and combine the building of a government under the rule of law with the efforts to cultivate a law-based, innovative, clean and service-oriented government.

It is the basic requirement of a government ruled by law to fully perform government functions according to law. In March 2015, the general office of the CCCPC and the general office of the State Council issued the *Guiding Opinions on the Implementation of the Power List System of Local Government Departments at all levels*, requiring that all administrative functions and powers exercised by local government departments at all levels and their basis, exercise subject, operation process, corresponding responsibilities, etc. be clearly listed in the form of a list, published to the public and subject to social supervision. According to the requirements, China has fully published a list of local government powers and responsibilities. In January 2016, the general office of the State Council issued the *Pilot Plan for the Preparation of the List of Partial Powers and Responsibilities of the State Council*, which determined to carry out the Pilot in The NDRC, the Ministry of Civil Affairs, the Ministry of Justice, the Ministry of Culture, the General Administration of Customs, the State Administration of Taxation and the China Securities Regulatory Commission (CSRC), so as to prepare for the preparation of the list of powers and responsibilities in the next step. By the end of 2017, items for administrative approval had decreased by 44 percent, and the licensing of matters not covered by the Law on Administrative Licensing had been completely phased out.

In addition, opinions including the following have been issued one after another: *Guiding Opinions on Deepening the Reform of Urban Law Enforcement System and Improving Urban Management, Decisions on Comprehensively Promoting Government Transparency, Opinions on the Implementation of the Legal Adviser System and the Government Lawyer Company Lawyer System, Provisions that Party and Government Leaders should Assume the Main Responsibility for the Work of Advancing the Rule of Law, Pilot Program to Implement the System of Public Notice of Administrative Law Enforcement,* the *System of Recording the Whole Process of Law Enforcement,* and the *System of Legal Audit of Major Law Enforcement Decisions, Guiding Opinions on the Full Implementation of the Administrative Normative Document Legality Audit Mechanism, Notice on Enacting Normative Documents and Supervising and Managing the Implementation of such Documents,* the *Provisional Regulations on Major Administrative Decision-making Procedures, Regulations on the*

Building of the Rule of Law Government and Responsibility for the Implementation of the Work of Inspection, Opinions on the Carrying out Demonstration Programs to Build the Rule of Law Government and etc,. China continues to make efforts to improve the system of administration according to law, promote the scientific, democratic and rule of law administrative decision-making, adhere to strict, fair and civilized law enforcement, strengthen the constraints and supervision of administrative power, effectively resolve social conflicts and disputes in accordance with the law, and comprehensively improve the ability of government staff to think and administer according to the rule of law, to promote the building of the rule of law government. By 2020, the goals and tasks set in the *Implementation Outline for Building a Law-based Government (2015–2020)* has been basically completed.

In order to further promote the building of a government under the rule of law, in August 2021, the CCCPC and the State Council issued the Outline for Building a Law-Based Government (2021–2025). The new outline sets a new goal for the construction of a government under the rule of law. It proposes that by 2025, government behavior will be fully integrated into the track of the rule of law, the government governance system with clear responsibilities and administration according to law will be increasingly improved, the administrative law enforcement system and mechanism will be basically improved, the quality and efficiency of administrative law enforcement will be greatly improved, the ability to respond to emergencies will be significantly enhanced, the construction of a government under the rule of law at all levels in all regions will be coordinated, and more regions will take the lead in making breakthroughs. This will lay a solid foundation for basically building a country, government and society ruled by law by 2035. This is a new programmatic document for the building of a government under the rule of law issued after the Outline in 2015. It is the road map and management chart for comprehensively promoting the building of a government under the rule of law during the 14th Five-Year Plan period. It is of great significance to better play the demonstration and driving role of the building of a government under the rule of law in the development of a country and a society under the rule of law.

A society ruled by law is a fundamental project and a fundamental move to comprehensively rule the country according to law. In April 2016, the CCCPC and the State Council forwarded the *Seventh Five-Year Plan (2016–2020) of the Publicity Department of the CCCPC and the Ministry of Justice on the Promotion and Education of the Rule of Law among Citizens* and began to implement the Seventh Five-Year Plan for increasing public knowledge of the law. The target of the publicity and education of the rule of law is all citizens who have the ability to receive education, with emphasis on leading cadres and young people. In the same month, the Organization Department of the CCCPC and other four departments jointly issued the *Opinions on Improving the System of Study and Use of Law by state staff*, making comprehensive arrangements for improving the system of studying and using law by state functionaries, to make a comprehensive deployment on the study and use of law by state functionaries. In May 2017, the general office of the CCCPC and the general office of the State Council issued the *Opinions on Implementing the Guideline on Adopting a Responsibility System for State Organs with the Principle that Law-Enforcing Departments Are Responsible for Publicizing the Law*, which proposed the establishment of a responsibility system for law popularization, requiring state organs to take law popularization as the basic work to promote the construction of the rule of law, formulate their own plans for law popularization, annual plans for law popularization and a list of responsibilities for law popularization, establish and improve the leadership and working institutions for law popularization. The specific responsible departments and personnel were clearly defined, and it was made sure that officials, though small in number, play a key role in implementing the rule of law. During the "Seventh Five-Year Plan" period of law publicizing, legal education was incorporated into the national education system. The state has formulated the Outline of Education on the Rule of Law for young people to strengthen the "Trinity" pattern of education on the rule of law among schools, families and society. By 2020, the Seventh Five-Year Plan for spreading public knowledge about law has been successfully completed.

In December 2020, the CCCPC issued the *Outline for Building a Law-Based Society (2020–2025)*, which proposed that by 2025, the implementation of the "Eighth Five-Year Plan" for increasing public knowledge of law will be completed, the concept of the rule of law will be deeply rooted in the hearts of the people, the system and norms in the social field will be more sound, the core socialist values will be integrated into the rule of law construction and social governance, and the results will be remarkable. The legitimate rights and interests of citizens, legal persons and other organizations will be effectively protected, and the level of social governance will be significantly better. We will create a lively situation in building a society under the rule of law that conforms to the national conditions, reflects the characteristics of the times, and is satisfactory to the people, and lay a solid foundation for basically building a society under the rule of law by 2035. In June 2021, the CCCPC and the State Council forwarded the *Eighth Five-Year Plan*

(2021–2025) of the Publicity Department of the CCCPC and the Ministry of Justice on the Promotion and Education of the Rule of Law among Citizens and began to implement the Eighth Five-Year Plan for increasing public knowledge of the law.

(4) Promote the Reform of the Judicial System.

Judicial justice is the lifeline of the rule of law. The Third Plenary Session of the 18th CCCPC put forward the task of judicial system reform, which involves ensuring the independent and fair exercise of judicial power and procuratorial power according to law, improving the operation mechanism of judicial power, and improving the judicial protection system for human rights. The Fourth Plenary Session of the 18th CCCPC emphasizes we should ensure fair justice and improve judicial credibility, and further clarifies the reform tasks in six aspects, including improving the system to ensure the independent and impartial exercise of judicial and procuratorial powers according to law, improving the allocation of judicial powers and responsibilities, promoting strict administration of justice, ensuring the participation of the people in the administration of justice, strengthening judicial protection of human rights, and strengthening supervision over judicial activities.

The reform of the judicial system, with the focus on enforcement of judicial accountability has been gradually promoted. China has reformed the category-based management of judicial personnel and job security for the judicial profession, promoted the unification of the management of staff, funds and properties of courts and procuratorates at and below the provincial level; improved the operation mechanism of judicial power, and improved the responsibility system for handling cases by the presiding judge and the collegiate bench, by which the judges hand down verdicts and the collegiate bench is responsible for carrying them out; set up circuit courts for the Supreme People's Court; explored setting up people's courts and people's procuratorates across administrative boundaries; explored the system of public interest lawsuits filed by procuratorial organs; further reformed the trial-centered litigation system. The adjudication documents of courts at all levels are available for public supervision on the China Judgment Online Website, and the Supreme People's Procuratorate has established a public system for legal documents such as decisions on non-filing, non-arrest, and non-prosecution; etc.

China has also strengthened the supervision of the implementation of laws to eliminate interference in law enforcement and judicial activities. In March 2015, the general office of the CCCPC and the general office of the State Council issued the *Regulations on Record, Notification and Accountability of Leading Cadres' Interference in Judicial Activities and Handling of Specific Cases*, which drew a red line for leading cadres' interference in judicial activities. In November of that year, the Central Political and Legal Affairs Commission publicly announced five typical cases of leading cadres interfering in judicial activities, intervening in the handling of specific cases, and interfering in cases involving internal personnel of judicial organs. Since then, relevant cases have been reported regularly every year, and a record, notification and accountability system for leading cadres to intervene in judicial activities and handle specific cases has been established.

Unjust, false and wrong cases are the focus of social attention. Correcting unjust, false and wrong cases is an important test of the achievements of the judicial system reform and a vivid reflection of the continuous strengthening of judicial justice. From 2013 to 2018, the people's court corrected 46 major criminal wrongs, including the Nie Shubin case, the Hugjiltu case, and the Zhang's uncle and nephew case through trial supervision procedures, involving 94 people, boosting the confidence of the whole society in judicial justice.

In November 2020, the central work conference on comprehensively administering the country according to law systematically summarized the historical achievements made in comprehensively administering the country according to law since the 18th National Congress of the CPC, emphasizing that the overall pattern of comprehensively administering the country according to law has basically taken shape, and significant progress has been made in the practice of comprehensively administering the country according to law. Since the 18th National Congress, the system of socialist rule of law with Chinese characteristics has constantly been improved, solid progress has been made in advancing the rule of law in China, the rule of law has played a greater role in consolidating foundations, ensuring stable expectations, and delivering long-term benefits, and the Party's ability to lead and govern the country through law-based methods has been notably enhanced.

4.2.4 Promoting Defense and Military Development in All Respects

(1) Clearly Define the Goal of Building a Strong Army in the New Era and Strengthen Political Building of the Army

A strong country must have a strong military, as only then can it guarantee the security of the nation. During a meeting with the leading cadres of the troops in Guangzhou above the division level in December, 2012, Xi Jinping proposed for the first time "the strong military dream." He stressed that, a strong military dream, to the military, is to make our forces strong. To achieve these aims we must strive both to enrich the country and build a strong national defense and powerful military. With this as the starting point, Xi Jinping made a series of important statements around national defense and military development. The 19th National Congress of the CPC summarized it as Xi Jinping's thinking on strengthening the armed forces, which is the fundamental leadership and scientific guidance for national defense and military development in the new era.

At the end of the year of 2012, Xi Jinping stressed at an enlarged meeting of the CMC that we should strive to build a people's army that follows the command of the CPC, is capable of winning battles, and has a fine style of work. In March, 2013, during the First Session of the 12th NPC, Xi Jinping made it clear that building such forces is the Party's goal for developing the military under the new circumstances. In February, 2016, Xi Jinping further put forward the requirements of achieving the goal of building the military and building the people's forces into world-class forces at an enlarged meeting of the CMC. In the new era, China has also formulated a new "three-step" strategy for the modernization of national defense and the armed forces, which aims to achieve the centenary goal of building the armed forces by 2027, basically realize the modernization of national defense and the armed forces by 2035, and comprehensively build a world-class armed forces by the middle of this century.

In 2014, the CMC formulated China's Military Strategic Guideline in the New Era. This guideline adheres to active defense, overall planning for war preparation and cessation, safeguarding rights and stability, deterrence and combat, war operations and the use of military forces in peacetime, and made winning local wars in the information age the focal point in preparation for military struggle, and strengthen military preparedness with emphasis on the sea, thus enhancing the enthusiasm and initiative of strategic guidance.

In order to implement the goal of strengthening the army in the new era, from October 30 to November 2, 2014, the first political work conference of the armed forces in the new century was held in Gutian Town, Shanghang County, Fujian Province. Xi Jinping made it clear in the conference that political work is the lifeline of the military, and the contemporary theme of our military's political work is to focus on realizing the Chinese Dream of national rejuvenation, and provide a solid political guarantee for achieving the Party's goal of building the military. The political work conference of the armed forces is an extremely important meeting held at an important juncture in the development of the Party, the state and the army, and it has opened a new journey in ideological and political building of the Party and the army. The CCCPC forwarded the *Decision on Issues Relating to the Military Political Work in the New Era* in December 2014. Since the end of 2014, the whole army has carried out in-depth four rectifications of rectifying ideology, personnel, organization, and discipline, as well as major inspection of cadre work and financial inspection and rectification. It has promoted political rectification and training in the spirit of the Yan'an Rectification Movement to govern the military with strict discipline in every respect and made resolute decisions to enforce political discipline within the military. In February 2015, the CMC formulated the *Overall Deployment Plan for the Implementation of the Spirit of the Political Work Conference of the Armed Forces*, and issued to the whole army the general plan and mission statement for the implementation of the general strategy of raising political awareness in the military.

The implementation of chairman assuming overall responsibility by the CMC is a fundamental system and a fundamental form of realization for upholding the Party's absolute leadership over the people's army. Comprehensively and thoroughly implementing this system is an inevitable requirement for raising political awareness in the military. In April 2014, the CMC issued the *Opinions on the Implementation of the CMC Chairman Responsibility System and the Establishment and Improvement of Relevant Working Mechanisms*, establishing the "three mechanisms" of request for instructions, supervision and inspection, and information services, and promoting the institutionalization of the requirements of the CMC Chairman responsibility system. In November 2017, the CMC issued the *Opinions on the Comprehensive and In-depth Implementation of the CMC Chairman Responsibility System* to promote the comprehensive and in-depth implementation of the CMC Chairman responsibility system.

(2) Deepen the Reform of National Defense and the Armed Forces and Strengthen Military Training and Combat Readiness

Reform is the only way to strengthen the army. In November 2013, the Third Plenary Session of the 18th CCCPC included the deepening of national defense and military reform as a separate part in the decision of the plenary session, which was incorporated into the overall layout of comprehensively deepening reform and elevated to the will and state behavior of the whole Party. In July 2015, Xi

Jinping presided over the Standing Meeting of the CMC and the Standing Committee Meeting of the Political Bureau of the CCCPC, respectively, to consider and finalize the *General Plan for Deepening Reform of National Defense and the Military*, forming a set of reform designs that address deep-rooted contradictions, have major innovative breakthroughs and are distinctive to the people's army. In November 2015, the reform work conference of the CMC was held to make overall arrangements for deepening the reform of national defense and the military. After the meeting, the CMC issued the *Opinions on Deepening the Reform of National Defense and the Armed Forces*, which clearly defined the guiding ideology, basic principles and overall objectives of the reform. Starting from the end of 2015, the reform of the leadership and command system took the lead, focusing on breaking down institutional obstacles. Since the end of 2016, the reform of scale structure and strength composition has been pushed forward, focusing on solving structural contradictions. By the 19th National Congress of the CPC, historic breakthroughs had been made in the reform of national defense and the military, forming a new pattern in which the CMC was in charge of general affairs, the theater was in charge of war, and the branches of the armed forces were in charge of construction. This represents a revolutionary restructuring of the organization and the services of the people's armed forces. the people's army had been revolutionized.

Law-based governance of the military and strict enforcement of discipline is an important part of the people's army's deepening reform. In October 2014, the Fourth Plenary Session of the 18th CCCPC incorporated law-based governance of the military and strict enforcement of discipline into the overall layout of a comprehensive framework for promoting the rule of law. In December, at an enlarged meeting of the CMC, Xi Jinping stressed that law-based governance of the military and strict enforcement of discipline is the basic strategy. The more modernized and informationized the military is, the more the rule of law is required. It is necessary to facilitate a fundamental change in the command and control of the military in accordance with the requirements of the rule of law and strive to achieve "three fundamental changes," that is, a fundamental change from relying solely on administrative orders to administering according to law, a fundamental change from relying solely on habits and experience to relying on laws, regulations and systems to carry out work, and a fundamental change from the assault and movement style of work to acting according to rules and regulations. In February 2015, the CMC issued the *Decision on Further Promoting Law-based Governance of the Military and Strict Enforcement of Discipline Under the New Situation*, making comprehensive arrangements for strengthening the rule of law in the military. In November 2015, the reform work conference of the CMC made a decision to stop the armed forces from providing paid services to foreign countries. In February 2016, the CMC issued the *Notice on the Complete Cessation of Paid Service Activities of the Armed Forces and the Armed Police Force*, which clearly planned to stop all paid service activities of the armed forces and the armed police force step by step in about three years. In May 2017, the *Regulations on Military Legislation* came into force, providing a legal basis and basic compliance for the military legislative work in the new era.

We must build strong armed forces through science, technology as well as talents. In 2016, the Science and Technology Commission of the CMC was established. In 2017, the Academy of Military Sciences, the National Defense University and the National University of Defense Technology were adjusted and established. In 2021, the CMC held a talent work conference. Subsequently, it issued the *Decision on Strengthening the Work of Military Talents in the New Era*, and vigorously implemented the strategy of strengthening the military with talents in the new era.

Proceeding from the needs of actual combat, the people's army has paid great attention to practical combat oriented military training and adhered to the principle that training should be guided by combat, combat should be promoted by training, and combat and training should be consistent. In March 2014, the CMC issued the *Opinions on Improving the Combat Ability of Military Training* and made systematic deployment. In the same month, a leading group for the military training supervision of the armed forces was established to supervise and inspect the military training. At the end of 2015, the CMC and the Theater Commands, the theater, military branches and the armed police forces set up training supervision departments, formally establishing the military training supervision system. In November 2016, the CMC issued the *Interim Provisions on Enhancing Simulation-based Training*, which put forward rigid measures and rigid norms for the implementation of practical military training. The accountability of units and individuals with lax military training has promoted the improvement of the actual combat training ability of the troops. In November 2020, the CMC issued the *PLA Joint Operations Program (Trial)*, which promoted the PLA to upgrade its joint operations capability to a new stage. In February 2021, the CMC issued the *Decision on Building a New Military Training System* to accelerate the construction of a new military training system.

In the new era, under the strong leadership of the CPC, the people's army has achieved a revolutionary restructuring on the whole, and the unity between the military and the government, the military and the people has been further consolidated. China's national defense strength and economic strength have been improved simultaneously, and the construction of an integrated national strategic system and capability has been accelerated.

4.2.5 Continue to Promote an All-Out Effort to Enforce Strict Party Discipline

(1) Making Plans and Arrangements for Ensuring Full and Strict Governance over the Party

Since the reform and opening-up, great achievements have been made in Party building. The Party has enhanced its governing capabilities, preserved and improved its pioneering nature and purity, and strengthened and improved its leadership. However, in view of the need to manage changes in domestic and international conditions, and to accomplish its historic mission, there is still considerable room for our Party to improve its art of leadership, governing capacity and organization, and the quality, competence, and practices of its members and officials. In addition, since the reform and opening-up, previously lax and weak governance has brought many problems. However, there have remained many problems within the Party with respect to upholding its leadership such as a lack of clear awareness and vigorous action as well as weak, ineffective, diluted, and marginalized efforts in implementation. There is a serious lack of political conviction among some Party members and officials, misconduct in the selection and appointment of personnel in some localities and government departments, a blatant culture of pointless formalities, bureaucratism, hedonism, and extravagance, and a prevalence of privilege-seeking attitudes and behavior. Political and economic problems are intertwined and the seriousness of corruption is alarming. These issues damaged the Party's image and prestige and severely undermined relations between the Party and the people and between officials and the people, arousing the discontent and indignation of many Party members, officials, and members of the public.

Faced with the above problems, in November 15, 2012, Xi Jinping, who was elected to his new role as the General Secretary pointed out at the press conference by members of the Standing Committee of the Political Bureau of the 18th CCCPC. "A happy life comes from hard work. Our responsibility is to bring together and lead the whole Party and the people of all ethnic groups to free their minds, carry out reform and opening-up, further unfetter and develop the productive forces, solve the people's problems in work and life, and resolutely pursue common prosperity.

In January, 2016, at the speech at the Sixth Plenary Session of the 18th CCDI of the CPC, Xi Jinping systematically expounded on the connotations and requirements of ensuring full and strict governance over the Party. He pointed out that the core of ensuring full and strict governance over the Party is to strengthen the Party's leadership. The foundation is comprehensive, the key is strict, and the core is governance. "Comprehensive" means managing and administering the whole Party. It is oriented to more than 87 million Party members and more than 4.3 million Party organizations, covering all fields, aspects and departments of Party building. The focus is on grasping the "critical minority." We need to integrate the requirement of strict governance throughout all processes in the running of the Party, carrying out a genuine, brave, and constant effort to govern the Party. "Governance" means that from the Party Central Committee to the provincial, city and county Party committees, from the Party groups (Party committees) of the central ministries and commissions, state organs and departments to the grass-roots Party branches, all should shoulder the main responsibility. The Party committee secretary should regard doing a good job in Party building as his own duty and must assume the responsibility; discipline inspection commissions at all levels should shoulder the responsibility of supervision, dare exercise oversight, enforce discipline, and ensure accountability.

In October 2016, the Sixth Plenary Session of the 18th CCCPC studied the issue of ensuring full and strict governance over the Party, and made new major arrangements for strengthening Party building under the new situation. The plenary session deliberated and adopted the *Regulations for Political Activities Within the Party in the New Era* and the *Regulations of the CPC on Internal Scrutiny*, which provide basic guidelines for the serious intra-party political life and the improvement of the intra-Party supervision system under the new situation, and provide important institutional guarantees for an all-out effort to enforce strict Party discipline.

In October, 2017, the report to the 19th National Congress of the CPC has included the following content into the "It makes clear that the defining feature of socialism with Chinese characteristics is the leadership of the Communist Party of China; the greatest strength of the system of socialism with Chinese characteristics is the leadership of the Communist Party of China; the Party is the highest force for political leadership. It sets forth the general requirements for Party building in the new era and underlines the importance of political work in Party building. It sets forth the general requirements for Party building in the new era and underlines the importance of political work in Party building. It considered adherence to enforcing strict Party self-governance as one of the basic strategies for upholding and developing socialism with Chinese characteristics in the new era. The Congress also put forward the general guidelines for Party building in the new era. The general requirements for Party building for the new era have made a top-level design and comprehensive deployment for promoting Party building, and pointed out the way forward for upholding the Party's comprehensive leadership and improving the quality of Party building.

In January, 2018, at the opening ceremony of a study session on implementing Xi Jinping Thought on Socialism with Chinese Characteristics for a New Era, Xi Jinping put forward A New Great Project of Party Building in the New Era. From Mao Zedong's "great undertaking" of Party building to the "new great project" of Party building proposed by the Fourth Plenary Session of the 14th CCCPC to the "new great project of Party building in the new era" proposed by the Party Central Committee with Xi Jinping as the core, the CPC has deepened its understanding of self-revolution and reached an unprecedented new height in the new era.

In October 2019, the Fourth Plenary Session of the 19th CCCPC made important arrangements to uphold and improve the Party's leadership system, especially made important deployment on enforcing strict Party self-governance. Focusing on upholding and improving the Party's leadership system, the plenary session proposed to establish a system that remain true to our original aspiration and keeps the mission firmly in mind, improve various systems that firmly safeguard the CCCPC's authority and centralized, unified leadership, improve the Party's comprehensive leadership system, improve various systems that govern for the people and rely on the people, improve the system that improves the Party's governance ability and leadership, and improve the system of ensuring full and strict governance over the Party. The plenary session made a systematic exposition on improving the system of ensuring full and strict governance over the Party.

In November 2021, the Sixth Plenary Session of the 19th CCCPC summed up the major achievements in Party building in the past 100 years, especially the important achievements in upholding overall Party leadership and enforcing strict Party self-governance in the new era, and summarized the historical experience of the Party's struggle in the past 100 years, especially the experience of adhering to self-revolution in the past 100 years. It issued an important call to continue to the great new project of Party building in the new era on the new journey of realizing the second centenary goals, and pointed out the direction for further deepening an all-out effort to enforce strict Party discipline.

In the process of an all-out effort to enforce strict Party discipline, the Party Central Committee, with Xi Jinping as the core, has creatively put forward a series of new ideas and opinions and assertions around the major issue of the times: what kind of Marxist party to build for long-term governance and how to build a Marxist Party for long-term governance. In January 2022, Xi Jinping proposed the "six must insist" and "nine insist" at the Sixth plenary session of the 19th CCDI of the CPC. Among them, "six must insist" includes: we must adhere to the political construction of the party as the leader, adhere to the fundamental political direction of self-revolution; we must adhere to the ideological construction as the basic construction of the party, and harden the sharp ideological weapon of self-revolution; The need to persevere in implementing the Party Central Committee's Eight Rules, with strict discipline to rectify the style of work, to enrich the effective way of self-revolution; we must fight corruption and punish wrongdoing with firm resolve; we must insist on enhancing the political function and organizational cohesion of Party organizations, and forging officials that are bold and adept at struggle and courageous in self-revolution; we must adhere to the self-purification, self-completion, self-renovation, self-improvement system of institutional norms to provide institutional safeguards to promote the great self-revolution. The "nine insist" are: adhere to the centralized and unified leadership of the Party Central Committee, uphold and strengthen overall Party leadership and ensure that the Party exercises effective self-supervision and practices strict self-governance in every respect, insist on taking the party's political construction as the command, unswervingly adhere to the practice of rigorous self-governance, insisting on keeping our shoulder to the wheel of every task to improve the work style, insist on continuing to combat corruption with zero tolerance, insist on taking resolute measures to punish and rectify improper conduct and corruption that harm people's interests, insist on putting the spotlight on leading officials, the "key few," insist on improving the supervisory systems of the Party and the state to form a comprehensive coverage, permanent and long-lasting supervision synergy. The "six must insist" and "nine insist" clarify the core meaning of General Secretary Xi Jinping's strategic thought of the Party's self-revolution, marking a new height of our Party's understanding of the regularity of the construction of long-term ruling Marxist parties, with great theoretical and practical significance. Under the guidance of this thinking, various arrangements for ensuring full and strict governance over the Party were carried out in an orderly manner, and great new project of strengthening the Party in new era was solidly advanced.

(2) Uphold and Strengthen the Overall Leadership Role of the CCCPC
In December 2013, Xi Jinping pointed out at the Central Economic Work Conference that socialism with Chinese characteristics has many features and characteristics, but the defining feature is adherence to the leadership of the CPC. On July 1, 2016, at the ceremony marking the 95th anniversary of the founding of the CPC, Xi Jinping noted, the most essential feature of the socialist society with Chinese characteristics is the leadership of the CPC. The greatest advantage of the socialist system of China is also the leadership of the CPC. In October 2017, the report of the 19th National Congress of the CPC further mentioned "the defining feature" and "the greatest advantage" together with "the highest force for political leadership." It made clear that the leadership of the CPC is the defining feature of socialism with Chinese characteristics and the greatest strength of the system of socialism with Chinese characteristics, and that the Party is the highest force for political leadership. It stressed that the Party exercises overall leadership over all areas of endeavor in every part of the country. This has theoretically clarified the issue of overall Party leadership.

In order to strengthen the overall Party leadership, the CCCPC has further improved the relevant systems and mechanisms to ensure that the ruling party plays a leading role in various organizations. In terms of leadership over non-Party organizations, in June 2015, the CCCPC issued the *Regulations on the Work of the Party Group of the CPC (for Trial Implementation)*, which is the first special inner-party regulation on the work of the Party group of the CPC, strengthening the leadership of the ruling party over the non-Party organizations. In 2019, the CCCPC revised this regulation to further improve the relevant systems and mechanisms. In terms of leadership over SOEs, in July 2015, the general office of the CCCPC issued *Several Opinions on Upholding Party Leadership and Strengthening Party Building in Deepening the Reform of SOEs*. In October 2016, the National Conference on Party building in SOEs was held to make systematic arrangements for solving the problems of weak, ineffective, diluted, and marginalized Party leadership and Party building in SOEs. Subsequently, the *Regulations of the CPC on the Work of Grassroots Organizations of SOEs (for Trial Implementation)* and the *Opinions on Strengthening the Party's Leadership in Improving Corporate Governance of Central Enterprises* were successively issued, further strengthening the leadership of the ruling party over SOEs. In terms of leadership over colleges and universities, in October 2014, the general office of the CCCPC issued the *Implementation Opinions on Upholding and Improving the President Taking the Overall Responsibility System Under the Leadership of the Party Committee of Institutions of Higher Learning*. Since then, the introduction of documents such as the *Opinions on Strengthening and Improving the Ideological and Political Work in Colleges and Universities under the New Situation* and the revision of inner-Party regulations such as the *Regulations of the CPC on the Work of Grassroots Organizations in Colleges and Universities* have further strengthened the leadership of the CPC over colleges and universities. In terms of leadership over social groups, in January 2015, the CCCPC issued the *Opinions on Strengthening and Improving the Work of the Party's Social Groups*. In the same month, the first meeting of the Party's social groups was held to promote the implementation of the opinions and strengthen and improve the Party's leadership over social groups. In terms of the leadership of local Party committees over their own localities, in December 2015, the CCCPC issued the newly revised *Regulations on the Work of Local Commissions of the CPC*, further improving the institutional basis for local Party committees to play the core role of leadership and improving the operation mechanism of local Party committees. In addition, a large number of important documents have also been issued or revised one after another, effectively upholding and improving the overall party leadership in all aspects. The documents include: *Regulations on the Rural Work of the CPC, Regulations on the United Front Work of the CPC, Regulations on the Work of the Socialist Academy, Regulations on the Political and Legal Work of the CPC, Regulations on the Administrative Organization of the CPC, Regulations on the Publicity Work of the CPC, Regulations on the Work of the CPC Leading the National Security, Regulations on the Central Ecological Environment Protection Supervision Work*, and *Regulations on the Party Building of the CPC, Regulations Concerning Political Work of the Army*.

To uphold and strengthen the overall Party leadership, the most important thing is to safeguard the authority of the CCCPC's authority and centralized, unified leadership. In January 2014, at the Third Plenary Session of the 18th CCDI of the CPC, Xi Jinping pointed out: the Central Committee, the Central Political Bureau and the Standing Committee of the Central Political Bureau are the core of the Party's leadership and decision-making. The speech clearly defined the connotation of the "Party Central Committee," that is, the Central Committee, the Political Bureau of the Central Committee and its Standing Committee, and put forward the basic requirements for safeguarding the authority of the CCCPC's authority and centralized, unified leadership. On January 16, 2015, the Standing Committee of the Political Bureau of the CCCPC specially hear the work reports of the Standing Committee of the NPC, the State Council, the National Committee of the Chinese people's Political Consultative Conference, the Supreme People's Court and the Supreme People's Procuratorate. The Standing Committee of the Political Bureau of the CCCPC hear the work reports of the party leading groups of relevant departments, which is an important institutional arrangement to ensure the centralized and unified leadership of the Party Central Committee, which stands as a shining example. In September 2020, the CCCPC issued the *Regulations on the Work of the CCCPC*, taking "ensuring Party leadership over all work and ensuring the centralized and unified leadership of the CCCPC" as the first principle that the Central Committee must grasp in carrying out its work, and emphasizing that the Central Committee, the Political Bureau of the CCCPC and the Standing Committee of the Political Bureau of the CCCPC are the brain and center of the Party's organizational system. The *Regulations* focus on strengthening the work of the Central Committee, and make comprehensive provisions on the leadership position, leadership system, leadership authority, leadership style, decision-making and deployment, and self-building of the CCCPC. It provides a basis for ensuring the centralized and unified leadership of the CCCPC over the Party and state undertakings. The CCCPC has also continued to improve the institutional mechanisms for maintaining centralized and unified leadership, especially strengthening the development of decision-making, discussion and coordination institutions. This is an important institutional arrangement to ensure that the CCCPC leads major work. For example, on the basis of the existing institutions, the Central Committee for Deepening Overall Reform (later changed to the Central Committee for Deepening Overall Reform), the National Security Commission, the Central Leading Group for Cyberspace Affairs (later changed to the Central Cyberspace Affairs Commission), the Central Military-Civilian Integration Commission, and the Commission for Overall Law-based Governance of the CCCPC have been established. The establishment of these decision-making, discussion and coordination bodies plays a vital role in strengthening the leadership and overall coordination of the CCCPC on relevant work.

The core of the Party is the crucial element for maintaining the Central Committee's authority and centralized, unified leadership. In October 2016, the Sixth Plenary Session of the 18th CCCPC has established Comrade Xi Jinping's core position on the Party Central Committee and in the Party as a whole. The plenum called on all party comrades to unite closely around the Party Central Committee with Comrade Xi Jinping at its core, enhance their political integrity, develop a better understanding of the general picture, and unswervingly safeguard the CCCPC's authority and centralized, unified leadership. In October, 2017, the Political Bureau of the CCCPC adopted the *Regulations of the Political Bureau on Upholding and Strengthening the Centralized, Unified Leadership of the Central Committee*, requiring the Political Bureau to maintain political integrity, think in big-picture terms, follow the leadership core, and keep in alignment with the central Party leadership, and firmly uphold General Secretary Xi Jinping as the core of the CPCCC and the whole Party. The document also stipulates that all comrades of the Political Bureau of the CCCPC report in writing to the CCCPC and General Secretary Xi Jinping once a year, which has become an important institutional arrangement. In November 2021, the Sixth Plenary Session of the 19th CCCPC put forward "Two Establishment" and stressed: the Party has established Comrade Xi Jinping's core position on the Party Central Committee and in the Party as a whole, and defined the guiding role of Xi Jinping Thought on Socialism with Chinese Characteristics for a New Era. This reflects the common will of the Party, the armed forces, and Chinese people of all ethnic groups, and is of decisive significance for advancing the cause of the Party and the country in the new era and for driving forward the historic process of national rejuvenation.[77] The "two establishment" has further highlighted the importance of maintaining the core, which is an important achievement and valuable experience in ensuring full and strict governance over the Party.

(3) In Some Sectors Misconduct and Corruption Are Still a Common
Since the 18th National Congress of the CPC, the CCCPC with Comrade Xi Jinping at its core has incorporated exercising full and strict governance over the

Party into its comprehensive strategy, started from improving the work conduct and focused on implementing the eight-point decision on improving Party and government conduct. In December 2012, just over half a month after the 18th National Congress of the CPC, the Political Bureau of the CCCPC held a meeting to adopt adopted *Eight Rules to Improve the Party's Conduct and its Ties with the People* (hereinafter referred as the *Rules*). The *Rules* put forward clear requirements for comrades of the Political Bureau of the CCCPC in eight aspects, including carrying out more investigations and studies, improving the organization of meetings, improving the style of writing, standardizing overseas visits, improving security work, improving news reports, strict manuscript publication, and practicing economy. In October 2017, the first meeting of the Political Bureau of the CCCPC after the 19th National Congress of the CPC put improving the work conduct on the agenda and reviewed the *Implementation Rules of the Political Bureau of the CCCPC for Eight-Point Decision on Improving Party and Government Conduct*. According to the new situations and problems encountered in the implementation of Eight-Point Decision on Improving Party and Government Conduct, the rules for implementation have further standardized, refined and improved the contents of carrying out more investigations and studies, improving the organization of meetings, improving the style of writing, standardizing overseas visits, improving security work, improving news reports, strict manuscript publication, and practicing economy.

Xi Jinping has always conducted himself in an exemplary fashion, taken the lead in improving his conduct, and kept his promise to implement the eight-point decision on improving Party and government conduct. According to the deployment and arrangement of the CCCPC, discipline inspection organs at all levels regard the supervision and implementation of the spirit of the eight-point decision on improving Party and government conduct as a regular work. At the Dragon Boat Festival, they pay attention to the purchase of zongzi and other festival gifts with public funds, at the Mid Autumn Festival, at the Spring Festival, they pay attention to the purchase of moon cakes and other festival gifts with public funds, and at the Spring Festival, they pay attention to the purchase of firecrackers and other new year's products with public funds. They also always maintain a tough stance in oversight, taking immediate action to investigate and deal with related issues and prevent minor wrongdoings from growing into major ones. In August 2013, the Discipline Inspection Commission of the CCCPC established and implemented the monthly report system, followed by weekly briefings and public exposure of typical problems, which formed a strong deterrent force. Between the 18th and 19th National Congress of the CPC, 176,100 cases of spiritual problems violating the eight-point decision on improving Party and government conduct were investigated and dealt with, 239,000 Party members and cadres were dealt with, and 128,000 of them were given Party and government disciplinary sanctions. On average, about 140 people were dealt with every day. The eight-point decision have endeavored to improve the work style and government discipline, driving the overall change of Party conduct and social morality. A telephone survey of public opinion conducted by the National Bureau of Statistics in June 2017 showed that 94.8% of the respondents affirmed the effectiveness of the eight-point decision on improving Party and government conduct formulated and implemented by the CCCPC with Comrade Xi Jinping at its core.

In the process of implementing the eight-point decision and carrying out work style improvement, the CCCPC has gradually focused on the "four forms of decadence," namely formalism, bureaucracy, hedonism and extravagance.

According to the deployment of the 18th National Congress of the CPC, the whole party began to carry out the campaign to educate party members about the mass line in May 2013. The educational practice activities focused on the "Four Malfeasances" which refer to going through the motions, excessive bureaucracy, self-indulgence, and extravagance. Through comprehensive examinations, over-hauls, and clean-ups, these efforts aim to halt the spread of these detrimental practices. Through educational practice activities, more than 586,000 meetings were canceled in various regions and departments, with a decrease of 24.6%; more than 386,000 cases of damage to the interests of the masses were investigated and dealt with; 663 "image projects" and "political achievements projects" were stopped; problems such as "naked officials," "freeload," "collecting bribes" and shopping cards, participating in high price training, and Party and government leading cadres taking part-time jobs in enterprises have been rectified.

Since the 19th National Congress of the CPC, the CCCPC has insisted on promoting the comprehensive and strict management of the Party by rectifying the "Four Malfeasances." Formalism and bureaucracy have been put in a prominent position in the "Four Malfeasances." In September 2018, the General Office of the Discipline Inspection Commission of the CCCPC issued the *Opinions on Implementing the Spirit of General Secretary Xi Jinping's Important Instructions to Focus on Rectifying Formalism and Bureaucracy*, emphasizing that rectifying formalism and bureaucracy is an important political task, is the primary and long-term task of working ceaselessly to improve Party conduct and enforce Party discipline, and eliminating the "Four Malfeasances," and it should be placed in a more prominent position. In March 2019, the general office of the CCCPC issued the *Notice on Solving the Prominent Problems of Formalism and Reducing the Burden of Grassroots Units*, which clearly proposed that 2019 should be regarded as the "year of reducing the burden of grassroots units," and that the fight against formalism and bureaucracy should be an important part of the education on the theme of "remaining true to our original aspiration and keeping the mission firmly in mind" carried out by the whole party. In April 2020, the general office of the CCCPC issued the *Notice on Continuously Solving the Formalism Problems that Beset the Grassroots and Providing a Strong Style Guarantee for the Decisive Victory in Building Moderately Prosperous Society in an All-Round Way* to deepen and expand the work of burden reduction at the grassroots level. In 2021, the general office of the CCCPC issued the *Main Measures and Division of Labor Plan on Further Solving the Formalism Problem and Doing a Good Job in Reducing the Burden on the Grassroots in 2021*. It investigated and laid out the old formalism problems and new manifestations of transformation, and put forward solutions one by one. From 2019 to 2021, the number of inspection and assessment items of central and state organs was reduced from nearly 900 to 47 items listed in the plan, a decrease of 94.8%; at the provincial, district and municipal level, the number of items has been reduced from 12,700 to 1,187, a decrease of 90.6%, and important achievements have been made in relevant work.

If we say that the improvement of work style is the entry point for an all-out effort to enforce strict Party discipline, then the counter-corruption struggle is the breakthrough point for it. In the face of a period of time when the party corruption problem is in more serious situation, the CCCPC with Comrade Xi Jinping at its core has followed the principle that no refuge has been excluded from the scope, no ground left unturned, and no tolerance shown in the fight against corruption, with coordinated efforts to "hunt down tigers," "swat flies" and "chase foxes."

In the face of major and important corruption cases, we will not be soft hearted. From 2012 to 2017, the CCCPC seriously investigated and dealt with Zhou Yongkang, Bo Xilai, Guo Boxiong, Xu Caihou, Sun Zhengcai, Ling Jihua cases and other cases of serious violations of discipline and law. In addition, the CCCPC also investigated and dealt with the problems of systematic and corrupt practices in Shanxi, and seriously dealt with the Hengyang bribery case involving local elections in Hunan, a election bribery case in Nanchong, Sichuan Province, and the systematic election canvassing and bribery case in Liaoning Province. Since the 18th National Congress of the CPC, as of October 2021, the discipline inspection and supervision organs throughout the country have filed 4.078 million cases and 4.379 million people, including 484 senior officials, and 3.998 million people were given Party discipline and administrative sanctions.

Severely punish corruption around the masses. The CPC and the Chinese government attach great importance to solving the unhealthy tendencies and corruption problems that occur around the masses, focus on the areas of poverty alleviation, intensify the punishment of "small officials and big corruption," and seriously investigate and deal with such problems as embezzlement, withholding and sharing these out privately, favoritism of relatives and friends, creating false accounts for receiving state subsidies, forcible occupation and predatory behavior. In 2020, a total of 124,000 corruption and work style problems in the field of people's livelihood were investigated and dealt with, and 38,000 cases of criminal syndicate-related corruption and protection rackets were investigated and dealt with.

China has strengthened international cooperation against corruption, and organized a series of "Sky Net" operations. The CPC and the Chinese government have elevated the anti-corruption pursuit of fugitives and stolen goods to the national political and diplomatic level and included it in the overall deployment of counter-corruption work. The central and provincial counter-corruption coordination groups set up international fugitive and stolen goods recovery offices, issued red arrest warrants for 100 fugitives, and continuously organized the "Sky Net" operation. From 2014 to October 2020, 8,363 fugitives were brought back from more than 120 countries and regions, including 2,212 Party members and state functionaries, 357 people on the red notice list, and 54 on the list of 100 most-wanted fugitives, and illegal assets worth RMB 20.84 billion were recovered.

Thanks to the joint efforts of all CPC members, a strong momentum has been fostered in the anti-corruption campaign, with discipline deterrence showing initial results, institutional checks improving and the aversion to corruption growing, which formed a strong deterrent force in an all-out effort to enforce strict Party discipline.

(4) Take Raising Political Awareness Among Party Members as the Guide to Promote Various Constructions

It is the CPC's fine tradition and unique advantage to stress politics with a clear-cut stand. Since the 18th National Congress of the CPC, the Party Central Committee, with Comrade Xi Jinping at its core, has always put the principle of "stress politics with a clear-cut stand" in the first place in the process of promoting the strategic layout of an all-Out effort to enforce strict Party discipline. While emphasizing a clear-cut emphasis on politics, the CCCPC also keenly raised the Issue of political activities within the Party. In October 2016, the Sixth Plenary Session of the 18th CCCPC formulated the *Regulations for Political Activities Within the Party in the New Era*, which comprehensively standardized the seriousness of political activities within the Party and the purification of Intra-Party Political Ecology, and provided basic guidelines for strengthening and regulating political activities within the Party in the new period.

In October 2017, the report of the 19th National Congress of the CPC clearly put forward the major proposition of "Raising Political Awareness in the Military," included reinforcing the Party's political foundations in the overall layout of Party building and put it in the first place in the history of the CPC, and made it clear that the Party's development in the new era should be led by raising political awareness in the military, thus grasping the fundamental principle of enforcing strict Party self-governance. The report also clearly defines the specific requirements for the raising political awareness among Party members, and stresses that ensuring that the whole Party obeys the Central Committee and upholds the authority and centralized and unified leadership of the CCCPC is the primary task to reinforce the Party's political foundations.

In January 2019, the CCCPC adopted the *Opinions on Raising Political Awareness among the Party*, which made a systematic interpretation and comprehensive deployment of the raising political awareness among the Party in the new era. It stressed that the purpose of it is to strengthen political belief, strengthen political leadership, improve political ability, purify the political environment, and achieve unity and consistency of the whole Party. We must uphold the Party Constitution as our fundamental rules, and implement the Party's nature and purpose, guiding ideology and objectives, line and program clearly defined in the it. We should highlight the fundamental position of the raising political awareness among the Party and focus on the Party's political attributes, political missions, political goals and political pursuits. It is necessary to take raising political awareness among the Party as the guide, put political standards and political requirements throughout the ideological work, organizational work, work conduct, discipline construction, system construction, and counter-corruption struggle of the Party, and use political strengthening to promote the in-depth development of comprehensively and strictly administering the Party, and lead and drive the overall improvement of the quality of Party building. It is necessary to adhere to the problem-oriented approaches, pay attention to "targeted treatment," and improve areas of weakness of prominent problems such as weak political awareness, unstable political position, insufficient political ability and improper political behavior. It is necessary to integrate raising political awareness among Party members into the whole process of formulating and implementing major decisions and plans of the Party and the state, and ensure that raising political awareness among Party members and all professional work, especially the central work, are closely integrated and mutually promoted. This is the first central document in history to systematically explain and deploy raising political awareness among Party Members. It is of great significance to to reinforce the Party's political foundations in the new era.

In order to reinforce the Party's political foundations in practice, in August 2018, the CCCPC issued the revised *Regulations of the CPC on Disciplinary Action*, which added the contents of "Four Consciousnesses" and "Two Upholds." In February 2019, the CCCPC issued the *Regulations on the Request for Instructions and Reports on Major Issues of the CPC*, further improving the institutional mechanism for practicing the "Four Consciousnesses" and "Two Upholds." In September 2020, the CCCPC issued the *Regulations on the Work of the CCCPC*, which proposed that the members of the Central Committee, the Political Bureau of the CCCPC and the Standing Committee of the Political Bureau of the CCCPC must take the "Two Upholds" as the fundamental political requirement. This is a landmark achievement in strengthening the institutional guarantee of "Four-Sphere Confidence" and "Two Upholds." The Sixth Plenary Session of the 19th CCCPC put forward the "two establishment," which is not only a centralized summary of the achievements of raising political awareness among Party members, but also puts forward new requirements for it. Through continuous efforts, the political standing, political consciousness and political ability of Party members and cadres have been significantly improved, the unity of the Party have been consolidated, and the authority of the CCCPC has been ensured.

Theory is fundamental to Party building. Strengthening ideals and convictions is the primary task of ideological work. Party organizations at all levels persist in taking ideals and convictions as an important political task, constantly grasp them, incorporate relevant contents into the cadre education and training plan and annual work plan, strengthen work guidance, supervision and inspection, and realize the institutionalization, normalization and scientization of ideals and convictions education.

Equipping ourselves with Xi Jinping Thought on Socialism with Chinese Characteristics for a New Era is a major political task of the whole Party. From 2014 to 2016, the Publicity Department of the CCCPC compiled *A Book on General Secretary Xi Jinping's Major Policy Addresses* and *A Book on General Secretary Xi Jinping's Major Policy Addresses (2016 edition)* and other books. After the 19th National Congress of the CPC established the guiding position of Xi Jinping Thought on Socialism with Chinese Characteristics for a New Era, from 2018 to 2021, the Publicity Department of the CCCPC compiled tutorials such as *Thirty Lectures on Xi Jinping Thought on Socialism with Chinese Characteristics for a New Era, Learning Outline of Xi Jinping Thought on Socialism with Chinese Characteristics for a New Era* and *Q&A on learning Xi Jinping Thought on Socialism with Chinese Characteristics for a New Era.* In order to study and implement the Party's innovation theory, Party schools, schools of administration and cadre academies have included the above-mentioned guidance books in the training and teaching contents, and colleges and universities have taken them as theoretical learning materials for teachers and students to equip their minds, guide their initiatives, and advance their work.

Intra-Party study and education activities are important carriers of the ideological work of the CPC. From June 2013 to September 2014, the CCCPC deployed to carry out the mass line education and practice movement of the Party throughout the Party, highlighting the improvement on work conduct and resolutely eliminating the "Four Malfeasances." In 2015, special education program of the "three stricts and three earnests" was carried out among officials at and above the county level. In 2016, the "Two Studies and One Action" Education Campaign was carried out among all Party members. In 2017, arrangements and deployments were made to promote the normalization and institutionalization of the "Two Studies and One Action" Education Campaign. In 2019, the whole Party launched a top-down education on the theme of "remain true to our original aspiration, and keeping the mission firmly in mind." The Fourth Plenary Session of the 19th CCCPC proposed to establish a system that remain true to our original aspiration, and keeping the mission firmly in mind to promote the normalization and long-term development of education. In 2021, we carried out activities to study the history of the CPC throughout the Party. While doing a good job in the education programs within the Party, the CCCPC also insists on integrating learning and education into daily life.

The Party draws its strength from its organization. Since the 18th National Congress of the CPC, the Party Central Committee, with Comrade Xi Jinping at its core, has conducted a series of important explorations around the organizational work of the Party. On this basis, in July 2018, Xi Jinping proposed the Party's organizational line for the new era at the National Conference on Organizational Work: it is important to comprehensively implement the Thought on Socialism with Chinese Characteristics for a New Era, focus on the construction of the organizational system, and focus on training loyal, clean and responsible high-quality cadres; it is important to cultivate a constant stream of talented people who are dedicated to the country and have the courage to break new ground; it is important to adhere to the criterion of evaluating officials in terms of both political integrity and professional capability, with priority given to integrity; it is important to appoint people on their merits without regard to their origins. It is to provide a strong organizational guarantee to adhere to and strengthen the overall Party leadership and adhere to and develop socialism with Chinese characteristics. For the first time in history, the organizational line of the Party in the new era has made a complete description of the Party's organizational line, which provides a scientific basis for strengthening the party's organizational development in the new era and is of great pioneering significance. In May 2021, the CCCPC issued the *Regulations on the Organizational Work of the CPC* (hereinafter referred as the *Regulations*), which comprehensively regulated the organizational work of the Party. The *Regulations* is the first general and comprehensive basic and main law on organizational work in the history of the CPC. It is of great significance to deeply implement the Party's organizational line in the new era, promote the scientific, institutionalized and standardized organizational work, and comprehensively improve the quality of organizational work.

The key to enforcing strict Party self-governance is to administer officials strictly. In June 2013, Xi Jinping proposed the standard of good officials for the new era at the National Conference on Organizational Work: be firm in their ideals and convictions, willing to serve the people, diligent in work, ready to take on responsibilities, honest and upright. In order to implement this standard, the CCCPC revised the *Regulations on the Selection and Appointment of Party and Government Leading Cadres* twice in 2014 and 2019, effectively eliminating the tendency of relying on votes, points, GDP and age, and clearly establishing a political yardstick in the selection and appointment of personnel. In July 2015, the general office of the CCCPC issued *Several Provisions on Promoting the Ability of Leading Cadres to be Promoted and Demoted (for Trial Implementation)*, which played an important role in promoting the formation of an employment orientation and a political environment in which the competent are promoted, the excellent are rewarded, the mediocre are demoted, and the inferior are eliminated. In August 2016, the general office of the CCCPC issued the *Opinions on Preventing Unqualified Officials from being Promoted* to ensure that the officials are loyal, clean and responsible. In 2017, the general office of the CCCPC and the general office of the State Council issued the newly revised *Provisions on the Disclosure of Personal Matters by Officials* and the newly formulated *Measures on the Handling of the Results of the Review of Disclosure on Personal Matters by Officials* to continuously strengthen the supervision over them. In 2019, the general office of the CCCPC issued the *Planning Outline for the Construction of the National Party and Government Leading Bodies from 2019 to 2023*, making a comprehensive plan for the construction of the National Party and government leading bodies at all levels from 2019 to 2023.

Fourth, the CCCPC attach much importance to the Party building at the grassroots level, promotion an all-out effort to enforce strict Party discipline at the grassroots. We should uphold and improve the Party's leadership over talent work, thoroughly implement the strategy to make China a talent-strong country, deepen the reform of the talent development system and mechanism, and accelerate the construction of an important talent center and innovation highland in the world.

Discipline building is the fundamental policy for ensuring full and strict governance over the Party. The CCCPC upholds discipline and rules in the front, stresses strict political discipline and rules, and focuses on strengthening political and organizational discipline. In 2015 and 2018, the CCCPC twice revised *Regulations of the CPC on Disciplinary Action*, making specific classification and description of violations of discipline according to the "Six Disciplines," adding the "Four Consciousnesses" and "Two Upholds" to make the Party's discipline clearer and more powerful. Disciplinary inspections have cut like a blade through corruption and misconduct, which is highly valued by the Central Committee. In

2015 and 2017, the regulations on inspection work were revised twice, and the inspection work achieved full coverage of one term for the first time. In 2016, the Sixth Plenary Session of the 18th CCCPC revised the *Regulations of the CPC on Internal Scrutiny*, and formally included "four forms" of scrutiny, action, and accountability in the general regulations. In 2017, the 19th National Congress of the CPC included discipline building in the overall layout of Party building for the first time in the history of the CPC. In 2018, according to the plan for deepening the reform of Party and State institutions, the State Supervision Commission was established to work together with the Discipline Inspection Commission of the CCCPC to strengthen discipline inspection and supervision. In 2021, the Political Bureau of the CCCPC held a meeting to review the Regulations on the Work of the CPC Discipline Inspection Commission, which established systems and rules for discipline inspection and supervision.

The system is fundamental and long-term. In 2013, the Third Plenary Session of the 18th CCCPC creatively proposed to deepen the reform of the Party building system, and regarded it as an important part of comprehensively deepening the reform, planning the Party's institutional development from the perspective of the overall situation of the Party and the state. In 2013 and 2018, the CCCPC formulated the Five-Year Plan and the Second Five-Year Plan for the formulation of Party regulations within the CCCPC. This is the first time in the history of the CPC to compile a Five-Year Plan for the formulation of Party regulations, and the two outlines have become important guidelines for the formulation of Party regulations. In December 2016, the CCCPC held the first national Party regulation work conference in history, which clearly proposed to form a relatively complete intra-Party laws and regulations system by the 100th anniversary of the founding of the party. On this basis, the whole Party formulated and revised a large number of Party regulations. At the same time, from 2012 to 2019, the CCCPC completed two centralized cleaning up of Party regulations and normative documents. As of July 1, 2021, there were 3615 effective Party regulations, forming the basic framework of the "1 + 4" Party regulations system, namely, the Party Constitution plus the Party's organizational laws and regulations, the Party's leadership laws and regulations, the Party's self-building laws and regulations, and the Party's supervision and protection laws and regulations. Xi Jinping announced at a Ceremony Marking the Centenary of the CPC that: The CPC has formed a relatively complete system of Party regulations. At the same time, the CCCPC has paid more attention to improving the enforcement Party regulations, and promoted the implementation of the Party regulations to be really intensified.

Summary

In the new ear, broader and deeper reform across the board has been consistently promoted. The system of socialism with Chinese characteristics is now more mature and stable, and the modernization of China's system and capacity for governance has reached a higher level. The cause of the Party and the country now radiates with fresh vitality. In the new era, we have made sweeping progress in improving the institutions, standards, and procedures of China's socialist democracy, and given better play to the strengths of the Chinese socialist political system. As a result, our political stability, unity, and dynamism have been reinforced and grown stronger. In the new era, the system of socialist rule of law with Chinese characteristics has constantly been improved, solid progress has been made in advancing the rule of law in China, the rule of law has played a greater role in consolidating foundations, ensuring stable expectations, and delivering long-term benefits, and the Party's ability to lead and govern the country through law-based methods has been notably enhanced. This represents a revolutionary restructuring of the people's armed forces. The Party Central Committee's authority and its centralized, unified leadership have remained robust, the Party's leadership systems have improved, and the way in which the Party exercises its leadership has become more refined. There is greater unity among all Party members in terms of thinking, political resolve, and action, and the Party has significantly boosted its capacity to provide political leadership, give guidance through theory, organize the people, and inspire society. The Party Central Committee with Comrade Xi Jinping as the core, with unprecedented courage and determination to ensure full and strict governance over the Party, leading the Party to overcome persistent and chronic problems, explore a successful way to rely on the Party's self-revolution to jump out of the historical cycle, fundamentally reversing the situation of laxity and softness in the management of the Party, eliminating serious hidden dangers within the Party, the state and the military. The Party has become stronger in its revolutionary forging, and its self-revolution has made historic and groundbreaking achievements, producing an all-round and profound impact, providing strong political assurance for the comprehensive construction of a modern socialist country and the realization of the Chinese Dream of the great rejuvenation of the Chinese nation.

SECTION 3

The Chinese Economy Has Been Transitioning from a Phase of Rapid Growth to a Stage of High-Quality Development

4.3.1 Put Forward Economic Development in the New Normal and Promote Supply-Side Structural Reform

(1) From "Three Phase Superposition" to the New Normal

Since the launch of reform and opening-up, China has brought about a miracle of rapid growth. China's economic strength has thus risen by a significant margin. However, there existed problems such as undue emphasis on the rate and scale of growth in some localities and sectors and an extensive growth model. They, combined with the impact from sluggish world economy in the aftermath of the global financial crisis, led to a stack-up of institutional and structural problems in China's economy. Imbalanced, uncoordinated, and unsustainable development hence became a glaring issue.

In view of the changes in China's economy, the ruling party and government have strengthened their leadership over economic work. In November, 2012, Xi Jinping pointed out: following the general guideline of making steady progress, the economy should maintain sustained and sound development.

In December, the central economic work conference clearly pointed out that it is necessary to strengthen the Party's leadership over economic work. Since then, the CCCPC has continuously improved the system and mechanism of the Party's leadership over economic work, formed a system of regularly analyzing and studying the economic situation and major economic issues, strengthened the analysis and grasp of the overall situation of development, timely formulated major policies and strategies, made major decisions, and deployed major work to ensure that the Party's leadership over economic work is implemented, and provided an important guarantee for promoting all parties to jointly do economic work well. Since the 18th National Congress of the CPC, the Party Central Committee, with Comrade Xi Jinping at its core, has put forward a series of important ideas around major theoretical and practical issues of economic development, which were summarized in the Central Economic Work Conference in December 2017 as Xi Jinping's Economic Thought on Socialism with Chinese Characteristics for a New Era.

Since 2012, China's economic growth rate has ended the high-speed growth of 10%, and has entered the speed shift period. According to the data of the National Bureau of statistics, China's economic growth rate was 7.8% in 2012 and 7.7% in 2013. After in-depth research and analysis, Xi Jinping put forward the major judgment that China's economy is at the stage of "Three Phase Superposition." In December 2013, Xi Jinping stressed at the Central Economic Work Conference that in the face of the complex situation of the continued downturn in the world economy, in the face of the fact that China's economic development is at a stage of shifting the growth rate, restructuring the economy, and addressing the impact of previous stimulus policies, the economic situation can be described as unpredictable and ever-changing. He also proposed the concept of "new normal" for the first time at the meeting.

In May 2014, Xi Jinping pointed out during a visit to Henan Province, China's development is still in an important period of strategic opportunity, we need to enhance confidence, from the current phase of China's economic development, adapt to the new normal and maintain a normal mindset on strategy.

In November, 2014, Xi Jinping at his speech at the APEC CEO Summit, Bali, Indonesia, made a systematic explanation on "new economic normal" for the first time. Second, the economic structure has been continuously optimized and upgraded, the tertiary industry and consumer demand have gradually become the mainstay, the gap between urban and rural areas has gradually narrowed, the proportion of residents' income has increased, and the development achievements have benefited more people; third, from factor driven and investment driven to innovation driven.

The Central Economic Work Conference was held in December 2014, shortly after Xi Jinping's systematic elaboration of the "new economic normal." The meeting pointed out: understanding the new normal, adapting ourselves to the new normal, and guiding the new normal are major tasks in the present and future stages of our economic development.[78] The meeting also put forward nine major trends brought about by the "new economic normal": (1) From the perspective of consumption demand, in the past, China's consumption had obvious characteristics of imitative wave expelling. Now, the stage of imitative wave expelling consumption is basically over, and personalized and diversified consumption has gradually become the mainstream. The importance of ensuring product quality and safety and activating demand through innovative supply has significantly increased. It is necessary to adopt correct consumption policies to release consumption potential, so that consumption will continue to play a fundamental role in promoting economic development. (2) From the perspective of investment demand, now, through over 30 years of high-intensive and large-scale development and construction, investment in traditional industries and real estate has reached capacity. But infrastructure connectivity, new technologies, new products, new industries, and new business models present new investment opportunities, and demand new means of investment and financing. We must find the right direction and eliminate barriers for investment, so that investment can continue to boost economic growth. (3) Exports and balance of payments. Before the global financial crisis, international markets were expanding rapidly. Exports were a major engine for China's rapid economic growth. Now, since global aggregate demand is sluggish, China's comparative low-cost advantage is receding. At one and the same time China is going out on a greater scale, and bringing in products of higher technology. We must foster new comparative edges, so that our exports can continue to support economic growth. (4) Production capacity and industrial structure. China's main problem used to be undersupply. Now the supply capacity of traditional industries has exceeded demand. we must upgrade our industrial structure, merge and reorganize enterprises, and promote concentration of production. Small and micro businesses are playing a more prominent role; small-scale, intelligent, and specialized production will become a new feature of industrial structure. (5) The comparative advantages of production factors. Our low labor cost was our biggest advantage; introduced technology and management were quickly transformed into productivity. Now, due to population aging, rural surplus labor is decreasing and we suffer from weakened influence of production factors. Economic growth will rely more on the quality of human capital and progress in technology, so innovation must become a new growth engine. (6) Market competition. Increases in quantity and price competition used to dominate. Now, it is turning to competition in quality and product differentiation. Therefore, a single national market and high resource allocation efficiency are essential to economic development. We must drive deeper reform and opening-up, and develop a single, transparent, well-organized, and procedure-based market environment. (7) Resource and environment constraints. China used to have sufficient energy and resources and extensive eco-space. Now, the carrying capacity of our environment is approaching or has reached the limit. We must meet the public demand for a good eco-environment, and promote a new eco-friendly and low-carbon development model. (8) The accumulation and defusing of risks. Now, as the growth rate slows down, hidden risks are becoming evident. The risks confronting us are under control, but we need some time to defuse threats in the form of high leverage and economic bubbles. We must "find the correct prescriptions to treat both symptoms and root causes," establish and improve the mechanisms. (9) The resource allocation model and the means of macro-economic control. The marginal effects of comprehensive stimulus policies are diminishing. We should resolve overcapacity on the one hand, and use market mechanisms to identify the future direction for industrial development on the other. We must conduct reasonable macroeconomic control.

"New economic normal" is the sober judgment and important definition of China's economic situation by the CPC and the Chinese government since the 18th National Congress of the CPC. The proposal of this concept is of great significance to correctly understand the characteristics of China's economy in the new era, meet the opportunities and challenges faced by China's economy, and formulate economic policies consistent with the new normal.

(2) Promote Supply-Side Structural Reform
During the new normal, restructuring the economy, and addressing the impact of previous incentive policies, the problems hindering growth are not only about economic aggregate but also structural conflicts. If we blindly stimulate demand, we will only accumulate more risks and overdraw future growth. In response, Xi Jinping first proposed supply-side structural reform at the sixth meeting of the Central Leading Group on Financial and Economic Affairs in November 2015. It is a major strategic deployment of the CCCPC to take supply side structural reform as the main line of economic work and adapt to and lead the new economic normal with supply side structural reform. In December, in his speech at the Central Economic Work Conference, Xi Jinping made a comprehensive elaboration on the supply-side structural reform from theory to practice, emphasizing the five major tasks of cutting overcapacity, reducing inventory, deleveraging financing, reducing costs, and strengthening weak links, and clarified the five policy pillars that we must ensure that macro-level policy maintains economic stability, industrial policy is targeted, micro-level policy injects dynamism into the economy, reform policy delivers results, and social policy sees that basic needs are met.

In January, 2017, the 30th group study session of the Political Bureau of the 18th CCCPC studied on the theme of the stepping up of supply-side structural reform. Xi Jinping made a comprehensive analysis on the current constraints on

China's economic development and stressed that there are cyclical, aggregate, but mainly structural constraints. China's economic development is facing and will encounter problems on both the supply side and the demand side, while major problems exist in the former. Supply-side structural reform is a crucial battle that has a bearing on the overall situation and the long-term development. On the basis of our existing work and achievements, we need to deepen the implementation of our goals, tasks, methods, policies, paths and measures, and constantly make substantive progress. To promote the supply-side structural reform, we must properly handle several major issues. He pointed out that it is necessary to properly handle the relationship between the government and the market, the relationship between short-term and long-term, the relationship between subtraction and addition, and the relationship between supply and demand.

In December 2018, the central economic work conference further have formulated the eight-character policy of readjusting, restructuring, consolidating and improving China's economy, which pointed out the direction for further adhering to the supply side structural reform as the main line and promoting high-quality development.

With the "cutting overcapacity, reducing excess housing inventory, deleveraging, lowering costs, and strengthening areas of weakness" as the starting point, the state has vigorously promoted the supply side structural reform. We have intensified efforts to cut overcapacity, prioritizing industries such as steel and coal; and a fund for rewards and subsidies has been put in place by the central government to support efforts to assist affected employees. We have Upheld the principle that housing is for living in, not for speculation. Thanks to city-specific policies and category-specific guidance, clear progress has been made in reducing commercial residential housing inventory in third- and fourth-tier cities, and the growth of housing prices in the most popular cities has been brought under control. We have taken active and prudent steps to deleverage, control the scale of debts, and expand equity finance. The debt-to-asset ratio of industrial enterprises has been consistently declining. Macro leverage ratio is increasing by much smaller margins and is generally stable. We sped up the trial program of replacing business tax with VAT. We have used a combination of measures to bring down costs: much of government-managed funds and fees have been cut. Some fees and charges levied on businesses by the central government have been abolished. The ratio of enterprise contributions to old-age pension, medical insurance, unemployment insurance, and maternity insurance, workers' compensation, and housing provident fund schemes has been reduced for the time being, and work has been done to lower energy, logistics, and telecommunications costs. During the 13th Five-Year Plan period, the supply side structural reform achieved remarkable results. The goal of reducing production capacity in key industries such as steel and coal has been achieved, a number of backward production capacity and zombie enterprises have been cleared, the supply-demand relationship in key industries has changed significantly, and the transformation and upgrading of traditional industries have been accelerated. Structural deleveraging was steadily promoted. The institutional transaction costs and production and operation costs of enterprises have been continuously reduced. More efforts were made to make up for weaknesses in key areas. Major scientific and technological innovation achievements are emerging, strategic emerging industries and modern service industries are developing at a faster pace, and new technologies, new industries and new forms of business are growing rapidly. They have played an important role in responding to the COVID-19 epidemic and promoting the restoration of economic and social order.[79]

4.3.2 We Should Speed Up Improvements to the Socialist Market Economy

China's economic and social development is driven by reform. In the new era, China has constantly improved the top-level design and promoted the reform of the socialist market economy to continue to develop in depth. The Third Plenary Session of the 18th CCCPC pointed out that economic structural reform is the focus of continuing the reform comprehensively. The key to economic reform lies in striking a proper balance between the role of the government and that of the market, so that the market can play a decisive role in allocating resources and the government can play its own role more effectively. From "fundamental role" to "decisive role," although only one word was altered, the market's role was redefined. This is a new breakthrough in the Party's understanding of the laws of socialist construction. The plenary session made comprehensive arrangements for the socialist market economy around the basic economic system, the modern market system, the transformation of government functions, the reform of the fiscal and taxation system, the integrated development of urban and rural areas, and the new open economic system.

Based on the important achievements of the reforms deployed by the Third Plenary Session of the 18th CCCPC, in October 2019, the Fourth Plenary Session of the 19th CCCPC adopted the *Decision on Major Issues Concerning Upholding and Improving the System of Socialism with Chinese Characteristics and Modernizing China's System and Capacity for Governance* (hereinafter referred as the *Decision*), making new plans and arrangements for reforms. The *Decision* points out that the basic socialist economic systems, such as public ownership as the mainstay, the common development of various forms of ownership, distribution according to work as the mainstay, and the coexistence of various modes of distribution, and the socialist market, not only embody the superiority of the socialist system, but also adapt to the development of social productive forces at the primary stage of socialism in China. They are great creations of the Party and the people. We must adhere to the basic socialist economy, give full play to the decisive role of the market in the allocation of resources, give better play to the role of the government, comprehensively implement new concept for development, adhere to the supply-side structural reform as the main line, and accelerate developing a modernized economy. The *Decision* has deployed relevant work in the five aspects: with the public sector as the core of our economy, the government encourages, supports, and guides the development of the non-public sector; based on the system in which distribution according to work is dominant and a variety of modes of distribution coexist; the government improves the socialist market economy; the government improves the institutional mechanism of science and technology innovation; the government builds an economy with high-level opening-up. The *Decision* points out that the basic socialist economic systems, such as the following three systems: public ownership as the mainstay, the common development of various forms of ownership, distribution according to work as the mainstay, and the coexistence of various modes of distribution, and the socialist market economy. It is a new overview of the basic socialist economy, which develops and deepens the connotation of the basic socialist economy.

In order to further refine the relevant requirements, in May 2020, the CCCPC and the State Council adopted the *Opinions on Speeding up the Improvement of the Socialist Market Economy in the New Era* (hereinafter referred as the *Opinions*), which systematically designed the goals, directions, tasks and measures for speeding up the improvement of the socialist market economy in the new era, and provided action guidance for promoting reform of the economy at a higher starting point, at a higher level and at a higher goal. The *Opinions* put forward reform measures in seven key areas, focusing on the outstanding problems in the system and mechanism of China's current economic and social development and the goal of building a high-level socialist market economy. First, we will ensure that public ownership is dominant and that economic entities under diverse forms of ownership develop side by side. We will strengthen the dynamism of micro entities. Second, we should consolidate the basic system of market economy and ensure fair competition in the market. Third, we will build a more complete system and mechanism for the market-oriented allocation of factors to further stimulate the creativity and market vitality of the whole society. Fourth, we should innovate government management and service methods and improve the macroeconomic governance. Fourth, we should ensure and improve people's wellbeing and uphold social fairness and justice. Sixth, we should build a new system of an open economy at a higher level and promote reform and development through opening-up. Seventh, we should improve the legal system of the socialist market economy and strengthen the guarantee of the rule of law. These key and fundamental reform measures are highly targeted. Under the guidance of the above top-level design, various reform measures were carried out in an orderly manner.

We will uphold and improve the basic economic system. Property right is the core of ownership. In November 2016, the CCCPC and the State Council issued the *Opinions on Improving the Property Rights Protection System and Protecting Property Rights* according to Law, which made arrangements for the protection of property rights according to law in the form of a central document for the first time. On this basis, the modern property rights system is improved to ensure clear ownership, well-defined rights and obligations, strict protection, and smooth transactions in China. It stresses that such an economy, with cross-shareholding by and integration of state-owned capital, collective capital and non-public capital, is important to materialize the basic economic system of China. Relevant departments have issued important documents such as *Opinions on the Development of Mixed Ownership Economy by SOEs* and *Opinions on the Reform and Improvement of the State-Owned Assets Management System* to improve the state-owned assets management system and actively develop the mixed ownership economy. State owned enterprises are an important force to promote the development of ownership. In August 2015, the CCCPC and the State Council issued the *Guiding Opinions on Deepening the Reform of SOEs*, which proposed that by 2020, decisive achievements should be made in important fields and key links of the reform of SOEs, a state-owned asset management system, a modern enterprise system, and a market-oriented operation mechanism that are more in line with China's basic economic system and the development of the socialist market economy should be formed. We should support a large number of outstanding entrepreneurs who have both political integrity and ability, are good at business and are full of vitality. We should cultivate a large number of key SOEs with innovative ability and international competitiveness. The vitality, control, influence and risk resistance of the state-owned economy should be significantly enhanced. The Opinions also made arrangements for deepening the reform of SOEs in terms of promoting the reform of SOEs by categories, improving the modern enterprise system, improving the state-owned assets management system, developing the mixed ownership economy, strengthening supervision to prevent the loss of state-owned assets, strengthening and improving the Party's leadership over SOEs, and creating good environmental conditions for the SOE reform. In June 2020, the 14th Meeting of the CCCPC for Deepening Overall Reform adopted the *Three-Year Action Plan for SOE Reform (2020–2022)*, which is a programmatic document for deepening SOE reform in China at the new development stage. The "road map" and "management chart" of the SOE reform are gradually clearer, and the relevant reform is steadily advancing. In the new era, the overall Party leadership in SOEs has been strengthened in an all-round way. For the first time, the functions of central enterprises have been defined and classified. The company system reform of central enterprises has been completed in an all-round way, and the number and quality of mixed ownership enterprises have been greatly improved.

We will improve the modern market system. Market rules are the basis for the orderly operation of the market system. In October 2015, the State Council issued the *Opinions on the Implementation of the Negative List System for Market Access*, to explore the implementation of a unified market access system, and accelerate the construction of a new market access management system that is open, fair, standardized and orderly, where enterprises make independent decisions and compete on an equal footing, where the government has clear rights and responsibilities and strong supervision. China has also reformed the market supervision system, established and improved the social credit system, and gradually established fair, open and transparent market rules. Price mechanism is the core of market mechanism. In October 2015, the CCCPC and the State Council issued *Several Opinions on Promoting the Reform of the Price Mechanism* to comprehensively deepen the price reform, improve the price formation mechanism in key areas, improve the government pricing system, and improve the mechanism that mainly determines prices by the market. In addition, a sound unified rural-urban market should be created for land designated for construction purposes, allowing rural collective land designated for business-related use to be transferred, leased, and bought into shares, establishing a mechanism for distributing land value-added income that takes into account the state, the collective, and the individual, and improving the secondary market for land leasing, transfer, and mortgage. We will improve the financial market, expand the opening-up of the financial industry to the outside world, promote the reform of policy oriented financial institutions, improve the multi-level capital market system, improve the insurance economic compensation mechanism, develop inclusive finance, enrich the financial market levels and products, improve the mechanism for the marketization of the RMB exchange rate, establish and improve the foreign debt and capital flow management system under the framework of macro prudential Management, implement the reform measures and sound standards for financial supervision. We will establish a deposit insurance system, strengthen the construction of financial infrastructure, and ensure the safe and efficient operation and overall stability of the financial market. In order to continuously deepen the reform, in January 2021, the general office of the CCCPC and the general office of the State Council issued the *Action Plan for Developing a High-Standard Market System*, which proposed to basically build a unified and open, orderly competition, complete system and perfect governance high standard market system through about five years of efforts, so as to lay a solid foundation for promoting high-quality economic development, accelerating the construction of a new development pattern, and modernizing the national governance system and capabilities. At the end of 2021, the general office of the CCCPC and the general office of the State Council issued the *Opinions on Strengthening Anti-Monopoly and Further Promoting the Implementation of Fair Competition Policy*, which formed the top-level design policy framework for fair competition in China for the first time. In December of the same year, the central economic work conference proposed to set up a "traffic light" for capital, strengthen the effective supervision of capital according to law, and prevent the wild growth of capital. In April 2022, the CCCPC and the State Council issued the *Opinions on Accelerate Moves to Build a Unified Domestic Market*, which defined the overall requirements, main objectives and key tasks for accelerating the building of the national unified market from the overall and strategic perspective, and provided an action program for the construction of the national unified market in the future. In the new era, a national unified market with high efficiency, standardization, fair competition and full opening is accelerating.

We will step up efforts to transform government functions. A sound macro-control system is an important foundation for the government to perform its duties. China will gradually improve the macro-control system guided by the national development strategy and planning and with fiscal policy and monetary policy as the main means, promote the formulation of macro-control objectives and the institutionalization of the use of policy means, strengthen the coordination of fiscal policy, monetary policy, industry, price and other policy means, improve the level of discretionary choice, and enhance the forward-looking, targeted and coordinated macro-control. China will form a mechanism for participating in international macroeconomic policy coordination and promote the improvement of the international economic governance structure. China will deepen the reform of the investment system and establish enterprises as the main investors. China will improve the assessment and evaluation system for development achievements and correct the bias of assessing political achievements based solely on the rate of economic growth. Comprehensive and correct performance of duties is the key to the transformation of government functions. In March 2013, the first executive meeting of the new State Council focused on the *Plan for the Reform of Bodies of the State Council* (part I), and handed over a reform timetable and mission statement to the society. Later, reforms designed to streamline administration, delegate power, improve regulation, and upgrade services are carried out in a comprehensive way. From 2013 to 2018, items for administrative approval had decreased by 44 percent, and the licensing of matters not covered by the Law on Administrative Licensing had been completely phased out. Enterprise investment projects subject to approval by central authorities have been substantially reduced by 90%, intermediary services subject to administrative examination and approval have been substantially reduced by 74%, and licensing and recognition of professional qualifications have been substantially reduced. At the same time, the government should strengthen the formulation and implementation of development strategies, plans, policies and standards, strengthen the supervision of market activities, and strengthen the provision of all kinds of public services. The government has been advancing reform of public institutions based on different categories, encouraged an increase in government procurement, promoted the rationalization and de-administration of public institutions and authorities, and created conditions to gradually eliminate the administrative level of schools, research institutes, hospitals and other units.

We should continue structural fiscal and tax reforms. In June 2014, the Political Bureau of the CCCPC reviewed and approved the *Overall Plan for Deepening the Reform of the Fiscal and Taxation System*. The goal of deepening the reform of the fiscal and taxation system is to establish a sustainable modern fiscal system that is unified, complete, standardized by law, open and transparent, and operates efficiently, which is conducive to optimizing the allocation of resources, maintaining the unity of the market, promoting social equity, and achieving the long-term stability of the country. The reform focuses on three aspects: (1) Improving the budget management system, strengthening budget restraint, standardizing government behavior, achieving effective supervision, and accelerating the establishment of a comprehensive, standardized, open and transparent modern budget system; (2) Deepening the reform of the taxation system, optimizing the structure of the taxation system, improving the function of taxation, stabilizing the macro tax burden, promoting the rule of taxation in accordance with the law, establishing a taxation system conducive to scientific development, social equity and market unity, and giving full play to the function of taxation in raising fiscal revenue, regulating distribution and promoting structural optimization; (3) Adjusting the financial relationship between the central and local governments, further rationalizing the division of income between the central and local governments on the premise of maintaining the general stability of the income pattern between the central and local governments, reasonably dividing the affairs and expenditure responsibilities between the governments, promote the unification of authority and responsibility, work and spending, and establishing a system in which affairs and expenditure responsibilities are compatible. In 2016, the key work and tasks were basically completed. By 2020, various reforms will be basically in place and the modern financial system will be basically established. In the process of reform, the national and local tax collection and management system has undergone historical changes. In 2018, the national and local tax authorities at and below the provincial level merged to implement a management system under the dual leadership of the State Administration of Taxation and the provincial (District, municipal) people's government. From 2012 to 2021, the national general public budget revenue increased from 11.73 trillion yuan to 20.25 trillion yuan, with a total of 163.05 trillion yuan over the past decade, with an average annual growth of 6.9%, providing a solid financial guarantee for the realization of the First Centenary Goal.

We must improve the system and mechanisms for integrating rural and urban development and embark on a new path of urbanization. Since the 18th National Congress of the CPC, policy documents such as the *Opinions on Guiding the Orderly Transfer of the Management Rights of Contracted Rural Land and Developing Agricultural Moderate Scale Operation, Opinions on Improving the Method of Separation of Rural Land Ownership Contracting Rights, Management Rights and Operation Rights, Guidelines on Reforming the Rural Collective Property Rights System, Opinions on Accelerating the Construction of a Policy System to Foster New Types of Agribusiness.* In April 2019, the CCCPC and the State Council adopted the *Opinions on the Setup of Robust Institutions, Mechanisms, and Policy Systems to Promote Integrated Urban-Rural Development,* and put forward the "three-step" strategy, that is, by 2022, the institutional mechanism for urban and rural integrated development will be initially established. The institutional channels for the free flow of urban and rural factors have been basically opened, the restrictions on urban settlement have been gradually eliminated, a sound unified market for urban and rural land that may be used for construction purposes has been basically completed, the ability of financial services to implement the strategy of rural revitalization has been significantly improved, the framework of rural property rights protection transaction system has basically formed, equal access to basic public services has been enhanced, the rural governance system continues to improve, and economically developed regions, metropolitan areas and suburban areas take the lead in making breakthroughs in institutional reforms. By 2035, the system and mechanism of urban-rural integrated development will be more perfect. Urbanization will enter a mature stage. Disparities in urban-rural development, in development between regions, and in living standards are significantly reduced. The system of orderly migration between urban and rural areas will be basically established, the unified urban and rural construction land market has been fully formed, a sound unified market for urban and rural land that may be used for construction purposes will be fully completed, urban and rural inclusive financial services system will be fully completed, the equalization of basic public services will be basically achieved, agricultural modernization will have been realized. By the middle of the century, the system and mechanism of urban-rural integrated development will be more perfect. The comprehensive integration of urban and rural areas, the comprehensive revitalization of rural areas, and the common prosperity of all people will have been basically realized. Guided by the above-mentioned policy documents, China will accelerate the development of a new agricultural management system, adhere to the basic position of family management in agriculture, adhere to the collective ownership of rural land, give farmers the right to occupy, use, make profit, transfer and mortgage and guarantee the contracted land. We will allow farmers to contract management rights into shares to develop agricultural industrialization, encourage contract management rights in the open market to professional households, family farms, farmers' cooperatives, agricultural enterprises, and develop a variety of forms of large-scale operations. We will give farmers more property rights, actively develop farmers' share cooperation, give farmers the right to share ownership, income, paid withdrawal, mortgage, guarantee and inheritance of collective assets, reform and improve the rural land designated for housing system, explore ways for farmers to increase their property income, establish a rural property rights transfer and transaction market, and promote the open, fair and standardized operation of rural property rights transfer and transaction. We will promote the equal exchange of urban and rural factors and the balanced allocation of public resources, safeguard the rights and interests of farmers in production factors, improve the agricultural support and protection system, improve the agricultural insurance system, encourage social capital to invest in rural development, and promote the equal access to basic public services in urban and rural areas. We will improve the system and mechanism for the healthy development of urbanization, adhere to the new path of urbanization with Chinese characteristics, promote innovation in urban development and management, speed up the reform of the registered residence system, fully relax the restrictions on settling in towns and small cities, orderly release the restrictions on settling in medium-sized cities, reasonably determine the conditions for settling in large cities, strictly control the population size of mega cities, and promote full coverage of urban basic public services and permanent residents. We will improve the mechanism linking the transfer payments a local government receives to the number of former rural residents granted urban residency in its jurisdiction and continue to grant permanent urban residency to people who move to cities from rural areas.

Mechanisms for Scientific and Technological Innovation. In September, 2015, the general office of the CCCPC and the general office of the State Council issued the *Implementation Plan for Deepening Reform of the Science and Technology Management System* (hereinafter referred as the Implementation Plan). According to the *Implementation Plan*, by 2020, breakthroughs will be made in important fields and key links of the reform of the scientific and technological system, and a national innovation system with Chinese characteristics that meets the requirements of the Innovation-Driven Development Strategy and conforms to the laws of the socialist market economy and the innovation-driven development will be basically established, and China will become a country of innovators. The ability of independent innovation will have been significantly enhanced, the market-oriented mechanism for technological innovation will have been improved, the innovation subjects such as enterprises, scientific research institutes and colleges and universities are full of vitality and efficiency, the integration of military and civilian science and technology has developed in depth, the flow of innovation elements such as talents, technology and capital has been smoother, the scientific and technological management system and mechanism will have been improved, the allocation of innovation resources has been optimized, the enthusiasm and creativity of scientific and technological personnel will have been fully stimulated. The atmosphere of mass entrepreneurship and innovation will become stronger, and the efficiency of innovation will have been significantly improved, laying a solid foundation for building a more complete national innovation system and entering the forefront of innovative countries by 2030. In view of the institutional mechanisms, policies and institutional obstacles in scientific and technological innovation and driving development, the *Implementation Plan* proposes 32 reform measures in 10 aspects, 143 policies and specific results. On the basis of successfully completing the reform tasks in the early stage, in November 2021, the 10th meeting of the CCCPC for Deepening Overall Reform adopted A *Three-Year Action Plan for the Reform of the Science and Technology Management System (2021–2023)*, and made arrangements for the next stage of reform. Since the 18th National Congress of the CPC, China's basic system in the field of science and technology has been basically established, substantive progress has been made in the reform of some important fields and key links, and the ability to systematize scientific and technological innovation has been continuously improved.

4.3.3 Clarify the New Concept for Development and Formulate and Implement the 13th Five-Year Plan

(1) Propose and Clarify New Concept for Development
Based on the strategic judgment that China's economy has entered a new normal, the Fifth Plenary Session of the 18th CCCPC held in October 2015 pointed

out that in order to achieve the objectives for the 13th Five-Year Plan period, resolve difficulties encountered during development, and cultivate strengths for further development, we need to firmly establish and put into practice a new philosophy of innovative, coordinated, green, open, and shared development. This is the prescription formulated by the CPC and the Chinese government for China's economic development entering the new normal and the sluggish recovery of the world economy. Among them, innovation is the first driving force to lead development, innovation and development focus on solving the problem of development drive. Coordination: an integral quality of sustained and healthy development. Coordinated development aims to solve the imbalance in development. Green: both a necessary condition for ensuring lasting development and an important way in which people can work to pursue a better life. Green development highlights the harmony between humanity and nature. Opening-up is vital for China's prosperity and development. Open development prioritizes interactions between China and the international community. Sharing: the essence of Chinese-style socialism. Shared development underpins social equality and justice.

In January 2016, the Political Bureau of the 18th CCCPC conducted the 30th group study on the strategic focus of China's economic and social development during the 13th Five-Year Plan period. On how to implement the new concept for development, Xi Jinping pointed out that the concept of innovation, coordination, green, open, shared development, concentrating on the "13th Five-Year Plan" and even a longer period of China's development ideas, development direction, development focus, underline our overall direction for the long term. It is necessary to grasp the key work that can drive the implementation of the five concepts for development, and promote the implementation of the five concepts for development as a whole. For each development concept, we should also focus on the key areas to promote the breakthrough of each concept in practice. This requires us to conduct in-depth investigation and research, not only to analyze the overall situation, but also to think in depth, and put forward feasible policy measures and work plans. The new concept for development is the baton and the traffic light.

Due to the different social and historical conditions and historical tasks, the development concepts of the CPC and the Chinese government have different characteristics in different periods. Since the reform and opening-up, from "taking economic development as the central task" to "development is the top priority of the Party and our country," to the Scientific Outlook on Development, and to the Five Concepts for Development, each enrichment of development concepts has promoted China to achieve new development. The change of China's development concept not only reflects the uniqueness of China's development path, but also conforms to the change of the world's development concept. The proposal of the five development concepts is a major contribution of China to the world development theory, and enriches the connotation and practice samples of development theory.

(2) Formulate and Implement the 13th Five-Year Plan

In October 2015, the Fifth Plenary Session of the 18th CCCPC adopted the *proposal of the CCCPC on Formulating the 13th Five-Year Plan for National Economic and Social Development.* Guided by the new concept for development, the "Proposal" clarifies China's development ideas, development direction and development focus during the 13th Five-Year Plan period. The proposal points out that building moderately prosperous society in all respects by 2020 is the First Centenary Goal of the Two Centenary Goals set by the CPC. The 13th Five-Year Plan period was the decisive stage in building a moderately well-off society. The "13th Five-Year Plan" must be closely focused on achieving this goal. The Proposal summarizes the major achievements made in China's development during the 12th Five-Year Plan period, analyzes the basic characteristics of China's development environment during the 13th Five-Year Plan period, expounds the main objectives and basic concepts of economic and social development during this period, and makes work arrangements for adhering to innovative development, coordinated development, green development, development for global progress and development for the benefit of all. The Fourth Session of the 12th NPC adopted the *Outline of the 13th Five-Year Plan for National Economic and Social Development* in March, 2016. The 13th Five-Year Plan is the First Five-Year Plan for socialism with Chinese characteristics to enter the new era and China's economy to enter the new normal. It is the specific blueprint for the CPC and the Chinese government to build a moderately prosperous society in an all-round way.

During the 13th Five-Year Plan, in the face of the complicated international situation and formidable domestic issues related to advancing reforms and development while maintaining stability, particularly under the grave impact of the COVID-19 pandemic, the of the CCCPC with Comrade Xi Jinping at the core, has stayed true to the CPC's original aspiration and kept the Party's missions firmly in mind. It has united and led the entire Party and the Chinese people of all ethnic groups to pioneer and forge ahead, and worked hard to advance various undertakings of the Party and the country.

From 2016 to 2020, overall, China's economy has performed stably and its structure has been consistently improved, with the country's GDP now exceeding RMB 100 trillion. China has accomplished much towards becoming an innovative country and has made major advances in manned spaceflight, lunar exploration, deep-sea engineering, supercomputing, quantum information, "Fuxing" high-speed trains, large aircraft manufacture, and other fields. We have attained a decisive victory in the fight against poverty and the rural poor residents, 55.75 million in total, have been lifted out of poverty. Agricultural modernization has been steadily advanced, and the annual grain output has surpassed 650 million tons for several years. The goal of granting urban residency to 100 million people from rural areas and other permanent residents without local household registration has also been met. Solid steps have been taken to implement major regional development strategies. Pollution prevention and control efforts have been intensified, the target of reduction in the discharge of major pollutants has been exceeded, resources and energy have been used more efficiently, and there has been a notable improvement in the environment. Important progress has been made in addressing financial risks in this period. China continued to open its door wider to the world; the joint pursuit of the Belt and Road Initiative yielded solid outcomes. The living standards of the Chinese people have increased significantly. Considerable headway was made in ensuring the provision of equitable, quality education. Higher education is becoming universal. Over 60 million urban jobs were added, and the world's largest social security system was established. China's basic medical insurance covers 1.3 billion people and its basic old-age insurance covers nearly 1 billion people. More than 23 million housing units in urban shanty towns have now been renovated. The country has had major strategic success in the response to COVID-19, and the preparedness and capacity for coping with emergencies have been substantially improved. The country's public cultural services have been consistently improved, and the cultural sector flourished. Notable advances have been made in the development of national defense and the armed forces, and the organizational structure of the military has undergone major changes. China's national security was enhanced on all fronts, and social harmony and stability were maintained across the country.

4.3.4 Implement the Coordinated Regional Development Strategy

After the 18th National Congress of the CPC, the CPC and the Chinese government put forward and implemented a series of major development strategies including innovation-driven development strategy, the coordinated regional development strategy, new urbanization strategy, rural revitalization strategy, and so on.

With regard to the innovation-driven development strategy, in March 2015, the CCCPC and the State Council adopted *Opinions on Deepening Institutional Reform and Accelerating Implementation of Innovation-driven Development Strategy*, proposing to accelerate the implementation of the innovation-driven development strategy and defining the development goal: by 2020, the institutional environment and policy and legal system that meet the requirements of innovation-driven development will be basically formed, providing a strong guarantee for entering the ranks of innovative countries. Talent, capital, technology and knowledge flow freely. Enterprises, scientific research institutes and colleges and universities cooperate in innovation. Innovation vitality bursts out, innovation achievements are fully protected, the value of innovation is more obvious, the efficiency of innovation resource allocation is greatly improved, and innovative talents share the innovation income reasonably, so that the innovation-driven development strategy can be truly implemented, so as to create a new engine to promote economic growth, employment and entrepreneurship, build new advantages in participating in international competition and cooperation, promote the formation of a new pattern of sustainable development, and promote the transformation of economic development mode. In May 2016, the CCCPC and the State Council issued the *Outline for the National Innovation-Driven Development Strategy*, which defined the "three-step" strategy, that is, the first step is to enter the ranks of innovative countries by 2020, basically build a national innovation system with Chinese characteristics, and effectively support the realization of the goal of building a moderately prosperous society in all respects. Second, by 2030, China will become one of the most innovative countries, achieve a fundamental transformation in the driving force of development, and substantially improve the level of economic and social development and international competitiveness, thus laying a solid foundation for building an economic power and a society of common prosperity. The third step is to build a world power in science and technology innovation by 2050, and become a major scientific center and innovation highland in the world, so as to build China into a modern socialist country that is prosperous, strong, democratic, culturally advanced and harmonious, and realize the Chinese Dream of the great renewal of the Chinese nation. On this basis, the outline also puts forward the overall deployment for implementing the innovation-driven strategy. With the implementation of the strategy, China's innovation quality has ranked first among the middle-income economies for consecutive years, and the main scientific and technological innovation indicators have steadily improved. By the end of June 2020, the effective number of invention patents in China (excluding Hong Kong, Macao and Taiwan) had reached 1.996 million, ranking first in the world for consecutive years.

As for the coordinated regional development strategy, first is to implement the coordinated regional development strategy focusing on relieving Beijing's non-capital functions. April 01, 2017 CCCPC and State Council made a decision to establish the *Xiong'an New Area in Hebei Province*. A model of high-quality development at the forefront of reform and opening-up in the new era comparable to Shenzhen Special Economic Zone and Shanghai Pudong New Area came into being. Second is to facilitate the development of the Yangtze Economic Belt by promoting well-coordinated environmental conservation and avoiding excessive development. The Yangtze Economic Belt covers 11 provinces and cities along the Yangtze River and spans the three major plates of East, West and central China. In September 2016, the CCCPC and the State Council issued the *Outline of the Development Plan for the Yangtze River Economic Belt*, which focuses on the following aspects to depict the grand blueprint for the development of the Yangtze River economic belt: the planning background, overall requirements, vigorously protecting the ecological environment of the Yangtze River, accelerating the development of a comprehensive three-dimensional transport corridor, innovation-driven industrial transformation and upgrading, actively promoting new urbanization, striving to build a new pattern of all-round opening, innovating the system and mechanism of regional coordinated development as well as safeguard measures and other aspects. Third is the Development of Guangdong-Hong Kong-Macao Greater Bay Area. In February 2019, the CCCPC and the State Council issued *Outline Development Plan for the Guangdong-Hong Kong-Macao Greater Bay Area*, which pointed out that Guangdong, Hong Kong and Macao Bay area should not only be built into a dynamic world-class city cluster, an international scientific and technological innovation center, an important support for the construction of the "Belt and Road" and a demonstration area for deep cooperation between the mainland and Hong Kong and Macao, but also be built into a high-quality living circle suitable for living, business and tourism, and become a model of high-quality development. Fourth is to promote the development of the Yangtze River Delta. In December 2019, the CCCPC and the State Council issued the *Plan for Integrated Regional Development of the Yangtze River Delta*, emphasizing the promotion of the integrated development of the Yangtze River Delta, the enhancement of the innovation capacity and competitiveness of the Yangtze River Delta, and the improvement of the degree of economic agglomeration, regional connectivity and policy coordination efficiency, which is of great significance to leading the country's high-quality development and building a modernized economy. Fifth is to promote ecological protection and high-quality development in the Yellow River Basin. In October 2021, the CCCPC and the State Council issued the *Overall Plan for the Ecological Protection and High-Quality Development of the Yellow River basin*, proposing to promote the a holistic approach to conserving mountains, rivers, forests, farmlands, lakes, and grasslands, strive to ensure the long-term stability of the Yellow River, improve the ecological environment of the Yellow River Basin, optimize the allocation of water resources, promote the high-quality development of the whole basin, and improve the people's livelihood, strive to protect, inherit and carry forward the Yellow River culture and make the Yellow River a happy river for the people. In addition, we will give stronger support to see faster development in old revolutionary base areas, areas with large ethnic minority populations, border areas, and poor areas. We will strengthen measures to reach a new stage in the large-scale development of the western region; deepen reform to accelerate the revitalization of old industrial bases in the northeast and other parts of the country; help the central region rise by tapping into local strengths; and support the eastern region in taking the lead in pursuing optimal development through innovation. To this end, we need to put in place new, effective mechanisms to ensure coordinated development of different regions.

As for the new urbanization strategy, in December 2013, the central urbanization work conference was held, which defined the guiding ideology, main objectives, basic principles and key tasks of promoting new urbanization. In March 2014, the CCCPC and the State Council issued and implemented the *National New Urbanization Plan (2014–2020)*, which defined the development path, main objectives and strategic tasks of urbanization. By the end of 2020, China's new urbanization has reached a record high, with the urbanization rate of permanent residents reaching 63.9%.

With regard to the rural revitalization strategy, in January 2018, the CCCPC and the State Council issued the *Opinions on Implementing the Rural Revitalization Strategy*, which clearly defined the objectives and tasks of implementing the rural revitalization strategy: by 2020, important progress will be made in rural revitalization, and the institutional framework and policy system will be basically formed. By 2035, decisive progress will be made in rural revitalization and agricultural modernization will be basically realized. The agricultural structure has been fundamentally improved, the quality of farmers' employment has been significantly improved, relative poverty has been further alleviated, and solid steps have been taken towards common prosperity; the equalization of basic public services between urban and rural areas has been basically realized, and the system and mechanism for urban-rural integrated development have been further improved; The fostering social etiquette and civility in the countryside has reached a new height, and the rural governance has been further improved; the rural ecological environment has taken a fundamental turn for the better, and the beautiful and livable countryside has been basically realized. By 2050, the rural areas will be revitalized in an all-round way, and agriculture will be strong, rural areas will be beautiful, and farmers will be rich. In January 2021, the CCCPC and the State Council issued the *Opinions on Accelerating the Modernization of Agriculture and Rural Areas and Comprehensively Promoting Rural Revitalization* and stated clearly that we must continue to make solving problems relating to agriculture, rural areas and farmers the top priority in the Party's work, make comprehensively promoting rural revitalization a major task of realizing the great rejuvenation of the Chinese nation, and mobilize the efforts of the whole Party and society to accelerate the modernization of agriculture and rural areas so that farmers can live a better life. In the same year, the *National Rural Revitalization Administration* was officially listed, and the *Rural Revitalization Promotion Law* was promulgated. On January 4, 2022, the CCCPC and the State Council issued the *Opinions on the Key Areas of Comprehensive Promotion of Rural Revitalization* in 2022, making major arrangements for comprehensively promoting rural revitalization in 2022. Rural Revitalization and poverty alleviation have been seamlessly linked.

In addition, China has also implemented the national strategy for food safety of basic self-sufficiency in grain and absolute security in rations, and the new energy security strategy of promoting energy consumption, energy supply, energy technology, energy system revolution and strengthening international cooperation in energy. China have formulated and implemented the action plan for building a strong manufacturing country, established a national venture capital guidance fund for emerging industries, promoted the development of big data, implemented the "Internet +" action plan, accelerated the technological transformation of traditional industries, accelerated the cultivation of emerging industries, and accelerated the development of modern service industries. China have encouraged Chinese companies with advantages to participate in overseas infrastructure development projects and engage in cooperation with their foreign counterparts in building up production capacity. These major strategies have had a profound impact on China's economic development and reform.

4.3.5 Pursue Higher-Level Opening-Up

In the new era, relying on its advantages in the super large-scale market, China is implementing a more proactive opening strategy, actively promoting the transition from commodity and factor flow opening to institutional opening, and striving to build an open pattern of linkage between land and sea, and two-way mutual assistance between East and West.

A high level of opening-up cannot be separated from high-quality top-level design. In November 2013, the Third Plenary Session of the 18th CCCPC adopted the *Decision of the CCCPC on Some Major Issues Concerning Comprehensively Continuing the Reform*, which emphasized that in order to adapt to the new situation of economic globalization, it is necessary to promote mutual promotion of domestic and foreign opening, make more efforts in combining attracting foreign investment and "going global," promote orderly and free flow of international and domestic factors, efficient allocation of resources, and deep integration of markets, and accelerate the cultivation of new advantages in participating in and leading international economic cooperation and competition, to promote reform through opening-up. Facing the domestic and international situation, in November, 2020, the Fifth Plenary Session of the 19th CCCPC pointed out: at present, China is speeding up the implementation of a new dual-cycle development pattern with the domestic cycle as the mainstay and the domestic and international cycles reinforcing each other. It is a major strategy decision made by the Party Central Committee, with Comrade Xi Jinping at its core faced with the changes the international and domestic economic situations. In January, 2021, at a study session on implementing the decisions of the Fifth Plenary Session of the 19th CCCPC, attended by officials at the provincial ministerial level, Xi Jinping stated that to build a new development pattern and implement a high level of openness to the outside world, we must have a strong domestic economic cycle system and a solid base. It is necessary to create new advantages for China to participate in international cooperation and competition, attach importance to improving the efficiency and level of domestic large-scale circulation through international circulation, improve the quality and allocation level of China's production factors, and promote China's industrial transformation and upgrading.

Committed to Building New systems for an Open Economy. On the basis of the strategic deployment made by the Third Plenary Session of the 18th CCCPC on building a new open economy, in May 2015, the CCCPC and the State Council adopted *Several Opinions on Building a New Open Economy System*, which defined the basic principles, overall objectives and key tasks of building a new open economy system, and highlighted the strategic, systematic and operable nature. It is a programmatic document in the field of China's opening-up in the new era. The Opinions put forward that the overall goal of building a new open economic system is to accelerate the cultivation of new advantages in international cooperation and competition, more actively promote the balance of domestic and foreign demand, import and export; attract foreign investment and promote the balance of foreign investment; gradually realize the basic balance of international payments, form a new pattern of all-round opening, realize the modernization of the open economic governance system and governance capacity, uphold justice while opening-up, earnestly safeguard national interests, safeguard national security, promote common development between China and other countries in the world, and build a new open economy that is mutually beneficial, diversified, balanced, safe and efficient. Subsequently, the requirements of the Opinions were gradually implemented. China vigorously innovated the foreign investment management system, established a new system to promote the "going global" strategy, built a new mechanism for sustainable development of foreign trade, optimized the regional layout of opening-up, accelerated the implementation of the "Belt and Road" strategy, expanded new space for international economic cooperation, built an open and safe financial system, and built a stable, fair, transparent and predictable business environment, strengthened the construction of support and guarantee mechanisms and established and improved an open economic security system.

Guided by this, in June 2017, China launched a nationwide negative list of foreign investment access for the first time. Since then, China has reduced the negative list of foreign investment access for five consecutive years, and the list items have been reduced to 31. In March 2019, the Second Session of the 13th NPC voted to adopt the *Foreign Investment Law of the PRC*, which is the first unified basic law in the field of foreign investment in China and is of great significance in making new ground in pursuing opening-up on all fronts. In January 2022, the general office of the State Council issued the *Opinions on Promoting the Integrated Development of Domestic and Foreign Trade*, to making arrangements for promoting the integration of domestic and foreign trade, forming a strong domestic market and ensuring the unimpeded domestic and international circulations. According to the Opinions, by 2025, we will better coordinate the laws and regulations, regulatory systems, business qualifications, quality standards, inspection and quarantine, certification, and accreditation in both areas. We will further enhance the level of integrated development of domestic and foreign trade of the market players, make internal and external connectivity network more perfect, continue to optimize the government management services, make the integration of domestic and foreign trade regulation and control system more sound, and achieve efficient operation of domestic and foreign trade, and integrated development. As measured by the World Bank's *Doing Business 2020 report*, China ranked the 31st place, up 15 places from the previous year, and joined the ranks of the world's top ten most improved economies for ease of doing business for the second year in a row. This is a vivid portrayal of China's efforts to improve the business environment and continuously expand its opening-up to the outside world. In 2021, China's actual use of foreign capital exceeded trillion yuan for the first time, achieving double-digit growth.

Build a New Highland for China's Opening-up. In September 2013, China (Shanghai) Pilot Free Trade Zone was officially established. In August 2016, the State Council decided to establish seven pilot free trade zones in Liaoning, Zhejiang, Henan, Hubei, Chongqing, Sichuan and Shaanxi. In October, 2017, we will grant more powers to pilot free trade zones to conduct reform, and explore the opening of free trade ports. In September 2018, the State Council issued the *Approval of the establishment of China (Hainan) Pilot Free Trade Zone*, which covers throughout Hainan Island. Since the establishment of the first pilot free trade zone in 2013, after several rounds of expansion, China now has 21 pilot free trade zones and Hainan Free Trade Port, forming a pilot pattern covering the East,

West, North and South and a comprehensive reform and opening-up situation in multiple fields. Building a pilot free trade zone is a strategic measure to promote reform and opening-up in the new era, and it has milestone significance in the process of reform and opening-up in China.

Implement the Free Trade Area Strategy. In December 2015, the State Council issued Several *Opinions on Accelerating the Implementation of the Free Trade Zone Strategy*. The opinions have made plans on the layout of China's free trade zone construction at three levels of the surrounding areas, the "Belt and Road" and worldwide. First is to accelerate the construction of the surrounding free trade zones, strive to establish free trade zones with all countries and regions adjacent to China, constantly deepen economic and trade relations, and build a win-win surrounding market. Second is to actively promote the "Belt and Road" free trade zone, combine the construction of surrounding free trade zones and promote the international cooperation on production capacity, actively negotiate and build free trade zones with countries along the "Belt and Road," form the "Belt and Road" market, and build the "Belt and Road" into an unimpeded road of commerce and opening-up. Third is to gradually form a global network of free trade zones, strive to establish free trade zones with most emerging economies, large developing countries, major regional economic groups and some developed countries, and build a large market for BRICs countries, emerging economies and developing countries. This is the first strategic and comprehensive document since China started the process of free trade zone development. It has made a "top-level design" for the development of China's free trade zone and put forward specific requirements. With the active promotion of China, the *Regional Comprehensive Economic Partnership (RCEP)* was signed in November 2020 and officially entered into force on January 1, 2022. The RCEP agreement is the most important free trade agreement of the largest scale which is under negotiation in the Asia Pacific. Its coming into effect marks the formal launch of a free trade area featuring the largest population, biggest economic and trade scale and greatest development potential. At present, China has signed 19 free trade agreements with 26 countries and regions. The free trade partners cover Asia, Oceania, Latin America, Europe and Africa, and the trade volume with the free trade partners accounts for about 35% of the total foreign trade.

Host the China International Import Expo. In November, 2018, the First China International Import Expo (CIIE) was held in Shanghai. The first CIIE, which was successfully concluded in Shanghai just a week ago, was attended by

172 countries, regions and international organizations, and 3,600-plus companies and over 400,000 Chinese and foreign buyers who sealed 57.8 billion U.S. dollars worth of deals. Attending the Second CIIE are 181 countries, regions and international organizations, more than 3,800 companies, and more than 500,000 Chinese and foreign buyers who are here to explore business deals. In 2020, the global epidemic continued to spread, and many large international exhibitions pressed the "pause" button. However, the third CIIE was held as scheduled, with a cumulative intended turnover of 72.62 billion U.S. dollars, an increase of 2.1% over the previous one. China's hosting of the CIIE not only made important contributions to promoting the recovery of the world economy, but also demonstrated China's firm determination to continue to expand its opening-up. In 2021, China's total trade in goods reached 6.05 trillion U.S. dollars, and the trade in services exceeded 800 billion U.S. dollars, up 56% and 70% respectively over 2012. Since 2017, China has maintained its position as the largest trader of goods.

Summary

In the new era, China's economy has entered a special stage of "three phases superimposition" due to complex external and internal reasons, and a new normal of economic development has emerged. How to achieve the set development goals under the new normal has become a major historical issue facing the CPC and the Chinese government. Under this situation, the ruling party and government put forward the concept of innovation, coordination, green, open, shared development, accelerated the improvement of the socialist market economy, carried out supply side structural reform, formulated and implemented a series of important development strategies, formulated and implemented the 13th Five-Year Plan, and continued to promote high-level opening-up. Through unremitting efforts, our economic development has become much more balanced, coordinated, and sustainable. China's GDP has exceeded 100 trillion yuan, while per capita GDP has topped 10,000 U.S. dollars. China's economic strength, scientific and technological capabilities, and composite national strength have reached new heights, and our economy is now on a path of higher-quality development that is more efficient, equitable, sustainable, and secure.

SECTION 4

Enhance Cultural Confidence and Build a Socialist Cultural Power

4.4.1 Put Forward Cultural Self-Confidence and Strengthen the Development of Socialist Ideology

Since the launch of reform and opening-up, the Party has attached equal emphasis to material progress and cultural-ethical progress. As a result, socialist culture has thrived, the national spirit has been lifted. At the same time, Chinese society is in an era of vigorous thinking, great collision of ideas and great integration of cultures, and many problems have arisen. One of the most prominent problems is the lack of cultural confidence. At the Seminar on Philosophy and Social Sciences May 17, 2016, Xi Jinping pointed out our confidence in our path, in our theories and in our system all boil down to our confidence in our culture—the essential, underlying and enduring strength of a nation.[80] On June 28, Xi Jinping put forward the "Four-Sphere Confidence," namely our confidence in our path, in our theories and in our system, our confidence in our culture with Chinese characteristics, during the 33rd group study of the Political Bureau of the 18th CCCPC, and explicitly included our confidence in culture into the "four-sphere confidence." On how to strengthen our confidence in culture, Xi Jinping stressed we must develop a socialist culture with Chinese characteristics, inspire the cultural creativity of our whole nation, and develop a great socialist culture in China.

Ideology is the concentrated embodiment of the social mainstream consciousness and the spirit of the times. The situation of ideological development directly affects the level of our confidence in culture. Under the conditions of socialist market economy, as the independence, selectivity, variability and diversity of people's ideological activities are obviously enhanced, the public opinion ecology, media pattern and communication mode have undergone profound changes, and the domestic and international environment facing ideological work has become more complex. In intensifying its efforts to improve communication and outreach, the CCCPC has convened a national conference on communication and outreach, as well as forums on literature and art, the Party's press and public communications work, cybersecurity and IT application, philosophy and social sciences, and ideological and political work at institutions of higher learning. During the period, Xi Jinping delivered a series of important speeches, which profoundly answered the major theoretical and practical issues of propaganda, ideology and culture work under the new historical conditions.

In August 2013, Xi Jinping pointed out at the national propaganda and ideological work conference, to enhance the cause of Chinese socialism we must promote material, cultural and ethical progress, strengthen the nation materially, culturally and ethically, and improve the material, cultural and ethical lives of the people of all ethnic groups. He stressed, our publicity and theoretical work aims to consolidate Marxism as the guiding ideology in China, and cement the shared ideological basis of the whole Party and the people. Five years later, in August 2018, Xi Jinping pointed out at the second national propaganda and ideological work conference since the new era that our publicity and theoretical work is to win over more people, and that it should be an important duty to foster a new generation capable of shouldering the mission of national rejuvenation. The most important thing is to build a solid spiritual foundation with firm ideals and convictions, strengthen faith in Marxism, socialism and communism, and confidence in the path, theory, system and culture of socialism with Chinese characteristics.

In October 2014, Xi Jinping chaired a national conference on literature and art and made an important speech, profoundly elaborating a series of major issues of fundamental and directional importance to the prosperity and development of literature and art, and making a comprehensive deployment of the work of literature and art under the new historical conditions. He pointed out that the realization of the great rejuvenation of the Chinese nation requires the Chinese culture to flourish. The Chinese spirit is the soul of socialist literature and art. We should create excellent works worthy of the times, adhere to the people-centered orientation, and strengthen and improve the Party's leadership over literary and art work.

In December 2015, Xi Jinping proposed at the National Conference on the Work of Party Schools that the premise of Party schools identifying themselves with the Party, which is the fundamental principle of Party school work, and is also the fundamental guidance of good Party school work. He stressed, the premise of Party schools identifying themselves with the Party is upholding the Party's ideals and convictions. Marxism and communism come above all else.

In February, 2016, Xi Jinping chaired a national conference on the Party's press and public communications work and stressed: publicity through media is an important responsibility of the CPC. It is of great significance to the governance and stability of the country. We should adapt to changes in the domestic and international situations, and identify the role of media in the Party's overall work. In this field, we must uphold the leadership of the Party, keep the correct political orientation, maintain a people-centered work ethic, follow the rules of news dissemination, and develop innovative methods. In this way can we effectively improve the coverage, guidance, and influence of the Party's news media, and increase its public trust.

In October 2014, Xi Jinping chaired a national conference on cybersecurity, and stressed that cyberspace is a common virtual home for millions of people. Having a clear sky and crisp air, having a good ecology in cyberspace conforms to the people's interests. A pestilent atmosphere and a deteriorating ecology in cyberspace do not conform to the people's interest. Inspired by a sense of duty to society and the people, we must step up our law-based governance of cyberspace, develop better online content, strengthen positive publicity, and work to foster a positive, healthy, upright online culture. We need to use our core socialist values and profit from the best achievements of human civilization to nurture people's minds and nourish society, ensuring that positive energy and mainstream values prevail. By doing so, we will be able to create a clean and upright cyberspace for internet users, especially young ones. Two years later, in April 2018, the national conference on cybersecurity was held in Beijing, where Xi Jinping attended and emphasized that we should strengthen positive publicity, and work to foster a positive, healthy, upright online culture, adhere to the correct political direction, public opinion guidance, value orientation, with the socialism with Chinese characteristics in the new era and the spirit of the 19th National Congress of the CPC to unite hundreds of millions of Internet users, conduct in-depth education on ideals and beliefs, deepen the socialism with Chinese characteristics in the new era and the Chinese Dream education, and actively cultivate and practice the core values of socialism, promote innovation in concept, content, genre, form, methods, and means of publicity, grasp the timing and effectiveness, build concentric circles online and off, better social consensus, consolidate the common ideological basis for the unity of the whole Party and the people.

In May 2016, Xi Jinping chaired a national conference on philosophy and social science, and pointed out that the role of philosophy and social science is irreplaceable. The roles of philosophy and social sciences and the workers in the fields are irreplaceable. Adhering to Marxism as the guidance is the fundamental sign that contemporary Chinese philosophy and social sciences are different from other philosophy and social sciences, and we must take a clear-cut stand to adhere to it.

In December 2016, Xi Jinping stressed at the national conference on ideological and political work in colleges and universities that building strong moral character should be taken as the central task of higher education. We should integrate moral and political education into every aspect of the entire education process, striving to elevate China's higher education to a new level.

Under the guidance of the above ideas, the ruling party and the government have made a series of decisions and arrangements and promoted a series of important work. We have strengthened Party leadership over ideological work. We promulgate the *Regulations on the Propaganda Work of the CPC, the Measures for the Implementation of the Responsibility System for Ideological Work of Party Committees (Party groups)*, and other intra-Party laws and regulations, uphold and improve the leadership of the ruling party over ideological propaganda work, improve the responsibility system for ideological work, and promote the whole Party to do propaganda and ideological work. We will distinguish between matters of political principle, issues of understanding and thinking, and academic viewpoints, but we must oppose and resist various erroneous views with a clear stand.

The second is the importance of Marxism as a guiding ideology is better appreciated. The Fourth Plenary Session of the 19th CCCPC explicitly put forward the guiding position of Marxism in the ideological field as a fundamental system for the first time. This is a major institutional innovation that has a bearing on the long-term development of the Party and the state, and on the direction and development path of Chinese culture. In order to adhere to this fundamental system, the CPC and the Chinese government have formulated a series of important documents, including the *Opinions on Strengthening and Improving the Ideological and Political Work in Colleges and Universities under the New Situation, the Opinions on Working Faster to Develop Philosophy and Social Sciences with Chinese Characteristics*, and *Opinions on Strengthening the Construction of Marxist Colleges in the New Era*. We will improve the work system of arming the whole Party and educating people with the Party's innovation theory, and improve the Party committee (Party group) theoretical study center group and other levels of learning system. We will thoroughly implement the research and construction project of Marxist theory, promote the construction of the discipline system, academic system and discourse system of philosophy and social sciences with Chinese characteristics, and comprehensively implement Marxism as the guidance in ideological and theoretical construction, philosophy and social sciences research, education and teaching. We will strengthen and improve ideological and political education in schools, and establish a system and mechanism for educating all personnel, in the whole process, and with all-round personnel.

Third is to promote the construction and innovation of communication means. We will accurately grasp the profound changes in the public opinion ecology, media pattern and communication mode, and issue policy documents such as the *Guiding Opinions on Promoting the Integrated Development of Traditional and Emerging Media*, and *Implementation Opinions on Promoting the Development of Deep Integration of Publishing*, and we will promote integrated development of media, and work to strengthen the penetration and credibility of the media and its ability to guide and influence. We will strengthen the guidance of public opinion, actively promote the positive energy of society, and lead the criticism of such erroneous trends of thought as money worship, hedonism, extreme individualism and historical nihilism.

Fourth is to promote the ideological struggle on the Internet. We have attached great importance to the Internet as the main front, main battlefield and forefront of ideological struggle, formulated the *Cybersecurity Law of the PRC*, issued important policy documents such as the *Opinions on Implementing the Network Content Construction Project* and the *Opinions on Strengthening the Construction of Network Civilization*, and established a leadership system and working mechanism under the unified leadership of the Party committee, the joint management of the Party and the government, the respective responsibilities of the relevant departments, and the active participation of the whole society; We have strengthened the ideological leadership of cyberspace, cultural cultivation, moral construction, behavior, ecological governance, civilization creation, governing the network by law to create a clear cyberspace

Through unremitting efforts, the situation in China's ideological field has undergone an overall and fundamental change, and a good situation of people's cohesion and unity has been increasingly formed.

4.4.2 Cultivating and Observing Core Socialist Values

In October 2006, the Sixth Plenary Session of the 16th CCCPC adopted the *Resolution of the CCCPC on the Development of Socialist Harmonious Society*, which clearly put forward the major proposition and strategic task of "the system of socialist core values" for the first time. The 18th National Congress of the CPC held in 2012 put forward for the first time that we should promote prosperity, democracy, civility, and harmony, uphold freedom, equality, justice and the rule of law and advocate patriotism, dedication, integrity, and friendship, so as to cultivate and observe core socialist values.

In December 2013, the general office of the CCCPC issued the *Opinions on Cultivating and Practicing Socialist Core Values*, which made overall arrangements for the construction of socialist core values. The Opinions clearly defines the important significance, guiding ideology and basic principles of cultivating and practicing socialist core values, and proposes to integrate the cultivation and practice of socialist core values into the whole process of national education, implement the cultivation and practice of socialist core values into economic development practice and social governance, strengthen the publicity and education of socialist core values, and carry out practical activities to cultivate socialist core values, so as to strengthen the organization and leadership of cultivating and practicing socialist core values. In April 2015, the Propaganda Department of the CCCPC and the Central Commission for Guiding Cultural and Ethical Progress issued the *Action Plan for Cultivating and Practicing Socialist Core Values*. The Action Plan is a supporting document with the Opinions on Cultivating and Practicing Socialist Core Values. Focusing on cultivating and practicing the socialist core values, it puts forward clear and specific requirements on strengthening the practice, the guidance of laws and regulations, deepening the popularization, setting role models, and developing a culture. The introduction of the opinions and the action plan has clarified the basic direction and practical path of the construction of socialist core values, and relevant work has been carried out in an orderly manner on this basis.

We will strengthen publicity, education and practical activities on core values. In October 2019, the CCCPC and the State Council issued the *Citizen Ethics Construction Program in the new era*. The outline consists of seven parts, mainly including the general requirements, key tasks, deepening moral education and guidance, promoting the formation of moral practice, grasping the moral construction in cyberspace, giving play to the role of system guarantee, and strengthening organizational leadership in the construction of citizens' morality in the new era. This is another *Citizen Ethics Construction Program* issued 18 years after the one in 2001. It is the basis of citizen's moral construction in the new era. Since the 18th National Congress of the CPC, various activities have been gradually carried out to guide people to consciously practice the socialist core values, such as: patriotic education, public activities to promote cultural and ethical advancement, volunteer service activities to promote the spirit of Lei Feng, credibility building, nationwide initiatives to promote morality and frugality, impartial and civilized law enforcement and judicial activities, the Peaceful China initiative, activities to foster ethnic unity and progress, tourism activities, activities to increase the population's understanding of science, activities to care for others, help the poor, the weak and the disabled, activities to improve public sanitation, activities to promote the civilized running of websites and civilized surfing, activities to set public figures as role models, the education program of the "three stricts and three earnests."

Strengthen the Publicity of Typical Demonstration. In December 2015, the CCCPC issued the *Opinions on Establishing Sound Systems of Party and State Awards and Honors, of the Party and the state.* Subsequently, the *Regulations on the Awards and Honors within the CPC*, the *Regulations on Systems of State Awards and Honors*, the *Regulations on the Military Awards and Honors*, the Methods on the Conferment of Awarding the "Medal of the Republic" and the National Honorary Title, the Measures on the Conferment of the "July 1 Medal," the Measures on the Conferment of "August 1 Medal" and the Measures on the Conferment of the "Friendship Medal" were successively issued. China established the Party, State and military merit books, and established a unified, standardized and authoritative merit honor recognition system with "five medals and one book" (the "five medals" refers to the "Medal of the Republic,""July 1 Medal,""August 1 Medal,""Friendship Medal" and national honor titles, and the "one book" refers to the merit book as the mainstay. By affirming the historical achievements of meritorious models, the state publicizes the models of the times, the most beautiful people, and the good people around us, selects and commends moral models, establishes and improves a long-term mechanism for the role of advanced models, sets up benchmarks and flags, and promotes the whole society to form a good atmosphere of learning from the good, advocating the heroes and striving to be pioneers.

To Integrate the Socialist Core Values into the Whole Process of National Education In November 2019, the CCCPC and the State Council issued *Implementation Outline of Patriotic Education in the New Era*, which proposed to focus on cultivating new people of the times who are responsible for national rejuvenation, cultivate and practice the core socialist values, extensively carry out education in patriotism, collectivism and socialism, and help our people raise their political awareness and moral standards, foster appreciation of fine culture. On this basis, the whole society has generally carried out patriotic education activities and mass spiritual civilization building activities. The socialist core values have been incorporated into the national education system, and the socialist core values have been promoted into textbooks, classrooms and students' minds.

In addition, the CPC and the Chinese government have also implemented the cultivation and practice of socialist core values in the practice of economic development and social governance, and implemented the requirements of socialist core values in all major policies.

4.4.3 We Will Deepen Reform of the Cultural System and Develop Cultural Undertakings and Cultural Industries

(1) We Will Deepen Structural Reform of the Cultural Sector
In November 2013, the Third Plenary Session of the 18th CCCPC took deepen structural reform of the cultural sector as an important aspect of comprehensively deepening the reform, and made major strategic deployment for promoting the innovation of cultural system and mechanism. The plenary session emphasized that we should adhere to the people-centered work orientation, put social benefits in the first place, integrate social benefits with economic benefits, and further deepen the reform of the cultural system with the stimulation of the creativity of the whole nation as the central link. The plenary session also made arrangements for improving the cultural management system, establishing and improving the modern cultural market system, building a modern public cultural service system, and improving the level of cultural openness.

In February 2014, the central leading group for comprehensively deepening reform deliberated and adopted the *Implementation Plan for Deepening the Cultural Restructuring*. This is an important top-level design of the cultural system reform, which marks that the new round of cultural system reform has entered the stage of comprehensive implementation. The plan lists 25 items, including 104 important reform measures, and defines the progress requirements according to the three time nodes of 2015, 2017 and 2020. The new round of cultural system reform will focus on one core goal, namely, cultivating and carrying forward the socialist core values and building a socialist cultural power. We will focus on two key links, namely, improving the cultural management system and deepening the reform of state-owned cultural units, and accelerate the construction of five systems, namely, the modern public cultural service system, the modern cultural market system, the excellent traditional cultural inheritance system, the foreign cultural communication and the foreign discourse system, the cultural policy and legal system.

In May 2017, the general office of the CCCPC and the general office of the State Council issued the *Outline of the National Cultural Development and Reform Plan for the 13th Five-Year Plan Period*. The outline establishes the main objectives of cultural development and reform during the 13th Five-Year Plan period from eight aspects: theoretical construction, literary and art creation, media construction, public culture, cultural industry, traditional culture, cultural opening, and cultural system reform. These objectives are both qualitative and quantitative, both prospective and binding. They are focused on each other and are interrelated. The general consideration is to link up with the overall goal of comprehensively deepening reform, so as to ensure that the socialist cultural system with Chinese characteristics will become more mature and more fixed by 2020.

On the basis of the gradual implementation of the above reforms, in October 2019, the Fourth Plenary Session of the 19th CCCPC made new plans and arrangements for the reform. The plenary session stressed that the development of advanced socialist culture and the extensive cohesion of the people's spiritual strength are the profound support for the modernization of China's system and capacity for governance. We must strengthen our cultural self-confidence, firmly grasp the direction of advanced socialist culture, focus on the mission and task of holding the banner, rallying the hearts of the people, cultivating new people, promoting culture and developing our image, persist in serving the people and socialism, persist in following the principle of "letting a hundred flowers bloom and a hundred schools of thought contend," encourage creative transformation and development, stimulate the creativity of the whole nation, and better bolster the Chinese spirit, Chinese values, and Chinese strength. Focusing on upholding and improving the system for the prosperity and development of advanced socialist culture, the plenary session started with the fundamental system of upholding the guiding position of Marxism in the ideological field, the system of guiding cultural construction with socialist core values, the system of safeguarding people's cultural rights and interests, the work mechanism of guiding public opinion with correct guidance and the cultural creation and production system and mechanism that integrate social and economic benefits.

Under the guidance of the above top-level design, various reform measures were carried out in an orderly manner.

Improving the Leadership and Management System for Services and Arms. In 2018, the Third Plenary Session of the 19th CCCPC made arrangements for the reform of the cultural leadership and management system, and assigned the State Administration of Press, Publication, Radio, Film and Television of China to the Publicity Department of the CCCPC; integrated the responsibilities of the Ministry of Culture and the National Tourism Administration (NTA) of China to establish the Ministry of Culture and Tourism (MCT); established the National Radio and Television Administration on the basis of The State Administration of Press, Publication, Radio, Film and Television, integrated CCTV, China National Radio (CNR) and China Radio International (CRI), and established the China Media Group. In addition, in accordance with the principle of the separation of the functions of the government from those of enterprises, China has also promoted the transformation of government departments from running culture to managing culture, and further straightened out the relationship between Party and government departments and their cultural enterprises and institutions. We will establish a management organization for the Party committee and the government to supervise state-owned cultural assets, and integrate the management of personnel, affairs, assets and guidance. We will improve the linkage mechanism of basic management, content management, industry management, prevention and crackdown on Internet crimes, improve the mechanism for handling network emergencies, and form a network public opinion work pattern that combines positive guidance with legal management. We will strictly enforce the professional qualification system for journalists, attach importance to the use and management of new media, and standardize the order of communication.

Improve the Modern Market System. When the pilot cultural system reform was first launched in 2003, the general office of the State Council issued a series of special supporting policies involving land, assets, income distribution, personnel placement, social security, finance and taxation. In 2014, the general office of the State Council issued the *Provisions on the Transformation of Operational Cultural Institutions into Enterprises in the Reform of the Cultural System* and the *Provisions on Further Supporting the Development of Cultural Enterprises*, and the supporting policies were continued. In 2018, the general office of the State Council issued these two documents again, extending the comprehensive supporting policies for cultural system reform for another five years, and persistently supporting the transformation of cultural enterprises. In September 2015, the general office of the CCCPC and the general office of the State Council issued the *guiding opinions on promoting state-owned cultural enterprises to put social benefits in the first and realize the unification of social benefits and economic benefits*, which took the realization of "the unification of double effects" as a system to be solidified in the enterprise development process, laying a solid foundation for the formation of an asset organization form and operation management mode that reflects the characteristics of cultural enterprises and meets the requirements of modern enterprise systems. In addition, the state also encourages the development of non-public cultural enterprises, lowers the threshold for social capital to enter, and supports the development of small and micro-cultural enterprises in various forms; establish a multi-level cultural product and factor market, and encourage the combination of financial capital, social capital and cultural resources; improve cultural and economic policies, expand government cultural subsidies and cultural procurement, and strengthen copyright protection.

Accelerate the Construction of the Modern Public Cultural Service System. In 2014, the Ministry of Culture led the establishment of the national public cultural service system construction coordination group, marking the official operation of the public cultural service coordination mechanism at a national level. At the beginning of 2015, the general office of the CCCPC and the general office of the State Council issued the *Opinions on Accelerating the Construction of the Modern Public Cultural Service System*, which carried out a top-level design for the construction of a modern public cultural service system. The state has formulated and promulgated the *Public Cultural Service Guarantee Law*, which, for the first time, regulates and defines the responsibilities and obligations of governments at all levels and relevant departments in public cultural services in the form of law, and brings public cultural construction into the track of rule of law and standardization. A series of important laws related to public cultural services, such as the *Film Industry Promotion Law*, the *Cybersecurity Law*, and the *Law on Public Libraries*, have also been introduced, and relevant laws and policies have been further improved. At the end of 2015, the general office of the CCCPC and the general office of the State Council issued the *Opinions on the Reform of the National Literary and Art Award System*, which required that the disadvantages of too many awards, overlapping awards, nonstandard procedures, and individual works separated from the masses should be eliminated, and the quantity should be reduced to improve the quality, and the standard evaluation should be used to support fine works and guide innovation. In the cultural field, we should gradually establish a mass evaluation and feedback mechanism to promote the effective connection between cultural projects benefiting the people and the cultural needs of the masses. The state has also introduced a competition mechanism, encouraged social forces and social capital to participate in the construction of the public cultural service system, and cultivated cultural non-profit organizations.

(2) We Will Develop Cultural Programs and Industries
Since the 18th National Congress of the CPC, China's cultural construction has made remarkable achievements.

A lot of fruitful achievements have been reaped in Culture. On October 15th, 2014, Xi Jinping chaired a national conference on literature and art and made an important speech, and made it clear that we must adhere to the people-centered orientation in the creation of literature and art. In October 2015, the *Opinions of the CCCPC on Prosperity and Development of Socialist Literature and Arts* was issued. The Opinions elevates the development of literature and art to the height of national strategy, and makes specific strategic, targeted and operable arrangements for the prosperity and development of China's literature and art undertakings from six aspects and 25 items. It draws a clear road map for the development of literature and art and provides strong policy and institutional guarantees. Since the 18th National Congress of the CPC, focusing on the themes of building moderately prosperous society in an all-round way, poverty alleviation, rural revitalization, strengthening the country through science and technology, and fighting the epidemic, the national state-owned literary and art troupes have created and arranged more than 4,000 excellent realistic theme works, carrying forward the main theme and expanding the positive energy.

Significant Progress was Made in Developing a System of Public Services. During the 13th Five-Year Plan period, the standardization and equalization of basic public cultural services were further promoted, and the network of public cultural facilities was increasingly improved. 3,196 public libraries, 3,326 public cultural centers and 5,132 public museums were built. The free opening of public cultural facilities such as public libraries, cultural centers (stations) and museums has continued to expand, and the construction of public digital culture has achieved remarkable results, further improving the accessibility and convenience of public cultural services. By June 2020, 560,000 grass-roots comprehensive cultural service centers had been built, with a coverage rate of more than 95%. Mass cultural activities have been carried out in depth, the coverage of cultural volunteer services has been further expanded, and the results of benefiting the people through culture have been more remarkable. The operation mechanism of public services has been constantly innovated, and social forces have participated in public cultural services extensively, and the efficiency of public cultural services has been further improved.

The quality and benefits of the development of the cultural industry have become more prominent. The state drafted the Cultural Industry Promotion Law, promulgated the Film Industry Promotion Law and other relevant laws, and further promoted the supply side structural reform in the cultural field. On this basis, new products, new formats and new models of the cultural industry have emerged in an endless stream, and the effect of integrated development has been constantly manifested, and the development quality and efficiency have been further improved. Under the influence of COVID-19, such "cloud" cultural projects as "cloud performance," "cloud museum," "cloud recording," "cloud tourism," "cloud concert" and "cloud forum" have become highlights, and new consumption and upgrading consumption have gradually developed. In the new era, the cultural industry has become an important engine to expand domestic demand, increase employment and promote economic growth. According to the data of the fourth national economic census, there are 2.103 million legal entities in the cultural industry in China, an increase of 129% over the previous census. As of the first half of 2020, there were 59,000 cultural and related enterprises above designated scale in China, an increase of 9,000 compared with 2016.[81] In 2020, the added value of national culture and related industries accounted for 4.43% of GDP, an increase of nearly one percentage point over 2012.

We accelerated the development of culture and sports. In October 2014, the State Council issued *Opinions on Accelerating the Development of Sports Industry and Promoting Sports Consumption*, which elevated "national fitness" to a national strategy. In March 2022, the State Council issued *Guidelines for the development of a higher-level service system for promoting general fitness and exercise*. By the end of 2021, there were 3.971 million sports venues nationwide covering an area of 3.41 billion square meters, or a per capita area of 2.41 square meters. These figures represented growth of 134.3 percent, 71.2 and 65.1 percent over 2013. From February 4 to 20, 2022, China overcame the impact of the epidemic and successfully hosted the 24th Winter Olympics. With 9 gold, 4 silver and 2 bronze medals, the Chinese delegation set a new record for the number of gold medals and the number of medals won in a single Winter Olympics, ranking third in the gold medal list, creating the best record in history since it participated in the Winter Olympics in 1980.

4.4.4 We Will Implement the Programs to Keep Fine Traditional Chinese Culture Thriving

In the new era, the CCCPC attaches great importance to the inheritance and development of China's excellent traditional culture, understands China's excellent traditional culture from the strategic height of realizing the great rejuvenation of the Chinese nation and socialist modernization, and promotes the creative transformation and innovative development of China's excellent traditional culture.

In January 2017, the general office of the CCCPC and the general office of the State Council issued the *opinions on the Implementation of Programs to Carry on the Best of Chinese Cultural Traditions and Heritage,* which promoted the inheritance and development of Chinese excellent traditional culture in the form of a central document for the first time, and pushed the inheritance of Chinese traditional excellent culture to a new historical height. The Opinions pointed out that the implementation of the project for the inheritance and development of Chinese excellent traditional culture is a major strategic task for building a socialist cultural power. It is of great significance for inheriting the Chinese culture, comprehensively improving the people's cultural literacy, maintaining national cultural security, strengthening the national cultural soft power, and modernizing the national governance system and capabilities. The opinions put forward the general objective of implementing the project of inheritance and development of Chinese excellent traditional culture, that is, by 2025, the system of inheritance and development of Chinese excellent traditional culture will be basically formed, and important achievements will be made in research and interpretation, education popularization, protection and inheritance, innovation and development, communication and exchange. Cultural products with Chinese characteristics, Chinese style and Chinese elements will be more abundant, and cultural awareness and cultural confidence will be significantly enhanced, the foundation of the country's cultural soft power will be more solid, and the international influence of Chinese culture will be significantly increased. The Opinions also clarify the key tasks of the project in terms of in-depth interpretation of cultural essence, throughout national education, protection of heritage, nourishing literary creation, integration into production and life, increasing publicity and education, and promoting cultural exchanges and mutual understanding between China and abroad. In 2021, the Propaganda Department of the CCCPC issued the *"14th Five-Year Plan" key project planning for the inheritance and development of Chinese excellent traditional culture*, and made plans and arrangements for the next five years.

In order to promote the implementation of the project of inheritance and development of Chinese excellent traditional culture, the Propaganda Department of the CCCPC established the joint meeting system of the project of inheritance and development of Chinese excellent traditional culture. Relevant departments issued supporting documents such as the *Guidelines on the Reform to Better Protect Cultural Relics* and *Opinions on Strengthening the Protection and Inheritance of Historical Culture in Urban and Rural Construction*, launched important projects such as the general survey of Chinese cultural resources to promote the development of key areas of heritage and key works to be interlinked, forming a synergy.

Find out the "Family Background" of Cultural Resources. The state has launched the general survey of Chinese cultural resources, completed the general survey of movable cultural relics, ancient books, art museum collections and opera types, and effectively improved the comprehensiveness and accuracy of the basic data of national cultural heritage resources. According to statistics, there are 766,700 immovable cultural relics and 108 million movable cultural relics (sets) in the state. A national, provincial, municipal and county intangible cultural heritage list system has been established throughout the country. At present, more than 100,000 representative intangible cultural heritage projects have been identified, including 1,372 cultural items to date in China's intangible cultural heritage list and 3,068 Representative inheritors of National Intangible Cultural Heritage. China has 42 intangible cultural heritage projects listed in the UNESCO list, ranking first in the world, and has successfully declared 56 world heritage projects, ranking second in the world. By 2020, China had completed more than 2.7 million census and registration data of ancient books, accounting for 94% of the total task; a total of 72,000 digital resources of ancient books were released. In addition, the national art collection database has been basically formed, and the national census of local opera types has been completed.

Strengthen Protection of Our Cultural Heritage. China has continued to strengthen the protection of cultural heritage. Taking the project of inheritance and development of Chinese excellent traditional culture as the general focus, it has identified 15 key projects such as the protection of national ancient books, the reading of Chinese classics, the inheritance and development of intangible cultural heritage, the inheritance and dissemination of Chinese national music, and the protection of Chinese traditional villages as the specific focus. An inter ministerial coordination group led by relevant central departments has been established to achieve this goal. Under the framework of the inter-ministerial coordination group, the coordination mechanism for intangible cultural heritage application, the inter-ministerial joint meeting mechanism for national cultural parks, the inter-ministerial coordination mechanism for the recovery and return of lost cultural relics, and the coordination mechanism for the special work of UNESCO flagship projects have been established and improved, forming a working force. During the "13th Five-Year Plan" period, China has continuously strengthened the awareness of cultural relics protection in the whole society, strengthened the protection of precious heritage resources such as world cultural heritage, cultural relics protection units, large sites, national archaeological sites parks, important industrial sites, historical and cultural cities, towns and villages, and intangible cultural heritage, and promoted the rational utilization of heritage resources. We should bolster the protection and restoration of the collection of state-owned cultural relics. We should establish and improve the national cultural relics supervision system and the cultural relics registration system. We should regulate the circulation market of cultural relics and intensify the search for Chinese cultural relics illegally lost overseas. We should improve the intangible cultural heritage protection system, strengthen the construction of national cultural and ecological protection experimental areas, and promote the productive protection of intangible cultural heritage. Some endangered traditional arts have been rescued, some ancient handicrafts have been inherited, some cultural relics that are sleeping in history and displayed on the earth have regained their luster, and some damaged cultural ecosystems have been gradually repaired, optimized and upgraded. China's cultural heritage protection has reached a new level.[82]

Strengthen archaeological excavation and research. In September 2020, the Political Bureau of the 19th CCCPC held its 23rd group study on the topic of the latest archaeological discoveries in China and their significance. Xi Jinping stressed that archaeological work is an important cultural undertaking and a work of great socio-political significance. Archaeological work is an important work to display and construct the history of the Chinese nation and the treasures of Chinese civilization. Understanding history is inseparable from archaeology. Historical and cultural heritage not only vividly describes the past, but also profoundly affects the present and future; it belongs not only to us, but also to future generations. To protect and inherit the historical and cultural heritage well is to be responsible for history and the people. We need to strengthen archaeological work and historical research and we need to bring all collections in our museums, all heritage structures across our lands and all records in our classics to life to enrich the historical and cultural nourishment of the whole society. In the new era, China has made major breakthroughs in field excavation, underwater archaeology, scientific and technological research and theoretical research. Important archaeological discoveries such as Shuidonggou in Ningxia, Shangshan in Zhejiang, Niuheliang in Liaoning, Liangzhu in Zhejiang, Shimao in Shaanxi, Erlitou in Henan and Sanxingdui in Sichuan have emerged one after another.

We need to promote the integration of China's excellent traditional culture into production, life and national education. The state has promoted the construction of 106 inheritance and development of Chinese excellent traditional culture bases in colleges and universities, and nearly 3,000 excellent traditional Chinese culture and art inheritance schools in primary and secondary schools across the country. It has promoted the integration of excellent traditional Chinese culture education into all aspects of the whole process of school education. More and more traditional classics, operas, calligraphy and other contents have entered the classroom and campus. We need to bring all collections in our museums, all heritage structures across our lands and all records in our classics to life and play its important role of promoting the excellent Chinese traditional culture.

4.4.5 Accelerating the Construction of the Ability to Communicate with International Audiences

In 2013, Xi Jinping pointed out at the national propaganda and ideological work conference, "We should enhance our foreign-oriented publicity work through trying methods with new concepts, domains and expressions that are understood by both China and the rest of the world, telling the true story of our country and making our voice heard."[83] Subsequently, the Party Central Committee, with Comrade Xi Jinping at its core, put forward a series of important ideas around international communication capacity building, such as emphasizing strengthening top-level design and research layout, building a strategic communication system with distinctive Chinese characteristics, and focusing on improving the influence of international communication, the appeal of Chinese culture, the affinity of China's image, the persuasiveness of Chinese discourse, and the guiding power of international public opinion; elaborately constructing the external discourse system; supporting the major media of the central government to go global, participating in the international media market competition, and creating a flagship media with strong international influence; accelerating the construction of the disciplinary system, academic system and discourse system of philosophy and social sciences with Chinese characteristics, and improving China's discourse power in the world and so on. Under the guidance of the above ideas, the CPC and the Chinese government have taken a series of important measures to speed up the construction of international communication capacity.

Straighten out the internal and external publicity system. In March 2014, the CCCPC decided to merge the International Communication Office, CCCPC (the Information Office of the State Council) into the Central Propaganda Department. The Central Propaganda Department attached the brand of the Information Office of the State Council to the outside world, and assigned six responsibilities from the original the International Communication Office, including guiding and coordinating foreign publicity work, organizing news release work, and contacting foreign government news management agencies, major news media and think tanks.[84]

Further Open Up the Cultural Sector. China adheres to the principle of government leadership, enterprise participation, market operation and social participation, expands cultural exchanges with foreign countries, and strengthens the construction of international communication capacity and foreign discourse system. We should make good use of the mechanism to promote cultural and people-to-people exchanges between China and the rest of the world and deepen cultural exchanges between governments. We should encourage international exchanges in Chinese studies and think tanks at home and abroad. We should support non-governmental forces to participate in cultural exchanges with foreign countries and give play to the positive role of overseas Chinese. Social organizations and Chinese funded institutions are encouraged to participate in the construction of overseas Chinese cultural centers and Confucius Institutes. We should expand cultural exchanges with other countries. We should help strengthen cultural exchanges and cooperation between the two sides of the Straits, work together with Taiwan in promoting Chinese culture, and enhance our common cultural and national identity. By 2020, China has established 45 overseas Chinese cultural centers in the world, 541 Confucius Institutes and 1,170 Confucius Classrooms in 162 countries (regions).

Promote the "going out" of Chinese culture through the "Belt and Road." In November 2016, the Central Committee adopted the *Guidelines on Further Strengthening and Improving the Work of Chinese Culture Going Out*, which clearly proposed to explain and introduce more excellent culture with Chinese characteristics, reflecting Chinese spirit and containing Chinese wisdom to the world, and improve the country's cultural soft power. In December 2016, the Ministry of Culture issued the *"Belt and Road" Cultural Development Action Plan of the Ministry of Culture (2016–2020)*, which proposed to accurately grasp the spirit of the "Belt and Road" initiative, comprehensively improve the opening-up of China's cultural field, adhere to the concept of cooperation based on the surrounding areas, radiating the "Belt and Road" and facing the world, and build a community of shared future for cultural integration. The Action Plan also specifies the key tasks, namely, improving the cultural exchange and cooperation mechanism, improving the cultural exchange and cooperation platform, building the cultural exchange brand, promoting the prosperity and development of the cultural industry, and promoting the cultural trade cooperation of the "Belt and Road." During the 13th Five-Year Plan period, focusing on the construction of the "Belt and Road," China has basically established a China-foreign cultural exchange and cooperation mechanism covering major countries and regions in the world. A modern external communication system has taken shape. The construction of overseas Chinese cultural centers and tourism offices has been accelerated. Brand activities such as the Silk Road International Art Festival and the Silk Road International Tourism Expo have been carried out in depth. Cultural and tourism brands such as "Happy Spring Festival," "Beautiful China" and "Unimaginable China" have become increasingly prominent, playing an important role in promoting people to people bonds. Cultural exchanges between Hong Kong, Macao and Taiwan have been continuously promoted, and cultural and emotional identity has been enhanced.

Improve the international communication capacity of key media. In 2016, China Global Television Network (CGTN) under CCTV was officially established, becoming an important channel for China's external communication. In the new era, China has initially established a multi-body and three-dimensional foreign publicity pattern by building a media cluster with international influence.

Promote theoretical innovation, academic innovation and expression innovation. China has promoted the interpretation of Xi Jinping's thought on socialism with Chinese characteristics in the new era through various forms such as news reports, think tank exchanges and cultural activities, published the first, second and third volumes of Xi Jinping: The Governance of China in multiple languages, and carefully planned and launched the documentary China: Time of Xi, to promote the formation of a correct view of China at the international level. In the new era, China's international voice and influence have significantly increased.

Summary

In the new era, in the face of the complex situation in the ideological field and the mutual stirring of cultures, the Party Central Committee with Comrade Xi Jinping at the core proposes confidence in culture and the construction of the Chinese spirit, the Chinese values and the Chinese power. We should focus on addressing the issue of lax Party leadership in the ideological sphere, strengthen the Party's leadership over ideological work, and strengthen propaganda and ideological work from the root. We should work harder to study and develop Marxist theory, adapt Marxism to China's realities, keeping it up to date and enhance its popular appeal, and further consolidate the guiding position of Marxism in the ideological field. We should adhere to the socialist core values to guide cultural development, pay attention to using advanced socialist culture, revolutionary culture and excellent traditional Chinese culture to cultivate the soul. Putting social benefits first while also stressing economic returns, the Party has advanced all-around development of cultural programs and industries and public cultural services have improved. For this purpose, we have launched projects to pass on and develop our fine cultural traditions, promoted their creative transformation and development. We have accelerated work to strengthen our international communication capacity, with the goal of telling well China's stories and the Party's stories, making China's voice heard. Our cultural soft power and the appeal of Chinese culture have increased significantly. Through the unremitting efforts, we have seen a sweeping and fundamental shift in the ideological domain, a notable boost in confidence in our culture among all Party members and all Chinese people, and a major increase in cohesiveness throughout society. All of this has provided solid ideological guarantees and powerful inspiration for the development of the socialism with Chinese characteristics in the new era.

SECTION 5
Improving People's Livelihood and Perfecting Socialist Social Governance System with Chinese Characteristics

4.5.1 Ensure and Improve People's Livelihood and Solidly Promote Common Prosperity

(1) Promoting Social Development to Ensure and Improve the Wellbeing of Our People

Since the launch of reform and opening-up, the Chinese people have witnessed notable improvements in their living standards and in social governance. Meanwhile, in pace with the changing times and social progress, they have developed an increasingly strong desire for a better life. In the new era, the ruling party and the government adhere to the people-centered principle, regard improving the people's well-being as the fundamental goal of development, focus on using development to strengthen areas of weakness, and make steady progress in ensuring people's access to childcare, education, employment, medical services, elderly care, housing, and social assistance, and enable all people to enjoy more benefits of reform in a more equal manner.

Worked to achieve fuller and higher-quality employment. In the face of structural employment pressure, the ruling party and the government have deeply implemented a pro-employment strategy and more active employment policies, introduced and improved various preferential policies for entrepreneurship, vigorously developed vocational education and vocational training, and increased efforts to help enterprises stabilize their jobs. In the face of changes in the domestic and international economic situation, in July 2018, the meeting of the Political Bureau of the CCCPC proposed to do a good job in the "stabilizing the six fronts" work, that is, to do a good job in stabilizing the employment, the financial market, foreign trade, foreign investment, domestic investment, and expectations, of which the first one is "stabilizing employment." At the end of the same year, the central economic work conference put forward the employment-first policy for the first time. The 2019 Report on the Work of the government further clarified that the employment-first policy is one of the three macro-policies, and the it is fully implemented. In April 2020, in order to cope with the impact of COVID-19, the meeting Political Bureau of the CCCPC proposed that while strengthening "stabilizing the six fronts" work, we should maintain security in six key areas, namely, to ensure the employment of residents, the basic livelihood of the people, the market main body, the food and energy security, the stability of the supply chain of the industrial chain, and the operation of the grass-roots. The employment is also the priority. The CCCPC and the State Council have also formulated a series of policies to help enterprises in distress, and introduced a number of measures to strengthen employment priority. On this basis, China's employment situation remained generally stable, with the total employment increasing from 180 million in 1949 to 750 million in 2020; by the end of 2020, the registered urban unemployment rate in China was 4.24%, which remained at a relatively low level; during the 13th Five-Year Plan period, more than 64 million new urban jobs were created, and the average annual new urban jobs remained at more than 10 million for many consecutive years. The employment structure has been continuously optimized, and the tertiary industry has become the industry that absorbs the most jobs. The proportion of urban employees increased from 48.4% in 2012 to 53.4% in 2016. The number of urban employees exceeded that of rural areas. The employment pattern in urban and rural areas has undergone a historic change. The labor force in the central and western regions has an obvious tendency to find jobs nearby and return to their hometown to start businesses. The quality of employment has been continuously improved, the wages of employees have been gradually raised, the protection of labor rights and interests has been strengthened, the employment behavior of enterprises has been increasingly standardized, and the coverage of social insurance has been continuously expanded. The ruling party and the government have continuously improved the mechanism for coordinating labor relations and mediating contradictions, resolutely prevented and corrected employment discrimination, established a long-term mechanism for resolving wage arrears of migrant workers, and promoted the whole society to jointly build harmonious labor relations.

Increase urban and rural incomes. We must ensure that personal income grows in step with economic growth and that wages increase in step with increases in labor productivity, and continuously work to grow personal incomes. We will improve primary income distribution, intensify efforts to regulate income redistribution, adjust and optimize the pattern of national income distribution, and work to bridge income gaps throughout the whole of society. We will improve the mechanisms allowing the market to evaluate factor contribution and base distribution on contribution. We will establish sound mechanisms for determining wage levels, ensuring regular pay increases, and guaranteeing payment; implement a system for collective wage bargaining within companies;

and improve the mechanism for increasing minimum wages. We will make pay systems for government offices and public institutions better adapted to the specific characteristics of these organizations. We will strengthen differentiated regulation over salary distribution in SOEs. We will give emphasis to the incentive role of income distribution policies and expand channels through which knowledge, technology, and management factors can take part in income distribution.

Personal property income will be increased through a variety of means. In terms of redistribution, we will narrow the income distribution gap by "expanding the middle, raising the low, adjusting the high, and cracking down on illegal incomes" and narrow the gap in income distribution. We will accelerate the establishment of a personal income tax system based on both adjusted gross income and specific types of income. We will bring certain luxury consumer items and high-expenditure activities under the scope of excise tax. We will improve tax policies which encourage giving back to society and helping to alleviate poverty. We will improve dynamic social security mechanisms aimed specifically at groups in difficult circumstances to ensure their basic needs are met. We will increase budgetary allocations for improving people's wellbeing, ensure that more of the earnings from the transfer of public resources go toward improving wellbeing, and gradually raise the proportion of revenue from state capital that is turned over to public finance. From 2013 to 2021, the per capita disposable income of Chinese residents increased from RMB 18,311 to RMB 35,128, and the income gap between urban and rural residents has continued to narrow.

We put education high on the development agenda. The ruling party and the government have closely implemented the fundamental task of building an education system to foster virtue and nurture a new generation of capable young people with the moral grounding, intellectual ability, physical vigor, aesthetic sensibility, and work skills. The main framework of the socialist education system with Chinese characteristics has been basically established. We will focus on reform and innovation to drive education development, focus on promoting education and teaching reform, deepen the reform of the examination and admission system, and stimulate the vitality of school operation. We will adopt a coordinated approach to developing world-class universities and disciplines. We will strengthen the construction of university innovation system, promote and regulate the development of private education, and actively develop "Internet + education." We will coordinate and promote the adjustment of education structure, promote the coordinated development of regional education, optimize the layout of basic education in urban and rural areas, accelerate the development of modern vocational education, adjust the structure of higher education, vigorously develop continuing education, and accelerate the training of talents urgently needed by modern industries. We will comprehensively improve the sharing level of education development, based on winning the battle of poverty alleviation through education, comprehensively promote targeted poverty alleviation and poverty elimination through education, comprehensively improve the basic school running conditions of schools with weak compulsory education in poor areas, implement the nutrition improvement plan for rural compulsory education students, the action plan for vocational education to realize the dream, and the pairing action for poverty alleviation through education, and achieve full coverage of the education stage through the funding policy system. We will promote the balanced and high-quality development of compulsory education, promote the balanced development within the county, accelerate the unification of the construction standards of compulsory education schools in urban and rural areas within the county, the unification of the teacher establishment standards, the unification of the standard quota of public funds per student, the unification of the basic equipment allocation standards, and the full coverage of the Two Cost-frees and One Subsidy policy in urban and rural areas, basically realize the balanced allocation of inter-school resources within the county. The provincial government will strengthen the overall planning to narrow the gap in the development of compulsory education within the province, work hard to improve the quality of education in rural, remote, poverty-stricken and ethnic areas where dropouts are concentrated, accelerate the development of preschool education, popularize high school education, and accelerate the development of ethnic education. We will continue to expand the coverage of high-quality education resources, and strive to solve the problems of "school selection fever" and "difficulty in entering kindergartens" strongly reflected by the people. During the "13th Five-Year Plan" period, China achieved the goal of "dynamic zero" of the 200,000 students who dropped out of school with poverty registration at the national compulsory education stage from the beginning of the establishment of the standing book, with a total of 391 million poor students and a total of 773.9 billion yuan. In 2021, the gross enrollment rate of preschool education reached 88.1%, the consolidation rate of nine-year compulsory education reached 95.4%, the gross enrollment rate of high school education reached 91.4%, and the gross enrollment rate of higher education reached 57.8%, realizing a historic leap from mass access to universal access. Efforts have been made to build a stronger team of teachers, and the establishment of a complete system of teacher ethics construction covering primary, middle and primary schools has been accelerated. China's education has leapt to the top of the world. The average length of education of the working age population has increased from 7.18 years in 2000 to 10.9 years in 2021. Basic education has been consolidated and developed, and higher education has entered the stage of popularization.

We will step up development of the social safety net. The ruling party and government adhere to the principle of full coverage, basic protection, multi-level and sustainable development, put the construction of the social security system in a more prominent position, constantly deepen the reform of the social security system, and promote the construction of China's social security system into the fast lane. The following important documents have been issued, and the system design has been continuously improved: Opinions on the Establishment of a Unified Basic Pension Insurance System for Urban and Rural Residents, Decision on the Reform of the Pension System for Employees of Party and Government Offices and Public Institutions, Opinions on Accelerating the Development of Commercial Pension Schemes, Opinions on the Integration of the Basic Medical Insurance System for Rural Residents with that for Non-Working Urban Residents, Opinions on Comprehensive Implementation of Serious Illness Insurance for Urban and Rural Residents, Opinions on Improving the Insurance System and Social Assistance for Serious and Major Diseases. On this basis, China has gradually unified the Basic old-age Insurance for urban and rural residents, brought government office and public institution pension schemes into line with enterprise schemes, and established a central system for enterprise employees' basic old-age pension funds to be used inter-provincially. We will continue to make progress in aligning basic medical insurance schemes for rural residents and non-working urban residents and fully implement serious illness insurance for urban and rural residents, and establish National Healthcare Security Administration. We will promote the universal coverage of social security, reduce social insurance premiums, and continue to appropriate a portion of state capital to replenish social security funds. We will actively develop welfare services such as old-age care, child care, and assistance for the disabled. The people, regardless of urban and rural areas, regions, gender, and occupations, have corresponding institutional guarantees in the face of risks such as old age, disease, unemployment, industrial injury, disability, and poverty. China's social security system, with social insurance as the main body, including social assistance, social welfare, social special care and other systems, has been basically completed. By 2020, the number of people covered by basic medical insurance has been 1.36 billion, and the number of those covered by basic old-age insurance has now been about 1 billion. China has established the world's largest social security system.

We should implement the Healthy China strategy. In August 2016, the National Health Conference was held. The conference put forward: we will focus on the grassroots, pursue reform and innovation as a driving force and disease prevention as the priority, give importance to both traditional Chinese medicine and western medicine, incorporate health into all policy-making, and strive for participation by all and benefits to all. In October, the CCCPC and the State Council issued the Outline of the Healthy China 2030, which made comprehensive arrangements for the construction of a healthy China. This is the action program for promoting the construction of a healthy China in the next 15 years. The Outline put forward that "collaboration and sharing, and health for all" is the strategic theme of building a healthy China; Co-construction and sharing is the basic path to build a healthy China; A healthy population is the fundamental goal of building a healthy China. The Outline defines the strategic goal of a healthy China, that is, by 2020, a basic medical and health system with Chinese characteristics covering urban and rural residents will be established, the level of health literacy will be continuously improved, the health service system will be perfect and efficient, everyone will enjoy basic medical and health services and basic sports and fitness services, and a health industry system with rich connotation and reasonable structure will be basically formed. Main health indicators will be generally higher than the average level of middle- and high-income countries. By 2030, the system for promoting the health of the whole people will be improved, the development of the health sector will be more coordinated, the healthy lifestyle will be popularized, the quality of health services and the level of health protection will be continuously improved, the health industry will flourish and develop, and the health equity will be basically realized. The main health indicators will enter the ranks of high-income countries. By 2050, we will build a healthy country compatible with a modern socialist country. According to this policy and deployment, the reform of the medical and health system should advance coordinated reform of medical services, medical insurance and the medicine industry, raising the public's awareness to prevent and control epidemics, and striving to provide the public with life-cycle healthcare services to continuously promote the transformation of disease treatment to health management. In the new era, China is making every effort to make progress in building a healthy China, shifting the focus from treating ailments to healthcare. The basic medical and health system with Chinese characteristics has been basically established, the public health service system covers the whole people, and the overall strength of health services has been significantly improved. The average life expectancy of Chinese people has risen from 76.3 years in 2015 to 77.3 years. The main health indicators of the Chinese are generally higher than the average level of middle- and high-income countries. Personal health expenditures as a percentage of total health costs dropped to 28.4%. The building of a healthy China has made a good start.

Adjust Family Planning. At the beginning of the founding of new China, China did not study and formulate clear policies of population and family planning. In the 1950s, with the rapid increase of China's natural population growth rate, the country began to have the idea and efforts of population control and family planning. However, under the influence of the "left" thinking, the family planning work that has not yet been carried out universally has been forced to stop. Facing the pressure of sustained and rapid population growth, since the 1970s, the ruling party and government have gradually strengthened family planning work, incorporated population growth indicators into the national economic plan, and began to implement a stricter family planning policy with the one-child policy as the core content. Historically, family planning has played a great role in solving China's own population and development problems. However, in recent years, with China's transformation from high fertility rate to low fertility rate, the disappearance of the population dividend, the approaching of ultra-low birth rate, the aging of the population, the gender imbalance in babies and other issues have gradually become prominent, and the family planning policy has reached a historical point that has to be adjusted. In November 2013, the Third Plenary Session of the 18th CCCPC proposed to implement the policy of that married couples can have a second child if one of the parents is a single child. In December of the same year, the Sixth Meeting of the Standing Committee of the 12th NPC agreed to start the implementation of this policy. In October 2015, the Fifth Plenary Session of the 18th CCCPC proposed to fully implement the policy that all couples can now have two children, that is, the "universal two-child policy." In December 2015, the 18th Meeting of the Standing Committee of the 12th NPC passed the amendment to the Population and Family Planning

Law, which clearly defined the unified implementation of the two-child policy throughout the country. In June 2021, the CCCPC and the State Council adopted the Decision on Improving the Family Planning Policy so as to Promote Balanced Development of the Population over the Long Term, implementing the policy that allows families to have up to three children. In August of the same year, the Standing Committee of the NPC adopted the draft the amendment to the Population and Family Planning Law. The newly revised law stipulates that the state promotes age-appropriate marriage, healthy childbirth and child rearing, and that a couple can have up to three children.

(2) Solidly Promote Common Prosperity

Common prosperity is the essential requirement of socialism and an important feature of Chinese modernization. In the new era, China has placed the promotion of common prosperity of all its people in a more important position.

In October 2020, the Fifth Plenary Session of the 19th CCCPC listed "achieving well-rounded human development and common prosperity for all" as an important part of the long-term goal of basically realizing socialist modernization in 2035, and proposed that we should adhere to the starting point and foothold of development of achieving, safeguarding and developing the fundamental interests of the broadest masses of people, do our best and do what we can, improve the basic public service system, improve the social governance system of co-construction, common governance and sharing, promote common prosperity in a down-to-earth manner, constantly enhance the people's sense of gain, happiness and security, and promote well-rounded human development and social progress.

In August 2021, Xi Jinping elaborated on solidly promoting common prosperity at the 10th meeting of the Central Finance and Economics Commission On why we should promote common prosperity in a down-to-earth manner, he pointed out, "Now, we are working towards the Second Centenary Goal—to build China into a modern socialist country that is prosperous, strong, democratic, culturally advanced, harmonious, and beautiful by the centenary of the PRC in 2049. To adapt to the principal challenge facing Chinese society as it evolves, and to meet the growing expectation of the people for a better life and work for happiness for all of our people, we must focus on promoting common prosperity, which will in turn strengthen the foundations of our Party's long-term governance. High-quality development requires a high-caliber workforce. Only by promoting common prosperity, raising urban and rural income levels, and boosting human capital, can we increase total factor productivity and create the driving force for high-quality development. Currently, income inequality has become a glaring problem worldwide. In some countries, the wealth gap is widening and the middle class is shrinking, resulting in social disintegration, political polarization, and a surge of populism. This is a profound lesson. China must prevent polarization between the rich and the poor, promote common prosperity, and ensure social harmony and stability." On what is common prosperity, he stressed, "The common prosperity that we pursue, both material and cultural, is for all of our people; it is not for a small minority, nor does it imply an absolute equality in income distribution that takes no account of contribution." As for the steps to achieve common prosperity, he proposed that "Based on thorough research, we should map out phased goals of common prosperity for different development stages: By 2025, the end of the 14th Five-Year Plan period (2021–2025), a solid step will have been taken towards common prosperity, steadily narrowing the gap between people's income and consumption. By 2035, more substantial progress will have been made in promoting common prosperity, ensuring equal access to basic public services. By the middle of the 21st century, common prosperity for all will have largely been achieved, narrowing the gap between people's income and consumption to a reasonable level." On the way to achieve common prosperity, he pointed out that, "The overarching principle is to uphold the people-centered development philosophy and promote common prosperity through high-quality development. We must balance efficiency and fairness in income distribution and devise an institutional framework within which distribution, redistribution and third distribution are coordinated and operate in parallel. Efforts should be intensified to improve the role of taxation, social security and transfer payments in adjusting income distribution, particularly for targeted social groups. The proportion of the middle-income group in the entire population should be increased, the low-income group should have their incomes raised, the high-income group should have their incomes reasonably readjusted, and illicit income should be confiscated, so as to form an olive-shaped distribution structure. The goal is to increase social fairness and justice, promote well-rounded development of the individual, and enable the people to make solid progress towards common prosperity." "achieving common prosperity for all is a holistic concept similar in nature to realizing moderate prosperity in all respects. Common prosperity is a goal for all of society, and therefore we should not break it up into separate goals for urban and rural areas, or for eastern, central and western regions. Instead, we should adopt an overall perspective. In order to enable 1.4 billion people to realize common prosperity, we must maintain a realistic attitude and make a sustained effort. We cannot make everyone wealthy at the same time, nor bring all regions to the same level of wealth simultaneously. There will be different levels of prosperity among different groups of people and different regions, realized on a different time scale. It should be a dynamic process where consistent efforts result in steady progress."[85]

In May 2021, the CCCPC and the State Council issued the Opinions on Support Zhejiang Province in Pursuing High-Quality Development and Building Itself into a Demonstration Zone for Common Prosperity, which is a major decision made by the ruling party and government to place greater emphasis on promoting common prosperity for all. Closely focusing on promoting common prosperity and promoting well-rounded human development, the Opinions has made plans and arrangements for supporting Zhejiang's high-quality development and building a common prosperity demonstration zone around the construction of institutional mechanisms and policy systems conducive to common prosperity. Proceeding from the goal orientation, the Opinions focuses on people-centered common prosperity in an all-round way, and focuses on planning and deployment in terms of people's material life, spiritual life, ecological environment, social environment and public services. It is proposed that by 2025, Zhejiang Province will make significant substantive progress in promoting high-quality development and building common prosperity demonstration areas. The quality and efficiency of economic development will have been significantly improved, the per capita GDP will have reached the level of moderately developed economies, and equil-access to basic public services will have been realized; the gap between urban and rural areas in regional development, the gap between urban and rural residents in income and living standards will continue to narrow, the income increasing ability and social welfare of low-income groups will be significantly improved, the olive type social structure with middle-income groups as the main body will be basically formed, the living standard of the province's residents will reach a new level, and social etiquette and civility will be significantly enhanced; new achievements will have been made in the construction of a beautiful Zhejiang, the governance capacity will have been significantly improved, and the people's life will become better; the institutional mechanism and policy framework for promoting common prosperity will have been basically established, and a number of successful experiences that can be replicated and popularized will have been formed. By 2035, Zhejiang Province will make greater achievements in high-quality development and basically achieve common prosperity. The per capita GDP and the income of urban and rural residents will strive to reach the level of developed economies, the coordinated development of urban and rural areas will be higher, the pattern of income and wealth distribution will be more optimized, the construction of a rule of law and a safe Zhejiang will reach a higher level, the modernization of China's system and capacity for governance will be significantly improved, and the material, political, spiritual, social and ecological civilizations will be comprehensively improved. The system of common prosperity will be improved. The Opinions clearly defined the major measures in six aspects. First, improve the quality and efficiency of development and consolidate the material foundation for common prosperity. Second, deepen reform of the income distribution system and increase the income channels of urban and rural residents. Third, narrow the development gap between urban and rural areas and realize high-quality sharing of public services. Fourth, create a new era of cultural heights and enrich people's intellectual and cultural lives. Fifth, practice the concept that green mountains and lucid waters are indeed mountains of gold and silver, and create a beautiful and livable living environment. Sixth, adhere to and develop the "Fengqiao Experience" in the new era, and build a comfortable social environment. Common prosperity in a big country with a population of more than 1.4 billion is an endeavor never undertaken in the history of mankind.

In July of the same year, Zhejiang printed and issued the Implementation Plan for High-Quality Development and Construction of Common Prosperity Demonstration Zones in Zhejiang (2021–2025), which proposed to promote high-quality development and construction of common prosperity demonstration zones to achieve significant substantive progress by 2025, and form phased and landmark achievements. Guided by the reform of "expanding the middle" and "raising the low," Zhejiang has set up the overall framework of "1 + 5 + n" major reform, focusing on narrowing the regional development gap, narrowing the development gap between urban and rural areas, sharing high-quality public services, achieving common prosperity in spiritual life, and achieving common prosperity as the basic unit of modernization, and has made efforts to form a number of advanced demonstration experiences. In addition, Zhejiang has also completed the selection of the first batch of pilot projects for the construction of the common prosperity demonstration zones, and identified six major areas with a total of 28 pilot projects, including narrowing the regional gap, narrowing the urban-rural gap, narrowing the income gap, promoting the sharing of high-quality public services, building a highland of spiritual civilization, and building a basic unit for the modernization of common prosperity. At present, the pilot work is progressing in an orderly manner.

4.5.2 We Should Establish a Social Governance Model Based on Collaboration, Participation, and Common Interests

Since the reform and opening-up, with the rapid development of China's economy, profound changes have taken place in China's economic structure and social structure, and profound changes have taken place in the way of social organization, social behavior norms and values. It is an important task for China to innovate social governance methods and accelerate the formation of a scientific and effective social governance system.

Defining the top-level design is the primary task to improve the social governance system. In November 2012, the report of the 18th National Congress of the CPC proposed: to strengthen social development, we must accelerate social structural reform. In November 2013, the Third Plenary Session of the 18th CCCPC further proposed the concept of "social governance." The Decision of the CCCPC on Some Major Issues Concerning Comprehensively Continuing the Reform adopted at the plenary session puts forward that "to innovate social governance, we must focus on safeguarding the fundamental interests of the broadest masses of the people, maximize the factors of harmony, enhance the vitality of social development, improve the level of social governance, comprehensively promote the Safe China Initiative, safeguard national security, and ensure that the people live and work in peace and contentment and social stability and order."[86] Focusing on "making innovation in the social management system," the plenary session made arrangements for such important work as improving the social governance mode, stimulating the vitality of social organizations, innovating the system for effectively preventing and resolving social conflicts, and improving the public security system. The change from social management to social governance reflects the new concepts and new thinking of the CPC and the Chinese government in dealing with social problems and solving social contradictions under the new historical conditions. In October 2015, the Fifth Plenary Session of the 18th CCCPC further put forward the new requirements of "strengthening and innovating social governance, promoting the refined social governance, and establishing a social governance model based on collaboration, participation, and common interests."

Later, the Fourth Session of the 12th NPC adopted the Outline of the 13th Five-Year Plan for National Economic and Social Development in March, 2016. A special section on "strengthening and innovating social governance" puts forward specific requirements for strengthening and innovating social governance. On the basis of remarkable achievements in innovating the social governance system, in October 2019, the Fourth Plenary Session of the 19th CCCPC made new arrangements for improving the effective mechanism for correctly handling contradictions among the people under the new situation, improving the social security prevention and control system, improving the public security system and mechanism, building a new pattern of grass-roots social governance and improving the national security system, focusing on upholding and improving the social governance system of joint construction, governance and sharing.

Improving the government's governance ability and level is the key link of social governance. In September 2016, the State Council issued the Guidelines on Making Progress with the Internet Plus Government Services, which proposed that by the end of 2017, the people's governments of all provinces (autonomous regions and municipalities) and relevant departments of the State Council should build an integrated online platform for government services, fully publicize government affairs, and significantly improve the standardization and networking of government services. By the end of 2020, we achieved the indepth integration of the Internet and government services, and build an "internet Plus government services" system that covers the whole country with overall linkage, departmental coordination, provincial-level coordination, and access via one website. We will significantly improve the level of intelligent government services, make government services smarter, and make it more convenient, faster, and more efficient for enterprises and the masses. In June 2018, the general office of the State Council issued the Reform Implementation Plan on Further Deepen the "Internet + Government Services" to "Promote Government Services Done through a Single Website at a Single Window within a Specified Time," to promote governments at all levels to accelerate the transformation of government functions and improve the efficiency and transparency of government services.

Extensive participation of social forces is a prominent feature of social governance. Policy documents such as Guiding Opinions on the Government's Purchase of Services from Social Forces "Measures for the Administration of the Government's Purchase of Services (for the time being)" have been issued one after another to speed up the improvement of the way the government providing public services, gradually change the traditional practice of the government taking the lead, build a diversified public service supply system, reasonably definine the functional roles of the government, the market and society, and fully release the great energy of micro-entities. In August 2016, the general office of the CCCPC and the general office of the State Council issued the Opinions on Reforming the Management System of Social Organizations to Promote the Healthy and Orderly Development of Social Organizations, so as to promote them to play a better role and realize the benign interaction between government governance, social regulation and residents' self-governance. According to statistics, there are more than 800,000 social organizations registered with the Ministry of Civil Affairs and the civil affairs departments in various places. Many areas have established incubation institutions for community social organizations to support the sound system of community social organizations. A law-based social management system featuring Party committee leadership, government execution, nongovernmental support and public participation is basically established in China, and a social governance model based on collaboration, participation, and common interests has taken shape.

Social credit construction is an important part of social governance. In June 2014, the State Council issued *Outline of Social Credit System Construction Plan (2014–2020)*, marking the beginning of a new stage of the social governance revolution with the construction of the social credit system as the core. In March 2022, the general office of the CCCPC and the general office of the State Council issued the *Opinions on Promoting the High-Quality Development of Social Credit System Construction and Promoting the Formation of a New Development Pattern*, further making relevant arrangements for promoting the high-quality development of social credit system construction. Since 2016, the Supreme People's Court has launched a three-year battle to solve the difficulty of enforcement. Courts at all levels have accepted 20.435 million enforcement cases, concluded 19.361 million cases, and implemented 4.4 trillion yuan, up 98.5%, 105.1% and 71.2% respectively year on year. The Supreme People's Court, together with the NDRC and other 60 units, promoted the construction of the disciplinary mechanism for dishonesty, adopted 150 disciplinary measures in 11 categories, promoted 3.66 million people to perform their obligations automatically under pressure, and promoted the construction of the rule of law and social integrity.[87]

Grass roots governance is an important cornerstone of social governance. In August 2017, the national standard of Urban and Rural Community Grid-Based

Service Management Norms was released, which provides more standardized guidance for a grass-roots governance system. In April 2021, the CCCPC and the State Council issued the *Opinions on Strengthening the Modernization of the Grass-Roots Governance System and Governance Capacity*, which proposed to strive to establish a grass-roots governance system with unified leadership of Party organizations, the government performing its responsibilities by law, active coordination of various organizations, broad participation of the masses, and the combination of self-governance, rule of law and rule of virtue in about five years, and improve the grass-roots governance mechanism with dynamic connection between normal management and emergency management, build a grass-roots management service platform with grid management, fine service, information support and open sharing; Party building has led to the comprehensive improvement of the grass-roots governance mechanism, the grass-roots political power is strong and powerful, the grass-roots self-governance is full of vitality, the grass-roots public services are accurate and efficient, the Party's governance foundation is more solid, and the modernization level of the grass-roots governance system and governance capacity is significantly improved. On this basis, we will strive to basically modernize the grass-roots governance system and governance capacity in another 10 years, and fully demonstrate the advantages of the grass-roots governance system with Chinese characteristics. This is a programmatic document for promoting the modernization of grassroots governance in the new era. In the new era, the focus of China's social governance has moved down to the grass-roots level, and more resources, services and management have been delegated to the grass-roots level. China's grass-roots governance system and mechanism have been continuously improved. The government governance, social regulation and residents' autonomy have achieved a positive interaction. The socialization, rule of law, intellectualization and specialization of grass-roots governance have been steadily improved.

4.5.3 Promote the Safe China Initiative

Social stability is the premise and foundation of economic development and an important guarantee for people's happy life. In the new era, the CPC and the Chinese government attach great importance to the issue of public security, and put the Safe China Initiative in the overall development of the cause of socialism with Chinese characteristics. In November 2012, the report of the 18th National Congress of the CPC proposed: we should intensify efforts to ensure law and order, improve the multi-dimensional system for crime prevention and control, strengthen the infrastructure of judicial bodies, and prevent and punish criminal and illegal activities in accordance with the law to protect the people's lives and property. In January 2013, Xi Jinping gave an important instruction on doing a good job in political and legal work under the new situation, proposing to "make every effort to promote the Safe China Initiative." Subsequently, he made important instructions many times, comprehensively expounded the major theoretical and practical issues of overall, strategic and fundamental significance in the Safe China Initiative, and promoted Initiative. In October 2017, the report of the 19th National Congress of the CPC clearly put forward: We will continue the Peaceful China initiative, strengthen and develop new forms of social governance, and ensure social harmony and stability. We must work hard to see that our country enjoys enduring peace and stability and our people live and work in contentment.[88] The Congress attached great importance to the Safe China Initiative and included it as an important content in the eighth aspect of the "14 insist" and made it an important content of the basic strategy of upholding and developing socialism with Chinese characteristics in the new era. When planning the social governance system, the Third Plenary Session of the 18th CCCPC and the Fourth Plenary Session of the 19th CCCPC also made comprehensive arrangements for the development of the Safe China Initiative. The Fifth Plenary Session of the 18th CCCPC and the Fifth Plenary Session of the 19th CCCPC respectively included "the Safe China Initiative" and "building a higher level of safe China" in the 13th Five-Year Plan proposal, the 14th Five-Year Plan and the 2035 long-term goal proposal. Subsequently, they were written into the 13th Five-Year Plan Outline, the 14th Five-Year Plan and the 2035 long-term goal outline through legal procedures, which became China's national will. On the basis of increasingly perfect top-level design, the Safe China Initiative has been steadily promoted.

A sound environment of public security is the prerequisite for a safe China. In April 2015, the general office of the CCCPC and the general office of the State Council issued the Opinions on Strengthening the Public Security System for Crime Prevention and Control, which made comprehensive arrangements for the construction of the social security prevention and control system, and proposed to form a working pattern of the social security prevention and control system led by the Party committee, led by the government, coordinated comprehensive management, coordinated by all departments, and actively participated by social forces, improve the operation mechanism of social security prevention and control, and weave a social security prevention and control network, improve the rule of law, socialization and informatization of the construction of the social security prevention and control system, enhance the overall prevention and control capacity of social security, strive to effectively curb violent terrorist crimes and individual extreme violent crimes that affect public security, effectively prevent multiple cases and public security accidents that affect the people's sense of security, significantly improve the people's sense of security and satisfaction, and make society more harmonious and orderly. With the implementation of the Opinions, the public security system for crime prevention and control has been gradually improved. More and more security networks, such as the crime prevention and control network, the security prevention and control network of key areas, and the security prevention and control network of townships and villages, provide comprehensive and multi-level security protection for the masses. "Dama in Xicheng District" and "Chaoyang people" and other brands that combine the efforts of both professionals and the people have been constantly emerging. The incentive mechanisms such as reporting rewards, substituting awards for subsidies, volunteer service points, and issuing Wechat red envelope (containing money) as a gift have been continuously improved. The network, telephone, Small Message Service (SMS), app, Weibo, wechat and other channels for expressing and reflecting social conditions and public opinions have been continuously improved. In January 2018, the CCCPC and the State Council issued the Notice on Launch a Campaign to Crack Down on Organized Crime and Local Mafia, which launched a three-year special struggle against organized crimes and local mafia. According to statistics, a total of 3,644 mafia related organizations have been eliminated in the special struggle to eliminate the local mafia, 1.3 times the total of the previous 10 years; 89,742 cases of criminal syndicate-related corruption and protection rackets were investigated and dealt with, 115,913 people were placed on file, 80,649 people were given party discipline and administrative sanctions, and referred cases involving 10,432 of them to the judiciary for prosecution. Criminal syndicates and vicious crimes have been fundamentally curbed, which has effectively promoted the continuous improvement of the social security situation and further enhanced the people's sense of security. In May 2021, the general office of the CCCPC and the general office of the State Council issued the Opinions on Consolidating the Achievements of the Struggle to Crack down on Organized Crime and Root out Local Criminal Gangs on an Ongoing Basis, and made arrangements for the regular fight against organized crime and root out local criminal gangs. By 2020, the total number of criminal cases filed in China had decreased for five consecutive years, and the number of eight major criminal cases and the number of public security cases investigated and dealt with had decreased for six consecutive years; according to the survey of the National Bureau of statistics, the people's sense of security has increased year by year, reaching 98.4% by 2020.

Preventing and resolving social conflicts is an important foundation for the Safe China Initiative. In March 2014, the general office of the CCCPC and the general office of the State Council issued the *Opinions on Settling Complaints Involving Law Violations and Lawsuits Made in the Form of Letters and Visits in Accordance with the Law,* which comprehensively elaborated the main contents, supporting measures and work requirements of the establishment of a system for settling complaints involving law violations and lawsuits made in the form of letters and visits in accordance with the law and deal with them by law. The "Opinions" not only compels the political and legal organs to improve the quality and level of law enforcement from the perspective of system and mechanism, but also create an environment of respect for the rule of law in which all of our people work in accordance with the law, look to the law when meeting difficulties, and rely on the law to resolve problems, so as to better protect the people's legitimate rights and interests and contribute to social stability and harmony. In October 2015, the 17th meeting of the central leading group for comprehensively deepening reform adopted the Opinions on Improving Mechanisms for Settling Tensions and Disputes through Multiple Means. The diversified dispute resolution mechanism has gradually been elevated from the diversified dispute resolution mechanism of the court system to the strategic action of modernizing the national governance system and capabilities. In February 2021, the 18th meeting of the Central Committee for Deepening Overall Reform adopted the Opinions on Strengthening the Governance of the Sources of Litigation and Promoting the Resolution of Conflicts and Disputes. It stressed the need to adhere to and develop the "Fengqiao Experience" in the new era, put the non-litigation dispute resolution mechanism in the front, promote more legal forces to guide, strengthen the prevention of conflicts and disputes at the source, the front-end resolution, and the control at the gateway, and improve the preventive legal system, and reduce litigation increment from the source. In the new era, China's social contradictions have been effectively resolved. In recent years, the total number of letters and visits across the country has decreased significantly, and the total number of group visits has decreased for 11 consecutive years. In 2020, the total number of litigation cases and civil litigation cases accepted by the courts in the country achieved a "double drop" for the first time after 15 years of continuous growth.

Public security is an important part of the Safe China Initiative. In terms of production safety, in December 2016, the CCCPC and the State Council issued the Opinions on Promoting Reform of Safe Production, which is the first programmatic document on production safety issued in the name of the CCCPC and the State Council since the founding of new China. The "Opinions" stipulates the safety production responsibility system of "both Party committees and governments assume responsibility, officials perform their duties while also taking responsibility for workplace safety, and those who fail to uphold safety standards are held accountable." It requires the establishment of a mechanism for enterprises to implement the main responsibility for safety production, the establishment of a rectification and supervision system for accident exposure problems, the establishment of a system for safety production supervision and law enforcement personnel to perform their statutory duties according to law, and the implementation of the "one vote against meaning veto" against the risk of major accidents. It points out the direction and path for the reform and development in the field of production safety in China at present and in the future. On this basis, relevant departments have formulated policy documents such as the Regulations on the Responsibility System for Safe Production of Local Party and Government Leading Cadres, to create a sound workplace safety and management responsibility system to establish systems for the investigation of potential public safety hazards and for safety-oriented prevention and control, and carried out a three-year drive to promote workplace safety since 2020. In terms of emergency management, in 2018, China set up a Ministry of Emergency Management to establish an emergency management system with unified command, both special and regular functions, sensitive response and linkage between the upper and lower levels. On this basis, 461 rescue teams for earthquake disasters and 27 rescue teams for geology, mountains and waters were newly established to continuously improve the national emergency management capacity and enhance the ability of disaster prevention, mitigation, resistance, and relief. In terms of food and drug safety, the outline of the "13th Five-Year Plan" proposes to implement the food safety strategy, raising the food safety issue to the national strategic level. In May 2019, the CCCPC and the State Council issued the Opinions on Deepening Reform and Strengthening Food Safety Work, which is the first programmatic document on food safety work issued in the name of the CCCPC and the State Council to accelerating the establishment of a modern governance system in the field of food safety. In May 2021, the general office of the State Council issued the Opinions on Comprehensively Strengthening the Building of Drug Regulatory Capacity to promote the establishment of a scientific, efficient and authoritative drug regulatory system for the protection of people's health and life safety.

The construction of the public security contingent provides an important guarantee for the Safe China Initiative. In February 2015, the Central Committee adopted the Framework Opinions on Several Major Issues of Comprehensively Deepening Public Security Reform and relevant reform plans, which defined the guiding ideology, objectives, tasks, basic principles, policy measures and work requirements of comprehensively deepening public security reform, and pointed out the way forward and provided important guidance for comprehensively deepening public security reform. The Opinions clearly define the overall objectives of comprehensively deepening public security reform as follows: to improve the modern police operation mechanism and law enforcement power operation mechanism compatible with modernizing the national governance system and capabilities and the construction of a socialist legal system with Chinese characteristics, to establish a public security organ management system that conforms to the nature and tasks of public security organs, and to establish a people's police management system that reflects the professional characteristics of the people's police and is different from other civil servants. By 2020, we basically formed a systematic, scientific, standardized and effective public security work and public security team management system, realized basic informatization, practical policing, standardized law enforcement and regularization of the team, and further enhanced the people's sense of security, satisfaction and public security organs' credibility in law enforcement. This is a comprehensive, systematic and fundamental reform. The reform measures include seven major tasks and more than 100 specific measures, covering almost all levels and fields of public security work and public security team building. Through reform, the overall efficiency and core combat effectiveness of public security work in the new era have been continuously improved, and social harmony and stability are more guaranteed.

In December 2021, the commendation conference for the Safe China Initiative was held in Beijing. 140 outstanding groups and 129 outstanding individuals of the Safe China Initiative were commended, 60 demonstration cities of the Safe China Initiative and 160 demonstration counties of the Safe China Initiative were named, and 73 cities and counties were awarded "Chang'an Cup." In the new era, the Safe China Initiative has made historic achievements, and constantly opened up a new realm of the "sound governance."

4.5.4 China's National Security Is Better Safeguarded

In the new era, China is faced with more acute national security challenges, as evidenced by unprecedented external pressure, intertwined traditional and non-traditional security threats, and frequent "black swan" and "grey rhino" events.

In view of the new security situation, the ruling party and government put forward and explained a holistic approach to national security. In April, 2014, at the first meeting of the National Security Commission, Xi Jinping put forward for the first time a holistic approach to national security. He stressed that, therefore, we must maintain a holistic view of national security, take the people's security as our ultimate goal, achieve political security as our fundamental task, regard economic security as our foundation, with military, cultural and public security as means of guarantee, and promote international security so as to establish a national security system with Chinese characteristics. In July 2015, the 15th Meeting of the Standing Committee of the 12th NPC voted to adopt the new National Security Law, which includes cybersecurity, ecological security, resource security, nuclear security, overseas interests security, outer space security, international seabed area security, and polar security into the overall national security. In October 2017, the report of the 19th National Congress of the CPC made a systematic elaboration: we must put national interests first, take protecting our people's security as our mission and safeguarding political security as a fundamental task, and ensure both internal and external security, homeland and public security, traditional and non-traditional security, and China's own and common security. We must improve our systems and institutions and enhance capacity-building for national security, and resolutely safeguard China's sovereignty, security, and development interests. At the same time, a holistic approach to national security is written in the newly revised Party Constitution as the basic policy to uphold and develop socialism with Chinese characteristics in the new era. After the outbreak of COVID-19, biosafety was also included in the national security system.

Under the guidance of a holistic approach to national security, China will continue to improve national security system. First, improve the national security leadership system. The Third Plenary Session of the 18th CCCPC established a National Security Committee as circumstances change. The main responsibilities of the National Security Commission are to formulate and implement national security strategy, promote national security legislation, design principles and policies for national security work, discuss and resolve key issues concerning national security, improve the centralized, high-performing, and authoritative leadership system for national security. In January 2014, the Political Bureau of the CCCPC held a meeting to study and decide on the establishment of the National Security Committee. In April, Central National Security Commission launched its first meeting. Second, improve the national security system. The Party Central Committee, with Comrade Xi Jinping at its core, attaches great importance to the construction of the national security legal system, and has put forward clear requirements for the construction of the national security legal system, namely, to strive to basically form a set of national security legal system with Chinese characteristics that is based on China's national conditions, reflects the characteristics of the times, and is adapt to the strategic security environment in which China is located, with coordinated content, strict procedures, complete support, and effective operation.[89] The Central National Security Commission, in accordance with its responsibilities, has actively promoted national security legislation, and China has developed and revised a series of laws, such as the Counter-Espionage Law of the PRC, the State Security Law of the PRC, the Law of the PRC on Administration of Activities of Overseas Nongovernmental Organizations in the Mainland of China, the Cybersecurity Law of the PRC, the Nuclear Safety Law of the PRC, the Counter-Terrorism Law of the PRC, National Intelligence Law of the PRC. The National Security Law stipulates that April 15 of each year is the National Security Education Day for the whole people. Since the 18th National Congress of the CPC, China has initially established the main framework of the national security system, improved the national security legal system, strategic system and policy system, and established the national security coordination mechanism and emergency management mechanism. Third, consolidated the public line of defense for national security, enhance the national security awareness of all people, and improve mechanisms for assessing national security risks, and coordinating efforts to prevent, control, forestall, and fend off these risks.

While strengthening the construction of the national security system, China has gradually strengthened its national security work and enhanced its national security capacity. In December 2016, the meeting of the Political Bureau of the CCCPC adopted the Opinions on Strengthening National Security Work, which requires that we must adhere to the overall national security concept, take people's security as the purpose, coordinate the domestic and international overall situation, coordinate the development of two major security issues, effectively integrate all forces, comprehensively use various means, maintain national security in all fields, build a national security system, and take the path of national security with Chinese characteristics. In November 2021, the Political Bureau of the CCCPC held a meeting to review the National Security Strategy (2021–2025). The meeting pointed out that to safeguard national security under the new situation, we must firmly establish a holistic approach to national security and accelerate the construction of a new security pattern. We must uphold the Party's absolute leadership, improve the centralized, unified, efficient and authoritative leadership system for national security work, and achieve the unity of political security, people's security, and national interests; adhere to safeguarding national sovereignty and territorial integrity, and maintain stability and order in the border areas, borders and surrounding areas; adhere to safe development, promote high-quality development and high-level safety dynamic balance; adhere to overall war and make overall planning for traditional and non-traditional security; should adhere to the path of peaceful development and promote coordination between our own security and common security. In the new era, the Party and the Chinese government has incorporated security imperatives into all areas throughout the process of national development, placed emphasis on guarding against and defusing major risks that may affect China's modernization process, and resolutely safeguarded political, institutional, and ideological security. The Party has enhanced efforts to raise public awareness about the importance of national security and national defense and consolidated the public line of defense for national security. Solid steps have been taken to boost development, raise living standards, and ensure stability in border areas and to strictly prevent and crack down on infiltration, sabotage, subversion, and separatist activities by hostile forces. The Party has withstood and pushed back against extreme external pressure, stood up on issues such as those related to Hong Kong, Taiwan, Xinjiang, Xizang, and territorial waters, and moved faster to build a strong maritime country. Through all these efforts, we have effectively safeguarded national security.

4.5.5 The Fight against COVID-19

Last year was an extraordinary year in the history of the PRC. In the past six months, the world was swept up in an unexpected coronavirus epidemic disrupted the normal order of production and life. The novel coronavirus disease (COVID-19) epidemic is a major public health emergency that has spread the fastest caused the most extensive infections and been the hardest to contain since the founding of the PRC in 1949 and the most serious pandemic in the past century.

In the face of the sudden epidemic, the CCCPC implemented centralized and unified leadership immediately. The Standing Committee of the Political Bureau of the CCCPC and the Political Bureau of the CCCPC held meetings on many occasions to study and make decisions. They put forward the general requirements to stay confident, stand united, and adopt both a science-based approach and targeted measures. A central leading group for coordinating the epidemic response was established and a central guidance team was dispatched. Full play was given to the functions of the State Council interdepartmental task force.

On January 20, 2020, Xi Jinping gave instructions on the coronavirus epidemic outbreak, calling for resolute containment of the spreading momentum of the epidemic. On the afternoon of January 22, the CCCPC, with Comrade Xi Jinping at its core, took stock of the situation and called for the immediate imposing of the most stringent closure and traffic control on the movement of people and exit routes in Hubei Province and Wuhan City. It is conceivable how difficult it is to close the passage of a large city with a population of 10 million. This decision requires great political courage. The WHO Expert delegation to China agreed that the measures taken by China were very timely and effective, which not only prevented the spread of the epidemic in China, but also bought time for the world.

Under the strong leadership of the CPC and the Chinese government, the whole country has rapidly formed a strategic layout of unified command, comprehensive deployment and three-dimensional prevention and control. It has launched a people's war, an overall war and a blockbuster war against the epidemic, effectively curbing the large-scale spread of the epidemic and effectively changing the dangerous process of virus transmission. In the fight against the epidemic, China basically controlled the spread of the virus within more than 1 month, capped daily increase of new local cases to single digits within 2 months, achieved decisive victory in freeing Wuhan and Hubei from the clutch of the virus within 3 months. The decisive result of the defense of Hubei, followed by several successive battles to destroy the epidemic in localized areas, secured major strategic outcomes in the domestic fight against the virus. On September 8, 2020, the meeting to commend role models in China's fight against the COVID-19 epidemic was solemnly held. The Congress commended the outstanding individuals and groups, the outstanding communist party members and the outstanding grass-roots party organizations in the fight against COVID-19. At the meeting, Xi Jinping spoke highly of the spirit of combating the COVID-19 epidemic, which features putting people's lives first, nationwide solidarity, heroic self-sacrifice, respecting science, and a sense of mission for humanity. He pointed out that: "The great spirit that we have forged in the battle against Covid-19 is deeply rooted in the character of the Chinese nation and our cultural genes. It carries and builds on patriotism, collectivism, and socialism, and illustrates and enriches the ethos of both our nation and our times."[90] On this basis, we shifted the focus of our national response to guarding against inbound cases and domestic resurgence, and changed from an emergency response mode to one of routine epidemic control. China developed nucleic acid test reagents for the first time, and the vaccine research and development is in the leading position in the world. The vaccines and vaccination costs are borne by the state budget, and people are vaccinated in batches. By April 2022, a total of 3,283.586 million doses of covid-19 vaccine had been vaccinated nationwide, with a total number of 1.278724 billion people vaccinated. 1.243226 billion people had been vaccinated throughout the whole process, accounting for 88.18% of the total population of the country. 75,693,000 people were vaccinated with the booster vaccination. The number of people over 60 years old covered by vaccination reached 224.182 million.

In 2021, the Delta variant with rapid transmission and rapid replication in humans posed a severe challenge to epidemic prevention and control. At most, there were more than 200 medium and high-risk areas in China, and it once affected more than 20 provinces. With the goal of strictly preventing import, China has quickly extinguished more than 30 local epidemic cases. On the basis of summing up experience, in August of the same year, China launched the "dynamic-zero" of the whole chain of precision prevention and control, and a series of precision prevention and control measures such as efficient and orderly nucleic acid test, scientific and accurate flow regulation traceability, and classified and graded prevention and control management were rapidly implemented.

In the fight against the epidemic, mainland, Taiwan and Hong Kong have been supporting and helping each other. After the outbreak of the epidemic, local governments arranged medical treatment and covid-19 vaccination for Taiwan compatriots in the mainland to help Taiwan funded enterprises return to work. After the outbreak in Macao was under control, the governments of Guangdong and MSAR established a mechanism for mutual recognition and exchange of "health codes" and nucleic acid test results, and the normal contacts between Macao and the mainland are gradually restored. In 2022, at the request of the government of the HKSAR and under the overall planning and command of the central government, the mainland set up a nucleic acid test support team to assist medical materials such as HUO-YAN laboratories, mobile testing vehicles and rapid test kits, and build 20,000 beds in six shelter hospitals to ensure the supply of living materials and help Hong Kong fight the epidemic.

In the face of enormous pressure from the epidemic, China has always adhered to the concept of a community with a shared future for mankind, actively carried out international and regional cooperation in the fight against the epidemic, and advocated building a global community of health for all. By the beginning of 2022, China had provided 150 countries and 13 international organizations with a large number of anti-epidemic supplies such as masks, protective clothing, respirators and testing equipment, sent 37 medical expert teams to 34 countries, and provided more than 2.1 billion doses of vaccines to more than 120 countries and international organizations, helping other countries improve their epidemic prevention and emergency treatment capabilities.

At the same time, the ruling party and government have endeavored to both contain the virus and speedily bring production and life back to normal, thus maintaining economic and social development. On February 23, 2020, President Xi Jinping stressed at a meeting to advance the work on coordinating the prevention and control of the COVID-19 and economic and social development, we should adopt a holistic, dialectical with firm confidence when we look at the development of China. Efforts should be made to turn pressure into impetus, turn crises into opportunities. We should intensify policy adjustments to fully unleash the huge potential and strong momentum of China's development. On March 6th, Xi Jinping stressed at a symposium on securing a decisive victory in poverty alleviation: we should coordinate to promote epidemic prevention and control and poverty alleviation, promote poverty alleviation with greater determination and strength, support the restoration of production in poverty alleviation industries, prioritize support for employment of poor laborers, and do a good job in helping people returning to poverty due to epidemic. In April, the meeting of the Political Bureau of the CCCPC proposed that while strengthening "stabilizing the six fronts" work, we should maintain security in six key areas, namely, to ensure the employment of residents, the basic livelihood of the people, the market main body, the food and energy security, the stability of the supply chain of the industrial chain, and the operation of the grass-roots. We have done a good job in the "stabilizing the six fronts," maintained security in six key areas, stabilized the basic economic situation, won time and created conditions for overcoming difficulties, and provided an important guarantee for coping with various risks and challenges. The CCCPC and the State Council have also formulated a series of policies to relieve poverty and benefit enterprises, introduced a number of measures to strengthen employment priority, promote investment and consumption, stabilize foreign trade and foreign investment, stabilize the industrial chain and supply chain, promote the development of new business forms, promote the orderly recovery of transportation, catering, supermarket, cultural tourism and other industries, implement a package of policies to support Hubei's development, and return to school and classes in batches. Under the effect of a series of policies, China's economic growth rate changed from negative to positive in the second quarter, and continued to turn positive in the third quarter. It took the lead in the global recovery and became the only major economy in the world to achieve positive growth in 2020.

Summary

Since the 18th National Congress of the CPC, China's social construction has been strengthened in an all-round way. The ruling party and government have focused on ensuring and improving people's livelihood, focused on solving the most immediate and realistic interests of the people, highlighted employment as the largest livelihood of the people, adjusted social income, promoted the comprehensive development of education, basically completed a fully functional social security system, comprehensively Carried Out the Healthy China Initiative, and improved people's lives in all aspects. We must remain committed to the people-centered philosophy of development and promote common prosperity in high-quality development. The social governance system has been further improved. The level of socialization, rule of law, intellectualization and specialization of social governance has been greatly improved, and the overall social stability has been ensured. We must put the construction of a safe China in the overall situation of the development of the cause of socialism with Chinese characteristics, plan and promote it, reach a higher level in building a safe China, and constantly increase the people's sense of gain, happiness and security. We have formed a holistic approach to national security, and we have enhanced national security on all fronts and overcome many political, economic, ideological, and natural risks, challenges, and trials. This has helped ensure that the Party and the country thrive and enjoy lasting stability. We have successfully responded to the COVID-19 epidemic, safeguarded people's lives, and fully demonstrated the superiority of the socialist system with Chinese characteristics. In the new era, we have continued to develop a sound atmosphere in which people are able to live and work in peace and contentment and social stability and order prevail. As a result, China's miracle of long-term social stability has continued.

SECTION 6

Vigorously Promote the Construction of Ecological Civilization with Chinese Characteristics

4.6.1 Establish the Concept of "Clear Waters and Green Mountains Are Invaluable Assets"

Building an ecological civilization is vital for sustaining the development of the Chinese nation. Since the launch of reform and opening-up, China has paid increasingly greater attention to ecological conservation and environmental protection, a major area in which we are still falling short. Since the 1980s, the CPC and the Chinese government have implemented environmental protection as a basic national policy. Over the years, China has vigorously promoted ecological and environmental protection and made remarkable achievements. China faces increasingly grave problems in the form of tightening environmental and resource constraints and ecological degradation. In particular, environmental pollution and ecological damage of various kinds are becoming increasingly commonplace, impairing our country's development and people's wellbeing. We will pay an extremely heavy price unless we reverse the trend of ecological and environmental deterioration as soon as possible.

In response to this situation, on August 15, 2005, Xi Jinping, then secretary of the Zhejiang Provincial Party Committee, first put forward the important thesis that "mountains and rivers green are mountains of silver and gold" during his research in Yu Village, Anji County, Zhejiang Province. In September 2013, General Secretary Xi Jinping further elaborated on this concept when he gave a speech and answered questions at Nazarbayev University in Kazakhstan: "We want to have not only mountains of gold, but alos mountains of green. If we must choose between the two, we could rather have the green than the gold. And in any

601

case, green mountains are themselves gold mountains."[91] Since the 18th National Congress of the CPC, Xi Jinping stressed: Clear waters and green mountains are as good as mountains of gold and silver. This has become an important concept to lead our country to the road of green development. Under the guidance of this concept, the ruling party and the government have constantly improved the top-level design of ecological civilization construction.

In November 2012, the 18th National Congress of the CPC took the construction of ecological civilization as an important part of the overall layout of the "the Five-Sphere Integrated Plan' for the first time, and made the strategic decision of "vigorously taking forward ecological conservation." The congress put forward: promoting ecological progress is a long-term task of vital importance to the people's wellbeing and China's future. Faced with increasing resource constraints, severe environmental pollution and a deteriorating ecosystem, we must raise our ecological awareness of the need to respect, accommodate to and protect nature. We must give high priority to making ecological progress and incorporate it into all aspects and the whole process of advancing economic, political, cultural, and social progress, work hard to build a beautiful country, and achieve lasting and sustainable development of the Chinese nation. We must follow the basic state policy of resource conservation and environmental protection, and give high priority to conserving resources, protecting the environment and promoting its natural restoration. We must make efforts to promote green development, circular development, low-carbon development, the formation of resource conservation and environmental protection of the spatial pattern, industrial structure, mode of production, lifestyle, and reverse the trend of ecological and environmental degradation from the source, to create a good working and living environment for our people and respond to global climate change. The congress also made comprehensive arrangements for the construction of ecological civilization around optimizing the national spatial development pattern, comprehensively promoting resource conservation, strengthening the protection of natural ecosystems and the environment, and strengthening the construction of ecological civilization system. Bringing the construction of ecological civilization into the overall layout of socialism with Chinese characteristics marks the further deepening of China's understanding of the laws of socialist construction.

In October 2017, the 19th National Congress of the CPC further elevated the issue of ecological civilization construction to the height of the core essence and basic strategy of Xi Jinping Thought on Socialism with Chinese Characteristics for a New Era to be recognized. The Congress summarized the basic strategy of upholding and developing socialism with Chinese characteristics in the new era as the "14 insist," of which the ninth is "ensuring harmony between human and nature." The congress stressed: "Building an eco-civilization is vital to sustain the Chinese nation's development. We must realize that lucid waters and lush mountains are invaluable assets and act on this understanding, implement our fundamental national policy of conserving resources and protecting the environment, and cherish the environment as we cherish our own lives. We will adopt a holistic approach to conserving our mountains, rivers, forests, farmlands, lakes, and grasslands, implement the strictest possible systems for environmental protection, and develop ecofriendly growth models and ways of life."[92] This systematically expounds the great significance of ecological civilization construction and the basic concepts, basic path, basic state policies and basic systems that should be adhered to in carrying out ecological civilization construction. Subsequently, the "ten clarifications" proposed by the Sixth Plenary Session of the 19th CCCPC also included relevant contents of ecological civilization construction. The 19th National Congress of the CPC also made comprehensive arrangements for the in-depth work related to the construction of ecological civilization, focusing on promoting green development, solving outstanding environmental problems, strengthening ecosystem protection, and reforming the ecological environment supervision system. "Ecological civilization construction," "green development" and "building a beautiful China" have been written into the Party Constitution and the Constitution, and have become the will of the whole Party, the will of the state and the common action of the whole people.

In May 2018, the National Conference on Environmental Protection was held in Beijing. Xi Jinping delivered an important speech at the meeting. It reviews the situation and tasks facing the construction of ecological civilization in China, and is a profound exposition of the significance, important principles, the main initiatives of strengthening the construction of ecological civilization. He stressed that although environmental quality in China is continuing to take a turn for the better and showing trends of steady improvement the results are still tenuous. Our efforts to build an ecological civilization are now in a crucial phase in which we must carry forward despite heavy strain and immense pressure, a decisive stage in which we will supply more high-quality ecological goods to meet the growing demands of the people for a pristine environment, and also a period of opportunity in which we have the conditions and abilities necessary to resolve prominent environmental issues. He stressed that the environment is a major political issue which bears upon the mission and purpose of the CPC as well as a major social issue which bears upon public wellbeing. The broad masses of the people are eager to speed up the improvement of the ecological and environmental quality. We must actively respond to the people's desires, hopes, and anxieties, vigorously advance development of an ecological civilization, provide more high-quality ecological goods, and consistently meet the people's growing demands for a beautiful environment. He put forward develop an ecological civilization in the new era, the following principles must be upheld. First, we must adhere to achieving harmony between man and nature, giving priority to conservation, protection and natural recovery. We must protect the ecosystems as preciously as we protect our eyes and cherish the environment as we cherish our own lives, to ensure that pristine natural vistas are never too far away, and preserve the serenity, harmony, and beauty of nature. Second, green mountains and lucid waters are indeed mountains of gold and silver. We must implement principled development that is innovative, coordinated, green, open, and shared, and accelerate the formation of spatial patterns, industrial structures, modes of production, and lifestyles conducive to resource conservation and environmental protection. We must also give the environment the time and space that it needs to rest and recuperate. Third, there is no welfare more universally beneficial than a sound natural environment. We must ensure that the environment benefits the people, stressing the resolution of prominent environmental problems that impact public health and consistently meet the people's growing demands for a beautiful environment. Fourth, mountains, forests, fields, lakes and grasses are a community of shared life. we must make plans that take all factors into consideration and simultaneously implement multiple comprehensive measures to ensure that our efforts to build an ecological civilization permeate all fields, regions, and processes. Fifth, the strictest regulations and laws must be applied in protecting the environment. We must accelerate innovation of regulations, ensuring that they are rigorously enforced. By doing so, we will turn our regulations into rigid and inviolable constraints. Sixth, joint efforts must be made in building a global ecological civilization. We must be deeply involved in global environmental governance, and create solutions for environmental protection and sustainable development around the world and take an active role in international cooperation on climate change. The congress put forward Xi Jinping's thought on ecological civilization, a powerful ideological weapon for advancing ecological civilization and building a beautiful

China, and clearly defined two milestones for achieving a beautiful China, namely: by 2035, the objective of building a beautiful China will be basically achieved. By the middle of the century, we will reach our objective of building a strong and modern socialist country that is prosperous, democratic, civilized, harmonious, and beautiful, and complete all-round improvements in the material, political, intellectual, social, and ecological domains. At that time, environmentally friendly ways of living and developing will be fully formed, humans and nature will coexist in harmony, modernization of our national governance systems and capacity in the environmental field will be fully realized, and our efforts to build a beautiful China will be successful. The meeting also put forward a series of important measures to promote the construction of ecological civilization, in particular, it proposed to accelerate the establishment and improvement of an ecological civilization system including an ecological culture system, an ecological economy system, a target responsibility system, an ecological civilization system and an ecological security system.

In April 2021, the Political Bureau of the 19th CCCPC conducted the 29th group study on strengthening China's ecological civilization construction under the new situation. Xi Jinping pointed out that the "14th Five-Year Plan" period, the construction of ecological civilization in China has entered a critical period with the reduction in carbon emissions as a major strategic goal, to decrease the emissions of both pollution and carbon, to promote a comprehensive transition to green and low-carbon economic and social development, to bring a fundamental change to its eco-environment by accumulating small changes. It is necessary to fully, accurately and comprehensively implement the new development concept, maintain strategic concentration, plan economic and social development from the perspective of harmonious coexistence between man and nature. We must follow the basic state policy of resource conservation and environmental protection, and give high priority to conserving resources, protecting the environment and promoting its natural restoration. We should preserve our geographical space and improve our industrial structure, way of production and way of life in the interest of conserving resources and protecting the environment. We should coordinate pollution control, ecological protection, and climate change, promote continuous improvement of the ecological environment, and strive to build a modernization in which people and nature live in harmony. This clarifies the tasks and measures of China's ecological civilization construction at the new development stage.

4.6.2 Deepen Reform of the System for Developing an Ecological Civilization

Most of China's outstanding problems in environmental protection are related to inadequate systems, lax regulations, imperfect laws, lacking enforcement, and ineffectual punishment. In this regard, China has strengthened the system design and actively planned and promoted the reform of the ecological civilization system.

In 2012, the 18th National Congress of the CPC proposed: we should move faster to set up a system for ecological progress, improve institutions and mechanisms for developing geographical space, conserving resources and protecting the ecological environment and promote modernization featuring harmonious development between man and nature.

In November 2013, the Third Plenary Session of the 18th CCCPC incorporated the "reform of the system of ecological civilization" into the target system of comprehensive deepening reform and proposed to deepen the reform of the system of ecological civilization closely around building a beautiful China. We should move faster to set up a system for ecological progress, improve institutions and mechanisms for developing geographical space, conserving resources and protecting the ecological environment and promote modernization featuring harmonious development between man and nature. The Decision of the CCCPC on Some Major Issues Concerning Comprehensively Continuing the Reform adopted at the plenary session, proposed to accelerate the construction of the ecological civilization system, and made arrangements for improving the property rights system of natural resource assets and a system of control over the purposes of use, drawing a "red line" for ecological protection, implementing a system of compensated use of natural resources and the eco-compensation system, and reforming the management system of ecological environment protection.

In October 2014, the Fourth Plenary Session of the 18th CCCPC made work arrangements for the construction of ecological civilization system from the perspective of ruling the country by law in all respects. The plenary session stressed that we should protect the ecological environment with strict rule of law, accelerate the establishment of an ecological civilization legal system that effectively restricts development activities and promotes green, circular and low-carbon development, strengthen the legal responsibility of producers for environmental protection, and significantly increase the cost of violations. We should establish and improve the legal system for the property rights of natural resources, improve the legal system for the development and protection of land and space, formulate and improve laws and regulations on ecological compensation, prevention and control of soil, water and air pollution, and marine ecological environment protection, and promote the construction of ecological civilization.

In April 2015, the CCCPC and the State Council issued the Guidelines on Accelerating Ecological Civilization, which is the first document of the Central Committee's special deployment on the construction of ecological civilization. It fully reflects the great importance that the ruling party and government attach to the construction of ecological civilization. According to the opinions, by 2020, major progress will be made in the construction of a resource-saving and environment-friendly society, the layout of main functional areas will be basically formed, the quality and efficiency of economic development will be significantly improved, the mainstream values of ecological civilization will be implemented in the whole society, and the level of ecological civilization construction will be compatible with the goal of building a moderately prosperous society in an all-round way. Focusing on this goal, the Opinions put forward "Five-Sphere Integrated Plan, five insists, four tasks and four guarantee mechanisms." Among them, the "five in one" is to put forward specific implementation paths and integration methods around the requirements of the 18th National Congress on "integrating ecological civilization construction into all aspects and the whole process of economic, political, cultural and social construction." The "five insists," which made the overall requirements of the central government on the construction of ecological civilization clear and detailed, includes the following: follow the basic state policy of resource conservation and environmental protection, and give high priority to saving resources, protecting the environment, and promoting its natural restoration; follow the basic approach to promote green development, circular development, low-carbon development; take deepening reform and opening-up and the innovation drive as the fundamental driving force; Insist on cultivating ecological culture as an important support; adhere to the key breakthroughs and overall promotion as a way of working. The "four tasks" are to define the four key tasks of optimizing the spatial development pattern of land, promoting technological innovation and structural adjustment, comprehensively promoting resource conservation, recycling and efficient utilization, and strengthening natural ecosystem and environmental protection. The "four guarantee mechanisms" put forward four guarantee mechanisms, namely, improving an ecological civilization system, strengthening the statistical monitoring and law enforcement supervision of ecological civilization construction, accelerating the formation of a good social trend to promote ecological civilization construction, and effectively strengthening organizational leadership. With regard to the construction of ecological civilization system, according to the overall thinking of source prevention, process control, damage compensation and responsibility investigation, the Opinions put forward the following ten mechanisms: improving laws and regulations, improving the standard system, improving the control system of property rights and uses of natural resources assets, improving the ecological environment supervision system, strictly observing the ecological red line of resources and environment, improving economic policies, promoting the market mechanism, improving the mechanism of compensation for ecological conservation, the performance evaluation system and the accountability system. The Opinions has specified the overall requirements, objectives, vision, key tasks and the system of ecological civilization construction, highlighted the strategic, comprehensive, systematic and operable nature, and clarified the timetable and road map for implementing the deployment of the Third and Fourth Plenary Sessions of the 18th CCCPC. It is a programmatic document for promoting China's ecological civilization construction in a period.

In September 2015, the CCCPC and the State Council issued the *Integrated Reform Plan for Promoting Ecological Civilization*. The plan clarifies the guiding ideology, basic concepts, main principles, work objectives and important measures of the reform of the ecological civilization system, and proposes that by 2020, the following eight systems of ecological civilization will constitute a complete system of ecological civilization that is of a clear property right, diversified participation, incentives and constraints, including the property right system for natural resources, the territorial space development and protection system, a system of integrated plans for space, a system of overall resource management and comprehensive conservation, a system of compensated use of natural resources and the eco-compensation system, the environmental governance system, the environmental governance and ecological protection market system, the ecological civilization performance evaluation and assessment and accountability system. We will promote the modernization of China's system and capacity for governance in the field of ecological civilization, and strive to move towards a new era of socialist ecological civilization. These eight systems actually jointly put up the pillars to support the ecological civilization system. The proposal to build these pillars made clear the direction and path of the reform of the system for developing an ecological civilization. In line with this, relevant departments have also issued such documents as the *Environmental Protection Supervision Scheme (Trial)*, the *Ecological and Environment Monitoring Network Construction Scheme*, the *Pilot Scheme for Carrying out Audit of Natural Resource Assets at the end of the Tenure of Leading Officials*, the *Measures for Investigating the Ecological Environment Damage Responsibilities of Party and Government Leading Cadres (Trial)*, the *Pilot Scheme for the Creation of Balance Sheets for Natural Resources and Trials to Reform the Ecological Damage Compensation System*, forming a raft of policies to implement the reform of the system of ecological civilization.

In October 2015, the Fifth Plenary Session of the 18th CCCPC further put forward the "Five Concepts for Development," taking "green" as an important concept of economic and social development during the 13th Five-Year Plan period and even longer. The session also made clear the objectives and requirements of ecological civilization construction during the 13th Five-Year Plan period.

On the basis of the gradual implementation of the above reforms, in October 2019, the Fourth Plenary Session of the 19th CCCPC made new plans and arrangements for the reform of the system of ecological civilization, and proposed to adhere to and improve the system of ecological civilization and promote the harmonious coexistence of man and nature. The plenary session further highlighted the systematic integration of the construction of ecological civilization system, and summarized the ecological civilization system into four aspects, namely, the ecological and environmental protection system, the resource utilization system, the ecological protection and restoration system, and the ecological and environment protection responsibility system, and deployed relevant work around these aspects.

Under the guidance of the above system design, the reform of the system of ecological civilization has been steadily promoted.

Put in place the most stringent ecological and environmental protection regime. In 2014, the pilot of "a system of integrated plans" was launched in cities and counties. In 2017, the pilot of provincial spatial planning was launched. In 2019, the Opinions on Establishing a Land Spatial Planning System and Supervising its Implementation were issued, which marked the basic formation of the top-level design of the land spatial planning system and the supporting pillars, and the continuous improvement in the system for developing and protecting China's geographical space. The Measures for Managing Natural and Ecological Space (for Trial Implementation) was implemented, and the system for regulating the use of all territorial space was further improved. The Guideline on Coordination in Setting Limits in Territorial Spatial Planning was formulated, and the three control lines of ecological conservation, designate permanent basic cropland and demarcate the boundaries of urban development were defined and implemented as a whole. Policy documents such as Guidelines for Establishing the Green Financial System and the Opinions on Accelerating the Establishment of a Legal and Policy System of Green Production and Consumption were issued to improve the legal system and policy guidance for green production and consumption. China became the first economy in the world to establish a relatively complete a policy system of green finance. Such documents as the Implementation Plan of a Permit System for Pollutant Emission Control and the Implementation Plan of Building of a System of Institutions for the Oversight of Fixed Pollution Sources based on Emissions Permits were issued. The construction of the pollutant emission permit system was basically completed, and the pollutant emission permit for fixed pollution sources was fully covered. In 2014, the Guiding Opinions on Improving the Living Environment of Poor Villages was issued. In 2018, the three-year campaign to improve rural living environments was launched, and in 2021, a five-year campaign to improve rural living environments was launched. The rural environmental governance system and mechanism were established to strengthen the prevention and control of agricultural and rural environmental pollution.

Mechanisms for efficient use of resources. In April 2019, the general office of the CCCPC and the general office of the State Council issued the Guiding Opinions on Comprehensively Promoting the Property Rights System of Natural Resource Assets, and in 2022, issued the Pilot Scheme of a Unified Responsibility Mechanism for People Who Act on Behalf of the Public to Manage Public Natural Resource Assets. The reform of the property rights system of natural resource assets was comprehensively promoted and continuously deepened. We issued the Interim Measures for Unified Registration of Natural Resource Rights, and comprehensively implemented the unified registration of natural resources. The Opinions on Expanding the Paid Use of State-Owned Land, Guidelines on Reforming Paid Use of Natural Resource Assets Owned by the Whole People, and the Opinions on the Systems for Paid Use of Sea Areas and Uninhabited Islands were formulated. Since July 2016, the resource tax reform has been comprehensively promoted, and the reform of systems for paid use of shoreline resources has been continuously deepened. The regulations on the efficient and intensive use of land resources and the opinions on the enforcement of the strictest water resources management system were issued to continuously strengthen the total resource management and the comprehensive resource conservation system. The Circular Economy Promotion Law was revised, and documents such as the circular development action plan and the guiding opinions on the establishment of a recycling system for waste and used materials were issued. The policy system of conserving, recycling, and efficiently using resources and the resource recycling system was improved. We have formulated such documents as the Plan for the Compulsory System of Garbage Sorting (draft for comments), the Implementation Plan for the System of Domestic Garbage Sorting, and the Guiding Opinions on Promoting the Recycling of Sewage, so as to generally implement the garbage sorting and recycling system. The 14th Five-Year Plan for Modern Energy System and other documents were issued to promote the energy revolution and build a clean, low-carbon, safe and efficient energy system. We have enacted and revised laws such as Law on the Exploration and Development of Resources in Deep Seabed Areas and the Marine Environment Protection Law, formulate Several Opinions on Promoting the Sustainable and Healthy Development of Marine Fisheries and other documents, and improved the marine resources development and protection system. We have formulated Several opinions on the Establishment of Long-Term Monitoring and Warning Mechanisms on the Carrying Capacity of Resources and the Environment and the Overall Plan for Building a Natural Resources Investigation and Monitoring System, and accelerated the establishment of a unified investigation, evaluation and monitoring system for natural resources. In 2018, the Ministry of Natural Resources was established to improve the natural resources regulatory system.

We have improved the ecological protection and restoration system. We have issued documents such as the Plans for the System for Protecting Natural Forests, Several Opinions on Strengthening Grassland Protection and Restoration, the System Plan for Closing off Decertified Land for Protection, Cultivated Land, Grassland, Rivers and Lakes Rest and Recuperation Plan (2016–2030), to strengthen ecological protection of forests, grassland, rivers, lakes, wetlands, oceans and other natural resources, We have formulated the "Yangtze River Protection Law of the PRC," promoted the Yellow River protection legislation, and strengthened the ecological protection and systematic management of the Yangtze River, the Yellow River and other major rivers. The Circular on Protecting Coastal

Wetlands and Strictly Controlled and Regulated Coastal Reclamation Activities was issued, and land reclamation was prohibited except for major national projects.

We have strictly enforced the responsibility system for ecological and environmental protection. In December 2016, the general office of the CCCPC and the general office of the State Council issued Measures for Assessing Progress Made in Ecological Improvement, establishing an evaluation and assessment system for the objectives of ecological civilization construction. We will introduce documents such as the Reform Plan for the Release of Environment-Related Information in Accordance with the Law, improve the information disclosure mechanism of evaluation of the environmental effects of a construction project, improve the system of environmental news spokesperson, improve the system of public participation, establish the system of environmental protection network reporting platform and reporting, and improve the reporting, hearing, public opinion supervision and other systems. We formulated such documents as the Pilot Scheme for Carrying out Audit of Natural Resource Assets at the end of the Tenure of Leading Officials and the Regulations on Audit of Natural Resource Assets at the End of the Tenure of Leading Officials (for Trial Implementation). We launched the relevant pilot work in 2015 and comprehensively promoted the off-office auditing of natural resource assets of leading cadres from 2018. The Measures for Investigating the Ecological Environment Damage Responsibilities of Party and Government Leading Cadres (Trial) and other documents have been issued, and the system of "officials perform their duties while also taking responsibility for workplace safety" for the construction of ecological civilization among leading members of local Party committees and governments has been implemented. Leading cadres who have major ecological environment damage after leaving their posts and are determined to be responsible for it will be subject to lifelong accountability. The Ministry of Ecology and Environment and the coordinated law enforcement teams for environmental protection have been established, the environmental protection responsibilities scattered in various departments have been adjusted to one department, and an authoritative and unified environmental law enforcement system have been established. The inspection system for environmental protection was established and two rounds of central ecological and environmental protection supervision were carried out from 2015 to 2020, which played a key role in solving outstanding ecological and environmental problems. We have formulated policy documents such as the Ecological and Environmental Monitoring and Planning Outline (2020–2035) and improved the ecological and environmental monitoring and evaluation system. The Opinions on Improving the Mechanism of Compensation for Ecological Conservation and the Opinions on Deepening the Reform of the System of Compensation for Ecological Conservation were formulated to explore the establishment of a diversified compensation mechanism. Trials to Reform the Ecological Damage Compensation System and the Reform Scheme for the Ecological Damage Compensation System were formulated. In 2016, the reform of the ecological damage compensation system was piloted in 7 provinces and cities, and in 2018, it was fully piloted nationwide. An eco-compensation system with clear responsibilities, smooth channels, technical specifications, strong guarantees, adequate compensation and effective repair was initially established. In March 2020, the general office of the CCCPC and the general office of the State Council issued the Guidelines for Establishing the Modern Environmental Management System, which proposed that by 2025, we should establish and improve the leadership responsibility system, enterprise responsibility system, national action system, regulatory system, market system, credit system, laws, regulations and policy system for environmental management, implement the responsibilities of various subjects, improve the enthusiasm of market subjects and the public, and form an environmental management system with clear guidance, scientific decision-making, strong execution, effective incentives, diversified participation and benign interaction.

In the new era, the supporting pillars of the ecological civilization system have been established. An ecological civilization system covering the whole process of ecological civilization from the source, process to the consequences, including ecological environment protection, efficient utilization of resources, ecological protection and restoration, and ecological environment protection responsibility, is accelerating its formation.

4.6.3 Solve Outstanding Environmental Problems and Strengthen Ecosystem Protection

(1) Make Solid Gains in the Battle against Pollution
The philosophy and system of ecological civilization should ultimately be implemented into practice for development. In October 2017, the 19th National Congress of the CPC listed the battle against pollution as one of the three major battles to win the victory in building a moderately prosperous society in all respects.

On this basis, the ruling party and the government concentrated their efforts on tackling the outstanding problems of the ecological environment.

Make our skies blue again. In September 2013, the State Council announced the Action Plan for Preventing and Controlling Air Pollution, which proposed that after five years of efforts, the air quality in the country would be improved as a whole, and the heavy smog would be greatly reduced; the air quality in Beijing Tianjin Hebei, Yangtze River Delta, Pearl River Delta and other regions improved significantly. We will strive to gradually eliminate the heavily polluted weather in another five years or more, and significantly improve the air quality throughout the country. This is known as the most stringent atmospheric control plan in history, making China the first developing country in the world to carry out PM2.5 control on a large scale. In June 2018, the State Council further prepared the Three-Year Action Plan for Keeping Our Skies Blue, which plans to continue to carry out air pollution prevention and control actions in key areas such as Beijing, Tianjin, Hebei and surrounding areas, the Yangtze River Delta, and the Fenwei Plain. It proposes that after three years of efforts, the total amount of major air pollutants will be significantly reduced, greenhouse gas emissions will be reduced in a coordinated manner, the concentration of fine particles (PM2.5) will be further significantly reduced, and the number of days with heavy pollution will be significantly reduced, the air quality throughout the country will be significantly improved and people's happiness will be enhanced. Therefore, China has strengthened comprehensive treatment to reduce the discharge of multiple pollutants, especially to strengthen the comprehensive treatment of air pollution in industrial enterprises, deepen the treatment of non-point source pollution, and strengthen the prevention and control of mobile source pollution; adjust and optimize the industrial structure, promote industrial transformation and upgrading, strictly control new production capacity in high energy consuming and high pollution industries, accelerate the elimination of backward production capacity, reduce excess production capacity, and resolutely stop the construction of projects under construction in industries with serious excess production capacity; speed up technological transformation of enterprises, improve scientific and technological innovation ability, strengthen scientific and technological research and development and promotion, comprehensively promote clean production, vigorously develop circular economy, and vigorously cultivate energy-saving and environmental protection industries; speed up the adjustment of the energy structure, increase the supply of clean energy, control the total consumption of coal, accelerate the replacement and utilization of clean energy, promote the clean utilization of coal, and improve the efficiency of energy use; actively adjust the transport structure and develop a green transport system; create strict access to energy conservation and environmental protection, optimize the industrial spatial layout, adjust the industrial layout, strengthen the constraint of energy conservation and environmental protection indicators, and optimize the spatial pattern; give play to the role of market mechanism and improve environmental and economic policies; implement major special actions to significantly reduce pollutant emissions; improve the system of laws and regulations, and strictly supervise and manage according to law; establish regional cooperation mechanism, strengthen regional joint prevention and control, and coordinate regional environmental governance; establish a monitoring, early warning and emergency system to properly deal with heavy smog; clarify the responsibilities of the government, enterprises and society, and mobilize the whole people to participate in environmental protection. In Beijing, Tianjin, Hebei and the surrounding areas and Fenwei Plain, China has completed the reduction in the use of about 25 million bulk coal, eliminated more than 24 million high-emission and old vehicles throughout the country, and 229 iron and steel enterprises have completed or are implementing ultra-low emission transformation of 620 million tons of crude steel. In many places, backward production capacity such as steel and coal has been eliminated. In 2020, the proportion of excellent days in cities at prefecture level and above increased by 5.8 percentage points over 2015, exceeding the target of the 13th Five-Year Plan by 2.5 percentage points.

Make our skies blue again. In April 2015, the State Council issued the Action Plan for Preventing and Controlling Water Pollution, which proposed that by 2020, the water environment quality of the whole country will be improved in stages, the seriously polluted water bodies will be reduced by a large margin, the drinking water safety guarantee will be continuously improved, the groundwater overexploitation will be strictly controlled, the trend of groundwater pollution will be initially curbed, the environmental quality of the coastal waters will be steadily improved, and the water ecology in Beijing Tianjin Hebei, Yangtze River Delta, Pearl River Delta and other regions improved significantly. By 2030, we will strive to improve the overall water environment quality and preliminarily restore the water ecosystem functions. By the middle of this century, the quality of the ecology and environment will be improved in an all-round way, and the ecosystem will realize a virtuous cycle. Therefore, China has comprehensively controlled the discharge of pollutants, paid close attention to the prevention and control of industrial pollution, strengthened the treatment of urban domestic pollution, promoted the prevention and control of agricultural and rural pollution, and strengthened the control of ship and port pollution; strived to conserve and protect water resources, control the total amount of water used, improve the efficiency of water use, and protect water resources scientifically; effectively strengthened water environment management, strengthened the management of environmental quality objectives, deepened the control of total pollutant discharge, strictly controlled environmental risks, and comprehensively implemented pollutant discharge permits; made every effort to ensure the safety of the water ecological environment and drinking water sources, deepened the prevention and control of pollution in key river basins, strengthened the environmental protection of coastal waters, renovated black and odorous water bodies in cities, and protected water and wetland ecosystems. In addition, the state has also promoted the transformation and upgrading of the economic structure, strengthened scientific and technological support, given full play to the role of the market mechanism, solidly promoted the river chief and lake chief systems, clarified and implemented the responsibilities of all parties, strengthened public participation and social supervision, and continued to focus on winning the key campaigns like promoting the protection and restoration of the Yangtze River, the comprehensive treatment of the Bohai Sea, and the protection of water sources. By 2020, the main stream of the Yangtze River will achieve Grade II or better water quality, the water quality of the Pearl River Basin will be improved from good to excellent, and the water quality of the Yellow River, Songhua River and Huaihe river basins will be improved from mild pollution to good. The proportion of black and odorous water bodies in cities at or above the prefecture level has reached 98.2%, and state-controlled water sections with good-quality surface water will exceed the target of the 13th Five-Year Plan by 13.4 percentage points.

Clean up and preserve our soil. In May 2016, the State Council issued the Action Plan for Preventing and Controlling Soil Pollution, which proposed that by 2020, the aggravating trend of soil pollution in the country will be initially curbed, the soil environmental quality will remain stable in general, the soil environmental safety of agricultural land and construction land will be basically guaranteed, and the soil environmental risks will be basically controlled. By

2030, the soil environmental quality of the whole country will be stable and good, the soil environmental safety of agricultural land and construction land will be basically guaranteed, and the soil environmental risks will be basically controlled. By the middle of this century, the quality of the soil environment will be improved in an all-round way, and the ecosystem will realize a virtuous cycle. To this end, the state has carried out in-depth investigation of soil environmental quality, built a monitoring network of soil environmental quality, improved the information management level of soil environment, and mastered the status of soil environmental quality; promoted the legislation of soil pollution prevention and control, established and improved the system of regulations and standards; implemented classified management of agricultural land to ensure the safety of agricultural production environment; implemented construction land access management to prevent human settlement environment risks; strengthened the protection of unpolluted soil, strictly controlled new soil pollution, strengthened the environmental management of unused land, prevented new pollution of construction land, and strengthen the control of spatial layout; strengthened the supervision of pollution sources, done a good job in soil pollution prevention, strictly controlled industrial and mining pollution, controlled agricultural pollution, and reduced domestic pollution; carried out pollution control and remediation to improve the quality of regional soil environment. By 2020, the rate of the safe use of contaminated farmland and the rate of safe use of other plots of land that have been polluted will both exceeded 90%, successfully achieving the goal of the 13th Five-Year Plan. Since the 18th National Congress of the CPC, a total of 960 million mu of afforestation has been completed, the forest coverage rate has increased by 2.68 percentage points, and the area of artificial forests has steadily ranked first in the world.

(2) Bolster the Protection and Restoration of Ecosystems
Since the 18th National Congress of the CPC, the Party Central Committee, with Comrade Xi Jinping as the core, has put forward the assertion that mountains, rivers, forests, farmlands, lakes, and grasslands are a community of shared life from the overall perspective of ecological civilization construction, and has continuously strengthened the protection and restoration of ecosystems. Xi Jinping stressed that "to improve the quality and stability of the ecosystem, we should adhere to the system concept, adopting a holistic approach to the protection and conservation

of mountain, river, forest, farmland, lake, grassland, and desert ecosystems, and strengthen comprehensive, systemic, and source-targeted governance."[93]

The spatial planning system has been continuously improved. In 2011, China issued the Planning of Main Function Zones, which planned the main functional areas of all territorial space, as well as the inland water and territorial sea (excluding Hong Kong, Macao and Taiwan). In August 2015, the State Council issued the National Plan for Marine Functional Areas. The promulgation and implementation of the Plan marks that the national functional area strategy has realized the full coverage of land and sea territory, and is of great strategic significance to promote the formation of a land-sea coordination, efficient, coordinated and sustainable national spatial development pattern. In January 2017, the State Council formulated the National Land Planning Outline (2016–2030). This is China's first national strategic, comprehensive and basic plan for land development and protection. The scope of the plan covers all China's land and sea territory (not including Hong Kong, Macao and Taiwan areas for the time being). It plays a guiding and regulatory role in various activities related to developing and protecting China's geographical space, protection and renovation, and plays a leading and coordinating role in relevant special land space planning.

We should build a nature reserve system with a focus on national parks. In November 2013, the Third Plenary Session of the 18th CCCPC proposed to establish a national park system, and regarded it as an important part of the construction of ecological civilization system. In September 2017, the general office of the CCCPC and the general office of the State Council issued a master plan for the establishment of a national park system, which proposed that by 2020, the pilot project for the establishment of the national park system would be basically completed, a number of national parks would be integrated and established, a unified management system at different levels would be basically established, and the overall layout of the national parks would be initially formed. By 2030, the national park system will be more perfect, the unified management system at different levels will be more perfect, and the protection management efficiency will be significantly improved. In 2018, the CCCPC issued the Plan for Deepening the Reform of Party and State Institutions, established the State Forestry and Grassland Administration, and added the title of National Park Administration to it. Since then, there have been unified management institutions for various nature reserves in China. In June 2019, the general office of the CCCPC and the general office of the State Council issued the Guiding Opinions on the Establishment of a System of Protected Natural Areas with State Parks as the Main Element, which proposed that by 2020, the general layout and development plan of national parks and various nature reserves should be put forward, the national park system pilot should be completed, a number of national parks should be set up, the demarcation of nature reserves should be completed and connected with the ecological protection red line, a negative list of construction projects in nature reserves should be formulated, and the multi-category and a unified multi-level management system should be established in the natural reserves. By 2025, we will improve the national park system, complete the integration and optimization of nature reserves, improve the laws and regulations, management and supervision systems of the nature reserve system, improve the natural ecological space carrying capacity, and initially build natural reserves with national parks as the main part. By 2035, the management efficiency of nature reserves and the supply capacity of ecological products will be significantly improved, the scale and management of nature reserves will reach the world's advanced level, and the system of nature reserves with Chinese characteristics will be fully established. Nature reserves account for more than 18% of the land area. This is the fundamental follow and guidance for the establishment of a nature reserve system with national parks as the main body, and it marks that China's nature reserves have entered a new stage of comprehensively deepening reform. In June 2020, the NDRC and the Ministry of Natural Resources issued the Master Plan for Major Conservation and Restoration Projects Relating to Ecosystems (2021–2035). This is the first comprehensive plan in the field of ecological protection and restoration after the 19th National Congress of the CPC, which defines the main objectives of national ecological protection and restoration by 2035, and details the key tasks at the three time nodes of the end of 2020, 2021–2025 and 2026–2035. In recent years, China has actively promoted the establishment of a nature reserve system with national parks as the main body, nature reserves as the foundation and various natural parks as the supplement, laying a foundation for protecting habitats, improving the quality of the ecological environment and maintaining national ecological security. Since 2015, 10 national park system pilots including Sanjiangyuan have been launched, and relevant natural reserves have been integrated into the scope of national parks to implement unified management, overall protection and systematic restoration. China has taken the lead in putting forward and implementing the ecological protection red line system in the international community. It has drawn ecological protection red lines in key ecological functional areas, ecological environment sensitive areas and vulnerable areas, and carried out strict protection. The initial designated area is no less than 25% of the land area. At present, China has established nearly 10,000 nature reserves at all levels, accounting for about 18% of the land area.

Biodiversity protection has been strengthened. In 2010, China issued and implemented the China National Biodiversity Conservation Strategy and Action Plan (2011–2030). On this basis, since the 18th National Congress of the CPC, China has incorporated the implementation of major biodiversity protection projects and the construction of biodiversity protection networks into the national economic and social development plan. In the past 10 years, the state has promulgated and revised more than 20 laws and regulations related to biodiversity, including the Forest Law, the Grassland Law, the Fisheries Law, the Wild Animal Conservation Law, the Environmental Protection Law, the Marine Environment Protection law, the Seed Law, the Yangtze River Protection Law and the Biosafety Law, providing a solid legal guarantee for biodiversity conservation and sustainable utilization. We have revised and adjusted the list of wildlife and plants under special state protection to lay a foundation for saving rare and endangered wild animals and plants and maintaining biodiversity. In October 2021, the general office of the CCCPC and the general office of the State Council issued the Opinions on Further Strengthening Biodiversity Protection, which defined the guiding ideology, working principles and overall objectives of further strengthening biodiversity protection, and proposed the following measures: accelerate the improvement of biodiversity protection policies and regulations, continue to optimize the spatial pattern of biodiversity protection, build a complete biodiversity protection monitoring system, strive to improve the level of biosafety management, innovative biodiversity sustainable use mechanism, increase law enforcement and supervision and inspection efforts, deepen international cooperation and exchange, comprehensive promotion of public participation in biodiversity protection and improve biodiversity protection measures, which are the basic principles for comprehensively promoting biodiversity protection in the future. In the new era, China adheres to ecological priority and green development. The legal system of ecological and environmental protection is improving, the regulatory mechanism is continuously strengthened, and the basic capacity is greatly improved. The new pattern of biodiversity governance has basically taken shape, and biodiversity protection has entered a new historical period.

4.6.4 Put Forward "Peaking Carbon Emissions" and "Carbon Neutrality" and Promote Green Development

At their roots, environmental problems are problems with the ways in which we live and develop. At the general debate of the 75th Session of the United Nations General Assembly on September 22, 2020, President Xi Jinping announced that China would scale up its NDCs by adopting more vigorous policies and measures, strive to peak CO_2 emissions before 2030, and achieve carbon neutrality before 2060. To achieve the goals of peaking carbon emissions and subsequent carbon neutrality is one of China's major strategies, defined after careful consideration. This is a must-do in order to relieve the serious constraints imposed by resources and the environment on China's economic growth, and to achieve sustainable development. It is also a solemn commitment towards building a global community of shared future.

Improve the guiding ideology of to achieve peak carbon emissions and carbon neutrality. After carbon peaking and carbon neutrality was proposed, the Party Central Committee, with Comrade Xi Jinping as the core, has repeatedly elaborated on related work. In January 2022, Xi Jinping stressed during the 36th group study of the 19th Central Political Bureau of the CPC that achieving the carbon peaking and carbon neutrality goal is a broad and profound change that cannot be achieved easily. We should improve our strategic thinking ability, put the system concept throughout the whole process of the carbon peaking and carbon neutrality, and pay attention to handling four pairs of relations: first, the relationship between development and emission reduction. Second, the relationship between overall and regional interests. Third, the relationship between short-term and long-term goals. Fourth, the relationship between the government and the market. He pointed out that to promote the whole process of the carbon peaking and carbon neutrality, we must adhere to the principles of national overall planning, prioritizing conservation, two wheels drive, smooth domestic and international flow, and risk prevention, give better play to China's institutional advantages, resource conditions, technological potential, and market vitality, and accelerate the formation of an industrial structure, production mode, lifestyle, and spatial pattern that saves resources and protects the environment. (1) Strengthen overall coordination. (2) Promote the energy revolution. (3) Optimize and upgrade the industrial structure. (4) Accelerate the green and low-carbon scientific and technological revolution. (5) Improve the green and low-carbon policy system. (6) Take an active part in and leading global climate governance. He proposed to strengthen the Party's leadership over the whole process of the carbon peaking and carbon neutrality, strengthen overall planning and coordination, strictly supervise and assess, and promote the formation of a working force. The Party and government should share the same responsibility, compact the responsibilities of all parties, incorporate the relevant indicators of the whole process of the carbon peaking and carbon neutrality into the comprehensive evaluation system of economic and social development in all regions, increase the weighting of performance indicators, and strengthen the constraint of indicators.[94] The speech deeply analyzed the major relationships and principles that need to be grasped in achieving peak carbon emissions and carbon neutrality, arranged and deployed the key tasks of the carbon peaking and carbon neutrality, and provided fundamental guidance for relevant work.

Accelerating work on "1 + N" policy for peaking carbon emissions and achieving carbon neutrality. In September 2021, the CCCPC and the State Council issued Working Guidance for Carbon Dioxide Peaking and Carbon Neutrality in Full and Faithful Implementation of the New Development Philosophy, which is the top-level design document of carbon peaking and carbon neutrality, and plays a leading role in a "1 + N" policy framework for carbon peak and carbon neutrality. The Opinions made systematic planning and overall deployment for the major work of carbon peaking and carbon neutrality, and defined the main objectives: by 2025, a green low-carbon circular development economic system will be initially formed, and the energy utilization efficiency of key industries will be greatly improved. The energy consumption per unit of GDP will decrease by 13.5% compared with 2020; carbon dioxide emissions per unit of GDP will be reduced by 18% compared with 2020; the proportion of non-fossil energy consumption will reach about 20%; the forest coverage rate will reach 24.1%, and the forest stock volume will reach 18 billion cubic meters, laying a solid foundation for achieving carbon peaking and carbon neutrality. By 2030, the comprehensive green transformation of economic and social development will achieve remarkable results, and the energy utilization efficiency of key energy consuming industries will reach the international advanced level. Energy consumption per unit of GDP will drop significantly; carbon dioxide emissions per unit of GDP will decrease by more than 65% compared with 2005; the proportion of non-fossil energy consumption will reach about 25%, and the total installed capacity of wind power and solar power generation will reach more than 1.2 billion kilowatts; the forest coverage rate will reach about 25%, the forest stock volume will reach 19 billion cubic meters, and the carbon dioxide emissions will reach the peak and achieve a steady decline. By 2060, a green, low-carbon and circular economic system and a clean, low-carbon, safe and efficient energy system will be fully established, the energy utilization efficiency will reach the international advanced level, the proportion of non-fossil energy consumption will reach more than 80%, the goal of carbon neutralization will be successfully achieved, and the construction of ecological civilization will have fruitful results, creating a harmony between man and nature. The Opinions also put forward 31 key tasks in 10 aspects and defined the implementation path of carbon peaking and carbon neutrality. On this basis, China is working on an action plan for peaking carbon emissions before 2030, with implementation plans for fields and sectors such as energy, industry, urban and rural construction, transport, and agriculture and rural areas. Support plans are being created in areas such as science and technology, fiscal funding, finance, pricing, carbon sinks, energy transition and coordination of pollution reduction and carbon emission reduction, with clearer timetables, roadmaps, and working plans. The country is shaping policies and actions with clear objectives, reasonable assignment of labor, effective measures, and sound coordination.

Establish and improve the working system of peaking carbon emissions and achieving carbon neutrality. In 2021, the Central Committee set up a special leading group to guide and coordinate the work related to peaking carbon emissions and achieving carbon neutrality. Provinces (regions and cities) have also set up corresponding leading groups to strengthen the coordination of peaking carbon emissions and achieving carbon neutrality from top to bottom.

Focus on the key work of peaking carbon emissions and achieving carbon neutrality. China made the expansion control of energy-intensive and high-emission projects a top priority in the effort to peak carbon emissions and achieve carbon neutrality. It required local governments to clearly identify all energy-intensive and high-emission projects, produce category-based management proposals, carry out special inspections, strictly punish any such projects constructed or operated in contravention of regulations, and implement list management, category-based handling, and dynamic monitoring of energy-intensive and high-emission projects. It has established working mechanisms on openly criticizing entities for wrongdoing, early warnings on energy use, regulatory talks, and accountability, gradually forming sound working and regulatory systems. China's carbon intensity in 2020 was 18.8 percent lower than that in 2015, a better result than the binding target set in the 13th Five-Year Plan (2016–2020). The figure was also 48.4 percent less than that in 2005, which means that China had more than fulfilled its commitment to the international community, to achieve a 40–45 percent reduction in carbon intensity from the 2005 level by 2020. The drop in carbon intensity translates to a total reduction of about 5.8 billion tons of carbon dioxide emissions from 2005 to 2020, and demonstrates that China has largely reversed the rapid growth of its carbon dioxide emissions.

In addition, the ruling party and the government have also issued policy documents such as Guidelines on Building a Sound Economic Structure that Facilitates Green, Low-Carbon, and Circular Development, which have significantly raised the ecological and environmental protection standards, forced the transformation and upgrading of traditional industries, continued to resolve the backwardness and excess capacity of heavy environmental pollution, large resource consumption and hopeless achievement, and accelerated the development of energy conservation and environmental protection industries and circular economy. It has encouraged the development of green credit mechanisms, green bonds, and green insurance, carried out pilot projects such as carbon emission trading and the cap-and-trade system for emissions, guided more social capital to invest in green industries, and supported major environmental protection infrastructure construction, ecological protection and restoration projects, and built a beautiful countryside. In 2020, the revenue of China's environmental protection industry was about 1.95 trillion yuan, becoming an important new growth point of the national economy.

With the continuous promotion of the green development mode, the green lifestyle has increasingly become the shared consensus and common pursuit of people. China encourages simple, moderate, green, and low-carbon ways of life, and oppose extravagance and excessive consumption to foster a culture of living green and living healthy. In the system of national education and training, the contents of cherishing the ecology, protecting resources and protecting the environment have been greatly strengthened. The supply of green products and services continues to increase. New business forms such as sharing economy, service leasing and second-hand trading are booming. Energy saving and environment-friendly renewable products are favored by consumers. Initiatives such as "Campaigns to oppose food waste" and low-carbon traveling have received positive responses from the whole society. As a result, the entire Party and the whole country have become more purposeful and active in pursuing green development, and there has been a clear shift away from the tendency to neglect ecological and environmental protection.

4.6.5 Actively Participate in Global Environmental Governance

Climate change is a challenge for all of humanity. As is stated in the State of the Global Climate 2020 released by the World Meteorological Organization, the global mean temperature for 2020 was around 1.2°C warmer than pre-industrial times, and the last 10-year average (2011–2020) was the warmest on record. Global climate change is affecting every region on our planet. Rising temperatures and sea levels and frequent extreme climate events pose a serious challenge for the very survival of humanity and are long-term major threats to the security of global food, water, ecology, energy and infrastructure, and to people's lives and property. Therefore, addressing climate change is a task of great urgency.

Actively promote international cooperation. In 2015, President Xi Jinping gave a keynote speech at the Paris Conference on Climate Change, making a historic contribution to the conclusion of the Paris Agreement on global climate action after 2020. In 2016, when the G20 Hangzhou Summit took place, President Xi Jinping submitted documents ratifying the Paris Agreement to the UN on behalf of the Chinese government. At critical moments when global climate governance is facing great uncertainties, President Xi has repeatedly expressed China's firm support for the Paris Agreement. In April 2021, Xi Jinping was invited to deliver an important speech at the Leaders Summit on Climate, and elaborated on the concept of "a community of life for man and ature" for the first time. He stressed: faced with unprecedented difficulties in global environmental governance, the international community should work together with unprecedented ambition and action, discuss ways to tackle this challenge and find a path forward for man and nature to live in harmony to foster a community of life for man and nature. We must be committed to harmony between man and Nature, green development, systemic governance, a people-centered approach, multilateralism, and the principle of common but differentiated responsibilities. These six initiatives are the core meaning of the concept of "a community of life for man and nature," and point out the direction for global environmental governance at the key node. China initiated the establishment of multilateral negotiation mechanisms such as the BASIC Ministerial Meeting (China, India, Brazil and South Africa) on Climate Change and the Ministerial on Climate Action. It actively coordinates the positions of countries within climate negotiation blocs such as the BASIC countries, the Like-Minded Developing Countries, and the Group of 77 and China. China actively participates in climate negotiations through the Group of 20, the International Civil Aviation Organization, the International Maritime

Organization, the BRICS meetings and so forth, promoting the synergy of multiple channels and multilateral processes.

Lead global governance with China's actions. In September 2014, the NDRC, together with relevant departments, organized the preparation of the National Plan on Climate Change (2014–2020), which put forward the guiding ideology, objective requirements, policy guidance, key tasks and guarantee measures for China's climate change response. In September 2015, Chinese President Xi Jinping attended the United Nations Sustainable Development Summit, and endorsed together with other heads of state the 2030 Agenda for Sustainable Development. This is another important global action determined by the United Nations in the field of sustainable development after the formulation of Agenda 21 and the millennium development goals. In 2016, China has shown great initiative through its release of China's National Plan on Implementation of the 2030 Agenda for Sustainable Development, and made comprehensive arrangements for the implementation. In December 2020, at the Climate Ambition Summit, President Xi announced China's further commitments for 2030 pertaining to matters such as the reduction of carbon dioxide emissions, the increase in use of non-fossil fuels, and the forest stock volume. In September 2021, at the general debate of the 76th session of the United Nations General Assembly, he stated that China will step up support for other developing countries in developing green and low-carbon energy, and will build no new coal-fired power projects abroad, manifesting China's sense of responsibility as a major country.

Help developing countries cope with climate change. China engages in South-South cooperation on climate change with other developing countries. It has done its best to help those countries, in particular small island states, the least developed countries, and African countries, to build capacity to fight climate change and reduce the adverse impact of climate change. Since 2011, China has allocated about RMB 1.2 billion for South-South climate cooperation and signed 40 cooperation documents with 35 countries. It has helped countries to build low-carbon demonstration zones and provided them with climate-related supplies such as meteorological satellites, (Photovoltaic) PV power generation and lighting equipment, New Energy Vehicles (NEVs), environmental monitoring devices, and clean cookstoves. It has trained about 2,000 officials and professionals in the field of climate change for nearly 120 developing countries.

Biodiversity protection has been strengthened. In October 2021, the high-level segment of COP15 concluded in Kunming, Yunnan Province, where the

Kunming Declaration was adopted, calling on all parties to take actions to build a shared future for all life on Earth. The declaration promises to ensure the formulation, adoption and implementation of an effective "Post-2020 Global Biodiversity Framework" to reverse the current trend of biodiversity loss and ensure that biodiversity is put on the path of recovery by 2030 at the latest, so as to fully realize the 2050 vision of harmony between man and nature. The Declaration sends a strong signal to show the world China's determination to solve the problem of biodiversity loss.

Summary

Since the 18th National Congress of the CPC, the CPC and the Chinese government have vigorously promoted the construction of ecological civilization from the strategic height of the Five-Sphere Integrated Plan of the cause of socialism with Chinese characteristics and from the height of the era of realizing the Chinese Dream of the great rejuvenation of the Chinese nation. We must stay true to the principle that lucid waters and lush mountains are invaluable assets, continue our holistic approach to the conservation of mountain, river, forest, farmland, lake, grassland, and desert ecosystems. Through all-out efforts in the areas of theory, law, institutions, organization, and conduct, the Party has strengthened ecological conservation and environment protection in all dimensions and regions and at all times. We have promoted the enforcement of red lines for ecological conservation, set benchmarks for environmental quality, imposed caps on resource utilization, and launched a whole raft of pioneering initiatives that will have fundamental and far-reaching significance. We have organized and implemented the main functional area strategy, optimized the pattern of territorial space development and protection. China has achieved initial success in the critical battle against pollution. Three major action plans on addressing air, water, and soil pollution have been fully implemented. We have carried out central government environmental inspections, strictly investigated and prosecuted a number of major representative cases of ecological damage, and addressed a number of environmental problems that have aroused strong public concern. Actively participate in global ecological environment governance with the goal of building a community of life for man and nature. Through unremitting efforts, the concept of ecological civilization has taken root in the hearts of the people. The entire nation have become more conscious and active in pursuing green development, and made significant progress in building a Beautiful China. The green development is making progress. Our environmental protection endeavors have seen sweeping, historic, and transformative changes.

SECTION 7

Advance Our Major-Country Diplomacy with Chinese Characteristics

4.7.1 Put Forward the Concepts of the Great Changes in the World That Have Not Been Seen in a Century, and Major Country Diplomacy with Chinese Characteristics

(1) The World Is Undergoing the Greatest Changes in a Century

In the 21st century, the world is fast becoming multipolar, economically globalized, information-oriented and culturally diverse. The international landscape and the international system are undergoing profound adjustments, the global governance system is undergoing profound changes, the contrast of international power is undergoing the most revolutionary changes in recent times, and the world is witnessing major developments that affect the course and trend of human history. As early as 2007, the 17th National Congress of the CPC already proposed that: the world today is undergoing tremendous changes and adjustments.[95] In the second decade of the 21st century, the evolution of unprecedented changes picked up speed. The relationship between China and the world has undergone profound changes, and China has never been closer to the center of the world stage. At the same time, the great rejuvenation of the Chinese nation has entered a critical period. The development and changes of the world and China are intertwined and surging with each other.

In December 2012, shortly after the 18th National Congress of the CPC, Xi Jinping introduced the concept of the Major Changes at an important meeting of the armed forces. Since then, he has talked about this issue many times. He stressed that "the international financial crisis has had a profound impact on the world economic pattern and the political and security situation in the past five years. The United States, the European Union and other countries have been caught in many crises and are in short supply. The collective rise of emerging market countries and large developing countries has had a major impact on the status of the West in the international landscape. The turmoil in West Asia and North Africa has triggered the largest geopolitical change since the drastic changes in the Soviet Union and East Asia. Non-state actions have emerged in large numbers and become increasingly important forces in the international arena. This great change can be said to be unprecedented."[96] In December 2017, Xi Jinping publicly used the concept of "once-in-a-century changes" for the first time at a meeting of overseas Chinese envoys. After that, he analyzed and explained the profound changes in a series of speeches. The most representative one is the speech delivered at the 23rd St Petersburg International Economic Forum in June. Xi Jinping said, "we live in a world of profound changes unseen in a century. The rising speed of emerging market countries and developing countries is unprecedented, the metabolism and fierce competition brought about by the new round of scientific and technological revolution and industrial transformation are unprecedented, and the global governance system is not adapted to and asymmetric with changes in the international situation."[97] He pointed out the core content and main characteristics of the world's unprecedented changes in a century with the concept of three "unprecedented."

In the midst of the profound changes in the world, China's sustained and rapid development and the great rejuvenation of the Chinese nation have continued to advance, becoming the main driving force behind the evolution of the global landscape. In 2020, the world was swept up in an unexpected coronavirus epidemic. China quickly brought the epidemic under control, successfully coordinated the prevention and control of the epidemic and economic and social development, and carried out the resumption of work and production in an orderly manner. China became the only major economy in the world to achieve positive economic growth that year, in sharp contrast to the panic and chaos of many western developed countries in the face of the epidemic. With this in mind, General Secretary Xi Jinping put forward that the world is undergoing changes unseen in a century. Economic globalization has run up against headwinds; protectionism and unilateralism are on the rise; the world economy is in the doldrums; and international trade and investment have slumped. The international economic, scientific and technological, cultural, security and political landscape is undergoing profound adjustments. The world has entered a period of turbulence and transformation."[98]

(2) Expound Major Country Diplomacy with Chinese Characteristics

Faced with major world changes unseen in a century, the CPC and the Chinese government has made careful planning of diplomatic work, and put forward the concept of major country diplomacy with Chinese Characteristics.

In November 2014, the Central Conference on Work Relating to Foreign Affairs was held in Beijing. Xi Jinping put forward in the conference: profound changes are taking place in China's relations with the rest of the world, with closer interactions between China and the international community. As China has increased its dependence on the world and its involvement in international affairs, so has the world deepened its dependence on China and had greater impact on China. Therefore, in projecting and adopting plans for reform and development, we must give full consideration to both domestic and international markets, both domestic and foreign resources, and both domestic and international rules, and use them judiciously. He stressed, "China must develop a distinctive diplomatic approach befitting its role as a major country. We should, summing up our past practice and experience, enrich and develop our diplomatic theories and practice, and conduct diplomacy with salient Chinese features and a Chinese vision."[99] He pointed out that we should uphold the CPC's leadership and Chinese socialism. We will stick to our development path, social system, cultural tradition and values. We should continue to follow the independent foreign policy of peace, always pursue the development of the country and the nation by relying on ourselves, and follow our own path unswervingly. While pursuing peaceful development, we will never relinquish our legitimate rights and interests, or allow China's core interests to be impaired. We will promote democracy in international relations, and uphold the Five Principles of Peaceful Coexistence. We are firm in our position that all countries, regardless of their size, strength and level of development, are equal members of the international community and that the destiny of the world should be decided by people of all countries. We will uphold international justice and, in particular, speak up for developing countries.

In March 2016, the Fourth Session of the 12th NPC held a press conference, and Foreign Minister Wang Yi made an interpretation to the major country diplomacy with Chinese characteristics: our goal is to help realize the Chinese Dream of national rejuvenation and build a community of shared destiny for all mankind. The strategic choice is to strive for peaceful development both at home and in the world. The basic principle is to seek win-win cooperation and, on that basis, build a new type of international relations. The main pathway is to establish various types of partnerships and choose partnership over alliance, dialogue over confrontation. The value we insist on is to adopt a balanced approach to friendship and interests, uphold justice in international affairs and put friendship before interests in state-to-state relations."[100] In May, he pointed out in an interview that the diplomatic theory of major country diplomacy with Chinese characteristics is a top-level design. Vividly speaking, this basic framework is supported by five aspects, that is, the goal is to build a community with a shared future for mankind, the strategic choice is to adhere to peaceful development, the basic principle is to seek win-win cooperation, the main path is to build partnerships, and the value orientation is to practice the correct concept of righteousness and interests.[101]

At the Central Conference on Work Relating to Foreign Affairs in June 2018, the most important outcome of this meeting is that Xi Jinping Thought on Diplomacy was established as our guideline, providing fundamental principles and action guidance for China to implement the major-country diplomacy with Chinese characteristics.

4.7.2 Build a Global Community of Shared Future

The new era calls for new ideas. In November 2012, the report of the 18th National Congress of the CPC put forward the idea of "advocating a global community of shared future." In March, 2013, in his speech at the Moscow State Institute of International Relations, Moscow, Russia, for the first time, Xi Jinping openly expounded this concept to the world, conveying China's judgment to the world on the direction of human civilization. He stressed:It is a world where countries are linked with and dependent on one another at a level never seen before. Mankind, by living in the same global village in the same era where history and reality meet, has increasingly emerged as a community of shared future in which everyone has in himself a little bit of others.[102]

Later, on a series of major international occasions, Xi Jinping elaborated on the concept of building a community of human destiny, which has had a wide impact on the international community.

Chinese President Xi Jinping addresses the annual high-level general debate of the 70th session of the UNGA at the UN headquarters in New York, the United States in September, 2015. He stressed, in today's world, all countries are interdependent and share a common future. We should renew our commitment to the purposes and principles of the *UN Charter*, build a new model of international relations featuring mutually beneficial cooperation, and create a community of shared future for mankind. The speech closely linked the building of a new type of international relations with win-win cooperation as the core and the building of a community with a shared future for mankind, and initially clarified that promoting the building of a new type of international relations is the basic path to building a community with a shared future for mankind. Later, the 19th National Congress of the CPC clarified the meaning of a new type of international relations, featuring mutual respect, equity, justice and win-win cooperation.

On Jan. 18, 2017, President Xi Jinping delivered a speech at the United Nations Office at Geneva. Faced with the question of "What has happened to the world and how should we respond?" Xi Jinping put forward: the Chinese approach building a community of shared future for mankind and achieving inclusive and win-win development. He profoundly expounded the rich connotation of the important concept of building a community with a shared future for mankind from the aspects of partnership, security pattern, economic development, cultural exchanges, and ecological construction. He stressed that we should adhere to dialogue and consultation to build a world of lasting peace; adhere to co-construction and sharing to build a universally safe world; adhere to win-win cooperation and build a world of common prosperity; adhere to exchanges and mutual learning and build an open and inclusive world; adhere to green and low-carbon development, and build a clean and beautiful world. This important concept guides the world at a crossroads.

In 2017, the 19th National Congress of the CPC listed building a community with a shared future for mankind as an important element of Xi Jinping Thought on Socialism with Chinese Characteristics for a New Era and included it in the Party Constitution. In 2018, the First Session of the 13th NPC promoted the inclusion of building a community with a shared future for mankind into the Constitution.

In the new era, promoting the building of a community with a shared future has become a clear banner of China's diplomacy. Focusing on the general theme of building a community with a shared future for mankind, the CPC and the Chinese government have also put forward many sub-themes, such as the bilateral community with a shared future of China and Pakistan, China and Laos, China and Cambodia, China and Vietnam, China and Myanmar, the Asian community with a shared future, China-ASEAN, China-Africa, China-Arab States and other regional communities with a shared future, as well as the community with a shared future for nuclear security, the community with a shared future for oceans, a community of life for man and nature, the community with a shared future for cyberspace, the community with a shared future for human health, the community of a shared future for global development and other fields, which have formed an all-round idea of a community of a shared future for mankind, covering different levels of the world, regions, and bilateral, as well as different fields such as economy, security and ecology.

China's proposals have won wide recognition of the international community. In February 2017, the 55th session of the United Nations Commission for Social Development adopted the Resolution on the Social Dimension of the New Partnership for Africa's Development. The concept of "building a community with a shared future for mankind" was first written into the United Nations resolution. Subsequently, this concept was also written into a series of other important documents of the United Nations. On April 28, 2019, China and Cambodia signed the action plan of building a China-Cambodia community with a shared future. This is the first action plan for a community of shared future signed by China and countries with different social systems. In April 30, General Secretary and President Xi Jinping and Lao President and General Secretary of the Lao People's Revolutionary Party (LPRP) Central Committee Bounnhang Vorachit signed an action plan to build the China-Laos community with a shared future. This is the first bilateral cooperation document signed in the name of the Party to build a community of human destiny in China. This document is not only a programmatic document to usher in a new era of China-Laos relations, but also has important leading and exemplary significance in promoting the construction of a community with a shared future for mankind at the regional and international levels.

4.7.3 We Should Advance International Cooperation under the Belt and Road Initiative

The Belt and Road cooperation is a major platform for building a global community of shared future. In September, 2013, when President Xi Jinping visited Kazakhstan, he proposed to build a Silk Road Economic Belt. In October of the same year, he proposed "the 21st Century Maritime Silk Road." during his visit to Indonesia. The two have jointly formed the major initiative of the "Belt and Road." After this initiative was put forward, it was quickly identified as a national strategy.

In November 2013, the Third Plenary Session of the 18th CCCPC proposed to accelerate the construction of infrastructure connectivity with surrounding countries and regions, promote the construction of the Silk Road Economic Belt and the Maritime Silk Road, and form a new pattern of all-round opening-up.

From 2013 to 2018, the overall layout of the "Belt and Road" was completed and the painting the broad strokes was completed. In June, 2014, at the sixth ministerial conference of the China-Arab States Cooperation Forum, Xi Jinping for the first time, officially used the term "Belt and Road," and elaborated the spirit of the Silk Road and the principles that should be adhered to in the construction of the "Belt and Road." In November of the same year, Dialogue on Strengthening Connectivity Partnership was held in Beijing. Xi Jinping pointed out at the meeting that the interconnection we want to build should be a three-way combination of infrastructure, institutions and people-to-people exchanges and a five-way progress in policy communication, infrastructure connectivity, trade link, capital flow, and understanding among peoples. He also put forward cooperation proposals focusing on Asian countries, relying on economic corridors, making breakthroughs in transportation infrastructure, building financing platforms, and people to people exchanges, further pointing out the direction and path of the "Belt and Road" construction. In the same month, the CCCPC and the State Council issued the Strategic Planning for the Building of the Silk Road Economic Belt and the 21st Century Maritime Silk Road. This year, the "Belt and Road" concept entered the stage of practical cooperation. In February 2015, the first meeting on promoting "Belt and Road" initiative was held in Beijing, and the leading group on the initiative formally appeared. In March, the NDRC and other departments jointly released the Vision and Actions on Jointly Building Silk Road Economic Belt and the 21st Century Maritime Silk Road, which defined the principles, framework ideas, cooperation priorities, cooperation mechanisms and other contents of the "Belt and Road," and the outline of the "Belt and Road" Initiative is clearer. Subsequently, the "Belt and Road" Initiative was included in the "13th Five-Year Plan" and became an important part of China's economic and social development. In August 2016, the Symposium on the Belt and Road Initiative was held, which put forward work requirements for continuing to promote relevant construction. In May 2017, the office of leading group on the initiative released the document "Building the Belt and Road: Concept, Practice and China's Contribution," which further explained the connotation, concept and essence of the Belt and Road Initiative, and summarized the rich achievements of jointly building the "Belt and Road" over the past three years. The document clearly puts forward a connectivity framework consisting of six corridors, six routes and multiple countries and ports. The "six corridors" are: new Eurasian Land Bridge, China-Mongolia-Russia, China-Central Asia-West Asia, China-Indochina Peninsula, China-Pakistan, and Bangladesh-China-India-Myanmar. The "six means of communication" are rail, highways, seagoing transport, aviation, pipelines, and aerospace integrated information network, which comprise the interconnection we want to build. "Multiple countries" refer to a number of countries along the Belt and Road that first joined the initiative. There are many countries along the Belt and Road. China will cooperate with them on the basis of equality and mutual benefit. But pragmatism requires a need to cooperate first with a number of particular countries, and try to achieve results with them that have a demonstrative impact and embody the concept of the Belt and Road, so that more countries will be attracted to participate in the initiative. "Multiple ports" refer to a number of ports that ensure safe and smooth sea passages. By building a number of important ports and key cities with countries along the Belt and Road, China works to promote maritime cooperation. The cooperation framework is the framework for joint building of the Belt and Road, giving a clear direction for countries involved to participate in the initiative. In the same month, the Belt and Road Forum for International Cooperation was successfully held in Beijing. This is the highest-level international activity under the framework of the Belt and Road Initiative. It is the highest level and largest multilateral diplomatic activity initiated and hosted by China since the founding of new China. The heads of state and government of 29 countries attended the forum, and more than 1,600 representatives from more than 140 countries and more than 80 international organizations attended the forum. The leaders' round table summit issued a joint communiqué, achieving broad consensus for working together to develop the Belt and Road Initiative. At this stage, financial cooperation represented by the Asian Infrastructure Investment Bank (AIIB) and the Silk Road Fund continued to deepen, and a number of influential landmark projects were gradually implemented. Among them, Asian Infrastructure Investment Bank is the first multilateral financial institution initiated by China, and the Silk Road Fund is an investment and financing platform based on medium and long-term equity investment. The two provide financial support for the infrastructure construction of countries along the "Belt and Road" and promote economic cooperation along the line.

After 2018, the Belt and Road Initiative has transformed from painting the broad strokes was completed to refining the details, and is moving towards high-quality development. In August 2018, a symposium was held to mark the fifth anniversary of the Belt and Road Initiative. Xi Jinping pointed out that after five years of efforts in laying the groundwork and establishing the comprehensive framework, the BRI was entering the phase of solid progress and sustained growth poised to achieve higher quality development. We should make every effort to make further progress. On the basis of maintaining the healthy and benign development momentum, we should promote the transformation of the Belt and Road Initiative to high-quality development. This is the basic requirement for working together to develop the Belt and Road Initiative in the next stage. In April, 2019, Belt and Road Forum for International Cooperation was successfully held in Beijing. The meeting produced 283 outcomes in six categories and adopted The Joint Communiqué of the Leaders' Roundtable of the Belt and Road Forum for International Cooperation. In 2020, in the face of global COVID-19, the High-Level Video Conference on Belt and Road International Cooperation reached a consensus on building a "Silk Road for health." In November 2021, the Third Symposium on the Belt and Road Initiative was held in Beijing. Xi Jinping pointed out at the meeting that, on the whole, the theme of the times of peace and development has not changed, the general direction of economic globalization has not changed, the international landscape has developed strategically in our favor, and there are still important opportunities for the Belt and Road Initiative. At the same time, the world today is undergoing momentous changes of a kind not seen in a century. The fierce competition brought about by the new round of scientific and technological revolution and industrial transformation are unprecedented. Global issues such as climate change and epidemic prevention and control have unprecedented impacts on human society. The international environment for the Belt and Road Initiative is becoming increasingly complex. We need to maintain strategic resolve, seize strategic opportunities, coordinate development and security, domestic and international, cooperation and struggle, stock and increment, overall and key, actively respond to challenges, seek benefits and avoid disadvantages, and forge ahead bravely. Thanks to the joint efforts of all of us involved in this initiative, a general connectivity framework consisting of six corridors, six connectivity routes and multiple countries and ports has been put in place. From 2013 to 2021, the annual trade volume between China and the countries along the line increased from 1.04 trillion U.S. dollars to 1.8 trillion U.S. dollars, an increase of 73%. China's direct investment in the countries along the line has accumulated 161.3 billion U.S. dollars, and the countries along the line have invested to build 32,000 enterprises in China, with an actual accumulated investment of 71.2 billion U.S. dollars.

"The Belt and Road" is an important public product provided by China to the world, which has attracted universal attention and response from the world, and its international influence has been expanding. On November 17, 2016, the 71th Session of the UNGA adopted resolution A/71/9 by consensus. This is the first time that the UNGA has included China's "the Belt and Road" initiative in the resolution. At present, China has signed more than 200 cooperation documents on the Belt and Road Initiative with 147 countries and 32 international organizations; signed third-party market cooperation documents with 14 countries including Japan and Italy; relevant cooperation concepts and propositions have been written into the outcome documents of the United Nations, the G20, the APEC, the SCO and other important international mechanisms. Since the Belt and Road Initiative was put forward, China has actively carried out development cooperation in accordance with the development needs of relevant countries, played a role in deepening policy communication, accelerating infrastructure connectivity, promoting unimpeded trade, promoting financial integration and enhancing people to people exchanges, and created space and opportunities for the development of all countries. By the end of 2021, Chinese enterprises had invested 43.08 billion U.S. dollars in overseas economic and trade cooperation parks in countries along the line, creating 346,000 local jobs, giving better play to the role of carriers and platforms, and promoting international production capacity cooperation. While injecting vitality into the world's development, the Belt and Road Initiative has also greatly improved the level of trade and investment liberalization and facilitation in China, promoted China's opening to the outside world from the coastal areas to the provinces and regions along the river, along the border and inland, and developing a new picture of all-around opening-up in which China is opened to the world through eastward and westward links and across land and sea.

4.7.4 Developing Global Partnerships

(1) Promote Coordination and Cooperation between Major Countries

Promoting the building of a new type of international relations is the basic path to building a community with a shared future for mankind. Chinese President Xi Jinping addresses the annual high-level general debate of the 70th session of the UNGA at the UN headquarters in New York, the United States on September 28, 2015 and put forward that we should renew our commitment to the purposes and principles of the UN Charter, build a new model of international relations featuring mutually beneficial cooperation, and create a community of shared future for mankind. A New Form of International Relations is "the Five-Sphere Integrated Plan," including partnerships based on equality, consultation, mutual understanding and accommodation; a security architecture featuring fairness, justice, joint contribution and shared benefits. We will pursue open, innovative, and inclusive development that benefits everyone; boost cross-cultural exchanges characterized by harmony within diversity, inclusiveness, and mutual learning; and cultivate ecosystems based on respect for nature and green development. In October 2017, the 19th National Congress of the CPC clearly defined the main connotation of the new type of international relations. The congress put forward: China will always hold high the banner of peace, development, cooperation and mutual benefit, adhered to the purpose of its foreign policy of safeguarding world peace and promoting common development, unswervingly developed friendly cooperation with other countries on the basis of the Five Principles of Peaceful Coexistence, and promoted the building of a new type of international relations featuring mutual respect, fairness, justice and win-win cooperation. To build a new type of international relations, China will actively develop global partnerships, expand the convergence of interests with other countries, to advance China's diplomatic agenda in a comprehensive, multilevel, multifaceted way, making friends across the world.

Major powers are the main actors in the international political arena and the main constructors of the international strategic environment. The relationship between major powers has a bearing on global strategic stability. We will contribute to a framework that ensures the overall stability and balanced development of relations between major countries.

China-Russia strategic coordination has become a cornerstone for global peace and stability and has been among the priorities of China's diplomacy all along. Our comprehensive strategic partnership of coordination is mature, stable and solid, enjoying the highest level of mutual trust and coordination and the highest strategic value. In March 2013, Xi Jinping met with Putin in Russia on his first overseas visit since assuming the presidency. Since then, China and Russia have maintained frequent high-level exchanges. From 2013 to early 2022, the heads of state of the two countries met 38 times on different occasions. On July 4, 2017, President Xi Jinping held talks with Russian President Putin at the Kremlin in Moscow and proposed to "firmly support each other in the four aspects," namely, firm support for each other's efforts to safeguard their core interests such as sovereignty, security and territorial integrity, firm support for each other's development path in line with their national conditions, firm support for each other's development and revitalization, and firm support for each other's efforts to get their own affairs in order. The heads of state of the two countries signed a Joint Statement between the PRC and Russia on the Establishment of a Comprehensive Strategic Partnership, making a comprehensive plan for the development of China Russia relations, and the comprehensive strategic partnership of coordination between China and Russia is constantly moving to a higher level. In June 2019, Xi Jinping paid a visit to Russia, where the two heads of state jointly announced China-Russia comprehensive strategic partnership of coordination in the new era and signed the Joint Statement on Strengthening Contemporary Strategic Stability. In February 2022, the two heads of state held talks in Beijing and attended the opening ceremony of the 24th Winter Olympic Games. The two sides issued a joint statement between China and Russia on international relations in the new era and global sustainable development, focusing on the common positions of China and Russia on the concept of democracy, development, security and order. Relevant departments of the two countries have also signed a series of cooperation documents in key areas, and China-Russia comprehensive strategic cooperation has become more stable. In 2021, the trade volume of goods between China and Russia reached 146.87 billion U.S. dollars, a year-on-year increase of 35.9%. The bilateral trade volume reached a new record. China has been the largest trading partner of Russia for 12 consecutive years.

China and the US are the world's largest developing country and largest developed country respectively. The China-US relationship is one of the most important bilateral relationships in the world. As for where we are and where we need to be in China-US relations, our position is consistent. As the largest developing country and the largest developed country, it is imperative for us to seriously and properly handle our relations out of a strong sense of responsibility to humanity, to history and to our peoples. In June 2013, Chinese President Xi Jinping visited the United States and met with American President Barack Obama. Focusing on the theme of developing a new model of major-country relations between China and the United States, the heads of state of China and the United States had a frank and in-depth exchange of views on bilateral relations and major international and regional issues. The two sides agreed to work together to build a new type of major country relationship featuring no conflict, no confrontation, mutual respect and win-win cooperation. In November 2014, US President Obama attended the informal meeting of APEC leaders held in Beijing and paid a state visit to China. In April 2017, Xi visited the United States again to meet with Trump, and the two sides established four high-level dialogue mechanisms concerning diplomatic and security issues, comprehensive economic issues, law enforcement, cyber security, and social, people-to-people and cultural exchanges. Since 2018, the US government has provoked trade friction by issuing Section 301 report on China and other ways. Subsequently, it was expanded to various fields such as science and technology, finance, and diplomacy to contain and suppress China in an all-round way. During the COVID-19 epidemic, some politicians in the United States tried their best to "stigmatize" China with the intention to deflect attention from their botched epidemic response, and shift the blame to China before the American people hold them accountable for their reckless actions. This year has witnessed the most challenging situation facing China-US relations since the establishment of diplomatic ties over four decades ago. In the face of the pressure from the United States, China has responded resolutely and rationally to unjustified moves by the United States. On the one hand, it has taken effective countermeasures to resolutely safeguard national sovereignty, security and development interests. At the same time, China is committed to resolving disputes through dialogue and consultation, to constructively handle and manage differences, work to stabilize bilateral relations, and maintain the strategic stability of the international system. In 2021, China-US trade volume increased by nearly 30% year-on-year, reaching 755.6 billion U.S. dollars, another record high. Facts have proved that win-win cooperation between China and the United States is the general trend.

Europe is an important pole in a multi-polar world and China's comprehensive strategic partner. China will unswervingly promote the healthy and stable development of China-EU comprehensive strategic partnership, and China-EU relations will continue to deepen and expand. In November 2013, at the invitation of China, President of the European Council Herman Van Rompuy and President of the European Commission Jose Manuel Barroso came to China to attend the 16th China-EU summit. China and the EU have jointly formulated and released the Strategic Agenda 2020 for China-EU Cooperation. This comprehensive strategic plan has set the common goal of strengthening cooperation between China and the EU in the fields of peace and security, prosperity, sustainable development and people to people exchanges, and has promoted the development of China-EU comprehensive strategic partnership. In March 2014, when he visited Europe and the headquarters of the European Union, he proposed China and Europe connect our strengths, markets and civilizations, and endeavor to promote a partnership for peace, growth, reform and civilization, pointing out the direction for the development of bilateral relations. In April 2019, China and the EU jointly issued the Joint Statement of the 21st China-EU Leaders' Meeting in Europe, and reached a series of new cooperation initiatives on deepening the comprehensive strategic partnership of mutual benefit and win-win results. In December, 2020, President Xi Jinping had virtual meetings with Chancellor Angela Merkel of Germany, President Emmanuel Macron of France, President Michel of the European Council and President Ursula von der Leyen of the European Commission. President Xi Jinping and European leaders have jointly announced the conclusion of negotiations on a China-EU investment treaty. While paying attention to investment protection, this investment treaty involves more market access and opening-up. It is the first comprehensive investment treaty signed between China and the EU, and also opens up new space for China-Europe economic and trade cooperation. China and the EU have established more than 70 consultation and dialogue mechanisms covering many fields. In 2021, despite the complex and severe situation, China-EU economic and trade cooperation continued to develop rapidly. The total value of imports and exports between the two sides reached 828.11 billion U.S. dollars, an increase of 27.5% over the previous year. China has continued to maintain its position as the largest trading partner of the EU.

(2) Deepen Relations with Neighboring Countries
China and its neighboring countries are interdependent and share a common destiny. China sees its neighboring countries as the foundation of its development and prosperity. It gives top priority to neighborhood diplomacy in foreign relations.

Improve the top-level design of peripheral diplomacy. In October 2013, the CCCPC specially held the first seminar on the work of neighborhood diplomacy since the founding of new China. Xi Jinping pointed out at the seminar that, China's diplomacy in this area is driven by and must serve the Two Centenary Goals and our national rejuvenation. To achieve these strategic aims, we must create and cement friendly relations and further mutually beneficial cooperation with neighboring countries, maintain and make the best use of the strategic opportunities we now enjoy, and safeguard China's state sovereignty, national security, and development interests. Together we must strive to build more amicable political relationships and closer economic ties, to further security cooperation and to encourage more cultural and people-to-people exchanges with neighboring countries. China's basic policy of diplomacy with neighboring countries is to treat them as friends and partners, to make them feel secure and to support their development. This policy is characterized by friendship, sincerity, reciprocity, and inclusiveness. Friendship is a consistent principle of China's diplomacy with its neighbors. In adherence to this principle, we need to help neighbors in times of crisis, treat them as equals, visit them frequently, and take actions that will win us support and friendship. In response, we hope that neighboring countries will be well inclined towards us, and we hope that China will have a stronger affinity with them, and that our appeal and our influence will grow. We must treat neighbors with sincerity and cultivate them as friends and partners. We should cooperate with our neighbors on the basis of reciprocity, create a closer network of common interests, and better integrate China's interests with theirs, so that they can benefit from China's development and China can benefit and gain support from theirs. We should advocate inclusiveness, stressing that there is enough room in the Asia Pacific region for all countries to develop, and promoting regional cooperation with an open mind and enthusiasm.[103] In November, 2014, at the Central Conference on Work Relating to Foreign Affairs, President Xi Jinping put forward the concept of a neighborhood community with a shared future. He stressed that we should promote neighborhood diplomacy, and turn China and its neighboring countries into a community of shared future. In this regard, we should continue to implement the principles of amity, sincerity, mutual benefit and inclusiveness in our relations with neighboring countries, promote friendship and partnership with our neighbors, foster an amicable, secure and prosperous neighborhood environment, and boost win-win cooperation and connectivity with our neighbors. President Xi Jinping have paid visits to many countries in

Southeast Asia, South Asia, and Central Asia and Northeastern Europe, covering almost all of China's neighbors.

Friendly and cooperative relations with Southeast Asian countries have progressed steadily. China put forward the "2 + 7" cooperation framework, and upgraded it into a "3 + X" cooperation framework, which is a new cooperation framework underpinned by the three pillars of political and security cooperation, economic cooperation and people-to-people exchange and supported by cooperation in multiple sectors. The two sides also formulated the Action Plan to Implement the Joint Declaration on China-ASEAN Strategic Partnership for Peace and Prosperity 2016–2020, signed the Strategic Partnership Vision 2030, and announced the establishment of China-ASEAN comprehensive strategic partnership.

Cooperation with South Asian countries has increased significantly. The leaders of China and India have met many times, and the two countries jointly issued the Joint Statement on the Decision to Build a Closer Developmental Partnership. India has joined the SCO, and China-India cooperation has developed steadily. China and Pakistan have successively issued a series of important documents, such as the Joint Statement on Establishing an All-Weather Strategic Cooperative Partnership and the Joint Statement on Further Strengthening the China-Pakistan All-Weather Strategic Cooperative Partnership and Forge a Closer China-Pakistan Community with a Shared Future in the New Era. The construction of the China Pakistan Economic Corridor has made constant progress, and the all-weather strategic cooperative partnership between China and Pakistan has developed in depth.

Closer relations with Central Asian countries. China has established strategic partnership with all Central Asian countries. The video Summit on the 30th anniversary of the establishment of diplomatic relations between China and the five Central Asian countries was held ceremoniously and a leaders' joint statement on the 30th anniversary of the establishment of diplomatic relations was issued, announcing to build a China-Central Asia community with a shared future.

Advance pragmatic cooperation with countries in Northeast Asia. China and Japan have continuously strengthened exchanges and cooperation in various fields. Since 2007, China has been Japan's largest trading partner. The friendly and cooperative relations between China and the ROK have continued to develop. The high-level leaders of the two sides have maintained close interaction and signed important documents such as the Sino-ROK Joint Statement for the Future and the China-ROK Free Trade Agreement. Cooperation in various fields has developed rapidly.

In addition, China has continuously deepened mutually beneficial cooperation and connectivity with neighboring countries to better benefit them through the Belt and Road Initiative. At the same time, China firmly upholds its territorial sovereignty and maritime rights and interests, insists on controlling differences through dialogue and cooperation, and peacefully resolving disputes through negotiation and consultation. For example, after a series of conflicts on the border between China and India, China has actively promoted border negotiations, and the border areas generally maintained peace and tranquility.

(3) Our Solidarity and Cooperation with Other Developing Countries Have Been Continuously Strengthened.

The vast number of developing countries are China's natural allies in international affairs. In China's foreign exchanges, developing countries have always been in a fundamental position. In the new era, our solidarity and cooperation with other developing countries have been continuously strengthened.

China Africa relations have to scaled new heights. In March 2013, President Xi Jinping visited three African countries, and attended the fifth BRICS Summit held in Durban. During this visit, he put forward the principles of China's African policy, namely, sincerity, real results, amity and good faith, achieving 20 important outcomes in economic and trade with the African side. In December 2015, at the Johannesburg Summit of the FOCAC, Xi Jinping proposed to upgrade China-Africa relations from "the new type of strategic partnership between China and Africa" to "a comprehensive strategic and cooperative partnership," and also proposed "ten cooperation plans" to meet the most urgent needs of Africa, covering industrialization, agricultural modernization, infrastructure, finance, poverty reduction and people's welfare, taking China-Africa cooperation to a new historical height. In September 2018, the Beijing Summit of the FOCAC adopted two outcome documents, namely, *Beijing Declaration*. Toward an Even Stronger China-Africa Community with a Shared Future and Forum on China-Africa Cooperation Beijing Action Plan (2019–2021), and proposed the implementation of eight major initiatives. In November, 2021, President Xi Jinping attended the opening ceremony of the Eighth Ministerial Conference of the FOCAC and delivered a keynote speech through video link. He summarized in his speech the spirit of China-Africa friendship and cooperation, which features sincere friendship and equality, win-win for mutual benefit and common development, fairness and justice, progress with the times, and openness and inclusiveness. The meeting adopted the Dakar Declaration, the Dakar Action Plan (2022–2024), the Declaration on China-Africa Cooperation on Combating Climate Change, and the China-Africa Cooperation Vision 2035. Among them, the China-Africa Cooperation Vision 2035 is the first medium- and long-term practical cooperation plan jointly formulated by China and Africa, which defines the overall framework for China-Africa cooperation in the next 15 years. China also announced at the meeting that it will jointly implement the "nine programs" with Africa.

A new phase of China-Arab relations. In 2014, the Sixth Ministerial Meeting of the CASCF opened up in Beijing. In the forum, President Xi Jinping put forward building a China-Africa community of shared interests and destiny, and proposed the China-Arab "1 + 2 + 3" cooperation network: take energy cooperation as the main axis, and infrastructure and trade and investment as the two wings, to make breakthroughs in the three high-tech areas of nuclear energy, aerospace satellites, and new energy. In January 2016, the Chinese government issued China's Policy Paper on Arab Countries. This is the first policy document for Arab countries formulated by the Chinese government. It sets forth the guiding principles for the development of China-Arab relations, draws up a blueprint for mutually beneficial cooperation between China and Arab countries, and promotes China-Arab relations to a higher level. In July 2018, the Eighth Ministerial Meeting of the China-Arab States Cooperation Forum (CASCF) was held in Beijing. The two sides agreed that China and Arab states would establish a future-oriented strategic partnership of comprehensive cooperation and common development. At the meeting, the two sides signed three documents: the *Beijing Declaration*, the implementation of plan for the CASCF events in 2018–2020, and an action declaration for joint implementation of the Belt and Road Initiative, presenting a clear, systematic and complete blueprint for the development of China-Arab States relations in the near future. In July, 2020, the Nineth Ministerial Meeting of the China-Arab States Cooperation Forum was held via video conference. In addition to the Joint Statement of China and Arab States on Solidarity Against COVID-19, the meeting also adopted the Amman declaration of the Nineth Ministerial Meeting of the China-Arab States Cooperation Forum (CASCF) and the execution plan for 2020–2022 of the China-Arab Cooperation Forum, to jointly forge a China-Arab community with a shared future for the new era.

Achieve a quantum leap in the relations between China and Latin America and the Caribbean. At the first China-Latin American and Caribbean Countries Leaders' Meeting in July 2014, President Xi Jinping and the leaders of regional countries issued a Joint Statement of the China-Latin America and the Caribbean Leaders' Meeting, jointly announced the establishment of Forum of China and the Community of Latin American and Caribbean States (China-CELAC Forum). From January 8 to 9, 2015, the first Ministerial Meeting of the China-CELAC Forum was held in Beijing. Three outcome documents were adopted, namely, the Beijing Declaration of the First Ministerial Meeting of the China-CELAC Forum, the China-Latin American and Caribbean Countries Cooperation Plan (2015–2019), and the Institutional Arrangements and Operating Rules of China-CELAC Forum, which marks a new period of overall cooperation between China and Latin America. In November 2016, the Chinese government issued a policy document on Latin America and the Caribbean, which is the second policy document on Latin America and the Caribbean issued by the Chinese government after the first policy document in 2008. The documents put forward that we will work together to build a five-dimensional relationship characterized by sincerity and mutual trust in the political field, win-win cooperation on the economic front, mutual learning and emulation in the cultural sphere, close coordination in international affairs, as well as synergy between China's cooperation with the region as a whole and its bilateral relations with individual regional countries. The two sides are ready to work together to push China-Latin America Comprehensive Cooperative Partnership forward for greater development and build a community of shared future. China and Latin American and Caribbean countries held a special foreign ministers' meeting on COVID-19 through teleconference in July, 2020. The meeting adopted the Joint Statement of the Special Video Conference of China and Latin American and Caribbean Countries' Foreign Ministers on COVID-19. China also established diplomatic relations with Panama in 2017, Dominica and El Salvador in 2018, and Nicaragua in 2021, constantly forging broader partnerships and further expanding our circle of friendship in Latin America.

In addition, China has continuously deepened exchanges and cooperation between political parties. From November 30 to December 3, 2017, a meeting of high-level dialogue between the CPC and world political parties was held in

Beijing. This is the first high-level dialogue between the CPC and various political parties around the world. In July 2021, video conference of the CPC and World Political Parties Summit was held. The CPC is celebrating the 100th anniversary of its founding this year. Leaders of more than 500 political parties, political and other organizations from over 160 countries as well as the ten thousand and more representatives of political parties and various circles, at this cloud event to discuss the important question of "working for the people's well-being and the responsibility of political parties," just as the CPC reaches its one hundredth anniversary. This is the highest and largest global political party summit ever hosted by the CPC. It is of milestone significance. In December 2021, 355 political parties, social organizations and think tanks from 140 countries and regions in the world contacted the International Department of the CCCPC in various ways and issued the Joint Statement on Independent Exploration of the Path to Democracy and Joint Efforts to Promote Common Development, opposing interference in the internal affairs of other countries in the name of democracy and calling for building a community with a shared future for mankind guided by the common values of all mankind. This is an important achievement of our country's intra-Party exchanges.

4.7.5 Take a Lead in Reforming and Developing the Global Governance System

The pattern of global governance depends on the international balance of power, and the transformation of the global governance system originates from changes in the balance of power. In today's world, with the increase in global challenges and constant changes in the international balance of power, there is a growing demand for strengthening global governance and transforming the global governance system.

Actively shape the course of reform of the global governance system. In March, 2014, at the third Nuclear Security Summit in The Hague, the Netherlands, President Xi Jinping proposed a rational, coordinated and balanced nuclear safety strategy. It lays out the principles and methods for addressing the fundamental issues of global nuclear safety governance and building a community of shared future for nuclear safety. When attending the Summits marking the 70th anniversary of the UN in September 2015, President Xi Jinping put froward that we uphold peace, development, equity, justice, democracy and freedom, which are all common values of humanity, which points out the common value basis for the future development of the world. In September, 2016, China hosted the 11th G20 Summit in the city of Hangzhou. In this summit, President Xi Jinping put forward: we need to build an innovative world economy to generate new drivers of growth; we need to build an open world economy to expand the scope of development; we need to build an interconnected world economy to forge interactive synergy; we need to build an inclusive world economy to strengthen the foundation for win-win outcomes. This is the first time that China has fully explained its view on global economic governance, and created the Chinese approach that treats both symptoms and root causes of the world economy and takes holistic approaches. China has also guided and coordinated all parties to formulate a series of guiding principles and indicator systems on such important issues as innovative growth, structural reform, multilateral investment, climate change and sustainable development, and issued the G20 Leaders' Communiqué of the Hangzhou Summit, to help it transform from a crisis-management body to a long-term and effective governance mechanism. In the face of the adverse current of economic globalization, in November 2018, China issued China's Position Paper on the Reform of the WTO, supporting the necessary reform of the WTO and promoting the building of an open world economy. Subsequently, he submitted the "China's Proposals on WTO Reform" to the WTO, proposing to solve the key and urgent problems that threaten the survival of the WTO, increase the relevance of the WTO in global economic governance, improve the operational efficiency of the WTO, and enhance the inclusiveness of the multilateral trading system. China has also actively promoted the signing and entry into force of the RCEP, demonstrating its confidence and determination to safeguard multilateralism and free trade. Since the outbreak of Covid-19 in 2020, China has been adhering to the vision of building a community of a global community of health for all. In combating Covid-19, China has engaged in international cooperation and launched the largest global emergency humanitarian operation since the founding of the People's Republic, providing supplies, medical support, and vaccine assistance for many countries, especially developing countries, and engaging in vaccine cooperation with a number of them. China has thus improved the global public health governance system. Faced with unilateral conduct such as withdrawing into isolation, China has worked to safeguard the international system centered on the UN, the international order underpinned by international law, and the basic norms of international relations based on the purposes and principles of the UN Charter. China has upheld and practiced true multilateralism, resolutely opposed unilateralism, protectionism, hegemonism, and power politics, and worked actively to make economic globalization more open, inclusive, balanced, and beneficial for all. When attending the Summits marking the 75th anniversary of the UN in September 2020, President Xi Jinping made four recommendations on how the UN should play its role in the post-epidemic era, namely, to do justice, enforce the rule of law, promote cooperation and focus on real action. In September 2021, President Xi Jinping attended the 76th session of the United Nations General Assembly via video conference, and put forward 6 initiatives: make development a top priority, stay committed to a people-centered development philosophy, staying committed to benefits for all, uphold an innovation-driven approach, achieve harmony between man and nature, stay committed to results-oriented actions. The initiatives inject confidence in international solidarity against the epidemic, guides the direction of global common development, and draws a blueprint for responding to the world's changes. In October, 2021, the Foreign Ministry released the position paper on China-UN cooperation, which sets forth China's positions and propositions on important international issues such as upholding multilateralism, promoting global development and rallying against the epidemic.

Promote creating governance rules in many emerging fields. China initiated the establishment of Asian Infrastructure Investment Bank, the Silk Road Fund, the New Development Bank, and the South-South Cooperation Assistance Fund to promote the accelerated development of relevant countries. Since 2014, China has held a World Internet Conference every year to promote transformation of the global internet governance system, and work together to foster a peaceful, secure, open, and cooperative cyberspace and put in place a multilateral, democratic, and transparent global internet governance system. In September 2020, China launched a Global Initiative on Data Security, which put forward a Chinese approach for promoting global data security governance. In addition, China has also actively participated in the formulation of rules in such emerging fields as polar regions, the deep sea, outer space and biosafety, and played an active role in poverty reduction and counter-terrorism.

Worked together for political solutions to regional and international flash-points. China has worked to promote the political settlement of the Korean Peninsula, Iran nuclear, Syria, Afghanistan, and Ukraine issues, and is committed to promoting dialogue and consultation and seeking solutions acceptable to all parties concerned. We have resolved respective concerns through dialogue and consultation, and advanced the political settlement process of the Korean

Peninsula issue. We have Promoted the relevant countries to reach a comprehensive agreement on the Iranian nuclear issue, and subsequently, at the critical stage of negotiations on the resumption of compliance with the Iran nuclear agreement, China coordinated all parties to maintain stability and build consensus. We have actively participated in the political settlement of the Syrian issue and provided multiple batches of humanitarian assistance to displaced persons and refugees in Syria and neighboring countries. We have successfully hosted important meetings such as the Foreign Ministerial Conference of the Istanbul Process on Afghanistan and the third Foreign Ministers' Meeting among the Neighboring Countries of Afghanistan to make an important contribution to the achievement of lasting peace in Afghanistan. After the outbreak of the crisis in Ukraine, we have actively urged peace and promoted negotiations. China has actively participated in international counter-terrorism actions, and promoted and implemented the United Nations Global Counter-Terrorism Strategy and the Security Council counter-terrorism resolutions. China firmly supports and participates in United Nations peacekeeping missions, and is the country with the largest number and the most comprehensive types of United Nations peacekeeping standby forces.

The Chinese government resolutely safeguards national sovereignty, security and development interests while proactively engaging in the reform of global governance. On the issue of the Diaoyu Islands, in the face of the farce of Japan's "island purchase," China has published statements or articles on many diplomatic occasions and some important national media that the patrol and law enforcement activities in the waters of Diaoyu Islands are legitimate and lawful measures to safeguard sovereignty. On the South China Sea issue, the Philippine government unilaterally put forward the so-called "South China Sea arbitration case," and the Chinese government issued a number of official statements and documents such as the Statement of the Government of the PRC on Territorial Sovereignty and Maritime Rights and Interests in the South China Sea, reiterating China's position on the South China Sea issue on many international occasions. At the same time, China has steadily advanced the consultation process on the Code of Conduct in the South China Sea and stabilized the maritime situation. In July 2014, Yongxing (town) Working Committee and Management Committee were inaugurated in Yongxing Island, Sansha City, to further declare China's sovereignty with political power organizations. On issues related to Xinjiang and Xizang, we have fought back against groundless accusations and won the understanding and support of most countries internationally. On the issue of security of overseas interests, we have comprehensively used political, economic, diplomatic and military means to protect the security and legitimate rights and interests of overseas Chinese citizens, organizations and institutions, and striven to form a strong security system for overseas interests. In September 2014, the Foreign Ministry's Global Emergency Call Center for Consular Protection and Services was launched, opening a green channel for consular protection and services between overseas Chinese citizens and the motherland. Since the 18th National Congress of the CPC, the Ministry of foreign affairs has taken the lead in organizing and implementing more than 10 emergency evacuations of overseas citizens, and handled more than 500,000 cases involving overseas citizens being kidnapped and attacked, involving nearly one million citizens. Since the outbreak of COVID-19, more than 300 temporary flights have been arranged to pick up more than 70,000 compatriots from more than 90 countries and help vaccinate nearly 1.5 million Chinese citizens in more than 160 countries.

Summary

Since the 18th National Congress of the CPC, there is a profound shift in the balance of international power. The world has entered a period of turbulence and transformation. In the face of the complex and severe international situation and unprecedented external risks and challenges, the CPC and the Chinese government have correctly studied and judged the global change on a scale unseen in a century, coordinated the domestic and international situations, closely focused on the main line of serving national rejuvenation and promoting human progress, improved the Party's leadership system and mechanism for foreign affairs, strengthened the top-level design of foreign affairs, and made strategic plans for the major-country diplomacy with Chinese characteristics. China has put forward the concept of a community with a shared future for mankind, clarified its connotation and path, and solidly promoted the construction of a community with a shared future for mankind. China has promoted high-quality development of the Belt and Road Initiative, and worked to build the BRI into an initiative of peace, prosperity, openness, green development, and innovation and a widely welcomed public good and platform for international cooperation in today's world. China has always held high the banner of peace, development, cooperation and mutual benefit. It has advanced and enhanced China's diplomatic agenda in a comprehensive, multilevel, and multifaceted way, actively developed global partnerships and promoted the building of a new type of international relations featuring mutual respect, fairness, justice and win-win cooperation. China will continue to play its part as a major and responsible country, take an active part in reforming and developing the global governance system, and keep contributing Chinese wisdom and strength to global governance. In the new era, China is increasingly approaching the center of the world stage. These efforts have resulted in a marked increase in China's international influence, appeal, and power to shape.

SECTION 8

Improve the System of "One Country, Two Systems" and Promote the Reunification of the Motherland

4.8.1 Maintain the Long-Term Prosperity and Stability of Hong Kong and Macao and Improve the System of "One Country, Two Systems"

(1) Maintain the Long-Term Prosperity and Stability of Hong Kong and Macao

"One Country, Two Systems" is a great initiative pursued by China. After their return to the motherland, Hong Kong and Macao were reincorporated into the national governance system and embarked on a broad path of complementarity and common development with other parts of the country. The practice of One Country, Two Systems has been a resounding success. As socialism with Chinese characteristics enters a new era, the great cause of "One Country, Two Systems" also enters a new era.

Xi Jinping made important remarks on the issue of "One Country, Two Systems" on a number of important occasions, including at the Gathering Marking the 15th Anniversary of Macao's Return to the Motherland and the Inauguration of the Fourth-Term Government of the MSAR in 2014, at the meeting celebrating the 20th Anniversary of Hong Kong's Return to the Motherland and the Inaugural Ceremony of the Fifth-Term Government of the HKSAR held in 2017. He pointed out: that is why 1 have made it clear that the central government will never waver in its commitment to "one country; two systems" and make sure that it is fully applied in Hong Kong without any distortion or alteration. This will enable us to keep advancing in the right direction. "One country" is like the roots of a tree. For a tree to grow tall and luxuriant, its roots must run deep and strong. To continue to advance this policy, we must remain committed to the fundamental purpose of "One Country, Two Systems," jointly safeguard national sovereignty, security and development interests, and maintain the long-term prosperity and stability of Hong Kong and Macao. We must continue to govern Hong Kong and Macao and implement the principle of "One Country, Two Systems" in accordance with the law. We must adhere to the one-China principle while respecting the differences of the two systems, uphold the power of the central government while ensuring a high degree of autonomy in the SARs, and give play to the role of the mainland as the staunch supporter of Hong Kong and Macao while increasing their competitiveness. At no time should we focus only on one side to the neglect of the other. These important expositions are the fundamental guidelines for the CPC and the Chinese government to further promote the practice of "One Country, Two Systems" in the new era.

The CPC and the Chinese government has attached great importance to administering Hong Kong and Macao by law, curb and crack down on "Hong Kong Independence" forces according to law, and resolutely safeguard the core interests of the state and the fundamental interests of the Hong Kong and Macao SARs.

In June 2014, in response to some people's vague views and erroneous remarks on the principles and policies of "One Country, Two Systems" and the basic law in Hong Kong, especially on the method of universal suffrage for the chief executive in 2017, the central government published the white paper on the Practice of the "One Country, Two Systems" Policy in the HKSAR for the first time on Hong Kong affairs. The white paper reviews and summarizes the practice of "One Country, Two Systems" in the HKSAR, comprehensively and accurately expounds the principles and policies of "One Country, Two Systems," and highlights such important viewpoints as the central government's overall governance over Hong Kong. It has played a role in rectifying the root cause and is conducive to continuing to promote the development of the practice of "One Country, Two Systems" along the correct track.

Articles 45 and 68 of the Hong Kong Basic Law provide for a comprehensive planning of the process of political reform in the HKSAR, and in Annex I of the Hong Kong Basic Law, Method for the Selection of the Chief Executive of the HKSAR and Annex II, Method for the Formation of the Legislative Council of the HKSAR and Its Voting Procedures, it specifies the "timetable" and "road map" for the HKSAR to promote political reform in the first ten years (1997–

2007) in accordance with the actual situation of Hong Kong and the principle of gradual and orderly progress. In December 2007, the 31st Meeting of the Standing Committee of the 12th NPC proposed that the election of the fifth Chief Executive of the HKSAR in the year 2017 may be implemented by the method of universal suffrage. After the chief executive was elected by universal suffrage, the Legislative Council of the HKSAR could be conducted by universal suffrage, which has set a "timetable" for the realization of "dual universal suffrage" for the chief executive and all members of the Legislative Council of the HKSAR. In August 2014, the 12th Meeting of the Standing Committee of the 12th NPC adopted Decision on Issues Relating to the Methods for Selecting the Chief Executive of the HKSARand for Forming the Legislative Council of the HKSAR in 2016, which determined the core elements and institutional framework of the system of universal suffrage for the chief executive of the HKSAR.

However, in September 2014, under the pretext of opposing the chief executive election method, some anti-China agitators both inside and outside Hong Kong carried out illegal "occupy central" activities. The central government fully supported the HKSAR Government in quelling the illegal "occupy central" activities that lasted 79 days according to law, thus safeguarding the overall stability of Hong Kong. In October 2016, when taking the oath of office, individual members of the Legislative Council of the HKSAR openly advocated "Hong Kong Independence" and said insulting words to the country and the nation. In November of the same year, the Standing Committee of the NPC adopted Interpretation Regarding the Second Paragraph in Article 104 of the Basic Law of the HKSAR of the PRC, clarifying the meaning and requirements of swearing in accordance with the law, providing a legal basis for the removal of the qualifications of relevant persons as members of the Legislative Council, and safeguarding the authority of the basic law and the rule of law in Hong Kong. In accordance with the interpretation of Article 104 of the basic law of Hong Kong by the Standing Committee of the NPC, the MSAR has also taken the initiative to add an "anti-independence" clause to the Legislative Council Election Law Amendment Bill, so as to prevent possible troubles. The central government has also taken corresponding measures in improving the chief executive's reporting system, exercising the substantive power to appoint the chief executive and principal officials according to law, and strengthening publicity and education on the National Constitution and the Basic Law.

The CPC and the Chinese government have planned and supported the economic and social development and the improvement of people's livelihood in Hong Kong and Macao from the perspective of the overall development strategy and the requirement of maintaining the long-term prosperity and stability of Hong Kong and Macao.

The realization of the Chinese Dream cannot be separated from the development of Hong Kong and Macao. President Xi Jinping has repeatedly stressed the importance of the long-term prosperity and development of Hong Kong and Macao to the realization of the Chinese Dream. In 2013, when he met with Leung Chun-ying, Fernando Chui Sai On, he stressed that Hong Kong, Macao and the Chinese mainland are closely linked by destiny. To realize the Chinese Dream—the rejuvenation of the Chinese nation—Hong Kong, Macao and the Chinese mainland must pool and share our strength, and seek common development. Moreover, the people of Hong Kong, Macao and the Chinese mainland must help each other to make progress.[104] In 2017, He pointed out in the Report of the 19th CPC National Congress that maintaining lasting prosperity and stability in Hong Kong and Macao and achieving China's full reunification are essential to realizing national rejuvenation.[105]

In many important decisions and arrangements adopted by the CPC and the Chinese government, Hong Kong and Macao have a place in maintaining long-term prosperity and stability. In March 2001, the Fourth Session of the Nineth NPC deliberated and approved the 10th Five-Year Plan. For the first time, the issue of "maintaining long-term prosperity and stability" in Hong Kong and Macao was included in the national overall development strategy. Since then, it has remained unchanged. In March 2011, the 12th Five-Year Plan reviewed and approved by the Fourth session of the 11th NPC for the first time made a separate chapter on the construction of "One Country, Two Systems" in the Hong Kong and Macao Special Administrative Regions, specifically discussing the issue of "maintaining long-term prosperity and stability" in the Hong Kong and Macao Special Administrative Regions, further highlighting the special status and role of this issue in the overall national development strategy. In March 2016, the Fourth Session of the 12th NPC approved the 13th Five-Year Plan, which once again included the contents of "supporting the long-term prosperity and stable development of Hong Kong and Macao" in a separate chapter, emphasizing the comprehensive and accurate implementation of the principles of "One Country,

Two Systems," "Hong Kong people administering Hong Kong," "Macao people administering Macao" and a high degree of autonomy, acting in strict accordance with the Constitution and the basic law, and giving play to the unique advantages of Hong Kong and Macao, enhancing the status and functions of Hong Kong and Macao in national economic development and opening-up, supporting Hong Kong and Macao in economic development, improving people's livelihood, promoting democracy and harmony.

In the new era, the central government has adopted a series of measures to promote the development of Hong Kong and Macao. In terms of promoting Hong Kong and Macao to be further integrated into the overall situation of national development, we support Hong Kong to hold the Belt and Road Forum for International Cooperation and join the Asian Infrastructure Investment Bank, support Macao to hold the Eighth APEC tourism ministers' meeting and the ministerial meeting of the Forum for Economic and Trade Cooperation between China and Portuguese-Speaking Countries, support Hong Kong and Macao to organize delegations to participate in the two Belt and Road Forum for International Cooperation, the China International Import Expo and other major activities to actively cooperate with countries along the "Belt and Road" in tourism, culture, sports, education and medical care. In 2019, the Outline Development Plan for the Guangdong–Hong Kong–Macao Greater Bay Area was issued and implemented. Since then, a series of preferential policies have been announced to facilitate Hong Kong and Macao investors and individual residents to participate in the development of the Greater Bay area. The construction of major cooperation platforms in Qianhai of Shenzhen, Nansha of Guangzhou and Hengqin of Zhuhai, has been steadily promoted, and infrastructure connectivity has been comprehensively promoted. In terms of deepening the cooperation and exchange between Hong Kong and Macao and the mainland, the mainland and Hong Kong and Macao signed the service trade agreement and the amendment agreement, the investment agreement, the economic and technological cooperation agreement, and the goods trade agreement under the Closer Economic Partnership Arrangements (CEPA)[106] framework, so as to achieve the CEPA upgrading goal in the 13th Five-Year Plan period ahead of schedule and basically realize the liberalization of service trade. Following the opening of the Shanghai-Hong Kong Stock Connect in 2014, the Shenzhen-Hong Kong Stock Connect and the Bond Connect were officially opened in December 2016 and July 2017, respectively. This not only steadily promoted the opening of China's financial market to the outside world, but also consolidated and enhanced Hong Kong's competitiveness as an international financial center. China has relaxed the restrictions on Hong Kong legal practitioners being employed by mainland law firms, expanded the scope of partnership of law firms, and launched pilot projects in the Greater Bay area of Guangdong, Hong Kong, Macao and nine cities in the mainland for Hong Kong and Macao legal practitioners to obtain mainland practice qualifications and engage in the legal operation. Exchanges and cooperation in the judicial field have been continuously strengthened. Hong Kong and Macao have signed agreements with relevant departments and institutions in the mainland to strengthen cooperation in innovation and technology, deepen closer cultural relations and cooperation, and build the Hong Kong Palace Museum. Relevant departments of the central government have issued a series of policies and measures to facilitate the development of Hong Kong and Macao residents in the mainland, regulate the enrollment of Hong Kong and Macao students in mainland universities, introduce measures for applying for residence permits for Hong Kong and Macao residents, allowed residents of Hong Kong and Macao to enjoy housing provident funds and take the examinations to determine the qualification of middle and primary school teachers and expanded cooperation in science, technology, culture, people's livelihood and other fields. After the outbreak of COVID-19, the mainland has also vigorously supported the fight against the epidemic in Hong Kong and Macao in terms of material support, equipment support, and cross-border assistance of medical personnel.

The overall situation of economic and social development in Hong Kong and Macao is good. In the 20 years since its return to China, Hong Kong's GDP has increased from HK$1.37 trillion in 1997 to HK$2.49 trillion in 2016, with an average annual growth of 3.2%, ranking among the top among developed economies; Macao's local economy has reversed its continuous negative growth. Its GDP has increased from 51.9 billion pataca in 1999 to 444.7 billion pataca in 2018, with an average annual growth rate of more than 10%, making it one of the fastest growing economies in the world. Hong Kong has maintained its position as the world's sixth largest banking center, the world's fifth largest stock market and the world's fourth largest foreign exchange market. In 2020, the total balance of the banking system exceeded HK$450 billion, breaking the historical record. The functions of the offshore RMB business hub and the international asset management center have been continuously enhanced; at the end of 2019, the scale of the offshore RMB capital pool was 658 billion yuan, and the average daily transaction volume of the RMB real-time payment and settlement system exceeded 1.1 trillion yuan; the cargo volume of the International Airport has ranked first in the world for 18 consecutive years, and the port container throughput ranked eighth in the world in 2019. The central government has gone all out to support the diversified development at a proper level by Macao. In 2016, Macao formulated its first five-year development plan, which clearly defined the development orientation of Macao in the next five years as "building a world tourism and leisure center," and based on this, it promoted the implementation of appropriate economic diversification, improved people's wellbeing, and promoted the comprehensive development of various construction projects in the SAR in a coordinated, balanced and orderly manner. Macao's moderately diversified economy has achieved initial results, and emerging industries such as exhibition, culture, traditional Chinese medicine, and characteristic finance have gradually grown. In 2017, the total added value of the above-mentioned emerging industries reached 32.08 billion pataca, accounting for 8.1% of the total added value of all industries. Compared with 2015, the total added value increased by 23.6%, accounting for 0.79 percentage points.

(2) Improve the Implementation of "One Country, Two Systems"
In June 2019, Hong Kong broke out in "the turbulence over the amendment bill." Under the pretext of opposing the amendment of the Fugitive Offenders Ordinance by the SAR government, some forces in Hong Kong have carried out various radical activities in the name of peaceful processions and assemblies. Even though the SAR government said that the work of amending the Fugitive Offenders Ordinance had been completely stopped, they still continued to use the "protest against the amendment bill" as a pretext to surround the police headquarters, attack the Legislative Council Building of the SAR, occupy the streets for illegal assemblies, block public transport, and constantly escalate violence and disrupt social order. Some people even openly advocate "Hong Kong Independence," surround and attack the central government's offices in Hong Kong, wantonly insult the national flag and national emblem, and openly challenge national sovereignty and the bottom line of the principle of "One Country, Two Systems." The practice of "One Country, Two Systems" in Hong Kong has encountered unprecedented challenges. The Party Central Committee, with Comrade Xi Jinping at its core, took stock of the situation and called for the

immediate actions and firmly supported the chief executives and governments as well as the police of Hong Kong to take measures in accordance with law to confront rioters to restore order.

In order to strengthen the centralized and unified leadership over Hong Kong and Macao work, in February 2020, the CCCPC decided to establish the central leading group for Hong Kong and Macao work to replace the original central coordinating group for Hong Kong and Macao work, and set up the office of the leading group, which was merged with the Hong Kong and Macao Affairs Office of the State Council. This is a major adjustment to the leading body of Hong Kong and Macao work, and has further strengthened the centralized and unified leadership of the CCCPC over Hong Kong and Macao work in terms of the arrangements for the establishment of relevant organs and institutional arrangements.

The "the turbulence over the amendment bill" has fully exposed the loopholes in Hong Kong's legal system and the lack of enforcement mechanism in safeguarding national security. It is urgent to strengthen national security legislation. In May 2020, the Third Session of the 13th NPC adopted the Decision on Establishing and Improving the Legal System and Enforcement Mechanisms for Safeguarding National Security in the Hong Kong SAR, and authorized the Standing Committee of the NPC to formulate relevant laws on establishing and improving the legal system and implementation mechanism of the HKSAR for safeguarding national security, so as to effectively prevent, suppress and punish any secession, subversion of state power, organizing and committing acts of terrorism, and other acts and activities that seriously endanger national security, as well as foreign and external interference in the affairs of the HKSAR. In June, The 20th session of the 13th NPC Standing Committee voted to adopt the Law of the PRC on Safeguarding National Security in the HKSAR, which was included in Annex III of the Hong Kong Basic Law. The law listed therein shall be applied locally by way of promulgation or legislation by the Region. This law has 6 chapters and 66 articles. It is a comprehensive law with the contents of substantive law, procedural law and organizational law. The law clearly stipulates the following contents: the responsibilities and institutions of the HKSAR for safeguarding national security, targeting four categories of acts as well as their punishment, namely secession, subversion of state power, organizing and committing acts of terrorism, and foreign and external interference in the affairs of the HKSAR; jurisdiction, applicable law and procedure; office for safeguarding national security of the Central People's Government in the HKSAR to establish and improve a legal system and enforcement mechanisms on upholding national security for the HKSAR. In July, according to the legislation on safeguarding national security in Hong Kong, the Committee for Safeguarding National Security of the HKSAR and the Office for Safeguarding National Security of the Central People's Government in the HKSAR were established one after another. According to the legislation on safeguarding national security in Hong Kong, the responsibilities of the Committee for Safeguarding National Security of HKSAR are: analysing and assessing developments in relation to safeguarding national security in the HKSAR; making work plans, and formulating policies for safeguarding national security in the Region; advancing the development of the legal system and enforcement mechanisms of the Region for safeguarding national security; coordinating major work and significant operations for safeguarding national security in the Region. The responsibilities of the Office for Safeguarding National Security of the Central People's Government in the HKSAR are: analyzing and assessing developments in relation to safeguarding national security in the HKSAR, and providing opinions and making proposals on major strategies and important policies for safeguarding national security; overseeing, guiding, coordinating with, and providing support to the Region in the performance of its duties for safeguarding national security; collecting and analysing intelligence and information concerning national security; handling cases concerning offence endangering national security in accordance with the law. Hong Kong National Security Law is an important landmark law for upholding and improving the system of "One Country, Two Systems" under the new situation. The promulgation and implementation of this law is the most important measure taken by the central authorities in handling Hong Kong affairs since the return of Hong Kong. It has consolidated the institutional barrier for safeguarding national security in Hong Kong and opened a major turning point in Hong Kong from chaos to rule.

In the same year, in view of the severe epidemic situation in Hong Kong, which has had a major impact on the election, the HKSAR's chief executive in Council, cited the Emergency Regulations Ordinance, decided to postpone the quadrennial LegCo General Election for one year. In August, the 21st Session of the Standing Committee of the 13th NPC made a decision that after September 30, 2020, the sixth LegCo of the HKSAR will continue to discharge its duties for no less than one year until the commencement of the seventh LegCo. The term of office of the Seventh Legislative Council of the HKSAR shall remain four years after it is elected according to law.

In November, the 23rd Meeting of the Standing Committee of the 13th NPC deliberated the proposal of the State Council to make a decision to allow Hong Kong authorities to dismiss disqualified lawmakers and made a decision to allow Hong Kong authorities to dismiss disqualified lawmakers. The above motion was moved at the request of the chief executive of the HKSAR. It is stated in the Decision expressly stated that a LegCo member does not fulfil the legal requirements and conditions on upholding the Basic Law and pledging allegiance to the HKSAR of the PRC if the member advocates or supports "Hong Kong independence," refuses to recognize the PRC's sovereignty over Hong Kong and the exercise of the sovereignty, solicits intervention by foreign or external forces in the HKSAR's affairs, or carries out other acts that endanger national security. When the member is so decided in accordance with law, he or she is immediately disqualified from being a LegCo member. At the same time, it is clear that the members of the seventh-term LegCo who were ruled to be invalid during the nomination period of the seventh-term LegCo election have been disqualified. This has further clarified the political rule of "those who love the country and Hong Kong should govern Hong Kong." According to the decision of the Standing Committee of the NPC, the government of the HKSAR subsequently announced that relevant personnel were disqualified from being members of the LegCo according to law, and the prestige of the Constitution and the basic law was fully demonstrated.

In March 2021, the Fourth Session of the 13th NPC adopted the Decision of the NPC on Improving the Electoral System of the HKSAR, which clearly stated that to improve the electoral system of the HKSAR, it is necessary to fully and accurately implement the principles of "One Country, Two Systems," "Hong Kong people administering Hong Kong" with a high degree of autonomy and effectively upholding the constitutional order in the HKSAR as prescribed by the Constitution and the Basic Law; it is necessary to ensure "Hong Kong people ruling Hong Kong" with patriots as the mainstay, effectively improve the governance efficiency of the HKSAR, and protect the right to vote and stand for election of permanent residents of the region. The decision stipulates that the HKSAR shall establish an election commission that is broadly representative, conforms to the actual situation of the region and reflects the overall interests of society. The election commission is responsible for electing the chief executive designate, some members of the Legislative Council, and nominating candidates for the chief executive and members of the Legislative Council. The election committee is composed of 1,500 members from five sectors, including the industrial and commercial, the financial, the professional, the grassroots, labour and religious sectors, members of the Legislative Council, representatives of regional organizations, deputies to the NPC of the HKSAR, members of the National Committee of the Chinese People's Political Consultative Conference from the HKSAR, and representatives of Hong Kong members of relevant people's organizations. The chief executive of the HKSAR shall be elected by the election commission and appointed by the Central People's government. The Legislative Council of the HKSAR shall have 90 members in each term. They shall be elected by the Election Committee, by functional constituencies and by geographical constituencies through direct elections. The decision authorizes the Standing Committee of the NPC to amend Annex I to the basic law of Hong Kong, Method for the Selection of the Chief Executive of the HKSAR, and Annex II, Method for the Formation of the Legislative Council of the HKSAR and Its Voting Procedures. On June 30, the 27th Meeting of the Standing Committee of the 13th NPC adopted the newly revised Method for the Selection of the Chief Executive of the HKSAR in Annex I of the Basic Law of the HKSAR of the People's Republic of China and Method for the Formation of the Legislative Council of the HKSAR and Its Voting Procedures in Annex II of the Basic Law of the HKSAR of the PRC. This is another major measure to administer Hong Kong by law after the formulation and implementation of the Law of the PRC on Safeguarding National Security in the HKSAR. It upholds and improves the system of "One Country, Two Systems," effectively promotes "patriots administering Hong Kong" and "patriots administering Macao," and is of milestone significance in the practice of "One Country, Two Systems."

In December 2021, the Information Office of the State Council issued a white paper titled "Hong Kong: Democratic Progress Under the Framework of 'One Country, Two Systems,'" further clarifying the central government's principled position on the democratic development of the HKSAR. The white paper points out that in recent years, the Anti-China and anti-Hong Kong forces have challenged the bottom line of the principle of "One Country, Two Systems," undermined the constitutional order of the SAR, undermined the rule of law in

Hong Kong, and carried out various activities endangering national security and harming Hong Kong's prosperity and stability with the aim of seizing the power to govern the SAR and implementing a "Color Revolution." Facts have repeatedly shown that the Anti-China forces and the external hostile forces behind them are the chief culprits hindering the democratic development of the HKSAR. The white paper stresses that developing and improving democracy in the HKSAR is of great significance to safeguarding the democratic rights of Hong Kong residents, realizing good governance, and ensuring long-term prosperity, stability, and long-term security in Hong Kong. "One Country, Two Systems" has provided a fundamental guarantee for the democratic development of the HKSAR. To ensure that the practice of "One Country, Two Systems" is stable and far-reaching and to continue to promote the democratic development of Hong Kong, we must resolutely implement the principle of "patriots administering Hong Kong." In accordance with the principle of "One Country, Two Systems" and the basic law, and in line with Hong Kong's political, economic, social, cultural and historical conditions, we must explore a path of democratic development with Hong Kong characteristics.

4.8.2 Promote the Peaceful Development of Cross-Strait Relations and Curb the Separatist Forces and Activities of "Taiwan Independence"

National rejuvenation and national reunification are the general trend of the times, where the great cause lies and what the people want. For more than 70 years, the CPC and the Chinese government have always taken the settlement of the Taiwan question and the complete reunification of the motherland as their unswerving historical tasks, united the Taiwan compatriots, and promoted the situation in the Taiwan Strait from tense confrontation to relaxation and improvement, and then embarked on the path of peaceful development. In the new era, China is keenly aware of the changes in the situation in the Taiwan Strait, remains committed to the major principles and policies on work related to Taiwan, and promotes important progress in cross-strait relations.

During the period when Ma Ying Jeou took office as the leader of the Taiwan region, the political mutual trust between the two sides of the Strait continued to increase, and economic and cultural exchanges gradually increased. In February, 2013, Xi Jinping met Lien Chan, honorary chairman of the KMT of China, and his delegation in Beijing. He stressed that it is the responsibility of the new CCCPC leading collective to continue to promote the peaceful development of cross-strait relations and promote the peaceful reunification of the two sides. In recent years, a series of major positive developments have been made in cross-strait relations, which have safeguarded peace in the Taiwan Strait and enhanced the well-being of compatriots on both sides of the Strait. This is in line with the common aspirations of the Chinese people on both sides of the Strait and the overall interests of the Chinese nation. Compatriots on both sides of the Strait are connected by blood and are a family. Safeguarding the rights and interests of the Taiwan compatriots and developing the well-being of the Taiwan compatriots are public declarations made by the mainland many times, and are also solemn commitments made by the new CPC central leadership. We have remained committed to the major principles and policies on work related to Taiwan, always adhered to the one China principle, continued to promote cross-strait exchanges and cooperation, strive d to promote the unity and struggle of compatriots on both sides of the Strait, and consolidated and deepened the political, economic, cultural and social foundation for the peaceful development of cross-strait relations.[107]

In June 2013, the Cross-Straits Trade and Service Agreement was signed in Shanghai. The two sides have 144 commitments to opening-up, involving more than 100 service industries, covering commerce, communications, architecture, distribution, environment, health and society, tourism, entertainment culture and sports, transportation, finance and other fields. The signing of the agreement has laid a foundation for the gradual reduction or elimination of restrictive measures on service trade covering many sectors between the two sides, promoted the liberalization of service trade, and also promoted the peaceful development of cross-strait relations.

In February 2014, through consultations between the two sides of the Strait, the Taiwan Affairs Office of the State Council and Taiwan's Mainland Affairs Council established a regular contact and communication mechanism on the basis of adhering to the common political basis of the "1992 Consensus." The heads of the two departments exchanged visits and opened hotlines to exchange views on the situation of cross-Strait relations and policies and measures to promote cross-Strait exchanges and cooperation in various fields, especially to communicate and prepare for the meeting of leaders on both sides of the Strait. This is the first "ice-breaking trip" of the heads of the departments in charge of cross-strait affairs of the two sides in decades. It opens a new page for cross-strait political dialogue and lays a foundation for mutual trust.

On the basis of the gradual increase in cross-strait exchanges, the leaders of the two sides of the Strait have achieved a historic meeting. On November 7, 2015, Xi Jinping met with the Taiwan region's leader Tsai Ing-wen in Singapore, and holding each others hand for 80 seconds. Xi Jinping stressed that the 66-year history of the development of cross-Straits relations shows that no matter what ordeals we have experienced, or how long we have been isolated from each other, no force can pull us apart. Bones may be broken but not sinews because we are fellow compatriot. Blood is thicker than water, and people on both sides of the Straits share the bond of kinship. Focusing on the theme of promoting peaceful development and national rejuvenation, the two sides had a frank exchange of views on cross-strait relations, and reached a positive consensus on upholding the "1992 Consensus" and further promoting the peaceful development of cross-strait relations. This is the first meeting between the leaders of the two sides of the Strait since 1949, creating a precedent for direct dialogue and communication between the leaders of the two sides of the Strait, turning a historic page in cross-strait relations, pushing the peaceful development of cross-strait relations and political interaction to a new height, and setting a new historical coordinate for promoting the process of peaceful reunification of the motherland. It has far-reaching historical significance.

During the period when Ma Ying Jeou took office as the leader of the Taiwan region, the economic exchanges between the two sides of the Strait gradually increased. From 2013 to the first half of 2017, the accumulated trade volume between the two sides reached 851.23 billion U.S. dollars, of which 19.3 billion U.S. dollars in 2014, a record high; 12,502 Taiwan funded projects were newly approved, and the actual utilization of Taiwan capital was 8.797 billion U.S. dollars; 327 investment projects in Taiwan were approved, with a total amount of 2.072 billion U.S. dollars. The Standing Committee of the NPC has amended "the Law on the Protection of Investment of Taiwan Compatriots" to create a more convenient and fairer legal environment for Taiwan compatriots to make investment and grow businesses. All localities and departments has actively supported the transformation and upgrading of Taiwan funded enterprises, participated in the Belt and Road Initiative and explored the market, established a currency clearing mechanism on both sides of the Strait, established a cross-strait Entrepreneur Summit, and promoted the deep integration of industries on both sides of the Strait. Social ties between the two sides of the Strait have also become closer. From 2013 to the first half of 2017, cross-strait personnel exchanges reached 40.967 million, of which 9.856 million in 2015, a record high, an increase of 1.888 million over 2012. The grass-roots people on both sides of the Strait have frequent exchanges, and the accumulated number of the Taiwan grass-roots people who participated in the Strait forum alone have been nearly 50,000 in the past five years. The mainland has set up 53 cross-strait youth employment and entrepreneurship bases and demonstration sites, attracting more than 1,000 Taiwan funded enterprises and teams. New progress has been made in cross-strait educational exchanges and cooperation, and the forms of cultural exchanges and cooperation have become more abundant. The State Council has revised the "Measures for the Administration of Chinese Citizens' Travel to and from the Taiwan Region," exempting Taiwan residents from the formalities of visa for travel to and from the mainland, and implementing electronic travel passes for Taiwan residents to enter or leave the mainland without registration. Relevant departments have issued more than 20 policies and measures to provide more convenience and create better conditions for Taiwan compatriots to study, work and live in the mainland.

The biggest threat to the peaceful development of cross-Straits relations now comes from the forces and activities for "Taiwan independence." In March 2014, an "Anti-Trade and Services Incident" occurred in Taiwan. A group of students forcibly broke into the legislative body of Taiwan under the name of opposing the cross-Strait service and trade agreement and have occupied the forum. In essence, this is an "Anti-China" incident instigated and supported by "Taiwan independence" and external forces. It is a premeditated and organized action that deliberately obstructs the development of cross-strait relations. The process and progress of the peaceful development of cross-strait relations have been affected to a considerable extent. In 2016, after the Democratic Progressive Party came to power, it refused to recognize the "1992 Consensus" reflecting the one China principle and carried out "Taiwan independence" separatist activities. Major changes have taken place in the internal situation of Taiwan Island, and the momentum of peaceful development of cross-strait relations has been seriously impacted.

Faced with the changes in the situation in the Taiwan Strait, the CCCPC with Comrade Xi Jinping at its core correctly studied the situation and clarified the basic attitude and policies in response to the changing situation. In March 2016, the Fourth Session of the 12th NPC, when President Xi Jinping is referring the proposals to the Shanghai delegation, he stressed that our major principles and policies on work related to Taiwan are clear-cut and consistent despite the change in Taiwan's political situation. We will adhere to the political basis of the "1992 Consensus" and continue to promote the peaceful development of cross-Strait relations. In November, Xi Jinping met with a delegation of the Chinese KMT from the mainland led by KMT Chairman Hung Hsiu-chu. He stressed that the two sides of the Strait are a community with a shared future that can never be separated. Our policy towards Taiwan is that we will stick to the political foundation of the 1992 Consensus, which embodies the one-China principle, uphold peace across the Taiwan Straits and peaceful development of cross-Straits relations and improve the well-being of people on both sides. It is the shared aspiration of all Chinese people and in the fundamental interests of the Chinese nation to safeguard China's sovereignty and territorial integrity. It is an irresistible historical trend to realize national rejuvenation and create a prosperous China. He also put forward six points of view on the development of cross-Strait relations, that is, to adhere to the "1992 Consensus" reflecting the one China principle, resolutely oppose the "Taiwan independence" separatist forces and their activities, promote the development of cross-Strait economic and social integration, jointly promote Chinese culture, improve the well-being of compatriots on both sides of the Strait, and work together to realize the great rejuvenation of the Chinese nation. In January, 2019, President Xi Jinping attended the 40th anniversary of issuing Message to Compatriots in Taiwan and made an important speech. He stressed that the historical and legal facts which prove that Taiwan is part of China and that both sides of the Taiwan Strait belong to one and the same China shall never be altered by anyone or any force! Compatriots who shared the same ethnic origin on both sides of the Strait are Chinese. Compatriots' recognition and feelings for the country and nation cannot be changed by anyone and any force! The situation in the Taiwan Strait is relaxing and improving and the forward development of cross-Strait relations is irresistible to anyone and any force! No individual or force could hold back the historical trend of reunification and revitalization of the Chinese that is growing stronger! He also put forward five proposals on promoting the peaceful development of cross-Strait relations and realizing the reunification of the motherland: first, working together to promote China's rejuvenation and its peaceful reunification; second, seeking a Two Systems solution to the Taiwan question and making innovative efforts towards peaceful reunification; third, abiding by the one-China principle and safeguarding the prospects for peaceful reunification; fourth, further integrating development across the Straits and consolidating the foundations for peaceful reunification; fifth, forging closer bonds of heart and mind between people on both sides of the Straits and strengthening joint commitment to peaceful reunification. The speech comprehensively expounds the major policy propositions of the CPC and the Chinese government to promote the peaceful reunification of the motherland in the great journey of national rejuvenation based on the new era. It is of epoch-making significance. President Xi Jinping has put forward a series of important ideas and major policy propositions on Taiwan-related work, thus helping to develop the Party's overall policy for resolving the Taiwan question in the new era.

The CPC and the Chinese government resolutely took measures to oppose and contain "Taiwan independence" and suspended the cross-Strait communication and negotiation mechanism based on the "1992 Consensus;" strengthened exchanges and interactions with relevant political parties, organizations and people from all walks of life on the island, and strengthened the strength and momentum of opposing "Taiwan independence" and safeguarding the peaceful development of cross-Strait relations; actively carried out public opinion struggle, expose and criticize the acts of the Taiwan authorities and "Taiwan independence" forces that undermine the political foundation and the status quo of cross-Strait relations; continued to promote cross-Strait exchanges and cooperation in all fields, and worked for the well-being of the Taiwan compatriots.

The Chinese government has also done extensive international social work to consolidate the pattern of one China in the international community. Adhering to the one China principle in handling Taiwan's external exchanges, Taiwan's participation in the activities of international organizations such as the International Civil Aviation Organization (ICAO) and the World Health Assembly (WHA) has encountered repeated frustration. We urge relevant countries to properly handle Taiwan related issues, resolutely oppose countries that have established diplomatic relations with China to enhance substantive relations with Taiwan, correct their wrong words and deeds on the Taiwan issue, and declare to the international community China's firm stance on safeguarding its core interests and urged Dominica, the so-called "country with diplomatic relations" with Taiwan, to "sever diplomatic relations" with it. In July, 2019, the white paper of China's National Defense in the New Era pointed out: the PLA will resolutely defeat anyone attempting to separate Taiwan from China and safeguard national unity at all costs. This once again shows the solemn stand of the CPC and the Chinese government against "Taiwan independence" separatism and interference by external forces, and clearly draws a red line that cannot be crossed. In May 2020, the Symposium on the 15th anniversary of the implementation of Anti-Secession Law was held in Beijing. The meeting emphasized that the "Anti-Secession Law" is based on the Constitution and implements the Party Central Committee's the major principles and policies on work related to Taiwan. It is an important part of the system of upholding "One Country, Two Systems" and promoting the peaceful reunification of the motherland. It is also an important follow-up to the political responsibility and mission requirements of opposing "independence" and promoting reunification. If the separatist forces of "Taiwan independence" persist in their willful acts and even take risks, we will, in accordance with the relevant provisions of the "Anti-Secession Law," take all necessary measures to resolutely smash the separatist plot of "Taiwan independence" and resolutely safeguard national sovereignty and territorial integrity. In August, in response to the negative trends of some major powers on the Taiwan related issues and the serious wrong signals sent to the "Taiwan independence" forces, the Chinese People's Liberation Army (PLA) Eastern Theater Command recently systematically sent troops from multiple military branches into multiple directions and organized consecutive, realistic drills in the Taiwan Straits and its northern and southern ends, to resolutely counter any provocative actions that could result in "Taiwan independence" and separate the country, creating a strong deterrent to "Taiwan independence" forces.

Summary

In the new era, the CPC and the Chinese government have studied the new situation, properly responded to the complex situation, eliminated all kinds of interference, fully and faithfully implemented the principle of "One Country, Two Systems," and ensured that the central government exercises its overall jurisdiction over Hong Kong and Macao as mandated by China's Constitution and the basic laws of the two special administrative regions; have thus boosted exchanges and cooperation between the mainland and the two regions and maintained prosperity and stability in Hong Kong and Macao; maintained long-term prosperity and stability in Hong Kong and Macao, leading the practice of "One Country, Two Systems" to achieve new successes in riding the waves. At the same time, the CPC and the Chinese government have taken a holistic approach to cross-Straits relations in keeping with changing circumstances, added substance to the theory on national reunification and the principles and policies concerning Taiwan, and formed the party's overall strategy for solving the Taiwan issue in the new era, thus helping to develop the Party's overall policy for resolving the Taiwan question in the new era. On this basis, we have strengthened the cross-straits exchanges and cooperation and firmly opposed separatist activities seeking "Taiwan independence" and firmly opposed foreign interference. We have maintained the initiative and the ability to steer in cross-Strait relations.

SECTION 9
Build a Moderately Prosperous Society in All Respects and Embark on a New Journey

4.9.1 We Won a Complete Victory in the Battle against Poverty

"Well-off society" is the Millennium dream and long cherished wish of the Chinese nation, and it is also the goal established by the CPC and the Chinese government in the early period of reform and opening-up. In December, 1979, when he met with Masayoshi Ohira, Prime Minister of Japan, Deng Xiaoping put forward: the four modernizations we are striving to achieve are modernizations with Chinese characteristics. Our concept of the four modernizations is different from yours. By achieving the four modernizations, we mean achieving a comparative prosperity. "A comparative prosperity" is the earliest formulation on the issue of moderately prosperous society. In September 1982, the 12th National Congress of the CPC officially listed the "well-off level" as the goal of China's economic development, and proposed that we should raise the people's material and cultural life to a well-off level. In November 2002, on this foundation, the 16th National Congress of the CPC in 2002 introduced the goal of comprehensively building and realizing a moderately prosperous society of a higher level for the benefit of more than one billion people in the first 20 years of this century. With regard to building a moderately prosperous society in all respects, in October 2007, the 17th National Congress of the CPC put forward "striving for building a moderately prosperous society in all respects," and emphasized that the grand goal of "building a moderately prosperous society in all respects" should be realized by 2020. In November 2012, the 18th National Congress of the CPC included "striving for building a moderately prosperous society in all respects" as the theme of the

Congress, and emphasized again that the grand goal of "building a moderately prosperous society in all respects" should be realized by 2020.

With regard to completing the building of a moderately prosperous society in all respects, the hardest and most arduous tasks lie in the fight against poverty in particular. Since the reform and opening-up, China has implemented large-scale, planned and organized poverty alleviation and development. It also enabled China to achieve the historic leap from a country with relatively backward productive forces to the world's second largest economy, and to make the historic transformation of raising the living standards of its people from bare subsistence to an overall level of moderate prosperity, and then ultimately to moderate prosperity in all respects. However, China's battle against poverty remains tough. By the end of 2012, there were 98.99 million rural poor population under the current national standards. By 2020, the poverty-stricken population should be lifted out of poverty in an all-round way. On average, more than 10 million poverty population need to be reduced each year. Faced with these major problems, China has entered the crucial stage of poverty reduction—this will prove a hard nut to crack. From the perspective of the composition of the poor population, it is difficult for many to shake off poverty by themselves, including some special poor groups such as the disabled and the elderly; from the perspective of the regional distribution of poverty, most of the severely impoverished areas are geographically remote, prone to natural disasters, and the foundation for poverty alleviation is even weaker. It can be said that it will be more difficult to shake off poverty in the end.

In the new historic circumstances, in terms of bringing about a moderately prosperous society in all respects, the Party Central Committee, with Xi Jinping as the core, has creatively put forward a series of new ideas and opinions and assertions. In terms of the basic connotation of finish building a moderately prosperous society in all respects, Xi Jinping stressed that to realize a moderately prosperous society in all respects, we must not only have in our mind "a moderately prosperous society" we must also focus on the issue of "in all respects"—the latter being more important and more difficult to achieve. "Moderate prosperity" refers to a standard of living, whereas "all respects" refers to balanced, coordinated, and sustainable development. To realize a moderately prosperous society in all respects, we must seek economic, political, cultural, social and ecological progress. To realize a moderately prosperous society in all respects, we must ensure that all the people are covered and share the fruits of development. To build a moderately prosperous society in all respects, we must ensure that every aspect is covered. With regard to the approach to building a moderately prosperous society in all respects, Xi Jinping stressed that we must take tough steps to forestall and defuse major risks, carry out targeted poverty alleviation, and prevent and control pollution, so that the moderately prosperous society we build earns the people's approval and stands the test of time. On the key task of building a moderately prosperous society in all respects, he said that the weak points in economic and social development, especially the main weak points, are the main factors that affect the achievement of the goal on schedule, and we must make up for them as soon as possible. Poverty alleviation and development work is a prominent weakness of our country. We need to do a good job with the efforts of the whole country to ensure that all the rural poor should be lifted out of poverty by 2020. These expositions systematically explain what is and how to finish building a moderately prosperous society in all respects and other important issues. They are the fundamental guidelines for striving to win this great victory in the new era. Under the guidance of the above ideas, the Central Committee have made a series of arrangements.

In October 2015, the Fifth Plenary Session of the 18th CCCPC made a strategic deployment for a comprehensive framework for completing the process of building a moderately well-off society in all aspects. The plenary session stressed that building moderately prosperous society in all respects by 2020 is the First Centenary Goal of the Two Centenary Goals set by the CPC. The 13th Five-Year Plan period was the decisive stage in building a moderately well-off society. The "13th Five-Year Plan" must be closely focused on achieving this goal. The plenary session put forward the goal of building a moderately prosperous society in all respects: to sustain medium-high growth; while working to achieve more balanced, inclusive, and sustainable development, we need to ensure that China's 2010 GDP and per capita personal income double by 2020; to move our industries to a medium-high level; to significantly increase contribution of consumption to economic growth; and to increase more quickly the proportion of those living in urban areas granted urban residency. Significant progress has been made in modernizing agriculture, and people's living standards and quality of life have generally improved. All the rural populations living below the current poverty threshold and all impoverished counties are lifted out of poverty, and to solve the problems of regional poverty. We must improve the overall caliber of the population and the level of civility in society Such efforts are expected to improve the environment. The modernization of China's system and capacity for governance is basically achieved. Institutions in all fields are further improved. The plenary session adopted the proposal on Formulating the 13th Five-Year Plan for National Economic and Social Development. In the Proposal, helping the impoverished rural population shake off poverty is regarded as a fundamental indicator of the realization of a moderately prosperous society in all respects. In the Proposal, emphasis is placed on enabling all the rural population living below the current poverty line shake off poverty, lifting all poor counties out of poverty, and eliminating overall regional poverty by 2020, and it is put forward that targeted approach to alleviating poverty emphasizes the implementation of targeted approach to alleviating poverty and the application of policies according to people and places to improve the effectiveness of poverty alleviation. Targeted Poverty Alleviation is an important concept put forward by President Xi Jinping in his visit to Shibadong Village in Hunan Province in 2013, and the formation of the concept marks the major shift in the methods of China's poverty alleviation.

In November of the same year, the "highest standard" Conference of the CCCPC on Poverty Alleviation and Development was held in Beijing. In the Conference, President Xi Jinping put forward that we should determine who must receive poverty relief, and identify the population and the poverty level of the truly impoverished and the root causes of their problems, so as to implement targeted polices for different households and individuals. We should determine who is to implement poverty relief, develop a working mechanism in which the central government makes overall plans, the governments of provinces and equivalent administrative units take charge, and governments at municipal, prefectural, and county levels implement the decisions. Governments at all levels should define a clear division of labor, clarify their own responsibilities, assign specific tasks to designated officials, and produce a thorough evaluation of their performance. He stressed that we should determine how to implement poverty relief. According to the different cases of poverty-stricken people and areas, we should adopt five measures: First, boosting the economy to provide more job opportunities. We should guide and encourage all people with ability to work for a better future with their own hands, and rely on local resources to end poverty. Second, relocating poverty-stricken people. Those who cannot escape from poverty locally can be relocated year by year in a planned and organized way. We should ensure smooth relocation and settlement, and make sure those involved have the means to better themselves. Third, providing eco-jobs for poverty-stricken people. We should strengthen ecological restoration and protection in impoverished areas, increase transfer payments in important ecological areas, expand the scope of those eligible for preferential policies, and enable impoverished people with the ability to work to serve as eco-workers, for example as forest rangers. Fourth, improving education in poverty-stricken areas. The best way to help the poor is to raise their educational level. National education funds should continue to be weighted towards poverty-stricken areas, for basic education and vocational education. We should improve the education services in impoverished areas, and direct particular attention to young children from impoverished rural households, especially children who stay in rural areas while their parents have gone to the cities as migrant workers. Fifth, improving social security for poverty alleviation. Among the poverty-stricken population, those who have completely or partially lost the ability to work should be guaranteed social security. We should readjust the rural poverty line and rural subsistence allowances, and provide other forms of social relief. We should increase medical insurance and medical aid for poverty relief, and ensure the rural poor are covered by the new type of rural cooperative medical care and serious illness insurance. We should increase efforts in poverty relief in the old revolutionary base areas of the CPC from before the founding of the PRC. At the conference, the heads of 22 central and western provinces (autonomous regions and municipalities) signed the letter of commitment on poverty alleviation with the central authorities, and made the pledge for poverty alleviation.

In the same month, the CCCPC and the State Council adopted the Decision on Winning the Tough Battle in Poverty Reduction. The Decision clearly defines the basic requirements and core indicators for poverty alleviation, and requires that by 2020, the state is committed to ensuring that the impoverished rural population has stable access to adequate food and clothing, compulsory education, and basic medical services and housing. We must ensure that the per capita disposable income of farmers in these areas increases faster than the national average and that indicators for the main types of basic public services there approach national averages. All rural residents falling below China's current poverty line will be able to lift themselves out of poverty, all poor counties will be able to rid themselves of poverty, and poverty alleviation will be achieved in all regions. The decision emphasizes the implementation of the targeted poverty alleviation strategy, accelerates the targeted poverty alleviation of the poor population, puts forward the requirements of "the "Six Precisions" in poverty alleviation (precision of target, measures to the household, use of funds, stationing of first village secretary, and effect of poverty alleviation)," and proposes a series of specific measures based on the Five Measures for Poverty Elimination project, such as developing characteristic industries to eliminate poverty, guiding labor export to eliminate poverty, and implementing relocation to remove poverty; in combination with ecological protection and poverty alleviation, making efforts to strengthen education and poverty alleviation, carry out poverty alleviation by providing medical insurance and aid, implementing the rural minimum living security system to help people out of poverty, exploring asset income poverty alleviation, and improving the system for supporting and caring for children, women, and elderly people left behind in rural areas and the disabled people. The decision also put forward a series of unconventional policies and measures in finance, finance, land, transportation, water conservancy, health, education and so on. It calls for strengthening the leadership responsibility system for poverty alleviation, implementing the working mechanism of central planning, provinces (autonomous regions, municipalities directly under the central government) taking overall responsibility, and cities (prefectures) and counties grasping implementation, and adhering to the principle of focusing on districts and accurately reaching villages and households; We will improve the poverty alleviation cooperation mechanism between the East and the west, intensify the poverty alleviation cooperation between the East and the west, and establish a precise docking mechanism so that the assistance funds will mainly be used in poor villages and households; We will improve the participation mechanism of social forces, encourage and support private enterprises, social organizations and individuals to participate in poverty alleviation and development, and achieve effective docking between social assistance resources and targeted poverty alleviation. The "decision" has made a comprehensive plan for the fight against poverty during the 13th Five-Year Plan period, issued a general order to win battle, and is a programmatic document guiding the battle for a period of time.

In March 2016, the Fourth Session of the 12th NPC deliberated and adopted the 13th Five-Year Plan, and the "full implementation of poverty alleviation" was included in the form of a special article. At the end of 2016, the State Council issued the 13th Five-Year Plan for poverty alleviation, which clarified the overall thinking, basic objectives, main tasks and major measures of the country's poverty alleviation during the 13th Five-Year Plan period, and put forward the timetable and road map for winning the battle against poverty.

In October 2017, the 19th National Congress of the CPC put forward that the period between now and 2020 will be decisive in finishing the building of a moderately prosperous society in all respects. In Congress stressed that we must focus on priorities, address inadequacies, and shore up points of weakness. In particular, we must be resolute in forestalling and defusing major risks, carrying out targeted poverty alleviation, and preventing and controlling pollution.

In June 2018, the CCCPC and the State Council formulated the guidelines on a three-year poverty-relief plan to win the fight against poverty, focusing on severely impoverished areas and laying out detailed plans to win the final battle against poverty In view of the fact that about 30 million rural poor people need to be lifted out of poverty in the next three years, the proportion of these people who are poor due to illness and disability remains high, and poverty is concentrated in deep poverty-stricken areas, etc., the Opinion clearly defines the work requirements of the Three-Year Action Plan of Winning the Battle against Poverty, and puts forward the "seven insist," that is, adhere to the strict implementation of the current poverty alleviation standards, adhere to the basic strategy of targeted poverty alleviation, adhere to putting improving the quality of poverty alleviation in the first place, adhere to combining poverty alleviation with intellectual support, adhere to integrating development-oriented poverty alleviation with social security poverty alleviation, adhere to integrating poverty alleviation with work style training, and adhere to mobilizing the enthusiasm of the whole society for poverty alleviation. This is a programmatic document guiding the work related to poverty alleviation in the next three years.

In October 2019, the Fourth Plenary Session of the 19th CCCPC proposed that "we should resolutely win the battle against poverty, consolidate our achievements in poverty alleviation, and establish a long-term mechanism to solve relative poverty."[108]

The above deployment involves principles and policies, institutional mechanisms, organizational structures, work requirements and other dimensions. It not only points out the direction of progress, but also clarifies the path and method, and draws a timetable and road map for winning the fight against poverty and building a moderately prosperous society in all respects. On this basis, the work related to building a moderately prosperous society in all respects has been carried out in an orderly and steady manner.

The Party Central Committee, with Xi Jinping as the core, has given top priority to the battle against poverty in its governance, and initiated the establishment of the systems of the responsibility, policies, investment, mobilizing, supervision, assessment for poverty alleviation, to achieve victory in the fight against poverty. In accordance with the system and mechanism of "a working mechanism whereby the central leadership makes overall plans, provincial authorities take overall responsibility, and city and county authorities ensure implementation," the implementation measures of the responsibility system for poverty alleviation were introduced, and a responsibility system was established in which each of them took its own responsibility and worked together to tackle key problems. All central departments and regions have issued supporting documents, policy documents or implementation plans to improve the series of "1 + N" (one over-all policy plus a number of supporting policies) poverty alleviation policies. We should adhere to the main and leading role of government investment, increase the investment of financial funds, and introduce the re-loan policy for poverty alleviation, so as to ensure that the investment in poverty alleviation is commensurate with the requirements of the fight against poverty. We have intensified poverty alleviation in the securities industry, insurance industry and land policy. We should intensify cooperation between the East and the West in poverty alleviation, strengthen pairing-off assistance in poverty alleviation, mobilize central enterprises to set up industrial investment funds in poverty-stricken areas, carry out the poverty alleviation action in counties and villages, mobilize private enterprises to carry out the targeted poverty alleviation program of 10,000 Enterprises Helping 10,000 Villages, set up national poverty eradication prize, award for outstanding contribution, award for dedication and award for innovation, and create a good public opinion atmosphere. We have promulgated the work methods for supervision and inspection of poverty alleviation, carried out supervision and inspection of the implementation of the decisions and arrangements of the central authorities in all localities, and put the requirements of ensuring full and strict governance over the Party through all links of the whole process of poverty alleviation. We will introduce measures for assessing the effectiveness of poverty alleviation and development work of provincial Party committees and governments, and implement the strictest examination and evaluation of poverty alleviation.

The ruling party and the government should firmly grasp the key links such as identification, assistance, exit precision and fund use, and strive to solve the problems of who to be supported, who should support, how to support and how to exit. We should carry out poverty registration to track on the conditions of the impoverished population through data. We should strengthen resident work teams in poor villages and strengthen the power of grassroots. We should implement the "five-pronged poverty alleviation measures" (developing production, relocation, ecological compensation, development of education, securing basic needs through social security) with differentiated and targeted measures. We should focus on key areas and improve the development environment. We should strengthen the supervision of funds and improve the use efficiency. We should standardize the withdrawal of poverty and ensure the quality of poverty alleviation.

The state has also organized and launched a massive people's fight against poverty. A total of 255,000 village-based working teams and over 3 million first secretaries of CPC village committees and village-based officials have been sent to the frontline of poverty alleviation, along with nearly 2 million township officials and millions of village officials. According to statistics, a total of more than 1,800 poverty alleviation cadres have fixed their lives on the journey of poverty alleviation. We should extensively mobilize people of all ethnic groups and all sectors of society to jointly declare war on poverty, and foster a society assistance mechanism where all are willing to and able to participate in the fight against poverty. We should continue to mobilize the enthusiasm, initiative and creativity of the broad masses of poor people, stimulate internal impetus for poverty elimination, and focus on the people's aspirations to live a better life into a powerful driving force for poverty alleviation. We should continue to invigorate people's confidence in their ability to eliminate poverty and help them develop the skills they need to do so, to enrich both their pockets and their heads, and to guide the poor people to rely on their hard-working hands and tenacity to get rid of poverty and change their fate.

The road to poverty alleviation is not a smooth one. In 2020, when the fight against poverty has entered the home stretch, the world was swept up in an unexpected coronavirus epidemic disrupted the normal order of production and life. The novel coronavirus disease (COVID-19) epidemic is a major public health emergency that has spread the fastest caused the most extensive infections and been the hardest to contain since the founding of the PRC in 1949 and the most serious pandemic in the past century. Under the influence of the COVID-19 epidemic, the income of poor labor force who found employment out of their hometown has decreased, the income increase from poverty alleviation by developing industries has decreased, and some poverty alleviation projects have not started on time. Winning the battle against poverty becomes a serious challenge. In the face of enormous pressure and difficulties, on the basis of unswervingly adhering to the poverty alleviation standard, the central government has clearly implemented the listing and supervision of 52 poor counties and 1,113 poor villages across the country with a large number of poor population and great difficulty in poverty alleviation. The seven provinces and regions involved have formulated the implementation plan to list all the counties and villages which had not yet eliminated poverty in order to oversee their poverty-alleviation efforts. All the counties have made special plans to ensure that the goal of poverty alleviation can be achieved on schedule.

By the end of 2020, we won a complete victory in the battle against poverty. We have lifted all 832 poor counties out of poverty, 128,000 poor villages were de-listed, and nearly 100 million rural poor people were lifted out of poverty. Since the 18th National Congress of the CPC, China has lifted over 10 million people out of poverty every year on average, equivalent to the population of a medium-sized country. The fight against poverty has changed China's rural areas in a historic and all-round way. It is another great revolution in China's rural areas. It has profoundly changed the backwardness of poor areas, vigorously promoted the overall development of China's rural areas, and filled the most prominent weaknesses in building a moderately prosperous society in all respects. Through the fight against poverty, the income and welfare of the poor have been greatly improved. The per capita disposable income of rural residents in poor areas has increased from 6,079 yuan in 2013 to 12,588 yuan in 2020, with an average annual growth of 11.6%. 28 ethnic groups with relatively small populations have shaken off poverty. After the founding of the PRC, some "the directly-entering-socialism ethnic groups" that have created a "thousand-year leap" to enter the socialist society have achieved the second historical leap from poverty and backwardness to moderately prosperous society in an all-round way. The fight against poverty has not only lifted all the rural poor out of poverty, but also enabled the economic and social development of the poor areas to catch up with others with great strides. The overall situation has undergone a historic change. The spiritual world of the poor people has been enriched and sublimated in the process of poverty alleviation. They have stronger confidence, more flexible minds and more sufficient morale, and profound changes have taken place from the inside out. The welfare of the group with special difficulties has been continuously improved, the right to survival has been fully guaranteed, and the opportunities for development have increased significantly. Winning the battle against poverty has also promoted the improvement of the national poverty governance system. The grass-roots governance system in impoverished areas has been further improved and the governance capacity has been significantly improved.

Poverty is a deep-seated problem of the human society. Poverty eradication is a challenging task for us all. Since reform and opening-up, China has lifted a total of 770 million rural poor people out of poverty, accounting for more than 70% of the global poverty reduction population in the same period. It has achieved the poverty reduction goal of the UN 2030 Agenda for Sustainable Development 10 years ahead of schedule, creating a miracle in the history of human poverty reduction. The complete elimination of absolute poverty in China, which accounts for nearly one fifth of the world's population, is not only a milestone event in the history of the development of the Chinese nation, but also a major event in the history of human poverty reduction and even human development. It has made great contributions to the development of global poverty reduction and human development.

The Party Central Committee, with Comrade Xi Jinping at its core, based on China's national conditions and grasping the patterns of poverty reduction, has introduced a series of extraordinary policy initiatives, built a set of effective policy system, institutional system and work system, and has blazed a development path that suits its national conditions. It has forged the spirit of "working with one heart, fighting with all sharpness, being precise and pragmatic, pioneering and innovative, overcoming difficulties, and living up to the people."

In December 2021, on the basis of the victory in poverty alleviation, the CCCPC and the State Council adopted the opinions on Combining Consolidating and Building on our Achievements in Poverty Alleviation with the Revitalization of Rural Area, making comprehensive arrangements to make sure that the positive results in poverty elimination are consolidated and become an integral part of rural revitalization.

While winning the battle against poverty, China has also paid attention to the fight against major risks and pollution. We should further advance the battle against major risks, focusing on strengthening the prevention and control of fiscal and financial risks. In the battle to prevent and resolve major risks, the Party Central Committee, with Comrade Xi Jinping at its core, has proposed "financial security" and made it a major issue in the governance of the country, constantly improving the top-level design. On this basis, China has established the China Banking and Insurance Regulatory Commission, deepened the reform of the financial regulatory system, constantly strengthened financial regulation, and maintained financial stability and security. China has also paid attention to preventing and resolving the "black swan" and "grey rhino" in the political, ideological, scientific and social fields. In terms of tackling tough problems in pollution prevention and control, the CCCPC and the State Council have successively issued The Decisions of the CCCPC and the State Council on Comprehensively Enhancing Eco-Environmental Protection to Completely Win the Battle Against Pollution and the Circular on Further Promoting the Nationwide Battle to Prevent and Control Pollution, proposing to resolutely win the three major battles to keep our skies blue, our waters clear, and our lands pollution-free. The government has issued Action Plan for Preventing and Controlling Air Pollution, Action Plan for Preventing and Controlling Water Pollution and Action Plan for Preventing and Controlling Soil Pollution to promote the three major defense wars with unprecedented strength, and the ecological environment has been significantly improved.

4.9.2　Fulfilling the First Centenary Goal of Building a Moderately Prosperous Society in All Respects as Scheduled

Through unremitting efforts, by the end of 2020, the main goals and tasks of the "13th Five-Year Plan" was successfully completed, China's economic strength, scientific and technological strength, comprehensive national strength and people's living standards has risen to a new level, and great historic achievements has been made in building a moderately prosperous society in all respects. On July 1, 2021, China announced that it would achieve the goal of building a moderately prosperous society in all respects as scheduled.

China's all-round well-off society reflects the balance, coordination and sustainability of development. It is moderately prosperous society with coordinated development of material civilization, political civilization, spiritual civilization, social civilization and ecological civilization; it is moderately prosperous society that continuously meets the people's growing diversified, multi-level and multi-faceted needs and constantly promotes people's all-round development; it is a multi-dimensional and all-round well-off society characterized by national prosperity, national rejuvenation and people's happiness.

An all-round well-off society is based on economic development.

Economic strength increased substantially. China's GDP jumped from 67.91 billion yuan in 1952 to 101.3 trillion yuan in 2020. Its total economic output accounted for more than 17% of the global economy, making it the second largest economy in the world. The per capita GDP increased from several tens of dollars in 1952 to more than 10,000 U.S. dollars in 2020, achieving a historic leap from a low-income country to an upper middle-income country. China has become the largest country in Global trade in goods, the second largest country in service trade, the second largest country in commodity consumption, and the first largest country in foreign exchange reserves. In 2020, China ranked the first in the world in terms of foreign capital utilization. Since 2010, China has ranked the first in the world in terms of manufacturing industry for 11 consecutive years, and has the place of the most promising growth market in the world.

We have a leapfrog development in our scientific and technological strength. In the early days of the founding of new China, even matches and iron nails had to be imported, and a series of major original achievements had been made in the frontiers of quantum information, iron-based superconductivity, neutrinos, stem cells, brain science, and a large number of strategic high-tech fields such as developing manned spacecraft and exploring the moon, the construction of the global network of the Bei Dou Navigation Satellite System, manned deep-sea submersibles, high-speed railways, fifth-generation mobile network technology (5G), and supercomputers. China has become an innovative country, moving from a big country in science and technology to a powerful country in science and technology. Science and technology are widely used in the production field, and innovation driven development has achieved remarkable results, with the contribution made by advances in science and technology estimated to account for more than 60% of economic growth. Science and technology have significantly improved governance and profoundly changed people's lives.

We have accelerated the optimization and upgrading of the industrial structure. China has built the most complete industrial system in the world, and its industrial development continues to move towards the medium-high level. The value added of the three industries has increased from 50.5:20.8:28.7 in 1952 to 7.7:37.8:54.5 in 2020. From a traditional agricultural power to an industrial power and a service industry power, the economy has shifted from relying on a single industry to relying on the common drive of the three industries. Notable progress should be made in modernizing agriculture with an increased grain production capacity. We have built a complete and independent modern industrial system, expanded the scope and depth of the integration of industrialization and informatization, transformed and upgraded from "made in China" to "invented by China," and further promoted the modernization of the industrial chain and supply chain. Strategic emerging industries represented by the new generation of information technology, biotechnology, high-end equipment and green environmental protection have developed rapidly and become an important engine leading high-quality development. The digital economy has stimulated new vitality of economic development, and the trend of digital industry and transforming industries with digital technologies has been accelerated. The modern service industry has accelerated its development, and new business forms and models marked by "Internet +" have emerged in an endless stream. People's personalized and diversified needs are constantly met.

The modern infrastructure network continued to improve. The information is unimpeded, the roads are networked, the railways are dense, and the bridges are towering, turning a deep chasm into a thoroughfare. The "five vertical and five horizontal" connecting the main transport corridors are basically connected. The total operating mileage of high-speed railway, expressway and urban rail transit and the number of deep-water berths in ports rank first in the world. The total turnover of civil aviation transportation ranks second in the world for many years. China has accelerated its progress towards becoming a country with a strong transport industry. China has consistently increased its capability in securing energy supply and energy development technology, improved its water infrastructure, and promoted the construction of Internet infrastructure.

Moderately prosperous society in an all-round way not only effectively protects the people's economic rights, but also effectively protects the people's political rights.

The people enjoy extensive democratic rights. All rights of the state belonged to the people. All the people exercise democratic election, democratic consultation, democratic decision-making, democratic management and democratic supervision. The links of democratic election, democratic consultation, democratic decision-making, democratic management and democratic supervision are interlinked and interconnected, achieving democracy in terms of both process and outcomes, both formal democracy and substantive democracy, direct democracy and indirect democracy, and ensuring the people's rights of information, participation, expression, and scrutiny.

The people's democratic life is rich and colorful. Democracy has become the norm, injecting great vitality into Chinese society and people are happy. People's opinions and suggestions can be expressed through democratic channels, on areas from food, clothing, housing and transportation, medical treatment and education to community management and social governance, to major policies and development plans. Democratic practices and one grassroots democratic forms have been emerging one after another including: democratic discussions and hearings, online discussion of government affairs, remote consultations, "legislative through train," "courtyard discussions," "neighborhood meetings," and so on. Civil people's discussion, civil people's decision and civil people's running have gradually become a common practice. Chinese style democracy made the people's aspirations and voices expressed, heard and responded to. It can truly solve the problems that the people want to solve, and truly integrate the thoughts and aspirations of more than 1.4 billion people into national development, forming a situation of unity and struggle.

People's democracy is guaranteed by systems. The main ones are people's congresses, which form the fundamental political system of China, CPC-led multiparty cooperation and political consultation, regional ethnic autonomy, and grassroots self-governance. These systems have laid a firm institutional foundation for protecting the fundamental interests of the people. The socialist legal system with Chinese characteristics, with the Constitution at its core, has been constantly improved, providing a solid legal system to guarantee people are the masters of the country.

Social fairness and justice have been constantly highlighted. The basic strategy of ruling the country by law has been fully implemented. The pursuit of the value of the rule of law of social fairness and justice has gradually penetrated the whole process and all aspects of legislation, law enforcement, justice and law-abiding. The concept of justice for the people has been fully implemented, and the judicial credibility has been significantly enhanced. We must make every effort to let fairness and justice shine on the people, and ensure that the people feel that justice is served in every court case.

Moderately prosperous society in an all-round way is moderately prosperous society that keeps the coordinated development of material civilization and spiritual civilization.

We must consolidate the common ideological basis for concerted efforts of all the Chinese people. Socialism with Chinese characteristics and the Chinese

Dream have been deeply rooted in the hearts of the people. The main theme of the times, that is, the Communist Party is good, socialism is good, reform and opening-up is good, the great motherland is good, and the people of all ethnic groups are good, hold greater appeal. The confidence of the whole people in the path, theory, system, and culture has been significantly enhanced. The core socialist values have been disseminated and practiced, the spirit of patriotism, reform and innovation, and the spirit of struggle in the new era have been widely promoted, and the national mentality has become more mature by of being proactive, open, inclusive, rational and peaceful. Revolutionary heritage has been vigorously promoted, red stories have been widely spread, and red tourism has become a fashion. The news media and other media adhere to the correct guidance of public opinion, and the whole society is full of positive energy for beauty and goodness. We have built the common spiritual homeland of the Chinese nation, and the sense of community for the Chinese nation.

The people's cultural life has become increasingly rich and colorful. From rural libraries and township cultural facilities to urban public libraries, museums, cultural centers and art galleries, the network of public cultural facilities covering both urban and rural areas has been continuously improved, and basically free or low-cost opening has been realized. The richness, convenience and equality of public cultural services have been significantly enhanced. The cultural industry continued to develop in a healthy manner, and new cultural enterprises, cultural formats, and cultural consumption patterns were accelerated. The chaos in the cultural and entertainment fields has been effectively rectified, and a law-abiding conduct is taking shape. Cultural exchanges between China and foreign countries are expanding day by day. People can enjoy world-class literary and artistic performances without going abroad. The national fitness craze is quietly rising, and China is transforming from a sporting nation to a leading sporting nation.

Take forward the transmission and development of the fine traditions of Chinese culture The Chinese civilization carries on the spiritual, ethical lineage of the Chinese nation and its people. It must be passed down from generation to generation, keep abreast of the times through innovation, and get rid of the stale and bring forth the fresh to brighten up the well-off life. A lot of fruitful achievements have been reaped in archaeological research and proved the historical lineage and splendid achievements of the origin and development of Chinese civilization. The ideological concepts, humanistic spirit and moral norms in the excellent traditional culture of China are inherited and carried forward, and the excellent characters of the Chinese nation, such as collective consciousness, unity spirit, struggle quality and family and country feelings, are carried forward, and the spiritual strength of the Chinese people is condensed.

Chinese culture is constantly accelerating its speed of going global. Traditional Chinese medicine, martial arts, Peking Opera, tea ceremony and other excellent traditional Chinese cultures have gone global. Chinese films have gone out of the country, food and beautiful Chinese sceneries are popular, and film and television variety shows, web literature and pop music enjoy a wide range of popularity. 56 world heritages sites in China show the world a comprehensive and real ancient China and modern China. The affinity and charisma of Chinese culture in the international community are constantly improving.

We must build moderately prosperous society, which is people-oriented and puts people's livelihood first.

Living standards have been significantly improved. The income of residents continued to increase. The per capita annual disposable income of residents nationwide increased from 171 yuan in 1978 to 32,189 yuan in 2020, and the quality of life of urban and rural residents continued to improve. After the problem of food and clothing has been solved, people have a higher pursuit of life quality and taste, and the clothing, food, housing and transportation have been continuously upgraded. The consumption structure has gradually transitioned from survival type to development type and enjoyment type.

China's employment situation remained generally stable for a long time, and the quality of employment has been significantly improved. The total employment increased from 180 million in 1949 to 750 million in 2020, with the scale of employment continued to expand; the vast majority of workers depend on agriculture for their livelihood in the past, but now the number of people employed in the tertiary industry accounts for 47.7%, and the number of people employed in cities and towns accounts for 61.6%, and the employment structure has been constantly optimized; workers are generally illiterate and semi-illiterate in the past, but now the average number of years of education of the working age population is 10.8 years, the total number of skilled personnel is about 200 million, and the quality of employees has been greatly improved. From planned distribution to market employment, free choice of employment and independent entrepreneurship, and from traditional employment mode to new employment mode, workers' concept of employment has been profoundly changed, the employment space is broader, and the employment modes are increasingly diversified. The legitimate rights and interests of workers have been protected, the remuneration for labor has increased, and the income from labor has been protected. People are working more and more with dignity and happiness, and relying on their own hands to create a better life. The belief that work is what is most honorable, most sublime, most magnificent and most beautiful have become the public's consensus and wisdom in action. The trend in the society is to be diligent at work and be decent to get rich, love labor and respect labor.

Education is flourishing. From a large illiterate and semi-illiterate country to a large educational country, and from a large population country to a large human resource country, China has built the largest education system in the contemporary world, including preschool education, primary education, secondary education and higher education. The overall level of education modernization has entered the ranks of average level of middle- and high-income countries. Vocational and technical education continues to develop, special education has been developed from scratch, and the construction of a networked, digital, personalized and lifelong learning system has been accelerated. China's education has unblocked the upward flow channel, changed the destiny of countless people, realized the dreams of countless people, and given people more opportunities to shine in life.

Social security benefits all the people. China has basically built the world's largest social security system, with social insurance as the main body, including social assistance, social welfare, social special care and other systems, and is moving towards the goal of full coverage, basic protection, multi-level and sustainable development. By the end of June 2021, the number of people participating in basic old-age pension, unemployment insurance and work-related injury insurance nationwide had reached 1.014 billion, 222 million and 274 million respectively, and the number of people covered by basic medical insurance exceeded 1.3 billion. Maternity insurance covers all employers and employees in accordance with the law. Housing security has been strengthened. It is a national strategy to actively respond to the aging of the population. The protection of the rights and interests of the disabled has become more powerful, and the child welfare and juvenile protection systems have been continuously improved. We will build an increasingly dense social security safety net, give full play to the sustainable role of the foundation, and make people feel more comfortable at work, in life, and more confident in the future.

We can achieve moderate prosperity in all respects, only when we can ensure the people's health. Since the founding of the PRC, from the spread of epidemic diseases to it is preventable and controllable, from lack of medical treatment to medical treatment, from local reimbursement to gradual settlement in different places, and from simple hospital treatment to contracted services by family doctors, the coverage of China's medical and health system has been gradually improved, and the allocation of medical resources has been further optimized. The problem of access to and affordability of medical services has been gradually resolved. The level of medical technology and service capacity have been continuously improved, the equalization of basic medical public services in urban and rural areas has been continuously promoted, and the Healthy China initiative has been accelerated. The people's health has been continuously improved, and a historic change has been achieved from being at the world average level at the beginning of the founding of new China to being at the forefront of middle-income countries. China has made major strategic achievements in combating the COVID-19 epidemic. The superiority of China's medical and health system has been further demonstrated, and people's lives and health have been effectively safeguarded.

All these steps will ensure people's security. From social management to social governance, from accelerating the formation of a scientific and effective social governance system to a social governance model based on collaboration, participation, and common interests, the socialization, rule of law, intellectualization and specialization of social governance have been constantly improved, and remarkable achievements have been made in reaching a higher level in building a safe China. The social security prevention and control system has been continuously improved, a campaign to crack down on organized crime and local mafia has been carried out in depth, the ability to prevent and resolve social conflicts at the grass-roots level has been significantly enhanced, and the overall effectiveness of social governance has been significantly improved. The people's sense of security has reached 98.4% by 2020. China has long maintained social harmony and stability, and its people live and work in peace and contentment. China has become one of the most secure countries recognized by the international community.

There is no welfare more universally beneficial than a sound natural environment. It is the brightest color of moderate prosperity in all respects.

Formulate and implement strict ecological civilization system. We have promoted the construction of ecological civilization with the concept and method of the rule of law, implemented the "strictest environmental protection law in history," formulated and revised a series of laws and regulations, basically formed a framework system of ecological environmental laws and regulations, and basically covered all major areas of environmental element supervision. From the system of ecological and environmental protection and the system of efficient utilization of resources, to the system for protecting and restoring ecosystems, a lifelong accountability system for ecological and environment damage, to the goal responsibility system and assessment system, and the inspection system of the central government for environmental protection, China has promoted development and transformation, promoted habit formation, and improved the efficiency of ecological and environmental protection and governance with the strictest system and the most rigid constraint. The system of public participation in environmental protection has been further improved, and a new situation is formed in which all the people participate in ecological and environmental protection.

Remarkable achievements have been made in pollution prevention and control. We must continue to fight the battles to defend blue skies, clear waters and clean land. By 2020, the proportion of days with good air quality in cities at and above the prefecture level would be 87.0%; the average concentration of PM2.5 in cities at and above the prefecture level that did not meet the standard decreased by 28.8% compared with 2015; the proportion of quality water reached 83.4%, and the drinking water sources that met the standard reached 94.5%, and black, malodorous bodies of water in the urban districts of cities at or above the prefectural level have been basically eliminated; the rate of the safe use of contaminated farmland reached 90% and the rate of safe use of other plots of land that have been polluted reached 93% and the goal of zero import of solid waste was achieved as scheduled. The Chinese people's satisfaction with the quality of the ecological environment reached 89.5%.

The quality and stability of the ecosystem have been continuously improved. By the end of 2020, the forest coverage reached 23.04 percent, the comprehensive vegetation coverage of natural grassland grew to 56.1 percent, and the wetland area totaled 6.53 million hectares and the wetland protection rate reached 50% or more. At present, China has established nearly 10000 nature reserves at all levels, accounting for about 18% of the land area. The creation of national forest cities continues to advance. The green space in urban built-up areas reached 36.44% of the total area, and with a per capita area of 14.78 square meters. A beautiful China that is kind to nature, with green mountains, green water, fresh air and harmonious coexistence between people and nature is becoming clearer and clearer.

Green development model and green way of life is gradually formed. The concept of "lucid waters and lush mountains are invaluable assets" has become more and more popular. Ecological priority and green and low-carbon development have gradually become the development path generally followed, and the spatial pattern, industrial structure, production mode and lifestyle conductive to resource conservation and environmental protection have taken shape quickly. China has become the world's largest country in the use of new energy and the country with the fastest progress in energy conservation. In 2020, the energy consumption per unit of GDP decreased by 13.2%, and carbon emission was cut by 18.8%, respectively from the 2015 level. The urban and rural living environment is cleaner, more comfortable and more beautiful. A simple and moderate, green and low-carbon, civilized and healthy lifestyle has become a new social trend.

As a populous country long plagued by weak economic foundations, it is extremely unusual and difficult for China to build moderately prosperous society that benefits more than one billion people in all respects. The CPC and the Chinese people have made long and arduous efforts. Building a moderately prosperous society in all respects is a great and glorious accomplishment for the Chinese nation, for the Chinese people, and for the CPC. Building a moderately prosperous society in all respects has boosted China's development and benefited the rest of the world. The growing affluence of the Chinese people and the continuous development and progress of China have injected positive energy into safeguarding world peace and promoting common development, and demonstrated China's strength in building a community with a shared future for mankind and a better world.

4.9.3 A New Journey Towards a Modern Socialist Country

Moderately prosperous society is not the end, but the starting point of a new life and a new struggle. On the basis of building a moderately prosperous society in all respects, the strategic goal of China's development has been transformed into building a great modern socialist country in all respects.

Since modern times, generations of people with lofty ideals have gone one after another to explore the path of China's modernization. During the New Democratic Revolution period, the CPC consciously shouldered the historical mission of realizing modernization and put forward the goal of realizing national industrialization and agricultural modernization. After the founding of new China, China gradually put forward the important proposition of socialist modernization. In 1964, Zhou Enlai clearly put forward the goal of realizing the "four modernizations" in his Report on the Work of the Government, that is, "modernizing our agriculture, industry, national defense and science and technology within the present century, and maintaining our economic growth ranking the first in the world."[109] In October 1987, the 13th National Congress of the CPC put forward the three-step development strategy, emphasizing that by the middle of the 21st century, the per capita GNP will reach the level of moderately developed countries, the people's lives will be relatively prosperous, and modernization will be basically realized. In October 2017, standing at a new and higher historical starting point, the 19th National Congress of the CPC put forward the new goal of basically realizing socialist modernization by 2035, building China into a rich, strong, democratic, civilized, harmonious and beautiful socialist modern country by the middle of the 21st century, and establishing the goal of building a great modern socialist country in all respects as the Second Centenary Goal. In October 2020, against the background that the goal of building moderately prosperous society in an all-round way is about to be realized, the Fifth Plenary Session of the 19th CCCPC proposed to "win a new victory in building a socialist modern country in an all-round way" and develop "building moderately prosperous society in an all-round way" in "the Four-Pronged Strategy" into "building a socialist modern country in an all-round way."

The period covered by the 14th Five-Year Plan will be the first five years during which China begins its march towards the Second Centenary Goal of building a modern socialist country by building on the success of achieving the First Centenary Goal of building a moderately well-off society.

In October 2020, the Fifth Plenary Session of the 19th CCCPC was held in Beijing. The Congress adopted the Proposal of the CCCPC on Formulating the 14th Five-Year Plan for National Economic and Social Development and the Long-Range Objectives through the Year 2035. The proposal puts forward a set of long-range objectives for China to basically achieve socialist modernization by 2035, which is: our economic and technological strength, and comprehensive national strength will increase significantly. We will make new strides in economic aggregate and the per capita income of urban and rural residents. Making major breakthroughs in core technologies in key areas, we will be a global leader in innovation, and will also achieve new industrialization, enhanced IT application, urbanization, and agricultural modernization, and complete building a modern economic system. we will promote the modernization of the national governance system and governance capacity; the rights of the people to participate and to develop as equals will be adequately protected. The rule of law for the country, the government, and society will be comprehensively in place; China will become a powerful country in terms of culture, education, human capital, sports, and health. The well-rounded development of the people and social etiquette and civility will be significantly enhanced. China's cultural soft power will grow much stronger; Eco-friendly work and lifestyle will be advanced to cover all areas of society. Carbon dioxide emissions will steadily decline after reaching a peak, and there will be a fundamental improvement in the environment after the goal of building a Beautiful China is met; the opening-up will reach a new stage with substantial growth in the country's capabilities for participating in international economic cooperation and competition; the per capita GDP will reach the level of moderately developed countries and the size of the middle-income group will be significantly expanded. Equitable access to basic public services will be ensured. Disparities in development between urban and rural areas and between regions, and in living standards will be significantly reduced; the Peaceful China initiative will be pursued at a higher level. The modernization of national defense and the military will be achieved; people will lead a better life, and more notable and substantial progress will be achieved in well-rounded human development and in common prosperity for all. The proposal also puts forward the main objectives of economic and social development during the 14th Five-Year Plan period, that is, new achievements are made in economic development, new steps are achieved in reform and opening-up, new progress is made in social civilization and ecological civilization construction, new levels are achieved in people's wellbeing, and new improvements are made in achieving more effective national governance. For the first time, the plenary session formally developed "the four-pronged strategy" into building a great modern socialist country in all respects, comprehensively deepening reform, advancing "ruling the country by law," and ensuring full and strict governance over the Party. While establishing the long-term goal of basically realizing modernization, the plenary session mapped out the guiding principles, basic principles, and main objectives of economic and social development during the "14th Five-Year Plan" period, pointing out the direction building a great modern socialist country in all respects. It is of great significance to make a good start in building a great modern socialist country in all respects.

Subsequently, the Fourth Session of the 13th NPC deliberated and adopted the Outline of the 14th Five-Year Plan (2021–2025) for National Economic and Social Development and the Long-Range Objectives Through the Year 2035 of the PRC. The Outline is divided into three parts, with 19 parts, 65 chapters and 192 sections. It puts forward strategic tasks and major measures in 17 aspects, and deploys 102 major engineering projects such as major breakthrough projects in the future, world-class landmark projects in the field of infrastructure, and important livelihood security projects, which involve all aspects of economic and social development.

In January 2021, Xi Jinping delivered an important speech at a study session on implementing the decisions of the Fifth Plenary Session of the 19th CCCPC, attended by officials at the provincial ministerial level, in which he gave an in-depth explanation of a series of important issues on China's economic and social development and pointed out the way forward for the new journey of building a great modern socialist country in all respects.

President Xi Jinping pointed out that we should ensure that we have an accurate understanding of the new development stage This new stage of development is a historical stage in which we march toward the Second Centenary Goal on the basis of achieving the First Centenary Goal. It is a stage in which we have reached a new starting point after decades of accumulation. It is a new stage in which the Party leads the people to make a great historical leap forward from standing up to becoming prosperous and strong. The new development stage is also an important stage in the process of China's socialist development. Building a great modern socialist country in all respects and basically realizing socialist modernization is not only a requirement for China's development at the primary stage of socialism, but also a requirement for China's socialism to move from the primary stage to a higher stage. China's modernization is a modernization with a large population, a modernization for the common prosperity of all the people, a modernization for the coordination of material civilization and spiritual civilization, a modernization for the harmony between man and nature, and a modernization for the path of peaceful development. This is the direction that China must adhere to in its modernization drive.

On the in-depth implementation of new concept for development, Xi Jinping stressed that the whole Party must implement the new concept for development completely, accurately and comprehensively. Since the 18th National Congress of the CPC, we have put forward many important theories and concepts for economic and social development, of which the new concept for development is the most important one. The new concept for development is a systematic theoretical system, which answers a series of theoretical and practical questions about the purpose, motive force, mode and path of development, and clarifies major political issues such as our party's political position, value orientation, development mode and development path. We must grasp the new concept for development from the fundamental purpose, from the problem-oriented approaches while staying alert against potential dangers.

On accelerating the construction of a new development pattern, Xi Jinping proposed that this is a strategic layout and first move to grasp the initiative of future development, is a new development stage to focus on promoting the completion of major historical tasks, and is also a major initiative to implement the new concept for development. Accelerating the construction of a new development pattern is to enhance our survivability, competitiveness, development and sustainability in the midst of various foreseeable and unforeseeable storms and turbulent waves, and to ensure that the process of the great rejuvenation of the Chinese nation will not be delayed or even interrupted. It is necessary to strengthen the leading role of the domestic circulation in the double circulation and shape China's new advantages in international cooperation and competition. It is necessary to attach importance to improving the efficiency and level of domestic large-scale circulation through international circulation, improve the quality and allocation level of China's production factors. It is necessary to enhance the competitiveness of China's export products and services by participating in international market competition, promote China's industrial transformation and upgrading, and enhance China's influence in the global industrial chain, supply chain and innovation chain.

Entering the new development stage, implementing the new development concept and constructing the new development pattern are determined by the theoretical logic, historical logic and practical logic of China's economic and social development, which are closely related. Entering the new development stage has clarified the historical orientation of China's development, implemented the new concept for development, clarified the guiding principles of China's modernization, and constructed a new development pattern to clarify the path choice of China's economic modernization. Understanding the new development stage is the realistic basis for implementing the new development philosophy and creating the new development paradigm. Implementing the new development philosophy provides a guide for understanding the new development stage and fostering the new development paradigm. Building the new development paradigm is a strategic choice in response to the opportunities and challenges in the new development stage and for implementing the new development philosophy.

The year of 2021 marks the 100th anniversary of the founding of the CPC and China held a host of celebrations. Thursday, July 1, 2021, General Secretary Xi Jinping declared at the ceremony marking the centenary of the CPC that through the continued efforts of the whole Party and the entire nation, we have realized the First Centenary Goal of building a moderately prosperous society in all respects. This means that we have brought about a historic resolution to the problem of absolute poverty in China, and we are now marching in confident strides toward the Second Centenary Goal of building China into a great modern socialist country in all respects.[110] In November, the Sixth Plenary Session of the 19th CCCPC was held in Beijing. The Plenary Session adopted the Resolution of the CCCPC on the Major Achievements and Historical Experience of the Party over the Past Century, which has systematically summarized the major achievements and historical experience of the CPC in its century of struggle. The Plenary Session focused on socialism with Chinese characteristics in the new era and summarized the historical achievements and changes in the new era from 13 aspects. This plenary session summarizes the historical experience of the Party in 10 aspects: upholding the Party's leadership; putting the people first; advancing theoretical innovation; staying independent; following the Chinese path; maintaining a global vision; breaking new ground; standing up for ourselves; promoting the united front; and remaining committed to self-reform. These ten aspects are not only the historical experience accumulated over a long period of time, but also the important experience guiding the new journey of building a great modern socialist country in all respects. They will be constantly enriched and developed in the new era. The plenary session also issued a call to the whole party to make unremitting efforts to for the realization of the Second Centenary Goal and the Chinese Dream of the great rejuvenation of the Chinese nation. It is important in both a practical and historical sense to have a comprehensive review by the Resolution adopted at the Sixth Plenary Session of the 19th CCCPC of the major achievements and historical experience of the Party over the past century as we celebrate its centenary and the fulfillment of the First Centenary Goal of building a moderately prosperous society in all respects and move on toward the Second Centenary Goal of building China into a great modern socialist country in all respects. This review will help build a broader consensus and stronger unity in will and action among all members and rally and lead Chinese people of all ethnic groups in achieving new and great success in building socialism with Chinese characteristics in the new era.

Summary

Since the 18th National Congress of the CPC, the CPC has led the people of the whole country to forge ahead, organized and implemented the largest and most powerful poverty alleviation campaign in human history, historically solved the problem of absolute poverty, and created a miracle in the history of poverty reduction. From "small well-off family" to "well-off society," from "overall well-off society" to "comprehensive well-off society," and from "comprehensive construction" to "comprehensive completion," the dream of well-off society has become a reality, and the centenary goal of building moderately prosperous society in all respects has been realized as scheduled. On this basis, the CPC and the Chinese government have actively planned, deployed and promoted the new journey of building a socialist modern country in an all-round way according to the changes in the situation, based on the new development stage, implementing the new development concept, building a new development pattern, and promoting high-quality development, so that our country is striding with confidence toward the Second Centenary Goal of building China into a great modern socialist country in all respects. Right now, changes of the world, of our times and of history are unfolding in ways like never before. On the one hand, we should see that China's development environment is facing profound and complex changes, and China will face no less risks and tests on its way forward than in the past. On the other hand, we should also see that China's economic fundamentals of strong resilience, sufficient potential, wide room for manoeuvre, and long-term improvement will not change. We will continue to move forward bravely along the path of Chinese style modernization successfully opened up in reform and opening-up. The CPC and the Chinese people will build upon the great glories and victories of the past hundred years with even greater glories and victories on the new journey that lies before us in the new era.

Notes

1. "Learn Documents Well and Grasp the Outline." *People's Daily* 1, February 7, 1977.
2. Party Literature Research Centre, CCCPC, *Selection of Important Literature Since the Third Plenary Meeting of the Central Committee of the Communist Party of China* (Beijing: People's Publishing House, 1982), 838.
3. Party Literature Research Centre, CCCPC, *Selection of Important Literature Since the 13th National Congress of the Communist Party of China* (Beijing: People's Publishing House, 1986), 3.
4. Ibid., 1991, 4–61.
5. Party Literature Research Centre, CCCPC, *Chronicle of Deng Xiaoping's Thoughts (1975–1997)* (Beijing: Central Party Literature Press, 2011), 401.
6. Deng Xiaoping, *Selected Works of Deng Xiaoping (Vol. 2)* (Beijing: People's Publishing House. 1992), 396.
7. Jiang Zemin, *Selected Works of Jiang Zemin (Vol. 1)* (Beijing: People's Publishing House, 2006), 138.
8. Deng Xiaoping, *Selected Works of Deng Xiaoping (Vol. 2)* (Beijing: People's Publishing House, 1994), 355.
9. Chen Yun, *Selected Works of Chen Yun (Vol. 3)* (Beijing: People's Publishing House, 1995), 282.
10. *The Complete History of the People's Republic of China (Vol. 5)* (Beijing: Unity Press, 1996), 5908.
11. Deng Xiaoping, *Selected Works of Deng Xiaoping (Vol.2)* (Beijing: People's Publishing House, 1992), 40–49.
12. Party Literature Research Centre, CCCPC, *Selection of Important Literature Since the 12th National Congress of the Communist Party of China* (Beijing: People's Publishing House, 1986), 15.
13. Party Literature Research Centre, CCCPC, *Selection of Important Literature Since the 12th National Congress of the Communist Party of China* (Beijing: People's Publishing House, 1986), 662.

14. Deng Xiaoping, *Selected Works of Deng Xiaoping (Vol. 3)* (Beijing: People's Publishing House, 1993), 409.

15. Ye Jianying, *Selected Works of Ye Jianying* (Beijing: People's Publishing House, 1996), 540.

16. Deng Xiaoping, *Selected Works of Deng Xiaoping (Vol. 3)* (Beijing: People's Publishing House, 1993), 291.

17. Xing Bisi, ed., *The Dictionary of Selected Works of Deng Xiaoping* (Beijing: Central Party School Press, 1994), 996.

18. Party Literature Research Centre, CCCPC, *Chronicle of Deng Xiaoping's Thoughts (1975–1997)* (Beijing: Central Party Literature Press, 2011), 675.

19. Party Literature Research Centre, CCCPC, *Chronicle of Jiang Zemin's Thoughts (1975–1997)* (Beijing: Central Party Literature Press, 2010), 66.

20. Party Literature Research Centre, CCCPC, *Selection of Important Literature Since the 14th National Congress of the Communist Party of China* (Beijing: People's Publishing House, 1996), 1–47.

21. Party Literature Research Centre, CCCPC, *Selection of Important Literature Since the 15th National Congress of the Communist Party of China* (Beijing: People's Publishing House, 2000), 1–51.

22. Party Literature Research Centre, CCCPC, *Selection of Important Literature Since the 14th National Congress of the Communist Party of China* (Beijing: People's Publishing House, 1997), 1743–1749.

23. Jiang Zemin, *Jiang Zemin's Remark on Strengthening and Improving the Construction of the Ruling Party (Special Extracts)* (Beijing: Central Party Literature Press & Yan Jiu Press, 2004), 192.

24. Party Literature Research Centre, CCCPC, *Selection of Important Literature Since the 15th National Congress of the Communist Party of China* (Beijing: People's Publishing House, 2000), 30–31.

25. Ibid., 808.

26. Party Literature Research Centre, CCCPC, *Selection of Important Literature Since the 14th National Congress of the Communist Party of China* (Beijing: People's Publishing House, 1996), 29.

27. Party Literature Research Centre, CCCPC, *Selection of Important Literature Since the 15th National Congress of the Communist Party of China* (Beijing: People's Publishing House, 2000), 32.

28. Deng Xiaoping, *Selected Works of Deng Xiaoping (Vol.3)* (Beijing: People's Publishing House, 1993), 148.

29. Ibid., 373.

30. Party Literature Research Centre, CCCPC, *Selection of Important Literature Since the 14th National Congress of the Communist Party of China* (Beijing: People's Publishing House, 1997), 1466–1467.

31. Party Literature Research Centre, CCCPC, *Selection of Important Literature Since the 15th National Congress of the Communist Party of China* (Beijing: People's Publishing House, 2000), 27.

32. Ibid., 28.

33. Jiang Zemin, *Selected Works of Jiang Zemin (Vol.3)* (Beijing: People's Publishing House, 2006), 295.

34. Ibid., 462.

35. Party Literature Research Centre, CCCPC, *Selection of Important Literature Since the 14th National Congress of the Communist Party of China* (Beijing: People's Publishing House, 1996), 1–47.

36. Jiang Zemin, *Selected Works of Jiang Zemin (Vol.2)* (Beijing: People's Publishing House, 2006), 132.

37. Deng Xiaoping, *Selected Works of Deng Xiaoping (Vol.3)* (Beijing: People's Publishing House, 1993), 290.

38. Party Literature Research Centre, CCCPC, *Selection of Important Literature Since the 12th National Congress of the Communist Party of China* (Beijing: People's Publishing House, 1986), 580.

39. Party Literature Research Centre, CCCPC, *Selection of Important Literature Since the 14th National Congress of the Communist Party of China* (Beijing: People's Publishing House, 1996), 535.

40. "Jiang Zemin and Li Peng Respectively Meeting with the U.S. Secretary of State," *People's Daily* 4, February 25, 1997.

41. Jiang Zemin, "Speech at a Meeting with the Scientific Community in Novosibirsk Science City," *People's Daily* 1, November 25, 1998.

42. "Jiang Zemin Meeting with Ryutaro Hashimoto," *People's Daily* 6, November 25, 1996.

43. Jiang Zemin, "Speech at the Celebration of the Establishment of the Macao Special Administrative Region of the People's Republic of China," *People's Daily* 2, December 21, 1999.

44. Jiang Zemin, *Selected Works of Jiang Zemin (Vol.2)* (Beijing: People's Publishing House, 2006), 127–128.

45. "Taiwan Affairs Office and Information Office of the State Council of the People's Republic of China, One-China Principle and The Taiwan Question," *People's Daily* 3, February 22, 2000.

46. Jiang Zemin, *Selected Works of Jiang Zemin (Vol. 3)* (Beijing: People's Publishing House, 2006), 2.

47. Ibid., 129.

48. Ibid., 272–279.

49. Ibid., 536–537.

50. Hu Jintao, *Selected Works of Hu Jintao (Vol. 2)* (Beijing: People's Publishing House, 2016), 67.

51. The Literature Research Office of the CPC Central Committee, ed., *Selection of Important Literature Since the 17th National Congress of the Communist Party of China* (Beijing: Central Party Literature Press, 2009), 10–11.

52. Ibid., 9.

53. The Literature Research Office of the CPC Central Committee, ed., *Selection of Important Literature Since the 15th National Congress of the Communist Party of China* (Beijing: People's Publishing House, 2001), 1369.

54. Hu Jintao, *Speech at the National People's Congress 50th Anniversary Meeting in the Capital* (Beijing: People's Publishing House, 2004), 9.

55. Hu Jintao, *The Remarks at the Conference of Celebrating the 55th Anniversary of the Founding of Chinese People's Political Consultative Conference* (Beijing: People's Publishing House, 2004), 2.

56. The Literature Research Office of the CPC Central Committee, ed., *Selection of Important Literature Since the 17th National Congress of the Communist Party of China* (Beijing: Central Party Literature Press, 2009), 501.

57. "A meeting was held by The Political Bureau of the CPC Central Committee to discuss the documents to be submitted to the Third Plenary Session of the 16th Central Committee for consideration to study the revitalization of the old industrial bases in the Northeast Region, September 30, 2009," *People's Daily* 1.

58. Party Literature Research Center of the CPC Central Committee. *Selected Important Documents since the Sixteenth National Congress I* (Beijing: Central Party Literature Press, 2005), 471.

59. Hu Jintao, *Selected Works of Hu Jintao (Vol. 2)* (Beijing: People's Publishing House, 2016), 430.

60. Hu Jintao, *Selected Works of Hu Jintao (Vol. 3)* (Beijing: People's Publishing House, 2016), 539.

61. "The Measures for the National Annual Festival and Commemorative Day Holiday (issued by the State Council on December 23rd, 1949) was revised for the first time according to the Decision of the State Council on Amending the Measures for the National Annual Festivals and Memorial Day Holidays on September 18th, 1999, and for the second time according to the Decision of the State Council on Amending the Measures for the National Annual Festivals and Memorial Day holidays on December 14th, 2007," *People's Daily* 2, December 17, 2007.

62. Hu Jintao, "China's Development Asia's Opportunity," *People's Daily* 1, April 25, 2004.

63. "Information Office of the State Council, China's Peaceful Development," *People's Daily* 14–15, September 7, 2011.

64. Hu Jintao, "Build Towards a Harmonious World of Lasting Peace and Common Prosperity," *People's Daily* 1, September 16, 2005,

65. "China US Joint Statement," *People's Daily* 2, January 20, 2011.

66. "Information Office of the State Council, China's Peaceful Development," *People's Daily* 14–15, September 7, 2011.

67. Hu Jintao, "Remarks at the Gathering Marking the 15th Anniversary of Hongkong's Return to the Motherland and the Inauguration of the Fourth-term Government of the Hongkong Special Administrative Region," *People's Daily* 2, July 2, 2012.

68. Hu Jintao, "Speech at the Congress to Celebrate the 10th Anniversary of Macao's Return to the Motherland and the Inauguration Ceremony of the Third Government of the Macao Special Administrative Region," *People's Daily* 2, December 21, 2009.

69. Hu Jintao, "While attending the deliberations of the Taiwan delegation, stressed the importance of unswervingly adhering to the basic policy of 'peaceful reunification and One Country, Two Systems' and striving for the early resolution of the Taiwan issue and the completion of the great cause of reunification of the country," *People's Daily* 1, March 12, 2003.

70. Hu Jintao, *Selected Works of Hu Jintao (Vol. 3)* (Beijing: People's Publishing House, 2016), 190.

71. Hu Jintao, *Selected Works of Hu Jintao (Vol. 2)* (Beijing: People's Publishing House, 2016), 302.

72. "When Hu Jintao visited the members of the Revolutionary Committee of the Chinese Kuomintang, Taiwan Democratic Self-Government League and All-China Federation of Taiwan Compatriots who participated in the CPPCC National Committee, he stressed that we should firmly grasp the theme of the peaceful development of cross-strait relations and work for the well-being of compatriots on both sides of the Taiwan Strait and peace in the Taiwan Strait region," *People's Daily* 1, March 5, 2008.

73. Hu Jintao, "Work together to promote the peaceful development of cross-strait relations and achieve the great rejuvenation of the Chinese nation with one heart," *People's Daily* 2, January 1, 2009.

74. Xi Jinping attended the Central People's Congress Work Conference and made an important speech Adhering to and Improving the System of People's Congresses and Continuously Developing the Whole-Process People's Democracy, *People's Daily* 4, October 15, 2021.

75. The Literature Research Office of the CPC Central Committee, ed., *Excerpts from the Discourse on Socialist Political Construction* (Beijing: Central Literature Publishing House, Research Press, 2017), 27–28.

76. Xi Jinping, *The Governance of China (Vol. 1)* (Beijing: Foreign Language Press, 2018), 141–142.

77. "The Resolution of the CCCPC on the Major Achievements and Historical Experience of the Party over the Past Century (adopted at the Sixth Plenary Session of the 19th CCCPC on November 11, 2021)," *People's Daily*, November 17, 2021.

78. Xi Jinping, *The Governance of China (Vol. 2)* (Beijing: Foreign Language Press, 2017), 233.

79. "Huang Shouhong: Continue to Pursue Supply-Side Structural Reform as our Main Task," *People's Daily* 7, December 11, 2020.

80. Xi Jinping, *The Governance of China (Vol. 2)* (Beijing: Foreign Language Press, 2017), 339.

81. "Fan Zhou and Song Lifu: the 13th Five-Year Plan Period—Cultural Industry Opens the Curtain of Transformative Development," *People's Daily* Overseas Edition, October 21, 2020.

82. "Fu Kaihua: Promoting Innovative Transformation and Development of Traditional Chinese Culture," *Guangming Daily* 6, November 25, 2021.

83. Xi Jinping, *The Governance of China (Vol. 1)* (Beijing: Foreign Language Press, 2018), 156.

84. The Propaganda Department of the CCCPC, ed., *The Brief History of the Propaganda Work of the Communist Party of China* (Beijing: People's Publishing House, 2022), 633.

85. Xi Jinping, "Take Solid Steps toward Common Prosperity," *Qiushi Journal* 20, 2021.

86. The Party Literature Research Center of the CCCPC. *Selected Works of Important Documents since the Eighteenth National Congress I* (Beijing: People's Publishing House, 2014), 539.

87. Xu Jun, "During the 13th Five-Year Plan period, China Accelerated the Construction of a Social Governance Pattern of Joint Construction, Common Governance and Sharing," *People's Daily* 1&13, November 30, 2020.
88. Xi Jinping, *The Governance of China (Vol. 3)* (Beijing: Foreign Language Press, 2020), 19.
89. Zhi'an, "Improving the National Security System," *Guangming Daily* 2, December 12, 2019.
90. Xi Jinping, "Speech Delivered at the Meeting to Commend Role Models in China's Fight against the COVID-19 Epidemic on September 8, 2020," *People's Daily* 2, September 9, 2020.
91. The Literature Research Office of the CCCPC. *Excerpts from the Discourse on Socialist Ecological Civilization Construction by Xi Jinping* (Beijing: Central Literature Publishing House, Research Press, 2017), 20–21.
92. Xi Jinping, *The Governance of China (Vol. 3)* (Beijing: Foreign Language Press, 2020), 19.
93. "Xi Jinping stressed during the twenty-ninth group study of the Political Bureau of the CPC Central Committee to maintain the strategic determination of ecological civilization construction and strive to build a modernization in which man and nature live in harmony," *People's Daily* 1, May 2, 2021.
94. "Xi Jinping Stressed during the 36th Group Study of the Political Bureau of the Communist Party of China (CPC) Central Committee that the Situation and Tasks Facing the Work of Achieving Peak Carbon Emissions and Carbon Neutrality should be Analyzed in Depth and that the Decisions and Deployments of the CPC Central Committee should be Put into Practice," *People's Daily* 1&3, January 26, 2022.
95. The Party Literature Research Center of the CPC Central Committee. *Selected Works of Important Documents since the Seventeenth National Congress I* (Beijing: Central Literature Publishing House, 2009), 35.
96. Qu Qingshan, "The Century of CPC and the Great Changes in the Past Century, Research Office of the CPC Central Committee," 2021.
97. Xi Jinping, "We must Commit to Sustainable Development and Jointly Create a Better World the Speech Delivered at the 23rd St Petersburg International Economic Forum on June 7, 2019," *People's Daily* 2, June 8, 2019.
98. Xi Jinping, "Speech at the Celebration Convention for the 40th Anniversary of the Shenzhen Special Economic Zone on October 14, 2020," *People's Daily* 2, July 2, 2020.
99. Xi Jinping, *The Governance of China (Vol. 2)* (Beijing: Foreign Language Press, 2017), 443.
100. "In the Press Conference of the Fourth Session of the 12th National People's Congress, Foreign Minister Wang Yi answered questions from domestic and foreign media on China's foreign policy and external relations," *People's Daily* 3, March 9, 2016.
101. Hu Zexi, "Act in Accordance with the Vision of Major-Country Diplomacy with Distinctive Chinese Features and Serve the Goal of Building Moderately Prosperous Society in an All-Round Way," *People's Daily* 14, May 4, 2016.
102. Xi Jinping, *The Governance of China (Vol. 1)* (Beijing: Foreign Language Press, 2018), 272.
103. Xi Jinping, *The Governance of China (Vol. 1)* (Beijing: Foreign Language Press, 2018), 297–298.

104. Xi Jinping, *The Governance of China (Vol. 1)* (Beijing: Foreign Language Press, 2018), 227.

105. Xi Jinping, *The Governance of China (Vol. 3)* (Beijing: Foreign Language Press, 2020), 20.

106. "In order to support the development of Hong Kong and Macao, from June to October 2003, the mainland signed the Closer Economic Partnership Arrangement with both Hong Kong and Macao. The English names and abbreviations of both are CEPA."

107. "General Secretary Xi Jinping met with Lien Chan and his delegation," *People's Daily* 1, February 26, 2013.

108. "Decision on Major Issues Concerning Upholding and Improving the System of Socialism with Chinese Characteristics and Modernizing China's System and Capacity for Governance (adopted at the fourth plenary meeting of the 19th CCCPC on October 31, 2019)," *People's Daily* 6, November 6, 2019.

109. The Party Literature Research Center of the CPC Central Committee, *Selected Works of Important Documents since the Founding of the People's Republic of China (17)* (Beijing: Central Literature Publishing House, 1998), 483.

110. Xi Jinping, "Speech at a Ceremony Marking the Centenary of the Communist Party of China," *People's Daily* 2, July 2, 2021.

Bibliography

1. Basic Documents

Chen, Yun. *Selected Works of Chen Yun (Vol. 2–3)*. Beijing: People's Publishing House, 1995.

Deng, Xiaoping. *Selected Works of Deng Xiaoping (Vol. 2, Ver. 2)*. Beijing: People's Publishing House, 1994.

Deng, Xiaoping. *Selected Works of Deng Xiaoping (Vol. 3)*. Beijing: People's Publishing House, 1993.

Hu, Jintao. *Selected Works of Hu Jintao (Vol. 1–3)*. Beijing: People's Publishing House, 2016.

Jiang, Zemin. *Selected Works of Jiang Zemin (Vol. 1–3)*. Beijing: People's Publishing House, 2006.

Lenin, Vladimir Ilyich Ulyanov. *V. I. Lenin Collected Works (Vol. 1–4, Ver. 2)*. Beijing: People's Publishing House, 2009.

Liu, Shaoqi. *Selected Works of Liu Shaoqi (Vol. 2)*. Beijing: People's Publishing House, 1984.

Mao, Zedong. *Collected Works of Mao Zedong (Vol. 5–8)*. Beijing: People's Publishing House, 1999.

Marx, Karl, and Frederick Engels. *Marx & Engels Collected Works (Vol. 1–4, Ver. 3)*. Beijing: People's Publishing House, 2012.

The Institute of Party History and Literature of the Central Committee of the Communist Party of China. *Mao Zedong, Deng Xiaoping, Jiang Zemin, Hu Jintao's Excerpts on the History of the Communist Party of China*. Beijing: Central Party Literature Publishing House, 2021.

———. *Selected Importance Documents Since the 19th National Congress of the CPC (Vol. 1–2)*. Beijing: Central Party Literature Publishing House, 2019–2021.

The Party Literature Research Center of the CPC Central Committee. *Manuscripts of Mao Zedong Since the Founding of the People's Republic of China (Vol. 1–13)*. Beijing: Central Party Literature Publishing House, 1987–1998.

The Party Literature Research Center of the CPC Central Committee, The Institute of Party History and Literature of the Central Committee of the Communist Party of China,

The State Archives Administration of the People's Republic of China. *Manuscripts of Liu Shaoqi Since the Founding of the People's Republic of China (Vol. 1–12)*. Beijing: Central Party Literature Publishing House, 2005–2018.

The Party Literature Research Center of the CPC Central Committee, The State Archives Administration of the People's Republic of China. *Manuscripts of Zhou Enlai Since the Founding of the People's Republic of China (Vol. 1–13)*. Beijing: Central Party Literature Publishing House, 2008–2018.

The Party Literature Research Center of the CPC Central Committee. *Selected Importance Documents Since the Founding of the People's Republic of China (Vol. 1–20)*. Beijing: Central Party Literature Publishing House, 2011.

———. *Selected Importance Documents Since the Third Plenary Session (Vol. 1–2)*. Beijing: People's Publishing House, 1982.

———. *Selected Importance Documents Since the 12th National Congress of the CPC (Vol. 1–3)*. Beijing: People's Publishing House, 1986–1988.

———. *Selected Importance Documents Since the 13th National Congress of the CPC (Vol. 1–3)*. Beijing: People's Publishing House, 1991–1993.

———. *Selected Importance Documents Since the 14th National Congress of the CPC (Vol. 1–3)*. Beijing: People's Publishing House, 1996–1999.

———. *Selected Importance Documents Since the 15th National Congress of the CPC (Vol. 1–3)*. Beijing: People's Publishing House, 2000–2003.

———. *Selected Importance Documents Since the 16th National Congress of the CPC (Vol. 1–3)*. Beijing: Central Party Literature Publishing House, 2008.

———. *Selected Importance Documents Since the 17th National Congress of the CPC (Vol. 1–3)*. Beijing: Central Party Literature Publishing House, 2009–2013.

The Party Literature Research Center of the CPC Central Committee, The Institute of Party History and Literature of the Central Committee of the Communist Party of China. *Selected Importance Documents Since the 18th National Congress of the CPC (Vol. 1–3)*. Beijing: Central Party Literature Publishing House, 2014–2018.

The State Archives Administration of the People's Republic of China, The Party Literature Research Center of the CPC Central Committee. *Selected Documents of the CPC Central Committee (October, 1949–May, 1966) (Vol. 1–50)*. Beijing: People's Publishing House, 2013.

Xi, Jinping. *The Governance of China (Vol. 1)*. Beijing: Foreign Languages Press, 2018.

———. *The Governance of China (Vol. 2)*. Beijing: Foreign Languages Press, 2017.

———. *The Governance of China (Vol. 3)*. Beijing: Foreign Languages Press, 2020.

———. *The History of the Communist Party of China*. Beijing: Central Party Literature Publishing House, 2021.

Zhou, Enlai. *Selected Works of Zhou Enlai (Vol. 2)*. Beijing: People's Publishing House, 1984.

2. Chronicle and Biography

The Party Literature Research Center of the CPC Central Committee. *A Biography of Deng Xiaoping (1904–1974) (Vol. 1–2)*. Beijing: Central Party Literature Publishing House, 2014.

———. *A Biography of Mao Zedong (1949–1976) (Vol. 1–2)*. Beijing: Central Party Literature Publishing House, 2003.

———. *A Biography of Liu Shaoqi (Vol. 2)*. Beijing: Central Party Literature Publishing House, 1998.

———. *A Biography of Zhou Enlai (1898–1976) (Vol. 3–4)*. Beijing: Central Party Literature Publishing House, 2008.

———. *Chronology of Chen Yun's Life (Vol. 1–3)*. Beijing: Central Party Literature Publishing House, 2000.

———. *Chronicle of Deng Xiaoping Thought (1975–1997)*. Beijing: Central Party Literature Publishing House, 1998.

———. *Chronology of Deng Xiaoping's Life (1975–1997) (Vol. 1–3)*. Beijing: Central Party Literature Publishing House, 2004.

———. *Chronicle of Jiang Zemin Thought (1989–2008)*. Beijing: Central Party Literature Publishing House, 2010.

———. *Chronology of Mao Zedong's Life (1949–1976) (Vol. 1–6)*. Beijing: Central Party Literature Publishing House, 2013.

———. *Chronicle of Mao Zedong Thought (1921–1975)*. Beijing: Central Party Literature Publishing House, 2011.

———. *Chronology of Mao Zedong's Life (Vol. 2)*. Beijing: Central Party Literature Publishing House, 1996.

———. *Chronology of Zhou Enlai's Life (1949–1976) (Vol. 1–3)*. Beijing: Central Party Literature Publishing House, 1997.

3. Chronicles and Reference Books

China Statistical Yearbook. Beijing: China Statistics Press, 1982–2021.

Deng, Liqun. *Encyclopedia of the History of the People's Republic of China (1949–1999)*. Beijing: Encyclopedia of China Publishing House, 1999.

Department of Comprehensive Statistics of National Bureau of Statistics. *China Compendium of Statistics 1949–2008*. Beijing: China Statistics Press, 2010.

Domestic Data Group of Xinhua News Agency. *Chronicle of the People's Republic of China (1949–1980)*. Beijing: Xinhua Publishing House, 1982.

———. *Chronicle of the People's Republic of China (1981–1984)*. Beijing: Xinhua Publishing House, 1985.

Faculty of History, Nankai University. *Chronicle of the People's Republic of China (Vol. 1–4)*. Shijiazhuang: Hebei People's Publishing House, 1958–1960.

Huang, Daoxia, et al. *40 Years of Chronicle of the People's Republic of China (1949–1989)*. Beijing: Guangming Daily Publishing House, 1989.

Liu, Haipan. *The Complete History of the People's Republic of China (Vol. 1–15)*. Beijing: Central Party Literature Publishing House, 2005.

Party History Research Center of the CPC Central Committee. *Chronicle of the People's Republic of China (1949–2009)*. Beijing: People's Publishing House, 2009.

Party History Research Center of the CPC Central Committee, National Museum of China. *Historical Atlas of the People's Republic of China*. Shanghai: Shanghai People's Publishing House, 2009.

The Institute of Contemporary China Studies. *Chronicle of the History of the People's Republic of China (1949–2018)*. Beijing: Contemporary China Publishing House, 2004–2021.

The Institute of Party History and Literature of the Central Committee of the Communist Party of China. *Chronicle of the Communist Party of China*. Beijing: People's Publishing House, 2021.

———. *Chronicle of the People's Republic of China (October 1949–September 2019)*. Beijing: People's Publishing House, 2019.

The Party Literature Research Center of the CPC Central Committee. *Chronicle of the People's Republic of China (October 1949–October 2009)*. Beijing: Xinhua Publishing House, 2009.

The People's Republic of China Yearbook. Beijing: The People's Republic of China Yearbook Press, 1981–2020.

Xinhua Daily. *30 years of China's Reform and Opening-Up, (Vol. 1–2)*. Beijing: People's Publishing House, 2008.

Xu, Jin, et al. *Chronicle of the People's Republic of China (1989–1994)*. Beijing: Scientific and Technical Documentation Press, 1995.

You, Lin, et al. *General Guide to the History of the People's Republic of China (Vol. 1–4)*. Beijing: Red Flag Press, 1993.

Zhang, Jinpan, et al. *Dictionary of the History of the People's Republic of China*. Harbin: Heilongjiang People's Publishing House, 1992.

4. Research Monograph, General Introduction and General History

Chen, Shu. *History of the People's Republic of China*. Beijing: People's Publishing House, 2009.

Cheng, Zhongyuan. *The History of Faith in the Establishment of the State: A Discussion on the Study of Contemporary Chinese History*. Shanghai: Shanghai People's Publishing House, 2015.

Concise History of the People's Republic of China Writing Group. *A Concise of the People's Republic of China*. Beijing: People's Publishing House, Contemporary China Publishing House, 2021.

———. *A Concise History of Reform and Opening-Up*. Beijing: People's Publishing House, China Social Sciences Press, 2021.

———. *A Concise History of the Communist Party of China*. Beijing: People's Publishing House, History of Chinese Communist Party Publishing House, 2021.

Gu, Anlin. *Twenty-eight Lessons of the History of the Communist Party of China*. Beijing: People's Publishing House, 2006.

Guo, Dehong. *Thematic History of the People's Republic of China (Vol. 1–5)*. Chengdu: Sichuan People's Publishing House, 2004.

Hu, Sheng. *70 Years of the Communist Party of China*. Beijing: History of Chinese Communist Party Publishing House, 1991.

Jiao, Chunrong, et al. *Research on the History of People's Republic of China*. Beijing: China Archives Publishing House, 1989.

Jin, Chunming. *A Concise History of the People's Republic of China (1949–1981)*. Beijing: History of Chinese Communist Party Publishing House, 2008.

———. Commentary on *Cambridge History of the People's Republic of China*. Wuhan: Hubei People's Press, 2001.

Li, Jie. *Meditation Record of National History*. Beijing: China Social Sciences Press, 2009.

Liao, Gailong, and Zhuang Puming. *Chronicle of the People's Republic of China (1949–2009)*. Beijing: People's Publishing House, 2009.

Liao, Gailong. *Chronicle of New China (1949–1989)*. Beijing: People's Publishing House, 1989.

Liu, Dejun. *Commentary on the History of the People's Republic of China*. Jinan: Publishing House of Jinan, 2010.

Liu, Guoxin. *History of the People's Republic of China*. Tianjin: Tianjin People's Publishing House, 2010.

Mac Farquhar, Roderick, and J. K. Fairbank, et al. *The Cambridge History of China Vol. 14: The People's Republic, Part1, The Emergence of Revolutionary China, 1949–1965*. Translated by Xie Liangsheng et al. Beijing: China Social Sciences Press, 1990.

———, *The Cambridge History of China (Vol. 15): The People's Republic, Part 2, Revolutions Within the Chinese Revolution, 1966–1982*. Translated by Yu Jinyao et al. Beijing: China Social Sciences Press, 1992.

Pang, Song. *The Development History of the People's Republic of China*. Qingdao: Qingdao Publishing House, 2009.

Party History Research Center of the CPC Central Committee. *90 Years of the Communist Party of China*. Beijing: History of Chinese Communist Party Publishing House, Party Building Reader Publishing House, 2016.

———. *A Concise History of the Communist Party of China*. Beijing: History of Chinese Communist Party Publishing House, 2001.

———. *History of the Communist Party of China (1949–1978) (Vol. 2)*. Beijing: History of Chinese Communist Party Publishing House, 2011.

Qi, Pengfei, and Yang Fengcheng. *Chronicle of Contemporary China (October 1949–October 2004)*. Beijing: People's Publishing House, 2007.

Teng, Fangwei, and Xu Haiqing. *Introduction to History of the People's Republic of China*. Beijing: Central Party School Press, 2013.

The Institute of Contemporary China Studies. *A Concise History of the People's Republic of China (1949–2019)*. Beijing: Contemporary China Publishing House, 2019.

The Institute of Contemporary China Studies. *The History of the People's Republic of China: (Prologue, Vol. 1–4)*. Beijing: People's Publishing House, 2012.

Wang, Haiguang. *Time Passes by without Moving: A Homesick Warrior, Contemporary Chinese History*. Chengdu: Sichuan People's Publishing House, 2014.

Wu, Li. *40 Years of Reform and Opening-Up: History and Experience*. Beijing: Contemporary China Publishing House, 2020.

Yang, Kuisong, and Lin Yunhui, et al. *History of the People's Republic of China (1949–1981) (Vol. 2–6, 8, 10)*. Hong Kong: The Chinese University of Hong Kong Press, 2008.

Zhang, Shujun. *Historical Records of the People's Republic of China*. Yinchuan: Ningxia People's Publishing House, 2009.

Zheng, Qian. *History of the People's Republic of China (Vol. 1–6)*. Beijing: People's Publishing House, 2010.

5. Research Monographs, Chronological History and Thematic History

Bo, Yibo. *Review of Several Major Decisions and Events (Vol. 1–2)*. Beijing: Central Party School Press, 1991, 1993.

Cao, Pu. *Some Important Problems in the Study of the History of Reform and Opening-Up*. Fuzhou: Fujian People's Publishing House, 2014.

Chen, Gang. *A History of Contemporary Chinese Advertising (1979–1991)*. Beijing: Peking University Press, 2010.

Chen, Guoen. *History of Chinese Contemporary and Modern Literature*. Wuhan: Wuhan University Press, 2011.

Chen, Jingliang. *History of Contemporary Chinese Legal Thoughts*. Zhengzhou: Henan University Press, 1999.

Chen, Mingxian. *History of Political Institutions of the People's Republic of China*. Tianjin: Nankai University Press, 1998.

Cheng, Kai. *History of Contemporary Chinese Educational Thoughts*. Zhengzhou: Henan University Press, 1999.

Chi, Fulin. *History of the Political System of the People's Republic of China*. Beijing: Publishing House of the Party School of the Central Committee of the CPC, 1998.

Cong, Jin. *Years of Tortuous Development*. Zhengzhou: Henan People's Publishing House, 1989.

Dong, Fureng. *Economic History of the People's Republic of China*. Beijing: Economic Science Press, 1999.

Fan, Shouxin. *History of the National Economic Recovery of the People's Republic of China (1949–1952)*. Beijing: Qiushi Press, 1988.

Guo, Zicheng, and Shen Xiaorong. *Planning History of the People's Republic of China*. Shijiazhuang: Hebei People's Publishing House, 1993.

Han, Yanlong. *General History of the Legal System of the People's Republic of China (1949–1995)*. Beijing: Publishing House of the Party School of the Central Committee of the CPC, 1998.

He, Dongchang. *The Education History of the People's Republic of China*. Haikou: Hainan Publishing House, 2007.

Huang, Anyu. *Diplomatic History of the People's Republic of China*. Beijing: The People's publishing House, 2005.

Huang, Yanqiu, and Yang Dongjie. *History of Contemporary Chinese Commercial Advertising*. Zhengzhou: Henan University Press, 2006.

Institute of Military History, Academy of Military Sciences. *Essentials of Military History of the People's Republic of China*. Beijing: Military Science Press, 2005.

——. *History of the War to Resist US Aggression and Aid Korea*. Beijing: Military Science Press, 2014.

Jiang, Jiannong, and Xiao Jie. *History of Contemporary Chinese United Front Thought*. Zhengzhou: Henan University Press, 1999.

Jiang, Xuchao. *The Marine Economy History of the People's Republic of China*. Beijing: Economic Science Press, 2008.

Jin, Chunming. *Exploration in the Age of Great Changes*. Beijing: China Social Sciences Press, 2009.

Li, Chun. *History of Chinese Contemporary Communication Studies*. Guilin: Lijiang Publishing House, 2014.

Li, Jinshan, et al. *History of the Chinese People's Political Consultative Conference*. Harbin: Heilongjiang Education Press, 1991.

Li, Mingshan. *History of Contemporary Chinese Academic Thought*. Zhengzhou: Henan University Press, 1999.

Li, Zhenghua, and Zhang Jincai. *The Political History of the People's Republic of China*. Beijing: Contemporary China Publishing House, 2021.

Li, Zongzhi, and Zhang Runjun. *Economic History of the People's Republic of China*. Lanzhou: Lan Zhou Univeisity Press, 1999.

Liu, Cuixiao. *The History of the People's Republic of China's Social Security Rule of Law* (1949–2011). Beijing: Commercial Press, 2014.

Liu, Zhengshan. *History of Contemporary China's Land System*. Dalian: Northeast University of Finance and Economics Press, 2015.

Long, Guan. *Economic History of the People's Republic of China*. Beijing: Economy and Management Press, 2010.

Luo, Pinghan, *History of Rural People's Commune*. Fu Zhou: Fujian People's Publishing House, 2006.

Lü, Peng. *History of Chinese Contemporary and Modern Art*. Hangzhou: China Academy of Art Press, 2011.

Party History Research Office of the Central Committee of the Communist Party of China. *A Brief History of the New Era of the Communist Party of China*. Beijing: Communist Party History Press, 2009.

Pei, Jianzhang. *The Diplomatic History of the People's Republic of China (1949–1956)*. Beijing: World Affairs Press, 1994.

Qi, Pengfei, and Li Baozhen. *A Concise History of the People's Republic of China*. Beijing: The People's Publishing House, 2014.

Qin, Yingjun. *History of Contemporary Chinese Philosophy*. Zhengzhou: Henan University Press, 1999.

Qu, Xing. *China's Diplomacy in Five Decades*. Nanjing: Jiangsu People's Publishing House, 2000.

Shi, Zhifu. *History of Foreign Relations of the People's Republic of China* (1949–1989). Beijing: Peking University Press, 1994.

Si, Youhe. *Development of the Public Communication of Science and Technology of the PRC*. Chongqing: Chongqing Publishing Group, 2005.

Song, Yuehong, and Wang Aiyun. *Theory and Method of Research on the History of the People's Republic of China*. Beijing: Contemporary China Publishing House, 2021.

Sun, Jian. *Economic History of the People's Republic of China*. Beijing: China Renmin University Press, 1992.

Sun, Youkui, et al. *History of Construction and Reform of the People's Republic of China*. Changchun: Jilin People's Press, 1990.

Sun, Youkui. *The Diplomatic History of the People's Republic of China*. Harbin: Heilongjiang Education Press, 1989.

The Third Research Department of the Party History Research Office of the CCCPC. *30 years of Reform and Opening-up in China*. Shenyang: Liaoning People's Publishing House, 2008.

Tian, Zengpei. *China's Diplomacy in 40 years Since the Reform and Opening-up*. Beijing: World Affairs Press, 1993.

Wang, Haibo. *Economic History of the People's Republic of China (October 1949–1998)*. Taiyuan: Shanxi Economic Publishing House, 1998.

Wang, Hongmo, et al. *The Course of Reform and Opening-Up*. Zhengzhou: Henan People's Publishing House, 1989.

Wang, Nianyi. *The Age of Turbulence*. Zhengzhou: Henan People's Publishing House, 1989.

Wang, Qiaorong. *The Diplomatic History of the People's Republic of China*. Beijing: Contemporary China Publishing House, 2021.

Wang, Ruifang. *History of Contemporary China's Water Conservancy (1949–2011)*. Beijing: China Social Sciences Publishing House, 2014.

Wang, Taiping. *The Diplomatic History of the People's Republic of China (1957–1969)*. Beijing: World Affairs Press, 1998.

———. *The Diplomatic History of the People's Republic of China (1970–1979)*. Beijing: World Affairs Press, 1999.

———. *The Diplomatic History of the People's Republic of China*. Beijing: World Affairs Press, 1999.

Wang, Yizhou, and Tan Xiuying. *Sixty Years of China's Foreign Affairs (1949–2009)*. Beijing: China Social Sciences Publishing House, 2009.

Weng, Youwei, Xi Fuqun, and Zhao Jinkang. *History of Political Thoughts of Contemporary China*. Zhengzhou: Henan University Press, 1999.

Wu, Chengming, and Dong Zhikai. *Economic History of the People's Republic of China*. Beijing: Social Science Academic Press, 2010.

Wu, Li. *Economic History of the People's Republic of China (1949–1999)*. Beijing: Economic Science Press, 1999.

Wu, Li. *People's Republic of China's Economic Brief History*. Beijing: China Social Sciences Publishing House, 2008.

Wu, Shaozu. *History of Sports of the People's Republic of China (1949–1998)*. Beijing: China Book Press, 1999.

Xi, Xuan, and Jing Chunming. *A Concise History of the Great Cultural Revolution*. Beijing: CPC History Publishing House, 2006.

Xia, Yanjing. *History of Chinese Contemporary and Modern Arts*. Nanjing: Nanjing University Press, 2011.

Xiao, Donglian, et al. *Seeking China: The History of the First Decade of the Cultural Revolution*. Beijing: Hongqi Publishing House, 1999.

Xiao, Donglian. *The Battle of Pathfinding: China's Economic Reform from 1978 to 1992*. Beijing: Social Science Literature Press, 2019.

Xiao, Guoliang, and Sui Fumin. *Economic History of the People's Republic of China*. Beijing: Peking University Press, 2011.

Xie, Chuntao. *Lushan Scenes: A Brief History of the 1959 Lushan Conference*. Beijing: China Youth Publishing House, 1996.

Xie, Yixian. *History of Contemporary Chinese Diplomatic Thoughts*. Zhengzhou: Henan University Press, 1999.

———. *The Diplomatic History of China (1979–1994)*. Zhengzhou: Henan People's Publishing House, 1995.

———. *The Diplomatic History of Contemporary China (1949–2009)*. Beijing: China Youth Publishing House, 2009.

Xu, Chongde. *Development of the Constitution of the PRC*. Fuzhou: Fujian People's Publishing House, 2003.

Xu, Guangchun. *A Brief History of Radio and Television in the People's Republic of China*. Beijing: China Radio and Television Press, 2003.

Yang, Kuisong. *Research on the History of the Founding of the People's Republic of China (1, 2)*. Nanchang: Jiangxi People's Publishing House, 2009.

Yang, Yifan, Chen Hanfeng, and Zhang Qun. *The Legal History of the People's Republic of China*. Beijing: Social Science Academic Press, 2010.

Ye, Zicheng, and Li Hongjie. *China's Diplomacy*. Beijing: Contemporary World Press, 2009.

Yu, Huamin, and Hu Zhefeng. *History of Contemporary Chinese Military Thoughts*. Zhengzhou: Henan University Press, 1999.

Zhang, Jingfeng. *History of China's Higher Education*. Beijing: Higher Education Press, 2010.

Zhang, Jingru, and Zhao Chaofeng. *History of Contemporary Chinese Society*. Beijing: Publishing and Media, 2011.

Zhang, Lili. *A Concise History of Contemporary China*. Shanghai: Shanghai People's Publishing House, 2009.

Zhang, Tao. *History of Journalism and Mass Communication of the People's Republic of China*. Beijing: Economic Daily, 1992.

Zhao, Xiaolei. *The Evolution of Economic Thoughts*. Beijing: Capital University of Economics and Business Press, 2009.

Zheng, Yougui. *The Economic History of the People's Republic of China*. Beijing: Contemporary China Publishing House, 2021.

Zhu, Jiamu. *China's Industrialization and Contemporary History*. Beijing: China Social Sciences Publishing House, 2009.

Zhu, Xun. *History of Geology and Mineral Resources of the People's Republic of China*. Beijing: Geology Press, 2003.

6. Textbooks

Chen, Mingxian. *A Course Book on History of the People's Republic of China*. Beijing: China Renmin University Press, 2009.

Chen, Mingxian. *History of the People's Republic of China*. Beijing: Beijing Institute of Technology Press, 1993.

Compilation Group of the History of the People's Republic of China. *History of the People's Republic of China*. Beijing: Higher Education Press, 2013.

Department of History, Beijing Normal University, Hebei. *Historical Manuscripts of the People's Republic of China*. Beijing: People's Publishing House, 1958.

Gao, Pingping. *A Concise Course Book on History of the People's Republic of China*. Shanghai: Tongji University Press, 2005.

Guo, Binwei, and Tan Zongji. *Brief History of the People's Republic of China*. Changchun: Jilin Literature and History Publishing House, 1988.

He, Li, *History of the People's Republic of China*. Beijing: China Archives Press, 1995.

He, Qin. *The History of the People's Republic of China (Vol. 3)*. Beijing: Higher Education Press, 2015.

Jin, Chunming. *A Concise History of the People's Republic of China*. Beijing: CPC History Publishing House, 2004.

Jin, Dexing. *A Concise History of the People's Republic of China*. Zhengzhou: Henan University Press, 2005.

Li, Maosheng. *History of the People's Republic of China*. Beijing: China Radio and Television Press, 1991.

Lin, Fengming. *History of the People's Republic of China*. Guilin: Guangxi Normal University Press, 1998.

Ouyang, Guoqing, et al. *A Concise Course Book on History of the People's Republic of China*. Changsha: Hunan People's Publishing House, 2007.

Pang, Song. *A Concise History of the People's Republic of China*. Guangzhou: Guangdong Education Publishing House, 2001.

Qi, Pengfei. *A Course Book on History of the People's Republic of China*. Beijing: Higher Education Press, 2013.

———. *The History of the People's Republic of China (Vol. 2)*. Beijing: China Renmin University Press, 2021.

Qin, Yuqing. *History of the People's Republic of China*. Xi'an: Shaanxi Normal University General Publication House, Co, Ltd., 1994.

Sun, Ruiying, et al. *A Brief History of New China*. Xi'an: Shaanxi People's Publishing House, 1991.

Wang, Xiliang. *History of the People's Republic of China*. Xi'an: Shaanxi Normal University General Publication House, 1990.

Wu, Benxiang. *History of the People's Republic of China*. Beijing: Higher Education Press, 1999.

Yang, Qinwei, et al. *Outline of the History of the People's Republic of China*. Qingdao: University of Petroleum Press, 1990.

Yang, Xiancai. *New Edition of Chinese History · History of the People's Republic of China*. Beijing: Higher Education Press, 2015.

Zhang, Muochao. *History of the People's Republic of China*. Chongqing: Chongqing University Press, 1997.

Zhang, Qihua, et al. *A Concise History of the People's Republic of China*. Beijing: Contemporary China Publishing House, 1997.

Zhang, Yinlin. *Sixteen Lectures on National History*. Beijing: China Friendship Publishing Company, 2009.

Zhu, Jianhua, and Zhu Yang. *Historical Manuscripts of the People's Republic of China*. Harbin: Heilongjiang People's Publishing House, 1989.

Zhu, Yang, Ren Yongxiang, and Guo Yongjun. *Forty Years of the People's Republic of China*. Changchun: Jilin People's Publishing House, 1989.

Zhu, Yuxiang. *A Concise History of the People's Republic of China*. Fuzhou: Fujian People's Publishing House, 1991.

———. *Brief History of the People's Republic of China*. Fuzhou: Fujian People's Publishing House, 1991.

Zhu, Zongyu, et al. *Outline of the History of the People's Republic of China*. Fuzhou: Fujian People's Publishing House, 1988.

Index

ABOUT THE AUTHORS

Qi Pengfei is a vice secretary of the Party Committee, professor, and doctoral supervisor at Renmin University of China. He is a member of the 12th Committee of the Chinese People's Political Consultative Conference in Beijing. He is also involved in various academic and research organizations, including the Chinese Historians Association and the National Taiwan Research Association. Qi Pengfei specializes in teaching courses on the history of the Communist Party of China, contemporary Chinese history, and modern and contemporary Chinese history. He has contributed to the development of professional textbooks, such as *An Analysis of Key Issues in a Concise History of Modern China*, *History of the People's Republic of China*, and *Textbook of the History of the People's Republic of China*.

Zhou Jiabin is an associate professor of Marxism at Renmin University of China.